Germany at fifty-five

Published in our
centenary year
2004
MANCHESTER
UNIVERSITY
PRESS

ISSUES IN GERMAN POLITICS

Edited by

Professor Charlie Jeffery, Institute for German Studies
Dr Charles Lees, University of Sheffield

Issues in German Politics is a major series on contemporary Germany. Focusing on the post-unity era, it presents concise, scholarly analyses of the forces driving change in domestic politics and foreign policy. Key themes will be the continuing legacies of German unification and controversies surrounding Germany's role and power in Europe. The series includes contributions from political science, international relations and political economy.

Already published:

Annesley: *Postindustrial Germany: Services, technological transformation and knowledge in unified Germany*

Bulmer, Jeffery and Paterson: *Germany's European diplomacy: Shaping the regional milieu*

Green: *The politics of exclusion: Institutions and immigration policy in contemporary Germany*

Gunlicks: *The* Länder *and German federalism*

Harding and Paterson (eds): *The future of the German economy: An end to the miracle?*

Harnisch and Maull: *Germany as a Civilian Power? The foreign policy of the Berlin Republic*

Hyde-Price: *Germany and European order: Enlarging NATO and the EU*

Lees: *The Red–Green coalition in Germany: Politics, personalities and power*

Rittberger (ed.): *German foreign policy since unification: Theories and case studies*

Germany at fifty-five

Berlin ist nicht Bonn?

Edited by James Sperling

Manchester University Press
Manchester and New York

Distributed exclusively in the USA by Palgrave

Published by Manchester University Press
Oxford Road, Manchester M13 9NR, UK
and Room 400, 175 Fifth Avenue, New York, NY 10010, USA
www.manchesteruniversitypress.co.uk

Distributed exclusively in the USA by
Palgrave, 175 Fifth Avenue, New York,
NY 10010, USA

Distributed exclusively in Canada by
UBC Press, University of British Columbia, 2029 West Mall,
Vancouver, BC, Canada V6T 1Z2

British Library Cataloguing-in-Publication Data
A catalogue record for this book is available from the British Library

Library of Congress Cataloging-in-Publication Data applied for

ISBN 0 7190 6472 4 *hardback*

0 7190 6473 2 *paperback*

First published 2004

13 12 11 10 09 08 07 06 05 04 10 9 8 7 6 5 4 3 2 1

Typeset
by Carnegie Publishing Ltd
Printed in Great Britain
by Bell & Bain, Glasgow

This book is presented to
Professor Peter Merkl on the occasion of his 70th birthday

Contents

Conclusion

List of figures and tables

Figures

Tables

Foreword

Germany at fifty-five is dedicated to Professor Peter Merkl on the occasion of his seventieth birthday. Peter Merkl, recipient of the *Bundesverdienstkreuz* for his contribution to mutual understanding between Germany and the United States, has had (and continues to have) a distinguished and influential academic career, which began with his graduation from the University of California, Berkeley in 1959 and has continued uninterrupted after his retirement from full-time teaching at the University of California, Santa Barbara, in 1993. The chapters in this book cover six different dimensions of German politics – the founding of the Bonn and Berlin Republics; the legacies of national socialism; the evolving political culture of a unified Germany; policy and institutional adaptation in a unified Germany; the evolution of the German party system; and German foreign policy. The chapters constituting *Germany at fifty-five* required the talents and expertise of over twenty authors. The depth and breadth of Peter Merkl's academic writings and expertise not only encompass the topics covered in this book, but reach well beyond them.

His first impact on the field of political science was made in his analysis of the institutions and constitutional evolution of the fledgling Federal Republic of Germany, beginning with his landmark article, 'Executive–Legislative Federalism in West Germany', published in the *American Political Science Review* and followed by his *The Origin of the West German Republic*, described by Arthur Gunlicks as a 'classic in the study of the making of the Basic Law', and *Germany: Yesterday and Tomorrow*. These constitutional studies were eventually augmented by his study of local government in his edited collection, *New Local*

Centers in Centralized States, and several entries in the *World Book Encyclopedia*.

Peter Merkl has made a long-lived contribution to the comparative study of political parties and elections, beginning once again with an influential article published in the *American Political Science Review*, 'Equilibrium, Structure of Interests and Leadership'. This article was followed by a series of articles on political parties published in *International Organization*, *International Social Sciences Journal*, *Journal of Conflict Resolution*, *The Review of Politics*, *Rivista Italiana di Scienza Politica*, *West European Politics*, *The Western Political Quarterly*, and *World Politics*. In addition, Peter was a contributing editor to *Western European Party Systems* and *When Parties Fail: Emerging Alternative Organizations*. His interest in the comparative study of political parties was conjoined to a series of articles between 1963 and 1966 on methodology which appeared in the *Politische Vierteljahresschrift*. His subsequent *Modern Comparative Politics* soon found wide acceptance as a core textbook and went into multiple editions.

Peter Merkl undertook an early and sustained investigation into the problems and dynamics of racism and sexism in Germany and in comparative perspective. He published two articles in the early 1960s on the problem of American racism in the *Politische Vierteljahresschrift* as well as his *Rassenfrage und Rechtsradikalismus in den USA*. That work eventually led him to begin his work on the sociology of Nazis and comparative fascism, which in turn led him to begin an extended investigation of the problem of comparative terrorism and political extremism in western Europe. His best known works on the political sociology of National Socialism are *Political Violence under the Swastika* and *The Making of a Stormtrooper*. His contributions to the study of comparative terrorism and political extremism are best represented in *Political Violence and Terror: Motifs and Motivations* as well as in the coedited *Encounters with the Contemporary Radical Right* and *The Revival of Right-Wing Extremism in the Nineties*.

His *The Origin of the West German Republic* found a companion volume some forty years later in his *German Unification in the European Context*, which examined the process of German unification. These two books illuminate important junctures of twentieth-century German political history and each has shaped our understanding of how the Bonn and Berlin Republics came into being. These two books, which by necessity investigate the domestic and foreign policy aspects of German politics, complement his articles and books on German foreign policy, notably *German Foreign Policies, West and East*, and *West German Foreign Policy: Dilemmas and Directions*.

In addition to these contributions to specific aspects of German politics, Peter has contributed to our understanding of German politics through his role as editor of *The Federal Republic of Germany at Forty*, *The Federal Republic at Forty-Five*, and *The Federal Republic of Germany at Fifty*. These edited collections, in addition to their value as a source of scholarship on German politics, provided an opportunity for many young scholars to make their mark in their chosen field of study.

This bibliographic sketch has overlooked Peter's many chapters in edited volumes, his commentary and analysis in book review essays and individual book reviews for the major journals in history, sociology and political science, and works that fall outside easy classification, such as his recent *A Coup Attempt in Washington? A European Mirror on the 1998/1999 Constitutional Crisis* as well as the coedited, two-volume study of comparative political economy, *The Politics of Economic Change in Japan and West Germany*. This brief overview of Peter's scholarly output serves, I hope, to underscore the important contribution he has made to the study of German politics and comparative politics more generally.

On a personal note, I have known Peter as a teacher, mentor and friend since the early 1970s, when I was an undergraduate at the University of California, Santa Barbara. Peter subsequently served on my doctoral dissertation committee, provided me with my first opportunity to deliver a paper at a professional meeting, and asked me to contribute to *Germany at 45*, which turned out to be my first published paper. Peter's continuing personal and professional support of my academic career over the past few decades cannot be easily measured or put into words. My only hope is that this *Festschrift* reflects the high regard I hold for him as a scholar and, more importantly, as a friend.

James Sperling

Contributors

Andrew Baker is director of International Jewish Affairs, the American Jewish Committee.

Karl H. Cerny is professor of political science (*Emeritus*), Georgetown University.

William M. Chandler is professor of political science, University of California, San Diego.

Clay Clemens is professor of political science, the College of William and Mary.

Alice H. Cooper is associate professor of political science, University of Mississippi.

Dieter Fuchs is professor of political science, University of Stuttgart.

Lily Gardner Feldman is senior fellow in residence, the American Institute for Contemporary German Studies, Johns Hopkins University.

Arthur B. Gunlicks is professor of political science, University of Richmond.

Mary N. Hampton is associate professor of political science, University of Utah.

Jeffrey Herf is professor of history, the University of Maryland, College Park.

Michael Huelshoff is associate professor of political science, University of New Orleans.

Wade Jacoby is assistant professor of political science, Brigham Young University.

Karl Kaltenthaler is department chair and P. K. Seidman professor of political economy, Rhodes College.

Emil J. Kirchner is Jean Monnet professor of European integration, University of Essex, and executive editor of the *Journal of European Integration.*

Mary M. McKenzie is assistant professor of political science, Grossmont College.

Peter Merkl is professor of political science (*Emeritus*), University of California, Santa Barbara.

Joyce Marie Mushaben is professor of political science and director of the Institute for Women's and Gender Studies, University of Missouri, St Louis.

David F. Patton is associate professor of political science, Connecticut College.

Arthur R. Rachwald is professor of political science, United States Naval Academy and professorial lecturer at the Paul H. Nitze School of Advanced International Studies, the Johns Hopkins University, Bologna.

Robert Rohrschneider is professor of political science, Indiana University.

James Sperling is professor of political science, University of Akron.

Stephen F. Szabo is professor of European studies, the Paul H. Nitze School of Advanced International Studies, the Johns Hopkins University, Bologna.

Achim Truger is public finance economist at the Wirtschafts- und Sozialwissenschaftliches Institut in der Hans-Boeckler-Stiftung (WSI), Düsseldorf.

Leonard Weinberg is University of Nevada Foundation Professor, University of Nevada, Reno.

Thomas-Durell Young is European program manager, Center for Civil–Military Relations, Naval Post-Graduate School, Monterey.

Preface

The fifty-fifth anniversary of a democratic Germany in 2004 coincides with a number of other important anniversaries in German history: it is the fifteenth anniversary of the fall of the Berlin Wall and the events that set into motion the transformation of the European political space; the thirtieth anniversary of Chancellor Willy Brandt's resignation from office in the aftermath of a spy scandal and during one of the most serious postwar crises in German–American relations; the fortieth anniversary of the founding of the neo-fascist NDP; the fiftieth anniversary of Germany's accession to NATO; the sixtieth anniversary of the Normandy invasion and liberation of France; the seventieth anniversary of the Roehm *putsch* and the execution of the SA leadership; the eightieth anniversary of the Dawes Plan which ultimately failed to resolve the reparations question, and of Adolf Hitler's beer hall *putsch* trial and imprisonment; and the ninetieth anniversary of the start of the First World War, the settlement of which provided the political and psychological backdrop for the Second World War and the founding of the Federal Republic in 1949.

Germany at fifty-five examines how these pasts have placed and continue to place constraints on the domestic and foreign policy discourse and practices, how they have both shaped and misshaped the evolution of the German political culture and how they have hindered the reintegration of eastern and western Germany. The volume is divided into six parts which explore the founding of the Bonn and Berlin Republics, the legacies of national socialism, the evolving political culture of a unified Germany, policy and institutional adaptation in a unified Germany, the evolution of the German party system and

German foreign policy. In the Introduction James Sperling asks whether *Berlin ist nicht Bonn?* He provides a comparison of the Weimar, Bonn and Berlin Republics along four dimensions: the impact of the post-war peace settlement on German foreign policy ambitions; the domestic and international economic challenges faced by each postwar political elite; the institutions and practices of each constitutional order; and the foreign policy aspirations of each Republic.

Part I is intended to provide the reader with some historical understanding and basis for comparing the founding and subsequent evolution of both the Bonn and Berlin Republics. Bonn and Berlin were largely shaped by external forces. Karl H. Cerny in Chapter 2 examines how the Bonn Republic was founded within the context of the division, dismemberment and Allied occupation of Germany. His analysis demonstrates how the policies imposed on Germany during the occupation regime were an ever-present facet of postwar German domestic and foreign policies. Mary M. McKenzie in Chapter 3, in turn, provides a narrative of the Berlin Republic's founding. The Berlin Republic, which emerged from the end of the Cold War and was legitimised by the allied powers, demonstrates yet again how the external environment has intruded upon the evolution of Germany since 1945.

Part II focuses on the sources and continuing relevance of Germany's National Socialist legacy for the Berlin Republic. Andrew Baker in Chapter 6 discusses the history of German efforts to effect a *Wiedergutmachung* with its reparations payments to the victims of Nazism as well as the recent negotiations, of which he was a principal mover, over restitution to slave labourers. Jeffrey Herf in Chapter 4 presents an overview of the Bonn Republic's official memory of the National Socialist past, the different memories framing the eastern and western German understanding of that regime prior to unification and the politics of the Holocaust in the Berlin Republic. Chapter 5, by Lily Gardner Feldman, revisits the difficult relationship between Germany and the Jewish Diaspora in the post-unification period. The question arises: how has the move to Berlin affected the force and importance of Germany's relationship with Jewry in Europe, America and Israel?

Part III examines the elements of continuity and change in the German political culture. Each chapter focuses on these elements since the move to Berlin. Robert Rohrschneider and Dieter Fuchs in Chapter 7 raise an important question: what does it mean to be a German in a unified Germany and in a unifying Europe? Towards answering that question, they focus on the evolving pattern of democratic values in western and eastern Germany. Chapters 8 and 9, by Joyce Marie Mushaben and Alice H. Cooper, ask: are there one or two or many Germanies? Mushaben investigates how the differentiated status of women in Germany and persistent gender inequality compete with the regional animosities that persist between western and eastern Germans. She focuses on the practice of gender mainstreaming, which has contributed to the accretion of 'girl power' in contemporary Germany. Similarly, Cooper investigates the role played by social movements in the Berlin Republic, the marginalisation of protest groups in eastern Germany, and the instititutionalisation of protest movements in western Germany. In Chapter 10, Leonard Weinberg addresses the central question about Germany: has it shed its National Socialist past? In answering this question, he provides a comparative commentary on the role of the radical right in the domestic politics of Germany and her European neighbours. He finds that neo-fascism or neo-Nazism is no longer a German problem, but rather a source of concern outside of Germany. Berlin has so far escaped the neo-fascist blight evident elsewhere in Europe.

Part IV examines critical developments in the German party system. William M. Chandler in Chapter 11 analyses the changes that have taken place in the German party system since the move to Berlin within the larger context of the evolution of the Germany party system since 1949. Rather than focusing on the state or evolution of the individual political parties, the subsequent chapters focus on specific aspects of the German party system: the evolution in the relationship between the chancellor and the governing party; the socialisation role played by political parties in eastern Germany; and the pattern of coalition politics at the *Land* level and its implications for government at the national level. Clay Clemens in Chapter 12 examines the changing role of the Federal Chancellor and the dynamics of party support within the Bundestag. He compares Chancellor Schröder's relationship with the Social Democratic Party (SPD) with the relationships enjoyed by previous chancellors with their party, traces the policy consequences of different leadership styles, and searches for the sources of Schröder's power within the SPD. David F. Patton in Chapter 13 examines how and to what extent the Party of Democratic Socialism (PDS) has performed an integrative role in a unified Germany. He reasons that political parties in the new *Länder* not only contest elections but perform the important role of socialising the eastern Germans into the ways of western German democracy. Patton questions whether the PDS is a party of protest or disaffection with a limited future or whether it is likely to become a permanent fixture of the Berlin Republic's political landscape. Arthur B. Gunlicks in Chapter 14 provides a comprehensive view of party politics in the Berlin Republic's fifteen *Länder.* He outlines the dynamics of party competition and coalition politics towards understanding the role played by the parties at the *Länder* level, the consequences for governance in Berlin and the interdependence of *Bundestag* and *Landtage* elections.

Part V investigates the institutional and policy innovations that have animated the domestic and foreign policies of the Berlin Republic. The move to Berlin has also been accompanied by the innovation of two important German institutions: the Bundeswehr and the Bundesbank. Thomas-Durell Young in Chapter 15 examines the transition of the Bundeswehr from an institution that has been subordinated to the North Atlantic Treaty Organisation (NATO) and an American commander since 1955 to an institution that now possesses sovereign prerogatives. Moreover, the Bundeswehr has faced the difficult tasks of creating an autonomous military command, and of making the transition from a military force that was designed to defend German territory into a military force that can project power with its European Union (EU) partners or NATO allies. Karl Kaltenthaler in Chapter 16 sketches the journey made by the Bundesbank from the second most important central bank in the world to a regional bank of the European Central Bank (ECB) that enjoys at best the status of *primus inter pares.* He examines the consequences of that change in the Bundesbank's status for Germany and the management of the German economy. Chapters 17 and 18, by Michael Huelshoff and by Achim Truger and Wade Jacoby, examine the elements of change and continuity in the German economic model. Huelshoff addresses the issues underlying the *Standort Deutschland* debate, particularly the seemingly intractable problem of labour market reforms and persistent unemployment; Truger and Jacoby explicitly examine the impact of fiscal and tax policy changes on the underpinnings of *Modell Deutschland.*

Part VI of the book addresses the continuing problem of finding a role for Germany in Europe and the world. Chapter 19, by Stephen F. Szabo, is a foreign policy retrospective insofar as he reassesses the impact of German unification on the 'Problem'. His chapter questions whether the 'German Problem' is the best or even relevant starting point for understanding the future trajectory of either German foreign policy or Europe in the new century. Chapters 20, 21 and 22, by Arthur R. Rachwald, Emil J. Kirchner, and Mary N. Hampton, examine three important arenas of German foreign policy: German policy towards the East; Germany's role in the EU; and Germany's relationship within the Atlantic Community. Rachwald's chapter focuses on Polish–German relations as both a special case and emblematic of Germany's larger web of relations in central and eastern Europe. He raises and answers two questions: has Germany become a more normal actor in international politics; how would German normalcy matter to the European security order? Kirchner in Chapter 21 focuses on Germany's role in shaping the direction of the EU constitutional convention that will form the basis for the Intergovernmental Conference (IGC) that will decide the division of labour between the Union, the states and the regions as well as the distribution of power within the institutions of the EU itself. Hampton in Chapter 22 pursues the theme of identity formation within the Atlantic Community and asks whether the move to Berlin has strengthened or weakened the bond between two of the most important NATO member-states.

Peter Merkl's Chapter 23, which serves as the conclusion, treats the *Reformstau* as a three-act play, drawing a parallel between the travails of Chancellor Schröder and those of the title character in the 1999 film, *Run, Lola, Run*. Economic reform and recovery *are* the two most important tasks facing the Berlin Republic. Yet the challenges facing Germany today have forced Chancellor Schröder, metaphorically, to run faster and faster in order to avoid losing ground in the economic reform process. So far, Schröder has only been able to offer the Bundestag, in the form of Agenda 2010, what Merkl calls a 'Goldilocks' reform package – not too far to the left, not too far to the right. The fourth act in the play, the likely failure of the reform package to lift Germany out of the economic doldrums, may well see the introduction of both a new chancellor and a new coalition.

List of abbreviations

AA	Foreign Affairs Ministry
AJC	American Jewish Committee
BdL	*Bank Deutscher Länder*
BEG	*Bundesentschädigungsgesetz*
BIS	Bank for International Settlements
BMBF	Federal Ministry for Education and Science
BMVEL	Federal Ministry for Agriculture, Nutrition and Consumer Protection
BMVg	Federal Ministry of Defence
BMZ	Federal Ministry for Economic Cooperation
CAP	Common Agricultural Policy
CBC	Central Bank Council
CCJG	Central Council of Jews in Germany
CDU	Christian Democratic Party
CEE	Central and Eastern Europe
CENTAG	Central Army Group
CFE	Conventional Forces in Europe
CFM	Council of Foreign Ministers
CFSP	Common Foreign and Security Policy
CSCE	Conference on Security and Cooperation in Europe
CSU	Christian Social Union
DGB	Deutscher Gewerkschaftsbund
DM	Deutsche Mark
DP	German Party
ECB	European Central Bank
EJC	European Court of Justice

EMS	European Monetary System
EMU	European Monetary Union
EP	European Parliament
ESDP	European Security and Defence Policy
EU	European Union
FDP	Free Democratic Party
Fü H	Army Staff
Fü L	Air Force Staff
Fü M	Navy Staff
Fü S	Central Staff of the Armed Forces
FüZBw	Federal Armed Forces Operations Centre
G–7	Group of Seven
G–8	Group of Eight
GDP	Gross Domestic Product
GDR	German Democratic Republic
GSP	Growth and Stability Pact
IGC	Intergovernmental Conference
JHA	Justice and Home Affairs
KLK	Air Mobile Forces Command
KLL	Conceptual Guidelines for the Future Development of the Federal Armed Forces
KPD	Communist Party
LCB	*Landesbank*
LFA	*Länderfinanzausgleich*
NATO	North Atlantic Treaty Organisation
NGO	Non-Governmental Organisation
NOE	European New Order
NORTHAG	Northern Army Group
OdF	Victims of Fascism
OMGUS	Office of Military Government United States
PDS	Party of Democratic Socialism
PLO	Palestine Liberation Organisation
PRO	*Partei Rechsstaatliche Offensive*
QMV	Qualified Majority Voting
SED	Socialist Unity Party
SPD	Social Democratic Party
TEU	Treaty on European Union
UN	United Nations
VPR	Defence Policy Guidelines
VVN	Association of those Persecuted by the Nazi Regime

WAV	Economic Reconstruction Party
WEU	Western European Union
WUNS	World Union of National Socialists
Z	Centre Party

Introduction

rather than its concentration, would better serve the interests of individuals and society.[5] Second, the hyperinflation of the mid-1920s and depression beginning in late 1929 served as a cautionary tale about the fragility of democracy in an unstable economic environment. Third, Germany had to avoid the isolation which followed the end of the First World War and work within the framework of the peace settlement, rather than seeking to subvert it. The foreign policy of the Weimar Republic demonstrated that the maxim, *viele Feinde, viele Ehre* (many enemies, much honour), although it might well be true for a warrior, isn't particularly advisable for a great power.

The Bonn Republic learned all three lessons well. The postwar German political class was largely preoccupied with avoiding any domestic or international development that could unleash the forces that precipitated the rise of National Socialism. The demand for price stability, economic growth and full employment (in that order of preference) was embedded in the electoral calculations of citizenry and politicians alike. German foreign policy conditionally accepted and worked within the confines of the San Francisco peace settlement.[6] Germany aligned itself with the United States on issues of transatlantic security, and with France on issues pertaining to the European project. German unification and the changed international context that accompanied it raise the question of continuity and change in the domestic and foreign policies of the Berlin Republic. Thus, the query, *Bonn ist nicht Berlin?*, is not raised with alarm or a sense of disquiet. Instead, it recognises only that unification has brought about changes within the domestic political landscape and the external context of German foreign policy within and outside of Europe.

The Berlin peace settlement

The Treaty on the Final Settlement constitutes the legal framework of the Berlin peace. It consolidated the existing institutional security framework for Europe, located Germany within the European security order and provided for an interesting comparison with agreements reached at Versailles and San Francisco at the end of the First and Second World Wars, respectively. At the end of both world wars, the peace settlements were largely imposed upon Germany, with lasting complications for both Weimar and Bonn. Weimar politicians were forced to cope with the domestic myth of a *Dolchstoß* which produced Germany's defeat and recriminations over the acceptance of the war guilt clause and the reparations provisions of the Versailles Treaty. Similarly, Bonn was the product of unconditional surrender and the terms of the peace were dictated by the allies. In contrast, Germany was a full and equal partner in negotiating the post-Cold War peace settlement. Arguably, this Berlin peace settlement enjoyed a domestic legitimacy in Germany that was lacking in the case of Versailles and was grudging at best in the case of San Francisco (see table 1.1).

The legitimacy of each peace agreement may be linked to the territorial consequences of each treaty for Germany. With the conclusion of the Berlin peace agreement, Germany's size increased for the first time in the twentieth century after the end of a conflict, whereas in the case of Versailles and San Francisco, Germany was made smaller and German communities were dislocated in those territories formerly within the Reich. Just as those dislocations and sense of loss fuelled resentments and atavistic political demands that had to be attended to domestically, the Berlin settlement left Germany without any active territorial claims and with only a small number of outstanding legal disputes, notably with the Czech Republic.[7] The Berlin settlement also settled the status of German minorities (through a number of bilateral treaties) and thereby removed a potentially divisive issue from the diplomatic agenda. Germany no longer has any revisionist designs on the rest of Europe as it did after 1918 and again after 1945.

As important, these territorial changes altered Germany's geopolitical orientation and identity. Although the Versailles Treaty left that identity and orientation largely unaffected, the terms of the treaty transformed Germany into a victim with recognised grieveances. Still, Germany remained a central European power with global ambitions. The San Francisco and Berlin peace settlements, however, changed Germany's geopolitical orientation and identity. After 1949, Germany was redefined as a western European state with regional responsibilities and concerns; after 1990, Germany began the process of redefining itself as a central European power, with limited global responsibilities, just as Europe was once again subdivided into eastern, western and central Europe. Thus, the Berlin peace agreement, at least with respect to territory, provided for the first time a stable foundation for the evolution of amicable relations between Germany and her neighbours in the twentieth century.[8]

Reparations played a role at the end of the two world wars, but significant financial transfers to the Soviet Union prior to and immediately

Table 1.1 Three postwar peace settlements

	Versailles	*San Francisco*	*Berlin*
	Weimar	*Bonn*	*Berlin*
Was settlement imposed or negotiated?	Largely imposed	Imposed	Negotiated
What role did Germany play?	Supplicant	Supplicant	Full partner
Was the peace settlement viewed as legitimate or illegitimate?	Illegitimate	Largely legitimate	Fully legitimate
Did the territorial settlement:			
(a) serve as a source of future conflict?	Yes	Yes	No
(b) increase or decrease Germany's size?	Smaller	Smaller	Larger
(c) have an impact on Germany's geopolitical orientation?	Neutral: remained Central European	Change: became Western European	Change: became Central European
Was Germany an assimilated or excluded power?	Excluded	Assimilated	Assimilated
Was Germany isolated or part of alliance system?	Isolated	Part of alliance system	Part of alliance system
Was Germany defeated or victorious?	Defeated	Defeated	Victorious
Were there postwar restrictions on sovereignty?	Yes	Yes	No
Did those restrictions serve as a source of irritation/conflict?	Yes	Yes	No
Peace settlement: (dis)advantageous?	Disadvantageous	Relatively advantageous	Advantageous

after unification could be viewed as a final payment against the debt incurred for the Second World War. Reparations were a raw issue for Weimar in both the domestic and international contexts: domestically, the reparations were viewed as too burdensome and punitive; internationally, the reparations were seen as legally binding obligation assumed by the German government owing to its status as a defeated power. The initial consolidated reparations obligation for Weimar was set in January 1921 at 269 billion gold marks that was subsequently reduced to 132 billion gold marks in the spring of that year. The hyperinflation of 1923–24 required a renegotiation of Germany's reparations payments. Under the Dawes Plan (1924), the total amount of reparations was left unspecified, but included annual payments that would reach 1.75 billion marks by 1927–28. The Young Plan (1930), which superseded the Dawes Plan, specified reparations payments at around 2 billion marks annually until 1987–88. Reparations were in any event suspended in 1932 and amounted to a total payment of only 11.3 billion marks.[9] Even though the reparations made by Germany only amounted to less than 5 per cent of the original figure, it poisoned the well of Germany's relations with its European neighbours. After the Second World War, reparations were again extracted from Germany, but the dismantling and transfer of physical plant to the Soviet Union, France, Britain and others amounted to only $517 million (in 1938 dollars). That sum was offset by negotiations which forgave a significant portion of German debt as well as the European Reconstruction Programme (ERP) which enabled Germany to rebuild its stock of industrial plant.[10] German unification was accomplished without a formal reparations agreement, but large financial transfers were made to the Soviet Union in order to obtain favourable conditions in the Treaty on Final Settlement, notably unification itself and Germany's right to remain within NATO, to ensure the ratification of the Treaty in the Dumas and to accelerate the withdrawal of Soviet troops from eastern German soil.[11] In this instance, unlike the others, German 'aid' to the Soviet Union and Russian Federation, which exceeded DM 87 billion, was exchanged for a diplomatic outcome that provided a palpable benefit for Germany.

Another set of differences between Berlin, Bonn and Weimar is located in the impact the three twentieth-century peace settlements had on German sovereignty. Both Versailles and San Francisco placed specific restrictions on the exercise of German sovereignty, notably on the size of the armed forces and the categories of industry that were expressly proscribed by treaty. Versailles restricted the size of the

Reichswehr to a professional army of 100,000, the size of the Navy to 15,000, the abolition of the air force and placed a ban on the construction of tanks. Moreover, the Allied powers enjoyed the unrestricted right of inspection to ensure compliance. The Treaty of Versailles also provided for the demilitarisation of the eastern bank of the Rhine river for 50 km and the Allied occupation of its western bank for periods ranging from five to fifteen years.[12] After the Second World War, the demilitarisation of the German economy was perhaps the most pressing Allied concern.[13] Towards that objective, the Allied Control Council prohibited German production in fourteen industrial categories, restricted production in twelve industrial categories of industry and limited the general level of the economy to 55 per cent of the prewar level in 1938.[14] The Bonn Conventions of 1952 contained two annexes in a protocol that outlined restrictions on German armaments – despite the clear need for a rearmed West Germany. The first annex prohibited the German manufacture of atomic, biological and chemical weapons. The second annex, often overlooked, placed limits on the production of a large number of conventional weapons categories (long-range guided weapons, warships, bomber aircraft, tanks, etc.). These controls on conventional weapons and critical areas of the economy continued after end of the formal occupation in 1955 until 1990.[15]

The Treaty on Final Settlement removed all restrictions on German sovereignty remaining from the end of the Second World War, German adherence to the Non-Proliferation Treaty was reaffirmed and the size of the German armed forces was restricted to 370,000 individuals under arms in the Conventional Forces in Europe Treaty (CFE). The constraint on the manufacture of nuclear weapons leaves open the possession of those weapons within a politically unified EU, while the limitations placed on Germany by the CFE Treaty were neither onerous, punitive nor one-sided. Unlike Versailles and San Francisco, the Berlin peace settlement *removed* restrictions on German sovereignty and thereby eradicated a source of irritation in Germany's relations with Europe's other great powers.

Kalevi Holsti persuasively argues that the assimilation of the defeated power into the postwar political settlement is a key indicator of the system's legitimacy and longevity.[16] The Versailles agreement also differed from the San Francisco and Berlin agreements in this important respect. The Versailles agreement excluded Germany as an active participant in the postwar peace settlement. The war guilt clause, the demilitarisation and occupation of Rhineland and later the Ruhr, the reparations provision and Germany's initial exclusion from the League of Nations left Germany as an aggrieved party without a stake in the Versailles system. Moreover, Germany emerged from the First World War as a defeated power without the population being convinced that Germany was in fact defeated.

Germany emerged from the Second World War as an utterly defeated country that had surrendered unconditionally. Despite the occupation, the western zones of occupation were soon amalgamated, Germany was allowed (under Allied supervision) to write a provisional constitution (the *Grundgesetz*). The Federal Republic of Germany was soon admitted into the Council of Europe, was a founding member of the European Coal and Steel Community (ECSC) and the European Economic Community (EEC), and eventually became a member of the WEU and NATO. While the German population did not overwhelmingly admit to Germany's responsibility for the outbreak of the Second World War, there was a gradual acceptance that Germany was in fact the aggressor (from 37 per cent in 1949 to 62 per cent in 1967),[17] which no doubt facilitated Germany's readmission into the western society of states.

A unified Germany emerged from the end of the Cold War as a 'victorious' power insofar as the desired change in the postwar status quo – an end to the division of Germany – had been accomplished, although Chancellor Helmut Kohl initially balked at accepting the Oder–Neiße as the final border between Poland and Germany in deference to those Germans still hoping for the reintegration of Pomerania, Silesia and even eastern Prussia in a German state.[18] The Berlin Republic is unlike the Weimar Republic, which was systematically excluded from the Versailles system of conflict resolution, and the postwar Federal Republic, which had to demonstrate repeatedly its non-aggressive and democratic *bona fides* within the Atlantic and European institutions of security governance. The Berlin Republic has a secure place in the post-Cold War peace settlement, despite early fears of a renewed German hegemony in Europe; it is no longer a supplicant or reflexively suspect. It is slowly moving towards what can be perhaps best described as an 'abnormal normalcy'.[19]

The domestic and international economic contexts

Weimar provided a relatively simple rule of thumb for those reconstructing postwar Germany, the health and viability of democracy were positively correlated with monetary stability. The excessive debt inherited from the Second Empire, the hyper-inflation of 1923–24 that was largely caused by it, and the Great Depression were blamed in the collective memory for the rise of National Socialism and the tragedies of the Second World War, particularly the truncation and dismemberment of Germany itself. The early political leadership of the Federal Republic, preoccupied with avoiding the mistakes of the past, accepted that a necessary requirement for a stable democracy was an economy free from inflation and a parliament averse to incurring large and persistent government deficits. A combination of political determination and institutional design provided the foundation for the *Wirtschaftswunder* of the 1950s. An institutionalised aversion to inflation, guaranteed by central bank independence, was carried over into the institutional design for European Monetary Union (EMU). It also explains the subsequent German demand for a codicil to the Maastricht Treaty, in the form of the Growth and Stability Pact (GSP), which provided for sanctions levied against those governments failing to meet the Maastricht budgetary criteria after the completion of monetary union. The consequences of economic mismanagement prior to and during the Weimar Republic shaped public and official expectations of economic propriety most forcefully after 1945, but the lessons of Weimar remained central to the economic concerns of the Berlin Republic, both in terms of policy and institutional form (see table 1.2).

The political and economic leadership of Weimar, Bonn and Berlin faced quite different macroeconomic conditions, different international macroeconomic and trading regimes and quite different domestic economic challenges. Weimar faced a set of economic conditions that were highly disadvantageous and were exacerbated by the reparations burden and the underlying unwillingness of the government to live up to its reparations commitments. The Weimar Republic also began its political life with a highly disadvantageous set of macroeconomic variables in place: it inherited a national debt of Reichsmark (RM) 144,000 billion in 1919 (up from RM 5 billion in 1913); the money supply increased from RM 2 billion to RM 45 billion between 1913 and 1919.[20] Unemployment was not a pressing problem at the outset: the rate of unemployment ranged between 1.5 per cent (1922) and 3.8 per cent (1920) until the hyper-inflation of 1923–24, when the unemployment rate reached 13.5 per cent. The hyper-inflation of 1923–23 saw the price index rise to a staggering 7,765,100 (1914:100); it drove the external value of mark from RM 49,000:$1 in January

Table 1.2 The domestic and international economic contexts

	Weimar	*Bonn*	*Berlin*
Was the domestic macroeconomic context (un)favourable?	Unfavourable: high unemployment and hyperinflation	Favourable: *wirtschaftswunder* of high growth and low inflation	Unfavourable: recession/slow growth and high unemployment
Was the international economic context (un)favourable?	Mixed: boom then great depression	Favourable: uninterrupted economic growth until mid-1960s	Unfavourable: lack of economic growth in Eurozone
What were the major domestic economic challenges?	Meeting reparations obligations; hyperinflation and currency reform; unemployment and depression	Fighting imported inflation; establishing the social market economy; coping with labour shortages	Financing German unification; meeting fiscal criteria of Maastricht Treaty and Stability Pact; stubborn unemployment and anaemic economic growth

1923 to RM 4.2 billion:$1 in November 1923.[21] Only after the introduction of the *Rentenmark* in November 1923 were prices eventually stabilised, although the hyper-inflation did allow the government to repudiate its mark-denominated debt. Prior to the stock market crash of 1929 and the onset of the Great Depression, German unemployment was stuck at 8.8 per cent and reached 30.1 per cent in 1932.[22]

The fear of economic insecurity and the causal connection made by the German political elite between inflation, a global depression deepened by trade protectionism and currency blocs, high unemployment and the collapse of the Weimar democracy explains in large measure the postwar emphasis in the Federal Republic on a stable currency and the progressive liberalisation of the global trading system as central to the preservation of democracy in Germany.[23] The Bonn Republic had a good track record with respect to both inflation and employment, although the primary policy task of the *Bank deutscher Länder* (BdL, the precursor to the *Bundesbank*) was to protect the value of the Deutsche Mark (DM) after the currency reform of 1948, which was required by the Reichsmark's virtual loss of value as a means of exchange or store of value after 1945. Stable money, high rates of growth and declining

Table 1.3 Inflation in Weimar (1920–32), Bonn (1949–60) and Berlin (1991–2002)

Weimar[a]		*Bonn*[b]		*Berlin*[c]	
1920	1,065	1949	107	1991	87.10
1921	1,250	1950	100	1992	91.60
1922	5,392	1951	108	1993	95.60
1923	7,765,100	1952	110	1994	98.3
1924	128	1953	108	1995	100.0
1925	140	1954	108	1996	101.4
1926	141	1955	109	1997	103.3
1927	148	1956	113	1998	104.3
1928	152	1957	115	1999	104.9
1929	144	1958	118	2000	106.9
1930	147	1959	120	2001	109.6
1931	136	1960	120	2002	110.6
1932	121				

Notes: [a] 1914:100. Data for Weimar drawn from League of Nations, *International Statistical Year-Book* (Geneva: League of Nations, 1930), p. 241; and League of Nations, *Statistical Year-Book of the League of Nations*, 1933/34 (Geneva: League of Nations, 1934), p. 250.

[b] 1950:100. Data for Bonn drawn from Patrick Boarman, *Germany's Economic Dilemma: In Inflation and the Balance of Payments* (New Haven: Yale University Press, 1964).

[c] 1995:100. Data for Berlin drawn from Deutsche Bundesbank, *Monthly Report* (Frankfurt: Deutsche Bundesbank, various years).

unemployment all conspired to consolidate and legitimise Germany's second and ultimately successful experiment with democracy.

The Berlin Republic has not been as lucky as the Bonn Republic in its economic performance, with the notable exception of protecting the internal value of the DM and now the euro. Both the Bonn and Berlin Republics enjoyed a high level of price stability in their first decades, although Bonn experienced periods of zero inflation in the early 1950s (see table 1.3). The growth and unemployment records of the Bonn and Berlin Republics tell two different stories. The highest number of unemployed in the Bonn Republic (1.230 million in 1949) was 47 per cent of the lowest number of unemployed in the Berlin Republic (2.616 million in 1991); the lowest number of unemployed in the Berlin Republic was not exceeded in the Weimar period

Figure 1.1 Unemployment in Weimar, Bonn and Berlin

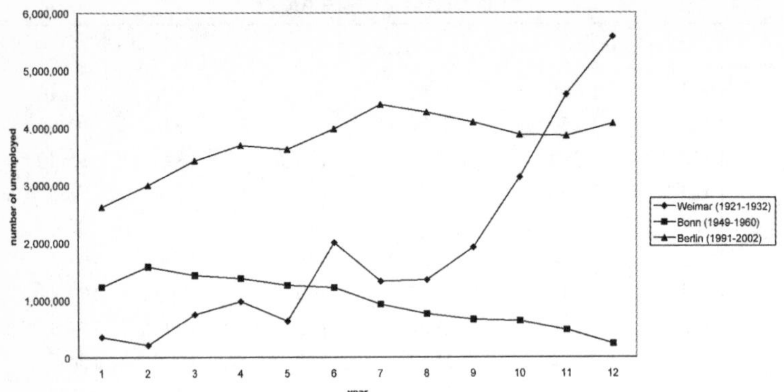

Source: *League of Nations, International Statistical Year-Book* (Geneva: League of Nations, 1930); League of Nations, *Statistical Year-Book of the League of Nations, 1933/34* (Geneva: League of Nations, 1934); IMF, *International Financial Statistics* (Washington, DC: IMF, various years); and Deutsche Bundesbank, *Monthly Report* (Frankfurt: Deutsche Bundesbank, various years).

until 1930 (see figure 1.1). Moreover, the number of unemployed steadily declined over the course of the 1950s until the number of unemployed in 1960 was only 237,000 (a number which continued to decline into the early 1960s). Likewise, there has been a more or less steady rise in the number of unemployed in unified Germany: in 2002, the number unemployed reached a staggering 4.071 million – a figure almost equal to the number of unemployed in 1931. The unemployment rate in the Bonn Republic declined from an early post-war high of 10.2 per cent (1950) to a low of 1.2 per cent (1960), while the unemployment rate reached 7.3 per cent in 1990, peaked at 11.5 per cent in 1997 and has remained stuck between 9 and 10 per cent since that time (see figure 1.2).

A comparison of the macroeconomic and fiscal performance of the Bonn and Berlin Republics also works to the latter's disadvantage: the rapid and continuous growth of the 1950s has been matched by the anaemic and sometimes negative growth of the 1990s and 2000s (see table 1.4). Total government debt as a share of GDP never rose above 1.5 per cent between 1949 and 1960, while that same ratio had risen from 21 per cent in 1991 to over 60 per cent by the end of the 1990s (see table 1.5); the budgetary balance of the Bonn Republic in its first

Figure 1.2 Unemployment rate in Weimar, Bonn and Berlin

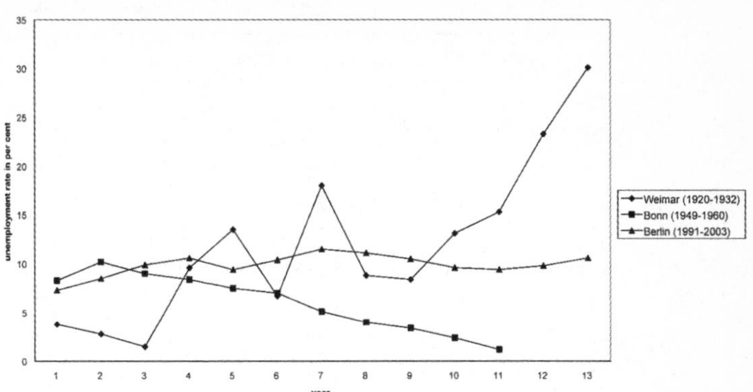

Source: League of Nations, *International Statistical Year-Book* (Geneva: League of Nations, 1930); League of Nations, *Statistical Year-Book of the League of Nations*, 1933/34 (Geneva: League of Nations, 1934) IMF, *International Financial Statistics* (Washington, DC: IMF, various years); and Deutsche Bundesbank, *Monthly Report* (Frankfurt: Bundesbank, various years).

decade ranged from a deficit of 2.16 per cent of GDP (1959) to a surplus of 1.04 per cent of GDP (1953), while the budgetary balance of the Berlin Republic has ranged from a surplus of 1.1 per cent of GDP in 2000 and multi-year deficits of over 3.0 per cent of GDP (see table 1.6). The current difficulties of the Berlin Republic have been attributed to market-distorting tax policies and rigid labour practices that have discouraged job creation and encouraged outward investment, but can also be traced to the consequences of the transition from the DM to the euro. Today, the euro is managed by an ECB servicing the macroeconomic requirements of the Eurozone, which are not coincidental with the needs of a German economy mired in slow growth and unemployment.

As important, the immediate economic challenges of the Bonn and Berlin Republics differ substantially. The postwar German political elite faced the relatively difficult problems of effecting monetary reform to lend confidence to German entrepreneurs, the banking sector, savers and consumers, and of creating a social market economy which would lend legitimacy to a market-based economy without violating the German social democratic and Catholic traditions. It also enjoyed a robust and progressively liberalised Atlantic and European economy, which by providing an outlet for German goods spurred economic

Table 1.4 GDP growth rate (%) in Bonn (1949–60) and Berlin (1991–2003)

Bonn[a]		*Berlin*[b]	
1949	–	1991	–
1950	12.5	1992	2.2
1951	26.4	1993	–1.2
1952	11.0	1994	2.9
1953	6.6	1995	3.9
1954	8.2	1996	0.8
1955	14.0	1997	1.5
1956	9.2	1998	2.2
1957	8.8	1999	1.8
1958	6.9	2000	0.2
1959	9.3	2001	0.6
1960	10.5	2002	2.9
		2003	nil

Notes: [a] Source: International Monetary Fund, *International Financial Statistics* (Washington, DC: IMF, various years).
[b] Sources: for 1991–2002, Deutsche Bundesbank, *Monthly Report* (Frankfurt: Deutsche Bundesbank, various years); 2003 forecast, *Economist*, 30 August – 5 September 2003, p. 72.

growth and progressively reduced the number of unemployed. The economic management challenge in the wake of the Korean War economic boom was meeting the danger posed to monetary stability by imported inflation, the very phenomenon fuelling Germany's postwar economic growth and exports.[24]

The *Wirtschaftswunder* of the 1950s gave way to the *Wirtschaft ohne Wunder* in post-unification Germany. Despite a global economic boom in the second half of the 1990s, German governments faced slow economic growth and unemployment attributed to structural rigidities in the economy. These structural rigidities were compounded by the mistakes of unification, particularly the rise in eastern German wages by government fiat and the undeserved purchasing power lent eastern Germans owing to the favourable rate of exchange between the west and east German marks. Moreover, the Kohl government assumed that the *Fonds Deutscher Einheit*, capitalised at DM 100 billion, would cover

Table 1.5 Total government debt as share of GDP (%) in Bonn (1949–60) and Berlin (1991–2002)

Bonn[a]		*Berlin*[b]	
1949	0.30	1991	23.8
1950	1.29	1992	27.5
1951	1.13	1993	48.0
1952	0.98	1994	50.2
1953	1.09	1995	58.0
1954	1.06	1996	60.4
1955	0.59	1997	61.1
1956	0.05	1998	61.5
1957	0.18	1999	61.2
1958	0.29	2000	60.2
1959	1.09	2001	59.5
1960	1.43	2002	–

Notes: [a] Source: IMF, *International Financial Statistics* (IMF: Washington, DC: various years).
[b] Source: Deutsche Bundesbank, *Monthly Report* (Frankfurt: Deutsche Bundesbank, various years).

the cost of unification. Instead, the costs of unification amounted to almost DM 100 billion per annum with a resulting sharp rise in the indebtedness of the German government. That unanticipated indebtedness has subsequently constrained the German government's ability to meet the challenges of slow economic growth and unemployment owing to the budgetary criteria of the Maastricht Treaty and the GSP. The fiscal straightjacket of the GSP may mean that the labour market reforms put forward by Chancellor Gerhard Schröder in his Agenda 2010 may be too little, too late. Berlin now faces a less promising domestic and international context than that which faced Bonn, particularly after the reconstruction process was well under way in the mid-1950s. Nonetheless, the Germany of 2004 is still a better place to live than the Germany of 1954. Both Bonn and Berlin, unlike Weimar, faced a domestic and international economic environment that was conducive to political stability.

Table 1.6 Central government fiscal balance, surfeit/deficit (+/-%), in Bonn (1950–59) and Berlin (1991–2003)

Bonn[a]		*Berlin*[b]	
1950	–1.06	1991	–3.3
1951	–0.59	1992	–2.8
1952	0.25	1993	–3.5
1953	1.04	1994	–2.6
1954	0.76	1995	–3.5
1955	1.10	1996	–3.5
1956	0.58	1997	–2.7
1957	–1.14	1998	–2.0
1958	–0.21	1999	–1.5
1959	–2.16	2000	1.1
		2001	–2.8
		2002	–3.8
		2003	–3.7

Notes: [a] Source: IMF, *International Financial Statistics* (IMF: Washington, DC: various years); author's calculations.
[b] Source: Deutsche Bundesbank, *Monthly Report* (Frankfurt: Deutsche Bundesbank, various years).

The domestic political context

The domestic political contexts of Weimar, Bonn and Berlin reveals the greatest degree of diversity among the three republics. Four aspects of the domestic political context are particularly relevant: the domestic and international origins of regime change; the breadth and depth of each republic's legitimacy; the sources and content of the national identity; and the nature and dynamics of the party system (see table 1.7).

Origins

The origins of the Weimar and Bonn Republics were similar in many respects. Both were the product of defeat, although in the case of Weimar the armistice left unresolved and ambiguous Wilhelmine Germany's position in the hierarchy of power in Europe. The contested nature of Germany's actual performance during the war and the circumstances contributing to the emergence of France, Britain and the United States as 'victors' festered and subsequently poisoned domestic political debates and thereby deepened the polarisation of an already polarised German society. In contrast, the defeat of the Nazi regime was unambiguous and unconditional. A relatively enlightened Allied occupation and the shame of Nazi war crimes not only delegitimised the radical right (and the left) as respectable and responsible political actors, but attenuated the domestic political debate over the war. The end of the Cold War, and the important role the Federal Republic played in the Atlantic security system, allowed the Berlin Republic not only to emerge from its conclusion as a victorious power, but as a country with its sovereignty fully and irrevocably restored.

The end of each war endowed the successor regime with a legacy: Weimar had to cope with the failure of the Kaiserreich, the *Dolchstoß* legend that attributed Germany's defeat on the Western front to domestic perfidy and the prospect of civil war owing to the miscarried German revolution of 1918–20.[25] The Nazi regime's legacy for Bonn was both positive and negative: it was positive insofar as the Nazi regime could not be looked upon nostalgically by the political elite as an alternative model of governance; it was negative insofar as it robbed the German political classes of any self-confidence it might have had in the sustainability of German democracy in difficult times.

The origins of the constitutional order also differed for Weimar, Bonn and Berlin. The Weimar constitution was indigenous in conception and execution, but it was also a response to President Woodrow Wilson's 'demand for the formation of a democratically legitimated government'.[26] The Bonn constitution was also subject to a set of Allied conditions. The Allies informed the Parliamentary Council, the body responsible for drafting the postwar constitution, that it should have the following features: a federal system with a bicameral legislature, a prescription of the powers held by the executive and any emergency powers would be subject to judicial review, an explicit separation of policy competencies powers between the central and *Land* governments and an independent judiciary with the right of judicial review.[27] The conditionality of the *Grundgesetz* was transformed into a permanency when the decision was made to forgo the calling of a constitutional convention after the Treaty on Final Settlement. While amendments were made to the *Grundgesetz* in order to accommodate unification, the constitution had clearly earned the legitimacy that was conditional in the early years of the Federal Republic. As important, the growing

Table 1.7 The domestic political context

	Weimar	*Bonn*	*Berlin*
System			
(a) *Origins*			
Was the political system the product of defeat or victory?	A contested defeat, revolution and partial occupation	Defeated and occupied	Victory and end of occupation
Was the preceding regime bankrupt or legitimate?	Second Empire discredited by defeat	Nazi regime was bankrupt	Bonn was fully legitimate
Was the constitutional order imposed or indigenous?	Indigenous, but conformed to allied requirements for democratic government	Framework of debate set by Allies	Indigenous
What was the legacy of the previous regime?	The Kaiserreich and the *Dolchstoß* legend	Nazi regime's barbarism; unconditional surrender; and a *Staat aus dem Nichts*	A democratically stable and legitimate Bonn Republic
(b) *Affect*			
Were the political classes *Staatsfremd?*	Yes	No	No
Was there significant opposition to the constitutional order?	Yes	SPD opposed to aspects of order until 1959	No
(c) *Political extremism*			
Was the political system polarised?	Yes: there was both a radical left and an arch-conservative right	No, but sporadic recurrence of radical right	No
Identity			
Was there a preexisting democratic identity?	No	No, but evolved over time	Yes, firmly established

What form did national self-definition take?	German and national	Search for alternative to national identity; eventually settled on a 'Europeanised' and democratic identity	'Europeanised' and democratic identity intact, but partial renationalisation
Party system			
Were the political parties extreme or catch-all parties?	Extreme and ideological; fragile coalitions	Catch-all and centrist coalitions	Catch-all, but a centre-left divide emerging
Was the party system resilient?	No	Yes, but doubts remained (1982)	Yes (1998 election)
Did the major parties accept the constitutional rules of game?	No	Yes, but provisionally	Yes
What was the nature of the party system?	Multi-party system	'Two-and-a-half' party system	Weak multi-party system
What was the nature of political competition?	Extremes against the middle	Competition to capture the centre	Left-centre/right-centre split

intersection and overlapping of EU, *Land* and Federal competencies led to a proposal for a constitutional commission charged with the task of redefining the nature of German federalism in order to cope with the expanded policy competencies and constitutional consolidation of the EU.[28] The eventual outcome of constitutional reform in Germany, should it occur, will be decided by the Germans themselves without outside interference, let alone an Allied *diktat* as in the cases of both Weimar and Bonn.

Affect and legitimacy

Each Republic has possessed a progressively deeper and broader legitimacy than its predecessor. A considerable portion of the Weimar political class was possessed of a '*Staatsfeindlichkeit*' (hostility to the State); the Republic suffered a contested legitimacy from both the left and the right.[29] On the right, there remained a significant minority of the population that considered the Republic to be 'anti-national' owing to its origins in defeat and preferred a continuation of a monarchy, even though Kaiser Wilhelm's regime was discredited by the war. On the left, the constitutional character of the Weimar Republic fell far short of the preferred socialist regime. As Allemann notes, Weimar was a 'republic of defeat' that had to cope with the internal and external legacy of the Reich, while Bonn instead enjoyed its status as a *Staat aus dem Nichts* (a state out of nothingness).[30] The bankruptcy of the National Socialist regime (and the failure of Weimar which made that regime possible) confronted Bonn with two equally unacceptable and failed pasts, which led to the acceptance of Bonn 'as a necessary evil'.[31] Yet Bonn was not unconditionally accepted: a sizeable minority of the population in the late 1940s and early 1950s still preferred the experience of national socialism to the experience of Weimar democracy.[32] Berlin, in contrast, was able to borrow and build upon the Bonn Republic's legitimacy in order to facilitate the democratisation of a unified Germany without the same fear of failure or the spectre of political extremism.

The problem of identity

There are two questions central to the definition of German identity. Is the German identity democratic or authoritarian? How 'German' is the German national identity? The definition of German identity during the interwar period is relatively unproblematic. Weimar did not enjoy or develop a particularly explicit democratic identity; Germans and the German political classes lacked a democratic tradition to draw upon. The constitutional position of the Weimar president went well beyond that of an '*Ersatzkaiser*' (substitute Kaiser); the constitution itself was a 'product of an authoritarian frame of mind'; and it 'remained committed to the primacy of the state (*Primat der Staatsräson*) and … denied the unity of state and society'.[33] A postwar democratic identity was purposefully created within the context of the Atlantic alliance. Since the German past was unusable as a source of identity formation, and in order to overcome the negative collective memories of Germany's past, American, British and West German policy makers cooperated in forging a new German national identity that was liberal democratic, irrevocably tied to the West and anti-Communist.[34] The democratic identity of Berlin is firmly established and embodies the genuine transformation of the postwar German political culture. When that identity is questioned, it merely reflects a lingering uncertainty about the long-term consequences of unification on German political culture. The absorbed eastern Germans (the 'Ossi') emerged from a political culture that was authoritarian at best from 1945 to 1989 and totalitarian from 1933 until the Second World War's end. While there is a noticeable gap between the understanding of democracy in the eastern and western portions of Germany as well as their assessment of the current form of German democracy, there is little reason to doubt that the political culture of the Berlin Republic is irrevocably democratic.[35]

Weimar Germans, despite the cosmopolitanism of 1920s Berlin, were possessed of a German national identity which was both national and unremarkable. The notion of a German national identity was contested only in the postwar period, when the idea of 'Germanness' was bankrupted by the behaviour and consequences of the National Socialist regime. Postwar Germans, while they retained a nominal understanding of themselves as 'German' also tried to fashion an alternative, untainted identity as Europeans. Some argue that there has been a thorough 'Europeanisation' of Germany and a conflation of the German national identity with a European identity.[36] This partial displacement of a national identity is most clearly manifested in the German dedication to European integration and the progressive willingness of individual Germans to define themselves as 'European' rather than as 'German'.

But the 'Europeanisation' of the German identity is being tested by a creeping renationalisation of the German identity (or perhaps the emergence of a national identity instrumentally suppressed prior to unification). In any event, national identities are not fixed, but are sticky. The transparent renationalisation of the German identity has progressed in parallel with persistent western ('Wessi') and eastern ('Ossi') identities that have not evaporated with the passage of time. A majority of West Germans believed that an alienation (*Entfremdung*) had emerged between the two Germanys in the mid-1960s, but many anticipated in the early 1990s that the eastern Germans would embrace and be readily assimilated into the western social, economic and political systems.[37] Instead, the divide between eastern and western Germans has persisted. This regional identity is of a different order than the north–south identities in western Germany; it is intensified by a palpable socio-economic inequality, a dissimilar political socialisation process and a muted Protestant–Catholic antagonism. This 'new' regionalism has added yet another layer to an alluvial German identity.

Party system

The precise correlation between the number of parties represented in a parliament and the stability of coalition cabinets is contested. It has been the conventional wisdom that two-party systems are stabler than multi-party systems; that single-party parliamentary coalitions are longer-lived than are multi-party coalitions; that catch-all parties better integrate society than do ideological parties; and that ideological extremism can lead to policy stasis and persistent constitutional crises.[38] The party systems found in Weimar and Bonn represent the two extremes in Germany's democratic experience.

The social and political cleavages in Weimar Germany produced a multi-party system. There were upwards of seven effective parties in the Reichstag and three of those parties were hostile to the Weimar constitution (the German Communist Party (DKP), German National People's Party (DNVP) and National Socialist German Workers' Party (NSDAP)).[39] Narrow parliamentary coalitions were challenged by extremist parties – on the left (DKP) and the right (DNVP and NSDAP) – that were not considered to be viable coalition partners by the centre. Cooperation between the extreme left and right was limited to their joint effort to force through votes of no confidence in order to bring down the existing government and erode the legitimacy of democratic governance. More problematically, the government lacked alternative partners in the Reichstag in the event of a disagreement between the coalition parties. The political parties contesting elections in Weimar were highly ideological and eschewed the electoral strategies of a catch-all party (no party received over 30 per cent of the vote until 1932). As a consequence of these factors, the centrist governing coalitions were relatively unstable (there were seven elections between 1920 and 1932). The deepening polarisation of politics in Weimar, the weakening of the centre and the eventual inability to form a sustainable governing coalition comprising parties supporting the Weimar constitution provided the conditions allowing the NSDAP to seize power. The collapse of Weimar democracy after the November 1932 election cannot be solely attributed to the large number of effective parties contesting parliamentary elections or occupying seats in the Reichstag. Rather, the collapse was caused in large part by the unwillingness of the parties on the far left and radical right to accept the constitutional order itself.

The Bonn Republic was blessed with a combination of ideological fatigue and constitutional law. The political party system in Bonn was dubbed a 'two-and-one-half' party system owing to the predominance of the SPD and the CDU/CSU with the relatively narrow centre occupied by the FDP. The complicated d'Hondt system of proportional representation limited the number of parties that could successfully contest an election; the *Grundgesetz* provided for the banning of parties hostile to German democracy. After the 1949 election, the number of effective parties contesting elections in Germany ranged from 2.18 in 1987 to 2.78 in 1953. The mean number of effective parties was 2.54; Bonn would appear to have had a 'two-and-one-half' party system. Both the CDU/CSU and the SPD (particularly after the Godesberg Programme of 1959) pursued the strategy of a catch-all party; politics was largely fought over a narrow range of economic and social issues. Political extremism was either legally proscribed (in the case of radical nationalists on the right) or lacked a significant constituency (the remnants of the DKP). Unlike Weimar, Bonn had elections on a four-year cycle as prescribed by the constitution, with the one exception of the 1983 election which was called after the successful vote of no confidence against the SPD/FDP government in October 1982. The party composition of the coalitions remained unchanged during these four year electoral cycles, but the FDP was considered a suitable coalition partner for either the right-of-centre CDU/CSU or the left-of-centre SPD. More remarkably, the SPD and the CDU/CSU formed a 'Grand Coalition' in 1966 to cope better with the deepest recession in postwar German history up to that time.

The party system in Berlin has retained all the virtues of the party system found in Bonn: the parties accept the constitutional order, there is a virtual absence of political extremism and the election of 1998 (the transfer of power from a right-of-centre to a left-of-centre coalition) demonstrated the continuing resiliency of German parliamentary democracy. The party system itself lies somewhere between Bonn and Weimar. The SPD and CDU/CSU remain catch-all parties. But the number of effective parties vying for power in the Bundestag now hovers between 2.8 (2002) and 2.9 (1994). The Berlin Republic's evolution towards a multi-party system has had an asymmetrical impact on the two major parties: the SPD has benefited owing to an increased range of coalition partners. The Greens/*Bündnis '90* and the FDP remain boutique political parties with a fairly narrow and volatile political base, but have together captured between 13 and 16 per cent of the vote in the three most recent elections (1994, 1998 and 2002). While the SPD views both of these parties as potential coalition partners, only the FDP is a realistic coalition partner for the CDU/CSU. Consequently, the SPD has a greater number of options as well as greater leverage with its junior coalition partner. Were the PDS to mature into a regional party of the left capable of capturing 5 per cent of the national vote, it too could eventually be viewed as a viable coalition partner for the SPD, but would also create the prospect for creating a permanent coalition of the left (PDS/Greens/SPD) vying with a permanent coalition of the centre-right (CDU/CSU–FDP) for control of the Bundestag. While such a development would make Germany more like her neighbours, it would disrupt the pattern of electoral politics and parliamentary compromise that served the Bonn Republic fairly well.

Foreign policy: what role for Germany?

Foreign policy has been central to the internal evolution of Weimar, Bonn and Berlin. The resentments and embitterments attending the Versailles peace treaty, manifested in continuing restrictions on German sovereignty, recurrent reparations crises and the occupation of the Rhineland and Ruhr, not only provided the grist for the rise of radical right-wing nationalist parties, but also fostered a revisionist foreign policy agenda embraced across the political spectrum. Likewise the foreign policy choices made by the Bonn Republic, particularly Adenauer's decision to bind the Federal Republic to the West, 'ultimately determine[d] the content and direction of the internal social order'.[40] West Germany's transformation into a liberal democratic and capitalist state positioned on the geopolitical periphery of the West sealed Germany's postwar division and truncation, but provided it with a kind of security and stability Germany had not yet enjoyed in the twentieth century. The foreign policy of the Berlin Republic currently remains in a process of redefinition. While the restitution of sovereignty has expanded the range of foreign policy choice, Germany remains nonetheless constrained by the foreign policy legacy of Bonn, particularly its membership in NATO and the EU (see table 1.8).

Weimar and Bonn were similar insofar as they were both revisionist powers. Weimar's foreign policy was directed towards invalidating the punitive provisions of the Versailles Treaty. Weimar sought to reestablish Germany's role as a great European power, which required an unencumbered rearmament, an acknowledged equality with the other European great powers, particularly the right to membership in

Table 1.8 Foreign policy

	Weimar	*Bonn*	*Berlin*
Foreign policy goals (revisionist or status quo?)	Revisionist (invalidate punitive provisions of Versailles)	Revisionist (regain legitimacy and unification)	Status quo (further European political unification; stabilise Europe politically and economically)
Primary foreign policy challenge	Equality with victorious Allied powers; reclaim position within Europe	Equality, legitimacy, and unification	Stability in central and eastern Europe; complete process of European unification
Role conception	Deprived great power	Economic giant, political dwarf; loyal transatlantic partner and dedicated European partner	European and civilian power; conditional transatlantic partner
Formal alliance	No	Yes, but compulsory membership (*Zwangsallianz*)	Yes, but voluntary
External threats	French, British and Soviet antipathy	Cold War	No traditional military threats; surrounded by friendly states

the League of Nations, and an end the occupation of the Rhineland and Ruhr. Bonn sought legitimacy and equality with the Allied powers, the right to rearm and the eventual unification of Germany, if not the reacquisition of eastern territories lost during the war. Prior to the war against Iraq, Berlin appeared to be following a qualified status quo foreign policy agenda: a deepening of European political integration, the stabilisation of central and eastern Europe and the consolidation of the NATO-sponsored security order. Germany's recent diplomatic alignment with France and Russia against the United States may well signal a change in foreign policy orientation or it may well signal nothing more than a deep disagreement about the nature of the problem presented by Saddam Hussein.

The role conception defining the foreign policies of Weimar, Bonn and Berlin provides a window for understanding the foreign policy trajectory of each republic. Role conception has two aspects: first, identity is partially derived from the role a state assumes in its foreign policy; second, roles define how actors become identified with each other. States are assumed to possess and to be assigned specific roles.[41] The Bonn Republic adopted and was largely assigned the roles of 'good European' and 'good Atlanticist'. Moreover, the progressive accretion of power over the course of the postwar period, as well as the presumed inability to wield that power baldly, led to the internal and external acceptance that Germany was an 'economic giant, but political dwarf'. The Weimar Republic saw itself as a unjustly deprived great power that was both excluded from the League of Nations and surrounded by states that were potential aggressors, particularly France and Russia. The Berlin Republic appears to have embraced the roles of a European and 'civilian' power, while remaining a conditionally loyal transatlantic partner of the United States.[42] Unlike Weimar, however, German military capabilities are seen as contributing to pan-European security and as safely embedded in NATO; unlike Bonn, German economic power has been largely muted by its participation in European monetary union.

Military power remains the *ultima ratio* of international politics. An effort was made under the Versailles Treaty to emasculate Germany militarily, primarily but not exclusively at the behest of France and in the service of French security interests. That effort failed and at the end of the Second World War the Allies agreed again to demilitarise Germany; the exigencies of the Cold War then forced a German rearmament in order to balance conventional power between the Warsaw Pact and NATO alliance. The postwar rearmament of Germany, however, took place within a formal alliance system in which Germany was not quite equal: the categories of armaments Germany could possess or manufacture were scrutinised by the allies within the framework of the WEU; only the German armed forces were responsible to a NATO commander rather than to a national general staff. The Berlin Republic remains embedded in NATO, although it now possesses the functional equivalent of a national general staff. Restrictions on the production or possession of conventional armaments are no longer in force. The crucial difference between Bonn and Berlin with respect to NATO, however, is that NATO is no longer a compulsory alliance (*Zwangsallianz*), but one in which Germany is a full, equal and voluntary partner.

The international environment offers the most significant category of difference for understanding the foreign policies of Weimar, Bonn and Berlin. As should be clear, in the immediate aftermath of the First World War the major European powers exhibited a corrosive antipathy towards the Weimar Republic that abated only with the Locarno Treaty (1925) and a ephemeral end to Franco-German enmity. Despite the sporadic multilateralism over the reparations issue, Europe's interstate relations remained largely bilateral and lacked an institutional basis critical to sustained cooperation in international affairs.[43] One lesson of Stresemann's foreign policy – cooperation with France was more profitable than a policy seeking to isolate her – was carried over into postwar foreign policy of the Bonn Republic.[44] The government of Chancellor Konrad Adenauer embraced a policy of Franco-German reconciliation that led to the founding of the ECSC as well as the EEC. Moreover, the Adenauer government prevented the military and diplomatic isolation of the interwar period by firmly aligning Germany with the United States. The decision to embrace both France and the United States, while it required an adroit diplomacy, prevented Germany's isolation and left only the Soviet Union as a putative military threat. Berlin has the luxury of (relatively) frictionless relations with her neighbours enmeshed in a dense web of institutions. For the first time since German unification in 1871, Germany not only has no immediate enemies, but faces no conventional military threat. That very absence of threat has complicated Germany's diplomacy with its erstwhile sponsor, the United States.

The 1998 German parliamentary election and the 2000 presidential election in the United States left both countries with a leadership less compatible with one another than any time since the rocky relationship between Chancellor Helmut Schmidt and Presidents Carter and Reagan in the late 1970s and early 1980s. The antipathy between Chancellor Gerhard Schröder and President George W. Bush was sealed during the 2002 parliamentary election when Schröder, out of conviction or electoral necessity, waged a campaign that took direct aim at the Bush administration's policy towards Iraq that culminated in the German Chancellor promising that even *with* a UN mandate, Germany would not join an American-led coalition to effect regime change in Iraq. This electoral gambit (if that indeed is all that it was) and the subsequent American pique largely eliminated any prospect for German-American cooperation on this issue, led the Germans (along with the Belgians and French) to veto the American request in the North

Atlantic Council to provide military assistance to Turkey in the run-up to the war in Iraq and left Germany aligned with France and the Russian Federation on the UN Security Council. It is difficult to know whether this crisis in German-American relations simply reflects a mismatch of personalities or is evidence of a growing divergence in German and American interests outside (and increasingly inside) Europe. What remains, however, is that the end of the Cold War provided the Berlin Republic with a greater degree of freedom in international affairs than that enjoyed by either Weimar or Bonn. Germany *is* drawn to both France and Russia as preferred partners in realising its foreign policy ambitions for Europe. But unlike the unsuccessful foreign policy of Weimar, the Berlin Republic is interested in consolidating the existing economic and security frameworks, rather than displacing them. Nonetheless, Germany's current Franco-Russian attraction may prove a fatal one if it pushes the United States out of Europe.

Conclusion

The Berlin Republic emerged in the most favourable external context than any other German state in the twentieth century and perhaps before. Just as the Versailles and San Francisco peace settlements placed German territorial claims on the diplomatic agenda, the Berlin peace settlement resolved the question of Germany's boundaries that had been open since 1871. The absence of restraints on German sovereignty, the full assimilation of Germany into the international system and its role as an author, rather than object, of the post-Cold War settlement also distinguishes Berlin from its two democratic predecessors.

Berlin has not been as lucky in its economic performance. While the 1950s and 1960s were periods of virtually continuous expansion, Berlin has not been able to do any better than very low rates of growth and has had live with the persistent threat of recession. The Berlin Republic, unlike Bonn, has been unable to stimulate growth or drive down unemployment. This failure can be attributed in part to an important institutional change – Germany can no longer conduct a monetary policy servicing the needs of the German macroeconomy – and in part to the German social welfare system and restrictive labour practices. The postwar consensus on the importance of inflation has not broken down; the causal connection between economic stability and the viability of democracy remains intact. Yet, the Berlin Republic does not face the disadvantages or dangers faced by Weimar, even though the lessons of Weimar remain embedded in the political calculations of the electorate and the elected.

Bonn left Berlin a generous domestic political legacy. The Berlin democracy (like its predecessor) enjoys a legitimacy that is both wide and deep. Political extremism, particularly in the form of parties that are anti-constitutional, is sporadic, largely limited to the radical right and inconsequential. While the Berlin Republic cannot be described as a politically polarised society, there remains the problem of integrating eastern Germans into the preexisting western German political and economic systems. This east–west divide has nurtured an alternative definition of identity which is 'German'. This development runs counter to the postwar construction of a 'Europeanised' identity that was designed to displace a suspect German national identity. While Berlin remains committed to the European 'ideal', there has been a partial renationalisation of government rhetoric. This development makes Berlin much less like Bonn, but the substance of policy has nonetheless remained fairly constant. One change that could upset the domestic balance and change the nature of German democracy is the transformation of the postwar 'two-and-a-half' party system into a post-Cold War multi-party system. This development has so far advantaged the SPD (in terms of potential coalition partners), but it may also create permanent coalitions along a left-centre/right-centre split with unknown consequences for German democracy and governability.

The foreign policy goals of the Berlin Republic are oriented towards the status quo. Both Weimar and Bonn actively pursued a revisionist agenda. Bonn's foreign policy ambitions were conditioned by a willingness to work within the San Francisco peace settlement, while Weimar's foreign policy ambitions were directed towards a fundamental revision of the Treaty of Versailles. Both Bonn and Weimar had territorial claims. Berlin does not. Instead, Berlin has adopted a policy which is aimed primarily at the milieu goals of solidifying European integration, stabilising eastern and southern Europe politically and economically, sustaining its relationship with France and the United States and drawing the Russian Federation into a constructive partnership. These foreign policy goals are not frictionless, as the recent rift between the United States and Germany testifies. The balancing of German interests with those of France, Russia and the United States has so far proven as difficult a task for Joschka Fischer as it was for his predecessors during the Cold War. There are two crucial differences, however: Germany is surrounded by friendly states and does not face imminent or latent military threat; and Germany enjoys a greater degree of freedom in the foreign policy options that can be considered. It is difficult to say whether these changes will allow Germany to pursue an even more constructive foreign policy in Europe or will lead Germany to make the same sorts of miscalculations that were made during the first half of the twentieth century.

There is little doubt that Germany is presently experiencing changes domestically and facing novel foreign policy challenges. It is the case that the historical experience of Bonn and Weimar have produced valid lessons for Berlin; it is also likely that some of the lessons carried over from Weimar have outlived their usefulness (for both Germany and her neighbours). German democracy should be treated as a given. German foreign policy will likely continue along the trajectory set for it in the early postwar period. Berlin is not Bonn. It's better.

Notes

1 Fritz René Allemann, *Bonn ist nicht Weimar* (Köln: Kiepenheuer & Witsch, 1956), p. 9.

2 Michael Kreile, 'Der Wandel des internationalen Systems und der Faktor "Macht" in der deutschen Europapolitik', in Heinrich Schneider, Mathias Jopp and Uwe Schmalz (eds), *Eine neue Deutsche Europapolitik? Rahmenbedingungen – Problemfelder – Optionen* (Bonn: Europa Union Verlag, 2001), p. 136; Mathias Jopp, 'Deutsche Europapolitik unter veränderten Rahmenbedingungen: Bilanz – Strategien – Optionen', in Heinrich Schneider, Mathias Jopp and Uwe Schmalz (eds), *Eine neue Deutsche Europapolitik? Rahmenbedingungen – Problemfelder – Optionen* (Bonn: Europa Union Verlag, 2001), p. 816; Lothar Rühl, 'Security Policy: National Structures and Multilateral Integration', in Wolf-Dieter Eberwein and Karl Kaiser (eds), *Germany's New Foreign Policy: Decision-Making in an Interdependent World* (New York: Palgrave, 2001), pp. 102–3; and Simon Bulmer, Charlie Jeffery and William E. Paterson, *Germany's European Diplomacy: Shaping the Regional Milieu* (Manchester: Manchester University Press, 2000), p. 3.

3 See Friedrich Meinecke, *Die deutsche Katastrophe: Betrachtungen und Errinerungen* (Wiesbaden: E. Brockhaus, 1949).

4 See Jochen Vogt, 'The Weimar Republic as the "Heritage of our Time"', in Thomas W. Kniesche and Stephen Brockmann (eds), *Dancing on the Volcano: Essays on the Culture of the Weimar Republic* (Columbia, SC: Camden House, 1994), pp. 21–8.

5 On the diffusion of power within Germany, see Bulmer, Jeffery and Paterson, *Germany's European Diplomacy.*

6 The postwar order is characterised as the San Francisco peace settlement in Kalevi J. Holsti, *Peace and War: Armed Conflicts and International Order, 1648–1989* (Cambridge: Cambridge University Press, 1991).

7 See Ann L. Phillips, *Power and Influence after the Cold War: Germany in East-Central Europe* (Lanham, MD: Rowman & Littlefield, 2000).

8 This development took place against the backdrop of three successive EU treaties (Maastricht (1992), Amsterdam (1997) and Nice (2001)) that cleared the way for deeper political and economic integration as well as the EU's eastward enlargement.

9 Detlev J. K. Peukert, *The Weimar Republic: The Crisis of Classical Modernity*, trans. by Richard Deveson (New York: Hill & Wang, 1989), pp. 196–7 and Hans Mommsen, *The Rise and Fall of Weimar Democracy*, trans. by Elborg Forster and Larry Eugene Jones (Chapel Hill: North Carolina University Press, 1996), p. 273.

10 The figures for reparations in the postwar period are found in Richard L. Merritt, *Democracy Imposed: US Occupation Policy and the German Public, 1945–49* (New Haven: Yale University Press, 1995), p. 360. On dismantling of German industrial plant, see John Gimbel, *The American Occupation of Germany: Politics and the Military, 1945–1949* (Stanford: Stanford University Press, 1968), pp. 174–85. For a brief outline of the postwar reparations agreements, see Beate Ruhm von Oppen, *Documents on Germany under Occupation, 1945–1954* (London: Oxford University Press, 1955), pp. 564–5. For a discussion of the ERP and Germany, see Alan S. Milward, *The Reconstruction of Western Europe, 1945–1951* (Berkeley and Los Angeles: University of California Press, 1984), pp. 92–133.

11 See Randall E. Newnham, *Deutsche Mark Diplomacy: Positive Economic Sanctions in German–Russian Relations* (University Park, PA: Pennsylvania State University Press), pp. 288–9.

12 See Peukert, *The Weimar Republic*, p. 46; Eberhard Kolb, *The Weimar Republic*, trans. by P. S. Falla (London: Unwin Hyman, 1988), p. 30 and Mommsen, *The Rise and Fall of Weimar*, p. 108.

13 The United States also presented the Allies with a draft treaty for the disarmament and demilitarisation of Germany in April 1946. The primary objective of the treaty was to 'ensure that the total disarmament and demilitarisation of Germany will be enforced as long as the peace and security of the world may require'. The draft treaty was to remain in force for twenty-five years, later extended to forty years. See 'Draft of Twenty-Five Year Treaty for the Disarmament and Demilitarization of Germany. Proposed to the Paris Session of the Council of Foreign Ministers by the United States Secretary of State' (29 April 1946) and US Secretary of State J. F. Byrnes, 'Restatement of Policy on Germany'

(6 September 1946), in Ruhm von Oppen, *Documents on Germany*, pp. 129–31, 158.

14 'Control Council Plan for Reparations and the Level of Post-War German Economy' (28 March 1946), in Ruhm von Oppen, *Documents on Germany*, pp. 113–18.

15 For a discussion of the controls placed on Germany, see James Sperling, 'Neither Hegemony nor Dominance: Reconsidering German Power in Post Cold War Europe', *British Journal of Political Science*, 31:2 (2001), pp. 394–408.

16 Holsti, *Peace and War*, pp. 340 ff. This argument is also found in G. John Ikenberry, *After Victory: Institutions, Strategic Restraint, and the Rebuilding of Order after Major Wars* (Princeton: Princeton University Press, 2001).

17 Merritt, *Democracy Imposed*, pp. 126–7.

18 In the mid-1960s, 34 per cent of the population still expected unification to be achieved with the inclusion of East Prussia, Pomerania and Silesia, which represented a drop from 66 per cent of the population in 1953. See Elisabeth Noelle and Erich Peter Neumann, *Jahrbuch der Öffentlichen Meinung, 1965–1967* (Allensbach: Verlag für Demoskopie, 1967), p. 388 and Elisabeth Noelle and Erich Peter Neumann, *Jahrbuch der Öffentlichen Meinung, 1947–1955* (Allensbach: Verlag für Demoskopie, 1956), p. 313.

19 For a review of contemporary German foreign policy, see James Sperling, 'The Foreign Policy of the Berlin Republic: The Very Model of a Post-Modern Major Power? A Review Essay', *German Politics*, 13:1 (2004), pp. 1–35.

20 See Kolb, *The Weimar Republic*, p. 40.

21 Mommsen, *The Rise and Fall of Weimar*, p. 144.

22 These number of unemployed in 1921 was 237,000, while that number climbed to over 5.5 million in 1932. See League of Nations, *Statistical Year-Book of the League of Nations, 1933/34* (Geneva: League of Nations, 1934).

23 The interwar experience also explains why individual Germans, when asked to choose, preferred economic security to political freedoms by a margin of 60 per cent to 30 per cent in the immediate postwar period. See Merritt, *Imposing Democracy*, pp. 338–9.

24 See Patrick Boarman, *Germany's Economic Dilemma: Inflation and the Balance of Payments* (New Haven: Yale University Press, 1964).

25 Mommsen, *The Rise and Fall of Weimar*, pp. 37 ff.

26 *Ibid.*, p. 20.

27 Merritt, *Democracy Imposed*, pp. 345–6.

28 Interestingly, while German federalism is upheld as a special and virtuous aspect of German governance (and a model for a politically unified Europe), Germans have not been particularly fond of federalism. Federalism, prior to the writing of the *Grundgesetz*, was the preference of

around 20 per cent of the population, while upwards to 50 per cent preferred a centralised system of government. That dissatisfaction with federalism persisted into the 1960s. See Merritt, *Imposing Democracy*, Figure 12.7, p. 340. In an elite survey conducted from Yale University at that time, 34 per cent of the respondents named federalism as a 'negative' aspect of the existing governmental system, the highest negative ranking for any of the 13 variables identified. See Karl W. Deutsch, Lewis J. Edinger, Roy C. Macridis, Richard L. Merritt and Helga Voss-Eckermann, *French and German Elite Responses, 1964: Code Book and Data* (New Haven: Political Science Research Library, Yale University, 1964), Appendix 2, p. 8.

29 Allemann, *Bonn ist nicht Weimar*, p. 425.

30 *Ibid.*, p. 428.

31 *Ibid*, p. 426

32 When Germans were asked to name the period when things were best for Germany, 45 per cent identified the Kaiserreich and 40 per cent identified the Third Reich (1933–38). Only 7 per cent had a positive view of Weimar. See Noelle and Neumann, *Jahrbuch der Öffentlichen Meinung, 1947–1955*, p. 126.

33 Mommsen, *The Rise and Fall of Weimar*, p. 58.

34 This argument is made in Mary Hampton and James Sperling, 'Positive/Negative Identity in the Euro-Atlantic Communities: Germany's Past, Europe's Future?', *Journal of European Integration*, 24:4 (2002), pp. 282 ff.

35 On pan-German attitudes toward democracy, see Robert Rohrschneider, *Learning Democracy: Democratic and Economic Values in Unified Germany* (Oxford: Oxford University Press, 1999). In 1946, 63 per cent of Germans agreed with the statement that 'very few Germans have shown understanding or inclination toward democracy'; in 2001, 75 per cent of western Germans believed that German democracy was the best system of democracy conceivable. See, respectively, Merritt, *Imposing Democracy*, p. 240 and Chapter 7 in this volume by Robert Rohrscheider and Dieter Fuchs, Figure 7.4, p. 169.

36 This argument is made by Bulmer, Jeffrey and Paterson, *Germany's European Diplomacy* and Adrian Hyde-Price, *Germany & European Order: Enlarging NATO and the EU* (Manchester: Manchester University Press, 2000).

37 In 1967, 54 per cent of those interviewed fully agreed with the statement that the alienation between eastern and western Germans was increasing, while another 25 per cent agreed with it in part. See, Noelle and Neumann, *Jahrbuch der Öffentlichen Meinung, 1965–1967*, p. 393.

38 For a good overview, see Arend Lijphart, *Patterns of Democracy: Government Forms and Performance in Thirty-Six Countries* (New Haven: Yale University Press, 1999), pp. 62 ff.

39 The number of effective parties contesting elections in Weimar ranged from a low of 4.30 parties in November 1932 to a high of 7.13 parties in May 1924. The mean number of effective parties was 5.96. By comparison, in the postwar period, only Papua New Guinea had a higher mean number of parties (5.98) and a higher number of parties in any single election (10.83). See Lijphart, *Patterns of Democracy*, Table 5.2, p. 76.

40 Wolfram F. Hanrieder, *West German Foreign Policy, 1949–1963: International Pressure and Domestic Response* (Stanford: Stanford University Press, 1967), p. 228. See also Thomas Banchoff, *The German Problem Transformed. Institutions, Politics, and Foreign Policy, 1945–1995* (Ann Arbor: University of Michigan Press, 1999).

41 Alexander Wendt, *Social Theory of International Politics* (Cambridge: Cambridge University Press, 1999), pp. 227–9.

42 The foreign policy of a civilian power is characterised by a willingness to transfer sovereignty to international or supranational institutions, opting for a policy of abnegation when faced with a conflict between norm-compliant behaviour and the maximisation of some material interest and the pursuit of 'civilised' international relations. For a recent treatment, see Sebastian Harnisch and Hanns W. Maull (eds), *Germany as a Civilian Power? The Foreign Policy of the Berlin Republic* (Manchester: Manchester University Press, 2001).

43 On the role of international institutions in solving problems of collective action, see Robert Keohane, *After Hegemony: Cooperation and Discord in the World Political Economy* (Princeton: Princeton University Press, 1984).

44 See Mommsen, *The Rise and Fall of Weimar.*

Part I

The origins of the Bonn and Berlin Republics

2

The origins of the Bonn Republic

Karl H. Cerny

The Bonn Republic can trace its origins to four successive developments: the breakdown of allied unity after the defeat of Germany in the Second World War; the governing of Germany in four separate occupation zones plus Berlin during the occupation period of 1945–49; the Western Allied initiative to invite the Germans to convene a constitutional conference in 1948 in order to provide a central government for their three zones of occupation; and the holding of elections for the new central legislature, the Bundestag, in August 1949. These four developments are not only chronologically related but also substantively interconnected, in the sense that events in the one laid foundations for the next. This is not to suggest some form of historical determinism. It would have been impossible to predict in 1945 the emergence of the Bonn Republic in 1949. Rather, events during 1945–49 were incrementally of pivotal importance.

The breakdown of Allied unity

In May 1945, Germany surrendered unconditionally to the United States, the Soviet Union, the United Kingdom and France.[1] As agreed upon at the Yalta Conference the previous February, Germany, after the transfer of some of its eastern territories to Poland and the Soviet Union, was to be divided into zones of occupation. France, a non-participant at Yalta, was nevertheless to receive a zone carved out of the British and American zones. To demonstrate Germany's complete defeat, its capital, Berlin, was to be separately administered and also divided into four zones of occupation.

Unconditional surrender granted total authority to the victorious allies. Policy decisions for all of conquered Germany were to be made by the Allied Control Council, composed of the military commanders of the four zones of occupation acting by unanimity. For Berlin, the Kommandatura, composed of the commandants of the capital's four military garrisons, was to perform a similar function. This institutional structure was not yet fully in play in late July 1945, when the governmental leaders of the victorious allies (still excluding France) met in Potsdam, Germany. The leaders this time were faced with reports from their deputies on the appalling conditions of conquered Germany. Cities were in ruins; communications and transportation systems were not functioning; food was in desperately short supply; millions of refugees and expellees were streaming into the western zones of occupation. Against this background, some of the tentative Yalta decisions on Germany's future could easily be reaffirmed; others were subject to controversy. As for the former, there was complete agreement on the need to outlaw the Nazi party and its affiliated organisations, to disarm and demilitarise the German war machine, to close down major armament-producing enterprises and to break up the business cartels held accountable for the rise and support of the Nazi party. More so than at Yalta, the Potsdam leaders were now also prepared to recognise the importance of encouraging the development of democracy in Germany.

Much more difficult were the Potsdam decisions regarding the devastated German economy. The Russians at Yalta had demanded $10 billion in reparations from defeated Germany. The United States had refused to accept a specific sum and instead postponed a decision until the condition of the German economy could be reviewed at the end of the war. This review proved to be most disturbing. Both the American and British zones of occupation lacked adequate food supplies to provide Germans with the bare minimum of daily calories. Matters were not helped by the decision at Potsdam to permit the expulsion of ethnic Germans from Poland, Czechoslovakia and Hungary, thereby adding to the flood of refugees. Moreover, the disputed unilateral Russian extension of the western Polish boundary to the Oder–Neisse line removed needed agricultural territory for the production of German food. Given these circumstances, neither the Americans nor the British could accept the Russian demand for reparations from their zones of occupation until important provisos were met. The principle had to be accepted that Germany be treated as a unit with the free flow of goods and persons across zonal borders. Surplus food resources from the Soviet zone would have to be made available to the American and British zones. Equally important, total German exports would have to be sufficient to cover total necessary imports. Otherwise, American and British leaders faced the prospect of their own national budgets paying for Soviet reparations as well as food shipments to their own zones of occupation.

The Potsdam Conference hammered out a package deal acceptable to the Americans and British. Germany was to be treated as an economic unit. Although no central government was established, a number of administrative agencies were to be set up to facilitate interzonal economic management. Determination of the total reparations sum was still postponed. Agreement was first to be reached on a level of industry production that would enable German exports to cover imports sufficient to maintain a standard of living no higher than that of other European countries. It would then be possible to determine surplus German productive equipment available for reparations from the American and British zones.

As General Lucius D. Clay, Military Governor of the Office of Military Government, United States (OMGUS), was quickly to discover, the Potsdam economic deal on Germany could not be put into practice. From the outset, France, not having been a participant at Potsdam, refused to be bound by its decisions until agreement could be reached on its own claims regarding the Saar, the Ruhr and the Rhineland. France, therefore, exercised its veto in the Allied Control Council to prevent the establishment of the central administrative agencies that were to carry out a common German economic policy. Despite Clay's repeated efforts, France would not budge. As for the Soviet Union, it had its own ways of sabotaging Potsdam. It stymied interzonal exchanges; it refused to provide information on the scope of its reparations from its own occupation zone; and it failed to send food shipments to the western zones. As early as May 1946, Clay stopped the dismantling of surplus German economic plants to be sent as reparations to the Soviet Union.

He, along with his British counterpart, General Sir Brian Robertson, could not, however, stop the mounting cost of providing adequate food for their respective zones. Moreover, the zonal division of Germany prevented economic revival and added to the costs of occupation. From

Clay's perspective, the need was to strengthen policy coordination within the American zone and to invite such other zones as wished to participate. Clay also continued to request that pressure be brought to bear on France to accept the establishment of central administrative agencies. In September 1946, Secretary of State James Byrnes, in a speech in Stuttgart in the American zone of Germany, indicated a more conciliatory occupation policy and reaffirmed Clay's offer of zonal cooperation. Only the United Kingdom continued to express interest and negotiated an agreement to establish Bizonia, the economic merger of the two zones on 1 January 1947.

In Washington, US authorities began to seek a solution to the German problem in a wider context. Relations with the Soviet Union had been deteriorating since the first quarrelsome Council of Foreign Ministers' (CFM) meeting in September 1945 in London. The cantankerous 1946 CFM meetings in Paris over peace treaties with Germany's wartime allies added to growing dissatisfaction. At the March 1947 CFM meeting in Moscow, George C. Marshall had replaced Byrnes as Secretary of State. Dismayed by continued inability to come to agreement with the Soviet Union on Germany, Marshall signalled the need for a new policy course. Not just Germany, but all of Western Europe was threatened with economic breakdown. The Truman doctrine of March 1947, involving military aid to Greece and Turkey, had to be supplemented by economic aid on a more inclusive basis. Eventually to be known as the Marshall Plan, the Secretary's vision, as sketched in his famous speech at Harvard University in June 1947, had important implications for Clay's problem in Germany. Not only were the western occupation zones to be included in the Marshall Plan, but also their economic revival was considered central to the revival of the entire West European economy. If Germany's economic revival was heretofore considered a threat, it was now seen as essential. With all participating countries jointly making decisions, a basis could now be laid for allaying French fears about a more united Germany. The way was possibly open as well to negotiate French claims to the Saar and the Ruhr, and to persuade the French to join with Bizonia.

On 1 July 1947, the Soviet Union refused the invitation to join the Paris Conference on Marshall Plan aid and also pressured Poland and Czechoslovakia not to participate. After another unsuccessful CFM meeting in December 1947 in London, the United States and United Kingdom, joined now by France and including the Benelux countries, met in early 1948 in London to negotiate outstanding German issues. The agenda included French economic and security interests, Germany's role in the Marshall Plan, and agreement on the procedure to form a common central government for a West German state. The Soviet Union responded by closing down Allied Control Council meetings. When the western occupation authorities then introduced German currency reform, heretofore blocked by the Soviet Union as well as France, the Soviet Union responded by cutting off all access to the western occupation zones of Berlin, thereby triggering the Berlin airlift crisis which lasted for almost a year. In effect, the effort at four-power unity over Germany had failed and was never revived, despite repeated attempts.

The occupation period, 1945–49

Since the Allied Control Council quickly ceased to function effectively, the political and economic revival of Germany after 1945 became the sole responsibility of the zonal military governments and their home governments.[2] Not surprisingly, each zone developed in its own way and at its own pace. This was obviously the case with the Soviet zone where Walter Ulbricht, the German leader chosen by Stalin, proceeded to establish his version of the communist system. But it was also the case with the three western zones. Unlike the Soviets, they may have shared a common understanding of goals, such as denazification, decartelisation and democratisation, but implementation led to variations in practice. Even when Bizonia was established, the fusion of the two zones was limited to specific economic policies and administration. By the time France joined this process in 1948, the three western allies along with the Benelux countries were negotiating the procedure to set up a full central government for a united West German state.

Prodded by early Soviet licensing of political parties, and increasingly aware of covert German meetings, the American and British occupation authorities began to license German political parties in August–September 1945.[3] The French followed suit in December. Unlike the Soviets, the western allies did not permit parties to organise immediately at the zonal level. Instead they began at the local and village, then on to the *Land* and finally, with the exception of the French, to the zonal level. The purpose was not simply to decentralise political activity; this was already assured by the independent structure of the zones. The purpose was also to promote the democratisation of the party system. The Americans went one step further in their licensing procedure: they insisted that the internal organisation of the parties be democratic, including election of party officials, public accountability of funding and independence of lower party organs.

The parties that emerged bore some resemblance to the Weimar party system. Like the Soviets, the western allies authorised four parties in all their zones: the SPD; the CDU and its Bavarian affiliate, the CSU; the FDP and the Communist Party (KPD).[4] Depending on the zone, the allies licensed additional parties, notably the Centre party (Z) and the German Party (DP) in the British zone; and the Bavarian Party (BP) and the Economic Reconstruction Party (WAV) in the American zone. The number of these parties was clearly reminiscent of Weimar. So too were the SPD, KPD and Z, which had been major Weimar competitors. Although the BP and DP were new organisations, they appealed to pre-Nazi regionalist sympathies.

Despite these similarities with Weimar, there were significant changes. The CDU, unlike Z, did not limit its appeal to Catholics. It deliberately combined the leadership of social reformist and conservative Catholic and Protestant organisations. At the same time, leaders such as Konrad Adenauer hoped to attract former conservative voters of the DNVP of Weimar days. In the same way, the FDP sought to widen its appeal. German liberals had been split between two parties in Weimar days: the German Democratic Party (DDP) and the German People's Party (DVP). For the first time since the 1860s, German liberals were attempting to join forces in the FDP. Still another difference from Weimar was a result of licensing: occupation authorities prevented the rise of extremist right-wing and revisionist refugee/expellee parties. Finally, unrelated to Weimar but of great importance for the future of West German politics, the SPD refused to join forces with the KPD as had occurred in the forced merger of the Socialist Unity Party (SED) in the Soviet zone in 1946.

An indication of the potential strength of the licensed parties had to await the holding of elections. In the American zone, local elections were held as early as January 1946; the British and French followed later in the year. Again the Americans were first with *Land* elections in 1946, to be followed by the British and the French in 1947. Voter turnout was quite high, reaching 86 per cent of the eligible electorate in some of the American and French and 79 per cent in the British local elections.[5] This turnout was largely unexpected since the assumption of most observers was that Germans were preoccupied with day-to-day needs and had little interest in politics. Rudimentary OMGUS polls revealed, however, that German attitudes were not at all apolitical. While there was poll evidence of continued attachment to authoritarian and Nazi ideology, 'most Germans had perspectives that were by and large democratic'. While the same polls revealed that Germans had little intention of joining parties or attending meetings, the act of voting was perceived differently.[6]

In any case, the results of these first elections provided a rough measure of relative party strength during the occupation period. The CDU/CSU and SPD were fairly evenly matched and were clearly the dominant parties in the multi-party spectrum. The FDP was the third most successful party but a distinct cut below the CDU/CSU and SPD. The KPD was a pale reflection of its former electoral strength during Weimar days. The Z party turned out to be no match in its competition with the CDU, not even in its former heartland of North Rhine-Westphalia. As for the other parties, they demonstrated regional strength sufficient to complicate coalition politics in a *Land* and possibly sufficient to do the same at the interzonal level.

Whatever their relative electoral strength, political parties after 1946–47 gained greater influence and increasingly limited the scope for manoeuvre of occupation authorities.[7] For example, American and British authorities met determined opposition from German political leaders who were unwilling to accept the occupation reform prohibiting recruitment of civil servants for political and elective positions. Kurt Schumacher of the SPD and Konrad Adenauer of the CDU were the dominant leaders in question. Schumacher, given his role in the Weimar party and his defiant principled opposition in Nazi concentration camps, had quickly risen to the leadership of the SPD in the British and other western zones. Adenauer faced much more serious challenges in 1945 from Karl Arnold, a former trade union leader of North Rhine-Westphalia, and Karl Kaiser, a leader of the CDU East in the Soviet zone. Both were outmanoeuvred by 1947, Arnold because of the CDU municipal election victory in September 1946 under Adenauer's leadership in the British zone, and Karl Kaiser because of the latter's summary dismissal by the Soviets in late 1947.

Neither Schumacher nor Adenauer was prepared to play consensus politics as a matter of principle. Everything depended on the issue at hand. An early opportunity presented itself with deliberations over constitutions for the *Länder* in elected *Land* constitutional assemblies during 1946–47 in the American and French zones. As several commentators have noted, convention members differed over the relative merits of majoritarian democracy and constitutional democracy.[8] Proponents of the former belonged to the SPD and like-minded supporters. They wanted to ensure that the majority elected to the legislature would face no obstacles in achieving reform of the socio-economic system. Implicit in this view was the assumption – and it was widely shared in the immediate postwar period – that the capitalist system had demonstrated its bankruptcy with the rise and support of Nazism. Given an opportunity to express themselves democratically, Germans would elect social democratic-minded representatives by a convincing majority. Proponents of constitutional democracy had a rather different view of postwar German society. Nazi totalitarianism had undermined society's commitment to moral values as it had also destroyed the associational life by means of which Germans had maintained their sense of identity. From this perspective, shared by Christian Democrats and like-minded supporters, German society had the features of a rootless mass society in which an elected majority would lack the restraints necessary to protect the values of minorities. Majority power therefore needed to be checked by proper constitutional means.

In the ensuing institutional debate, majoritarian democrats advocated a single parliamentary executive, namely a minister-president and cabinet, enjoying majority support in a single-house legislature. Constitutional democrats, concerned over the instability of cabinets, advocated the establishment of a second independent executive, capable of insuring continuity of government in times of crisis. Equally important, they sought the establishment of a second chamber to cope with the risks of majority tyranny in a single-house legislature.

In the event, none of the *Land* constitutional conventions provided for a second executive. Again none established a second chamber with effective veto power.[9] Although it is tempting to conclude that the majoritarian democrats carried the day, in fact the final constitutional documents were the product of compromise, with party leaders prepared to search for consensus. In the process, the *Land* constitutions introduced significant changes in the German tradition of parliamentary democracy. For example, constitutional democrats, concerned over cabinet instability, and majoritarian democrats, concerned over a dual executive, were able to compromise on the constructive vote of no-confidence, whereby the leader of a parliamentary cabinet cannot be voted out of office unless a legislative majority can also agree on a successor. The issue of the second chamber was also resolved to mutual satisfaction. Social Democrats had maintained all along that the exercise of rights for the purpose of destroying the constitutional order should be outlawed. If constitutional democrats were concerned over possible majority tyranny, then an acceptable compromise was the establishment of constitutional courts in all of the *Länder* with the power of judicial review. In addition to these compromises, it turned out that there was broad consensus among German parties on other constitutional matters drawn from the Weimar constitution. Thus not only civil and political but also economic and social rights were enumerated. Some of Weimar's direct democracy features, such as the initiative and the referendum, were retained. And understandably, given the mood of the times, most constitutions included various provisions permitting reform of the economic system.

Consensus and the search for compromise among party leaders had its limits. This became evident as the occupation authorities relied increasingly on Germans to deal with mounting economic difficulties. Initially, in order to improve coordination of efforts within their own zone, Americans had established a *Länderrat*, made up of the appointed leaders of their respective *Länder*. When Bizonia was put into place in January 1947, resistance to Bizonia decisions on the part of the now elected *Land* leaders and assemblies of the two zones led to several reorganisations. The final structure in 1947 amounted to a central economic government for Bizonia, including an Economic Council, composed of members chosen by the elected *Land* legislatures according to political party strength; a new *Länderrat*, composed of representatives of the *Länder* governments; and a quasi-cabinet of Executive Directors, elected by the Economic Council and responsible for individual administrative departments.[10]

In this new structure, political party conflict was no longer to be held in bounds. Disagreement emerged over the selection of an Economic Director in July 1947. The SPD insisted that their candidate be chosen in order to insure their type of socio-economic reform. They lacked a majority, however, refused to compromise and, at Schumacher's insistence, went into principled opposition. Adenauer, who was not a member of the Economic Council, worked behind the scenes to help forge the winning coalition of CDU/CSU, FDP and DP members. But their successful candidate was dismissed in January 1948 and the selection of a new Director led to renewed intense negotiations. The SPD maintained its opposition stance, the while the July 1947 coalition debated the merits of several candidates, including the FDP nominee, Ludwig Erhard. In the end, although relatively unknown, Erhard was the winning candidate.

Once in office, Erhard boldly removed price and wage controls in conjunction with the currency reform of the occupation authorities in June 1948. Despite the initially severe economic consequences of his policies, Erhard refused to change course. Significantly, the coalition that had elected him continued to support him. With the wisdom of hindsight, it can be argued therefore that the turnaround of the German economy had been launched. But that was not obvious in June 1948. More certain was that the days of Bizonia, or now Trizonia, were coming to an end. The London conferences of western allies and Benelux countries had reached agreement on the next stage of development in western occupied Germany: Germans were to be invited to convene a constitutional convention for the purpose of drawing up a constitution for a united West German state.

Deliberations of the parliamentary council

It was by no means self-evident that the Germans would accept the invitation.[11] They feared that the creation of a West German state might endanger the cause of eventual unification with the Soviet zone, not to mention Berlin which was to remain under continued four-power occupation. In late June, moreover, the Soviets had triggered the Berlin crisis. Apart from reenforcing fears of antagonising the Soviets, there was the constant uncertainty that the four powers would reach an agreement that would leave German constitutional participants out on a limb. This apprehension was reenforced by lack of information over the contents of an Occupation Statute that was to be promulgated at the same time as the new constitution. If the controls were to be as extensive as those practised during Bizonia then, as some Germans argued, it would be best to draw up provisional institutional arrangements for the administration of occupied Germany.

There were also important procedural reservations. In the absence of a united and sovereign country, Germans did not consider it appropriate to have popular elections for a constitutional convention. There were also objections to the Allied proposal that the completed constitutional document be submitted to popular referendum for approval. A unified German people would be unable to participate. Moreover, under the crisis conditions of the Berlin standoff between the

Soviets and western allies, a referendum risked becoming a populist electioneering opportunity for the communists.

The minister-presidents, the elected executives of the *Länder* of the three western zones who had received the invitation to convene a constitutional conference, requested information on the contents of the proposed Occupation Statute. In place of direct elections for the members of the constitutional convention, they suggested that the *Land* legislatures choose the members according to political party strength and that the deliberative body be called a Parliamentary Council. The final document should be termed a Basic Law (*Grundgesetz*), not a constitution. And instead of a popular referendum, ratification of the new document should depend on the approval of the *Land* legislatures.[12]

The minister-presidents finally did gain approval of their procedural recommendations. But they received little clarification on the Occupation Statute and there could be no assurance regarding the impact of their deliberations on German unification. In agreeing to convene the Parliamentary Council, therefore, the minister-presidents were from their perspective taking a most uncertain step. It was not clear what future decision making power Germans would have; it was also unclear how their electorate would react.

The Parliamentary Council, which met in Bonn on 1 September 1948, was no longer under the leadership of the minister-presidents. Admittedly, the most important constitutional draft to be considered by the Council had been prepared by constitutional experts on the initiative of the minister-presidents; still, the sixty-five members of the Council had been chosen by the *Land* legislatures to reflect political party strength and leadership. Significantly, Adenauer, not a CDU minister-president, was elected President of the Council and became the major liaison spokesman with the western allies. As was the case in the Frankfurt Economic Council, the CDU/CSU and SPD were evenly balanced in the Council. Unless they joined forces, each party needed support among the smaller parties, especially the FDP, the Z and the DP, to fashion a majority. Since two-thirds of the Parliamentary Council members had been participants in *Land* constitutional conventions, it should be no surprise that the deliberations of the *Land* conventions proved to be a dress rehearsal for the Council's deliberations.

There was broad agreement on parliamentary democracy, enumeration of basic civil and political rights, and denial of these rights to those intent on subverting the constitutional order. Consensus now also extended to the establishment of a federal system, but there were disagreements on its structure. Significantly, the Basic Law of the Parliamentary Council made no mention of three other items on the consensus list of the *Land* convention members: social and economic rights; direct democracy features, such as the initiative and referendum; and provisions permitting economic reform. That these items were missing was a consequence of negative consensus, reflecting conflicting aims and strategies. As for the socio-economic provisions, the SPD preferred to achieve the desired results via national legislation. Had they pushed for constitutional inclusion, they would have come up against a non-socialist majority. As for the direct democracy features, despite questionable references to Weimar experience, political party leaders were apparently guided less by principle than by pragmatic assessments of possible policy consequences.[13]

With respect to party differences, majoritarian democrats and constitutional democrats clashed over much the same institutional issues that had dominated their agenda at the *Land* constitutional conventions. Understandably, in light of adverse Weimar experience, the Council members paid considerable attention to the issue of a dual executive, i.e. the relationship between the president as head of state and the chancellor as cabinet leader in a parliamentary system. After much debate, the final compromise was to create a largely ceremonial presidency and to vest executive power in the chancellor. The chancellor's prerogatives would be strengthened in a twofold manner: his election by the legislature and the limited possibility of his removal by means of the constructive vote of no-confidence.[14]

The second chamber issue also reappeared in Council deliberations, this time as part of the broader issue of establishing a federal system. Unlike their opposition to the very existence of a second chamber at the *Land* level, the SPD accepted the need for its establishment at the new central governmental level. Federalism had traditional roots in Germany and the western allies, who themselves had required federalism as an element of the new German constitution, had laid the foundations for such a system by establishing *Land* governments in three quite independent occupation zones. As majoritarian democrats, however, the SPD wanted a second chamber that was directly elected and would be distinctly subordinate to the proposed lower chamber, the Bundestag. Constitutional democrats wanted a second chamber that would have equal legislative powers with the Bundestag, but were divided over the merits of a directly elected chamber and one composed in the German tradition of representatives of the *Länder* governments. The final solution was a compromise. Thanks to the south German *Länder*, especially Bavaria, the traditional form of second chamber was chosen. But the new Bundesrat was not to have equal power. On most legislation, it was to have a suspensive veto; only on bills directly affecting the role of the *Länder* in the federation would it have an absolute veto.

Apart from the Bundesrat issue, Germans quarrelled among themselves endlessly about the administration of federal finances. Majoritarian democrats argued that federal finances should be under central government administration. Constitutional democrats argued that the tradition of German federalism should be maintained, whereby the central government is given wide-ranging legislative powers and the *Länder* are responsible for administration. After much bitter debate, the Germans arrived at a compromise toward the end of their Council deliberations. But the western allies raised objections to the compromise (as well as other parts of the constitutional draft). In the ensuing negotiations, the entire work of the Council threatened to end in failure. Granted that the final solution on the federal issue was quite close to their original compromise, the Germans were forced to accept a mixed form of central government/*Land* administration of federal finances. More symbolically than substantively, the western allies had seriously interfered in the intra-German negotiating process.

The first Bundestag election, 1949

On 8 May 1949, the fourth anniversary of Germany's unconditional surrender, the Parliamentary Council passed the final version of the Basic Law by a four-fifths majority.[15] On 12 May, the day the Soviets lifted the blockade of Berlin, the military governors formally approved the constitutional document. Sent to the *Land* legislatures for their formal ratification, the Basic Law received the approval of ten legislatures; only the Bavarian legislature rejected it. Accordingly, on 23 May the Basic Law was officially promulgated, with Bonn as the provisional capital pending decision on the ultimate status of Berlin. Still, there was some unfinished business since agreement had not been reached on the electoral law for the new Bundestag. After earlier manoeuvering between Parliamentary Council, *Land* minister-presidents and the military governors, the Council in one of its last actions passed a bill over the objections of the CDU/CSU, establishing a system of personalised proportional representation. The military governors objected and, after further negotiations, ordered the adoption on 13 June of their amended version of the proportional representation system. Although the amendments were minor, the episode provided another example of Allied interference and also a rare example of the Council taking a majority rather than a compromise decision.

The date for electing the Bundestag was set for 14 August. Despite the apparent shortness of time, political party leaders had long since been campaigning. For the SPD and Schumacher, the task was essentially to mobilise the majority of the electorate for socio-economic reform that they assumed all along existed. For the CDU/CSU and Adenauer, the task was to provide a clear alternative to the socialist programme. As Adenauer came to realise in 1948, the most promising was Erhard's social market economy programme which had been supported in the Frankfurt Economic Council. The resulting socialist/anti-socialist debate dominated media coverage and at times became nasty and negative.

The results of the election were a disappointment for both major party leaders. Neither the SPD nor the CDU/CSU won a majority of the 402 seats. At most, Adenauer could take satisfaction in the CDU/CSU leading the SPD by 139 to 131 seats. In many ways, however, the real winners in the election were the minor parties which gained a total of 154 seats (not counting two independents). Ranging from fifty-two seats for the FDP to one seat for the South Schleswig Voters' Association (SSW), some eight additional parties won representation in the Bundestag. Understandably, the postwar German party system reminded commentators of the Weimar multi-party system.

In any event, for a chancellor to be elected by the newly elected Bundestag, a coalition of parties was unavoidable. The only way for the SPD to form a winning coalition was to join in a Grand Coalition with the CDU/CSU. But ever since the Frankfurt Economic Council, Schumacher had rejected a Grand Coalition and preferred to go into opposition. Adenauer also rejected a Grand Coalition and preferred a coalition with the FDP and DP, a continuation of the Frankfurt Economic Council coalition. Rallying supporters, however, was no easy task. Most CDU *Land* leaders were in coalition with the SPD and believed that a Grand Coalition was necessary to cope with the many problems facing the new government. Left-leaning members of the CDU, especially the trade union wing, also wanted a Grand Coalition. Adenauer's proposal to support Theodor Heuss, the FDP party leader, for the office of President triggered further discontent within CDU ranks. And to add to his problems, the CSU was notoriously split into several factions, each prepared to go its own separate way. Until 15 September, the very day of the election of a chancellor by the Bundestag, Adenauer was wheeling and dealing to garner support. That he just barely met with success was demonstrated by the 202 votes he received, the minimum one-vote margin needed to secure the required absolute majority for election.

By 20 September, Adenauer had completed the selection of his cabinet and the membership was officially sworn in. On 21 September, the Occupation Statute, reserving widespread powers to the western Allied governments, took effect; so too did the new Allied High Commission which replaced the military governors of the three occupation zones. The Bonn Republic was officially launched. Once again, with the wisdom of hindsight, it is tempting to conclude that the Adenauer era had begun. But such was certainly not obvious in September 1949. All that could reasonably be anticipated was that Adenauer could not easily be voted out of office, that the new government knew the economic policies it hoped to pursue successfully and that, given the new chancellor's known views, it would seek a role in the emerging pattern of Atlantic and West European cooperation. Whether it would be able to do so and in what manner were open questions. The new government had yet to be tested.

Conclusion

Overall assessments of the 1945–49 years have been mixed. One group of commentators has stressed that the occupation authorities played an essentially enabling role, setting the institutional stage for the Germans who so desired to renew the attempt to establish a democratic government. The *Land* governments and the Bonn Republic which eventually emerged were thus very largely German creations and in keeping with German traditions.[16] Another group of commentators has been much more critical and revisionist.[17] They have pointed to the widespread desire after unconditional surrender for thoroughgoing socio-economic and political reform. The western Allies, especially the Americans, had a similarly ambitious programme of reeducating Germans to acceptance of democratic ways. In the end, however, little was accomplished. Military governors modified much more stringent occupation guidelines and refused to sanction socialisation and codetermination measures. Despite efforts at denazification, the old Weimar elites, minus the more egregious Nazi offenders, were reinstalled. For all intents and purposes, what happened after May 1945 was not a real change, but a restoration of traditional German elites.

A third group of commentators, this author included, has attempted to provide a more balanced picture.[18] Western Allies did indeed ease occupation guidelines in mid-1947 and stymie attempts to introduce radical economic reforms. But their reasons were above all to avoid disruption of their desperate efforts to revive the badly damaged economy by introducing the still further dislocations of radical reforms. Moreover, their efforts were not so much to prevent, but rather to postpone the issue, until such time as the German electorate of a new central government would have a chance to make a final decision. In this respect, even in the earliest elections, it was questionable whether a majority of the German electorate voted for parties that supported radical reform. Growing awareness of conditions in the communist occupation zone as well as heightening tensions of the Cold War contributed to the decline of support for socialist solutions.

Was the result therefore a restoration of the old German elites? It is again certainly true that the elites which emerged after 1945 were heavily drawn from political activists of the Weimar era. In this sense, denazification, especially the more ambitious American version, did not bring about a new democratic leadership.[19] But a distinction has to be made between Weimar elites who had supported the republic and opposed the Nazis and those elites who had at best questionable commitments throughout the Weimar and Nazi eras. In choosing Germans for top political positions to help them run the occupation, the western Allies turned to those who had proven records of Weimar support and anti-Nazi convictions. They and the Germans had far less choice as they filled non-political positions, especially those requiring expertise. Besides they were trying to get the economy moving and were not out to reform radically. As a result, only the top political elites were significantly changed.

To conclude that the years 1945–49 brought about a restoration of the old Weimar regime is to ignore the ways in which both the western Allies and the Germans brought about changes. Granted, the Allies helped set the institutional stage for the Germans who wanted to reestablish a democratic government. But this formulation runs the risk of playing down the important degree to which the Allies changed the stage. After all, they redrew *Länder* geographical boundaries; they licensed and closely supervised the establishment of political parties, trade unions, as well as the printed and broadcast media. Their open interference in constitutional deliberations has generally been much criticised. And not to be forgotten are the countless undocumented ways in which Allied liaison officers interacted with Germans and helped influence the German decision making process.

The formulation that Germans followed their traditions in reestablishing their institutions also risks underplaying the degree to which Germans changed or, at the very least, reshaped their traditions. Admittedly, institutions, such as the civil service and the educational structure, harked back to Weimar days. But it was the Germans, not the Allies, who broke with the tradition of organising their parties and trade unions to reflect different religious and ideological interests. Institutionally, the constructive vote of no-confidence and the electoral system of personalised proportional representation were genuine German innovations. The constitutional provisions for judicial enforceability of civil and political rights and protection against their misuse marked distinct breaks with the Weimar tradition. Even in reestablishing parliamentary democracy and federalism, Germans combined old with new provisions whose functioning together had no precedent but at least offered the best promise since 1871 of functioning effectively.

The relationship between the western occupation powers and the Germans could hardly be called a partnership. But uneven as the relationship may have been, a division of labour did arise and with each passing year the Germans played a somewhat greater role. Launched in September 1949, the Bonn Republic had at least the potential of becoming a functioning democratic political system.

Notes

1 This section is based primarily on the following sources: Lucius D. Clay, *Decision in Germany* (Garden City, NY: Doubleday & Co., 1950); John Gimbel, *The American Occupation of Germany: Politics and the Military, 1945–1949* (Stanford: Stanford University Press, 1968); Jean Edward Smith, *Lucius D. Clay: An American Life* (New York: Henry Holt & Co., 1990); and W. R. Smyser, *From Yalta to Berlin* (New York: St Martin's Press, 1999).

2 For this section, the following sources were especially helpful: Theodor

Eschenburg, *Jahre der Besatzung, 1945–1949. Band I: Geschichte der Bundesrepublik Deutschland* (Stuttgart: Deutsche Verlags-Anstalt, 1983); Peter Graf Kielmansegg, *Nach der Katastrophe: Eine Geschichte des geteilten Deutschland* (Berlin: Siedler Verlag, 2000), pp. 80–130; Hans-Peter Schwarz, *Konrad Adenauer*, vol. 1 (Providence, RI: Berghahn, 1995), Part V.

3 See especially Daniel E. Rogers, *Politics after Hitler: The Western Allies and the German Party System* (New York: New York University Press, 1995).

4 The titles and initials of the CDU and the FDP were different in some of the *Länder* before they gained common interzonal usage.

5 Clay, *Decision in Germany*, Chapter 5. For early British elections, see Raymond Ebsworth, *Restoring Democracy in Germany* (London: Stevens & Sons, 1960), Chapter 3; for French elections, F. Roy Willis, *The French in Germany 1945–1949* (Stanford: Stanford University Press, 1962), Chapter 9.

6 Anna J. Merritt and Richard L. Merritt (eds), *Public Opinion in Occupied Germany: The OMGUS Surveys, 1945–1949* (Urbana: University of Illinois Press, 1970). The quote is on p. 41. The discussion on political participation can be found on pp. 43–50. In a subsequent study that also analyses OMGUS data, Richard Merritt comes to the interesting conclusion that Germans 'consistently supported US policy'. Richard L. Merritt, *Democracy Imposed: US Occupation Policy and the German Public, 1945–1949* (New Haven: Yale University Press, 1995), p. 392.

7 For excellent analyses of the changed and important role played by parties during the occupation, see Kenneth H. F. Dyson, *Party, State and Bureaucracy in Western Germany* (Beverly Hills: Sage, 1977) and Michaela W. Richter, 'From Occupation to Unification: Political Parties and Democratic Transformations in Germany', in *Transformation of the German Party System*, Working Paper 7.8 (Berkeley: Center for German and European Studies, University of California, 1996).

8 One of these terms, 'majoritarian democracy' is not exactly the commonly used German term 'soziale Mehrheitsdemokratie'. More extended discussion of both concepts and their application to constitutional deliberations can be found in Karlheinz Niclauss, *Der Weg zum Grundgesetz* (Paderborn: Schöningh, 1998). For an earlier and still very useful discussion of the general political intellectual climate in the immediate postwar years, see Peter H. Merkl, *The Origin of the West German Republic* (New York: Oxford University Press, 1963), Chapter 2.

9 Bavaria did make provision for a consultative chamber along corporate lines. For an extended discussion of the *Länder* constitutions, see Frank R. Pfetsch, *Ursprünge der zweiten Republik* (Opladen: Westdeutscher Verlag, 1990).

10 The Economic Council was also to be given the power to levy customs duties and excise taxes. In addition, a high court and a central bank were

to be established. The background and details of Bizonia reorganisation are covered in Gimbel, *The American Occupation*, Chapters 7, 11.

11 A good discussion of the invitation which came in three parts, known as the Frankfurt Documents, is found in Eschenburg, *Jahre*, pp. 462–70.

12 One of the Frankfurt Documents requested that the minister-presidents examine *Länder* boundaries and propose changes to be voted on at the same time as the electorate would be choosing constitutional convention members. The minister-presidents argued that, apart from concern over direct elections, the time allowed for deliberation was too short for such an important topic. An invaluable reference work for the verbatim proceedings of the minister-presidents is Der Bundestag und Bundesarchiv, *Der Parlamentarische Rat 1948–1949: Akten und Protokolle, Band 1* (Boppard-am-Rhein: Harold Boldt Verlag, 1975). This volume is part of a series covering all proceedings up to and including the constitutional convention which has appeared over the years and now comprises thirteen volumes.

13 The definitive work is Otmar Jung, *Grundgesetz und Volksentscheid* (Opladen: Westdeutscher Verlag, 1994). For a somewhat different interpretation, see Niclauss, *Der Weg*, pp. 192–202. It should be noted that the Basic Law does make provision for a referendum in the event of *Länder* boundary changes.

14 Apart from Niclauss, *Der Weg*, two earlier works on the institutional deliberations of the Council are still most useful: John Ford Golay, *The Founding of the Federal Republic of Germany* (Chicago: The University of Chicago Press, 1958); and Merkl, *The Origin of the West German Republic*, pp. 66–89.

15 This section is based on Eschenburg, *Jahre*, pp. 522 *passim*; and Schwarz, *Konrad Adenauer*, Part VI.

16 Golay, *The Founding*, belongs to this group; so too, Carl J. Friedrich, 'Rebuilding the German Constitution, I and II', *American Political Science Review*, 43:3 and 43:4 (1949), pp. 461–82, 704–20. Harold Zink had already criticised Allied preoccupation with organising elections rather than concentrating on reform, in Harold Zink, *American Military Government in Germany* (New York: Macmillan, 1947).

17 Representative would be Eugen Kogon, *Die unvollendete Erneuerung* (Frankfurt-am-Main: Europäische Verlagsanstalt, 1994). See also Merritt and Merritt, *Public Opinion*, pp. 50–8.

18 Merkl, in *The Origin of the West German Republic*, touches on many of the themes of this group. Good later representatives are Eschenburg, *Jahre* and Kielmansegg, *Nach der Katastrophe*.

19 Lewis J. Edinger, 'Post-Totalitarian Leadership: Elites in the German Federal Republic', *American Political Science Review*, 54:1 (1960), pp. 58–82.

3

The origins of the Berlin Republic

Mary M. McKenzie

The defeat of Germany in the Second World War led to the emergence of two German states in 1949. As Karl Cerny (Chapter 2 in this volume) notes, however, the events and policy decisions of the intervening years were crucial in determining the final shape and status of these two states. Likewise, a shock to the international system paved the way for the emergence of the Berlin Republic in 1990. This shock was the fundamental change in East–West relations brought about by the policies of Mikhail Gorbachev in the Soviet Union. At the time of his ascension to power in 1985, there was no way of predicting that his policies of *Glasnost* (opening) and *Perestroika* (restructuring) would in the end lead to Germany's unification. Rather, it was the events and policy decisions during the years 1989–90 which would determine the full impact of Gorbachev's policies for the two German states and for the configuration of Europe as a whole. Just as with the Bonn Republic, there was nothing inevitable about the emergence of the new united Federal Republic of Germany.

In fact, although the Federal Republic's Basic Law contained the call for eventual unification, by the late 1980s the existence of two German states was accepted by all but a small minority of West Germans. As Peter Merkl has written: 'Active engagement or calls for "tearing down the Wall" or for thoughtfully commemorating the East German workers' uprising of June 17, 1953 … had become the stuff of right-wing propaganda and of graffiti on public walls.'[1] Helmut Kohl's CDU-led government had continued – and in some instances, even enhanced – the *Ostpolitik* of its Social Democratic predecessor, hosting the German Democratic Republic's (GDR) chief of state, Erich Honecker, in Bonn in 1987. West German public opinion, too, generally saw unification as a moot issue. In responding to whether unification of the two German states was likely within a foreseeable time frame, only 3 per cent replied affirmatively in 1987, down from 13 per cent in 1968. And 72 per cent of the respondents thought it was 'unlikely'.[2] Indeed, even in November 1989, only 30 per cent of West German respondents believed that unification would occur within their lifetimes, while 46 per cent did not think so.[3]

But the winding down of the Cold War opened the path toward German unification and the founding of the Berlin Republic in 1990 just as its intensification had led to the founding of two separate German states in 1949. To explain the path and speed of German unification, however, one needs to assess the confluence of these international changes and domestic political pressures in both German states.[4] Hence, the chapter begins by assessing the impact of the changed international environment on the East German regime. The next section discusses the rapid emergence of unification as a viable political agenda item, and the third and fourth sections analyse the dual sets of negotiations necessary to regulate German unification, the internal and the external ones. Finally, the last section analyses the continuing domestic and foreign policy challenges of the unification process. As Karl Cerny writes of the Bonn Republic, each step of unification was temporally and substantively related to the preceding one.

Gorbachev's *perestroika* and the demise of the German Democratic Republic

In the late 1980s, the East German leadership had for the first time publicly acknowledged that its economy was stagnating. Instead of undertaking Soviet-style reforms, however, the regime clung to the rigid policies of a command economy. While the Soviet Union was expressly encouraging its eastern European allies to pursue their own reforms, a challenge undertaken by the governments in Warsaw, Budapest and, later, Prague, the East German leadership used the new room for manoeuvre to argue that the GDR already had achieved many of the goals of the proposed Soviet reforms. Erich Honecker distanced himself from the Soviet path, stating that: 'We have never considered copying others to be a substitute for our own thinking or political action.'[5] Ironically, the East German regime used the Soviet

Union's renunciation of the Brezhnev doctrine to repudiate the Soviet leadership. This isolation would prove fatal: in the end it was the Soviet anchor that had guaranteed the separate existence of an East German state.

Beginning in 1987 and continuing throughout 1989, the East German government was increasingly confronted with sporadic but significant internal dissent over its unwillingness to emulate Gorbachev's reform policies. It reacted with police raids against churches and citizen assemblies and refused to legitimise formal opposition. Further distrust was sewn by blatantly fraudulent communal elections held in May 1989. By summer of 1989, the growing dissatisfaction of the East German people led to a dramatic number of East Germans exercising their right to 'vote with their feet' and to seek refuge in the West German embassies in neighbouring states. Hungary had added to this pressure by opening its border to Austria in May, thereby allowing East Germans to flee westwards. By August 1989, 500 East Germans were arriving daily in Giessen, West Germany.[6] By October, 130,000 had fled – as many as in the preceding five years.[7] Confronted with the task of absorbing the East German refugees, the West German government continued to call on East Berlin to reform.

Throughout the autumn, demonstrations continued to grow in all of the major cities of East Germany. With the rallying cry of 'we are the people', the protesters demanded that the government in East Berlin institute democratic reforms, principally focusing on the right to travel freely. In addition, several opposition groups emerged echoing the call for political and economic change in the GDR. By November, 200,000 people had signed the manifesto of the largest of these groups, New Forum, which 'had become the symbol of change and rebellion'[8] since its founding in September. After Mikhail Gorbachev visited East Berlin on the occasion of the GDR's fortieth anniversary in October 1989, the East German leadership resigned, in what Erich Honecker considered fundamentally a *coup d'état*.[9] However, the government of SED Politburo member Egon Krenz lasted only until 6 November, when his government, too, resigned. A policy announcement of eased travel restrictions to the West resulted in the opening of the Berlin Wall on 9 November.

The West German government responded to these monumental events in late November 1989, when Chancellor Helmut Kohl announced his controversial 'Ten-Point Plan'. In it, Kohl outlined a path that would lead toward the gradual federation of the two German states, firmly embedded in European and international institutions. Coming without prior consultation, it caused an uproar in some Allied capitals and outright resistance in Moscow. A close advisor to Kohl, however, has asserted that the secrecy involved was intended more to trump his domestic opposition and his FDP coalition partners than to assert Germany's international independence.[10] One analyst observed, 'This is deliberately timed just before [the Malta summit between George Bush and Mikhail Gorbachev] so Mr. Kohl can show *the Germans* that he is in control of the process.'[11]

German unification is on the agenda

The Ten-Point Plan reflected the generally held belief that unification remained a distant prospect. It also reflected a broad consensus on the way that unification was to be achieved: stabilisation of the GDR, deepening of relations between the two Germanies, capped by a new national constitution for a unified Germany. In fact, it mirrored the 'contractual community' proposed by the new government of communist party reformer Hans Modrow in East Berlin. However, developments on the ground quickly challenged this nascent elite consensus. First, the East Germans continued to flee as the economy of the GDR crumbled. In January 1990 alone, 58,000 East Germans moved to West Germany. Second, the East Germans who remained continued to take to the streets in protest, calling in massive numbers for German unity with the call: 'We are one people.'[12]

The government of Hans Modrow recognised the extent of the economic, political and social crisis in the GDR. First, Modrow met with Kohl in December to promote a 'contractual community' between the two German states. Second, the East German government for the first time recognised a legitimate role for opposition groups and formed the Round Table in East Berlin. Consisting of SED members, opposition leaders, and the former SED bloc parties, the Round Table hoped to charter 'a dignified unification process', based on a new constitution.[13] And third, free elections for the East German *Volkskammer* scheduled for May were moved up to March 1990. A legitimate and democratic government in Eastern Germany was cited by Kohl as a prerequisite for further negotiations between the two German states.

By February 1990, two significant changes had occurred in the discourse about the future of Germany. First, all of the major parties in the West and the East had come to accept the goal of unification, including the successor to the SED, the PDS, and even the citizens' groups, such as New Forum, that had been holding out for some sort of 'third way' between capitalism and socialism. Political momentum 'had passed into the hands of the street demonstrators' who were no longer willing to settle for reform of the GDR.[14] Second, the consensus on how unification should occur was ruptured. There were now two distinct conceptions about the process: the gradual building of a 'contractual community' as outlined in the Ten-Point Plan and the speedy incorporation of the GDR into the institutions of the Federal Republic.

Thus, the March 1990 elections were not about whether unification would occur, but rather about how. The results were widely interpreted as a vote for rapid unification on West German terms. The conservative Alliance for Germany (forged by Kohl's CDU with the eastern CDU, the Democratic Awakening (DA) and the German Social Union (DSU)) received 48 per cent of the vote; the SPD, which had been widely favoured in the run-up to the elections, received 22 per cent. Alliance 90 and the Greens each received less than 3 per cent of the vote.[15] Lothar de Maizière of the eastern CDU became the new prime minister, heading a grand coalition government.

Now that German unification was undeniably on the political agenda, two broad sets of legal and political issues critical to the identity of the new German state had to be resolved. First, policy makers needed to define the internal process of unifying two separate states. Simultaneously, decision makers had to regulate how this new German state would fit in the international system. After all, the two German states not only had different political and economic structures, but they were also members of opposing alliances that had been central in the Cold War.

Defining the internal process of unification

The 'Two-plus-Four' diplomatic formula announced in February 1990 recognised the right of the Germans to negotiate the internal matters regarding unification as well as the right of the four Allied powers to participate in negotiations regarding its external aspects. The rapid collapse of the East German economy, under the weight of the continuing exodus of its people, compelled German leaders first to address the economic unification of the two separate states. These decisions, in turn, would fundamentally affect the course of political unification.

In the campaign for the March 1990 elections, Kohl not only had promised 'blossoming landscapes' for the East German economy but also had promised rapid unification and a currency reform based on a parity exchange between the West German and East German mark. Further, his campaign refrain included a 'no new taxes' pledge, reflecting the long shadow of the national elections scheduled for December 1990. Although this strategy is credited for the conservative electoral victory, the details were by no means clear in March 1990. In fact, the pledges belied two central questions regarding economic union. First, should the goal of such policy be to stabilise the GDR's economy or to hasten unification? Second, who would pay the costs?

It rapidly became clear the type of unification process Kohl envisioned, namely the rapid incorporation of the GDR into the Federal Republic. Currency union was proposed by the West German government as the best way to stabilise the faltering GDR. In February, Hans Modrow had travelled to Bonn where he was denied his request for a significant 'solidarity contribution' from the West German government. Again, economic and currency union was offered as 'an alternative to direct aid. [The Federal government] did not intend to bail out the GDR for the purpose of creating a stronger negotiating partner during unification.'[16] The meetings 'demonstrated to the East German people that Kohl not Modrow would decide what, if any, future the GDR possessed'.[17]

The debate over costs would come to a head only after the March elections. The opposition SPD in West Germany asserted that the goal of economic policy should be to alleviate any further hardship in the GDR and thus argued for a more gradual process. It further argued that Kohl's policies ignored the real costs of unification. The SPD claimed, correctly, that a rapid introduction of a market economy based on a 1:1 rate of exchange between the West and East German marks would drastically weaken the East German economy. Significantly, the prestigious head of the Bundesbank, Karl Otto Pöhl, spoke out against a 1:1 rate of exchange, as did Kohl's own economics minister, Helmut Haussman. The discussion in the Federal Republic provoked large demonstrations in East Germany, with people protesting the 'election deception'[18] of the promised 1:1 rate of exchange.

Although he was virtually alone in the West in his support for a parity exchange between the West German and East German mark,

Kohl went forward with the proposal in April. Wages, pensions, and savings worth up to 4,000 marks would be exchanged at a rate of 1:1; savings in excess of that amount would be exchanged at a rate of 2 East German marks to 1 West German mark. The treaty would transfer economic and monetary sovereignty to the Federal Republic and would open the eastern German economy to the pressures of the market effective on 1 July 1990. The costs of unification would be financed primarily through borrowing.

As David Patton has written, 'the treaty on currency union all but sealed a rapid unification' as it 'hastened East Berlin's decision to enter the [Federal Republic]'. The treaty also gave Bonn a pressing economic imperative to speed the unification process. In the words of Finance Minister Waigel (CSU), 'we don't want them to play "GDR" with our money any longer'.[19] It is important to recall as well that the GDR's loss of sovereignty in July was not accompanied by political representation in Bonn. In fact, the East German participants in the process had come to feel powerless to influence the substance of the negotiations.[20] As Peter Merkl observed: 'All hopes therefore began to focus on the day when East German representatives might receive seats and voting rights in the Bundestag and Bundesrat in Bonn.'[21] Thus, after monetary union, the discussion shifted to the issues of constitutional reform and the precise circumstances under which East Germany would become part of the Federal Republic.

The Basic Law of the Federal Republic stipulated two ways in which unification could occur. The first was Article 23 allowing for the accession of a German state to the existing Federal Republic. The second was Article 146, which called for a national plebiscite on a new constitution for what would be a new German nation-state. Although his Ten-Point Plan had recommended a gradual process beginning with the election of a new government in the GDR, by January Kohl had become a proponent of utilising Article 23 to facilitate a speedy unification process.[22] The victory of the conservative coalition in March assured the choice of Article 23 as the vehicle for unification.

Proponents of constitutional change hoped that the negotiations for the Unification Treaty might allow for some modification to the Basic Law in order to rescue 'some of the social protections of GDR life for the united German future'.[23] Although the eastern German negotiators were able to secure some protections for labourers and for pensioners, a number of controversial issues remained unsettled even after the two state treaties providing for unification. Abortion laws, property rights and the seat of government were left for a unified Germany to decide.[24] In August, the Unification Treaty was signed, and the East German *Volkskammer* voted for the accession of the entire GDR to the institutions of the Federal Republic (and with it, its own dissolution) to be effective on the Day of Unity, 3 October 1990.

Germany is at the table: the 'Two-plus-Four' talks

Although treated as analytically separate, in truth the internal and external processes of German unification were inextricably linked. Indeed, Kohl's Ten-Point Plan had made the relationship explicit, as he argued that German unification could occur only within the context of international institutions. In 1989, the Federal Republic was not fully sovereign. The four victorious Allies of the Second World War continued to have legal rights over matters pertaining to 'all of Germany'. Thus, constructing the international framework for German unity was going to require a complex act of international diplomacy that Karl Kaiser has since described as 'one of the greatest triumphs of leadership and diplomatic professionalism in the postwar period'.[25]

Despite its seeming modesty in retrospect, the Ten-Point Plan evoked strong dissension in Moscow and in some Allied capitals. In December, Gorbachev warned that the process should not be accelerated and even convened a meeting of the Allied Control Council in Berlin. Margaret Thatcher and François Mitterrand warned against rushing into the process. In a speech in the Soviet Union in early December, Mitterrand 'pointedly warned Bonn not to force the pace of unification, arguing that to do so could upset the political balance in Europe and have negative consequences for European integration ... He also tried to use the possible impact of unification on internal Soviet politics as leverage, telling Kohl in a private meeting some weeks later that Gorbachev had informed him on this trip that "the day German unification is announced, a two line communiqué will announce that a marshal is seated in my chair".'[26] Later in December, Mitterrand also chose to visit the beleaguered East German government 'as if to breathe life into the dying ancient regime'.[27] The French position mellowed only after the March 1990 election.

As was the case with the creation of the Bonn Republic, the role of the Soviet Union was particularly important to the unfolding of the unification process. As the Malta Summit with President Bush neared in early December 1989, Gorbachev continued to express a strong preference for two German states. However, after the summit, Gorbachev came to realise that the Cold War was at an end and that 'understanding and cooperation with the United States was now on the agenda'.[28] A few weeks later, Eduard Shevardnadze outlined to the European Parliament (EP) the conditions under which German unification might be acceptable to the Soviet Union, which included German demilitarisation and neutrality.[29] In January and February 1990, Gorbachev agreed in principle to German unification, acknowledging the right of the Germans to self-determination in separate meetings with Hans Modrow and Helmut Kohl.[30]

This sea change in Soviet pronouncements opened the way for a more constructive diplomatic process that would be announced in February: the 'Two-plus-Four' talks, consisting of the two German states and the four wartime Allies. While the two German states would regulate the internal matters of unification, the four Allied powers would negotiate with the Germans the external issues arising from German unity. Chief among these was the question of alliance membership. Until July 1990, the Soviets held that a united Germany could not be a member of NATO, a premise unacceptable to the other negotiating partners. Increasingly, however, the Soviets came to realise that their obstinacy on this issue risked the rapprochement with the West that they considered fundamental to the success of Gorbachev's policies inside the Soviet Union. Gorbachev also realised that he had significantly underestimated the speed with which German unification would unfold.[31]

The first of four sessions of the Two-plus-Four talks was held in May 1990. Soviet leaders remained adamant in their opposition to NATO membership for a united Germany. Shevardnadze stated: 'For us, NATO remains what it always was – an opposing military bloc with a doctrine based on the … possibility of a first [nuclear] strike … If there is any attempt to put us into a tight situation on issues affecting our security, this will lead to a position – and I say this quite openly – where the degree of our political flexibility will be strictly limited … Emotions [could] boil in our country, raising ghosts of the past, raising national complexes rooted in tragic pages of our history.'[32] Shevardnadze continued to argue for an all-European solution to the security problems arising from German unification. Specifically, he argued that a revamped Conference on Security and Cooperation in Europe (CSCE) could absorb the existing security arrangements in

'European non-aligned structures'.[33] At this meeting, Shevardnadze also briefly attempted to decouple 'the internal and external processes of unification, allowing internal unification to occur but postponing the external settlement for a transitional period during which a new pan-European security system could develop'.[34] This move was rejected by Kohl and the United States because they viewed the restoration of German sovereignty as a crucial step toward German 'normality'.

From the beginning, however, the Germans and the Americans had been sensitive to the legitimate security interests of the Soviet Union. Kohl, especially, thought it was in the West's best interest to support Gorbachev and minimise the opposition fallout he would face in the Soviet Union. Indeed, as Karl Kaiser has written: 'No other actor was faced with similar problems in making the outcome of the "two plus four" process acceptable domestically.'[35] Early on, both Foreign Minister Genscher and Secretary of State Baker floated the possibility of a significant restructuring of NATO military doctrine to accommodate Soviet concerns. For the same reason, the German government also favoured giving a stronger security mandate to the all-European CSCE.

Before the second round of Two-plus-Four talks in June, diplomacy focused on formulating the guarantees that could permit the Soviet Union to accept German membership in NATO. Based on ideas developed in the Bonn Foreign Ministry (the 'Genscher Plan'), the 'Nine Assurances' were delivered to Gorbachev at a summit with Bush in May 1990. These included the continued non-nuclear status of Germany, limitations on the size of the Bundeswehr, limitations on troop stationing in the territory of the former GDR and transitional arrangements for Soviet troops stationed there, a pledge to restructure NATO, a promise to institutionalise the CSCE, an affirmation by Germany of existing borders and significant German economic assistance to the Soviet Union. Gorbachev in turn agreed to work toward an agreement on conventional force reductions by the end of the year and reiterated his belief that a united Germany had the right to choose its own alliance affiliations based on the Helsinki Accords.[36]

NATO leaders, in the meantime, were making good on these promises to the Soviet Union. In June 1990, the North Atlantic Council sent out the 'Message from Turnberry' which emphasised the importance of multilateral arms reductions in the context of the negotiations on Conventional Forces in Europe (CFE); highlighted a growing role for the CSCE in European security; and pledged support for the ongoing reforms in central and eastern Europe (CEE). In July, the NATO

Summit released its 'London Declaration on a Transformed North Atlantic Alliance' which stated that 'the Atlantic Community must reach out to the countries of the East which were our adversaries in the Cold War, and extend to them the hand of friendship'. In addition to reiterating the commitments of Turnberry, NATO pledged to work with the Soviet Union to eliminate short-range nuclear weapons in Europe; that remaining nuclear weapons would be weapons of 'last resort'; and invited Soviet and eastern European governments to establish diplomatic liaisons with NATO.[37] Eventually, these proposals would lead to the creation of the Partnership for Peace initiative and to the membership of most eastern European states in NATO.

The European Community (EC), too, provided an essential institutional context for German unification. After the opening of the Berlin Wall, at a special EC summit, Kohl declared that European integration was 'now more than ever of prime importance'.[38] However, the element of surprise of the Ten-Point Plan spent much of the diplomatic goodwill that Kohl previously had achieved in his European policies. Kohl's European partners expected the German government to signal its renewed commitment to European Monetary Union (EMU) at the December 1989 Strasbourg summit. The French government especially called for a commitment to an IGC on the matter in 1990, a problematic issue politically for Kohl given the financial uncertainties surrounding German unification. For France, EMU had become 'the defining element and the touchstone of Franco-German relations after German unity, the very symbol of *Einbindung*'.[39] In the end, 'the German government accepted the French demand that an EMU conference would begin in the second half of 1990, while Paris conceded the German request to delay this until after the federal elections in early December … In addition to delaying the conference until after the federal elections, the Germans gained another concession – viewed as vital for domestic political reasons – by extracting from France and other EC countries a postsummit statement endorsing the idea of a single German state, as long as unification took place within the context of broader European integration.'[40]

By the time of the Special European Council in Dublin in April, Kohl and Mitterrand were once again working cooperatively to deepen European integration. Specifically, Mitterrand had agreed to Kohl's proposal to call for a second IGC to work toward European political union, 'so that Chancellor Kohl could claim to have extracted something in return for agreeing to surrender the D-mark and German monetary sovereignty'.[41] The summit also agreed on a framework for integrating the GDR (without having to sign a treaty of accession and with temporary exemptions from much EC law) and on EC relations with CEE states. At the end of June, a commitment was made to convene two separate IGCs, one on EMU and the other on political union. Although further debates erupted in autumn 1990 over their timetable, these IGCs would result in the Treaty on European Union (TEU) which went into effect in November 1993.

In this way, the actual negotiations of German unification went far beyond the Two-plus-Four process. In addition to the multitude of bilateral negotiations that occurred (especially involving representatives of the United States, the Soviet Union and West Germany),[42] the participation of NATO, the EU and the CSCE were crucial to the process of German unification. This was in part by design: while the Soviet Union had hoped to use the Two-plus-Four talks for broad-reaching security arrangements, the United States had insisted that the talks focus on restoring German sovereignty and on affirming Europe's existing borders.[43] If some European governments originally had felt the Two-plus-Four process was too narrow in membership, they were able to make their priorities known in these many other arenas. In fact, after France had come to accept German unification as inevitable in March, it chose to focus its diplomatic energies on working with Germany in the EC rather than in the venue of the Two-plus-Four talks or within NATO, where it had little influence.[44]

Ultimately, agreement was reached on NATO membership for Germany at the celebrated meeting between Kohl and Gorbachev in the Caucasus in July. Earlier in the month, the Gorbachev team had cleared a significant domestic hurdle when the 28th Congress of the Communist Party of the Soviet Union (CPSU) backed their policies toward Germany. The changes in NATO were clearly significant in enabling this outcome, as Shevardnadze argued, 'the construction of collective security structures on a pan-European scale had already begun'.[45] After the Caucasus meeting, Gorbachev explicitly recognised the importance of the London Declaration for the agreement.

The accord reached in the Soviet Union was essentially a modified version of the 'Nine Assurances' and the Genscher Plan. United Germany would remain in NATO, but no nuclear weapons or non-German NATO troops would be stationed on the territory of the eastern German states. Further, the overall number of German troops would be reduced to 370,000 (from a combined total of 700,000 in

1990) as part of the pending CFE Agreement and NATO restructuring. The Soviets would be given four years to withdraw their 380,000 troops from eastern Germany, during which time other Allied troops could remain in Berlin. Bonn also pledged to assume outstanding financial obligations of the GDR and an additional $7.5 billion to offset the costs of the Soviet troop withdrawal. Finally, Kohl promised Gorbachev a comprehensive bilateral treaty on cooperation.

The second major concern of the Two-plus-Four talks was the issue of Germany's recognition of its borders, specifically the Oder–Neisse frontier with Poland. Germany's constitution, the Basic Law, had stipulated that the border remained provisional until a final peace settlement officially ended the Second World War. Through the CSCE process of the 1970s, however, both Germanies had pledged to respect existing borders. But given the movement toward unification in 1989–90, a legal affirmation of the border became more important for Poland and the Soviet Union. For this reason, the absence of an 'eleventh point' in Kohl's Ten-Point-Plan addressing the border had already stirred controversy in November 1989.[46] In February 1990, Kohl had again significantly underestimated the importance of this issue when he refused to recognise Germany's eastern border with Poland, saying that it was a matter for a united Germany. After much internal and international debate, it finally was agreed that the Two-plus-Four talks would work toward a final recognition of the borders, with representatives of Poland participating in those sessions. In the meantime, the two German parliaments would also affirm their formal recognition of the Polish border.

After the successful meetings in the Caucasus, the July Two-plus-Four talks achieved an agreement on Germany's boundaries. It included a promise by

> East and West Germany that a united German government will negotiate and sign a border treaty 'as soon as possible'; a declaration that Germany has no territorial ambitions toward any other countries; agreement by West Germany that, after unification, a provision of the West German constitution allowing other German states to join the Federal Republic will be eliminated; a statement that West German laws that declare the border to be provisional pending a World War II peace treaty will no longer be considered valid; and a firm endorsement by the two-plus-four powers of the present German–Polish border along the Oder and Neisse rivers.[47]

On 14 November 1990, Germany and Poland signed a treaty

formalising the border; the following year, the two states signed a comprehensive agreement that protected the rights of ethnic Germans in Poland and committed Germany to supporting Poland in its bid for EU membership.[48]

The Berlin Republic

Early in the process, the six negotiating partners had agreed that the outcome of the Two-plus-Four process would not be a peace treaty which would confer the title of defeated power on a united Germany and possibly open Germany to a host of claims from a significant number of wartime adversaries. Rather, the talks would result in a 'Final Settlement' that would be presented to all of Europe at a CSCE summit in November. The 'Treaty on the Final Settlement with Respect to Germany' was signed on 12 September 1990, and the two Germanies became one on 3 October. The Berlin Republic was born. However, to say that the Treaty 'finally settled' the German question would be to overstate matters. As many analysts have noted, the German question always had two dimensions: the internal dimension pertaining to political stability or democratic viability, and the external one, concerning Germany's 'fit' in the European system. The Two-plus-Four talks were designed to address precisely these concerns.

Domestically, German unification was based on two state treaties providing for the economic and political union of two separate states. More than ten years after the Berlin Wall fell, there remain significant divisions of both kinds in the Berlin Republic, leading many observers to refer to the 'Berlin Wall in the head'. Economically, the costs of unification continue to preoccupy the Federal Republic. Over the years, the government has transferred approximately \$80–\$100 billion annually to the eastern German states to promote economic development and welfare. Financed by heavy borrowing on the part of both Federal and state governments, by 1991, Kohl's government was forced to renege on its 'no new taxes' pledge.[49] Using the demands of the first Gulf war as cover, the government raised gasoline and value-added taxes (VAT). The 'Solidarity Pact' of 1993 further increased financial assistance to the eastern states by imposing a 7.5 per cent solidarity surcharge on income taxes beginning in 1995; this was reduced to 5.5 per cent in 1998.[50] Despite these massive efforts, and despite a brief boom in western German production, the eastern German economy continued to crumble. In the wake of the currency union of 1990, the *Treuhand* was established to privatise firms, but instead tended to oversee their demise. What property remained tended to end disproportionately in western German hands.[51] Although wage levels have tended to equalise between the two parts of Germany, unemployment rates have remained dramatically disparate, with eastern Germany consistently suffering twice the rate of unemployment as the western states, even as recently as 2003.

Politically, unification was achieved by imposing the constitutional order of the old Federal Republic onto the new one. Although the new Article 146 retains the possibility of a referendum for a new constitution to replace the still-provisional Basic Law, post-unification constitutional reform commissions have vetoed any significant changes.[52] As such, political unification has tended to favour western Germans as well. Increasingly resented by many East Germans, the parliament, political parties, interest groups and the civil service have been dominated by those from the old Federal Republic.[53] As early as the March 1990 elections, the main western parties were calling the shots for their counterparts in the East.[54] Increasing numbers of East Germans began to feel like 'poor country cousins' in the new German state and voiced their discontent by voting for a purely eastern political party, namely, the PDS. In the March *Volkskammer* elections, for example, the PDS received 16 per cent of the vote nationally and 30 per cent in Berlin. In October 1999, 18 per cent of voters continued to cast their votes for the PDS in citywide elections in Berlin; in eastern Berlin, 40 per cent of voters did so.[55] The intractability of these problems eventually led to the defeat of Chancellor Kohl in the Federal elections of 1998.

The state treaties had also left open the question of the new state's seat of government. Although the Federal Republic's Basic Law had named Berlin as its capital, Bonn was designated the seat of government as the Cold War cemented the division of Germany and Berlin. The Unification Treaty retained the same sleight of hand in naming Berlin as the capital while leaving the final decision to a unified Germany's government. The ensuing debate was deeply coloured by questions of German history and identity: did Germany belong in the East or the West? Was it the Germany of 1949 or the Germany of 1891, 1933, or 1945? There were strong arguments on both sides: Bonn had served the Federal Republic well; it would continue to anchor Germany firmly with the West; the cost of moving the government would be exorbitant; and Berlin was haunted by too many historical ghosts. On the other hand, the eastern Germans had no ties to Bonn; Berlin was the historic capital; moving to Berlin would provide an economic jolt to the eastern states; and it was what the founding fathers of the Bonn Republic had desired. In June 1991, the Bundestag chose Berlin over Bonn in a very close vote.[56] Internationally, Germany's newly earned sovereignty compelled it more than ever to act as a 'normal' country. Whereas the Federal Republic that arose from the ashes of the Second World War was severely constrained in its foreign policy, united Germany rapidly had international responsibility thrust upon it. The first Gulf War was unfolding as Germany unified, and it was not long before war broke out in the Balkans. This forced the German government to face whether it was the 'partner in leadership' that US President George Bush had spoken of in May 1989. Although the Federal Republic did not send combat troops to the Gulf, it 'participated in the costs of the Gulf war to the tune of $6.5 billion. Logistical support was also provided.'[57] The wars in the Balkans compelled Germany to reassess its constitutional provisions prohibiting the use of force except for self-defence, and after a landmark decision of the Constitutional Court in 1994, it sent peacekeepers and AWACS aircraft to this region of the globe. It has subsequently sent peacekeepers to Cambodia, Somalia, Rwanda, Macedonia, Georgia and Afghanistan. In the context of the war against terrorism, Germany additionally has made available special forces and medical personnel and has sent troops to Kuwait and the Horn of Africa. The constrictions on Bundeswehr deployment felt by the Federal Republic during the Cold War have clearly dissipated.

The clear intersection of domestic and international politics during unification allowed Helmut Kohl to guide foreign policy, an arena in which previously the Foreign Ministry under Hans-Dietrich Genscher had acted authoritatively.[58] It had allowed the Kohl government to craft not only the internal arrangements for unification, but also, in large part, the external ones, so much so that Kohl has been credited with the rebirth of 'Chancellor-democracy' in the Federal Republic.[59] Although his electoral defeat to Gerhard Schröder's SPD in 1998 has dampened enthusiasm for Kohl, many analyses have pointed to the truly historic dimension of his contributions to German unification and European unity.[60]

As noted, the Kohl government frequently made explicit the necessary linkage between unification and European integration during the unification process. Post-unification politics have attested to the German commitment to Europe. With the signing of the Maastricht Treaty on European Union in 1991, Germany pledged to give up its DM, even though only a small minority of member states was in support of moving toward deeper political union which German leaders had considered part of the bargain. However, increased German calls for burden sharing in the EU, its insistence on the rigid independence of the ECB and on the strict criteria for joining the Eurozone led some observers to feel justified in their fears of a too-German Europe.[61]

Germany also has led the West's policy transformation toward eastern Europe and the Soviet Union and Russia. In addition to serving as the largest foreign investor in the reforms of these states, the German government has continued to press for the opening of both the EU and NATO to the states of the former communist bloc. German policy makers were at the forefront of the creation of the North Atlantic Cooperation Council (NACC), the Partnership for Peace, and the NATO–Russia Council, securing the bilateral relationship between Russia and NATO. These have been the substance of NATO's promise to 'reach out the hand of friendship' to these former adversaries. Additionally, Germany's post-unification foreign policy continued to lay heavy emphasis on the strengthening the pan-European Organisation for Security and Cooperation in Europe (OSCE) as a way to secure a role for Russia in Europe.

The importance of the German–Russian relationship was made especially clear during the process of unification, as Kohl consistently pressed other western governments for more financial support for Gorbachev's reforms. The 'Treaty on Good Neighbourliness, Partnership, and Cooperation', signed on 9 November 1990, has continued to serve as the basis for a greatly improved bilateral relationship. Despite the uncertainty surrounding the collapse of the Soviet Union and the shifts from Mikhail Gorbachev to Boris Yeltsin to Vladimir Putin, Germany remains Russia's most important trading partner, and German leaders have continued to emphasise the need to support the reform project there and to include Russia in international decision making.[62]

Conclusion

The revolution in international relations of the late 1980s opened the door for Germany's unification. However, the speed with which it occurred can be explained only by two concurrent domestic political processes: the inability of the East German regime to recognise the impact of these changes; and the ability of Helmut Kohl's government to guide them toward the goal of unification. The rush toward unity resulted in the absorption of the GDR into the institutions of the Federal Republic in less than one year. The process of unification, however, continues to confront the Federal Republic with enormous political and economic challenges which have strained the German budget and economy and resulted in some adjustments to the social market economy. The global recessions of the 1990s and early 2000s have exacerbated these problems and have resulted in labour strikes, budget cuts and tax hikes, but have not threatened the democratic fabric of the Federal Republic.

The international sea change begun in the late 1980s continues more than a decade after German unification, and the international institutions that embedded the process continue to be transformed. Fears that Germany would be so preoccupied with unification that it would neglect its international obligations or fears that a revitalised unified Germany would prove too strong for those same constraints have thus far proved unfounded. Instead, Germany's foreign policy continues much as it had developed throughout the 1980s, striving to merge the requisites of both its western and eastern policies by pursuing policies of integration and cooperation with all of Europe while maintaining its transatlantic anchor.[63]

It is equally true, however, that Germany's new-found sovereignty, together with the generational change symbolised by the transfer of power from Kohl to Schröder, have enabled Germany to act more self-assuredly in the international realm.[64] Most of Germany's foreign policies, however, have continued to be grounded firmly within the context of its international commitments, what some have labelled as a 'reflexive multilateralism'.[65] A notable exception occurred in early 2003, when Chancellor Gerhard Schröder rebuked George W. Bush for his policies toward Iraq. Although Schröder's challenge was made in the name of 'European sovereignty', most European governments had come out in support of Washington's policies.[66] This episode not only suggests trouble ahead for the NATO alliance as it expands its mandate, but it also illustrates the new Germany's desire to assert its own interests, as any other 'normal' state would. The Berlin Republic has taken the stage.

Notes

1 Peter H. Merkl, *German Unification in the European Context* (University Park, PA: Pennsylvania State University Press, 1993), p. 119.
2 *Ibid.*
3 *Ibid.*, p. 125. Merkl cites a poll by the Institut für Demoskopie.
4 David F. Patton examines this theoretical framework in *Cold War Politics in Postwar Germany* (New York: St Martin's Press, 1999), see especially the Introduction.
5 FBIS-EEU–880232, 2 December 1988.
6 'Bisher keine Lösung für die Flüchtlinge in Ost-Berlin', *Der Tagesspiegel*, 9 August 1989.
7 Patton, *Cold War Politics*, p. 109.
8 Merkl, *German Unification*, p. 111.
9 Reinhold Andert and Wolfgang Herzberg, *Der Sturz: Honecker im Kreuzverhör*, 3rd edn (Berlin, Weimar: Aufbau-Verlag, 1991).
10 Horst Teltschik, *329 Tage: Innenansichten der Einigung* (Berlin: Siedler, 1991).
11 Barbara Donovan, then a specialist on German politics at Radio Free Europe in Munich, is cited in 'Kohl Unveils Plan to Reunite Germany – Proposals Appear Designed to Quiet Political Foes and Influence Summit', *Wall Street Journal*, 29 November 1989, emphasis added.
12 See Patton, *Cold War Politics*, p. 113. Peter Merkl notes that the change in emphasis of the demonstrators had begun already on 22 November in Leipzig. *German Unification*, p. 124.
13 Patton, *Cold War Politics*, p. 116.
14 Merkl, *German Unification*, p. 108. Josef Joffe, then foreign editor of the prestigious daily *Süddeutsche Zeitung*, was quoted as saying: 'This is a real revolution of the streets. Control is sliding out of our hands. [West German Chancellor Helmut] Kohl doesn't want reunification now. Bush doesn't want it. The Russians don't want it. But the time is past for imploring the people to go slow. With the announcement of free travel, de facto reunification has already been proclaimed.' 'Revolution of the Streets: East German People Take Control of Reunification Question', *Houston Chronicle*, 7 December 1989.
15 'East Germany Tries Elections', *World Affairs*, 152:4 (1990), p. 217.
16 Patton, *Cold War Politics*, pp. 121–2.
17 Klaus Larres, 'Collapse of a State: Honecker, Krenz, Modrow, and the End of the German Democratic Republic', *European Review of History*, 1:1 (1994), pp. 79–84.
18 Patton, *Cold War Politics*, pp. 128–9.
19 Patton, *Cold War Politics*, p. 132. Waigel is cited from 'Dann wird der Kampf heiss', *Der Spiegel*, 21 (21 May 1990), p. 19.

20 'De Maizière's role was best characterised by a comment he himself made near the end of the unification process, comparing himself to a cuckolded husband, who was always the last one to know.' Stephen F. Szabo, *The Diplomacy of German Unification* (New York: St Martin's Press, 1992), p. 26.

21 Merkl, *German Unification*, p. 202.

22 Szabo notes that Kohl changed his mind as a result of his visits to the GDR in December where he heard East German crowds calling for unification. *Diplomacy*, p. 140, n. 38.

23 Merkl, *German Unification*, p. 170.

24 See Patton, *Cold War Politics*, pp. 132–4, 138–40.

25 Karl Kaiser, 'Germany's Unification', *Foreign Affairs*, 70:1 (1991), p. 179.

26 Michael J. Baun, 'The Maastricht Treaty as High Politics: Germany, France, and European Integration', *Political Science Quarterly*, 110:4 (1995/96), p. 614.

27 Kaiser, 'Germany's Unification'.

28 Gerhard Wettig, 'Moscow's Acceptance of NATO: The Catalytic Role of German Unification', *Europe-Asia Studies*, 45:6 (1993), pp. 953–73.

29 Merkl, *German Unification*, p. 311.

30 According to Peter Merkl, 'Kohl returned in triumph from Moscow, proclaiming he held the "key to German unification" in his hand'. Merkl, *German Unification*, p. 312.

31 Wettig writes that 'Political transformation in the USSR presupposed a stable international environment'.

32 'Will 2-plus–4 Talks equal German Unity?,' *Houston Chronicle*, 6 May 1990.

33 Richard E. Rupp and Mary M. McKenzie, 'The Organization for Security and Cooperation in Europe: Institutional Reform and Political Reality', in Mary M. McKenzie and Peter H. Loedel (eds), *The Promise and Reality of European Security Cooperation: States, Interests, and Institutions* (Westport, CT: Praeger, 1998), p. 127.

34 Szabo, *Diplomacy*, p. 83.

35 Kaiser, 'Germany's Unification'.

36 Szabo, *Diplomacy*, pp. 86–7.

37 For the text of NATO documents, see the website, www.nato.int.

38 Baun, 'The Maastricht Treaty', p. 611.

39 Simon Bulmer, Charlie Jeffery and William E. Paterson, *Germany's European Diplomacy: Shaping the Regional Milieu* (Manchester: Manchester University Press, 2000), p. 99.

40 Baun, 'The Maastricht Treaty', p. 613.

41 *Ibid.*, p. 616.

42 Horst Teltschik, for example, visited the Soviet Union six times between January and July 1990. See Szabo, *Diplomacy*, p. 25.

43 *Ibid.*, p. 70.

44 *Ibid.*, pp. 48–51.

45 *Ibid.*, p. 97.

46 Kaiser, 'Germany's Unification'.

47 'Poland, Germany Agree on Border, Reunification: The Settlement Removes the Last Big Obstacle to a Single German State', *Los Angeles Times*, 18 July 1990.

48 This agreement took the form of the 'Treaty on Good Neighbourly Relations and Friendly Cooperation'. See Marc Fisher, 'Germany and Poland Sign Border Treaty; Pact Assures Minority Rights, Cooperation', *Washington Post*, 18 June 1991.

49 Peter Merkl points out that voters supported Kohl and the CDU even though they did not believe this promise. See Merkl, *German Unification*, p. 397.

50 'Solidarity Pact II' will go into effect in 2005 and will transfer DM 306 billion to the eastern states through to 2019.

51 Patton, *Cold War Politics*, p. 141.

52 Lewis Edinger and Brigitte L. Nacos, 'From the Bonn to the Berlin Republic: Can a Stable Democracy Continue?', *Political Science Quarterly*, 113: 2 (1998), pp. 179–91.

53 Patton, *Cold War Politics*, p. 145.

54 See the discussion in H. G. Peter Wallach and Ronald A. Francisco, *United Germany: The Past, Politics, Prospects* (Westport, CT: Praeger, 1992), pp. 48–9. There are some notable exceptions to this pattern. Wolfgang Thierse, an East Berliner and founding member of New Forum, has served as president of the Bundestag since 1998. After Kohl's defeat in 1998, Angela Merkel, formerly of the East CDU, became General Secretary and then head of the CDU.

55 'Former Communists Surge In Berlin Municipal Voting', *New York Times*, 11 October 1999.

56 The vote was 338–320 for Berlin. For a discussion of the various positions taken on this issues, see Merkl, *German Unification*, pp. 223–33.

57 Rudiger von Rosen, 'The German Financial System after Unification', *Vital Speeches of the Day*, 58:4 (1991), pp. 114–18.

58 Szabo, *Diplomacy*, pp. 19–21.

59 Patton, *Cold War Politics*, pp. 151–3.

60 Among these are Jeffrey Gedmin, 'Helmut Kohl, Giant', *Policy Review*, 96 (1999), pp. 37–50 and Peter Norman, 'Emu's Broody Hen: Man in the News Helmut Kohl. Peter Norman Profiles the German Chancellor whose Dogged Pursuit of European Integration has Led to the Birth of the Euro', *Financial Times*, 2 May 1998.

61 Margaret Thatcher later stated: 'I was opposed to German unification from early on for the obvious reasons. To unify Germany would make her the dominant nation in the European Community. They are powerful and they are efficient. It would become a German Europe.' See Merkl, *German Unification*, pp. 385–94.

62 Adrian Hyde-Price, 'Berlin Republic Takes to Arms', *The World Today*, 55:6 (1999), pp. 13–15.

63 For a more thorough examination of this policy emphasis, see Mary M. McKenzie, 'Competing Conceptions of Normality in the Post-Cold War Era: Germany, Europe and Foreign Policy Change', *German Politics and Society*, 14:2 (1996), pp. 1–18. Some have suggested that this balancing act may no longer be possible in the post-Cold War era. See James Sperling, 'Germany and the Transatlantic Relationship after Enlargement', Paper presented at the German Studies Conference, San Diego, CA, 4–6 October 2002.

64 As Gerhard Schröder completed the government's move to Berlin in 1999, one account observed: 'German interests are now asserted by Schröder's government without the deference Kohl gave Paris on European unity and Washington on global issues. This is a generational change as much as a political one. And it must be taken into account as the Berlin Republic gives notice it is no longer the willing paymaster for European construction or a silent partner on NATO strategy.' 'New Era For the Old World', *Washington Post*, 27 December 1998.

65 See Peter Katzenstein, 'The Taming of Power: German Unification, 1989–1990', in Meredith Woo-Cumings and Michael Loriaux (eds), *Past as Prelude: History in the Making of a New World Order* (Boulder, CO: Westview Press, 1993) and Harald Müller, 'German Foreign Policy After Unification', in Paul Stares (ed.), *Germany and the New Europe* (Washington, DC: Brookings, 1992), pp. 126–60.

66 'When Squabbling Turns too Dangerous', *Economist*, 15 February 2003, pp. 23–5.

Part II
The legacies of National Socialism

4

Legacies of divided memory and the Berlin Republic

Jeffrey Herf

After more than a half-century, the memory of and debates over the Holocaust occupy an enduring and in some ways even larger place in German public discussion than was the case in the immediate postwar years. This discussion is not only an indicator of how willing or unwilling Germans have been to look honestly at the criminal past. As the historian Dan Diner has put it, 'the Holocaust might well be defined as an identity-forming foundational event'.[1] Despite repeated efforts to displace this memory and the guilt and shame bound up with it, it keeps returning in ways that Diner and others argue have shaped the emergence, legitimacy and persistence of liberal democracy in post-Nazi Germany. To the surprise of many, the memory of the Holocaust continues to shape the discussion of national policy and identity in unified Germany. Both memory and political lessons were decisively shaped by the postwar occupation and multiple restorations of past political traditions in the early postwar period. While early fears that a Berlin Republic would be marked by an end to the traditions of *Vergangenheitsbewältigung* ('mastering the past') were not realised, some disturbing trends have emerged. The voices of those who called for putting the memory of this past aside grew more strident. Anti-Israeli and anti-Semitic outbursts merged with anti-Americanism in places closer to the mainstream of political life. While the predominant tone continued in the traditions of *Vergangenheitsbewältigung*, the lessons drawn from the Nazi past became pluralised and contentious.[2] The memory of the Holocaust in German public life has been neither displaced nor repressed. The contemporary implications of its remembrance, however, remain a source of contention.

The broad outlines of the history of political memory of the Holocaust are now well known.[3] In the occupation era of 1945–49 the victorious Allies crushed remnants of the Nazi party and carried out trials for war crimes and crimes against humanity that led to over 5,000 convictions in the western zones between 1945 and 1949. De-Nazification was never popular with the Germans and the extent of their hostility to it was evident in the amnesty legislation passed by large majorities in the Bundestag as soon as the Federal Republic gained sovereign control over such matters. As Norbert Frei has recently demonstrated, a *Vergangenheitspolitik*, a politics toward the past oriented toward undoing the accomplishments of the occupation era, dominated the early years of the Adenauer era.[4] While avoidance of the whole Nazi period in favour of looking to the future was the dominant mood of the time, another reinforcing tendency was a not surprisingly selective memory of German suffering and victimisation.[5] Yet in the midst of this era of avoidance, silence and selective and self-regarding memory, a minority tradition of West German memory of the murder of European Jewry emerged among some politicians, writers and scholars. This tradition emerged in West Germany both because of restorations of previously defeated political traditions and leaders as well as by the successful destruction of Nazism as a major political force during the occupation years. While millions of Germans avoided discussion of the Holocaust because they were either implicated in crimes, knew others who were, still harboured anti-Semitic views or did not want to examine a criminal past, this same proximity to events drove some political leaders to speak out. For them proximity, personal experience and memory spurred them on to public memory.

The East German memory of the Holocaust

In the Soviet occupation zone and then in the GDR, orthodox Communists led by Walter Ulbricht focused on the connections between capitalism and fascism while giving short shrift to the specifics of anti-Semitism and the mass murder of the Jews. In East Berlin in the immediate postwar years, or the Nuremberg interregnum, the issue of where the mass murder of the Jews should fit into the general Communist memory was most passionately debated first within the organisation Victims of Fascism (OdF, *Opfer des Faschismus*) and later in the Association of those Persecuted by the Nazi Regime (VVN, *Verein des Verfolgten des Naziregimes*). The OdF was the first political organisation to stress, as one headline put it in September 1945, that 'Jews were also victims of fascism' and the first to organise *Gedenktäge* and commemorative events in which memory of the *rassisch Verfolgten* (those persecuted on grounds of race) – that is, Jewish victims, found a place. Though Communists clearly dominated this organisation of former prisoners of concentration camps and members of the anti-Nazi resistance, it also included Social Democrats, Protestant and Catholic clergy, and a large percentage of Jews. In these early years, leaders such as Franz Dahlem, who later fell victim to the anti-cosmopolitan purge of 1952–53, gave speeches that stressed Jewish suffering, as well as the persecution of political prisoners and the peoples of eastern Europe and the Soviet Union.[6] Commemoration had not yet entered the period of a clear, zero-sum game in which the memory of the Jews was marginalised or repressed. Yet even in this early period, and despite Dahlem's comparative inclusiveness, he and other former resistance leaders, such as Alfred Kantorowicz, made a clear and clearly invidious distinction between 'fighters against fascism' and 'victims of fascism'. The distinction broadly overlapped in the minds of leaders of the political resistance with the distinction between Jews and non-Jews, though many Jewish Communists accepted the distinction as well.[7]

The uneasy balance of the memory of Jewish suffering and of Communist martyrdom that one finds in the VVN's early ceremonies came to an end as a result of the anti-cosmopolitan campaign of 1949–53, which reached its high-point in the winter of 1952–53 with the arrest of Paul Merker and the purging of Franz Dahlem from the Central Committee. Merker, who had been a member of KPD Politburo and leader of the Communist emigration in Mexico City, was known for his insistence during and after the Second World War that the Communists placed central focus on fighting anti-Semitism and properly remembering the mass murder of European Jewry. He advocated these policies in the SED's administration during the postwar years but fell afoul of the party line as Stalin cast suspicion on all Communists who had been in western emigration and as the Soviet Union's policy towards Israel turned from initial support to growing hostility. His arrest in December 1952 was part of a broad repression of members of the SED who shared his views on these issues as well as of leaders of the small, remaining Jewish communities in East Germany. He was convicted on trumped-up espionage charges in a secret trial in the East German Supreme Court in 1955. Upon his release in 1956, the charges were dropped. In a statement to the East German Politburo in 1956, Merker emphasised the anti-Semitic nature of the purge.[8] The anti-cosmopolitan purge of the winter of 1952–53 was the decisive event in the history of East German public memory of the Holocaust. Thereafter, the memory of the Nazi crimes against the Jews remained marginalised in the context of an official anti-fascist memory. The contending voices of the early postwar months and years within the Communist Party now gave way to one unified Stalinist version. Further, the purges revived anti-Semitic stereotypes which pejoratively associated presumably powerful Jews with American capitalism and Israel.

Alexander Abusch, who had worked with Merker in Mexico City, endured the anti-cosmopolitan purge and reemerged as a leading cultural official only after a series of recantations of his deviations regarding the Jewish question in wartime Mexican exile, and subsequently served as the Minister of Culture during the planning stages of the major East German memorials to victims of fascism in Buchenwald and Sachsenhausen. East German President Otto Grotewohl chaired the planning committee.[9] In 1954 in memos to the committee, Grotewohl wrote that the memorials' most important goal was 'to place the shame and disgrace of the past before the young generation so that they can draw lessons from it'. Yet they must also 'indicate the path toward the future … give expression to the will for life and struggle that developed among the prisoners' in their 'resistance to Nazi barbarism'. They should combine remembrance of the past and warning for the present and future, while demonstrating that the resistance legacy continued in the policies of East German antifascism.[10] Though the memorials would show the victims' suffering, 'above all they bear witness to the indefatigable strength of the antifascist resistance fighter' and should be 'towering signs of victory over fascism'.[11] In other words, the memorials were Hegelian moments set in stone, intended to encourage optimism about the future based on memory of past heroism more than the reflection of unredeemable past tragedy and catastrophe.

The memorials had clear links to ongoing policy. The committee planning statement for the ceremony of 14 September 1958 convey Grotewohl's intended meaning. For the 'honour of the dead' and for the 'sake of the living', memory admonished 'all of us' to action.[12] The statement denounced West German plans to introduce atomic weapons and missiles into the hands of 'fascist murderers' and 'old Nazi generals'. The planning committee of the Buchenwald dedication demanded an immediate halt to nuclear weapons tests, the creation of a nuclear weapons free zone in central Europe, negotiations for disarmament and detente and peace.[13] Commemoration at Buchenwald was meant to focus attention on present politics and to lend the moral prestige of Communist martyrdom to East German foreign policy. Because it was thought to continue the legacy of Buchenwald's victims and martyrs, dissent from this policy was not only a political error but also held to be a desecration of their secular but sacred memory. The clear message of the memorials was that East Germany was the successor to the anti-fascist resistance fighters, while West Germany was the successor to the fascists and Nazis.[14]

Grotewohl gave the main speech at the dedication of the Buchenwald memorial on 14 September.[15] He praised the heroism of past resistance fighters and called 'the living to action; we urge you not to be paralysed in the struggle against fascism' and for peace. The SED regime used commemorative and other occasions to offer a more benign public view of the Germans and the GDR as heirs to a heroic legacy of resistance. At Buchenwald, 'resistance' to war and fascism now meant opposition to West German rearmament. Hence, fighting the Cold War was synonymous with *Vergangenheitsbewältigung*. Grotewohl's Buchenwald address lacked any public declaration of solidarity with the Jews, past or present. Rather he used the dedication of the first major East German memorial to the victims of fascism to signal East German support for the Arabs in the Middle East conflict.[16]

The most important commemorative event in the history of the GDR took place during the dedication of the memorial to victims of fascism in Sachsenhausen on 24 April 1961. An estimated 200,000 people from East Germany and twenty-three foreign countries attended. Walter Ulbricht delivered a classic, political funeral oration that connected the national past to the East German present and future. He extolled the heroism of 'our precious dead, the fighters against war, fascism and militarism, and to the victims of Nazi terror ... They were driven and tortured to death, and murdered only because they loved their people, because they loved freedom, peace and democracy more than their own life, because they were socialists, because they rejected hatred among peoples, and rejected genocide, and because they dedicated their lives to humanism and to friendship among peoples.'[17] The sacrifices of the anti-fascist resistance '*saved the future of the German nation*'.[18] Ulbricht then recalled the thousands of Communists, Social Democrats, Soviet prisoners of war, and citizens of Poland, Luxembourg, Yugoslavia,

Holland, Belgium, Denmark, Austria, Hungary, Czechoslovakia and France as well as British prisoners of war who had been murdered in Sachsenhausen. He did not mention that Jews were killed in Sachsenhausen or anywhere else.

To be sure, there was some truth in what Ulbricht had to say. There had been 'martyrs and heroes' who were murdered 'only' because of their political convictions and activities. Many did die heroic deaths 'in the struggle' against fascism. Yet the untruths in his statement were even more important. In Sachsenhausen and other concentration camps, the Jews were not murdered because of their political actions or beliefs but simply because they were Jews. Yet Ulbricht clearly privileged 'our precious dead' – the minority of Nazism's victims that was comprised of political opponents, as well as the members of the nations of Europe, especially eastern Europe and the Soviet Union. Ulbricht's Sachsenhausen address was less about mourning for past losses than it was a plea for redemption for the dead.[19] The Holocaust was a mass death that could not be placed or that Ulbricht chose not to place in the service of his ongoing political goals. At the same moment that he laid claim to the mantle of anti-fascism, Ulbricht pushed the memory of the Holocaust to the far margins of official commemorative practice.

In the 1960s, East Germany worked to establish diplomatic and economic ties to the Arab states. During the 1967 Six Day War, the GDR offered resounding support to the Arabs and denounced 'Zionist aggression'. East German hostility to Israel extended to opening a consulate of the Palestinian Liberation Organisation (PLO) in East Berlin in 1970, supporting the 1975 UN resolution equating Zionism with racism, and giving increasing military assistance to the PLO in the decades in which it was openly using terrorism in an effort to destroy the Jewish state. The irony of an 'anti-fascist' regime lending support to states and terrorist organisations at war with the Jewish state will stand as one of the most bizarre features of the East German regime.[20]

The West German memory of the Holocaust

In West Germany a very different kind of commemorative practice emerged in the postwar years. Though Chancellor Konrad Adenauer supported financial restitution for Jewish survivors and for Israel as part of West Germany's responsibility to accept the burden of the Nazi past, his own public comments about the murder of European Jewry were few and far between. He approved a West German national day of mourning (*Volkstrauertag*) in 1952, in which distinctions between perpetrators, bystanders and victims were obliterated.[21] Indeed, at this early stage, some West German politicians included among the 'victims of fascism' those German soldiers who died at the front, civilians killed by allied bombing of German cities and the *Vertriebenen*, Germans who fled and were expelled from eastern Europe in the last year of the war and in the early postwar years. Yet, as has been frequently noted, the Adenauer era was also one of undoing the effects of postwar Allied purges as a result of which many former officials of the Nazi regime were able to recover pensions and in many cases careers in the Federal Republic. The shortcomings of West German de-Nazification are well known. Yet Adenauer initiated a programme of financial restitution to Jewish survivors which disbursed over $90 billion in the postwar decades, and he established a relationship of friendship with and support for Israel that was of considerable importance in the 1950s and 1960s. This was no mean accomplishment for a conservative business leader given the desires of German big business to curry favour with Arab oil interests.[22]

The distinctive West German form of Holocaust commemoration was established by Theodor Heuss, the first President of the Federal Republic, Kurt Schumacher, the first postwar leader of the SPD, as well as by two SPD leaders, Ernst Reuter, the mayor of West Berlin in the early postwar years and Carlo Schmid, the leader of the SPD in the Bundestag.

In the early years, Kurt Schumacher and the SPD were the major political force pushing to include the memory of Jewish suffering in West German public commemoration. Schumacher was the political figure most admired and cherished by Jewish survivors. He was the first German politician in the postwar period to support financial restitution to Jewish survivors and to give prominence to the murder of the Jews in postwar public memory. Indeed, had it not been for Social Democratic support, Adenauer would not have been able to pass the early restitution measures. Following Schumacher's death in 1952, Ernst Reuter and Carlo Schmid took the most prominent roles in continuing the Social Democratic contribution to the West German memory of the Nazi murder of Europe's Jews.

On 19 April 1953, at a memorial for the tenth anniversary of the Warsaw Ghetto's destruction, Reuter delivered his most impassioned statement regarding the genocide of European Jewry. It remains one of the most moving and powerful statements of its kind in postwar German political culture:

> Ten years ago today, on April 19, 1943, following Hitler's orders, the attack on the Warsaw Ghetto began. Its goal was, as totalitarian discourse put it, liquidation of the ghetto. And then something began in the history of these awful years that indeed are behind us but still today burden our souls as a nightmare. It was something that the world had not seen before: Hitler's victims rebelled. They stood together. They fought to their last breath. They defended their lives. But by sacrificing their lives to the last person, they defended more than a short span of their lives. They defended their honour. They defended their rights. They defended everything that is sacred to every one of us in this room: the right of every human being to be free, free to live and free to raise his head to the heavens …
>
> We live in a time that is inclined to forget all too quickly. But in this hour we want to say that there are things which we are not permitted to forget, and which we do not want to forget: As Germans – I speak to you here as well as to my Jewish fellow countrymen as a German – we must not and we cannot forget the disgrace and shame that took place in our German name.[23]

Reuter's commemorative evocation of Jewish heroism and martyrdom was unusual then – and it has remained unusual – in the canon of official expressions of postwar memory. Perhaps for postwar Germans, Reuter's comments expressed a discomforting commonality between non-Jewish anti-Nazis and the Jews; they broke with stereotypes of passive Jewish victimisation. Or, perhaps most German politicians were simply reluctant to praise Jews in the Warsaw ghetto who took up arms against German soldiers.

In the same speech, Reuter dramatically underscored his solidarity with Hitler's Jewish victims. That solidarity came both from moral and political convictions and his personal experience of imprisonment in 1933–34.[24] Proximity to events and personal memories drove many of Reuter's contemporaries to keep their heads down and mouths shut. Proximity impelled him to speech and political action. In contrast to the famous historical optimism of Social Democracy before 1914 Reuter, as Schumacher before him, was driven less by confident theories of future happiness than by the memory of past injustice and cruelty. A German intellectual and moral renewal was essential in order to ensure that those who died in the Warsaw ghetto 'did not die in vain. For they moved our conscience, and our conscience has not and will not let us sleep until we have reached this great and beautiful goal.'[25] Reuter was one of the first West German political leaders to evoke Jewish martyrdom and heroism as an inspiration for a democratic renewal in the Federal Republic.

From the earliest moments, postwar political memory included efforts to balance and weigh the relative suffering and victimisation of different groups, including the Germans themselves. Carlo Schmid made a number of important yet rarely noted public contributions to West German commemorative practices. Schmid was a leading voice in favour of restitution payments to Jewish survivors.[26] In the Federal Republic, no less than in the GDR, the issue of restitution required making determinations about who was and who was not a victim of National Socialism, who among these victims had suffered most and who had a moral claim to restitution. The *Wiedergutmachung*, or restitution, debates entailed making distinctions among the kinds and extent of suffering during the Nazi era. In the February 1951 Bundestag restitution debates, Schmid argued against an undifferentiated view of past suffering which transformed everyone into a victim of Nazism:

> Certainly, there are many victims of the Third Reich. One could say that almost all of those who survived the period are victims. But one shouldn't make this all too easy and forget that there are distinctions among them. People are beginning to forget. Indeed, things are getting to the point that even former SS and SD men are beginning to regard themselves as victims of National Socialism ... [rumbling among the SPD] ... and those who were given a negative classification by the denazification counsels are already beginning to consider themselves to be victims of National Socialism![27]

Schmid warned against forgetting just who 'the really special victims of National Socialism' had been.[28] Generalising the victim category went hand-in-hand with obscuring the special features of the extermination of the Jewish people:[29]

> Among all that the Nazi regime brought about, the crimes committed against our Jewish fellow human beings were the most awful, not only because of the extent of murder, not only because it was a matter of millions of victims, not only due to the methodical mercilessness of the gassing in Auschwitz and Maidanek, not only because these acts of butchery also fell on women and children, but also because the whole Third Reich at its basis, at its core was set up to exterminate the Jews! [vigorous

> applause]. The Third Reich was integrated very much more around antisemitism than around, one is ashamed to use the term 'pro-German' sentiment.[30]

Schmid rejected an apolitical remorse for past victims that made no distinctions between perpetrators and victims. Such a stance was not a sign of higher morality. Rather, it represented an enduring failure to think clearly about politics and morality, or about the nature of the Nazi regime. In contrast to those who wished to place the Holocaust on the fringes of the Nazi era, Schmid insisted that it lay at the core of what the Nazi regime was about, and that Germans understood this to be so at the time. Hence to equate all victims was both morally unacceptable and historically inaccurate. It rested on a distorted and apologetic understanding of the Nazi regime.

Theodor Heuss, the first *Bundespräsident*, founded the distinctive West German governmental tradition of memory. His singular accomplishment as President was to make the memory of the crimes of the Nazi era a constitutive element of national political memory and to associate it with a redefined understanding of national honour, even patriotism. To his critics, he was the cultured veneer obscuring the failures of denazification in the Adenauer era. His efforts to keep the memory of Jewish persecution before the West German public never extended to similar efforts to bring about timely justice. Yet in speeches about German history, extensive private correspondence with Jewish survivors, resistance veterans and West German and foreign intellectuals, Heuss planted the seeds within the West German political and intellectual elites for subsequent, broader public discussion and action. He evoked German liberal aspirations and honoured those who had stood for democracy and human rights in German history. He expressed a sense of loss for the destruction of the German–Jewish country in which he had come of age, and used commemorative occasions to urge postwar West Germans to face the Jewish catastrophe directly. He defined courage as the willingness to truthfully confront a disastrous past.

Just as Grotewohl in Buchenwald and Ulbricht in Sachsenhausen both defined the East German commemorative style, so Heuss' speech in Bergen-Belsen on 30 November 1952 was the defining commemorative speech of West German practice. The Bergen-Belsen ceremonies reflected the realities of divided memory. It was a very western event. Attending were government representatives from Britain, the United States, Denmark, Belgium, the Netherlands, Switzerland, Sweden,

France, Yugoslavia, Israel and the Jewish communities in Germany, Europe and the United States. None of the Communist states was represented. Nahum Goldmann spoke on behalf of the World Jewish Congress. The speeches were broadcast over national radio.[31]

The Jewish catastrophe, which had been marginalised in official East German anti-fascist narratives, came to the fore at the Bergen-Belsen ceremonies. Though Jewish survivors had gathered at the former concentration camps since 1945 for memorial services, the 30 November 1952 ceremony at Bergen-Belsen was the first occasion on which they were joined by the ceremonial head of state of the Federal Republic. In the presence of Heuss and the assembled officials, Goldmann delivered a powerful narrative of Jewish suffering:[32]

> Speaking in the name of Jews around the world I repeat in this hour our pledge never to forget these dead. For all time, we will carry the memory of these martyrs, who died only because they were Jews, in our hearts and in the hearts of our children and children's children. With the inextinguishable memory that is the characteristic of our people, we will forever keep reflection on the Jewish victims of Nazi terror in our history. The ten thousand who are buried here symbolize for us all the millions who found their tragic end in Auschwitz, Treblinka, Dachau, and in Warsaw, and Vilna and Ballistics and in countless other places.[33]

Goldmann's speech in Bergen-Belsen was the fullest account of the Holocaust presented at a political memorial ceremony in the first postwar decade in West Germany. Had he delivered it in East Berlin, it could have landed him in prison. Yet Goldmann, who fitted the image of the Jewish cosmopolitan denounced by the Communists, drew attention to the *eastern geography* of the Jewish catastrophe. His memory of the Holocaust did not fit within the constraints of divided memory. In Bergen-Belsen, Goldmann broke the barriers of Cold War memory to recall the millions who were murdered in places then in the Soviet bloc, namely, Auschwitz, Treblinka, Warsaw and 'countless other places'. At the same time that Stalinists such as Hermann Matern denounced the Jews as a source of western influence, Goldmann pointed out that the geography of memory did not fit easily into the political fault lines of the Cold War. Memories of Nazi barbarism on the Eastern front in the Second World War were not at all common in the western anticommunist narratives of the time. Memory of the Holocaust remained an uncomfortable, troubling often inconvenient accompaniment to West German elite recollection. Though most of the Holocaust took place in eastern Europe and the Nazi-occupied Soviet Union, it was in the West during the bitterest days of the Cold War that the memory of the Holocaust first found adequate public expression. Those generally left-of-centre political figures, who were most inclined to reflect on anti-Semitism and the Holocaust, were also those most willing to recall the suffering of the non-Jewish peoples of eastern Europe and the Soviet Union. That said, in Bergen-Belsen, the memory of the Holocaust was largely separated from memory of German race war on the Eastern front as a whole. In the era of divided memory, the separation of the memory of the Holocaust from the memory of non-Jewish victims was common in the commemorative practices in both Germanys.

Heuss' speech in Bergen-Belsen became known by its most famous sentence: 'No one, no one will ever lift this shame from us'. It was the most extensive public reflection to come from a leading official of the West German government regarding the crimes of the Nazi era. It was broadcast on radio, and then reported in the West German press, especially the liberal press. The West German government press office reprinted the text.[34] Heuss' speech marked a watershed for several reasons. He affirmed the inclusion of memory of Jewish suffering in postwar West German political memory.[35] He rejected efforts to obscure distinctions among victims, to equate Jewish suffering with that of other groups, or to divert attention from German culpability by pointing to the misdeeds of others. He rejected the arguments of postwar Germans concerning what 'the others' had done in the Allied internment camps of 1945–46, the camps in the Soviet zone or the East German show trials in Waldheim. Such balancing of accounts 'endangers the clear, honourable feeling for the fatherland of everyone who consciously knows our history' and faces up to it. Violence and injustice were not things to 'be used for mutual compensation'.[36] In Bergen-Belsen, there were many victims of other countries and many Germans as well. But this place had a 'deep meaning, which Nahum Goldmann expressed for everyone'. Economic competition and religious fanaticism had made their contributions to the Nazi crimes. But it was the 'breakthrough of biological naturalism', that led to the 'pedantry of murder as a sheer automatic process … No one, no one will lift this shame from us.'[37] He also rejected appeals to leave the past in the past. 'The Jews will never forget, they cannot ever forget what was done to them. The Germans must not, and cannot ever forget what human beings from their own people did in these years so rich in shame.' He replied to those who pointed to the misdeeds of 'the others': 'It seems to me that the scales of virtue (*Tugendtarif*) with which the peoples defend themselves by comparison with others, is a corrupting and banal affair. It endangers a clear, honourable feeling for one's country which everyone who consciously places himself or herself in its history carries.'[38] Heuss spoke up for a patriotism self-confident enough to face honestly the dark past. 'Honourable feeling for one's country' was not composed of comforting myths and resentment at others. Heuss sought to place the language of patriotism in the service of memory rather than avoidance and resentment. For Heuss, the moral imperative to recall the crimes of the Nazi era was not a burden imposed by the occupiers and victors but an imperative demanded by the better traditions of a still existing 'other Germany'.

Heuss placed Jewish suffering at the centre of official West German memory of the Nazi era. He put the conservative forces in the Federal Republic on notice that he would oppose those who sought to equate amnesia and avoidance with the national interest or national honour, or again to misuse the discourse of patriotism for their own purposes. For him, memory, not avoidance, of a difficult past was a matter of national honour. He initiated an often unpopular but never completely extinguished component of the Federal Republic's identity.

Generational change, the Eichmann trial in Jerusalem, the efforts of state attorneys general such as Fritz Bauer in Hessen culminating in the Frankfurt Auschwitz Trial and Bundestag debates over extension of statutes of limitation on prosecution of crimes of murder all contributed to expansion of public discussion of the crimes of the Nazi era.[39] The emergence of the new left and the reemergence of Marxism as a potent influence in West German intellectual life – not long after the SPD had distanced itself from Marxism in mainstream politics at the Bad Godesberg congress in 1959 – had an ambiguous impact on memory of the Holocaust. On the one hand, the political and moral impulse of the 1960s new left was to break away from the culture of forgetting of the first postwar decades. On the other hand, the Marxist categories in which it sought to place the Nazi era undermined an effort to grasp the particulars of anti-Semitism and the Jewish experience, rooted as these were in ideological postulates not derivable from analyses focused on class and capitalism.[40] By generalising the events in Germany into universal features of capitalism/fascism, the Marxist discussion also had an ironic unburdening impact while intending at the outset to do just the reverse.[41] Things became so confused and contorted in parts of the West German leftist scene that by 1975, West German terrorists were involved in an airplane hijacking in Entebbe that entailed threatening the lives of Jewish, not only Israeli, passengers.[42]

With the election of Willy Brandt in 1969, his implementation of *Ostpolitik*, his bended knee in 1970 at the memorial to the Jews of the Warsaw Ghetto and repeated public assertions of the need to remember the suffering inflicted by Nazi Germany on the Eastern front in the Second World War, the West German tradition of memory of the Holocaust received its most powerful boost ever from a sitting West German Chancellor. What had been an elite, minority tradition now diffused into broader spheres. With Brandt, West Germany had a Chancellor who viewed memory of the crimes of the Nazi era less as an embarrassing burden than as an indispensable component of the Federal Republic's effort to regain trust which had been smashed by Nazi Germany's crimes and aggressions. By 1979, when the American docudrama 'Holocaust' was broadcast in West Germany it touched a nerve regarding the specific fate of the Jews so that for the first time the elite discussion of this crime spread beyond political and intellectual elites to a broader public audience.[43]

The history of the memory of the Holocaust in West Germany is also the history of opposition to that memory. By no means the first but one of the most important chapters of that opposition cam from some conservatives in the 1980s who were reacting against the Social–Liberal era. Part of that reaction sought a greater focus on German victimisation similar to that which Carlo Schmid had criticised in the 1950s. In the 1980s, this impulse led to the ill-fated visit by President Ronald Reagan to the military cemetery in Bitburg. Another enduring theme of opposition to the traditions of *Vergangenheitsbewältigung* was the effort to compare the Holocaust to other terrible crimes, deny its uniqueness or even to suggest it was modelled on and a reaction to previous Soviet events. When the historian Ernst Nolte put forward such a thesis in the wake of the Bitburg affair and the social theorist Jürgen Habermas rejected Nolte's arguments, the *Historikerstreit*, the 'historians' debate', flared up in the cultural pages of West Germany's major newspapers.[44] Observers of the dispute agreed that a consensus emerged that efforts to diminish the uniqueness of the Holocaust or to diminish its singularity had failed. At the level of broad public opinion, the speech of *Bundespräsident* Richard von Weizäcker on 8 May 1985 was of even greater and more enduring importance.

Weizsäcker's speech reaffirmed and deepened the tradition which

Heuss and Schumacher had begun, made all the more powerful as it came from a political figure of the centre-right.[45] 8 May 1945 represented the defeat of the Nazi Germany, but it 'was a day of liberation' from 'the inhumanity and tyranny of the National Socialist regime'. In response to Germans who regarded 8 May as the beginning of flight, expulsion and dictatorship in the East, von Weizäcker insisted that the cause of Germans' postwar problems 'goes back to the start of the tyranny that brought about war. We must not separate May 8, 1945, from January 30, 1933.'[46] Rather than remember the sufferings of one group at the expense of another, he urged Germans to mourn for 'all the dead of the war and the tyranny'.[47] He listed the victims in the following order: 6 million Jews; 'countless citizens [in the] Soviet Union and Poland'; German soldiers, German citizens killed in air raids, captivity or during expulsion; the Sinti and Gypsies; the homosexuals and mentally ill; those killed due to their religious or political beliefs; hostages; members of resistance movements 'in all countries occupied by us', and also 'the victims of the German resistance – among the public, the military, the churches, the workers and trade unions, and the Communists'.[48] This was the most comprehensive listing of Nazi victims yet made by a West German *Bundespräsident*, and was one that crossed the Cold War fault lines which had distorted memory in Bitburg.

The narrative structure of the speech dispensed with a happy ending, whether it be Ulbricht's victorious socialism in Sachsenhausen in 1961, or the reconciliation of former enemies of Reagan and Kohl in Bitburg. Memory meant the ability to mourn and to grieve about 'the endless army of the dead' and the suffering of those who survived.[49] Like Heuss, Weizsäcker presented a most unHegelian narrative of unredeemed suffering and tragedy and he placed anti-Semitism and the Holocaust at the centre of discussion.[50] While hardly any country was free of violence in its history, 'the genocide of the Jews is, however, unparalleled in history'. Though 'the perpetuation of this crime was in the hands of a few people' and was concealed from the public, 'every German was able to experience what his Jewish compatriots had to suffer, ranging from plain apathy and hidden intolerance to outright hatred. Who could remain unsuspecting' after the persecutions of the Jews in the 1930s. Anyone who 'opened his eyes and ears and sought information could not fail to notice that the Jews were being deported'.[51]

As the dispute over euromissiles in the early 1980s had demonstrated, in West German political culture, with a few exceptions, the lessons of genocide at Auschwitz and appeasement in Munich had been neatly apportioned between left and right. Weizsäcker brought together the memories of appeasement in the 1930s with those of genocide and war in the 1940s. Though he stressed that Hitler had been 'the driving force' on the road to disaster, he recalled the failure of the western powers to stop Hitler, as well as the non-aggression pact with the Soviet Union in 1939. Yet, while some West German politicians had pointed to these episodes to point the finger of blame at others, Weizsäcker emphasised that the failures of the other powers do 'not mitigate Germany's responsibility for the outbreak of the Second World War'. Moreover, he traced the postwar division of Germany to the policies of Nazi Germany.[52] Weizsäcker's speech showed the impact of Brandt's challenge to the political culture of the Adenauer era. By insisting that 8 May 1945 must not be separated from 30 January 1933, Weizäcker placed postwar history into a longer chronological causal sequence. He named the Nazis' victims, and included the Communists within the anti-Nazi resistance. He asserted that many Germans knew that genocide was taking place and that too many members of his own generation either remained silent or refused to learn more about what was taking place. He stressed that the postwar division of Europe and Germany had its roots in the Nazi seizure of power and the Second World War, and called 8 May 1945 a day of liberation. These assertions angered and provoked some West German conservatives.[53] However, especially because it came only days after Bitburg, the response to Weizsäcker's speech both in West Germany and abroad was overwhelmingly favourable. The distinctive West German tradition inaugurated by Heuss and Schumacher emerged from the debates of the mid-1980s stronger, more widespread and more explicit in its willingness not only to discuss the genocide of the Jews but to place this crime in the centre of West German memories of the Nazi era.

Memory in a unifying Germany

As of 1989–90, West Germany's traditions of memory of the Holocaust, though repeatedly attacked, had emerged stronger and more resilient with more advocates than in earlier decades. To be sure, the euphoria unleashed by German unification included nationalist excesses as well as the emergence of a violent, neo-Nazi scene. Yet the leitmotif of

Helmut Kohl's diplomacy surrounding German unification was the need to embed the new, larger Germany into European institutions.[54] Germany needed to reassure Europe that its unification did not signal an era of forgetfulness and nationalist bluster.

Just as the marginalisation of the Jewish question had been a chapter in the consolidation of the East German dictatorship, its return to prominence in East German politics was also an important chapter in the reemergence of democracy. Surprisingly, the first act of East Germany's first democratically elected government ended forty years of Communist denial and evasion regarding the Holocaust and its consequences. On 12 April 1990 the Volkskammer voted 379 to 0, with 21 abstentions, to approve a resolution that accepted joint responsibility for Nazi crimes, and expressed a willingness both to pay reparations and to seek diplomatic ties with Israel.[55] On 14 April 1990 the headline of the left-liberal *Frankfurter Rundschau*, the West German daily which had most carefully reported on the anti-Jewish purges of the 1950s, firmly established the link between democratisation and discussion of the Holocaust.[56] The Volkskammer statement broke with the view West Germans alone should bear the burden of the crimes of the Nazi era, or that it was a marginal event in the history of Nazism and the Second World War. Gone were the arrogance and lack of historical self-consciousness which led East German political leaders to lend support to Israel's armed adversaries. Gone was a forty-year legacy of anti-Semitic code words clothed in Marxist–Leninist slogans and denials that anti-Semitism could exist in an officially anti-fascist regime.[57]

Yet, throughout the 1990s, calls for a 'line to be finally drawn under the past' (a *Schlußstrich*) continued. They came from unrespectable neo-Nazis and skinheads as well as from respectable conservative intellectuals. In the autumn of 1998 the German novelist Martin Walser unleashed a tempest in the German establishment in a speech on the occasion of the reception of the Peace Prize of German Publishers. He attacked the public culture of German commemoration of the Holocaust as a 'moral cudgel' thereby unleashing yet more public controversy.[58] In turn, Ignatz Bubis, then chairman of the Central Conference of Jews in Germany, sharply criticised Walser's speech as an effort to displace the memory of the Holocaust in German public discourse, one which had previously been the prerogative of the fringe, hard right in German politics and culture. Chancellor Kohl continued to oppose changes in Germany's ethnically based citizenship laws, and refused to adopt as high a profile as he could have in support of foreigners subject to violence from right-wing extremists. On the other hand, rather than returning to the facile comparisons of Bitburg, Kohl in the 1990s emerged as one of the strongest supporters of the proposed Berlin memorial to Europe's murdered Jews. In short, despite repeated pleas to 'finally' put the past behind, the long conservative chancellorship of Helmut Kohl did not usher in a new era of forgetfulness. The postwar tradition of public memory survived.

Ironically, Chancellor Gerhard Schröder, the leader of the SPD–Green coalition elected in 1998, initially sounded the themes of leaving the past behind and looking to the future in ways that would have been sharply criticised had they come from the lips of Helmut Kohl. Conventional wisdom had it that members of the generation of 1968, having broken in the 1960s with the apologia and silence of the postwar era, would continue to remember publicly what conservatives had previously sought to forget, cover up, and relativise when they had the opportunity to govern in the 1980s and 1990s. Yet, in the summer and fall of 1998, SPD chancellor candidate Schröder and his nominee for the new position of cultural minister, Michael Naumann, struck very different tones in speaking of the need for Germans to look to the future rather than succumb to the burdens of the past. Beginning in the early 1990s, an initiative of intellectuals and public figures in Berlin had supported construction of a Holocaust memorial in the heart of the Berlin, the new capital of a unified Germany.[59] Naumann's initial reservations about the proposal elicited significant protest from across the domestic political spectrum.[60]

Supporters of the Berlin Holocaust memorial, notably the television journalist Leah Rosh, and the historian Eberhard Jaeckel, argued that such a memorial in Berlin's centre was morally and politically essential because: the genocide of European Jewry was central in Nazi policy and war aims; this genocide had been directed from the government offices in Berlin; the existing concentration camp memorials within Germany were not the places at which the mass murder of European Jewry had taken place and in any case were comfortably out of sight and out of mind in Berlin; and the movement of the German government from Bonn to Berlin must not be accompanied by a desire to push the difficult past from view. Construction of such a memorial was a powerful signal to Germans and observers outside Germany that unification had not brought about a forgetful Germany. Chancellor Kohl, in the heat of the autumn 1998 election campaign, strongly supported the construction of a memorial. Schröder, however, struck a decidedly more ambiguous tone while stressing the need to look to the future. While some left-leaning intellectual veterans of 1968 expressed their doubts, the Bündnis 90/Green *Fraktion* in Bonn was particularly emphatic in its support for the memorial.[61]

In January 1999, Chancellor Gerhard Schröder stepped away from the equivocations of the summer and autumn of 1998 and embraced a proposal to build a slightly modified version of Peter Eisenman's design for a Berlin Holocaust memorial in combination with an archive and museum on the same site. Efforts of the last half of 1998 to focus on the future at the expense of memory failed just as previous efforts to do so in postwar West Germany had. As in years past, there were too many 'other Germanys', too many fellow Europeans, too many survivors of the Holocaust and their children and grandchildren – and now, more than ever, too many other German politicians and citizens who had incorporated and deepened the founding traditions of postwar memory to accept its displacement. On 25 June 1999, following over a decade of debate first in Berlin and then nationwide, the members of the Bundestag by a large majority of 314 to 209, with 14 abstentions, voted in favour of building the national memorial in Berlin.[62] Construction is now under way.

The memory and ascribed meaning of the Holocaust changed the content and direction of German foreign policy. In 1998 and 1999, the new German Foreign Minister, Joschka Fischer, surprised and irritated many members of his own Green Party when he spoke out in favour of, albeit belated, German armed intervention to help to put an end to murder and violence accompanying Serbia's policies of war and ethnic cleansing in the Balkans. Sweeping aside arguments that Germany should not support NATO intervention in the Balkans because of what the Nazi armies did in Yugoslavia during the Second World War, Fischer made the case that because of the memory of the Holocaust, Germany had a particular responsibility to intervene, with force if necessary, to prevent ongoing acts of mass murder and gross violations of human rights.[63] The memory of the Holocaust, he and others argued, must not become an excuse for permanent non-intervention when faced with ongoing crimes in the present. Fischer's arguments of 1998–99 stood in a striking contrast to those he had made in the contentious debates in the Bundestag during the dispute over the euromissiles. In spring of 1983, he compared the logic of Western nuclear deterrence to 'the logic of the modern' that had led to Auschwitz. He made these comments in response to the arguments of Heiner Geissler, a leading figure of the Christian Democratic Union, who had no less provocatively said that it was the peace movements of the 1930s which had first made Auschwitz possible by their support of Britain's policy of appeasement.[64] In the polarised climate of the spring of 1983, the lessons of the past seemed to divide, with some exceptions, neatly on political lines. Conservatives recalled the Churchillian lessons of the danger of appeasing dictatorships, while liberals and leftists evoked the memory of Auschwitz to denounce Western nuclear deterrence. Perhaps as a result of the ferment of the Historians' dispute, the Weizäcker speech and the debates over the Berlin Holocaust Memorial, the lessons of the Holocaust in Germany by 1998–99 had become more complex, crossing political lines in unexpected ways. The call for armed intervention to stop ethnic cleansing in Kosovo from liberals and left-of-centre figures indicated that, at least in this instance, the memory of Auschwitz did not have the pacifist and neutralist implications it had in the early 1980s.

Conclusion

Allied victory, postwar occupation and multiple restorations of previously defeated, pre-1933 German anti-Nazi traditions all made decisive contributions to the emergence of public memory of the Holocaust in the immediate postwar decades. Yet at the same time, from the East German purges from 1949 to 1956 to the bitter West German attacks on the American 'East Coast press' (i.e. *New York Times*) during the Bitburg affair, those in both postwar Germanys who opposed public memory of the Holocaust have repeatedly attributed efforts to give it prominence to foreign – primarily Israeli, American, or simply Jewish – influences. At times, such arguments have been associated with old stereotypes about the power of international Jewry. The statement during the Bundestag debate over the Berlin memorial by SPD member and Bundestag President Wolfgang Thierse is of interest in this regard:

> Today we must decide. After a debate lasting nine years, do we want to build a memorial to the murdered Jews of Europe in Berlin? Again and again, I hear that all of the arguments have been made. But I also hear that we, the Germans, are no longer free in our decision. The public as well as the international pressure is so great that the decision has in effect already been made. To that I say: this is our, yes, our decision to make,

> one that we take from our sense of responsibility with a view to our own national history and to the conditions of its memory.[65]

Thierse went on to reject calls for a *Schlußstrich* and praised the founders of the citizens' initiative supporting the memorial in Berlin. Then, in phrases reminiscent of Heuss and Schumacher, Thierse concluded as follows: 'The memorial that is the subject of today's decision aims at future generations with the message: Shame is a moment of our human dignity. Moral duties in the present and capacity to master the future grow from political and practical reflection on our history, one bound up with unimaginable injustice.'[66]

Had the Allies not fought the war to an unconditional surrender, arrested and put on trial the Nazi regime's leading figures, and ensured through the occupation that Nazism would not return to postwar German politics as a major factor, the prospects for any public memory of the Holocaust or any other crimes of the Nazi regime would have been slim to none. Those Allied policies made possible the emergence of postwar memory, first in Schumacher and Heuss' public pronouncements. The collapse of the GDR and its official anti-fascism, in which the specifics of the Jewish catastrophe could find little or no room, was another precondition for the persistence of Holocaust memory in unified Germany. The oft defeated and then revived indigenous traditions of democracy and human rights were evident in the Bundestag vote of 1999. Thierse's comments indicate that for the still dominant segment of the national political establishment, public acknowledgment of a criminal and shameful past was the result of outside pressures. Rather, as some of the founders of democracy hoped, and as odd as it may seem to many, such acknowledgement itself has been and remains one source of a distinctive sense of honour and moral obligation in now longstanding and not easily dislodged postwar traditions. The memory of the Holocaust had become part of what Dolf Sternberger and Jürgen Habermas had called 'constitutional patriotism', a conception of citizenship in which memory of the Nazi past played a key role.[67]

As time passes, a new era of indifference and relieved break from the burdens of German memory of the Holocaust past is always possible. Certainly, such desires will remain part of German public life in the future as they have in the past. Should such a new era of forgetfulness emerge, it will have to fight what has so far been an uphill and unsuccessful battle to displace the centrality of the memory of what the German political establishment beginning with Heuss and Schumacher recognised as 'an identity forming foundational event'.

One of the striking features of history and memory in unified Germany has been the examination of the East German dictatorship. Parliamentary investigations, trials, the opening of access to Stasi files and a flood of historical scholarship have subjected the East German regime to a level of scrutiny beyond that of any other former Communist regime.[68] A certain intellectual freedom, and willingness to examine differences but also similarities between fascist, Nazi and the Communist dictatorships has reentered German scholarly and intellectual life, pushing somewhat to the side the ideological polarisation which at times distorted intellectual work during the Cold War. Working through the memory and history of this second German dictatorship has become an important feature of historical scholarship in Germany. Scholars, writers and political actors examining East German history have explored the vexing questions of anti-Semitism and the memory of the Holocaust, the mix of fact and fiction in the official formulæ of anti-fascism, as well as the grim details of the apparatus of terror and surveillance as they affected political, religious, educational and economic spheres. The impetus to confront the past honestly in the spirit of von Weizsäcker's speech of 1985 survived in the work of Joachim Gauck and his staff which worked to make the files of the Stasi accessible to scholars, journalists and to its former victims.[69] As the only major country in Europe to experience dictatorships of both the right and the left, Germany looks back on the twentieth century with an understandably strong interest in coming to terms with these difficult pasts. Indeed, this theme has become one of the defining ones of its intellectual and scholarly life.

Postscript

Chancellor Gerhard Schröder's refusal in summer 2002 to support a war against Saddam Hussein's Iraq, even if it was approved by the UN Security Council, to ride the 'peace' issue against American policy to electoral victory in the autumn elections and to join France and Russia in opposition to American policy in the United Nations and then during the war with Iraq all raise issues of direct relevance for the memory of the Holocaust in Germany. There is little doubt that Schröder's position was popular with a majority of Germans and judging from editorials in leading newspapers and comments by leading politicians, much of the German establishment as well. This turn of events, and the deep tensions in American–German relations that resulted, put the lessons of the Holocaust into a rather different light.

The axiom that changes in political culture and basic mentalities proceed more slowly than does the pace of political events has been borne out by the German response to the Iraq crisis. For faced with the Ba'ath party and regime in Iraq with deep ideological connections to the European fascist past – especially France's *Action Française* of the 1930s and 1940s – Chancellor Schröder, Foreign Minister Fischer and the majority of the German political establishment (not only its left-of-centre component) rejected all of the arguments for going to war should the Iraqi regime refuse to disarm as required by UN resolutions whether the arguments were made by American President George Bush or British Prime Minister Tony Blair. Where Blair and his Foreign Minister, Jack Straw, repeatedly made arguments in the Churchillian tradition warning of the dangers of allowing Iraq to accumulate weapons of mass destruction and/or to give support to terrorism, the German leadership remained adamant that these lessons of appeasement did not apply in this instance.[70] When the United States and Britain warned that the United Nations was in danger of losing credibility just at the League of Nations had when faced with Italian and German aggression in the 1930s, the German leadership followed the French in dismissing Anglo-American fears and warned instead that war would only make a bad situation worse. Schröder focused on successful disarmament through peaceful measures.[71] The ideological links and structural similarities to the fascist and totalitarian dictatorships of Europe's mid-century were dismissed in the German discussion as historically unfounded. Saddam Hussein's threats against Israel seemed to leave most German commentators unmoved, as if the memory of the Holocaust had no implications for thinking about real threats to the Jewish state in the present.

Only a minority of German political and intellectual public figures connected the memory of the Holocaust in Germany to the need to resort to force against the threat posed by totalitarianism in Iraq.[72] Indeed, one German cabinet member had to resign after comparing President Bush's tactics to Hitler's while a more prevalent mood was that the United States, not Iraq, posed the greatest threat to world peace. There were also ugly rumblings about excessive Jewish influence on American foreign policy. The evidence of German public discussion suggests that Germans after Nazism, to the extent to which they have thought about the Holocaust, have thought about German perpetrators and Jewish victims far more than they have about why the Second

World War could take place to begin with and then how it was that the Allies defeated the Axis powers. The memory of the Holocaust remains a key element of German national self-understanding and commitment to liberal democratic values and individual human rights. Especially when compared with the avoidance and myth making of other nations facing difficult pasts, the German public record of confronting the criminal past, with all of its well-known shortcomings and missed opportunities, is impressive. But one aspect of that memory and its attendant lesson, namely the need for liberal democracies to resort to force when the world is made dangerous by totalitarian dictatorship, had not yet, in 2003, become a major component of the German confrontation with the Nazi past.

Notes

1 Dan Diner, *Beyond the Conceivable: Studies on Germany, Nazism and the Holocaust* (Berkeley and Los Angeles: University of California Press, 2000), p. 218.

2 On this complex, see, among others, Dan Diner, *Feindbild Amerika: Über die Bestädigkeit eines Ressentiments* (Munich: Propylaen Verlag, 2002).

3 Jeffrey Herf, *Divided Memory: The Nazi Past in the Two Germanys* (Cambridge, MA: Harvard University Press, 1997).

4 Norbert Frei, *The Adenauer Era and the Nazi Past*, trans. by Joel Golb (New York: Columbia University Press, 2002).

5 See Robert G. Moeller, *War Stories: The Search for a Usable Past in the Federal Republic of Germany* (Berkeley and Los Angeles: University of California Press, 2001).

6 For Dahlem's description of the treatment of prisoners in the concentration camp in Mauthausen, see Franz Dahlem, 'Einige Probleme unserer künftigen Arbeit in Deutschland: Rede vor ehemaligen Häftlingen des KZ Mauthausen', in Franz Dahlem, *Ausgewählte Reden und Aufsätze 1919–1979. Zur Geschichte der Arbeiterbewegung* ((East) Berlin: Dietz Verlag, 1980), pp. 251–69. On Mauthausen, see Gordon J. Horwitz, *In the Shadow of Death: Living Outside the Gates of Mauthausen* (New York: Free Press, 1990).

7 On the compromises, myth-making and strategies of survival of Dahlem and other leading German Communists in the East German government, see Catherine Epstein, *The Last Revolutionaries: German Communists and Their Century* (Cambridge, MA: Harvard University Press, 2003).

8 For a full account of the anti-cosmopolitan purges and the Marker case, see Herf, *Divided Memory.*

9 See SAPMO-BA, ZPA NL Otto Grotewohl 90/553.

10 Otto Grotewohl, 'Mahn- und Gedenkstätte Buchenwald' (13 January, 1958), SAPMO-BA, ZPA NL Otto Grotewohl 90/553, p. 95.

11 *Ibid.*, p. 96.

12 'Aufruf des Komitees für die Einweihung der Mahn- und Gedenkstätte Buchenwald', SAPMO-BA, ZPA NL Otto Grotewohl 90/553, p. 46.

13 *Ibid.*

14 There are parallels to postwar myths of both the Gaullists and Communists regarding France as supposedly a nation of resistance. On this see Henry Russo, *The Vichy Syndrome: History and Memory in France Since 1944*, trans. by Arthur Goldhammer (Cambridge, MA.: Harvard University Press, 1991).

15 Otto Grotewohl, 'Buchenwald mahnt! Rede zur Weihe der nationalen Mahn- und Gedenkstätte Buchenwald, 14 September 1958', in Otto Grotewohl, *Im Kampf um Die Einige Deutsche Demokratische Republik: Reden und Aufsätze, Band VI, Auswahl aus den Jahren 1958–1960* ((East) Berlin: Dietz Verlag, 1964), pp. 7–8.

16 Also see Otto Grotewohl, 'Zur Suezfrage: Erklärung vor ägyptischen Journalisten in Berlin 14. September 1956', in Grotewohl, *Im Kampf um die Einige Deutsche Demokratische Republik*, pp. 66–8. Grotewohl expressed solidarity with the Egyptians in the face of the British and French intervention, but avoided public attacks on Israel.

17 Walter Ulbricht, 'Von der DDR wird stets der Frieden ausstrahlen: Rede des Genossen Walter Ulbricht', *Neues Deutschland*, 24 April 1961.

18 *Ibid.* (emphasis in the originals).

19 *Ibid.*

20 On this, see Herf, *Divided Memory* and Angelika Timm, *Hammer, Zirkel, Davidstern: Das gestörte Verhältnis der DDR zu Zionismus und Staat Israel* (Bonn: Bouvier Verlag, 1997).

21 On this, see Jeffrey Herf, 'Abstraction, Specificity and the Holocaust: Recent Disputes over Memory in Germany', *Bulletin of the German Historical Institute* (London), 22:2 (2000), pp. 20–35 and Peter Reichel, *Politik mit der Erinnerung: Gedächtnisorte im Streit um die nationalsozialistischer Vergangenheit* (Munich: Hanser Verlag, 1995).

22 On West Germany and Israel under Adenauer and after, see Inge Deutschkron, *Israel und die Deutschen: Das schwierige Verhältnis* (Cologne: Verlag Wissenschaft und Politik, 1983); Lily Gardner Feldman, *The Special Relationship between West Germany and Israel* (Boston: Allen & Unwin, 1984); and Michael Wolffsohn, *Eternal Guilt: Forty Years of German–Jewish Relations*, trans. by Douglas Bukovoy (New York: Columbia University Press, 1993).

23 Ernst Reuter, 'Ansprache auf der Gedenkfeier des Bezirksamtes Neukölln am 10. Jahrestag der Vernichtung des Warschauer Ghettos am 19. April 1953', in *Ernst Reuter: Schriften, Reden*, 4 (Berlin: Propyläen Verlag, 1972), p. 714.
24 *Ibid.*, p. 716.
25 *Ibid.*, p. 721.
26 See Carlo Schmid, 'Wir Deutschen und die Juden', *Politik als Geistige Aufgabe* (Bern, Munich, Vienna: Scherz, 1973), pp. 282–300.
27 Carlo Schmid, *Deutscher Bundestag, Stenographische Bericht*, 6, 120. Sitzung (22 February, 1951), p. 4592; reprinted as 'Zur Wiedergutmachung', in Carlo Schmid, *Bundestagsreden* (Bonn: AZ Studio, 1966), p. 52.
28 *Ibid.*
29 *Ibid.*, p. 53.
30 *Ibid.*
31 Theodor Heuss, 'Diese Scham nimmt uns niemand ab!: Der Bundepräsident sprach bei der Weihe des Mahnmals in Bergen-Belsen', *Bulletin des Presse- und Informationsamtes der Bundesregierung*, Nr. 189 (1 December 1952), pp. 1655–6. An abridged version appeared as 'Das Mahnmal', in Theodor Heuss, *Der Grossen Reden: Der Staatsmann* (Tübingen: Rainer Wunderlich Verlag, 1965), pp. 224–30. Also see Bundesarchiv Koblenz, NL Heuss B122, 2082.
32 Nahum Goldmann, 'Goldmann' (Speech at Bergen-Belsen, 30 November, 1952), BA Koblenz, NL Theodor Heuss, B122 2082, p. 1.
33 *Ibid.*, pp. 1–2.
34 Heuss, 'Diese Scham nimmt uns niemand ab!', pp. 1655–6; 'Heuss weiht Mahnmal in Belsen ein: Der Bundespräsident gedenkt der Opfer des ehemaligen Kz', *Frankfurter Rundschau*, 1 December 1952.
35 Heuss, 'Dies Scham nimmt uns niemand ab!', p. 1655.
36 *Ibid.*
37 *Ibid.*, p. 1656.
38 *Ibid.*
39 For an overview of all this issues, see Herf, *Divided Memory*. On the Auschwitz trial in Frankfurt, see Rebecca Wittmann, 'The Wheels of Justice Turn Slowly: The Pre-Trial Investigations of the Frankfurt Auschwitz Trial, 1963–1965', *Central European History*, 35:3 (2002), p. 378 and *Beyond Justice: The Auschwitz Trial, the Law and the Holocaust* (Cambridge, MA: Harvard University Press, 2003). On the debates about the Nazi past in the Bundestag, see Helmut Dubiel, *Niemand ist Frei von der Geschichte: Die nationalsozialistische Herrschaft in den Debatten des Deutschen Bundestages* (Munich: Hanser Verlag, 1999).
40 On the new left debates during and after the 1960s about these issues, see Anson Rabinbach and Jack Zipes (eds), *Germans and Jews Since the*

Holocaust: The Changing Situation in West Germany, (New York: Holmes & Meier, 1986).

41 On the issues of generalisation and particularity, see Jeffrey Herf, *Reactionary Modernism: Technology, Culture and Politics in Weimar and the Third Reich* (New York: Cambridge University Press, 1984) and Thomas Nipperdey, '1933 und die Kontinuität der deutschen Geschichte', in *Nachdenken über die deutschen Geschichte* (Munich: C. H. Beck Verlag, 1986), pp. 186–205.

42 On the background to this tortured tale, see Martin W. Kloke, *Israel und die deutsche Linke: Zur Geschichte eines schwierigen Verhältnisses* (Frankfurt: Haag & Herchen, 1990).

43 On the West German reaction to the broadcast, see the essays by Jeffrey Herf, Andrei Markovits and Rebecca S. Hayden, and Siegfried Zielinski, in Anson Rabinbach and Jack Zipes (eds), *Germans and Jews Since the Holocaust: The Changing Situation in West Germany* (New York: Holmen & Meier, 1986).

44 The debate and the issues it raised is excellently discussed in Charles Maier, *The Unmasterable Past: History, Holocaust and German National Identity* (Cambridge, MA: Harvard University Press, 1988). The documents of the dispute are published in *Forever in the Shadow of Hitler: Original Documents of the* Historikerstreit, trans. by James Knowlton and Truett Cates (Atlantic Highlands, NJ: Humanities Press, 1993).

45 Richard von Weizsäcker, *Reden und Interviews* (Bonn: Presse- und Informationsamtes der Bundesregierung, 1988), pp. 262–73.

46 *Ibid.*, p. 263.

47 *Ibid.*

48 *Ibid.*, pp. 263–4. On politics and the memory of the German Resistance, see David Clay Large, '"A Beacon in the German Darkness": The Anti-Nazi Resistance Legacy in West German Politics', in Michael Geyer and John W. Boyer (eds), *Resistance Against the Third Reich, 1933–1990* (Chicago: University of Chicago Press, 1994); and Jeffrey Herf, 'German Communism, the Discourse of "Antifascist Resistance", and the Jewish Catastrophe', in Michael Geyer and John W. Boyer (eds), *Resistance Against the Third Reich, 1933–1990* (Chicago: University of Chicago Press, 1994), pp. 257–94.

49 *Ibid.*, p. 264.

50 *Ibid.*

51 *Ibid.*

52 *Ibid.*, p. 267.

53 Norbert Seitz, 'Bemühter Umgang: 50 Jahre 8. Mai – eine deutsche Pathologie', *Süddeutsche Zeitung*, 15 April 1995.

54 On this see Condoleeza Rice and Phillip Zelikow, *Germany Unified and Europe Transformed* (Cambridge, MA: Harvard University Press, 1995);

Andrei Markovits and Simon Reich, *The German Predicament: Memory and Power in the New Europe* (Ithaca, NY, London: Cornell University Press, 1997) as well as the extensive document collection, Hanns Jürgen Küsters and Daniel Hofmann (eds), *Dokumente zur Deutschlandpolitik: Deutsche Einheit, Sonderedition aus den Akten des Bundeskanzleramtes 1989/90* (Munich: R. Oldenbourg, 1998).

55 'The East Germans Issue an Apology for Nazis' Crimes', *New York Times*, 13 April 1990.

56 The headline read 'Volkskammer bekennt Schuld am Holocaust: Erste freigewählte DDR-Regierung im Amt' ('Volkskammer Recognises Guilt for the Holocaust: First Freely Elected GDR-Government in Office'), *Frankfurter Rundschau*, 14 April 1990.

57 See 'Truth and Healing in Eastern Europe', *New York Times*, 14 April 1990 and 'East Germany accepts burden of Holocaust', *Jerusalem Post*, 13 April 1990. For the text of the *Volkskammer* declaration, see 'Dokumentation: Gemeinsame Erklärung der Volkskammer', *Deutschland Archiv*, 23:5 (1990), pp. 794–5.

58 See Martin Walser, *Erfahrungen beim Verfasser einer Sonntagsrede: Friedenspreis des Deutschen Buchhandels 1998* (Frankfurt-am-Main: Suhrkamp Verlag, 1998) and the abundant press reaction in the German prestige press. On the reaction of German intellectuals to German unification, see Jan Werner Müller, *Another Country: German Intellectuals, Unification and National Identity* (New Haven: Yale University Press, 2000).

59 See *Colloquium: Denkmal für die ermordeten Juden Europas: Dokumentation* (Berlin: Senatsverwaltung für Wissenschaft, Forschung und Kultur, 1997).

60 See Jeffrey Herf, 'Traditionsbruch: Rollenaustausch zwischen SPD und CDU', *Die Zeit*, 13 August 1998. For a more detailed discussion of this episode, see Jeffrey Herf, 'A New *Schlussstrichmentalität*? The Schröder Government, the Berlin Memorial and the Politics of Memory', in Carl Lankowski (ed.), *Germany After the 1998 Federal Elections* (Washington, DC: American Institute for Contemporary German Studies, 1999), pp. 57–62.

61 For an extensive collection of views on the Berlin Holocaust Memorial debate, see Michael Jeismann (ed.), *Mahnmal Mitte: Eine Kontroverse* (Cologne: Dumont, 1999).

62 The vote was the lead story in all of the major German newspapers. See the editions of 26–27 June 1999 of *Die Frankfurter Allgemeine Zeitung, Frankfurter Rundschau, Die Süddeutsche Zeitung* and *Der Tagesspiegel*. The official record of this and other Bundestag debates is now available for downloading from the website of the Deutscher Bundestag as well as in the published *Verhandlungen des deutschen Bundestages*.

63 For a most helpful overview of Fischer's evolution, see Paul Berman, 'The Passion of Joschka Fischer', *The New Republic*, 27 August 2001. For two

German intellectuals who viewed the Kosovo conflict from a position similar to Fischer's, see essays by Dan Diner and Peter Schneider in Frank Schirrmacher (ed.), *Der westliche Kreuzzug: 41 Positionen zum Kosovo-Krieg* (Stuttgart: Deutsche Verlags-Anstalt, 1999), pp. 159–68, 226–33.

64 On this, see Jeffrey Herf, *War By Other Means: Soviet Power, West German Resistance and the Battle of the Euromissiles* (New York: Free Press, 1991), pp. 164–95.

65 Cited in 'Scham ist ein Moment menschlicher Wurde', *Der Tagesspiegel*, 26 June 1999. The same edition includes excerpts from opponents as well as supporters of the memorial. One novel element in this long-standing debate was evident in several interventions from younger members of the Bundestag. In particular, see the text of twenty-eight-year-old SPD member, Michael Roth, 'Im Wortlaut: Das Denkmal dient der Zukunft', *Frankfurter Rundschau*, 26 June 1999.

66 *Ibid.*

67 On the idea of 'constitutional patriotism', see Muller, *Another Country*.

68 See for example, Ausstellung des Bundesministeriums der Justiz (ed.), *Im Namen des Volkes? Über die Justiz im Staat der SED* (Leipzig: Forum Verlag, 1994); Karl Wilhelm Fricke and Roger Engelmann, *Konzentrierte Schläge: Staatssicherheitsaktionen und politische Prozesse in der DDR 1953–1956* (Berlin: Ch. Links, 1998); Konrad H. Jarausch (ed.), *Dictatorship as Experience: Towards a Socio-Cultural History of the GDR*, trans. by Eve Duffy (New York: Berghahn, 1999); Jürgen Kocka (ed.), *Historische DDR-Forschung: Aufsätze und Studien* (Berlin: Akadamie Verlag, 1993); James P. McAdams, *Judging the Past in Unified Germany* (New York: Cambridge University Press, 2001); Sigrid Meuschel, *Legitimation und Parteiherrschaft zum Paradox von Stabilität und Revolution in der DDR, 1945–1989* (Frankfurt-am-Main: Suhrkamp, 1992); Anne Sa'adah, *Germany's Second Chance: Trust, Justice, and Democratization* (Cambridge, MA: Harvard University Press, 1998); Siegfried Suckut (ed.), *Das Wörterbuch der Staatssicherheit* (Berlin: Ch. Links Verlag, 1996); and Deutscher Bundestag, *Materialien der Enquete-Kommission 'Aufarbeitung von Geschichte und Folgen der SED-Diktatur in Deutschland'* (Baden-Baden: Nomos; Frankfurt-am-Main: Suhrkamp, 1995).

69 Joachim Gauck, *Die Stasi-Akten: Das unheimlich Erbe der DDR* (Hamburg: Rowohlt, 1992).

70 See British Prime Minister Tony Blair, 'Full Statement to the House of Commons', 18 March 2003, at www.britainusa.com/iraq.

71 See Jeffrey Herf, 'Die Appeaser: Schröder und Fischer haben nichts gelernt', *Frankfurter Allgemeine Zeitung*, Feuilleton, 11 February 2003.

72 See for example, Wolf Biermann, 'Brachiale Friedensliebe', *Der Spiegel*, 24 February 2003, at www.spiegel.de/spiegel/o,1518,237393,00.html.

5

A three-dimensional view of German history: the weight of the past in Germany's relations with Jews in Germany, Israel and the Diaspora

Lily Gardner Feldman

In July 1949, just before the founding of the Federal Republic, John McCloy as US Military Governor suggested that the viability of the new Germany would be determined by the way in which it encountered Jews: 'The world will watch carefully the new West German state, and one of the tests by which it will be judged will be its attitude towards the Jews and how it treats them.'[1] Over fifty years later, this litmus test still seems relevant, as Foreign Minister Joschka Fischer noted to the November 2002 conference of the Anti-Defamation League on 'Global Anti-Semitism':

> The origins and the identity of democratic Germany can only be understood against the background of my country's responsibility for the crimes against humanity of the Holocaust. An important gauge for our capacity to be an open and tolerant society are the Jewish communities in Germany. The question of whether German Jews feel safe and at home in Germany is the test of our credibility as a democracy.[2]

The German–Jewish relationship that has developed over the more than five decades since McCloy's admonition has been highly complex and multi-layered. The following analysis tries to do justice to this complexity within the confines of a chapter by focusing on a three-dimensional perspective with respect to both the non-Jewish German actors and the Jewish recipients of their behaviour in Germany and abroad. The chapter's emphasis on policies leads us to a primary examination of decision makers and those who help shape policy debates, but all-important societal actors will also appear. Consideration of attitudes and behaviour toward Jews on the part of Chancellor Gerhard Schröder,

Foreign Minister Joschka Fischer and the late Bundestag Deputy Jürgen Möllemann opens three windows onto the Nazi legacy in the Berlin Republic. The analysis will address two principal themes: the motives of the actors in terms of morality and pragmatism; and the issue of continuity and change.

Since 1989, open debates, such as the controversy between the novelist Martin Walser and the German Jewish leader Ignatz Bubis, the deliberations on the Berlin memorial to the Jewish victims of the Holocaust or the Bundestag discussion on anti-Semitism all testify to the reality that German Jews have become a feature of public life. The growth of the Jewish community (increasing from 29,000 before unification to some 100,000 in 2002) through immigration from the former Soviet Union, the community's increased public visibility and verbal and physical attacks on Jews and their institutions have provoked Germans to look inside German society in their effort to confront the past. Such introspection, however, is new; in the past Germany preferred first Israel (from 1949 through today) and then the American Jewish community (beginning in the mid-1980s) as vehicles for addressing Germany's National Socialist legacy. All three actors feature here.

Gerhard Schröder: an equilibrium between morality and pragmatism

As the first Chancellor of the Federal Republic with no direct experience of the Second World War and Nazism, Gerhard Schröder could have been expected to forge a new set of relationships with Jews involving only a faint imprint of the past. In fact, new accents have emerged, but they move in two directions: relegating the past, and honouring the Third Reich's Jewish victims. Overall, Schröder has maintained the balance between morality and pragmatism, between historical obligation and contemporary national interest that has characterised the Federal Republic's relationship to Jews since 1949.[3] On this subject more than any other, statements are as important as actions. What are Schröder's public views on German history, and his policies *vis-à-vis* Jews in Germany, Israel, and elsewhere?

History: responsibility and interests

In a number of pronouncements over the last five years on the occasion of events of deep significance to Jews, six elements have emerged for Schröder's view of history and its contemporary import: opposition to a closing or endpoint of history (*Schlußstrich*); objection to 'mastering' history (*Bewältigung der Vergangenheit*); acceptance of historical facts; rejection of collective guilt; importance of the future; and reference to German rescuers.[4] The first three are clear moral responses to the past, whereas the last three begin to suggest more pragmatic interests that reach beyond the victims. The *Schlußstrich* debate erupted in full in the mid-1980s with Chancellor Helmut Kohl's decision to visit with President Ronald Reagan the Bitburg cemetery where SS officers are buried. For much of the last fifty years, while many German leaders were not actively closing off the past, they philosophically believed they could temper its force by the 'mastery of history'. Like President Richard von Weizsäcker in his famous 8 May 1985 speech to counter the Bitburg visit, Schröder has argued against the dilution of history, and following Theodor Adorno's 1977 dictum, has preferred a continuing encounter (*Aufarbeitung* or *Auseinandersetzung*):

> History is never over in the sense that one can draw a line under it. It's just as impossible to master the past. Only through an ongoing confrontation with our history, only when we are capable of accepting history, will we be able to draw lessons for the present and the future.[5]

Following the pattern set by Chancellor Adenauer and pursued by his successors, for Schröder the acknowledgment of history does not mean accepting the concept of collective guilt. Echoing von Weizsäcker, disavowal of collective guilt does not entail, however, the absence of individual guilt or a collective moral position of responsibility.[6] Schröder insists on maintaining historical memory first out of respect for the victims and their heirs; he then proceeds to note the pragmatic reason that: preserving the robustness of German society and the German polity through memory of the Holocaust is especially important for the next generation. Some analysts argue that this attempted balance between past and future will inevitably tip in favour of the latter over time.[7] Moreover, the Chancellor is keen for young Germans to learn about the past and the victims of the Third Reich, but wants them to appreciate the 'civic courage' of Germans who helped Jews. Unlike his predecessors who tended to talk about German 'opposition' to Hitler in general terms or with reference to the well-known cases of resistance, Schröder has sought to personalise the experience of 'average' German rescuers by telling individual stories.[8]

Schröder's statements are a first public indication of his orientation toward history. The Chancellor's actions in his dealings with Jews in Germany, with Israel, and with the Jewish Diaspora both validate and challenge this first impression.

Jews in Germany

Two areas reveal the enactment of Schröder's ideas about history: his responses to anti-Semitism in Germany and to efforts to impair Jewish life; and his signing of the federal agreement with the Central Council of Jews in Germany (CCJG), an act to solidify and perpetuate Jews' institutional representation.

A sporadic phenomenon throughout the life of the Federal Republic, anti-Semitic acts appeared to increase beginning with the new millennium as part of a radicalisation of extreme-right behaviour.[9] According to a report on the government's activities to counter right-wing extremism (including xenophobia and anti-Semitism), extreme-right criminal acts in general mushroomed by some 50 per cent between 1998 and 2000 and had jumped from 2,031 cases in 1990 to 15,951 cases in 2000.[10] The report cited the 1998 effort to blow up the grave of Heinz Galinski, the former head of the Jewish Community in Berlin, as the beginning of a new form of right extremism.

An increase in anti-Semitic attitudes was also registered in the same period by the Frankfurt Sigmund Freud Institute and the University of Leipzig whose survey indicated a rise in anti-Semitic answers, from 20 per cent of respondents in 1999 to 36 per cent in 2002, a result borne out by an Anti-Defamation League poll in summer 2002. A poll by *Der Spiegel*, however, suggested a small decline in anti-Semitic attitudes compared to a decade earlier.[11] The American Jewish Committee's office in Berlin concluded that while the numbers overall may not have surged, the manifestation of anti-Semitism was moving into new territory.[12]

Schröder has been vigorous in his condemnation of anti-Semitism. After the October 2000 attack on the Düsseldorf synagogue, the Chancellor visited the scene together with Paul Spiegel, the President of the CCJG, who saw the visit as a sign of solidarity with the Jewish community.[13] Schröder's call for an 'uprising of the decent', to fight anti-Semitism and xenophobia seemed to resonate with significant parts of the German public.[14] Speaking to the CCJG in September 2000, Schröder outlined a three-pronged strategy for dealing with right extremism: defence of the rule of law; communication with German youth and their integration into society; and mobilisation of civil society.[15] Shortly thereafter, during Schröder's visit to Israel, Prime Minister Ehud Barak thanked the Chancellor personally for his engagement against anti-Semitism and right extremism.[16] In a report of government activities two years later, this 'multi-dimensional' approach was embellished with concrete details and expanded to include other preventive measures such as human rights policies and support for the integration of foreigners, and transformative activities, such as a ban on the *Nationaldemokratische Partei Deutschlands* (NPD) and efforts to convert right extremists.

Schröder's public stand against anti-Semitism and for 'decency' was put into question for the CCJG on 8 May 2002, the fifty-seventh anniversary of the end of the Second World War, when the Chancellor commemorated the occasion by engaging in an organised discussion about 'Nation, Patriotism, Democratic Culture' with the author Martin Walser, who in 1998 had decried the use of the Holocaust as a 'moral cudgel' against Germans.[17] Moreover, the moderator of the 8 May event was Christoph Dieckmann, who earlier had indulged in anti-Jewish clichés. On this occasion, Walser argued that the First World War peace settlement was the cause of Nazism. The CCJG indicated that it was 'irritated and bewildered' by the Chancellor's initiative. Michel Friedman, the vice-president of the Central Council, deemed the Chancellor's behaviour 'contradictory' and 'relativising'. Non-Jewish voices joined Jewish opposition to the 8 May discussion, for example those of *Aktion Sühnezeichen* (the Sign of Atonement Movement), the organisation founded in 1958 by the Evangelical church to encourage young Germans to volunteer in countries that had suffered under Nazism.

Comparison of Schröder's response with his predecessors' is difficult owing to the changing nature of anti-Semitism, although Jewish leaders have both praised and criticised his initiatives. The notion of departure is much easier to identify in the second area of interaction with the Jewish Community, the signing of the federal agreement with the CCJG.

At the November 2002 announcement of the agreement with Chancellor Schröder and Interior Minister Otto Schily, Paul Spiegel deemed the plan an 'historic event', for while there were agreements at the *Land* level, this state treaty at the Federal level was a first.[18] Although it took five decades for the treaty to emerge, Spiegel noted the speed with which the Chancellor acted upon presentation of the idea.[19] At the signing of the treaty on 27 January 2003, the national day of remembrance for the liberation of Auschwitz, Spiegel noted that the agreement went further than financial support (€3 million) by emphasising a commitment to the reconstruction of Jewish life in Germany now and in the future as a 'duty to [honour] the past', and by reflecting a Jewish sense of 'trust' and 'hope'.[20]

The Jewish community will now be legally recognised at the Federal level as equal with Christian religious communities in Germany. Schröder recognised the trust of the Jewish community in German democracy manifested in the agreement, and committed himself to helping institutionalised Jewry – now eighty-three local communities – face the challenges of growth and change attendant on being Europe's third largest Jewish community.[21]

In his relations with Jews in Germany, Chancellor Schröder has often been pro-active, seeking new ways to instil Jewish confidence in the strength of German democracy and its capacity to draw lessons from the past, but on occasion also has been insensitive to Jewish concerns about the dilution of history. Similarly, with Israel, he has maintained Germany's commitment to a 'special relationship', but has not always understood Jewish sensitivities to the past.

Israel

Schröder's statements and actions regarding the Middle East reflect continuity, both in Germany's special commitment to Israel, and in the limits of preference. Schröder's public support for Israel was demonstrated in his autumn 2000 visit to the region. While Schröder has not travelled to Israel with the frequency of Kohl or Foreign Minister Fischer, he has not declined to visit, as did Helmut Schmidt in the 1970s to signal his disapproval of Israeli Middle East policy. Barak used the occasion of Schröder's visit to proclaim Germany one of Israel's close friends, and sought the Chancellor's help in gaining the release of Israeli prisoners in Lebanon. The same themes of friendship and appreciation for Germany's intermediary role in the north were reiterated when Israel's President, Moshe Katsav, visited Germany in December 2002.

The two years between those trips witnessed some of the greatest tension and violence ever between Israelis and Palestinians, culminating in the spring 2002 Passover massacre in Israel and Israeli reoccupation of parts of the West Bank and Gaza. The period, in which Israel felt its daily existence threatened and was frequently condemned by international opinion (except from the United States) for its action against Palestinians, became a test of what Germany would and would not do to protect Israel's security. The 25 April 2002 Bundestag debate on the Middle East highlighted four aspects of German policy toward Israel: overall political support; advocacy for Israel in the EU; military engagement; and the right to criticise.

Noting first how a spiralling Middle East conflict could endanger Germany's economic and political interests, Schröder proceeded to reaffirm the Federal Republic's commitment to Israel.[22] Yet, the Chancellor also wanted to fix the relationship with Israel not only in the past, but in the present and future by emphasising the democratic values that bind the two countries. Relying on the EU's Berlin March 1999 declaration for a Palestinian state, the chancellor also stressed the need to view the Palestinians as 'equal neighbours and negotiating partners'.[23] This 'even-handed' (*ausgewogen*) policy was hardly new, for the language was first used by German officials in the second half of the 1960s.[24] Markus Weingardt, for example, has characterised the overall policy of the Red–Green coalition in this domain as one of essential 'continuity'.[25] Even if German official acceptance of a Palestinian state is now more open than in the past, it has conformed to international (EU and US) and Israeli (Barak government) practice.

Schröder's bifurcated approach dictated concrete 'consequences'. Because of the past and shared common values, Germany would not join most of the EU members in calling for economic sanctions against Israel.[26] The German role as Israel's benefactor is well established, ranging from support for Israel's membership application to the EC in the 1960s to pushing for the 1975 Free Trade Agreement, to limiting the pro-Palestinian language of the 1980 Venice Initiative and arguing for Israel's special status at the 1994 Essen European Council. At the same time in April 2002, Germany supported Israel at the UN Human Rights Commission by voting against a resolution condemning Israel.

Germany's special commitment to Israel, according to the Chancellor's April statement in the Bundestag, would not mean German participation in an international security force in the Middle East. Schröder was in fact reversing his position of a few weeks earlier when he had suggested German involvement and found himself in a hail of criticism from inside and outside his party, including from Edmund Stoiber, for his insensitivity to Holocaust survivors and the descendants of those who perished.[27] The fact that he floated the idea on the eve of Israel's Day of Remembrance for the Holocaust added to the derision. Schröder's verbal and symbolic clumsiness when dealing with Israel was reminiscent of Helmut Kohl's 1983 reference to the *Gnade des späten Geburts* (the blessing of being born late) and the Brandt government's 1971 opening of Germany's first Culture Week in Israel on the anniversary of *Kristallnacht.*

Non-participation in an international security force hardly means an absence of military relations more generally with Israel: training and intelligence exchanges are part of the history of German–Israeli relations and remain vibrant.[28] The military supply relationship that began in the 1950s persists. The limits to Germany's help for Israel were activated in spring 2002. The stoppage of export licenses for security-related items to Israel, including tank parts, in early 2002 led Israel's Defence Minister to register a complaint with the government. Emphasising Germany's long-standing policy of no weapons to 'areas of tension', German officials denied media reports of an effective 'embargo'. Defence Minister Scharping insisted that exports had been 'interrupted but not stopped' and noted the purpose 'to send a signal [to Israel] that in the current situation we are interested in de-escalation'.[29] This 'interruption' confirmed that Israel previously received German military matériel in what one observer characterised as 'a flourishing but largely secret arms trade'.[30]

Germany's Federal Security Council (*Bundessicherheitsrat*), chaired by the Chancellor, makes a distinction between offensive and defensive weapons, enabling it to comply at the end of 2002 with Israel's long-standing request for Patriot anti-missile systems and to refuse its more recent request for Fuchs tanks to carry troops. In a press conference at the end of November 2002, Schröder invoked 'moral and historic reasons' for sending the 'purely defensive' Patriot missiles.[31] When he met with Israeli President Katsav two weeks later, he stressed that Germany would do 'everything permitted by law' to help.[32]

The final element of Schröder's *Bundestag* address of general significance was his insistence on Germany's right to criticise Israeli policy. The German government's caveat of friendship coupled with criticism of Israel was by now embedded in German–Israeli relations, the practice having been ushered in during the Schmidt–Genscher years.[33] Yet, outside the government novel language was used by mainstream politicians in spring 2002 to criticise Israeli policy. In utter distortion by analogy, the CDU Deputy and former cabinet minister Norbert Blüm referred to Israeli actions against Palestinians as a 'war of annihilation', a phrase used previously only to describe Nazi behaviour.[34] His party chastised him for intemperance; Möllemann's language reached an even higher level of distemper.

Criticism of Israel by this time was quite pervasive in both elite and mass opinion. A study of the German print media found that German reporting on Israeli policy 'activated anti-Semitic discourse', and was permeated by 'negative characterisations' and anti-Jewish stereotypes.[35] In mid-April 2002, over 30,000 Germans protested against Israeli policy; support for Israel drew far smaller numbers.[36] An April 2002 poll revealed that 46 per cent of German respondents questioned whether the relationship to Israel should be special given Israel's response to the intifada.[37] However, important organisations involved in German-Israeli relations since the 1950s, such as the Society for Christian–Jewish Cooperation (*Gesellschaft für Christlich-Jüdische Zusammenarbeit*), came to Israel's defence.[38]

Jewish leaders did not maintain that Israel could brook no criticism, but did draw boundaries. The President of the CCJG chided Germans for criticising Israelis from their comfortable seats in cafés that were not being blown up; while criticism was not 'sacrilegious', it should not be purely destructive and one-sided. Israel's President during his December 2002 visit acknowledged Germany's right to criticise, but said it should not be rooted in ignorance.[39]

As the millennium began, Chancellor Schröder, either through initiative or response, was forced to define what 'honouring the past' meant in concrete actions with respect to Jews in Germany and in Israel. Simultaneously, Schröder was preoccupied with Diaspora Jewry through the negotiations over compensation for slave and forced labour.

Diaspora Jews

Even though Jewish claimants constituted a minority of slave and forced labour survivors, they were an important focus for the Schröder government; it was largely their March–April 1998 lawsuits in American courts against German companies that prompted the talks on compensation for the victims.[40] Whereas Chancellor Kohl had insisted it was the companies' sole responsibility to respond to lawsuits,[41] Gerhard

Schröder already as Minister-President of North-Rhine Westphalia argued there was a role for government and began to mobilise industry leaders.

In his November 1998 inaugural address as Chancellor, Schröder signalled his support for compensation. By February 1999, the government and twelve German companies announced their commitment to creating a private and a public foundation (later rolled into one) to compensate victims. Schröder's motives were clear and twofold – Germany was moved by moral remorse, but also by a pragmatic goal to 'counter lawsuits, particularly class action suits, and to remove the basis of the campaign being led against German industry and our country'. The pragmatic emphasis met with irritation from the head of the American Jewish Committee's office in Berlin: 'If Schröder thinks there is a campaign against Germany, perhaps he does not totally understand the issue of people waiting 50 years for justice.'[42]

By the time of the February announcement, the German government and German industry were concerned about the efforts of Alan Hevesi, the comptroller of New York City, and the World Jewish Congress to block the merger of Deutsche Bank and Bankers Trust until Holocaust claims had been settled.[43] According to Bodo Hombach, the Chancellor's first negotiator in the slave and forced labour talks, Germany wanted to avoid the public relations nightmare the Swiss government and banks had suffered in responding to Holocaust victims' legal claims.[44] The second negotiator, Otto Graf Lambsdorff, reaffirmed the twin motives of 'morality and business'.[45] Stuart Eizenstat, the American government's negotiator, has attributed this same combination of moral obligation and material interest to the German companies.[46]

When the talks reached a difficult juncture in October 1999 over the amount of the German side's offer, which the claimants' lawyers rejected as insufficient, Jewish leaders looked to Schröder to be even more engaged. Schröder relieved the impasse in December by increasing the government's contribution. It took, however, another six months to finalise the details of the 'legal peace' (*Rechtssicherheit*) the Germans insisted upon: in exchange for compensation, the plaintiffs' attorneys agreed to dismiss their pending cases, and the US government committed itself in pending and any future cases to a 'Statement of Interest' that would advocate the foundation as a legal solution and recommend dismissal of any lawsuits.

The emphasis on the future identified earlier in Schröder's statements on history also appears regarding slave and forced labour, directly in the title of the Foundation: Remembrance, Responsibility and the Future (*Erinnerung, Verantwortung und Zukunft*). In his April 2000 speech introducing draft legislation for the creation of the Foundation, the chancellor confronted the issue of whether emphasising the future meant relegating the past: 'With the creation of this Foundation we are not drawing a line under the past. Just the opposite: Accompanying the overdue humanitarian gesture of justice to the victims is the promise not to let their fate be forgotten.'[47] The law establishing the Foundation went into effect in August 2000, but payments did not start until almost a year later.

During the first five years of Gerhard Schröder's chancellorship, on a variety of occasions history seemed to impel him to protect and honour Jews, whether in Germany, Israel, or in the Diaspora. At other times, the legacy of the Nazi past either vied with or was subordinated to Germany's national interest. Foreign Minister Joschka is of the same generation as the Chancellor, but for him history has been a constant companion. Where the Chancellor's attitudes and actions are quite complex, the Foreign Minister's are more straightforward. Where the Chancellor acted formally and with measured tones, the Foreign Minister acted emotionally and with personal conviction. Where the Chancellor expressed sympathy, the Foreign Minister demonstrated empathy. In terms of personal engagement and the respect he enjoys among Jews, Fischer operates in the tradition of Willy Brandt as Foreign Minister.

Joschka Fischer: a moral compass

Foreign Minister Fischer's views on the role of history in foreign policy revolve around four main elements: Germans are obliged to draw lessons from the past; German policy must be driven by principles and interests, but the latter must be bounded; German foreign policy should not strive for 'normalcy'; and the acknowledgment of history means feeling shame for the crimes of Nazism.

History and foreign policy

For Fischer, learning from the past does not mean a primary orientation to the future, but rather letting history shape contemporary action, as he noted in his early days as Foreign Minister: 'We must always take into account the present [impact] of our history. We, including our younger generation, can't be selective … We must live with the power of collective memory.'[48] History, according to Fischer, dictated that German foreign policy should be propelled by principles as well as a special, circumscribed brand of interests. The role of the past is so immutable in Fischer's view that German unification has not signified 'normalcy, but rather [the] freedom to assume international responsibility'.[49] Rather than shying away from history, Fischer has confronted it, especially in his many trips to Israel (six, for example, in the two-year period beginning June 2000) where he has been moved by the precariousness of daily existence, an awareness acutely reinforced by the June 2001 suicide bombing of young Israelis that coincided with one of his visits.

Israel

Fischer's view of history has led to specific accents in German foreign policy: constrained power, multilateralism and diplomacy, conflict prevention, force as a last and limited resort, human rights and European integration. It has also entailed a specific commitment to Israel. In a May 2002 speech to the heads of Germany's delegations abroad, outlining the 'four theses' of foreign policy after September 11 2001, Fischer emphasised Israel's place and the continuity of policy over fifty years: 'Germany assumes responsibility for its past, including its unshakeable special relationship to the State of Israel and its people. Israel's right to exist in peace and secure borders is an inviolable basis of German foreign policy.'[50] Support for Israel, described as a 'moral responsibility', precludes neither support for Palestinian rights, including a state, nor a concern for German and European pragmatic security interests, but it does mean standing up for Israel in difficult times. Such a position has become increasingly atypical in Germany. Four examples – mediation, diplomatic initiative, criticism of the detractors, military support – illustrate Fischer's approach in action during the spring of 2002 and validate his characterisation of Israel as 'friend' and 'partner' with whom 'remembrance and trust' are the basis of relations.[51]

As a result of witnessing first-hand the devastation at the discotheque in Tel Aviv in June 2001, which he deemed a 'terrible crime' and an act of 'cowardly terrorism', Fischer prolonged his stay in Israel, and shuttled between Prime Minister Ariel Sharon and Chairman Yasser Arafat. In no uncertain terms, he gave Arafat 'hours, not days' to condemn the violence and to express his willingness for a cease-fire and a return to negotiations, all of which transpired at the end of Fischer's meeting with Arafat. He persuaded Sharon to employ a measured response to the discotheque attack.[52] German officials before him, and Fischer himself prior to the trip, had been extremely reluctant to mediate owing to the special relationship with Israel and the desire not to be seen as meddling in EU and American efforts.[53] However, in Fischer's mind a boundary had been crossed by the Palestinians, requiring immediate personal action. His success was a testimony to his excellent *bona fides* with both the Israeli and Palestinian sides.[54]

Fischer was unwilling to be a regular mediator between Israelis and Palestinians, but did proffer ideas to resuscitate negotiations between the two sides in April 2002. His seven-point 'idea paper' essentially consolidated elements of extant peace plans: a balanced position of mutual recognition of statehood between Israelis and Palestinians; a guaranteeing role for the 'quartet' of the EU, the United States, the Russian Federation and the United Nations; and an international peace conference. However, Fischer was not willing to endorse the French Foreign Minister's proposal for immediate recognition of a Palestinian state. Fischer's approach was much more gradual, calling for a referendum on the peace process, acceptance of Israel and the end of the intifada; he proposed a provisional Palestinian state until the final status issues could be negotiated within a two-year period.[55]

Paul Spiegel, the President of the CCJG, welcomed the Foreign Minister's 'mediation efforts' in the Middle East, but expressed concern about anti-Israel sentiments elsewhere in Germany.[56] Fischer concurred with Spiegel, and on a number of occasions during the spring of 2002 vociferously opposed the 'one-sidedness' of criticism for Israel, which went 'completely against the grain' for him.[57] Speaking from his own experience on the political left, he warned how extreme criticism could go awry, how 'anti-Zionism turns into anti-Semitism'; he feared such a development in the spring of 2002, 'particularly on the right'.[58] Fischer recognised Israel's security needs, particularly that 'Israel is the only state whose existence is immediately called into question after a single strategic defeat'.[59] Consequently, Germany had a historically grounded and 'continuing duty to … solidarity', including a continuation of 'traditional' arms cooperation.[60] Christian Sterzing, a Green Bundestag member involved in foreign policy and defence issues, has referred to the military relationship as 'effectively outside the scope of the [general] arms export guidelines'.[61]

The Diaspora

Fischer has personalised his views about Israel by empathising with individuals. He has taken the same approach when addressing Jews elsewhere in the world, trying to put faces on the victims. Since 2000, Fischer has been a featured speaker at four major Jewish events: the September 2000 'Partners in History' dinner of the World Jewish Congress in New York; the May 2001 annual dinner of the American Jewish Committee in Washington; the November 2002 'Global Anti-Semitism' conference of the Anti-Defamation League in New York; and the November 2002 meeting of the Conference on Material Claims Against Germany (an umbrella organisation created in 1950 to negotiate with Germany over compensation and restitution), held for the first time in Germany. In addition to talking about Germany's special commitment to Israel, the Foreign Minister has elaborated three main themes: the victims of Nazism; slave and forced labour; and the relationship of American Jewry to Germany. Fischer insists that 'memory is about the victims … the six million murdered sons and daughters of the Jewish people'.[62] He also pays tribute to those who survived, but were lost to German culture and society through migration to other parts of the world. The memory of the victims has carved Fischer's approach of 'never again' (*nie wieder*), in which Auschwitz is the template for directing Germany's policies on human rights violations and racism at home and abroad. The murders and the losses have filled Fischer with shame, leading him in September 2000 to repeat President Rau's December 1999 request to Holocaust victims for forgiveness, and in November 2002 to talk about German guilt. Guilt, shame and forgiveness have not been the common formulas in Germany's post-war confrontation with the past, the preferred term being 'responsibility'.[63] Although compensation to slave and forced labour victims is one moral way to respond to the victims, Fischer would not allow that such compensation, and the attending 'legal closure', signified a 'moral closure' for Germany.[64]

In his speeches to American Jewish audiences, the Foreign Minister has underscored the importance of the transatlantic relationship and the American role in Germany's rebirth.[65] He has lauded the contribution to this partnership of the American Jewish Committee,[66] and its willingness to act as a 'bridge of understanding' with the new Germany to which it had given a 'second chance'. Fischer (and to some extent Schröder) has been a frequent interlocutor with the American Jewish

Committee, whether in Washington, New York or Berlin. The 1998 opening of the American Jewish Committee's office in Berlin further facilitated the dialogue between Diaspora Jewry and Germany. It is part of a triangulation of the discussion about the past, opening up the essentially separate bilateral relationships Germany has forged with Israel, American Jewry and German Jews. Israel and Diaspora Jewry as topics fall within Joschka Fischer's ambit as Foreign Minister, yet he has chosen also to extend himself personally in both cases. A German Foreign Minister's agenda has not typically included speaking out against anti-Semitism in Germany and expressing solidarity with German Jews, yet Fischer has done so forcefully, testifying once again to his commitment to drawing lessons from the past.

Jews in Germany

In response to a major article by Salomon Korn, a CCJG board member, regarding his concern for the future of Jews in Germany in light of anti-Semitic statements by German politicians, Fischer addressed the issue directly in a 11 May 2002 article in the *Frankfurter Allgemeine Zeitung*. He decried Möllemann's 'unspeakable utterances' (see p. 127), but also the lack of outrage on the part of Germans. And he shared Korn's view that something darker than legitimate criticism of Israel was brewing in Germany, and reminded Germans of the historically based special obligation to the security of Israel and its citizens. He cautioned that the search for 'normality' by some Germans and the desire to treat the heirs of the victims as perpetrators in the Middle East ('guilt transference') could easily descend into anti-Semitism.

Regarding Jews in Germany, Fischer was most concerned that once again the community felt alone. In the same *Frankfurter Allgemeine Zeitung* article, he emphasised their 'Germanness' as fully equal 'citizens' (*Bürger*), not 'fellow citizens' (*Mitbürger*). Here, and elsewhere, he insisted that they should not be held accountable for Israel's policies, or should their loyalty as Germans be questioned. Fischer concluded by warning against 'an instrumentalisation of the tragic conflict in the Middle East for domestic [German] purposes'.[67] Jürgen Möllemann clearly did not heed Fischer's warning; in the following months, he converted his statements of April and May 2002 into campaign material for the federal election.

Jürgen Möllemann: moral fog

Jürgen Möllemann belonged to the same generation as Gerhard Schröder and Joschka Fischer, but could not be more removed in terms of historical sensitivity. If the Chancellor is buffeted by the competing pressures of morality and pragmatism, and the Foreign Minister is guided by a moral compass, then the former Federal Economics Minister was shrouded in a moral fog that prevented him from seeing the past at all.

In the spring and summer of 2002, Möllemann, the vice-chairman of the FDP, took a number of actions deemed anti-Zionist and anti-Semitic by Jewish and non-Jewish Germans. At the beginning of April, in an interview with the *Tageszeitung*, Möllemann endorsed violence against Israelis in Israel: 'What would one do if Germany were occupied? I would also resist and resist by force. I am an officer of the paratroopers in the army reserve. It would then be my mission to resist. And I would do it not only in my own land, but also in the land of the aggressor.'[68] The Greens' leader saw this as 'legitimising suicide attacks'.[69]

Möllemann then invited Jamal Karsli, a former Green Party member in the North-Rhine Westphalian parliament, to join the FDP. Karsli had earlier characterised Israeli actions as 'Nazi' and decried the 'Zionist lobby' in Germany.[70] When the CCJG protested Karsli's membership in the FDP, Möllemann continued his verbal attacks on Jews, first in a mid-May interview with ARD-Television: 'I repeat my impression that the policies of Mr Sharon and the unbearable, arrogant handling by Mr Friedman of any critic of Sharon unfortunately are liable to awake anti-Israel and anti-Semitic resentment.'[71] Paul Spiegel responded to the attack on Friedman, his deputy, by identifying an anti-Semitic tradition: 'This claim shows anti-Semitic structures. Throughout history it has been said again and again that the Jews are themselves to blame for anti-Semitism.'[72] Foreign Minister Fischer had noted in early May the lack of outcry over Möllemann's *Tageszeitung* remarks, but now there was more of a response. Fischer himself observed that 'the most revolting brew is okay with [the FDP]' which in its electioneering was practicing 'shabby and dangerous' tactics.[73] Schröder emphasised Möllemann's 'lack of sensitivity' and urged him to apologise to Friedman. Möllemann did subsequently offer a lukewarm apology to Jews in Germany, but only later to Friedman.[74] The CDU's party leader, Angela Merkel, warned that her party would not countenance populism in the election campaign and questioned the leadership qualities of the FDP. Chancellor candidate Edmund Stoiber charged that 'playing with the fire of anti-Semitism for electoral reasons is deeply irresponsible'.[75]

The FDP was mixed in its response. Prominent FDP politicians such as Otto Graf Lambsdorff and Klaus Kinkel criticised Möllemann, and Hildegard Hamm-Brücher threatened to resign from the FDP if the party included Karsli.[76] However, it took the party chairman, Guido Westerwelle, some time to distance himself from Möllemann. The seriousness of Möllemann's behaviour was made clear to Westerwelle on a trip to Israel at the end of May.[77] Even after Karsli was not admitted to the FDP in reaction to these protests, he was permitted by the regional FDP to be a non-party member of the FDP caucus in the *Land* parliament. At this point, the FDP did not seek to remove Möllemann from his federal and regional leadership positions .

Möllemann ratcheted up the controversy in September when he introduced new attacks on Sharon and Friedman in a brochure for the federal election campaign, hoping to win Muslim voters and those on the extreme right.[78] Westerwelle chided Möllemann for the campaign brochure, but it was only after the FDP's poor performance in the election, for which it blamed Möllemann, that the party took serious action. In October, the FDP revealed that Möllemann had financed the brochure with illegal contributions. By the end of October, he had stepped down from all of his party leadership positions, but resigned from the Bundestag only in February 2003 on the eve of a caucus vote on whether to eject him.[79]

As the Möllemann controversy unfolded in 2002, analysts asked whether he was breaking a taboo in his criticism of Israel and German Jewish leaders. Möllemann himself had a long history of anti-Israel sentiment. For example, he met with Arafat in 1979 and 1980 when the PLO was committed in principle and practice to the destruction of the Jewish state. Shortly thereafter, he became Minister of State in the German Foreign Office, and his criticism of Israel did not abate. His criticism of an Israeli leader was hardly new, for he had called Prime Minister Menachem Begin a 'war criminal',[80] but his personal attack on a Jewish leader in Germany was a new departure. The fact that Möllemann was a mainstream politician (unlike the anti-Semites of the extreme right and left) and a party leader (unlike the minor CDU mayor Graf von Spee and the CSU Bundestag deputy Herbert Fellner) moved anti-Semitism into new territory, especially when he used prejudice for election purposes. Hildegard Hamm-Brücher saw

Möllemann's actions as rendering 'a new variation of anti-Semitism socially acceptable'.[81] Salomon Korn did not judge the anti-Semitism of 2002 as new, but rather as the unfolding of a latent condition, and as a portent.[82] Whether old or new, most mainstream German politicians have deemed anti-Semitism pernicious.

Conclusion

Ten main conclusions emerge from the analysis of history's role in the Berlin Republic:

- First, the past continues to be important and to shape contemporary policies, but not uniformly.
- Second, the Berlin Republic has interacted with all three Jewish actors – the Jewish community in Germany, Israel and Diaspora Jewry – simultaneously and vigorously.
- Third, the greatest continuity is evident in Chancellor Schröder's actions with respect to Israel, where the combination of moral and pragmatic motives etched by Konrad Adenauer over fifty years ago still defines German policy.
- Fourth, the genuine departure in terms of policy is the institutionalised relationship with the Jewish community in Germany, expressed in the 2003 Federal agreement with the CCJG and the conclusion of the forced and slave labour negotiations.
- Fifth, while relations with world Jewry have been significant owing to the negotiations over slave and forced labour, they may dissipate with the passage of time and a German perception that this area represents the last open issue from the Holocaust era.
- Sixth, ties to American Jewry are likely to remain more vibrant owing to the institutionalised presence of the American Jewish Committee in Berlin, and the probable increased significance of non-governmental actors, such as Jewish organisations, as the official transatlantic relationship continues to sour.
- Seventh, Foreign Minister Fischer's priority to take a moral imperative with all three actors, in which the past is always present, has echoes in the last five decades, but it continues to be a minority view.
- Eighth, anti-Semitism remains a fact of life in German society.

- Ninth, the new face of anti-Semitism is its utilisation in mainstream politics, a boundary breached by Jürgen Möllemann.
- Tenth, the German political elite and German society have confronted anti-Semites, even if at times with delay.

A sense of balance and boundaries still guides Germany's confrontation with the past, but this dynamic could be challenged as the war with Iraq heralds a new world order, in which Jews become targets, whether in Israel, worldwide, or in the United States. As in the past, Germany may extend itself for Jews with a view that history should not repeat itself and conveys a moral duty. However, the spring 2003 opposition to war with Iraq (even if there had been UN backing) may suggest a competing lesson from history, one of self-limitation.

Notes

1 *New York Times*, 1 August 1949.

2 The text is available at: www.auswaertiges-amt.de/www/de/aussenpolitik/ausgabe_ archiv? archiv_id=3701&type_id=3&bereich_id=17.

3 For an analysis of this balance in Germany's first three decades, see Lily Gardner Feldman, *The Special Relationship Between West Germany and Israel* (Boston: George Allen & Unwin, 1984). For a more recent summary along the same lines, see Markus A. Weingardt, *Deutsche Israel- und Nahostpolitik. Die Geschichte einer Gratwanderung seit 1949* (Frankfurt, New York: Campus Verlag, 2002).

4 See, for example, 'Erklärung von Bundeskanzler Schröder zum Holocaust-Gedenktag, 27. Januar 1999', at www.bundeskanzler.de/Reden-.7715.8158/a.htm?printView=y; 'Rede von Kanzler Gerhard Schröder zum Festakt am 9. November 1999 im Reichstag', at www.bundeskanzler.de/Findulin-Spiel-.8442.7466/a.htm?printView=y; 'Rede von Bundeskanzler Gerhard Schröder auf der Eröffnungsveranstaltung des internationalen Holocaust-Forums', 26 January 2000, Stockholm, Sweden, at www.bundeskanzler.de/Reden-.7715.6507/a.htm?printView=y; 'Rede von Bundeskanzler Gerhard Schröder anlässlich des Ausstellungseröffnung "Juden in Berlin 1938–45" in Centrum Judaicum', 8 May 2000, at www.bundeskanzler.de/Reden-.7715.6980/a.htm?printView=y; 'Ansprache von Bundeskanzler Gerhard Schröder anlässlich des Festaktes zum 50. Gründungsjubiläum des Zentralrats der Juden in Deutschland,' 21 September 2000, at www.bundeskanzler.de/Reden-.7715.13383/a.htm? printView=y; 'Ansprache von Bundeskanzler Gerhard Schröder anlässlich der Eröffnung der Internationalen Wanderausstellung "Anne Frank – Eine Geschichte

für heute" am Dienstag, 20. Februar 2001, in Prenzlau', at www.bundeskanzler.de/Europa-.7732.23933/a.htm?printView=y; 'Ansprache von Bundeskanzler Schröder bei der Gedenkfeier Bahnhof Grunewald anlässlich des Besuchs von Premierminister Sharon', 5 July 2001, Berlin, at www.bundeskanzler.de/Findulin-Spiel-.8442.38703/a.htm?printView=y; and 'Erklärung von Bundeskanzler Gerhard Schröder zum 60. Jahrestag der "Wannsee-Konferenz"', 18 January 2002, Berlin, at www.bundeskanzler.de/Kanzler-News-.7698.57027/a.htm?printView=y.

5 See 'Ansprache von Bundeskanzler Gerhard Schröder anlässlich der Eröffnung'.

6 See 'Rede von Bundeskanzler Gerhard Schröder anlässlich der Ausstellungseröffnung'.

7 See, for example, Eckhard Fuhr, 'The Heavy Burden of History. Can New Generation Claim "Normal" Identity?' *International Herald Tribune*, 22 April 1999.

8 See 'Ansprache von Bundeskanzler Gerhard Schröder anlässlich des Festaktes' and 'Erklärung von Bundeskanzler Gerhard Schröder zum 60. Jahrestag'.

9 The Stephen Roth Institute at Tel Aviv University, citing official German figures, notes a 100 per cent growth in anti-Semitic activities in Berlin in 2001. See 'Antisemitism Worldwide 2001/2', at www.tau.ac.il/Anti-Semitism/asw2001–2/germany.htm. For the period 1990–2000, see Werner Bergmann, 'Wie viele Deutsche sind rechtsextrem, fremdenfeindlich und antisemitistisch? Ergebnisse der empirischen Forschung von 1990 bis 2000', in Wolfgang Benz (ed.), *Auf dem Weg zum Bürgerkrieg? Rechtsextremismus und Gewalt gegen Fremde in Deutschland* (Frankfurt-am-Main: Campus Verlag, 2001).

10 Deutscher Bundestag, 'Bericht über die aktuellen und geplanten Maßnahmen und Aktivitäten der Bundesregierung gegen Rechtsextremismus, Fremdenfeindlichkeit, Antisemitismus und Gewalt', 14. Wahlperiode, 14 May 2002, *Drucksache* 14/9519.

11 The Stephen Roth Institute, 'Antisemitism Worldwide', pp. 8–9; American Jewish Committee Berlin Office, 'Perspectives from Berlin on Anti-Semitism', *AJC Briefing Paper* (Berlin: American Jewish Committee, 11 June 2002).

12 *Ibid.*

13 'Bundeskanzler fordert "Aufstand der Anständigen"' at www.bundeskanzler.de/Kanzler-News-.7698.14663/a.htm?printView=y.

14 The Stephen Roth Institute, 'Antisemitism Worldwide', p. 12.

15 *Ibid.*

16 'Nahost-Reise: Besuch des Bundeskanzlers in Israel', at www.bundeskanzler.de/Findulin-Spiel-.8442.16622/a.htm?printView=y.

17 See: *Agence France Presse*, 7 May 2002; *Berliner Morgenpost*, 8 May 2003;

Toby Axelrod, 'Germany Tries to Define Itself', *Jewish Telegraphic Agency*, 17 May 2002; Tony Czucka, 'German Post-Holocaust Taboos Come Under Attack in Politics, Books', *Associated Press*, 3 August 2002.

18 See 'Bundesregierung schließt Staatsvertrag mit dem Zentralrat der Juden in Deutschland', 14 November, 2002, at www.bundeskanzler.de/Kanzler-News-.7698.449488/a.htm?printView=y.

19 *Jüdische Allgemeine Wochenzeitung*, 20 November 2002.

20 'Ein Zeichen des Vertrauens', *Jüdische Allgemeine Wochenzeitung*, 29 January 2003.

21 *Jüdische Allgemeine Wochenzeitung*, 29 January 2003.

22 This emphasis on German interests in the Middle East was consistent with the open discussion of German pragmatism in the Schröder government. See, 'Rede von Bundeskanzler Gerhard Schröder zur offiziellen Eröffnung des Sitzes der Deutschen Gesellschaft für Auswärtige Politik – "Außenpolitische Verantwortung Deutschlands in der Welt"', at www. bundeskanzler. de/Reden-.7715.8181/a.htm?printView=y. See also, Deutscher Bundestag, 14. Wahlperiode, 233. Sitzung, Thursday, 25 April 2002, p. 23114. For motions on the Middle East by the main political parties for the debate, see Deutscher Bundestag, *Drucksache* 14/8904; *Drucksache* 14/8879; *Drucksache* 14/8271; *Drucksache* 148862, 14. Wahlperiode, 24 April 2002.

23 Deutscher Bundestag, 14. Wahlperiode, 233. Sitzung, Thursday, 25 April 2002, p. 23115.

24 See Gardner Feldman, *The Special Relationship*, pp. 163–76.

25 See Weingardt, *Deutsche Israel- und Nahostpolitik*, Chapter 7.

26 See, 'Germany to Block EU Sanctions against Israel', EUObserver.com, 12 April 2002, at www.euobserver.com/index.phtml; *Financial Times*, 15 April 2002.

27 Matthias Arning, 'Am Ende der Geschichte rückt die Bundeswehr an', *Frankfurter Rundschau*, 10 April, 2002; Nico Fried, 'The Tabubrecher', *Süddeutsche Zeitung*, 10 April 2002; and Jochen Siemens, 'Historische Ignoranz', *Frankfurter Rundschau*, 10 April 2002.

28 For the historical relationship, see Gardner Feldman, *The Special Relationship*. For the current, intensive relationship between German and Israeli armed forces, see Sebastian Engelbrecht, 'Nichts stört die Freundschaft der Uniformierten', *Frankfurter Rundschau*, 17 April 2002.

29 Quoted in *Agence France Presse*, 14 April 2002. Also see, 'Berlin weist Vorwurf des "Waffenembargos" zurück', *Frankfurter Rundschau*, 10 April 2002.

30 Roger Boyes, 'Missiles Highlight German Trade with Israel', *The Times*, 18 January 2003.

31 Quoted in *Guardian*, 28 November 2002.

32 'Treffen von Bundeskanzler Schröder und dem israelischen

Staatspräsidenten Katzav', at www.bundeskanzler.de/Kanzler-News-.7698.453781/a.htm?printView=y.

33 For their remarks, see Gardner Feldman, *The Special Relationship*, pp. 174–5.

34 Tony Czucka, 'Germany Takes New, Sharper Tone Toward Israel, Holds Back Military Spare Parts', *Associated Press*, 15 April 2002.

35 Duisburger Institut für Sprach- und Sozialforschung, 'Die Nahost-Berichterstattung zur Zweiten Intifada in der deutschen Printmedien, unter besonderer Berücksichtigung des Israel-Bildes. Analyse diskursiver Ereignisse im Zeitraum von September 2000 bis August 2001', *Kurzfassung* (Duisburg: Duisburger Institut für Sprach- und Sozialforschung, 2002), p. 30.

36 *Associated Press*, 10 April 2002; *New York Times*, 4 April 2002; *Agence France Presse*, 15 April 2002.

37 Lorne Cooke, 'Germany Carefully Carving Out a Role in the Middle East', *Agence France Presse*, 4 September 2002.

38 Matthias Arning, 'Rat rügt Vorwürfe gegen Israel', *Frankfurter Rundschau*, 13 April 2002.

39 Quoted in David McHugh, 'Head of German Jewish Community Decries Criticism of Israel', *Associated Press*, 10 April 2002; 'German Jewish Leader Stresses Country's "Special Responsibility" for Israel,' *BBC Monitoring International Reports*, 12 May 2002; and Katsav interview in *Der Spiegel*, 9 December 2002.

40 See Deputy Secretary of the Treasury Stuart E. Eizenstat, 'Remarks at the 12th and Concluding Plenary of the German Foundation, Berlin Germany, July 17, 2000'. For a detailed discussion of the compensation issue, see Chapter 6 by Andrew Baker in this volume.

41 Graham Bowley and John Authers, 'US Lawyers Prepare Nazi Labour Lawsuits', *Financial Times*, 27 August 1998.

42 Both statements are quoted in Roger Cohen, 'Citing "Campaign" Against Germany, Chancellor Announces Fund for Victims of Nazism', *New York Times*, 17 February 1999.

43 *Süddeutsche Zeitung*, 11 December 1998; *Süddeutsche Zeitung*, 25 January 1999; *Washington Post*, 5 February 1999; *Financial Times*, 15 April 1999.

44 David Sanger, 'Germans Approve New Plan to Pay Holocaust Victims', *New York Times*, 10 February 1999.

45 Quoted in *Spiegel Online*, 'Moral und Geschäft dicht beieinander', 8 October 1999, at www.spiegel.de/wirtschaft/politik/0,1518,45727,00.html.

46 Eizenstat, 'Remarks'.

47 'Rede von Bundeskanzler Gerhard Schröder zur Einbringung eines Gesetzentwurfes zur Errichtung einer Stiftung "Erinnerung, Verantwortung und Zukunft" vor dem Deutschen Bundestag', 14 April 2000, at www.bundeskanzler.de/Reden-.7715.6810/a.htm?printView=y.

48 'Interview des Bundesministers des Auswärtigen Joschka Fischer mit dem Tagesspiegel für die Ausgabe vom 05. November 1998', at www.auswaertiges-amt.de/www/deinfoser.../index_html?bereich_id=17&type_id=0&archiv_id=893&detail.

49 'Rede von Bundesaußenminister Fischer anlässlich des Festakts '50 Jahre Deutsche Gesellschaft für die Vereinten Nationen' am 19. März 2002', at www.auswaertiges-amt.de/www/deinfoser.../index_html?bereich_id=17&type_id=5&archiv_id=3601&detail.

50 'Rede von Bundesaußenminister Fischer zur Eröffnung der dritten Konferenz der Leiterinnen und Leiter der deutschen Auslandsvertretungen am 27. Mai 2002', at www.auswaertiges-amt.de/www/deinfoser.../index_html?bereich_id=17&type_id=5&archiv_id=3252&detail.

51 See 'Rede von Bundesaußenminister Fischer anlässlich der Entgegennahme der Ehrendoktorwürde der Universität Haifa am 29. Mai 2002 in Haifa/Israel', at www.auswaertiges-amt.de/www.deinfoser ... /index_html ?bereich_id=17&type_id=5&archiv _id=3600&detail.

52 Quoted in Ute-Marion Schnurrer, 'Lilien für die Toten – dann redet Fischer Tacheles mit Arafat', *Deutsche Presse Agentur*, 2 June 2001.

53 'Deutschland schaltet sich in Nahost-Gespräche ein: Keine Vermittlung', *Deutsche Presse Agentur*, 1 June 2001.

54 For Israeli and Palestinian perspectives on Fischer, see 'Fischer reist Freitag nach Israel – Auch Besuche bei Arafat, in Ägypten und Jordanien', *Agence France Presse*, 31 May 2001; *Associated Press*, 20 August 2001.

55 Richard Meng, 'Sieben-Punkte-Plan. Vom Rückzug bis zum Friedensschluss', *Frankfurter Rundschau*, 10 April 2002.

56 'German Jewish Leader Stresses Country's "Special Responsibility for Israel"', *BBC Monitoring International Reports*, 12 May 2002.

57 '"Israel Must Not Show Any Sign of Weakness" – Interview by Federal Foreign Minister Fischer with *Die Zeit* newspaper, 11 April 2002', at www.auswaertiges-amt.de/.../ausgabe_archiv?archiv_id=2989&bereich_id=27&type_id.

58 *Ibid.*

59 *Ibid.*

60 'Die Nahostkrise wird ihre Lösung erzwingen – oder eskalieren', *Frankfurter Rundschau*, 20 April 2002.

61 Christoph Sterzing, 'Deutsche Rüstungsexporte: Politik zwischen Moral und Interesse', in Volker Perthes (ed.), *Deutsche Nahostpolitik. Interessen und Optionen* (Schwalbach: Wochenschau-Verlag, 2001), p. 151.

62 '"A Second Chance? – Germany and the Jewish Community Today," Speech by Joschka Fischer, Federal Minister for Foreign Affairs at the Annual Meeting of the American Jewish Committee, 3 May 2001, Washington, DC', Embassy of the Federal Republic of Germany, Washington, DC, 4 May 2001.

63 Forgiveness features in 'Fischer: Rede anlässlich des "Partners in History"-Dinner des World Jewish Congress in New York', 11 September 2000, at www.auswaertiges-amt.de/www/deinfoser.../index_html?bereich_id=17&type_id=0&archiv_id=321&detail; shame, in 'A Second Chance?'; and guilt, in 'Rede von Bundesaußenminister Fischer anläßlich der Konferenz "Global Anti-Semitism" der Anti-Defamation League in New York am 1. November 2002', at www.auswaertiges-amt.de/www/deinfose ... /index_html?bereich_id =17&type_id=0&archiv_id=3701&detail.

64 See 'Fischer: Rede anlässlich der "Partners in History"'.

65 See, for example, 'Rede von Bundesaußenminister Fischer aus Anlass der fünfzigjährigen Wiederkehr der Unterzeichnung des Luxemburger Abkommens, gehalten im Rahmen eines Festakts in Berlin am 13.11.2002', at www.auswaertiges-amt.de/www/deinfose ... /index_html?bereich_ id=17&type_id=0&archiv_id=3745&detail.

66 This Diaspora Jewish organisation has by far the most extensive institutionalised ties to Germany. For the development of these relations, see Lily Gardner Feldman, 'The Jewish Role in German–American Relations', in Frank Trommler and Elliott Shore (eds), *The German–American Encounter. Conflict and Cooperation between Two Cultures, 1800–2000* (New York: Berghahn, 2001).

67 See *Frankfurter Allgemeine Zeitung*, 11 May 2002.

68 Quoted in *BBC Monitoring International Reports*, 16 April 2002; *Jerusalem Post*, 26 May 2002.

69 *BBC Monitoring International Reports*, 16 April 2002.

70 Quoted in *Die Tageszeitung*, 7 May 2002.

71 Quoted in *Deutsche Presse Agentur*, 27 May 2002; *Jerusalem Post*, 28 May 2002; *Frankfurter Allgemeine Zeitung*, 4 June 2002.

72 Quoted in *Deutsche Presse Agentur*, 27 May 2002.

73 *Ibid.*

74 See *Frankfurter Allgemeine Zeitung*, 4 June 2002; and *Handelsblatt*, 27 May 2002.

75 Quoted in *AFX European Focus*, 28 May 2002.

76 *Die Tageszeitung*, 17 and 27 May 2002.

77 *Frankfurter Rundschau*, 10 April 2002; *BBC Monitoring Reports*, 29 May 2002; and *Jerusalem Post*, 28 May 2002.

78 *Agence France Presse*, 19 September 2002.

79 *International Herald Tribune*, 20 September 2002; *Deutsche Presse Agentur*, 18 October 2002; *Agence France Presse*, 11 February 2003.

80 Quoted in Weingardt, *Deutsche Israel- und Nahostpolitik*, p. 298.

81 Quoted in *The Jerusalem Post*, 26 May 2002.

82 Salomon Korn, 'Ende der Schonzeit', *Frankfurter Allgemeine Zeitung*, 6 May 2002.

6

Restitution and the Berlin Republic

Andrew Baker

On 9 November 1988, ceremonies marking the 40th anniversary of *Kristallnacht* were held in many cities around the world. Yet, perhaps the most surprising commemoration took place at the centre of what had been the Nazi capital, on Oranienbürgerstraße in Berlin at the ruins of a former synagogue, whose golden domes had been a prominent feature of the prewar city's skyline. Presiding over the ceremony, which also included the announcement that the former synagogue would be rebuilt, was the unlikely figure of Erich Honecker, leader of the GDR. The GDR from its inception had declared itself to be the 'anti-Fascist' German State. The Federal Republic of Germany accepted from its founding in 1949 responsibility for the crimes of the Nazis. Its first Chancellor, Konrad Adenauer, entered into negotiated reparation agreements with the State of Israel and with the Conference on Jewish Material Claims Against Germany (more commonly known as the Claims Conference) on behalf of Holocaust survivors. But East Germany, which also claimed to be a 'victim' state, rejected any obligation to compensate Nazi victims. Now in 1988, Honecker – who calculated that Jewish support was key to a coveted invitation to Washington – seemed ready to reconsider his country's rejection of Holocaust claims. Among the foreign dignitaries in East Berlin were leaders of the Claims Conference, who held their first direct discussion with the East German leader.

A year later there were other things on the mind of East Berliners. The Berlin Wall had fallen. Honecker was out and on his way to prison. A democratically elected parliament, the *Volkskammer*, passed a motion accepting responsibility for the crimes of the Third Reich as its first order of business:

> The first freely elected parliament of the GDR accepts, on behalf of the citizens of this country, its share of the responsibility for the humiliation, expulsion and murder of Jewish women, men and children ... We declare that we will do everything we can to help heal the mental and physical wounds of the survivors and to bring about just compensation for material losses.[1]

The ground was set for opening compensation negotiations with the GDR. The Claims Conference, which considered the Federal Republic's payments as covering the debt of only two-thirds of the German people, was already prepared to calculate East Germany's new obligations.

Negotiations in Bonn

For a brief period, it appeared that a second, democratic German state might be a part of the European landscape. At first unification seemed neither inevitable nor desirable. Certainly, both Britain and France did nothing to hide their uneasiness. Even the Social Democrats in Bonn favoured only a gradual confederation of two independent nations. But, as a growing number of young East Germans crossed the intra-German border, and as Chancellor Helmut Kohl recognised the unique opportunity to move quickly, a rapid process of unification through incorporation into the Federal Republic became the politically desirable goal.

There were far more pressing questions at this time than the demands for further compensation to Nazi victims. Would a newly unified Germany remain a member of NATO or steer a neutral course? What of the thousands of Soviet troops in East Germany? Could the costs of unification be calculated, and were West Germans prepared to pay? Would the United States support German unification, particularly in light of French and British ambivalence? All of these issues would be addressed in the complex September 1990 'Agreement on the Enactment and Interpretation of the Unification Treaty', or the 'Two-plus-Four Agreement' as it was generally known. Responding to the intervention of US Secretary of State James Baker, German Foreign Minister Hans-Dietrich Genscher pledged that the Federal Republic would address the outstanding claims of Jewish victims against the former GDR.

Citing this exchange as an invitation to reopen negotiations, the Claims Conference pressed ahead with two main objectives. It sought to reopen the postwar programmes of indemnification payments to Nazi victims. Enacted between 1953 and 1965, these laws, known as the *Bundesentschädigungsgesetze* (BEG), provided for restitution payments to slightly more than 2 million Holocaust survivors. But there were many victims who had not secured these direct benefits from the German government before the programmes had been closed. Some Holocaust survivors had initially rejected any help from Germany in the immediate years after the war as a matter of principle. But, as they grew older, their financial needs, often exacerbated by physical maladies related to their Holocaust experience, made them reconsider. Additionally, a significant number of Nazi victims could be counted among those Jews leaving the Soviet Union and eastern Europe for Israel and other Western countries in the 1970s and 1980s. They were never afforded an opportunity to apply for indemnification benefits while living behind the Iron Curtain. Not only did these two groups represent a sizable and growing number of needy Holocaust victims, but they were a core constituency of the Claims Conference, which could not ignore their plight.

At the same time, the Claims Conference was well aware that the process of unification included important legislation governing the restitution and privatisation of property in the GDR. Although driven primarily by domestic, German politics – there were many West Germans who sought to reclaim properties they had once owned – the proposed legislation would obviously encompass former Jewish property, too, that had been Aryanised by the Nazis before being nationalised under the Communists. Thus, they maintained that all formerly Jewish-owned properties on the eve of the Holocaust that were without living claimants should be handed over to the Claims Conference as the beneficiary of the Jewish people. The small staff of the Claims Conference worked quietly but diligently to press these demands. It frequently sought support in Washington to help make its case with German leaders. It also enlisted the help of other Jewish organisations, such as the American Jewish Committee and B'nai B'rith, which had their own network of relations with German officials. It studiously avoided public attention, and even its Board of Directors – which met only once every two years – was unaware of the details of its negotiations.

In the end, the Claims Conference did not succeed in reopening the BEG to new applicants. However, the German government was not indifferent to the obvious plight of these uncompensated victims. It agreed to a new programme, established in 1993, that came to be known as the Article 2 Fund, a reference to the relevant section of the Two-plus-Four Agreement. This would provide modest, monthly pensions of DM 500 to Nazi victims who met several, strict conditions. Only those former victims who had received little or nothing from Germany in the past and who had suffered 'severely' (defined as a minimum of eighteen months in a ghetto or six months in a concentration camp) and who lived now only in Western countries would be eligible. The programme, however, would be administered by the Claims Conference itself, which would have the onerous task of examining Holocaust survivors and determining if they met the eligibility criteria. Despite the fact that literally tens of thousands of survivors would now receive pensions, it would be the task of the Claims Conference and not the German government to tell many others no.

It was a somewhat easier process for the Claims Conference to secure the designation as heir to unclaimed, former Jewish property in East Germany. A precedent had already been established in the early years of the Federal Republic (and even prior, in the American Zone of Occupation) that transferred such properties to the predecessor of the Claims Conference. At the time, most of the proceeds from the sale of those properties were used to aid in the resettlement of Holocaust survivors in Israel and elsewhere. As before, the German government made no effort to claim these properties for itself. It recognised that if private claimants did not exist, it was owing to the exterminationist policies of the Nazis. The Jewish community in Germany, although active and organised, officially numbered little more than 30,000. The Claims Conference, a broad umbrella of international Jewish organisations, was the proper recipient, and it had indicated its intention to use these new assets in large measure to alleviate the conditions of Holocaust survivors worldwide, many of whom were aging and in need. But that did not mean that the negotiations were without complications. Only after repeated sessions did the German government agree that a tax on restituted properties – intended to help pay for compensation where restitution was not possible – would not apply to the claimants of Holocaust victims. The real work, however, would begin after the legislation was adopted. The Claims Conference had only two years to research and submit claims for all possible former Jewish properties. If the claims of former owners or their heirs were also filed, the Claims Conference would withdraw its claims. But, if no claim were filed before the 1993 deadline, the property would remain with the German state.

Between the establishment of the Article 2 Fund and the designation as heir to unclaimed Jewish property, the Claims Conference succeeded in securing $2 billion in new benefits for Holocaust survivors. Yet, a decade later these achievements would lead to fractious debates within segments of the Jewish community itself.

The case of Hugo Princz

During the same period that Claims Conference officials were engaged in their quiet negotiations with Germany to secure these new benefits, a very different approach was being taken on behalf of a single Holocaust victim in the United States. It would eventually result in a new compensation agreement of relatively modest amounts, but it would come to change radically the dynamics of all future negotiations.

Hugo Princz was born to an American businessman living in Slovakia in 1922. Twenty years later he and his family were arrested by the Nazi SS as Jews and deported to Majdanek. From the beginning Princz was identified as an American citizen and was so registered throughout a three-year ordeal that took him to Auschwitz and from there on a death march to Dachau. In 1945 he was liberated by American soldiers, who saw the letters 'USA' on his prisoner uniform, and sent directly to a US military hospital for treatment. He came to America in 1946. In 1955, Princz applied for compensation under the German indemnification laws, but his claims were denied. Fellow survivors in America and Israel who received these BEG payments had been registered at displaced persons centres in Germany at the war's end. But since Princz was repatriated directly to the United States, he never passed through a displaced persons centre and was thus 'ineligible' to receive compensation. Ironically, his US citizenship prevented him from receiving the very same assistance given to stateless survivors who settled in America after the Holocaust or to survivors in (western) European countries, where state-to-state agreements had been reached with the Federal Republic.

In 1992, Princz brought suit against the German government in a Federal District Court in Washington. His attorneys argued that his was a unique case, perhaps the only identified American citizen to be caught up in the Holocaust and to be denied compensation by the post-war German government for precisely that fact. Surprisingly for the German government's attorneys and perhaps even those of Hugo Princz, the judge rejected a move for dismissal. Germany was certain that the doctrine of sovereign immunity, which protects a foreign government from facing suit in a US court, would shield it from any liability. While that was probably true, months would pass before an Appeals Court would consider reversing the lower court's decision. The Germans failed to understand that Princz really did not expect victory to be achieved in the courtroom. More often than not, a lawsuit in American courts is a prelude to a negotiated, out-of-court settlement. The lower court's refusal to dismiss the case outright was a signal from the judge to do just that. Princz's *pro bono* attorney was ready and eager to begin discussions with his German counterpart.

But those discussions did not follow. The Germans took the position that the matter would eventually be decided in the Appeals Court, where they would surely prevail. Princz's advocates claimed his case was *sui generis*, but who could really know for sure? The Germans reasoned that, if a single Holocaust survivor managed to secure new compensation benefits just by filing suit in an American court, there would be no end to such battles. All the carefully negotiated indemnification agreements worked out with the Claims Conference and other global partners would mean nothing. Despite the tragic circumstances of Hugo Princz's Holocaust suffering, the German government would stand firm on what it saw as a matter of principle.

They were not alone in this view, which was substantially shared by the negotiators of the Claims Conference. In fact, the very discussions taking place which eventually led to the Article 2 Fund pensions were intended to address the plight of survivors who were similar to Hugo Princz – people living in the West who, for whatever reason, did not receive BEG payments. For the Claims Conference, the Princz matter was not just a special pleading that ignored the many thousands of still uncompensated victims, it also threatened to complicate the long-standing relationship it maintained with Germany as the official representative of Holocaust survivors worldwide. But neither party realised that it was no longer under their control. The case for Hugo Princz would not be made in the private negotiating rooms of the Finance Ministry in Bonn or in a Washington, DC courtroom. Instead, it would be made to the American public and to official Washington.

Princz's attorney secured the *pro bono* help of the Washington office of an influential, Atlanta-based law firm with Democratic ties forged during the Carter Administration. Together they took the case to members of Congress and to officials in the Clinton White House. Senators and Representatives wrote letters to German Foreign Minister Klaus

Kinkel and Chancellor Helmut Kohl. Hugo Princz was the subject of sympathetic profiles in national magazines and on network television. Each one emphasised that this Holocaust survivor was repeatedly denied compensation from Germany precisely *because* he was an American citizen.

In July 1994, the DC District Court of Appeals – albeit in a split decision – ruled in favour of Germany, acknowledging its claim to sovereign immunity. (Germany's attorney pointed out that Princz was now eligible to receive an Article 2 Fund pension.) But the matter was far from over. The District Court permitted the case to continue, by allowing the substitution for the German state of several German companies who employed Princz as a slave labourer. If anything, support in the U.S. Congress only grew stronger. In October 1994, the House of Representatives passed legislation to amend the Foreign Sovereign Immunities Act. Similar legislation was introduced in the US Senate, which recessed before taking up the matter. Although deferred until a new Congress took office after the mid-term elections, Germany was put on notice. Only a handful of rogue states had been denied the benefit of sovereign immunity, but it appeared that Congress now was willing to add Germany to that small list.

All of us who had frequent contacts with German officials urged them to reach a settlement. It had long since ceased being a question of what Hugo Princz merited from the German government. Despite the many negotiated compensation agreements, this case had now become the most visible expression of how Germany addressed its Holocaust-era past despite the many negotiated compensation agreements. While no one wanted to see Germany actually brought into a US court to stand trial for its treatment of Holocaust survivors – and no one really imagined that the White House would in the end allow Germany's sovereign immunity to be repealed – it increasingly looked like a 'runaway train' that no one was prepared to stop. Frustrated diplomats at the German Embassy in Washington said they had repeatedly urged Bonn to settle the matter privately. Finally, in January 1995 it appeared that the message had been received. Asked about the Princz case at a press conference on the eve of a visit to Washington, German Chancellor Kohl replied that he was looking for a 'pragmatic solution'.

That pragmatic solution would still be months away. The German government decided that it would address Princz's claim through a global agreement with the United States. In this way the claims of any other individual who might be similar to Princz would also be resolved.

In fact, there were others, as well as several hundred American soldiers, who were eventually covered by the new agreement. Almost lost in the negotiations was the late addition of three German companies to Princz's suit. They agreed to an out-of-court settlement on the stipulation that the amount would not be publicly disclosed. Their concern for secrecy and fear of establishing a precedent were so great, that they refused to make any payment to Princz directly. The dilemma was resolved only when the American Jewish Committee agreed to accept the payment as a humanitarian gesture from the German companies and pass it on to Princz.

It was not until the fall of 1995 that Hugo Princz and his attorneys were able to celebrate their three-year struggle. They demonstrated that the combination of court suits, public appeals and pressure from Washington could achieve results, when private appeals and quiet negotiations failed. It was a lesson not lost on future efforts to secure help for Holocaust victims.

The double victims

As European Director for the American Jewish Committee, I travelled regularly to central and eastern Europe in the early 1990s. It was an exciting but unusual experience to be visiting Jewish communities in the now 'former' Communist world. Most of these communities had been decimated during the Holocaust, and the majority of those who survived left for Israel or America. During decades of Communist rule, Jewish communal life was severely restricted and carefully monitored by security officials. Only a fraction of even the remnant that survived openly associated themselves with the official community. With numbers so small and a postwar generation that was denied virtually any Jewish education, there were only a few optimists who believed that a revival of Jewish life was possible. But their optimism was not unfounded. A revival of Jewish life was soon evident in every country, with new religious, cultural and educational groups replacing the one official Communist-sanctioned body of former times. Most of these groups shared the same hopes of a better life in a democratic society that were held by their non-Jewish neighbours.

But one group stood apart. Each community included an association of ghetto and concentration camp survivors. They came to be known as 'double victims', since they had survived the Holocaust only to be subject to the rigors and oppression of Communism. They had never received any compensation for their suffering under the Nazis. In some places they were not even permitted to assert the singularity of their persecution as Jews, since all their fellow citizens were victims of the Fascist German state. Now they were pensioners in a suddenly free market economy where their pensions were quickly losing value.

Initially, these survivors had expectations that the indemnification benefits that Germany had been paying to survivors in the West would be extended to them, too. They knew it was not possible as long as totalitarian governments ruled the Soviet Union and its satellites. But that barrier had now been removed, and so they reasoned that compensation payments should soon follow. But they were wrong.

Helmut Kohl had promised a quick unification that would not significantly burden the West German taxpayer. But the costs would prove to be far more than anyone anticipated. Additionally, Germany was expected to aid in the economic rebuilding of its newly democratic neighbours to its east. There was also the problem of thousands of Soviet troops still stationed in eastern Germany, with a collapsing Soviet Union that could not afford to bring them home. With such pressing demands, the needs of the double victims were not high on the list of priorities.

In its negotiations, the Claims Conference focused on the plight of those Nazi victims who had received little or no help from Germany in the past, which would appear to describe precisely the double victims of eastern Europe and the Soviet Union. But the German Government insisted – and the Claims Conference could do little more than acquiesce – that only survivors living in western countries would be eligible. Many of those who would come to receive these Article 2 Fund pensions had in fact been double victims. Some had emigrated from the Soviet Union in the 1970s and early 1980s, while considerable numbers left at the end of the decade as the Soviet Union imploded. The Article 2 Fund obligations would alone be a considerable burden on the German budget. Although the Claims Conference presented itself as the representative of Holocaust survivors worldwide, its constituent members were limited to Jewish organisations in the West. There would be recipients of these new pensions from each country represented on its board, a genuine success in a difficult set of negotiations. And if there were some critical voices, they could report that Germany intended to provide direct funding to several states of the former Soviet Union to help Nazi victims living there.

It was true, but only up to a point. Germany had agreed to provide

DM 1 billion to the Soviet Union for a humanitarian foundation that would pay compensation to former Nazi victims. It was generally understood in Bonn that this was part of the price for removing Soviet troops from German soil. However, because the Soviet Union fell apart before the foundation could be created, the money was divided among three foundations established in Russia, Ukraine and Belarus. Little attention was paid to how these new foundations operated, and in some cases money was lost to private banks and shaky investment schemes. In making payments to individual claimants, the foundations applied a very broad definition of 'victim'. As a result, the one-time payments averaged only a few hundred dollars, and well over 95 per cent of the recipients were non-Jews. Nevertheless, Germany would now assert that it had addressed the needs of Nazi victims in the former Soviet Union through these humanitarian foundations.

Restitution battles had generally pitted Jewish groups such as the Claims Conference against the German government. But new allies emerged inside Germany that some thought might change these dynamics. Several members of the Greens/*Bündnis '90* Party took up the cause of Holocaust survivors in the Baltic States. They visited the survivor group in Latvia, which numbered only slightly more than 100. Its chairman, Alexander Bergmann, exemplified the inequality of German restitution policy. His brother, who had endured the same experiences in Nazi concentration camps, now lived in Frankfurt and received an Article 2 Fund pension, but he, living in Riga, received nothing. In Bonn these few Bundestag members sought, with only limited success, to move their colleagues to act. Meanwhile they took up private collections in order to offer at least some help to the most beleaguered among the Holocaust survivors, whose small pensions could not even cover the cost of winter heating oil.

When the German army entered Latvia in the summer of 1941, many Latvians greeted them as liberators, ending a brief but despised period of Soviet occupation. But for Latvia's Jewish population it heralded unspeakable horrors. On 4 July 1941, several hundred Jews were locked into Riga's main synagogue, which was then set on fire. Thousands of others were marched to the outskirts of town, where they were murdered and buried in mass graves. Many individual Latvians and Latvian Legionnaire members assisted the Nazis in their persecution and killing of Jews and later became members of the *Waffen SS*. In 1944, when Germany was defeated and Latvia was again incorporated into the Soviet Union, some of these Latvian war criminals were arrested and prosecuted. All of them recognised the prudence of keeping silent about this period in their lives. But that silence ended with Latvian independence in 1991. They pulled out their Legionnaire and *SS* uniforms from attic and basement chests and paraded in the centre of Riga. In these first organised 'reunions', the veterans learned to their surprise that they were eligible for German army disability payments. Though non-German, all former *Waffen SS* soldiers could submit applications to the German government. Provided they could demonstrate some health or medical infirmity that resulted from their wartime experience – and nearly all could make some such claim – they would be entitled to monthly 'war victims' pensions', as they were called. Unlike the BEG programmes, applicants for war victims' pensions faced no expiration date.

A production team from the German ARD television show, 'Panorama', filmed these gatherings of *SS* veterans in Latvia. Initially they were shocked that in the 1990s there actually people who would proudly march in Nazi uniforms, and they drew attention to the fact that the fledgling democratic government in Riga seemed to sympathise with them. But they also discovered that Germany's programme of disability payments for military veterans was easily accessible and without any examination of the wartime record. In fact, the German law had been written in such a way that even those who were convicted of war crimes could not be excluded. 'Panorama' also filmed interviews with the dwindling number of Holocaust survivors in Riga, who in 1995 had still received nothing from the German government. When the show ran, its producers hoped that the terrible contrast of the continued mistreatment of Holocaust victims in Latvia with the benefits being provided to *SS* veterans and possibly even war criminals would so arouse the German public that the government would be embarrassed into helping these Nazi victims. But, they were mistaken. On the night of the broadcast most of the phone calls coming into the station were not from Germans, but from Dutch citizens who were also frequent viewers of ARD. They all had the same question: as *Waffen SS* veterans in the Netherlands they did not know they were entitled to German army pensions, they wanted to know how they could apply.

In 1995 the American Jewish Committee took up the issue of the double victims in meetings with German officials. Foreign Minister Klaus Kinkel seemed genuinely sympathetic and promised to examine the subject himself. He instructed his ambassadors to meet Holocaust survivor groups in several countries and report to him on the situation. But he was unable to persuade his senior partner in the coalition government to change the current policy. In a candid exchange I had with him in March 1996 in Berlin, he shared his frustration and admitted that he probably could not do any more. American Jewish Committee (AJC) leaders had met German Chancellor Kohl on several occasions, and the organisation was held in high regard in Bonn as a partner in efforts to build German–Jewish dialogue and reconciliation. There was a network of close, personal ties with senior aides in the Chancellery, as well as with members of the CDU party leadership. Our goal was a simple one – merely to extend the programme of Article 2 pensions to Holocaust survivors still living in eastern Europe and the former Soviet Union. We had assumed that we would be able to press the issue forcefully – but quietly and privately – to achieve success. But, we were wrong.

Friedrich Bohl, minister of state in the Chancellery, also agreed to see me in March 1996 in Bonn to discuss this issue. We spent an hour together in a cordial but stiff exchange – a marked contrast to the friendly meetings that had taken place with the Chancellor in the same building.[2] Bohl recited the litany of compensation programmes that Germany had instituted throughout the history of the Federal Republic and went on to enumerate the various programmes that had been set up or were being contemplated to address the needs of victims in the former Communist world. I responded that none of them provided anything more than meagre one-time payments to individual survivors. Most of the money would go to non-Jews or to hospitals and old-age homes that served primarily non-Jews. At the end of our discussion he told me that the issue had come up in a meeting with the negotiating chairman of the Claims Conference the previous December. They had reached an agreement to liberalise the Article 2 Fund criteria that would enable more victims in the West to qualify for pensions. But in return, Bohl said, all the other demands – including compensation for the double victims – would be deferred for three years. Only four months had passed, and Bohl was obviously irritated that I sought to reopen the subject. We had hoped to resolve this issue quietly, I told him, but if necessary we were prepared to press it publicly.

Accounting for slave labour

As many as 10 million people were forcibly employed by the Nazis during the Second World War. About half were Jews, whose forced labour was often only a way station on their path to the gas chambers – *Vernichtung durch Arbeit* (annihilation through work), as it was understood by the Nazis. The others were primarily Poles, Russians and Ukrainians. Even though the indemnification programmes of the Federal Republic, which had come to total DM 100 billion, were intended to compensate victims for damage to health and loss of liberty, they pointedly excluded compensation for forced labour. A 1953 agreement deferred this issue, understood to be a matter for an international reparations agreement, until a final peace agreement was signed between Germany and all its neighbours. But the Cold War meant that such an agreement was never signed and, as a result, forced labourers were never compensated.

Nearly all major German companies made use of forced labour. Many of those companies played important roles in the postwar economic reconstruction of Germany, often with Nazi-era industrialists still at their helm. Despite their postwar commercial success, only a handful of companies offered some very modest payments to former forced labourers, usually in the form of a 'humanitarian fund' negotiated with the Claims Conference. The companies insisted that these were *voluntary* gestures made without obligation, but they still required that the Claims Conference relinquish any future claims. Some DM 52 million were paid to 15,000 survivors, as a result. When former forced labourers sought to file suit in a German court, the companies marshalled their attorneys and fought back vigorously. Not a single claimant succeeded. Although decades had passed, there were new legal and public relations tools that could be used to press the case of the former forced and slave labourers. This would eventually lead to the last major compensation agreement to be negotiated with the German government.

Though unknown in Germany, the class action lawsuit has frequently been employed in the American courtroom to win settlements for victims of various misfortunes, ranging from airline crashes to racial discrimination to defective products. Holocaust survivors – in particular those who were forced into servitude by the Nazis – were an obvious class of victims. And the obvious targets were those German companies with business interests in the United States. German automobiles and electronics were well known to American consumers. But in banking, insurance and pharmaceuticals, too, German companies had a growing stake in the American market. It was not too difficult to draw a line back to a Nazi-era predecessor that literally worked concentration camp inmates to death.

In early 1998, several lawsuits were filed in US Courts against German companies, including Volkswagen, Siemens and Daimler–Benz. Additional suits followed against banks and insurance companies. By the summer there were fifty suits in Federal and State courts from New York to California. It was estimated that some 250,000 (primarily Jewish) former slave labourers were still alive and over 1 million (primarily non-Jewish) forced labourers. Both were identified as plaintiffs in the suits.

Of course, it was not the intention of the attorneys to wait and fight the battle in the courtroom. Several were veterans of a previous fight with Swiss banks over the dormant accounts of Holocaust victims. In that case, they were joined by the World Jewish Congress and other groups in a campaign that included calls for boycotts, the threat of pension fund withdrawals and US Senate Banking Committee hearings. In the end the Swiss agreed to a $1.25 billion settlement, brokered by Under Secretary of State Stuart Eizenstat. There was little reason to doubt that a similar approach would also work against German industry. One attorney, with the assistance of B'nai B'rith International, would later follow up with a full-page advertisement in the *Washington Post* that read, 'German Industry's Shameful Offer to Slave Laborers' over a half-page photo of two pennies.

German industry was not of a single mind in how to respond to the lawsuits and the potential for adverse publicity. Some companies, for whom the American market was not important, were unconcerned. A few decided that they would act on their own. Volkswagen established its own humanitarian fund of DM 20 million to provide compensation to surviving forced labourers. Others were still being counselled to fight the suits in court. Most were expecting that the German government would intervene and take responsibility for finding a comprehensive solution. But Chancellor Kohl, who was in the midst of an increasingly difficult campaign for re-election, steadfastly refused. He argued that this was not something for the German taxpayer to shoulder, and in any case after fifty years and DM 100 billion the country had fulfilled its obligation to compensate Holocaust victims. But his opponent, Gerhard Schröder, who as Minister-President of Lower Saxony sat on the Board of Directors of Volkswagen when it created its new fund for forced labourers, took a different view. Following his election in September 1998, Schröder agreed to take up the issue. A few months later he dispatched his chief-of-staff, Bodo Hombach to the United States as his special emissary. In February 1999, Hombach told an audience assembled by the AJC in Washington that he hoped to have an agreement in place and payments being made to former slave and forced labourers within ninety days. It took nearly two years.

The Germans were prepared to negotiate an overall agreement that would resolve all outstanding Holocaust-era claims against all of German industry – not only those companies that employed forced labour, but all banks and all insurance companies as well. However, in return they wanted a guarantee of 'legal peace' in the United States – i.e. the withdrawal of all suits against German companies and the promise of the US government to prevent any future lawsuits. In order to achieve this, there would have to be direct negotiations with the American government, and Stuart Eizenstat, now Deputy Secretary of the Treasury, was the obvious person to lead them. But, he would first have to bring together the various class action attorneys, survivor groups and others so there could be a common representation of the victims' demands. When Hombach became entangled in a domestic political scandal, Chancellor Schröder turned to Otto Graf Lambsdorff, a former Economics Minister and past Chairman of the FDP, to represent the German government and German industry across the table from Eizenstat.

Although seven months would pass before it was signed, the negotiators announced they had reached an agreement in December 1999. The German government and German industry would together provide DM 10 billion to create the 'Remembrance, Responsibility and the Future Fund'. Most of the money would be used to provide individual payments of DM 5,000 to former forced laborers and DM 15,000 to former slave labourers. It would also include DM 350 million to cover any claims against German insurance companies, which were being addressed by the International Commission on Holocaust Era Insurance Claims, a joint creation of insurance companies, regulators and victims' representatives, chaired by former Secretary of State Lawrence Eagleburger, as well as money for outstanding property claims against German banks. The agreement also set aside DM 700 million for a 'Future Fund', an endowment intended to support unspecified projects in the area of education and reconciliation. Arguably, the last major restitution settlement between Germany and Holocaust victims had been concluded.

Unfinished business

Yet, it may still be premature to draw that final line under this chapter of Germany's reckoning with its Holocaust-era past. Claims

Conference negotiators have repeatedly said that, as long as a single survivor is still alive, they will continue to press the German government. Ongoing negotiations focus on cost of living adjustments in Article 2 Fund pensions and the inclusion of new applicants. Most of the debate at its July 2003 annual board meeting in New York centred on how it was using its own discretionary funds – money that came from restituted unclaimed Jewish property in the former GDR – which were being allocated for welfare projects to aid survivors, and education and research efforts to convey the memory of the Holocaust to future generations. The needs of aging survivors are becoming more acute, particularly in the area of home care and prescription drugs, and a vocal minority inside the Jewish community has chastised the Claims Conference for diverting any money toward education. One board member spoke passionately against being forced 'to choose between the needs of our parents and our children', and argued that this was Germany's responsibility.

The American courts will no longer serve as a venue to press Holocaust-related claims. But there are still outstanding legal challenges being pursued elsewhere. The Jewish Community of Slovakia has sought – so far without success – to use the German courts to try to reclaim the money that the Slovak puppet state took from its Jewish community in 1942 and paid to Nazi Germany for the deportation of 70,000 Jews to death camps. The Jewish Community of Thessaloniki has a record of payments made to the German occupying army in return for 'exempting' its members from forced labour in the Greek port city. The payments stopped when all the Jews in the city were deported to Auschwitz between mid-March and mid-May 1943; 95 per cent of Thessaloniki's 43,000 Jews subsequently perished in the death camps. Jewish leaders have sought an acknowledgement by Germany of its responsibility to repay the money and are considering pursuing their claim at the European Court of Human Rights (ECHR) in Strasbourg. Germany has ignored both these claims, and points to its extensive record of compensation and restitution.

These cases are not likely to succeed, and Germany may be safe to ignore them. But they illustrate a basic fact: no matter how many years have passed since the Holocaust and how much Germany may have done, for many it is not enough. Arguably, no nation has been pressed and has acceded to paying the degree of material compensation as the Federal Republic has to the victims of the Holocaust. But so complete and so utterly destructive were the crimes that no truly final settlement will ever be made. When the first restitution agreement was reached between the German Government and the Claims Conference in 1953, the Germans termed it *Wiedergutmachung*. Fifty years and innumerable agreements later, Jewish representatives still refuse to use that phrase.

Notes

1 See 'Dokumentation: Gemeinsame Erklärung der Volkskammer', *Deutschland Archiv*, 23:5 (1990), p. 794.

2 There was a marked contrast between this meeting with Bohl and much friendlier meetings with Kohl, which tended to have a more general focus on German–Jewish issues. In meetings with Kohl, the Chancellor would speak emotionally about the loss of German Jewry and his commitment to German–Jewish and German–Israeli relations.

Part III

The evolving political culture of the Berlin Republic

7

Public opinion and political issue divides

Robert Rohrschneider and Dieter Fuchs

The unification of Germany has fundamentally altered its political agenda. With historical hindsight, the issues of the 1980s appear almost mundane. The costs of the welfare states were debated, economic growth and unemployment dominated the concerns of parties, and the growth of an environmental movement added a 'green' dimension to the West German agenda. To be sure, these conflicts were serious. They pitted proponents of the welfare state against those who favoured a reduction in state-sponsored services; or defined the controversies between advocates of an economically centred strategy against those who favoured ecological policies. In general, however, the nature of these debates between political parties – the main agents of interest representation – indicated that Western Germany had come a long way from the fledgling democracy inaugurated in 1949. In short, before unification, West German politics was characterised by normal, democratic politics.

Germany's unification changed this tranquil picture, not necessarily for the worse, but did add a contentious aspect to German politics that had not existed beforehand. In part, this change results from the fact that unification exacerbated some problems that preceded Germany's unification. For example, the reconstruction of the eastern economy added a financial strain that did not exist before 1989, even though budget deficits already exerted pressures to downsize governmental services. Other policy domains acquired a new level of urgency after unification, such as the design of a new immigration policy, which accounts for the open borders in Europe.

A special place on this new agenda is occupied by the apparent ambiguity of eastern Germans about Germany's democracy; a topic that this chapter focuses on. The collapse of the Weimar democracy and the subsequent destruction caused by the Third Reich documented Germany's lack of commitment to a liberal democracy. This changed slowly, but steadily, after the current constitution was inaugurated in 1949. Political elites and ordinary citizens came to appreciate first the economic prosperity generated by the fledgling democracy, then the democratic nature of the constitution itself.[1]

In contrast to the growing familiarity with and support for a liberal democracy, eastern Germans were exposed to an authoritarian system that minimised the opportunities for citizens to engage in public discussions and controversies: processes that are at the core of a democratic polity. Moreover, the economy in the East nearly collapsed. Consequently, we ask: how supportive are eastern Germans of those values that underlie the regime in Germany? To what degree do eastern and western Germans hold different policy priorities? And to the extent that we find systematic East–West differences along these dimensions, do they affect mass evaluations of the existing regime?

This chapter addresses these questions and, in the course of it, hopes to make two contributions. First, we examine whether eastern and western Germans are beginning to converge in their views about ideological values and regime appraisals. While there are numerous studies that have addressed these questions,[2] these analyses show that the East–West gap over ideological values and political institutions remained surprisingly stable well into the second half of the 1990s. We now have data for over ten years which affords us an opportunity to update previous studies and, more importantly, to test whether a convergence over fundamental views about a democratic regime can occur within a decade. Second, as will become plain in the empirical section, we use a unique survey conducted in 1997 in eastern and western Germany. The survey was designed to test various arguments in the democratisation literature. It focuses on publics' appraisal of various performance dimensions, such as economic factors, but also including the regime's capacity to implement social and liberal rights.

The chapter is divided into three parts. We first discuss the theoretical backdrop of the study. We then provide evidence that Germany's constitution continues to be viewed sceptically by a surprisingly large number of citizens in the East. The next section conducts a series of multivariate analyses that document the strength with which citizens' perceived regime performance and ideological values affect their views about of the regime. The conclusion highlights the implications of this research.

The theoretical framework

Germany's constitution (the Basic Law) establishes a liberal-democratic order. Given the nature of the system, a congruence between citizens' values and the system exists if a majority holds liberal-democratic ideals; an incongruence would exist if a large number holds ideals reflecting a preference for a different order, such as socialist ideals. This, in a nutshell, is the congruence postulate which was developed by Almond and Verba in their pathbreaking *The Civic Culture.*[3] The postulate, then, raises the following issue: to what extent does a mismatch between citizens' ideological values and Germany's constitution lower support for the existing regime?

This question defines a major schism in the transition literature. In simplified form, *culturalists* assert that ideological values have an independent effect on how citizens evaluate institutions.[4] Because ideological values develop mainly during the formative socialisation years, they tend to be quite stable over time. Accordingly, if the institutional context in which values were initially formed changes, one would expect the value-legacy inherited from the old regime to structure evaluations of the new order. This perspective remains pessimistic concerning the stability of new democracies because several country studies point to the persistence of socialist values in post-communist societies.[5]

The logic underlying this view, however, is disputed by *institutionalists* who maintain that the importance of ideological values is overestimated by culturalists. Rather, so the argument goes, the stability of democratic institutions depends primarily on the performance of a system, in particular, the performance of the economy. If citizens evaluate it positively, this brings preexisting values presumably in line with the a new system.[6] In this view, then, ideological values and positive views about a democratic regime *result* from the performance of the institutional order and have little influence on a regime's support. This approach, too, can refer to country studies to corroborate its arguments.[7]

We think that the differences between culturalists and institutionalists are exaggerated and similarities downplayed. It seems overstated to argue that *only* ideological values or *only* economic performance affect mass evaluations of existing institutions. Instead, we maintain that both factors play a role, and that it is primarily an empirical question which of the two has a stronger impact in a given country at a given point in time.[8]

The model depicted in figure 7.1 begins to map the linkages among

Figure 7.1 Values, performance and regime support

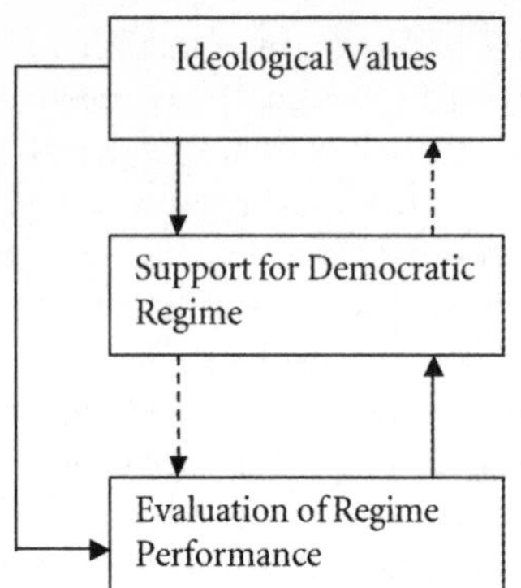

these conceptual categories. The model contains a level for individuals' values, appraisals of the structure about the regime, and their appraisals of the performance of the regime which includes economic perceptions, but also evaluations of its *democratic* performance. The linkages among these categories are likely multi-directional. For example, one could move from the 'top down' (from values to regime to performance appraisals) which would mean, for example, that positive or negative attitudes generated through value orientations affect perceptions at the 'lower' level. Another process moves 'bottom up' (from performance to values) and represents a generalisation of positive or negative experiences with a system to the higher levels. Further, we include a direct effect of the value level on the performance level because such judgments are usually formed on the basis of one's value predispositions (see figure 7.1).

Attitudes about all three dimensions are crucial in defining the sum of what constitutes a 'political culture'. Obviously, of particular import are the first and second level because they directly concern how citizens define their ideal-typical order, and how these preferences influence their evaluations of the existing constitutional framework. Disagreement with the specific performance of the regime, for example, is to some degree expected in a democratic polity, and would tell us less about the extent to which a nation's constitution is accepted than disagreement with the basic principles of a regime – or a rejection of the constitution itself. At the same time, if a regime falls short in supplying expected goods deemed important, this may affect views at the values and regime level. For this reason, we will consider various performance dimensions in this study.

How do citizens develop their views about these various regime dimensions – especially regime values and their evaluations? Our discussion thus far suggests that at least two factors contribute to their genesis. First, the performance of a regime affects how strongly citizens support a regime, at least in the short run. A well-performing system, in the economic domain, for instance, can generate a reservoir of support for a regime. And the perception that a regime delivers basic democratic goods, such as political liberties and social services, also tends to generate support for it.[9]

In addition to these performance dimensions, however, we would expect that individual evaluations of a regime depend to some degree on one's exposure to the political environment. There are multiple ways in which a regime affects how citizens perceive it. There is, of course, the performance of a regime in those domains deemed central. Moreover, exposure to a democratic process helps citizens develop the skills to navigate the complex political reality. Elsewhere, we referred to this process as 'institutional learning'.[10] Based on this model, we expected – and found – that eastern Germans are significantly less supportive of a range of citizenship qualities presupposed from a democratic public.

One central question is whether eastern Germans adjusted to the new regime in the 1990s. To put it differently, how quickly does a public develop the values underlying a constitutional framework? Similarly, given the import of a regime's performance in affecting mass support for it, we will examine whether western Germans have lowered their support for the existing system in light of persistent economic problems. Therefore, we examine the ideological values of citizens, after which we document the changes in policy focus resulting from unification. Thereafter, we will present evidence that the policy emphasis has changed, after which we explore whether values and various performance dimensions affect individuals' regime support.

Ideological values

We begin by examining the democratic ideals of citizens in both parts of Germany. To this end, we use an indicator that asks respondents to evaluate whether they believe that socialism is a good ideal that was poorly implemented. This indicator has been used in a variety of value

Figure 7.2 'Socialism is a good ideal that was poorly implemented'

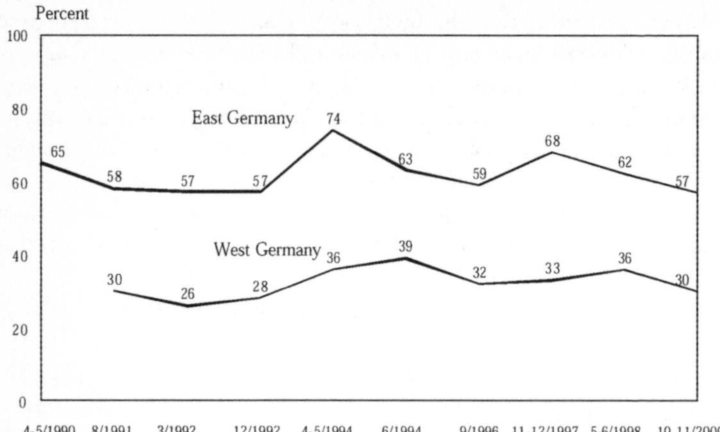

Note: Entries are percentages of respondents who agree with the statement.
Source: Allensbacher Instut für Denoskopie.

studies in eastern Germany and correlates strongly with central tenets of socialist beliefs in the East.[11]

A substantial proportion of eastern Germans agree with this statement (see figure 7.2). In 1991, 65 per cent of eastern Germans endorse it; and levels of support remain roughly at that plateau in late 2000. We find the swings typically found in opinion surveys; for example, we observe a peak of 74 per cent (in 1994) and a low of 57 per cent (in 1992 and 2000). On the whole, however, there is little systematic movement away from the endorsement of the statement by about two-thirds of the eastern German population.

Western German citizens are as consistent as their eastern counterparts – but at a much lower level of support for the idea expressed by the statement. Support fluctuates within a fairly narrow band between 30 and 39 per cent agreement. To some degree, it is surprising how *many* citizens in the West hold the view that socialism is a good ideal. However, analyses of responses to open-ended questions about citizens' understanding of democracy suggest that western Germans associate social security with the term 'socialism', whereas eastern Germans tend to attribute socialist elements to it, such as establishing an income ceiling.[12] In the past, this term has been interpreted differently across the former East–West boundary. Consequently, agreement with the statement tends to reflect a somewhat different set of social–egalitarian concerns. In the East, it connotes an expectation that the political process should produce egalitarian outcomes; in the West, it connotes a view that the political process should produce a material floor below which nobody should fall, but not to guarantee a ceiling above which no one may rise.

This interpretation concerning the different meanings is supported by an analyses of a different question which asks respondents to chose between freedom and social equality:

> Two people are talking about what is ultimately more important, freedom or as much equality as possible. Would you please read this and tell me which of the two comes closest to saying what you also think?
> A I think that freedom and equality are equally important. But if I had to choose between the two, I would say personal freedom is more important; that is, for people to be able to live in freedom and not be restricted in their development.
> B Certainly both freedom and equality are equally important. But if I had to choose between the two, I would consider as much equality as possible to be more important; that is, for no one to be underprivileged and class differences not to be so strong.

Figure 7.3 shows that eastern and western Germans stress different priorities, especially in the first half of the 1990s. Eastern Germans clearly prefer social equality over freedoms, especially at the later time points. Indeed, shortly after Germany's unification, citizens appeared to favour freedoms; a sentiment, however, that quickly gave way to more egalitarian preferences. The movement away from political freedoms illustrates a pattern found not only in eastern Germany, but in other post-communist societies as well. Shortly after citizens began to experience the rough and tumble of democratic politics, with all its uncertainties and social inequities, they begin to yearn for the greater social security that socialist systems provided. Given the economic hardship experienced by many eastern Germans, and especially the social and personal upheavals that the regime change brought for them, it appears natural to wish for a return of the predictability and stability that the authoritarian regime provided. Regardless of the specific reasons underlying this dynamic away from political freedom, we note that a central pillar of the liberal constitution – the stress on political freedoms – takes a back seat in the East when it conflicts with social equality.

In the West, with the exception of the 1998 survey, freedom comes

Figure 7.3 Freedom versus equality

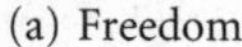
(a) Freedom

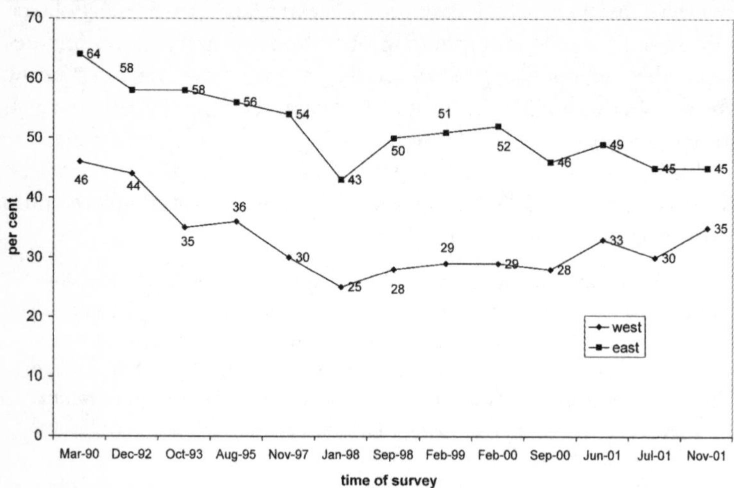

(b) Equality

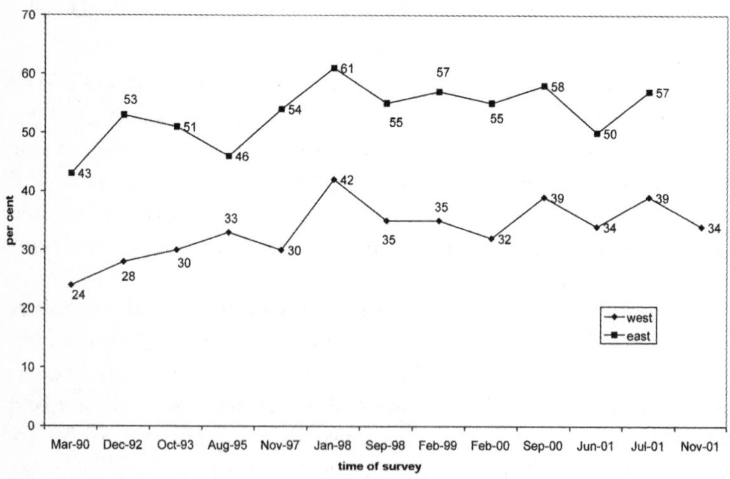

out ahead of social equality by a substantial margin until the late 1990s. We noted elsewhere that the first systematic reduction in support for freedom appeared in the late 1990s but were cautious not to over-interpret what might have been a temporary setback for political freedoms.[13] However, beginning with the onset of 2000 and up to mid-year

2001, there is an unmistakable increase in selecting social equality and a concordant decline in stressing political freedoms. It is still too early to firmly interpret this decline, but it does appear that the long-term economic problems may take a toll on the support for a key pillar of Germany's constitution. We hasten to add that this is a tentative 'explanation' because we do not have access to the micro-level data and thus cannot determine the individual-level predictors of these responses. But this surmise is consistent with other analyses which show that negative evaluations of the national economy increase individuals' endorsement of socialist ideals (see below).

Policy priorities

Given the argument made in the previous section, it is important to examine how citizens actually evaluate the economy – and whether economic problems are perceived to be central, both taken alone and relative to other policy domains. One question is thus to determine the salience of issues. Specifically, to what extent are economic issues more important than other policy domains?

The Politbarometer surveys provide a partial answer to this question. These surveys contain a question, asked several times a year, about which problems respondents believe to be the most important one (see table 7.1). Note first that the environment is the most important problem among western Germans shortly before unification, reflecting the 'postmaterial' orientation of western Germans.[14] However, shortly after the economic consequences of unification surfaced and became politicised, unemployment increasingly dominated the concerns of western and eastern Germans. While the category mentioning this problem is somewhat reduced in 2000–1, most surveys from 2002 suggest that unemployment once again trumps this list when over 70 per cent of eastern and western Germans mention it. In stark contrast, environmentalism is not at the forefront of citizens' policy concerns, in clear contrast to the period preceding unification.

When we use a simple, but powerful, summary indicator of policy priorities – Inglehart's measure of postmaterialism[15] – we find a systematic movement away from traditional bread-and-butter issues during the 1980s (see table 7.2) before unification. By 1989, nearly one-third of western citizens claimed to prioritise such postmaterial issues as environmentalism – the same year in which environmentalism

Table 7.1 'Current most important problem in Germany', 1986–2000, % of all respondents

	West Germany		*East Germany*	
Year	*Unemployment*	*Environmental protection*	*Unemployment*	*Environmental protection*
1986	31.1	14.1	–	–
1987	32.9	14.3	–	–
1988	30.9	14.2	–	–
1989	16.3	16.9	–	–
1990	6.9	11.5	32.5	2.2
1991	5.6	7.6	47.9	1.2
1992	6.7	6.3	48.0	1.4
1993	24.8	2.9	52.9	0.9
1994	48.4	3.7	66.0	0.7
1995	46.9	7.1	65.7	1.2
1996	66.3	2.1	76.0	0.6
1997	71.6	1.1	80.4	0.3
1998	77.1	1.0	85.8	0.4
1999	58.1	1.0	73.0	0.6
2000	39.2	1.6	57.5	0.9

Source: Politbarometer.

became the most important problem in western Germany. Shortly after unification, however, the proportion of postmaterial issues declines, although not to the same level as it was at the beginning of the time series in 1980. These patterns are consistent with an earlier analysis which shows that the influence of postmaterial values on vote choice systematically declines after 1990.[16]

In the East, we find a partially different pattern. There are always more materialists than postmaterialists, albeit by a small margin in 2000. High unemployment rates, the collapse of many companies and the long-term nature of economic reconstruction prevent a focus on non-material policy issues. Note also that the proportion of post-materialism is substantially lower in the East than the West. Overall, the East–West differences are to be expected in light of the significant variation in economic security, and postwar experiences.

Up to this point, we have focused on priorities. We know that unification and its resulting problems raised the salience of economic

Table 7.2 Postmaterialism in Germany, 1980–2000

	1980	*1982*	*1984*	*1986*	*1988*	*1990*	*1991*	*1992*	*1994*	*1996*	*1998*	*2000*
West												
Materialist	37.9	38.3	29.2	17.4	19.4	15.2	13.0	23.1	16.7	13.2	18.8	13.1
Mixed	48.6	47.5	48.3	56.5	52.9	53.3	57.0	53.7	60.6	61.3	61.0	58.6
Postmaterialist	13.4	14.2	22.5	26.1	27.7	31.5	30.0	23.2	22.6	25.6	20.2	28.4
East												
Materialist							26.6	28.5	25.0	19.8	28.2	17.7
Mixed							58.9	61.7	64.2	67.8	59.8	66.2
Postmaterialist							14.5	9.8	10.8	12.4	11.9	16.1

Source: Allbus (German nationality only).

Table 7.3 National economic assessment, 1982–2000

	1982	*1984*	*1986*	*1988*	*1990*	*1991*	*1992*	*1994*	*1996*	*1998*	*2000*
West											
Very good/good	14.0	20.4	38.6	–	75.6	66.5	44.4	11.4	13.4	19.9	36.7
Partly good, partly bad	52.0	54.7	49.2	–	21.7	30.7	47.1	49.3	47.6	47.0	54.0
Very bad/bad	34.1	24.9	12.3	–	2.8	2.9	8.5	39.2	39.0	33.1	9.3
East											
Very good/good						51.5	45.0	12.1	11.3	14.4	24.0
Partly good, partly bad						44.7	46.5	57.3	51.5	47.3	59.5
Very bad/bad						3.8	8.5	30.6	37.2	38.4	16.5

Sources: Allbus (German nationality only).

Table 7.4 Personal economic assessment, 1982–2000

	1982	*1984*	*1986*	*1988*	*1990*	*1991*	*1992*	*1994*	*1996*	*1998*	*2000*
West											
Very good/good	49.0	51.9	60.5	–	67.3	68.4	61.9	57.9	53.1	49.7	59.7
Partly good, partly bad	39.9	36.2	29.4	–	25.9	24.2	29.4	29.9	37.2	36.9	32.8
Very bad/bad	11.1	11.9	10.1	–	6.9	7.4	8.7	12.1	9.7	13.4	7.5
East											
Very good/good						35.1	34.7	48.2	42.3	43.1	43.9
Partly good, partly bad						44.7	44.9	33.7	43.6	39.8	42.4
Very bad/bad						20.2	20.5	18.1	14.1	17.1	13.7

Source: Allbus (German nationality only).

issues relative to others. However, given the import of economic issues, we also would like to know how citizens evaluate the economy. That is, how large is the group of citizens which evaluates the economy negatively?

We note that a majority usually give mixed marks to the present state of the national economy (see table 7.3). Except for the period between 1994 and 1998, when the costs of unification were intensely debated, the longitudinal patterns are fairly stable. We find a similar pattern in the East, albeit at a somewhat lower level. Consistent with macroeconomic conditions, publics in both parts view the conditions of the economy with a degree of ambiguity.

However, citizens are much more positive about their personal situation, not just in the West but also among eastern Germans (see table 7.4). In fact, the proportion of publics indicating that their economic situation is bad is surprisingly small. This no doubt reflects the enormous subsidies which the welfare state provides for the needy, and the considerable resources that went into temporary programmes to lower, for instance, unemployment rates. Thus, while Germans have not suffered in the short-run, they are worried about the severity of national economic problems.

All told, this evidence points to a partially different foundation for political conflicts across the former East–West divide. While western Germans continue to attach considerable weight to non-material issues, eastern Germans are preoccupied with the materialist dimension. However, we also note that there is a systematic movement away from a postmaterial emphasis in the West, both concerning broader value priorities as well as the more specific problems citizens stress. In short, the changed policy agenda of post-unification politics is clearly reflected in the changing salience of political issues to citizens. Likewise, publics in the East and the West perceive that the economy is not doing very well, although this does not severely affect how ordinary citizens perceive their own economic situation.

Regime evaluation

Given the East–West differences over ideological values and policy priorities, how do the eastern and western public evaluate the current system? Figure 7.4 suggests that a persistent gulf separates the two publics regarding their appraisal of the current regime. The question

Figure 7.4 'Do you think the existing democracy in Germany is the best system or is there something better?'

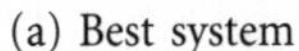

(a) Best system

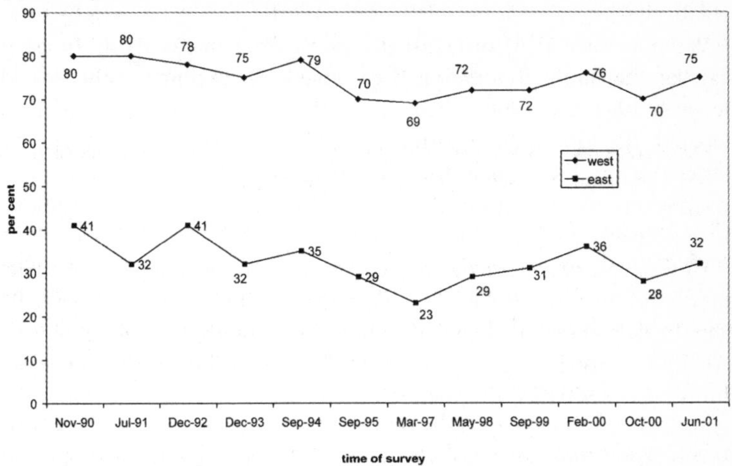

(b) There is a better system

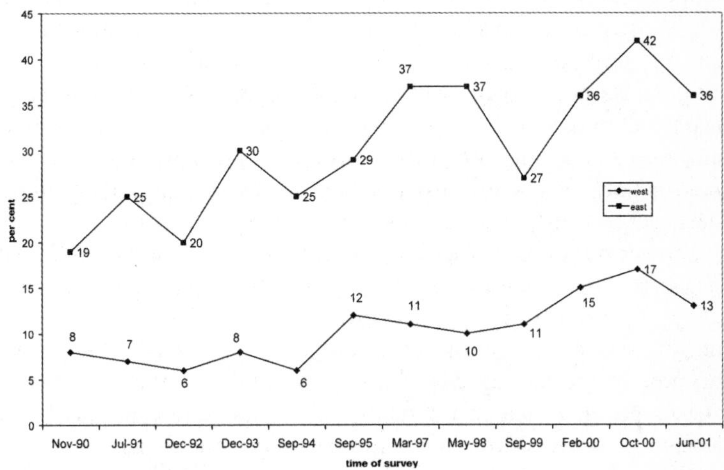

asks citizens to evaluate the existing system against a hypothetical alternative. The figures make plain the near-universal and steady acceptance of the existing democracy in the West. In contrast, in the East, the existing democracy is accepted by a little over one-third of the eastern

Germans public; another third rejects it and the remaining group is uncertain. There exists, in short, a substantial degree of ambiguity over the current form of democracy in the East.

This does not mean, of course, that eastern Germans reject any form of democracy; to the contrary. In a 1997 survey, respondents were asked two questions. The first question asked them to evaluate democracy as an ideal:

> Democracy may involve problems, but it's still better than any other form of government. Strongly agree, agree, disagree, strongly disagree.

This indicator focuses on democracy as an ideal, not on how it is implemented in Germany. A Forsa survey revealed that eastern Germans endorse democracy as an ideal – 84 per cent agree with the statement; only slightly below the approval found in the West (about 90 per cent). There is, in short, strong support for *some form* of democracy in both parts of Germany.

The second statement in the same survey was designed to solicit evaluations about the existing democracy: 'What would you say in general about the democratic system in Germany, that is, about our whole political system as laid down by the constitution? Are you very satisfied with it, satisfied, dissatisfied, or very dissatisfied?' In the East, about 55 per cent of respondents indicate their satisfaction with Germany's constitution; about 71 per cent of West Germans express satisfaction. Thus, nearly half of eastern Germans is not satisfied with the existing regime. However, even this fairly equivocal assessment probably underestimates the true levels of systemic dissatisfaction in the East, given the patterns that emerge over time in the Allensbach surveys.

Another indicator focuses less explicitly on the constitution, but on the performance of the democratic process. The question asked is: 'How satisfied are you with the way democracy works?' This question contains a substantial performance component, of both the current incumbents and the capacity of the system to deliver those goods that citizens prefer. Although the nature of this measure continues to be debated controversially,[17] the meaning of the question's wording is actually quite straightforward in its focus on citizens' overarching evaluations of the democratic *process.*[18]

The responses clearly indicate that there is a substantial East–West difference over how the democratic process is appraised (see figure 7.5). About two-thirds of citizens in the West are satisfied with the process. And despite several dips during the tumultuous years in the mid-1990s,

Figure 7.5 Satisfaction with democracy, 1991–2000 (%)

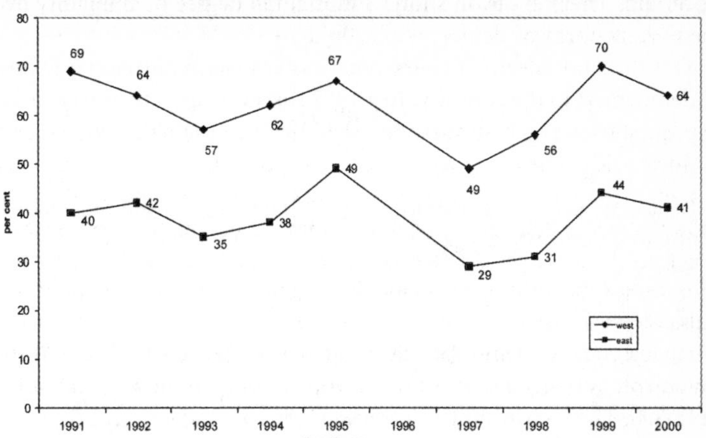

western Germans do not become systematically more negative about the process, although we do note that, in 1997, satisfaction levels drop below 50 per cent. In the East, responses produce a line with similar dips and peaks – except that this occurs around a substantially lower average. A little over one-third are satisfied, and the remaining proportion is at least ambiguous about the current democratic process.

Thus, while eastern Germans value democracy as an ideal, they are considerably more equivocal in their support for the current regime. This contrasts with the views of the western publics where both democratic ideals and reality receives substantial approval. The data also document that except for the apparent erosion of a preference for freedom, the longitudinal patterns evince a remarkable degree of stability. These patterns suggest that basic values and regime evaluations are fairly stable and do not change in short order after a new regime is established.

Values, performance and support for democracy

This section provides a systematic test of two central premises underlying the previous discussion. First, individuals' ideological values and their assessments of a regime's performance influence their support for a regime. Second, it examines whether the very fact that citizens reside in the East or the West substantially influences their support for a democratic regime beyond their evaluations of the performance and their ideological values.

Hypotheses

If we consider the controversy between culturalists and institutionalists in the light of our model (figure 7.1), the dominant effect on support for the democratic regime should, according to culturalists, be generated by ideological values and a regime's democratic performance. In contrast, institutionalists would emphasise a system's perceived economic performance.

Accordingly, we formulate five hypotheses. To begin with, a liberal democracy restricts itself to the constitutional guarantee of individual civil rights while a socialist democracy also provides a constitutional guarantee of social rights.[19] A liberal democracy is characterised by the representative organisation of political decision making, while a socialist democracy favours plebiscites. Similarly, we would expect that support for democratic ideals enhances support for the current regime. Thus, in light of the congruence postulate, we predict:

> *Hypothesis 1: support for socialist ideals reduces support for a liberal democracy; support for democratic ideals increases support for it.*

In addition, if individuals believe that a system implements civil rights, support for the current order should be increased:

> *Hypothesis 2: positive assessment of the implementation of liberal rights enhances support for the democratic regime.*

A third hypothesis applies primarily to eastern Germany. A voluminous body of literature indicates that a large number of eastern Germans prefer a socialist democracy.[20] Because these ideals are not congruent with the existing order, citizens in the East should be more dissatisfied than West Germans with the extent to which social rights are currently implemented. This, in turn, probably lowers East Germans' support for the current regime:

> *Hypothesis 3: a negative assessment of the implementations of social rights reduces support for the liberal-democratic regime in the East.*

A fourth hypothesis focuses on the effect of negative performance on institutional support. First, negative evaluations of the economy are expected to lower support for the existing system. Second, we also included a measure of how citizens evaluate the performance of the current government, with the expectation that negative evaluations lower institutional support. These two indicators capture the central tenet of institutionalists:

Hypothesis 4: negative assessments of economic and government performance reduce support for the liberal-democratic regime.

Finally, beyond individuals' ideological values and their performance assessment, the institutional learning argument predicts that eastern Germans are less likely to support a liberal democracy than western Germans:

Hypothesis 5: support for democracy is lower in the East than the West.

Measurement and multivariate analyses

Our dependent variables are the two indicators about various aspects of democracy, democracy as an ideal and the current German regime. They are located at different levels of abstraction (ideal and the material) and thus allow us test whether the various processes affect them differently. We identify three categories of independent variable: political values, political and economic performance, and sociodemographics (age, gender and education).

Political values

We include two value predictors for democratic ideals: the socialist ideals statement and the freedom versus equality measure. When we predict support for the current regime, we also include the democratic ideals measure.

Political performance

The system's political performance is measured by a liberal rights and a social rights indicator. The indicator for liberal rights measures the extent to which basic procedures as set forth in Germany's constitution are implemented. We asked respondents:

> In any country, the following goals can be more or less strongly realised. In Germany, in your opinion, has each of these goals been very strongly realised, strongly realised, not very strongly realised, or not realised at all: freedom of expression, freedom of assembly, freedom of religion and conscience, free and secret elections?

A large majority of eastern and western Germans believe that these constitutionally stipulated civil liberties are implemented in Germany, the percentages of respondents with a positive view ranging from 80 per cent to 94 per cent; few East–West differences exist concerning these assessments. There is, in short, near-universal agreement that basic civil liberties are secure.[21] We created an additive index based on these responses.

The social rights index, also based on four indicators, asks respondents to evaluate the state of social rights in Germany:

> In any country, the following goals can be more or less strongly realised. In Germany, in your opinion, has each of these goals been very strongly realised, strongly realised, not very strongly realised, or not realised at all: the right to work, the right to provision for old age, the right to health protection, the right to living accommodation?

In contrast to civil liberties, Germans are more equivocal in their assessments of social rights: positive responses in the East and West, respectively, are right to work (16 per cent and 37 per cent), old age (30 per cent and 48 per cent), health insurance (48 per cent and 57 per cent) and housing (44 per cent and 52 per cent). This indicator reveals more East–West variation than the civil liberties indicator, although western Germans also perceive shortcomings in the social safety net.[22] We created an additive social rights index based on these responses.

Economic performance

We use two indicators to measure a system's economic performance. A first indicator directly gauges respondents assessment of the general economic situation in Germany: 'How, in very general terms, do you judge the current economic situation in Germany? Very good, good, partly good/partly bad, bad, very bad?' A second, generalised performance indicator reads: 'How satisfied are you – all in all – with the current performance of the federal government? Very satisfied, satisfied, dissatisfied, or very dissatisfied?' The strength of the indicator is that it permits respondents to think of a variety of different performance aspects. They may think of any aspect of the economy they deem important. They may also consider their views about the situation concerning social and liberal rights. This entails that the ensuing multivariate analyses actually bias the analyses *against* finding significant results for the liberal and social rights indicators. Our analyses therefore constitute a conservative test of the democratic performance model.

Results

Table 7.5 shows the results when we predict citizens' support for democratic ideals. We note, first, that there is significant effect of prioritising equality over freedom in the East *and* the West. Those who prefer social equality are less likely to support the notion that some form of democracy is the best regime. While the significance of the coefficients in the western public is surprising, note that the large sample size in the West undoubtedly contributes to this – the magnitude of the standardised coefficients suggests that this effect is actually quite weak (beta = 0.07). Nevertheless, this finding, along with the declining preference for freedom over equality, may hint at the beginnings of an erosion of regime support in the West. In the East, the coefficient is highly significant despite the fairly small sample – and the unstandardised coefficient is about twice the size as in the West; a pattern that is consistent with the first hypothesis.

Another pattern, consistent with the second hypothesis, is that those who believe that liberal rights are respected in Germany are substantially more likely to endorse some form of democratic ideals. Indeed, this factor produces one of the largest standardised coefficients, indicating that the democratic performance of the current regime is vital in maintaining support for democracy as an ideal. This parallels findings from central Europe[23] and, beyond that region, the world[24] which point to the centrality of a regime's democratic performance in maintaining support for it.

As expected, those with higher education are more inclined to appreciate democracy as an ideal: a frequently found pattern in post-communist societies. Moreover, younger citizens are more likely to endorse this statement in the West (but not in the East), which is consistent with prior research documenting a process of generational change in western Germany.[25]

Table 7.5 Predicting support for democratic ideals, OLS

	East	*West*	*Pooled*
West Germany dummy variable	a	a	0.16**
			0.25
Political values			
Socialism is a good idea	–0.04	0.02	0.001
	–0.03	0.02	0.001
Equality over freedom	–0.12**	–0.07**	–0.08**
	–0.19	–0.09	0.12
Performance			
Political rights	0.22**	0.25**	0.23**
	0.08	0.09	0.08
Social rights	0.04	–0.05*	–0.02
	0.01	–0.02	–0.01
Government satisfaction	0.11*	0.02	0.04
	0.08	0.01	0.03
Economic perceptions	0.01	0.14**	0.11**
	0.01	0.11	0.09
Sociodemographics			
Gender (male)	0.05	0.01	0.02
	0.06	0.01	0.03
Age	–0.07	–0.12**	–0.09**
	–0.01	–0.01	–0.01
Education	0.12**	0.15**	0.14**
	0.06	0.06	0.06
R^2	0.11	0.14	0.23
N	525	1,561	2,086

Notes: + <0.05 level one-tailed; * p<0.05 level significance two-tailed; ** p<0.01 level significance two-tailed. 'a' denotes that a variable is excluded; the first entry in each cell is the unstandardised OLS coefficient, and the second entry is the standardised OLS coefficient.
Source: Forsa.

Finally, note that eastern Germans are significantly less likely to support democratic ideals even after controlling for their ideological values, performance appraisals and socio-demographic traits (the pooled model). This is consistent with an 'institutional learning' argument which attributes to individuals' exposure to the practices of a regime an independent effect on their readiness to support it. Recall, however, that this East–West effect represents difference in degree of support for some type of democracy, but does not divide Germans over the desirability of a democracy; remember that most eastern and western Germans support some form of democracy as an ideal (see p. 170).

Do the same patterns emerge when we predict the publics' satisfaction with the current democracy? Table 7.6 indicates that both ideological values are significant in the East and the West. Again, this pattern is expected among eastern Germans and less expected in the West. Despite the fact that the term socialism tends to connote partially different political visions across the East–West divide, this pattern is consistent with hypothesis 3 and suggests that the current regime is receiving negative evaluations, in part, because of the growing emphasis on social policies in the western public. Indeed, this is consistent with prior analyses which indicate that social issues are quite important to western Germans[26] – and it may eventually reach a centrality for western citizens where the perceived performance deficits in this domain begin to lower regime support not only in the East but also in the West. Again, as we noted earlier, this conclusion is speculative, though sufficiently substantiated that it ought to be monitored in the future.

The good news, for the current regime, is that positive evaluations of democratic ideals turn out be a substantial source of support for the regime in both publics. Similarly, higher education contributes to a greater acceptance of the regime. The strong support for democratic ideals thus partially offsets the negative influence of economic perceptions.

One noticeable difference between individual evaluations of democracy as an ideal and the current system concerns publics' satisfaction with the government. For the current regime, this has a strong impact on public approval of the regime in both parts. For democratic ideals, there is no linkage in the West; and the influence of government satisfaction on democratic ideals is substantially lower in the East, though it is significant. Importantly, residing in eastern Germany also reduces support for the current regime independently of the other variables. This, too, supports the notion that the current experience with one's regime independently of other predictors shapes how citizens think about it.

Overall, these patterns suggest that individuals' ideological values are central for their acceptance of democracy as an ideal form and for the

Table 7.6 Predicting support for the current regime, OLS

	East	*West*	*Pooled*
West Germany dummy variable	a	a	0.12**
			0.21
Political values			
Socialism is a good idea	–0.09**	–0.06*	–0.06**
	–0.07	–0.04	–0.05
Equality over freedom	–0.04	–0.04	–0.05**
	–0.07	–0.04	–0.07
Democracy as an ideal	0.21**	0.21**	0.21**
	0.21	0.22	0.22
Performance			
Political rights	0.07	0.16**	0.14**
	0.02	0.06	0.05
Social rights	0.10*	0.001	0.02
	0.03	0.001	0.001
Government satisfaction	0.24**	0.15**	0.17**
	0.17	0.12	0.13
Economic perceptions	0.06	0.001	0.12
	0.05	0.11	0.10
Sociodemographics			
Gender (male)	0.08*	0.13**	0.12**
	0.11	0.19	0.17
Age	0.002	0.02	0.02
	0.02	0.00	0.001
Education	0.04	0.01**	0.11**
	0.02	0.05	0.05
R^2	0.22	0.24	0.26
N	513	1,549	2,062

Notes: + <0.05 level one-tailed; * p<0.05 level significance two-tailed; ** p<0.01 two-tailed. 'a' denotes a variable that is excluded; the first entry in each cell is the unstandardised OLS coefficient, and the second entry is the standardised OLS coefficient.
Source: Forsa.

current system. This applies to the East, where we expected it, but also in the West, where we did not (though we do note that the magnitude of the values coefficients is quite low). Further, a regime's democratic performance also matters, especially regarding liberal rights but also pertaining to social rights. In contrast, economic appraisals, while statistically significant in some instances, are considerably weaker influences on citizens' constitutional views. In light of the negative economic evaluations, this is clearly an important finding as, for the time being at least, they do not undermine support for the basic constitutional framework. We note, however, that other analyses show that more performance-based measures of institutional appraisals, such as institutional trust, do reveal a strong linkage between economic evaluations and institutional trust.[27]

Conclusion

This chapter documents the persistent gulf between eastern and western Germany concerning various ideological and policy dimensions. While both publics are near-universal in their support for some form of democracy, East–West differences are considerably more noticeable when citizens evaluate the existing constitution: in the East, nearly half of the eastern public are dissatisfied with the current system, thereby revealing a substantial gap between acceptance of democracy as an ideal versus the current regime. In the West, in contrast, the gap is quite small, which illustrates the popularity of the current regime – it is evidently viewed by many as the ideal-typical democracy. Furthermore, both publics emphasise economic policies whereas postmaterial issues are taking a back seat on the policy agenda, albeit to a lesser degree in the West.

In part, these East–West differences are rooted in the different weight attached to socialist ideals. They are more valued in the East than the West, which reduces positive evaluations of the current regime. Moreover, publics' satisfaction with the current government has an especially strong influence in the East, though poor marks for incumbents also lowers support for the constitution among western citizens. Most eastern Germans at the time of the survey had experienced the new democracy for about seven years – not enough to appreciate the rough and tumble of any democratic polity which, in the case of a post-communist transition, imposes an unusual amount of hardship on most individuals. Finally, economic problems are especially severe in the East, which is reflected in negative evaluations of the national economy. The combination of values, poorer performance evaluations and institutional learning creates a powerful set of factors that reduces positive appraisals of the current regime in the East.

In fact, we find hints that the current regime may eventually begin to experience declining appraisal in the West as well. We noted that the increase in support for equality over freedom is unmistakable by the end of 2001. Note further that the multivariate analyses do produce a weak influence on current regime views of socialist ideals. While this decline in favour of freedom did not become visible in western appraisals of the current regime, it may simply be a question of time before the growing support for socialist ideals affects assessments of the current regime in the West as well. In this sense, eastern and western Germans may converge in the long run, but in a form not anticipated by many at the time of unification: citizens in the West may begin to adopt the views of their eastern counterpart regarding socialist ideals and the current regime.

Of course, we do not mean to suggest that there will be a full-fledged diffusion of distrust from the East to the West. After all, support for democratic ideals is very high in the East and West; and the current regime, by all accounts, receives positive evaluations, in both our analyses and others that examine the sources of institutional trust with different data.[28] Furthermore, the strong positive evaluations the constitution receives in the domain of political rights, combined with the resulting boost in mass support for the constitution, suggest to us that democratic ideals and the current regime will not be undermined in the short term. What we would like to stress is that the long-term repercussions of Germany's unification now warrants that the attention of social scientists not only be directed towards eastern Germans, but also towards western Germans in order to examine whether the enormous consequences of the fall of the iron curtain may just begin to unfold in western Germany.

Notes

1 Max Kaase, 'Demokratische Einstellungen in der Bundesrepublik Deutschland', in Rudolf Wildenmann (ed.), *Sozialwissenschaftliches Jahrbuch für Politik*, 2 (Munich: Gunter Olzog Verlag, 1971); Dieter Roth, *Zum Demokratieverständnis von Eliten in der Bundesrepublik Deutschland* (Frankfurt: Peter Lang, 1976); and Kendall L. Baker, Russell J. Dalton and

Kai Hildebrandt, *Germany Transformed: Political Culture and the New Politics* (Cambridge, MA: Harvard University Press, 1981).

2 Dieter Fuchs, 'The Democratic Culture in Unified Germany', in Pippa Norris (ed.), *Critical Citizens* (Oxford: Oxford University Press, 1999), pp. 123–45 and Robert Rohrschneider, *Learning Democracy: Democratic and Economic Values in Unified Germany* (Oxford: Oxford University Press, 1999).

3 Gabriel Almond and Sidney Verba, *The Civic Culture* (Princeton: Princeton University Press, 1963).

4 Gabriel Almond, 'Communism and Political Culture Theory', *Comparative Politics*, 15:1 (1983), pp. 127–38 and Harry Eckstein, 'A Culturalist Theory of Political Change', *American Political Science Review*, 82:3 (1988), pp. 789–804.

5 Ada W. Finifter and Ellen Mickiewicz, 'Redefining the Political System of the USSR', *American Political Science Review*, 86:4 (1992), pp. 857–74 and Donna Bahry, Cynthia Boaz and Stacy Burnett Gordon, 'Tolerance, Transition, and Support for Civil Liberties in Russia', *Comparative Political Studies*, 30:4 (1997), pp. 484–510.

6 Ronald Rogowski, *Rational Legitimacy* (Princeton: Princeton University Press, 1974); Giuseppe Di Palma, *To Craft Democracies* (Cambridge: Cambridge University Press, 1990); and B. Geddes, 'A Comparative Perspective on the Leninist Legacy in Eastern Europe', *Comparative Political Studies*, 28:2 (1995), pp. 239–74.

7 Brian Barry, *Sociologists, Economists, and Democracy* (London: Macmillan, 1970) and Peter McDonough, Samuel H. Barnes and Antonio Lopez Pina, 'The Growth of Democratic Legitimacy in Spain', *American Political Science Review*, 80:3 (1986), pp. 735–60.

8 William Mishler and Richard Rose, 'What are the Origins of Political Trust? Testing Institutional and Cultural Theories in Post-Communist Societies', *Comparative Political Studies*, 34:1 (2001), pp. 30–62.

9 *Ibid.*

10 Rohrschneider, *Learning Democracy.*

11 Frederick Weil, *The Effects of Diffusion, Nostalgia, and Performance on Democratic Legitimation in Unified Germany* (Frankfurt: Campus Verlag, 2000).

12 Frederick Weil, 'The Development of Democratic Attitudes in Eastern and Western Germany in a Comparative Perspective', in Frederick Weil (ed.), *Research on Democracy and Society: Democratization in Eastern and Western Europe* (Greenwich, CT: JAI Press, 1993), pp. 195–227.

13 Robert Rohrschneider and R. Schmitt-Beck, 'Trust in Democratic Institutions in Germany: Theory and Evidence Ten Years after Unification', *German Politics*, 11:3 (2002), pp. 35–58.

14 The problem categories in the Politbarometer surveys change somewhat

over time. However, the two items 'unemployment' and 'environment' remain identical, which make them ideally suited to trace the response patterns over time.

15 Ronald Inglehart, *The Silent Revolution: Changing Values and Political Styles among Western Publics* (Princeton: Princeton University Press, 1977).

16 Dieter Fuchs and Robert Rohrschneider, 'Postmaterialism and the Electoral Choice before and after German Unification', *West European Politics*, 21:2 (1998), pp. 95–116.

17 Damarys Canache, Jeffrey J. Mondak and Mitchell A. Seligson, 'Meaning and Measurement in Cross-National Research on Satisfaction with Democracy', *Public Opinion Quarterly*, 65:4 (2001), pp. 506–28.

18 Dieter Fuchs, 'Trends of Political Support in the Federal Republic of Germany', in Dirk Berg-Schlosser and Ralf Rytlewski (eds), *Political Culture in Germany* (London: Macmillan, 1993), pp. 232–70.

19 Robert A. Dahl, *Democracy and its Critics* (New Haven: Yale University Press, 1989).

20 Richard I. Hofferbert and Hans-Dieter Klingemann, 'Democracy and Its Discontents in Post-Wall Germany', *International Political Science Review*, 22:4 (2001), pp. 363–78.

21 *Ibid.*

22 *Ibid.*

23 William Mishler and Richard Rose , 'Learning and Re-Learning Regime Support: The Dynamics of Post-Communist Regimes', *European Journal of Political Research*, 41:1 (2002), pp. 5–36.

24 Richard I. Hofferbert and Hans-Dieter Klingemann, 'Remembering the Bad Old Days: Human Rights, Economic Conditions, and Democratic Performance in Transitional Regimes', *European Journal of Political Research*, 36:2 (1999), pp. 155–74.

25 Baker, Dalton and Hildebrandt, *Germany Transformed*; and Kaase, 'Demokratische Einstellungen in der Bundesrepublik Deutschland'.

26 Edeltraud Roller, *Einstellungen der Bürger zum Wohlfahrtsstaat der Bundesrepublik Deutschland* (Opladen: Westdeutscher Verlag, 1992).

27 Rohrschneider and Schmitt-Beck, 'Trust in Democratic Institutions in Germany'.

28 *Ibid.*

8

'Girl power': women, politics and leadership in the Berlin Republic

Joyce Marie Mushaben

Auf die Dauer hilft nur Mädchen-Power
(Button purchased at a 1987 Youth Festival in Stuttgart)

Something I have long had in common with Peter Merkl is a fascination with the processes of generational change, and a certain obsession with its consequences for gender relationships.[1] My exposure to German politics and society was grounded in the words and works of scholars forced to flee Germany in the late 1930s and 1940s. The older I become, the more I am in awe of the generations which lived through the most barbaric period of modern European history and yet emerged with such a deep faith in the 're-educatability' of human beings and the capacities of democratic institutions that they set aside personal grief, cleared out millions of cubic metres of rubble and generated unprecedented levels of peace and prosperity for generations to come.

I was particularly intrigued by Peter Merkl's comparison of political identities among the 'Angry Old Men' and 'Angry Old Women' of the 1940s and 1950s with those of the 'Angry Young Men' and 'Angry Young Women' of the late 1960s and early 1970s. Still preoccupied with the themes of national identity and generational change, this chapter reconsiders the trends, trajectories, and reconfigurations of women's political roles in the Federal Republic.

Feminism in five acts

Fifty-five years into its history, the Federal Republic of Germany has entered into a dramatically different phase of the life-cycle. Since unification, two more generations have been added to the national family, despite a dramatic plunge in birth rates since the 1980s. The September 1998 elections effected a demographic changing of the guard at the highest levels of governance. Not only did women secure over 30 per cent of the seats in the Bundestag, they also reached critical mass within the SPD–*Bündnis '90*/Greens (Red–Green) cabinet by capturing five of fifteen ministerial posts, supplemented by a number of Federal Commissioners and State Secretaries.

Women's increased presence in national government testifies to the completion of a gender-specific 'long march through the institutions'. By the late 1980s, women had already completed four acts in their efforts to move front and centre on the German political stage. Act One, played out through the 1950s, centred on a quiescent reconstruction of the patriarchal order. The 1960s witnessed a very turbulent Act Two, grounded in a growing consciousness of 'fine (biological) distinctions' leading to 'major (political–economic) consequences' and institutionalised sexual inequality (Article 3 of the Basic Law notwithstanding). Act Three saw a degree of feminist retrenchment throughout the 1970s, following a vehement yet unsuccessful campaign to decriminalise abortion. This era gave rise to radical, autonomous groups as well as to a plethora of feminist self-help projects, which reflected a loss of faith in male-normed institutions. Act Four, which commenced with the Conservative return to power in 1982, remobilised pragmatic feminists in the opposition parties and larger women's organisations. The Kohl government tried so hard to turn back the clock in some policy domains that even the CDU/CSU women protested. The 1990s, shaped by unification, accelerated European integration and economic globalisation, marked the beginning of Act Five: the onset of real empowerment and policy feminism. Two developments contributed heavily to this paradigm shift: the EU's 1995 adoption of gender mainstreaming in conjunction with the attainment of critical mass in the Bundestag (up from 27 per cent to 30.3 per cent).[2]

Gender mainstreaming is a strategy for incorporating equal opportunities for women and men into all EU policies, especially those tied to the allocation of community funds. The legal basis for its implementation rests in Articles 2 and 3 of the European Communities Treaty, as well as Article 23 (1) of the Charter of Fundamental Rights of the EU. Its purpose lies in

> not restricting efforts to promote equality to the implementation of specific measures to help women, but [in] mobilizing all general policies

> and measures specifically for the purpose of achieving equality by actively and openly taking into account at the planning stage their possible effects on the respective situation of men and women (gender perspective). This means systematically examining measures and policies and taking into account such possible effects when defining and implementing them.

Efforts to promote equality

> must not be confused with the simple objective of balancing the statistics: it is a question of promoting long-lasting changes in parental roles, family structures, institutional practices, the organization of work and time, their personal development and independence, but also concerns men and the whole of society, in which it can encourage progress and be a token of democracy and pluralism.[3]

The Commission has outlined a specific 'method' for achieving these goals, requiring *ex ante* gender impact assessments, the creation of gender mainstreaming units within each Directorate-General, formal training *qua* consciousness-raising among key personnel, benchmarking and a breakdown of data and statistics by gender.

The term *critical mass* defines the point at which women's ability to effect changes in the dominant political culture becomes non-reversible and self-sustaining. As of September 1998, women's share of mandates stood at 57.4 per cent for the Greens, 57.1 per cent for the PDS, 34.2 per cent for the SPD, 18.4 per cent for the Christian Democratic Union/Christian Social Union (CDU/CSU) and 20.5 per cent for the Free Democratic Party (FDP). Women initially hoped to constitute a full 40 per cent of the Cabinet but missed the mark when the Greens opted to appoint two males and one female.

The women in the first SPD/Green cabinet were Edelgard Bulmahn (SPD/Education, Science, Technology), Herta Däubler-Gmelin (SPD/Justice), Andrea Fischer (Greens/Health), Christine Bergmann (SPD/Family, Seniors, Women, Youth) and Heidemarie Wieczorek-Zeul (SPD/Economic Cooperation and Development). Marieluise Beck (Greens) was named the new Federal Commissioner for Foreigners. Two more women joined the governance team in 2000: the high-powered, organic-agriculture advocate, Renate Künast (Greens), replaced Karl-Heinze Funke (SPD) as the Minister for Agriculture and Consumer Protection amid the first bovine spongiform encephalitis (BSE) outbreak ('mad cow disease'); Health Minister Fischer was simultaneously replaced by SPD deputy caucus chair, Ulla Schmidt. Former GDR activist Marianne Birthler assumed another Federal Commissioner position, responsible for managing archived *Stasi* files, when Landsman

Joachim Gauck retired in 2001. In the Bundesrat, Heidi Simonis (SPD) remains the only woman found among the sixteen minister-presidents.

Another central player is Angela Merkel, the 'girl next door' promoted by Helmut Kohl from the position of average-GDR citizen-turned-activist to Federal Minister for Women in 1990 and then to Environmental Minister in 1994. Merkel found herself catapulted into a position of party prominence for a second time shortly after the CDU's 1998 electoral defeat, when campaign finance corruption charges were levelled against Kohl. She was elected CDU General Secretary, having taken a very public stance against her own patron in a December 1999 article in *Die Zeit.* Exiting the stage centre-right is former Bundestag President Rita Süssmuth (CDU), who chaired the Independent Commission on Immigration and Integration (2000–1). Last, but certainly not least, Jutta Limbach (SPD) retired in 2002 as Chief Justice of the Constitutional Court, but has taken on a new international role as President of the Goethe Institute.

In the late 1980s, SPD parliamentarian Peter Conradi predicted that it would not be long before several of these women would be given a direct opportunity to demonstrate their 'eminently ministerial qualities'.[4] With the exception of Bergmann and Birthler (both of whom spent 1968 on the other side of the Wall), the female Red–Green Cabinet members all stem from the so-called Student Movement Generation. Three women were active participants in protest events of that era, as were their male Cabinet counterparts, Foreign Minister Joschka Fischer (a 'Sponti' radical) and Gerhard Schröder (former head of the *Jusos* and a leftist defence lawyer). Since these SPD women joined the party between 1965 and 1972, they can be characterised as 'the daughters of Willy Brandt'. All spent their formative years being nourished by détente and a call 'to dare more democracy'. Except for Fischer, the Green members are roughly ten years younger than their SPD counterparts.[5] All, in fact, are women who pursue 'politics as a vocation' and who evince a wide variety of professional–political skills. The era of the 'coffin-hoppers' is over.[6]

Act Five: critical mass and policy feminism

The 1998 elections marked a great leap forward with respect to the number of women recruited into national governance. Reflecting on the Scandinavian experience, Drude Dahlerup uses the concept of critical mass to describe the point at which women might substantially influence public policy even from a 'minority' position. She focuses on fundamental changes that occur in the policy making environment when a group's size shifts from that of a 'small' to a 'large' minority.[7] Well before they accrue seats proportionate to their share of the population, women can exercise a qualitative, *self-sustaining* influence on the character and structure of decision making. Because human behaviour is self-conscious, women can pursue *critical acts* prior to achieving critical mass (roughly 30 per cent). Those critical acts, in turn, 'change the position of the minority considerably and lead to further changes'.[8]

Critical mass can be inferred from specific, observable institutional changes deriving from women's critical acts. The most important changes include: shifts from negative (or at best neutral) reactions to women's presence in decision making organs to gestures on the part of decision makers welcoming their input; improvements in the 'performance and efficiency' of individual female politicians, e.g. through the creation of 'old girl' networks that reduce the learning process for new recruits; and modifications in the political culture of the institution, fostering an acceptance of women's issues as a routine part of the agenda. Broader changes that follow include a gradual transformation of the prevailing political discourse, actual changes in policy substance and approaches to decision making, and perceived increases in the power of women working collectively.

Commensurate with the introduction of *Quotierung*, the number of female parliamentarians rose from forty-four in 1980 (pre-quota) to fifty-one in 1983 to eighty in 1987. Of the eighty-one *Mitglieder des Bundestages* (MdB) in the eleventh Bundestag, forty-six (56 per cent) acquired their mandates after 1983 and thirty-three (41 per cent) entered in 1987.[9] These individuals moved quickly into their respective party executives as a consequence of concerted efforts to bring more women into the leadership. They crossed the 30 per cent threshold in 1998 in terms of parliamentary seats, but *gender democracy* has yet to reach the SPD executive suite (see table 8.1).[10] Even though the Greens, for example, presented a 50–50 'electoral team' for the 2002 elections, they opted for a single *Spitzenkandidat*, Foreign Minister Joschka Fischer.

The supranationalisation of European foreign and domestic policies has had a particularly salutary effect on women's equal-treatment demands at the member-state level, especially since the embrace of gender mainstreaming in 1995. Gender mainstreaming is not an ideological

Table 8.1 Women in parliament, 1998–2002

Party	*Women*	*Seats*	*Share (%)*
SPD	105	298	35.2
CDU/CSU	45	245	18.4
Bündnis 90/Die Grünen	27	47	57.4
FDP	9	43	20.9
PDS	21	36	58.3
Total	207	669	30.9

Source: Ausdruck aus dem Internet–Angebot des Deutschen Bundestages © Deutscher Bundestag, 30 August 2002.

construct but rather a set of evaluation and implementation methods applicable at all levels of policy making. When Gregor Gysi joined the Berlin Senate as Finance Minister in 2002, his hand picked State-Secretary, Hildegard Marie Nickel, declared she would implement gender mainstreaming in all domains subject to the Economics Ministry. Nickel planned to extend the model to other ministries after a three-year learning-by-doing-period (both resigned from the government over other issues before their terms expired).[11]

Women's ability to reconfigure Federal policies along openly feminist lines has been curtailed by the increasingly dysfunctional nature of the German *Parteienstaat*, on the one hand, and by the vicissitudes of recession and mass unemployment, on the other. However, to the extent that these ministers have always tended towards pragmatic feminism, they have achieved a great deal more than meets the eye. They have established *policy-feminist frameworks* that will be nearly impossible to dismantle. Their initiatives enjoy broad support among the public at large, especially in the wake of the Pisa study, multiple outbreaks of mad cow disease and other assorted scandals – despite the arcane importunings of conservative male politicians, who demanded a return to 'traditional family values'.

Women coming to terms with the nation

Rather than inducing deep feelings of solidarity, the unification process precipitated disenchantment, frustration and some very hard feelings between East and West feminist groups. Western activists were accused of selling out eastern women over the abortion issue. Eastern women were deemed ungrateful and 'theoretically backward' for refusing to accept the advice their western counterparts hoped to offer on the patriarchal state, which had provided women in the GDR with the very support systems women in the Federal Republic lacked for 'reconciling family with career'.[12] Having long eschewed any particular responsibility for 'the German nation', women on both sides of the divide were ill-prepared for a coming to terms with two dictatorial pasts, with a present plagued by high unemployment and 'illegal but unpunishable' abortion and even with each other after forty years of diametrically opposed ideological paradigms.

Shortly after the formation of the Red–Green coalition, I predicted that one would witness more harmonious 'East–West' relations, as well as greater issue congruence between women in the Cabinet and their constituents, especially in the new *Länder*.[13] Indeed, for women at the top, neither coming to terms with the past nor with each other seems to have been a problem. All six Cabinet members identify themselves with gender-equality causes in ways that transcend old Federal Republic–GDR differences. As pragmatic feminists, they continue to demand more but always 'take what they can get'.

In contrast to their CDU government predecessors, Angela Merkel and Claudia Nolte, none of the current ministers has been politically defined in terms of her respective 'eastern' or 'western' identity. As a practicing Catholic from Thüringen, former CDU *Frauenminister* Claudia Nolte was particularly outspoken (and thus unabashedly instrumentalised by the Kohl government) for her opposition to reproductive choice and legal abortion. While Merkel initially supported women's right to choose, based on the GDR experience, she ultimately toed the party line in 1992. Despite majoritarian support, male and female, for freedom of choice, Nolte agitated for a tougher version of the 'illegal but unpunishable' abortion law that passed after the *Bundesverfassungsgericht* rejected the 1993 Group Resolution. Merkel was subsequently pushed upstairs as Environmental Minister for refusing to join in the Union's march to Karlsruhe.

As unhappy as she may have been with her *Cinderella-East* image of earlier elections, Merkel was not taken seriously by her male party colleagues until the party finance scandal overtook her 'stepfather' Helmut Kohl. Her move into the position of General Secretary has now rendered her a kind of 'deterritorialised *Vorzeigefrau*' (token woman) for the party as a whole, largely because there are so few CDU women to be found on the national political stage. Although biographical accounts attempt to reconstruct the eastern influences on Merkel's modest, north German, and Protestant demeanor, her talk-show appearances suggest a rapid learning curve in matters of western political style. As a GDR citizen she was just as conformist and apathetic as the rest, but was quick to take advantage of a new political opportunity structure. Ironically, that structure has shown little tolerance for former GDR dissidents, other than to draw on their visceral 'anti-communist' appeals in order to rally *western* voters.[14]

Christine Bergmann, by contrast, has consistently pursued a very East German emphasis on 'reconciling family and career'. During her tenure as Berlin's Senator for Labour and Women, Bergmann worked to limit the damage inflicted by the post-unity abortion law that Kohl had once promised would 'leave all women in a better position than before'. One westerner, Andrea Fischer (Greens), nonetheless took a curious turn once she was installed as the Minister of Health. She 'rediscovered' her own Catholic roots after assuming office, prolonging the government's long-planned move to permit the use of the abortifacient, RU 486. Despite heavy pressure placed on Schröder by the other female Cabinet members, the abortion drug mifegyne was not approved until July 1999.

Several PDS women have also emerged as potential political role models for the next generation. The PDS has become more attractive to young female voters, in part owing to its stances on equality issues; its spokespersons are also a decade or two younger than the SPD women. One is party chief Gabi Zimmer, who headed the PDS-*Landesverband* Thüringen between 1991 and 1998. Zimmer joined the national executive in 1995, became Deputy Chair in 1997 and rose to Chair following Gysi's resignation in October 2000. Petra Pau sat in the Berlin Assembly from 1995 to 1998, entered the Bundestag in 1998 and was deputy chair of the PDS caucus. Petra Bläss, who first joined the PDS in 1997 but had served in parliament since 1990, was named a Vice-President of the Bundestag in October 1998. Dr Barbara Höll shifted to the PDS in 1996 but had also held a Bundestag mandate since 1990. She was particularly outspoken during the 1993 abortion debate, favouring 'choice' along GDR lines. One of the youngest and openly 'orthodox-communist' PDS parliamentarians was Angela Marquardt, who sported a personal 'punk' style (despite the stodgy, elder-male nature of most PDS members) and entered the Bundestag in 1998.[15]

Despite many common causes, women are precluded from cooperating more openly with each other owing to limits imposed by party executives, worried about potential contagion effects that can be all too easily exploited by the conservative opposition. Here the party bosses at the national level are clearly out of synch with developments at the *Länder* level, particularly in the east. In at least three eastern *Länder*, the SPD has engaged in coalition politics with the PDS or has otherwise relied on PDS 'toleration' of a minority SPD government. The Greens, by contrast, are not afraid of Union condemnation but rather face direct competition from the PDS as a party of the left.

Just as the SPD constituted the party of fundamental opposition through the 1950s and 1960s, only to acquire an 'establishment' image once it assumed power under Willy Brandt, the fundamental opposition role passed to the Greens, self-defined as *the* anti-party party during the 1980s. Since then the Greens, too, have joined the ruling elite. It is only natural that the PDS will emerge as a voice of fundamental female opposition for the 2000s, since far-right parties are inherently misogynist in orientation. Whatever the parties in power are doing for women, it usually isn't enough. Once in power themselves, women face a classic *Realo versus Fundi* dilemma: they need to play by the male-normed rules of the game in order to bring about policy change, but in so doing, they come to be viewed by grassroots groups as coopted collaborators upholding the status quo.

'Girl power', policy domains and political change

For the most part, girl power has brought a more holistic approach to Federal policies, foreign and domestic, turning each woman into an advocate for the policies of her counterparts. The search for a theoretical *Gesamtkonzept* (comprehensive concept) from the late 1960s through the early 1970s, a period of intense ideological factionalisation, hurt the women's movement significantly more than it helped. The search for a practical *Gesamtkonzept* in response to crises involving education, immigration, demographics, development and national security has given rise to new networks, new partnerships and a willingness to compromise.

This section sketches core reforms undertaken in each ministerial domain. My aim is to show that gender-sensitive policies pursued by women have acquired a 'framework' character that will be very hard to dismantle, regardless of future changes in the ruling coalition. Paradoxically, perhaps, the interlocking and mutually reinforcing nature of some of these policies could shake the Federal Republic out of its deeply rooted *Reformstau.*[16] One striking example is the three-way push for *Ganztagschulen* (all-day schools): as one solution to poor educational-testing results; as a reaction to women's demands for quality child-care facilities; and as a response to the language-training needs of second- and third-generation migrant children.

Gender and justice

It would have not been inconceivable in 1998 to expect the first Red–Green coalition to work towards greater gender balance with respect to official appointments as well as to provide ongoing support for 'positive action' policies in line with the EU's Equality and Equal Treatment Directives. According to the Government's *Third Report on the Proportion of Women in Significant Organs within the Federal Sphere of Influence* (May 2002), women have made modest gains since the late 1990s. They have increased their share of seats from 12.2 per cent to 15.9 per cent in more than 300 commissions, committees and expert/advisory councils (from 1,058 women in 355 bodies in 1997 to 1,242 in 318 bodies in 2001). Correspondingly, the number of appointed bodies with no women fell from 28.7 per cent to 21.4 per cent. They now constitute over 50 per cent of ten entities focusing on consumer protection, sex trafficking and 'youth for Europe'. The *Law on Appointments to Federal Offices* now makes extensive use of an extraordinary network of equal opportunity officers at the state and local/communal levels in soliciting female nominees.

As further anticipated, the SPD–Green coalition government proposed many critical anti-discrimination laws after 1998, but securing Bundesrat approval has been a different matter. A broad anti-discrimination law that would adequately serve the needs of Germany's ethnic minorities and other disadvantaged groups, introduced in December 2001, has yet to be officially adopted. The *Law on the Prevention of Discrimination in Civil Law* would prohibit unequal treatment on the basis of national origin, gender, religion, age or disability with regard to housing, credit, access to services and membership in professional or occupational associations. The law would shift the burden of proof to the 'excluding party', grant financial awards for damages and warrant special services for sight- or hearing-impaired residents in juridical proceedings. A further law recognising same-sex partnerships, called *Homo-Ehen*, has been formally adopted, and even upheld in a July 2002 Constitutional Court verdict. The *Act on Registered Partnerships* (2001) allows gay and lesbian couples to register their partnerships with state authorities, affording both partners previously denied rights (and obligations) similar to those enjoyed by heterosexual couples joined by marriage.[17]

One reform that has transcended party lines pertains to domestic violence. The new rule of thumb reads: 'the beater goes, the beating victim stays'.[18] Enacted in January 2002, the law requires police and the courts to remove the perpetrator from a shared domicile, as opposed to the long-standing pattern of forcing some 40,000 women per year to seek shelter in community safe-houses. This law follows on an earlier ordinance giving children the right to a 'violence-free upbringing', which Union politicians have yet to embrace. The *Protection against Violence Act* (2002) adds added rights for abused children and partners.

Yet another woman-friendly reform is the *Victim Protection Law* introduced by the Greens in June 2002. Its threefold aim is to secure crime victims faster and better assistance, to expand the use of obligatory community service as punishment and to confront perpetrators directly with the impact of their actions; 10 per cent of all punitive fines will flow into a special fund for aiding victims, based on the services required by the latter. Victim compensation will not be slowed by the guilty party's 'inability to pay'; instead, the state will expedite the process and seek its own compensation from the convicted person. While the inability to pay has often led judges to convert fines into jail time, the new law foresees *Schwitzen statt Sitzen* ('sweating not sitting') to ease already overcrowded jail conditions. Judges now have the power to determine community service terms, but they will be accompanied by a registered conviction (*Verurteilung*) rather than the previous probationary 'warning'.

Surprisingly, former Justice Minister Däubler-Gmelin came out against a legalisation of stem-cell research and pre-implantation diagnostics, putting her at odds with her Educational/Science counterpart, Minister Bulmahn. Germany's reluctance to embrace biotechnologies with enthusiasm derives from its historical responsibility for eugenics *qua* race hygiene abuses perpetrated during the Nazi period. Rules on stem-cell research have been preempted, in part, by regulatory measures at the EU level. In January 2002 the Bundestag voted to permit the import of stem cells, even though the German *Law on Embryonic*

Protection precludes their extraction at home.[19] Bulmahn occupies a middle position, recognising the need for national research in this area. She insists that the full contingent of EU regulations be in place, however, before the research work can begin. Meanwhile, Britain's very liberal policy will make it virtually impossible for the Federal Republic to block such research. Otherwise Germany faces the prospect of losing even more of its top researchers to the United States and the United Kingdom.

Bulmahn actively rattled the foundations of the German university system when she introduced major changes in personnel policy (e.g. the creation of tenure-track junior professors), revised *BAfög* regulations (under a Federal law for the promotion of tertiary education) and broke new ground with her candid discussion of future tuition charges. The picture regarding women's position in German academic institutions remains quite bleak, however. As of 1999, women accounted for 53 per cent of all university admissions, 33.1 per cent of the completed PhDs, 28.3 per cent of the assistant positions, 15.3 per cent of the academic lecturers, 9.5 per cent of the professors, 5.9 per cent of the 'full professors' and 4.6 per cent of university Rectors. There is nonetheless a new joint *Bund–Länder* campaign to raise the share of female professors to 20 per cent by 2005. The states are being urged to fill 40 per cent of all recently vacated positions with female recruits.[20]

The Federal Ministry for Education and Science (BMBF) has set itself the 'priority task … of achieving equal opportunities for women in education and research'. It has established a division on Women in Education and Research, as well as a separate budget devoted to 'Strategies for achieving equal opportunities' in these domains. Gender mainstreaming is used 'as a goal and method in all its areas of work', including programme design, budget allocation, implementation and evaluation processes. One example of effective gender mainstreaming is the programme on 'Innovation and Workplaces in the Information Society of the 21st Century', initiated in 1999. By 2005, the programme expects to foster 50 per cent female participation with regard to Internet use, to raise women's share of information technology (IT) training places and first-semester enrolments in computer science or *Informatik* to a full 40 per cent and to increase the women's share of business start-ups to 40 per cent. The programme has moreover developed specific indicators, programme controls and mentoring through an expert group 'Women in the Information Society'.

In a joint venture with the Bundesanstalt für Arbeit, Deutsche Telekom and the magazine *Brigitte*, Bulmahn has sponsored free internet courses for over 40,000 women in more than 100 cities. Further 'high-tech' initiatives include a parallel programme for school-age girls (*LizzyNet*) as well as mentoring programmes for women in computer sciences and engineering. A new Centre of Competence, 'Women and Science', has already accumulated 8,000 entries for its databank, *Fem-Consult*, to ensure the availability of candidates for such positions. Bulmahn has persuaded the Max Plank Gesellschaft, the Helmholtz Gemeinschaft Deutscher Forschungszentren, the Deutsche Forschungsgemeinschaft and the Frauenhofer Gesellschaft to arrange child-care opportunities for their respective employees. Another programme, the International Women's University 'Technology and Culture' has given 900 young scientists from foreign countries the chance to conduct 100 days of interdisciplinary research with counterparts in the Federal Republic. At the symbolic level, the BMBF now sponsors a prize, the 'Total E-Quality Science Award', to motivate universities and research institutes to compete with each other over innovative ways to integrate female scientists into their organisations on an equal basis.

Reconciling family and career

Although the Federal Republic's financial resources for expanding social policies are strained, all of the female Ministers actively support programmes facilitating women's reentry into the paid labour force, an expansion of child-care options for working parents and equitable distribution of federal job-creation slots. By the time the Wall fell in 1989, 52 per cent of west German women had joined the paid labour force, despite their lack of all-day schools and daycare facilities. Over 90 per cent of the eastern German women engaged in paid employment prior to unity, but were backed by a wide array of 'social rights' eliminated since 1991. Today, the official long-term female unemployment remains disproportionately high at 16 per cent in the new eastern *Länder*.[21]

Male reluctance to recognise a dramatic transformation of 'family life' since the 1980s still constitutes the single most important barrier to policies promoting effective reconciliation of family responsibilities and equal employment opportunity. Western women, especially, have responded to the lack of support structures not by 'staying home', but by cutting out child-rearing: the number of marriages and births continues to decline every year. There were 6.8 per cent fewer marriages and 3.9 per cent fewer births in 2001 than in 2000. Jürgen Ruttger's admonition that what Germany really needs as a solution to its shortage of high-tech labourers, namely, *Kinder nicht Inder*, illustrates how completely out of touch conservative politicians are with the nation's women, over 60 per cent of whom now hold paying jobs.[22]

Directly confronted with many aspects of Germany's demographic deficit and its rapidly aging population, Minister Bergmann has responded with long-overdue changes in relation to maternal protection at the workplace before and after delivery. As of June 2002, women not only enjoy greater job security and income protection, but also extended pregnancy leaves of fourteen weeks (eighteen weeks for premature deliveries or multiple births). Small businesses can seek 100 per cent compensation for additional costs from the state insurance system. A second reform, advocated by the Greens, altered child-subsidy regulations under the 2002 *Bundeskindergeldgesetz.* Subsidies have been extended to child custodians living abroad, serving in NATO, or possessing EU citizenship but nonetheless residing in Germany.

Bergmann also worked with the Justice Ministry in passing the *Law on the Regulation of the Legal Status of Prostitutes* (2002). The law enables sex-workers to sign up for the social insurance system, guaranteeing them access to medical, unemployment and pension benefits. Prostitutes, who are already required to pay taxes on their earnings, are no longer subject to prosecution (according them equal treatment *vis-à-vis* 'free agents' and pimps); criminal charges will be limited to cases of exploitation of the prostitutes themselves. The aim is to eliminate the moral double standard that has traditionally punished women, but not the estimated 1.2 million men per year who take advantage of their services. By improving their legal security, officials hope to enable more women, no longer completely at the mercy of their pimps, to exit the profession.

Health-care and consumer protection

More intractable, and certainly more expensive than any of the services necessary for balancing family and work responsibilities, are the problems of health care and pension reform. Ironically, the 'greening' of Germany augurs the *greying* of Germany: demographic realities, not value change, are driving the current policy debate. By 2030, it is estimated that half of German voters will be over 55. The SPD–Green government quickly reversed penalties on women's early retirement at age sixty rather than sixty-five, accepted as constitutional by the High Court in 1992, owing to their triple burden of worker, wife and mother. The Kohl Government had imposed these penalties as part of its 1996 Savings Package (3.6 per cent subtracted from net benefits for one year, 10.8 per cent for three years, 18 per cent for retiring five years early). The proportion of citizens over sixty-five will rise from 21.6 per cent in 1987 to a projected 31.3 per cent and 35 per cent for the years 2010 and 2020, respectively. Women now comprise the overwhelming majority of persons over the age of eighty.

Minister Schmidt assumed her post after a number of purported cost-cutting reforms had already been implemented, all to no avail. Physicians and health-care providers have repeatedly circumvented new provisions (e.g. caps on physician expenditures) despite their growing complexity. Increasing life expectancies and the rapid aging of the population have left the new Health Minister between the proverbial rock and the hard place between the Labour and Finance Ministers. Schmidt advocates the use of mail order and e-commerce services as a means of inducing fair but effective 'cost-cutting' competition and promoting the dispensation of generic drugs. Schmidt has moved to create a national information system *qua* databank for registering medical products, devices and suppliers. The Health Ministry also backed the *Law to Secure the Quality and Strengthen Consumer Protection for Care-Dependent Persons* that took effect in January 2002. Additional legislation within Minister Schmidt's domain addressed the treatment of terminally ill children: parents are now permitted unlimited access to *Kinderkrankengeld* and unrestricted (unpaid) leave beyond the usual sick-leave provisions. Correspondingly, Schmidt has implemented a restructuring of treatment programmes for the chronically ill, especially for patients suffering from diabetes and breast cancer. The aim is to protect the dignity of the patient as well as broader human rights while allowing the pursuit of biomedical research in these areas.

Minister Schmidt not only had to navigate between the public's demand for intensified health-care needs and the government's need for fiscal self-restraint, but was caught between the extraordinary promise of genetic research and the perils of unwarranted genetic engineering. German law on biotechnologies seeks to regulate the use of genetically altered organisms within closed systems, to ensure that companies conducting such research are carefully monitored. No such organisms are to be 'set free' without adequate supervision , as defined by EU rules.

In an effort to meet these health-care challenges, Minister Schmidt has introduced one of the more innovative approaches to policy formulation – the use of the Round Table. Inclusive in nature, this approach brings together a wide spectrum of twenty-seven affected groups. The Round Table convenes every three months outside the normal policy making process and addresses the medium- and long-term problems affecting the health-care system. It relies on specialised work groups to generate detailed proposals (a model developed during the east German *Wende*). The object is to establish a broadly consensual, and thus easily implementable, framework that transcends the usual interest group lines.

No minister has been more directly confronted with the problems created by ineffective monitoring of substances harmful to human health than the indefatigable Renate Künast, Minister for Agriculture, Nutrition and Consumer Protection (BMVEL). Assuming office in the middle of the first BSE scandal, Künast quickly established herself as an outspoken proponent of organic agriculture. She defines the main advantages of this form of food cultivation in terms of 'achieving a closed nutrient cycle on the farm … and keeping animals in a particularly welfare-oriented manner'. This means eliminating synthetically produced 'plant-protecting' chemicals, growth regulators and hormones. Farmers are urged to avoid easily soluble mineral fertilisers, to adopt green manuring with nitrogen-fixing plants, and to adhere to strictly land-related stocking density. *Sustainability* as well as *biological diversity* are favourite themes of the BMVEL ministry. Towards those ends, Künast advocates stringently supervised eco-labels, an emphasis on fair trade and preventative consumer protection. Her quick and decisive responses arguably saved the traditional agricultural sector from itself. A few good Künast clones would go a long way in shaking up the Common Agricultural Policy (CAP) establishment in Brussels.

Sustainable development abroad: foreign aid

With more than a little support from her Foreign Minister colleague Joschka Fischer, Heidi Wieczorek-Zeul has infused the Ministry for Economic Cooperation (BMZ) with new policy priorities, including gender mainstreaming and the promotion of civil society. Gender needs now play a key role in structuring German developmental assistance to Third World countries in places ranging from Afghanistan to Zambia.

The Coalition Agreement of October 1998 embedded developmental assistance within the larger framework of German structural policies and peace-keeping activities. Several competencies were transferred to the BMZ, including responsibility for the administration of the EU's post-Lomé Accords, the transformation programmes in central and eastern Europe, and the 'Stability Package' for the Balkans. The Development Minister now holds a seat in the National Security Council as well.

Wieczorek-Zeul's policies derive their legitimation from international and supranational agreements, particularly the 1995 Beijing Platform, the Beijing + 5 Action Plan, the Copenhagen + 5 Initiative and the EU embrace of UN Action Plans. Conceptual frameworks include not only gender mainstreaming, empowerment, the rights of the girl-child and a rejection of all forms of violence against women (e.g. female genital mutilation); they also mandate an activist approach to the precept that women's rights *are* human rights.[23] Gender mainstreaming is applied to all bilateral programmes adopted by the Ministry, which does not preclude, for example, the use of women-specific initiatives to combat domestic violence and female genital mutilation (over 130 million women and girls have been thus mutilated). This requires women's participation in decision making, policy planning, programme implementation and benefit distribution in the receiving country. Programmes focus on expanding elementary and vocational education, micro-lending and small business creation.

Wieczorek-Zeul actively criticises neo-liberal forms of globalisation, calling for a restructuring of the International Monetary Fund (IMF), the World Bank, and the World Trade Organisation (WTO). She has challenged the credibility of developed states for retaining protective tariffs *vis-à-vis* the forty-eight poorest countries, the elimination of which would add $40 billion per year to their respective economies. The Cologne G–8 Summit of 1999 adopted a debt-forgiveness campaign amounting to $70 billion; at the Mexico Summit of March 2002, the Schröder government pushed to replace the so-called Washington Consensus on macroeconomic management ('let the market rule!') with the Monterrey Consensus of cooperation, good governance and new principles of ownership.

Indeed, despite her early credentials as an anti-capitalist, Wieczorek-Zeul has been surprisingly active in her pursuit of partnerships with 'free-marketers', more than 800 of them extending over sixty countries to date. Since 1999, they have sponsored over €3.2 billion's worth of pilot projects. Wieczorek-Zeul has tried to shape development policy through an adherence to new labour protection, social justice and environmental sustainability standards. She too adopted the Round Table model, which incorporates representatives from major companies, unions and non-governmental organisations (NGOs) to oppose forced and extreme forms of child labour, to foster union rights and collective bargaining practices and to guarantee anti-discrimination rules in the workplace.

Last but certainly not least, Wieczorek-Zeul has designated women 'the heart of a peaceful Afghanistan', expecting them to play a key role in the construction of a democratic civil society there. Wieczorek-Zeul hosted a parallel 'peace' summit for Afghan women during the 2002 Petersburg negotiations after the fall of the Taliban. The Red–Green government then provided organisational support for the 1,500 delegates who assembled in Kabul on 10–16 June 2002 to decide on a two-year interim government. Hoping to establish a minimum quota of 160 female participants in the Loya Jirga, the Friedrich-Ebert-Stiftung staged a Women's Congress in Kabul shortly before in order to promote nominations of female 'pioneers'.

Germany was also among the first countries to offer active assistance after the fall of the Taliban. One absolutely crucial measure was to reopen schools for girls, to the tune of €15 million.[24] Prior to 1990, women comprised 70 per cent of all teachers, 50 per cent of the civil servants and 40 per cent of all physicians in Afghanistan. The Federal Republic hopes to raise the share of female enrolments in co-ed schools from the post-Taliban rate of 3 per cent to 20 per cent by 2004. One Foreign Ministry (AA) official sent to aid in Afghan reconstruction is Ursula Mueller, formerly the *Frauenbeauftragte* responsible for gender mainstreaming within the AA itself.

Immigration, human rights and asylum policy

Soon after her appointment, Justice Minister Däubler-Gmelin insisted she would mount an active campaign against pornography, sex-trafficking and domestic violence, issues directly linked to the rights of migrant women in the Federal Republic. Foreign women (and men) are still denied 'equal protection' under both German and EU regulations. Women abused as the spouses of migrant workers or as mail-order brides, and even women forced into prostitution by mafia groups, have been routinely deported for violating immigration law before they can testify against their abusers. During her tenure as Berlin's Senator for Labour, Bergmann provided new financial support for projects offering language and job training to Asian women, particularly from Thailand, forced to flee abusive partners. The coalition's plans to reduce the number of years required for naturalisation, as well as its embrace of dual citizenship, promised to afford greater protection to second- and third-generation Turkish women regarding forced marriages, child-custody, and domestic violence.

Women were given special status in the 2002 *Law on Immigration and Integration*, which nonetheless limited the impact that the Green Federal Commissioner for Foreigners, Marieluise Beck, had on the legislation. Policy decisions in this policy area were controlled by Interior Minister Otto Schily (Green turned SPD). While Schily courted conservatives in the Bundesrat on immigration issues at the expense of his Green coalition partners, he did make one crucial concession during the final phase of negotiations in that he incorporated a provision recognising an independent right to asylum for women, based on gender-specific forms of oppression, including female genital mutilation. This policy shift was an outgrowth of the mass rape perpetrated against the women of Bosnia-Herzegovina and women's persecution under the Taliban in Afghanistan. Prior to a 2001 High Court ruling, the Federal Republic had refused to recognise asylum claims filed by Afghan women on the absurd grounds that they were not subject to persecution by state actors. According to legal purists, the Taliban regime that seized power in 1995 had been recognised only by two other governments. By contrast, the Federal Republic had been uncharacteristically liberal in extending full asylum rights to men fleeing persecution by the fundamentalist Islamic government in Iran since 1979, as well as in granting asylum to Turks who fled their country after the 1980 military *coup*.

Conclusion

Since 1998, women have clearly entered a new stage as regards their long march through the institutions, adding new weight to the adage, '*ohne Frauen ist kein Staat zu machen*'. While the impact of critical mass has been less apparent at the parliamentary level, owing to party-line voting, the years since 1998 provide concrete evidence of real political changes deriving from feminists' critical acts. Women's presence in decision making organs at the highest levels of governance is now a given. The 'performance and efficiency' of individual female politicians has increased dramatically within the Red–Green coalition. Gender mainstreaming has modified the institutional culture by requiring that women's issues be made a routine part of the agenda. The prevailing political discourse has been modified at a number of levels, beginning, literally, with the addition of the German feminine suffix form, *Innen*, to all job advertisements, political speeches, etc. The years since 1998 have also brought gender-sensitive changes in policy substance as well as in overall approaches to decision making in virtually every domain headed by a woman. Increases in the power of women working collectively are often easier to perceive through exercises like this one, that is, by tracing one's way back to the starting point. There is ample evidence that collective displays of girl power are beginning to reshape policy even in non-traditional arenas.

The EU has become a key shaper of regional, structural and environmental policies, although completion of the Single Market and the three pillars of Maastricht have had mixed consequences for women as workers. The 1997 Amsterdam Treaty provides a new constitutional foundation for pressuring national governments into more expansive anti-discrimination and comparable-worth legislation; it also offers a new foundation for combating racism and unequal treatment grounded in sexual orientation. The harmonisation of immigration, asylum and European defence policies has a long way to go, but the outcomes need not be detrimental to women – if women are included in all stages of the policy process with the aim of gender mainstreaming.

Having emphasised elsewhere feminists' personal involvement in the New Social Movements of the 1970s and 1980s, I am quite impressed at the extent to which ecological, peace and equality-oriented approaches have featured prominently in the domestic and foreign policy agendas of women leading the Berlin Republic.[25] The day-to-day battles – the never-ending budget crisis, party posturing, the verbal wrangling that turns molehills into mountains via the TV talk-shows – obscure many of the small steps forward that eventually culminate in a long march. Although the SPD–Green government as a whole has pursued more equality-oriented policies than its predecessors, pragmatic-feminist reforms continue to take a back seat to party politics, mass unemployment, and new burdens tied to Germany's changing role in regional and global security processes. The paradox here is that the holistic approach employed by these women would go a long way in overcoming the *Reformstau* born of the vested interests of the 'Angry Old Men'. The hot flashes of earlier decades have become the power surges of the new millennium, putting a new spin on the concept of critical mass.

Notes

1 This chapter is a fitting way to commemorate Peter Merkl's 70th birthday, insofar as he has always actively supported women in political science and often reflected in his own writings on the experiences of his mother and grandmother. Representative works are: 'The Women of West Germany', *The Center Magazine* (May–June 1974), pp. 68–9; 'The Politics of Sex: Western Germany', in Lynne Iglitzin and Ruth Ross (eds), *Women in the World: A Comparative Study* (Santa Barbara, CA: ABC-Clio Press, 1976), pp. 129–48; and 'West German Women: A Long Way from Kinder, Küche, and Kirche', in Lynne Iglitzin and Ruth Ross (eds), *Women in the World: The Women's Decade, 1975–1985* (Santa Barbara, CA: ABC–Clio Press, 1985), pp. 27–52.

2 Another trend rendering women's political strength greater than the sum of the individual national parts is the increasing transnationalisation of feminist networks and NGOs, e.g. in the field of women and development.

3 See the Equality Treatment section of the Directorate General on Employment and Social Policy, at www.europa.eu.int.

4 Joyce Marie Mushaben, *From Post-War to Post-Wall Generations. Changing Attitudes towards the National Question and NATO in the Federal Republic of Germany* (Boulder, CO: Westview Press, 1998), especially Chapter 6.

5 Biographical information can be gleaned from official ministerial homepages as well as from Johanna Holzhauer and Agnes Steinbauer, *Frauen an der Macht. Profile prominenter Politikerinnen* (Frankfurt-am-Main: Eichborn, 1994).

6 This was the derogatory term applied to the *Nackrückerinnen* from the 1950s through the early 1970s, women who moved up the party list and into the Bundestag to replace colleagues who had died or resigned in mid-term.

7 See Drude Dahlerup, 'From a Small to a Large Minority: Women in Scandinavian Politics', *Scandinavian Political Studies*, 11:4 (1988), p. 276.

8 *Ibid.*, p. 296.

9 Mushaben, *From Post-War to Post-Wall Generations*, p. 271 and Eva Kolinsky, 'Political Participation and Parliamentary Careers: Women's Quotas in West Germany', *West European Politics*, 14:1 (1991), p. 56 ff.

10 Beate Höcker, 'Geschlechterdemokratie im europäischen Kontext', *Aus Politik und Zeitgeschichte*, B31–32/2000 (28 July 2000), pp. 30–8.

11 Interview with Professor Nickel in Berlin, 13 June 2002.

12 Joyce Marie Mushaben, 'Second Class Citizenship and its Discontents: Women in the New Germany', in Peter Merkl (ed.), *The Federal Republic at Forty-Five. Union without Unity* (New York: New York University Press, 1995), pp 79–98 and Joyce Marie Mushaben, 'Coming to Terms with the Nation: The Political and Literary Voices of Women', *The Federal Republic at Fifty: The End of a Century of Turmoil* (New York: St Martin's Press, 1999), pp. 43–57.

13 Joyce Marie Mushaben, 'What the SPD–Green Coalition Means for German Women', in Carl Lankowski (ed.), *Germany After the 1998 Federal Elections* (Washington, DC: AICGS Research, December 1998), pp. 39–42.

14 Jörg Schindler, Thomas Kröter and Reinhard Voss, 'Gregor Gysi tritt zuruck', *Frankfurter Rundschau*, 1 August 2002.

15 The PDS-affiliated Rosa Luxemburg-Stiftung has pursued many feminist themes and generated major documents on topics like genetic research and biotechnology.

16 Peter H. Merkl, '*Reformstau* über alles: The FRG at 50', *Politik* (Newsletter of the Conference Group on German Politics) (Autumn 1999), pp. 8–9.

17 The Act upholds same-sex relationships 'as a perfectly natural part of society'. It guarantees the right to a joint name, upholds maintenance rights/duties, secures inheritance, tenancy and 'minor custody' rights for the registered partners.

18 In the United States, common law allowed husbands to 'discipline' their wives, as long as such action occurred within 'reasonable bounds'. The 'rule of thumb' meant that, until the 1870s, a man could beat his spouse, as long as the stick he used in the process was no thicker than his own thumb, by which point wife-beating was declared illegal in *most* American states. See Joyce Gelb, 'The Politics of Wife Abuse', in Irene Diamond (ed.), *Families, Politics and Public Policy: A Feminist Dialogue on Women and the State* (New York, London: Longman, 1983), pp. 250–62.

19 See 'Wir sind in einem moralischen Dilemma', *Berliner Zeitung*, 26–27 January 2002; Jörg Michel, 'Weg zum Import von Stammzellen endgültig frei', *Berliner Zeitung*, 26 April 2002; Jörg Michel, 'Bulmahn will Klon-Babys verhindern', *Berliner Zeitung*, 9 April 2002.

20 During State-Secretary Nickel's first year on leave of absence from the Humboldt University, I was technically the only female full Professor in the entire Social Science faculty for the seven months I spent in residence in 2002.

21 Renate Oschlies, 'Auch Mütter wollen arbeiten: Im Westen fehlen Kita-Plätze, im Osten fehlt Arbeit', *Berliner Zeitung*, 5 June 2002.

22 'Endlich ist es in den Köpfen drin', *Berliner Zeitung*, 15–16 June 2002.

23 'Ansprache von Bundesministerin Heidemarie Wieczorek-Zeul anlässlich der Verleihung des "Entwicklungsländerpreises 2000"', 26 October 2000, Gießen.

24 The German Foreign Ministry financed some 10,560 girls who entered grades 1–6 in fifteen special winter schools which opened in Kabul on 15 January 2001.

25 For detailed policy treatments across the decades, see Joyce Marie Mushaben, *From Post-War to Post-Wall Generations*; 'Concession or Compromise? The Politics of Abortion in United Germany', *German Politics*, 6:3 (1997), pp. 69–87; 'The Rise of *Femi-Nazis*? Women and Rightwing Extremist Movements in Unified Germany', *German Politics*, 5:2 (1996), pp. 240–75; 'Grassroots and *Gewaltfreie Aktionen*: A Study of Mass Mobilization Strategies in the West German Peace Movement', *Journal of Peace Research*, 23:2 (1986), pp. 141–54; 'Innocence Lost: Environmental Images and Political Experiences among the West German Greens', *New Political Science*, 14 (1986), pp. 39–66; and 'Anti-Politics and Successor Generations: The Role of Youth in the West and East German Peace Movements', *The Journal of Political and Military Sociology*, 12:2 (1984), pp. 171–90.

9
Social movements in the Federal Republic

Alice H. Cooper

Social movements accompanied every phase of West German development and, particularly from the mid-1960s on, transformed the face of politics. Organised outside of, and reflecting disappointment with, parliamentary and corporatist channels of policy making, left-libertarian social movements represented a widening of both the scope and the forms of political participation by ordinary citizens. Though initially feared by some as threats to Germany's democratic development, they are now widely seen as important contributions to democratic political culture.

As this chapter discusses, social movements put new and neglected issues on the political agenda and worked for political, social and cultural change. They eventually effected significant change in government policy, the policy stances of the established parties and, with the advent of the Greens, the composition and dynamics of the party system. Under very different conditions, social movements also arose in the former GDR and contributed significantly to the fall of the SED regime. After the *Wende*, however, these movements found themselves isolated from political developments. Since the 1980s, left-libertarian movements have undergone a process of institutionalisation and have developed stronger links to conventional politics. Social movements currently confront issues of globalisation and Europeanisation, although they remain largely wedded to the domestic arena.

Social movements in the Federal Republic, 1949–89

Scholars have linked the 'new' left-libertarian social movements of the 1960s and beyond to a variety of structural preconditions. For some, generational turnover, dissolution of traditional social milieux, the expansion of higher education and the tertiary sector and postmaterial values led to movements around 'new politics' issues.[1] For others, movements represent self-defence against state intervention into the 'life-world' and against threats to social and physical integrity posed by pollution and nuclear power, for example.[2] Social movements and Green parties have been facilitated, moreover, when corporatism excludes non-economic interests and/or mainstream left parties vacate political space on the left through centrist electoral strategies and participation in government.[3] In Germany, these conditions were amply fulfilled after the SPD's turn toward the centre in the late 1950s. In addition, the pacification of class and religious cleavages created space for mobilisation by new social movements. Similarly, the German state's specific institutional configuration and its (informally) exclusionary strategy have shaped social movements' choices of action forms.[4] Unresolved issues from Germany's painful past, German territorial division and West Germany's heightened military and political dependence on the United States all contributed to a highly problematic sense (or lack) of national identity, which increased the gap between wartime and postwar generations and heightened the latter's critique of the West German political system.[5]

Even in the 1950s, a time otherwise bleak for protest movements, there were large demonstrations against rearmament, NATO membership and nuclear weapons organised by the left in the SPD, unions, churches and elsewhere. These demonstrations became part of, and a vehicle for, opposition to the newly founded Federal Republic's political, economic and social order. Peace protest in the 1950s spoke to the costs of Adenauer's foreign policy of Western integration, including its reinforcement, given the Cold War context, of German division. The SPD and *Deutscher Gewerkschaftsbund* were the dominant forces of peace protest at its height, which collapsed when the two no longer deemed such protest politically expedient. Protest movements had not yet formed extra-parliamentary networks capable of sustaining action in the absence of the major institutional actors on the left.[6]

Starting in the 1960s, social movements came into their own. Propelled in part by their suspicion that West Germany's democracy was but a veneer superimposed on traditional authoritarianism in new guises, the student movement and the 'extra-parliamentary opposition' protested against the proposed 'Emergency Laws', the Vietnam war and the universities' antiquated governing structures and curriculum. The new social movements of the 1970s formed around issues of quality of life and social risk – such as ecology and nuclear power, feminism, security and peace, solidarity with developing countries as well as urban land use and housing. In addition, hard-core activists continued to question the very legitimacy of West German democracy, convinced that genuine democratic participation was impossible within the existing system. Instead of lobbying parliaments, social movements tried to create political space outside established institutions, and therefore emphasised grass-roots politics, mass mobilisation and direct action.[7] Beginning in the early 1960s, movements developed the networks necessary for autonomous extra-parliamentary action; some movements, e.g. feminism, worked to create infrastructure for alternative lifestyles and countercultural milieux.[8]

New social movements have had significant impacts on government policy, party stances and political culture. The peace movement, for example, helped alter the terms of debate on security policy. Despite its defeat on the Intermediate Nuclear Forces deployment in the early 1980s, the peace movement influenced the security policy positions of both major parties, and induced the Kohl government to push for arms control later in the decade.[9] The environmental movement has served as an agenda-setter for government, parties and even industry, while also shaping individual attitudes toward environmental issues.[10] Social movements have shaped political culture as well, moving it from a formalistic view of democracy to a more participatory conception, including a more liberal view of demonstration rights.[11]

Eastern German movements and the *Wende* of 1989

Social movements in the GDR had a profound impact on their regime, questioning its legitimacy, pushing for expanded citizen participation and eventually contributing to its demise. The East German state worked hard to repress or coopt dissent and thereby to restrict the development of a civil society capable of autonomous action, and it was reasonably successful in this endeavour for several decades. In the 1980s, however, small, informal grass-roots groups began to form and to establish networks. The Protestant Church and the universities provided crucial protection for these groups, as well as meeting spaces and libraries for alternative peace and environmental literature.[12] Ecological, human rights, peace and feminist activists formed informal networks, such as Women for Peace and its successor, the Initiative for Peace and Human Rights. These activists later helped create *Neues Forum* and *Demokratie Jetzt*, two pillars of the grassroots citizens' movement instrumental in bringing about the end of the socialist regime in 1989.[13]

Two factors undermined the regime's legitimation and set the stage for the citizen movements which contributed to its collapse. First, poor economic performance violated the informal 'social contract' exchanging popular accommodation with the regime for improving standards of living. Second, citizens' bitterness rose when the regime visibly avoided following the Soviet example of reform under President Mikhail Gorbachev.[14] During his visit to the GDR in October 1989, Gorbachev indicated that the Soviets would no longer use force to support eastern European regimes against indigenous opposition. In contrast to earlier Soviet behaviour, this significantly lowered the costs of protest for East German citizens.[15]

By the fall of 1989, the East German regime was under escalating pressure from citizen use of both 'exit' and 'voice'. Surging mass emigration of GDR citizens, via the recently opened Hungarian borders and occupation of West German embassies in Prague and Warsaw, expressed individual discontent and protest. Mass emigration not only encouraged further demands for exit visas, but also swelled the ranks of opposition groups which pressed for domestic change.[16] Spearheading the use of 'voice' were the informal networks of dissident groups discussed above. As people perceived the regime's vulnerability, 'voice' found expression in the ever-growing Monday demonstrations in Leipzig, Berlin and elsewhere. The combination of mass emigration and mass demonstration finally brought down the socialist regime and initiated a transition to German unification and democracy in eastern Germany.

Marginalisation of eastern German opposition groups in 1990 and beyond

Having contributed significantly to bringing down the socialist regime, East German citizen movements expected to have substantial influence on developments thereafter. Apart from participation in the central

Round Table of 1989–90, however, East German opposition groups soon found themselves marginalised. The rapid extension of West German institutions and practices into the former GDR changed the 'political opportunity structure' (the political context) of the citizen movements rapidly and for the worse, rendering their ideological appeal irrelevant and their organisational structures ineffective. Since 1990, the citizens movements' marginalisation has mirrored and contributed to a broader sense of eastern German marginalisation within the newly unified Federal Republic.

East German citizen movements originated in opposition to the GDR's socialist regime. They envisaged a reformed but autonomous GDR and the introduction of radical democracy from below. Developments, however, quickly rendered these goals obsolete as rapid unification soon dominated the agenda. This became apparent as early as the GDR-wide *Volkskammer* (People's Chamber) elections, moved from May to March 1990. Early *Volkskammer* elections pulled the citizen movements up short, as they necessitated a shift in focus from mass demonstrations to electoral politics, from the grass-roots to the national level, and from their identity as movements to the issue of forming political parties. Some citizen movement groups did nominate candidates, but they did so as three competing electoral groups (some with subgroups of their own) rather than one broad alliance. The *Volkskammer* elections soon came under the dominance of the West German parties, each with ties to their East German counterparts. The new electoral politics was highly westernised and oriented to the mass media rather than to the citizen movements' ideals of participatory democracy. New skills and resources were necessary for success and the previous achievements of the citizen movements were devalued.[17]

Citizen movements found themselves further impeded by their ideological stances and organisational forms. With their political identity formed by opposition to the old regime, movement activists were committed to democracy but also had strong interest in reformed socialism or a 'third way' between communism and capitalist democracy. Critical of the populace's desire for unification, movement activists presented a stark alternative between creating a democratic-socialist, autonomous GDR or selling out to the West. Both this ambivalence toward unification and their preoccupation with GDR-specific issues, such as the danger of a recreated *Stasi*, distanced citizen movements from the general population. The citizens movements' organisational forms, moreover, were equally outmoded in the new political context. Having been designed for survival in an authoritarian setting, citizen groups were small, informal and only loosely networked with each other. Wary of hierarchy and centralisation, they valued direct democracy and consensus reached through dialogue. Citizen groups lacked the experience and resources to form the larger, cohesive, organisations which were required as their membership temporarily surged and which might have been more effective in the new setting from 1990 on. In addition, groups wanted to experience pluralism and maintain their separate identities; they therefore even exaggerated their differences rather than creating effective alliances.[18]

Since unification, eastern German movements' experience of marginalisation has continued, and eastern and western German groups have had trouble cooperating on common issues such as the environment and women's concerns. Although the relative density of women's projects (an indicator of levels of feminism) in eastern Germany is about average for Germany as a whole and indeed higher than in Bavaria or Baden-Württemberg, the low absolute number of women's projects in eastern Germany is indicative of the minority status of eastern women's groups and projects in the German context as a whole. This means that eastern German women remain a minority in the national discussion, both quantitatively and structurally. In national debates, the context is set by western Germans, while the eastern German position is articulated as a deviation from this norm.[19] Moreover, in part because of differences in socialisation, the perspectives of eastern and western citizen groups differ sufficiently to hinder cooperation. Whereas eastern German women had positive orientations toward the democratic state and toward cooperation with men, the emphasis of the western women's movement on autonomous feminism meant a greater distance from both the state and men. In addition, eastern women emphasise feminist theory less than western women. Instead, eastern women's projects perform a significant amount of social work and offer an important source of employment via government-funded job creation measures.[20] Cooperation between eastern and western environmental movements has also proved problematic, at least in the early post-unification years, in part due to their different understandings of technology, the relationship between state and society, and the appropriate weight of experts in policy making.[21] Only a few eastern German environmental organisations formed in 1989 or the early 1990s have survived, most notably the *Grüne Liga*. Instead, the eastern German citizen movements that had formed *Bündnis '90* merged with the western Greens in 1993. In addition, some western groups, such as the *Bund für Umwelt und Naturschuzt*, expanded eastward by establishing regional and local branches.[22] Thus even the area of environmentalism may have contributed to the eastern German feeling of 'colonisation'.

Normalisation of protest and institutionalisation of movements?

If eastern German citizen movements have experienced marginalisation, what role do the (largely western) left-libertarian social movements now play in the Berlin Republic? Despite the relative absence of mass demonstrations reminiscent of the 1970s and early 1980s, the left-libertarian social movements of the Bonn Republic are not necessarily 'dead'. However, they have undergone significant institutionalisation and now play a larger 'insider' role in politics.

Some observers assume that protest has declined since the early 1980s. Clearly, this was partially true for the peace movement. After huge mass mobilisation in the early 1980s, its numbers dwindled significantly. Although the movement mobilised respectable protest against the Gulf war in 1991, it failed to mobilise against German participation in the NATO peace-keeping mission to Bosnia in 1995 and other instances of German military activity outside of NATO territory.[23] The end of the Cold War rendered obsolete ideological frames of reference tied to nuclear weapons and East–West confrontation. The post-Cold War situation has also confronted the movement with the issue of using military force to contain civil wars or genocide rooted in nationalism.

Overall levels of protest, however, apparently did *not* decline in (West) Germany during the 1980s and early 1990s. Several peaks of both demonstrative and violent protest between 1985 and 1992 equalled those attained in the early 1980s, measured in numbers of protest events, although levels of conventional and confrontational protest dropped.[24] Numbers of participants in overall protest did drop in the second half of the 1980s, but they rose again in the early 1990s. While protest concerning nuclear power, environmentalism, peace and women fell from high points in the 1980s, protest against foreigners but also against racism and racist violence contributed to the rise in protest in the 1990s.[25] And, after falling in the late 1980s and early 1990s, environmental protest rose during the rest of the 1990s.[26] On the organisational level, too, the environmental movement shows no signs of decline. Instead, membership, budgets and staff size have either held steady or grown for most groups in the 1980s and 1990s. Nor has the movement become markedly more centralised; newly created groups join decentralised networks that cannot be controlled by a few dominant organisations.[27]

Koopmans sums up the evolution of protest levels in the 1990s by noting that, despite a decrease in the number of truly huge protest demonstrations, the total quantity of protest has otherwise not declined.[28] Protest has, however, become more fragmented and ad hoc in character. In other ways too, the persistence of protest has not precluded change in the nature of protest since the 1970s and 1980s. One notable change is the relative absence of the fundamental critique of the 'system' which united the hard core of social movements in the 1970s and 1980s, when the movements and the Greens were 'the Federal Republic's most prolific critics'.[29] Since the later 1980s, or so, the tone has changed. The old 'Green' voter milieu, with its roots in the new social movements and a common notion of leftist opposition to the 'Republic' (*Systemverweigerer*), has shrunk dramatically. One reason for this change is the end of the Cold War, which provided the backdrop for so much of domestic (West) German politics. The collapse of communism in eastern Europe has spelled the end of utopian visions and grand designs and has forced the left to rethink its relationship to the United States and the German state, Europe and the global economy.[30]

The 'institutionalisation' of the new social movements serves as both further reflection of and further contributor to this change in the character and role of social movements, if not the extent of protest. In the course of the 1980s and 1990s, social movements gained access to the 'input' side of policy making, which dramatically increased their participation in institutional or conventional politics. Access to policy making, which was previously closed to movements, complements access to the 'output' or implementation side of the political system of which social movements have long made use (e.g. legal appeals in the courts to block construction of nuclear power plants).[31] Social movement institutionalisation has taken at least four forms: the emergence of the Greens as a 'movement party' and their subsequent 'domestication'; alliances between movements and various parties; an increase in lobbying and other forms of conventional activity; and the decreased weight of citizens' initiatives and the increased weight of more conventional interest groups.

One of the chief forms of movement institutionalisation is the formation of the Green party and the increased responsiveness of the established parties to movement concerns. As is well known, the Green party had its origins in the new social movements of the 1970s and 1980s, at a time when the state, other parties and interest associations all remained largely closed to the movements' policy positions and participants.[32] The Greens' presence in the Bundestag and subnational parliaments has given parliamentary representation to social movements since the early 1980s. It has also put considerable pressure on the other parties to reach some accommodation with their concerns. As the Greens' nearest competitor in the party space, and with its own internal New Left component, the SPD in particular opened itself to the New Social Movements (after 1983) and adopted 'new politics' concerns.[33] With the formation of the Greens, the New Social Movements thus made a major contribution to reorienting the Bonn Republic's 'two-and-a-half' party system, the policy reorientation of the other parties and the composition of coalition governments.

Institutionalisation in the form of the Greens, however, has meant good and bad news for the new social movements. Because of 'the overwhelming attractiveness of the institutional mode of normal politics',[34] Claus Offe regards the formation of the Greens as virtually inevitable because it permitted the most effective use of the movement's resources. Becoming a party meant access to the state financial subsidies and television/radio air time to which all German parties are entitled, and it increased pressure on other parties to respond to their concerns. Institutionalisation as a party, however, also brought about partial loss of the movement's identity and autonomy, loss of influence of their activist core and pressure to compromise their demands. The evolution of the Greens in the 1980s and 1990s bears witness to these dilemmas and to the extent to which the German political system has penetrated the Greens as much as they have penetrated it.

This change in the party system contributed to another manifestation of social movement institutionalisation, movement alliances with parties and state agencies. The women's movement, for example, initially refused to work within existing institutions and focused instead on the creation of a 'counter society' via 'projects' such as feminist bookstores and anti-authoritarian daycare. Since the mid-1980s, however, feminists developed a double strategy in order to increase women's influence on mainstream political decision making. While maintaining local projects which now enjoy a higher level of state financing, women have added an institutional strategy of integration into the political system. Responding to the new political opportunities afforded by changes in the party system, the women's movement has forged alliances with 'institutionalised' feminists in the Greens, the SPD and even other parties, as the parties have adopted more feminist policies such as quota systems for determining candidates for office. Autonomous feminists also found an ally in the *Frauenbeauftragte* offices within the administrative state apparatus. Women's affairs officers increased the flow of government funds to feminist projects, while also overseeing affirmative action within city and state governments. Moreover, women in autonomous feminist initiatives, universities, foundations of the political parties and private service sector agencies have generated a considerable body of expertise on gender issues, which they offer to parties, unions, private firms, etc.[35] Thus, German feminists have made considerable strides in pressuring their political system into more responsiveness to women as a distinct constituency. Institutionalisation has not come without costs, however, to the autonomy of women's organisations and particularly their projects. Institutionalisation has also led to demobilisation of the feminist movement on the streets, and, by increasing competition for resources, has encouraged segmentation and factionalisation within the movement.[36]

Another form of institutionalisation has been the increased use of lobbying and other conventional forms of action. German social movements had long made use of the court system in fighting their campaigns. During the 1980s, the West German women's movement added conventional action forms such as lobbying and petitions to its repertoire, while continuing to use civil disobedience and demonstrations on the non-conventional side.[37] The environmental movement also uses a dual strategy combining confrontational protest and institutionalised lobbying. Greenpeace, for example, engages in both spectacular actions at sea (involving activists in 'wet suits') and in tedious negotiations with firms and government agencies (involving experts in 'dry suits').[38] As a final example, there are few visible mass protests any more at World Bank or IMF meetings. Instead, citizens' initiatives now hold intensive talks with experts and politicians, and they have enjoyed visible success in getting poverty and debt-forgiveness onto meeting agendas.[39]

Parallel to, and consistent with, rising levels of conventional action forms was the growing importance of traditional interest associations

(*Verbände*) and NGOs. In the early years of the ecology movement (1970s), citizens' initiatives were the dominant organisational basis of environmental protests, loosely integrated into various networks and making decisions in a 'bottom-up' fashion. Traditional nature-conservation organisations existed but played an insignificant role, while parties and unions were closed to the movement. By the advent of the Berlin Republic, parties had adopted ecology-friendly positions and the ecology movement had become a 'social movement industry' with over 1 million members and hundreds of paid employees. Grass-roots involvement continues unabated, but it now shares the stage with parties and professional ecology movement organisations such as BUND and Greenpeace. The regional and national network infrastructure of citizens' initiatives, such as *Bund Bürgerinitiativen Umweltschutz* in the meantime has virtually collapsed.[40]

Institutionalisation of social movements in the 1980s and 1990s, however, was only partial and is only part of the story. Koopmans observes a dual tendency toward both institutionalisation and radicalisation in the later stages of protest cycles.[41] Although down from their peak in the early 1980s, the use of radical action forms by left-libertarian social movements stayed within a consistent range for the rest of the decade. The frequency of both light and heavy violence surged between 1984 and 1986 and again in the first half of the 1990s, this time on the extreme right as an expression of hostility against foreigners. On the left, radical actions were increasingly perpetrated by groups with a low level of organisation, 'small and nameless circles of activists' (*Autonomen*)[42] and they focused particularly on the struggle against nuclear power (e.g. the reprocessing plant proposed for Wackersdorf). In the 1990s, radical forms of action (such as occupation of rail lines) were also used to impede transport of nuclear wastes for reprocessing abroad (Castor transports).

Finally, in addition to the institutionalisation of social movements, protest itself has become institutionalised, with the tamer forms of protest becoming part of the conventional repertoire of participation. Germany has become, like many other advanced industrial societies, a 'social movement society'[43] with a 'culture of protest'.[44] Protest is so common among the middle class that it has become simply another political resource, used with greater frequency by more diverse constituencies than in earlier decades.[45] To some extent, protest has become separated from the social movements which traditionally made most use of it. Indeed the lines have blurred between the traditional social movement sector and conventional political actors, with tendencies toward both institutionalisation of social movement action and 'movementization' of politics.[46] Social movements combine disruptive and conventional activities, while institutional actors like interest groups and parties add contentious behaviour to their own, otherwise conventional, repertoire. Party elites are often at the forefront of movement activities, and movement activists and elites share similar beliefs and interests.[47] Perhaps most strikingly so far, the CDU/CSU used a petition drive to great effect against the SPD–Green government's proposed citizenship law reform in 1999. Not only did the petition drive indirectly bring about significant modifications of the proposed legislation, but it also swung the Hessen election in 1999 in favour of the CDU and robbed the new SPD–Green government of its Bundesrat majority.[48]

Globalisation and Europeanisation

Parallel to this process of institutionalisation at the national level, left-libertarian social movements have transferred a portion of their efforts to global arenas. Indeed, globalisation has had observable impacts on social movements in Germany and elsewhere. Despite the undeniable effects of globalisation, on the other hand, transferral to the supranational level has been uneven and much social movement activity remains focused, perhaps surprisingly, on the national level.

For German and other European social movements, the most relevant aspect of globalisation is the EU. As one might expect, there are incentives and opportunities for national-level social movements to become 'Euro-social movements'. As Marks and McAdam argue, the ongoing shift in the locus of institutionalised power from the nation-state to transnational forms of governance such as the EU should logically be accompanied by attendant changes in the forms and dynamics of interest articulation historically linked to the state, including social movements.[49] Policy making now takes place in a 'multi-level polity' with decision making shared among supranational, national and subnational levels of government. The increasing tendency of protest actors to target the EU results from new opportunities created by European integration. Social movements can use supranational arenas to bring pressure on their own national governments: for example, environmental movements have brought suits against their own governments for failing to live up to EU standards.[50]

For all of these reasons, transnational social movement activity should be increasingly prominent at the EU level. Indeed, despite relatively static overall levels of contentious politics in Europe in the 1990s, the proportion of protest related to European integration is growing.[51] However, although certain movements and public interest groups do indeed work at the EU level, the EU has by no means replaced the relevance of the national state.

For one thing, because of heterogeneity of policy regimes, the EU offers movements highly variable political opportunities. The opportunities available to any group depend in part on the EU's general policy receptivity to the group's issues. The environmental movement has found the EU Commission, Court (ECJ) and Parliament (EP) receptive to environmental issues and has aggressively taken advantage of these institutional channels by establishing a strong lobbying presence in Brussels (European Environmental Bureau, Greenpeace, etc.) and by appropriate legal and electoral strategies. Many national environmental movements, especially the German one, have long practised a combination of legal, electoral and lobbying strategies and were thus well positioned to adapt to EU-level opportunities. This was not true, however, for the anti-nuclear power movement. The EU has proved loath to undertake a common nuclear energy policy, in part because of extreme divergence among member-states with respect to nuclear power. Since the EU has not established its authority in this area, the EP and ECJ are not available to anti-nuclear activists for legal strategies or lobbying efforts.[52]

The effect of the EU's opportunity structure is further seen in social movement strategy, as social movements do not necessarily behave in Brussels as they do at home. Instead of mass demonstrations and attendant media coverage, movements lobby, write impact reports and so on. They thus behave much like traditional interest groups, or in this case public interest groups. There are several reasons why unconventional action forms seem poorly suited to the EU. First, it is far easier to lobby in Brussels than to transport activists over considerable distances from their various abodes. Second, the general populace remains far more attached to its local and national communities than to the EU, and public discourse is correspondingly deeper there than in Europe as a whole. Third, the mass media are still pitched primarily at distinct national audiences rather than at an overarching European one. Fourth, the EU's institutional structure is more open to conventional than to unconventional activity; the Commission, ECJ and EP all grant groups formal access. Only the EP occasionally provides a good target for unconventional action.[53]

Furthermore, a movement's ability to take advantage of EU-level opportunities depends on whether its own organisational structure and inherited ideologies permit adaptation. Labour movements, for example, tailored their strategies so consistently to national systems of interest representation that they have not effectively organised at the EU level.[54] Many other groups simply lack the resources, or see no reason to bear the costs, necessary to sustain EU-level campaigns, particularly those associated with the tasks of building collective identities and organising protest over large distances. Not surprisingly, therefore, 62 per cent of EU-related protest involves *domestic* action against EU policies.[55] This represents a logical strategic response to the multi-level nature of European policy making, Tarrow argues.[56] European states continue to provide suitable opportunities for domestic movements and groups, even when they oppose policies whose origins are supranational. Implementation of EU rules rests primarily with national administrations and courts. Therefore, domestic groups need not transfer their resources to Brussels but can instead pressure their national governments, through protest if necessary, to take their interests into account in the implementation phase. Groups which are weak at the supranational level can use domestic-level pressure and protest as the functional equivalent of European interest representation.

Just as the growth of supranational governance has not resulted in the transferral of most social movement activity to that level, so national social movements also remain considerably diverse even when responding to common internationally generated stimuli. The Gulf War might be called the first truly 'global war' in that it was backed by a large coalition of UN member states and it generated roughly the same media coverage in each country (based on CNN and information supplied by the US military). The Gulf War also witnessed diffusion of protest frames; 'no blood for oil' became the masterframe and the key opposition slogan across the globe. Nonetheless, national political and cultural contexts remained highly significant in shaping the anti-war movements that emerged in various countries. Germany had higher levels of mobilisation than France or the Netherlands, and the German movement made more use of confrontational action. These differences lay in the extent to which organisational networks left over from the 1980s were still intact, whether protest against the Gulf War could be linked to already sensitive issues such as arms exports, whether potential protestors had enjoyed success in previous campaigns and felt efficacious and whether significant allies such as parties and unions were available to the movement. Thus, despite the 'mother of all international, suddenly imposed grievances', the Gulf War showed that while globalisation is internationalising the themes at stake, the nation-state is still the principal frame of reference. Cross-national differences among movements were more striking than similarities.[57] Similarly, despite the existence of a supranational women's movement, abortion discourse remains heavily influenced by the national context. The divergence between the American and German abortion discourse confirms the limits to convergence despite globalisation.[58]

Conclusion: *Quo Vadis* social movements?

The advent and evolution of left-libertarian social movements played a significant role in the broader democratisation of German political culture after 1945. Whereas political culture in the early postwar period still reflected Germany's authoritarian past, Germany since then has evolved into a much more vibrant, participatory democracy. This change is demonstrated not only by rising levels of social movement participation, but also by changing attitudes toward protest as such. Protesters themselves, much of the wider population and political and scholarly observers all consider protest a fundamental component of democratic political culture, a sign of vitality rather than a threat to democracy.[59]

The left-libertarian social movements of the 1970s and 1980s have become increasingly 'established' in the politics of Germany at fifty-five. Although none of the movements has had the total impact to which they aspired, the environmental movement, the women's movment, and even the peace movement have made considerable progress. Social movements have had enormous impacts on popular attitudes and party positions. 'New politics' issues have to a large extent been folded into the party system. In their turn, large portions of the social movements have dropped their generalised radical critique of parliamentary democracy and capitalism, settling instead for focus on issue-oriented coalitions and limited reforms. On an organisational level, while protest itself continues, some observers think that Germany is moving away from the mass (physical) mobilisations of the social movements, conducted by informal networks of grass-roots groups with a bottom-up chain of decision making, and toward formalised lobbying and media-transmitted public campaigns professionally channelled by NGOs with a much more 'top-down' chain of command.[60] One benefit of this transformation is that institutionalisation of social movements makes them into a more permanent, long-term factor in politics and lets them avoid fading into insignificance. Social movements and NGOs are seen as contributing to a durable 'active civil society' (*aktive Bürgergesellschaft*).[61]

The SPD–Green government in power since 1998 marks one of the high points of this institutionalisation of left-libertarian social movements. And yet, within a year of taking office, the new government had already dashed many hopes for significant reform. Reforms of both nuclear power and citizenship law fell short of the hopes of their most avid supporters, while Germany's participation in NATO's use of armed force in the Kosovo conflict (and later in Afghanistan) met with great ambivalence among the Greens and SPD. Some observers feel that disappointment in the SPD–Green government contributed to social-movement malaise in the short term, and might also render them politically 'homeless' by detaching them from parties of the left.[62] The Greens' disastrous showings in *Land*-level elections in the first legislative period of the Red–Green government (1998–2002) lent apparent confirmation to this concern. Long-term detachment from parties could mean a partial deinstitutionalisation of left-libertarian social movements, as an institutional strategy presupposes that existing political institutions and actors are in fact capable of bring about reform.[63] On the other hand, in the 2002 Federal election the Greens recovered sufficiently to increase their vote share by 1.9 per cent (from 6.7 per cent in 1998 to 8.6 per cent in 2002), as left-libertarian voters returned to the fold when faced with the alternative of a CDU/CSU/FDP government with Edmund Stoiber as Chancellor.

Social movements, in whatever form, still seem to play an important role in picking up unresolved issues. Globalisation raises new twists on left-libertarian issues of justice, environmentalism, women's rights, etc. and it provides potential fodder for such movements. New cleavages, moreover, pit left-libertarian movements against the extreme right. Just as left-libertarian movements were reaching peaks of integration into the political system in the late 1980s and 1990s, right-extremist mobilisation and parties emerged as new challengers to mainstream politics. Although international developments have robbed the radical right of its traditional nationalist issue of reunification, those and other developments generated a new issue for extreme-right mobilisation – immigration.[64] In certain policy areas, extreme-right mobilisation represents a counter-movement to the left-libertarian movements.[65] Violence against foreigners and extreme-right mobilisation generated, in its turn, a counter-movement on the left – the anti-racism movement. Thus a new cleavage involving exclusion–inclusion of foreigners is developing, which pits left-libertarian and right-authoritarian movements against each other. However it may be evolving, the end of popular mobilisation does not yet seem to be at hand.

Notes

1 See Ronald Inglehart, *Culture Shift in Advanced Industrial Society* (Princeton: Princeton University Press, 1990); Russell Dalton, *Citizen Politics: Public Opinion and Political Parties in Advanced Western Democracies*, 2nd edn (Chatham, NJ: Chatham House Publishers, 1996); and Samuel Barnes, Max Kaase, *et al.*, *Political Action: Mass Participation in Five Western Democracies* (Beverly Hills: Sage, 1979).

2 See Jürgen Habermas, *Legitimation Crisis* (London: Heinemann, 1976); Jürgen Habermas, *The Theory of Communicative Action*, 2 (Boston: Beacon Press, 1987); Karl-Werner Brand, Detlef Büsser and Dieter Rucht, *Aufbruch in eine andere Gesellschaft: Neue Soziale Bewegungen in der Bundesrepublik* (Frankfurt: Campus Verlag, 1983); and Claus Offe 'New Social Movements: Challenging the Boundaries of Institutional Politics,' *Social Research*, 52:4 (1985), pp. 817–68.

3 Herbert Kitschelt, 'Left-Libertarian Parties', *World Politics*, 40:2 (1989), pp. 194–234.

4 See Hanspeter Kriesi, Ruud Koopmans, Jan Willem Duyvendak and Marco Giugni, *New Social Movements in Western Europe* (Minneapolis: University of Minnesota Press, 1995).

5 See Andrei Markovits and Philip Gorski, *The German Left: Red, Green and Beyond* (New York: Oxford University Press, 1993).

6 Alice Cooper, *Paradoxes of Peace: German Peace Movements since 1945* (Ann Arbor: University of Michigan Press, 1996).

7 Carol Hager, 'Environmentalism and Democracy in the Two Germanies', *German Politics*, 1:1 (1992), pp. 95–118.

8 Brigitte Young, *Triumph of the Fatherland: German Unification and the Marginalization of Women* (Ann Arbor: University of Michigan Press, 1999).

9 David Meyer, 'How the Cold War was Really Won', in Marco Giugni, Doug McAdam and Charles Tilly (eds), *How Social Movements Matter* (Minneapolis: University of Minnesota Press, 1999), pp. 182–203 and Steve Breyman, *Why Movements Matter: The West German Peace Movement and US Arms Control Policy* (Albany: State University of New York Press, 2001).

10 Dieter Rucht, 'The Impact of Environmental Movements in Western Societies,' in Marco Giugni, Doug McAdam, and Charles Tilly (eds), *How Social Movements Matter* (Minneapolis: University of Minnesota Press, 1999), pp. 204–24.

11 Donnatella della Porta, 'Protest, Protesters, and Protest Policing,' in Marco Giugni, Doug McAdam and Charles Tilly (eds), *How Social Movements Matter* (Minneapolis: University of Minnesota Press, 1999), pp. 66–96; and Hager, 'Environmentalism and Democracy in the two Germanies'.

12 John Burgess, *The East German Church and the End of Communism* (New York: Oxford University Press, 1997).

13 See Young, *Triumph of the Fatherland*; and Hager, 'Environmentalism and Democracy in the two Germanies'.

14 Dieter Rucht, 'German Unification, Democratization, and the Role of Social Movements: a Missed Opportunity?', *Mobilization*, 1:1 (1996), pp. 35–62 and Michaela Richter, 'Exiting the GDR: Political Movements and Parties between Democratization and Westernization', in Donald Hancock and Helga Welsh (eds), *German Unification: Process and Outcomes* (Boulder, CO: Westview Press, 1994), pp. 93–138.

15 Suzanne Lohmann, 'Dynamics of Informational Cascades: The Monday Demonstrations in Leipzig, East Germany, 1989–91', *World Politics*, 47:1 (1994), pp. 42–101.

16 Rucht, 'German Unification'; Richter, 'Exiting the GDR'; Lohman, 'Dynamics of Informational Cascades'; Albert Hirschman, 'Exit, Voice, and the Fate of the German Democratic Republic', *World Politics*, 45:2 (1993), pp. 173–202; and Christian Joppke, '"Exit" and "Voice" in the East German Revolution', *German Politics*, 2:3 (1993), pp. 393–414.

17 Lynn Kamenitsa, 'The Process of Political Marginalization: East German Social Movements after the Wall', *Comparative Politics*, 30:3 (1998), pp. 313–33 and Young, *Triumph of the Fatherland.*

18 Rucht, 'German Unification' and Kamenitsa, 'The Process of Political Marginalization'.

19 Ingrid Miethe, 'Women's Movements in Unified Germany: Experiences and Expectations of Eastern German Women', *AICGS Humanities*, 11 (2002), pp. 43–59.

20 *Ibid.*

21 Hager, 'Environmentalism and Democracy in the two Germanies'.

22 Dieter Rucht and Jochen Roose, 'Neither Decline nor Sclerosis: The Organizational Structure of the German environmental movement', *West European Politics*, 24:4 (2001), pp. 55–81.

23 Alice Cooper, 'When Just Causes Conflict with Accepted Means: The German Peace Movement and Military Intervention in Bosnia', *German Politics and Society*, 15:3 (1997), pp. 99–118.

24 Dieter Rucht, 'The Structure and Culture of Collective Protest in Germany since 1950', in David Meyer and Sidney Tarrow (eds), *The Social Movement Society: Contentious Politics for a New Century* (New York: Rowman & Littlefield, 1998), pp. 29–58.

25 Dieter Rucht, 'Linking Organization and Mobilization: Michel's Iron Law of Oligarchy Reconsidered', *Mobilization*, 4:2 (1999), pp. 151–69.

26 Christopher Rootes, 'Environmental Movements in Western Europe Compared: Accounting for British Exceptionalism ... Again!', Paper presented at the American Political Science Association, San Francisco, CA, 30 August–2 September 2001.

27 Rucht and Roose, 'Neither Decline nor Sclerosis'.

28 Rudd Koopmans, 'Globalisierung, Individualisierung, politische Entflechtung', *Forschungsjournal Neue Soziale Bewegung*, 13:1 (2000), pp. 26–31.

29 Markovits and Gorski, *The German Left*, p. 275.

30 *Ibid.*

31 Herbert Kitschelt, 'Political Opportunity Structures and Political Protest: Anti-Nuclear Movements in Four Democracies', *British Journal of Political Science*, 16:1 (1986), pp. 57–85 and Dorothy Nelkin and Michael Pollak, *The Atom Besieged: Anti-Nuclear Movements in France and Germany* (Cambridge, MA: MIT Press, 1982).

32 Markovits and Gorski, *The German Left* and Rudd Koopmans, *Democracy from Below: New Social Movements and the Political System in West Germany* (Boulder, CO: Westview Press, 1995).

33 Koopmans, *Democracy from Below* and Breyman, *Why Movements Matter*.

34 Claus Offe, 'Reflections on the Institutional Self-Transformation of Movement Politics: A Tentative Stage Model', in Russell Dalton and Manfred Kuechler (eds), *Challenging the Political Order: New Social and Political Movements in Western Democracies* (New York: Oxford University Press, 1990), p. 241.

35 Mechtild Jansen, 'Nebensache, Detailproblem oder grundlegende Herausforderung', *Forschungsjournal Neue Soziale Bewegung*, 12:3 (1999), pp. 54–7.

36 Young, *Triumph of the Fatherland* and Myra Marx Ferree, 'Thinking Globally, Acting Locally: German and American Feminism in the World System', *AICGS Humanities*, 11 (2002), pp. 13–29.

37 Young, *Triumph of the Fatherland*.

38 Christian Lahusen, 'International Campaigns in Context: Collective Action between the Local and the Global', in Donnatella della Porta, Hanspeter Kriesi and Dieter Rucht (eds), *Social Movements in a Globalizing World* (London: Macmillan, 1999), pp. 189–205 and Fouad Hamdan, 'Aufdecken und Konfrontieren: NGO-Kommunikation am Beispiel Greenpeace', *Forschungsjournal Neue Soziale Bewegung*, 13:3 (2000), pp. 69–74.

39 Harald Gesterkamp, 'Professionell auf der Weltbühne, verankert in der Region', *Forschungsjournal Neue Soziale Bewegung*, 13:1 (2000), pp. 92–6.

40 Koopmans, *Democracy from Below.*

41 *Ibid.*

42 *Ibid.*, p. 146.

43 Meyer and Tarrow (eds), *The Social Movement Society.*

44 Rucht, 'The Structure and Culture of Collective Protest in Germany Since 1950'.

45 Dalton, *Citizen Politics.*

46 Bert Klandermans, 'Mobilization Forum: Must We Redefine Social Movements as Ideologically Structured Action?', *Mobilization*, 5:1 (2000), pp. 25–30.

47 Beth Caniglia, 'Informal Alliances vs. Institutional Ties: The Effects of Elite Alliances on Environmental TSMO Networks', *Mobilization*, 6:1 (2001), pp. 37–54.

48 Alice Cooper, 'Party-Sponsored Protest and the Movement Society: The CDU/CSU Mobilizes against Citizenship Law Reform', *German Politics*, 11:2 (2002), pp. 88–104.

49 Gary Marks and Doug McAdam, 'Social Movements and the Changing Structure of Political Opportunity in the European Union', *West European Politics*, 19:2 (1996), pp. 249–78.

50 Doug Imig and Sidney Tarrow, 'The Europeanization of Movements? A New Approach to transnational contention', in Donnatella della Porta, Hanspeter Kriesi and Dieter Rucht (eds), *Social Movements in a Globalizing World* (London: Macmillan, 1999) pp. 112–33.

51 *Ibid.*

52 Marks and McAdam, 'Social Movements'.

53 Gary Marks and Doug McAdam, 'On the Relationship of Political Opportunities to the Form of Collective Action: The Case of the European Union', in Donnatella della Porta, Hanspeter Kriesi and Dieter Rucht (eds), *Social Movements in a Globalizing World* (London: Macmillan, 1999) pp. 97–111.

54 Marks and McAdam, 'Social Movements'.

55 Imig and Tarrow, 'The Europeanization of Movements?'

56 Sidney Tarrow, 'Europeanization of Conflict: Reflections from a Social Movement Perspective', *West European Politics*, 18:2 (1995), pp. 223–51.

57 Rudd Koopmans, 'Globalization or Still National Politics? A comparison of Protests against the Gulf war in Germany, France and the Netherlands', in Donnatella della Porta, Hanspeter Kriesi and Dieter Rucht (eds), *Social Movements in a Globalizing World* (London: Macmillan, 1999) pp. 57–70.
58 Myra Marx Ferree and William Gamson, 'The Gendering of Abortion Discourse: Assessing Global Feminist Influence in the United States and Germany', in Donnatella della Porta, Hanspeter Kriesi and Dieter Rucht (eds), *Social Movements in a Globalizing World* (London: Macmillan, 1999) pp. 40–56.
59 Rucht, 'The Structure and Culture of Collective Protest in Germany since 1950'.
60 Ingo Take, 'Transnationale Allianzen als Anwort auf die Herausforderungen des 21. Jahrhunderts', *Forschungsjournal Neue Soziale Bewegung,* 13:1 (2000), pp. 87–91 and Heike Walk and Achim Brunnengräber, 'Von Mobilisierungsschwächen und kosmopolitischen Grössen: NSBs und NGOs', *Forschungsjournal Neue Soziale Bewegung,* 13:1 (2000), pp. 97–100. Imgo Bode dubbed this development a '*virtuelles Bewegungshandeln*'. See Bode, 'Die Bewegung des Dritten Sektors und ihre Grenzen', *Forschungsjournal Neue Soziale Bewegung,* 13:1 (2000), pp. 48–52.
61 Jupp Legrand, 'Editorial', *Forschungsjournal Neue Soziale Bewegung,* 12:4 (1999), pp. 2–4.
62 *Ibid.*
63 Ansgar Klein, 'Soziale Bewegungen bleiben ein bedeutender politischer Faktor', *Forschungsjournal Neue Soziale Bewegung,* 13:1 (2000), pp. 36–42.
64 Roger Karapin, *Movements and Democracy in Germany: Conventional Participation, Protest and Violence on the Left and Right, 1969–1995,* unpublished book manuscript.
65 Herbert Kitschelt (with Anthony McGann), *The Radical Right in Western Europe* (Ann Arbor: University of Michigan Press, 1997).

10

Neo-nazism in comparative perspective: no longer Germany's problem?

Leonard Weinberg

The twentieth century witnessed the rise and fall of two major challenges to the values of liberal democracy. Marxism–Leninism, particularly as it found expression in the Soviet Union and elsewhere, was the first to come with the 1917 Bolshevik Revolution and the last to leave. After all, the Soviet Union imploded only in 1991. By contrast, European fascism came second, was to a significant extent a reaction against the emergence of communism and was the first to depart the scene; a departure hastened by the military collapse of Fascist Italy and Nazi Germany in the period 1943–45.[1] What is left of these two anti-democratic movements and principles today? What are the remains of the day?

In the case of Marxism–Leninism there is quite a bit to observe. China, the world's most populous country, is still governed by a communist regime which at least pays lip-service to this doctrine. The same may be said with respect to Cuba, Laos, Vietnam and perhaps a few other places as well. Armed insurgencies mounted in the names of Marx, Lenin and Mao are currently under way in Nepal, Peru and Colombia. 'Reformed' communist parties often perform well at the polls in the former eastern European Soviet Bloc countries as well the Russian Federation itself, a country whose present leader is a former officer in the Soviet KGB. Numerous intellectuals, academic and otherwise, continue to treat the ideology with the utmost seriousness, if not exactly as a blueprint for the future then at least as a tool for the analysis of their own societies. In short, Marxism–Leninism lingers on. What about the fascist phenomenon?

Opinions differ on this matter. Some writers contend that fascism or the fascist era, of which Nazism was a central part, ended in 1945. The movements, which brought Mussolini and Hitler to power, and mimetic movements' public visibility elsewhere in Europe were based on social and economic conditions unique to the interwar era.[2] Other observers believe that fascism is still with us today. It has simply undergone a change in location from Europe to places in the Third World where issues of national self-assertion and spiritual renewal seem to call forth charismatic leaders, para-military organisations and 'rogue' regimes, which some believe resemble their European predecessors. For example, in recent years writers have used interwar terminology in referring to Iran as presently dominated by 'clerico-fascism'.[3]

If we refocus our attention on Europe in the early years of the new millennium, what do we find? The answer is that in a number of countries, located in both the western and eastern Europe, there has been a revival of right-wing extremism or right-wing radicalism.

This revival has taken essentially two forms. First, in Austria, France, Italy, Belgium, the Netherlands and to some extent the Scandinavian countries, new or newly reformed parties of the far right have done well at the polls. Beginning in the 1980s and continuing into the next century, parties that Hans-Georg Betz and others have labelled 'right-wing populist' have developed significant constituencies for their views and, in some cases, blocs of seats in their respective parliaments.[4] In both Austria and Italy parties belonging to this family, the Austrian Freedom party and the Italian National Alliance and Northern League, have become part of their countries' ruling coalitions. Germany has been a conspicuous exception in this regard. If we identify Germany's far right as consisting of the Republikaners, National Democrats and the German People's Union, voter support for these parties increased by a total of 0.6 per cent of the vote, from 2.4 per cent to 3.0 per cent, between the 1990 and 1998 national elections.[5] This less than 1 per cent gain occurred at the time of German national reunification, with its concomitant social and economic dislocations.

Does this surge in support for parties of the extreme right indicate we are witnessing a Nazi revival? Or, are these neo-Nazi parties? For Peter Merkl and almost all serious analysts the answer is negative. If there is a consensus, it holds that the new right-wing 'populist' parties, especially the most successful ones, direct their attention to the contemporary issues and problems that confront their advanced industrialised countries rather than those of the interwar era. Concerns about Third World immigration, popular fears about the consequences of economic and cultural 'globalisation', a backlash or a 'silent counter-revolution' against the postmaterialism of Europe's highly educated youth and widespread voter resentments about the performances of the major parties have combined to create a political space for these new extreme-right parties. The latter appear to thrive when they come to be led by charismatic, or at least self-dramatising, figures able to catch the public's attention via their manipulation of electronic media, particularly television appearances. If they and their followers oppose constitutional democracy and capitalism, advocate biological racism or detect a Jewish world-conspiracy, they tend to keep these views to themselves.[6]

Radical right-wing parties have also emerged or reemerged in eastern Europe and the successor states of the former Soviet Union. Their views concerning liberal democracy and the economic benefits of the market place appear far more tenuous than Western Europe's new right-wing populists. According to Christopher Williams,

> Some people across East-Central Europe and the Soviet Successor states, faced with the dual edged sword of political and economic reform have also turned to radical right-wing parties and groupings. Since the collapse of communism in the period 1989–91, nationalists, anti-Semites, racists, xenophobic populists, and authoritarians of all types have competed for the attention of disillusioned voters.[7]

Some of the 'groupings' that Williams mentions might justifiably be called 'neo-Nazi' (although as readers are no doubt aware, authentic Nazis and their successors in the Federal Republic regard Slavic peoples with the utmost contempt – whether or not they dress in Nazi-era regalia and wave swastika-embossed banners), but the parties mentioned bear a closer resemblance to Eastern Europe's interwar far right, the clerico-fascist tradition of Slovakia, Hungary and Romania, than they do to German Nazism, neo or otherwise.

Where does this leave us with respect to neo-Nazism? Where are we to locate this phenomenon? The second form of expression the revival of right-wing extremism has taken involves the use of violence. In recent years and in European countries ranging from Sweden in the north to Spain and Italy in the south, and from Britain in the west to Russia in the east, small bands of young men (typically) have carried out literally thousands of attacks on Third World immigrants, asylum-seekers, foreign students, gypsies, as well as synagogues, cemeteries and other symbols of Jewish life, past and present. Nor is the violence confined to Europe. The United States has had more than its fair share of similarly motivated attacks.

In many instances these attacks have been carried out by inebriated young men (and a few women) simply out for a good time, but lacking any organised political affiliations. In other instances however, the violence has been the work of groups wearing the symbols of and claiming inspiration from the Nazi movement.[8] Some have maintained that these manifestations of racist and xenophobic violence and the new right-wing populist parties' successes among voters vary inversely. In other words, countries where the violence occurs frequently are likely to have parties of the extreme right that do poorly at the polls; and, conversely, places where the radical right does well are locales with rare occurrences of racist/xenophobic violence. We are dealing then, so the argument goes, with two sides of the same coin.[9] This interpretation hardly goes unchallenged – especially when evidence at the regional level is brought to bear on it. It will have to suffice to say, though, that today no European political party, or American for that matter, that takes its participation in the electoral process seriously is willing to express itself in terms which Nazis or neo-Nazis would find compatible.

If we are interested in expressions of contemporary neo-Nazism, the place to look for them is not among the contestants in European (or American) party political activity but among the numerous organisations on the far right that Roger Griffin labels 'groupuscules'.[10] It is among this extended milieu of small far-right groups that neo-Nazism makes its appearance today. At this point, it would be useful to note that by 'neo-Nazi' we have in mind groups or organisations that explicitly venerate the Nazi tradition and define themselves as continuing the work of Hitler and his national socialist movement, especially its racist and anti-Semitic agenda. In large measure, then, the groups involved largely define themselves. Where are such neo-Nazi 'groupuscules' to be found? What are they like? How are they unlike the original Nazi movement of the interwar era? And, finally, what are we to make of them?

In responding to the 'where' question, there is some danger of conveying a false sense of precision by applying numbers to situations where group membership is often volatile and where the groups involved are often ephemeral. Nonetheless, it is possible to make a few general observations. First, in Europe, Germany (and to a lesser extent Austria), Norway and Sweden stand out as countries with comparatively large numbers of explicitly neo-Nazi 'groupuscules'. Appropriately enough, Germany leads the way. Moreau and Backes estimate that in 1998 the Federal Republic had forty separate neo-Nazi groups with a combined membership of approximately 2,400 individuals.[11] At about the same time Austrian police estimate their nation had from 300 to 500 hard-core neo-Nazis with a few thousand fringe supporters.[12] All told there appear to be well over 100 neo-Nazi groups with some thousands of adherents and followers scattered from the Atlantic to the Urals.

The United States is also home to neo-Nazi 'groupuscules', the most prominent of which trace their origins to the late George Lincoln Rockwell's American Nazi Party.[13] At the turn of the new millennium, one estimate placed the number of active neo-Nazi groups in the United States at 130. The latter figure does not include the local branches of such nationally directed bands as the National Alliance and the World Church of the Creator. The figure also does *not* include such racist skinhead groups as the Angry Aryans (Michigan), Aryan National Front (Alabama) and Fourth Reich Skins (Arizona) whose understanding of national socialist doctrine and admiration of Hitler appears limited.[14] Like their counterparts on the other side of the Atlantic, American neo-Nazis have been quick to take advantage of the opportunities provided by the Internet. The Southern Poverty Law Center's *Intelligence Report* listed a total of sixty-three active neo-Nazi websites in 2000.

What are the European and American groups like? Opinions vary on this matter. William Pierce, the recently deceased leader of the National Alliance, noted that the individuals drawn to his cause seemed 'defective'. He apparently meant the word in a biological sense. Another American neo-Nazi, Harold Covington, made the following observation:

> Right now this movement is plagued with little self-appointed SS groups who spend huge bucks in assembling SS paraphernalia and putting it on for secret photographic sessions that almost smack of queers coming out of the closet – indeed in some cases that is exactly what it is. The fact is (and we had better start admitting some of these unpleasant facts) that this movement has a distinct tendency to attract faggots because of the leather-macho image that the System Jew media imparts to the SS uniform … And this is in Carolina, admittedly the best and most selective unit in the Party! The other units are even worse … drug addicts, tattooed women, total bums and losers, police informers, the dregs of urban life.[15]

Ingo Hasselbach, a former youth leader of Berlin's neo-Nazis, paints a similar picture of the individuals with whom he shared a 'Brown House' in that city during the early 1990s.

Based on these assessments, it is easy enough to develop a dismissive caricature of the individuals involved in neo-Nazi activities in recent years. But to do so would be to ignore such figures as the late Michael Kuhnen (Germany), Jürgen Rieger (Germany), William Pierce (United States), Gottfried Kussel (Austria) and Christian Worch (Austria), individuals possessing considerable organisational skill and other intellectual qualities helpful to the cause. The problem they and other aspiring neo-Nazi leaders have is the 'material' with which they have to work. In thinking about the ways in which neo-Nazism differs from the original interwar phenomenon, a number of things come to mind immediately. Let us take them into consideration and then see where these differences take us in developing an overall appraisal of neo-Nazism in the western world.

First, interwar German Nazism was or became a mass movement with a large para-military formation, a movement able to mobilise thousands of individuals onto the streets to participate in parades, ceremonies and various emblematic events. Neo-Nazism, by contrast, operates within the context of a 'cultic milieu' consisting of some hundreds of 'groupuscules' often functioning on a clandestine or semi-clandestine basis.[16] In Germany, Italy and other European democracies, groups which too openly express their support for National Socialism will face legal proscription. In Germany, for example, the public display of the swastika constitutes a crime in and of itself.

Next, for both Nazis and neo-Nazis violence is never far below the surface. But there is a large difference between those early Nazis Peter Merkl defines as 'Marcher-Fighters' and the contemporary violent neo-Nazis.[17] The latter hardly seem exponents of the order, hierarchy, discipline and other martial values of interwar Germany. In the various countries in which they are active, neo-Nazis commit acts of violence often in the manner and style of politicised youth gangs rather than as a disciplined para-military force. Another important difference is evident: certainly in the United States and perhaps elsewhere as well, neo-Nazi marchers often require police protection. When it becomes known there is to be a public demonstration by a neo-Nazi group, the event usually brings out far more anti-Nazi protestors than neo-Nazis. Local law enforcement authorities frequently have to intervene to prevent the neo-Nazis from being pummelled (or worse) by those opposing their public appearance. In Weimar Germany, by contrast, the storm-troopers rarely sought or needed police protection.

Musical preference is another way in which neo-Nazis differ from the originals. Wagnerian operas and military marches hold little attraction for today's neo-Nazi youth. Instead, as Helene Loow describes it, neo-Nazis these days are drawn to 'white power rock 'n' roll' and especially 'white noise' music. The appeal is to youth in rebellion against the establishment. But unlike other music of this genre, the rebellion and the appeal is based on Aryan racial superiority, hatred of Jews and all non-whites and the romance of violent racial conflict. In fact neo-Nazi activists use the music as a recruiting tool through such vehicles as Resistance Records and Nordland:

> White noise recordings, concerts, music magazines, and so on, are the key instruments that have enabled the activists to reach large numbers of young people beyond their 'normal' recruiting ground ... Matti Sundquist, the singer in *Svastika*, remarked: 'The music is very important, both as entertainment, to keep the flame burning, and to recruit people. We have noticed that a lot of people become interested because of the music'.[18]

Third, the interwar Nazi movement was built around the idea of Aryan or Nordic racial superiority. Hitler and his followers had something specific in mind. Not all people with white skin were included in the racially superior category. People of Italian, Spanish, French ethnic origin were defined as 'children of a lesser God'. Virtually all people from Eastern Europe and the Russian regions were defined as *Untermenschen*, incapable of achieving a high level of civilisation. Their lands and later lives were to be forfeit as a consequence of their biological inferiority. These views continue to be widely held among Germany's neo-Nazis as well as their cohorts in the Nordic countries.[19] For instance, after visiting like-minded figures in Spain and elsewhere in Mediterranean Europe, Hasselbach and other German neo-Nazis concluded that fascism was the highest world-view to which these young radical right-wingers could aspire. Racially they were not good enough to be Nazis. Kuhnen always said that national socialism was a 'natural science'. It was about biological facts and hierarchies, while fascism was purely a political and social concept. Spanish Fascists, he went on, might be sympathetic, but 'Our doctrine predetermined all place by race, so they could never be anything but the helpers of our race.'[20]

But this racially exclusionary standard does not prevail in the United States. Early on, George Lincoln Rockwell and other founders of American-style neo-Nazism made a decision to make all whites eligible for membership in their organisations. In ethnically and racially diverse

America, neo-Nazi 'groupuscules' opened their arms to individuals from 'racial' backgrounds that would make them ineligible for neo-Nazi recruitment in Germany and other northern European countries. The United States continues to be a melting pot even for its neo-Nazis.

This is not to say, however, that neo-Nazis in the United States or other countries outside Northern European do not perceive the world in racial terms. They do. However, they have reconceptualised the problem. Their contemporary world-view is one which the 'white race', in general, is in imminent danger of extinction. Whites are to be found in Europe, North America, South Africa, Australia and New Zealand. The white race is the sole source of human creativity and progress. Its members represent a shrinking proportion of the world's population. Inter-racial marriage, abortion and birth control measures are accelerating the decline of the white population. Jews, as expected, are behind these malignant developments.[21] On the basis of a common and threatened racial identity, 'whites' need to overcome various national differences, forge a common inter-continental identity and wage a struggle to save their race from destruction.

These ideas of course bear a resemblance to the national socialist originals. But they have undergone a significant transformation. The conspiratorial role of the Jews remains constant. In place of Aryans waging a struggle against Slavs for living space in Eastern Europe, or ideas about pan-Germanism, the neo-Nazi outlook stresses a worldwide struggle of all whites against the growing demographic menace of non-whites.

The role of Germany in contemporary neo-Nazism is curious. Today neo-Nazis venerate the original Nazi German tradition. Rudolph Hess Day, for example, continues to be celebrated among the various neo-Nazi 'groupuscules' in Europe. Hitler himself is often not merely venerated but often worshiped as a racial saviour. On the other hand, the centre of gravity for contemporary neo-Nazism appears to have moved elsewhere.

During the Nazi era, spokesmen for the 'new Germany' sought to export their ideas to ethnic German communities in European countries and the Americas. For instance, during the 1920s and 1930s, the Nazi party's Foreign Division promoted a succession of organisations in the United States, including the Teutonia Society, Friends of the New Germany and the German-American Bund.[22] Their purpose was to convert German-Americans to the cause of National Socialism.

Today the situation is radically different. Instead of exporting neo-Nazi ideas elsewhere, Germany has become the largely inadvertent importer of these ideas. Officials of the German Federal Criminal Police and the Office for the Protection of the Constitution complain that such neo-Nazi figures as the Nebraskan Gary Lauck are able to take advantage of the American First Amendment to publish and print neo-Nazi propaganda which they then attempt to smuggle into Germany – in violation of its own domestic law. According to Jeffrey Kaplan:

> European governments take a dim view of National Socialist propaganda and the German government in particular has gone to great lengths to outlaw such material. For almost two decades in the United States, however, Lauck, protected by the First Amendment, produced tremendous quantities of such propaganda, translated it into German ... and smuggled it into Germany with apparent ease ... German neo-Nazi leader Ingo Hasselbach went so far as to claim that the German neo-Nazi network would collapse without Lauck.[23]

Other figures from Europe and Latin America have joined Lauck in efforts to export Nazi propaganda material from their countries of origin to the Federal Republic.

In recent years the propaganda has found a new medium for its expression: the internet, and the world wide web, in particular. The advantages to neo-Nazis (and others) are evident. The internet offers, or seems to offer, a low-cost way to reach a significant audience. Second, it provides a way of communicating directly to an audience without the message being filtered through other, usually hostile, means of mass communication. Next, the message may be conveyed in a format involving online games and music so as to make it attractive to younger audiences, obviously a prime target for recruitment. Also, since the internet cuts across national jurisdictions, efforts to combat neo-Nazi propaganda requires significant cooperation among the countries involved in the dissemination and receipt of these cyberspace communications.[24]

Neo-Nazis and other racists have been quick to take advantage of the web and the possibilities offered by chat rooms. A report submitted to the Council of Europe's Parliamentary Assembly indicated there were approximately 600 racist websites in 1997 and that by 2001 the figure had risen to 4,000.[25] As in the case of the print format for neo-Nazi propaganda, so too in this instance the United States stands apart. German law is prohibitive while the American courts have not been willing to impose limits on freedom of expression short of messages containing 'fighting words'. As a result many German neo-Nazi propagandists and Holocaust deniers have shifted their websites to American servers in order to evade prosecution. In any case, the overall pattern ultimately involves the importation into Germany of propaganda originating elsewhere.

The centre of gravity of contemporary neo-Nazism has shifted from Germany in another way. Since the demise of the Third Reich various attempts have been made to form a neo-Nazi international, a peak organisation which could pull together like-minded groups in Europe, North and South America, South Africa, Australia and New Zealand. In the immediate aftermath of the Second World War, these efforts were undertaken by German ex-patriots, *SS* veterans hoping to keep the flame alive. Martin Lee, for instance, pays particular attention to such third- or forth-echelon Nazi figures as Otto Remer, Reinhard Gehlen and Otto Skorzeny.[26]

With the passage of time, the initiative shifted elsewhere. During the 1950s a European Social Movement was organised in Malmo (Sweden) by French, Italian and Swedish neo-fascists who hoped to save the continent from Bolshevism. Another and more explicitly anti-Semitic and racist international, the European New Order (NOE), was formed in Zurich (Switzerland). NOE hoped to promote a common European identity by, among other things, prohibiting marriages between Europeans and non-Europeans.

The 1960s witnessed still more attempts to create neo-Nazi internationals. The war in Algeria over the continuation of French domination as well as Belgium's departure from the Congo, led Jean Thiriat, the Belgian neo-Nazi optometrist, to promote *Jeune Europe* to rally support for a European 'Third Way' between America and the Soviet Union. In this regard he echoed the views of the American ex-patriot and neo-Nazi Francis Parker Yockey, who organised the European Liberation Front in order to expel both the Americans and Soviets from the continent.[27] The most ambitious of these neo-Nazi internationals was the World Union of National Socialists (WUNS). WUNS was the creation of George Lincoln Rockwell and Colin Jordan, the English neo-Nazi leader. To quote Rockwell's biographer Frederick Simonelli:

> From its founding in 1962 to the European neo-Nazi resurgence following the fall of communism ... the World Union of National Socialists played a key role in preserving the ideology, mythology, and rhetoric of Nazism and in transferring that belief system to subsequent generations of adherents. WUNS was the organizational bridge between the leading

> neo-Nazi movement in post-war America … and the fragmented and disparate national neo-Nazi cells in post-war Europe.[28]

WUNS was created at a meeting in the Cotswolds in Gloucestershire (England) and subsequently developed links to like-minded groups in Iceland, Denmark, Belgium, France, South Africa, Australia, Chile and Argentina – not to mention Britain and the United States. The point to be emphasised or reiterated is that WUNS and the other neo-Nazi internationals may have venerated Hitler and celebrated the Third Reich retrospectively but they were not centred in the contemporary Germany of the Federal Republic. Neo-Nazism became and has continued to be a more global though infinitely weaker version of the original.

Two more points need to be stressed in the effort to reach an overall assessment of the neo-Nazi phenomenon. First, many of those who hope to achieve a National Socialist revival, to make contemporary neo-Nazism more than a collection of 'groupuscules' on the fringes of social and political life in the democracies, have needed to deal with the barrier posed by the Holocaust. While some among the neo-Nazis regard the extermination of European Jewry with relish and lament the fact that Hitler was not able to complete the job, the record of mass murder restricts the potential appeal to a wider audience. As a consequence, neo-Nazi groups and publicists have devoted an enormous amount of time and effort to Holocaust denial.[29] The transparent neo-Nazi purpose in falsifying the historical record, typically claiming that 'the Jews' were the original distorters, is to cleanse Hitler and his regime of the genocidal crime and in so doing make them more attractive to European and North American audiences.

Finally, whatever else may be said, Hitler and the other leaders of the original Nazi movement articulated concrete plans and objectives concerning the economic and political reorganisation of the Fatherland. Celebration of the country's Nordic racial heritage certainly played a role. Despite the cant and histrionics, for the most part the movement was in touch with reality. Contemporary neo-Nazism, on the other hand, exhibits strong elements of fantasy and unreality. Not uncommonly the 'groupuscules' belong to a 'cultic milieu', a curious religious environment of pre- or anti-Christian worship of Wotan and the other gods of the Norse pantheon. Satanism has also developed some appeal for those within this 'cultic milieu'.[30] Instead of Nazi 'science' and social Darwinism, contemporary neo-Nazis often emphasise the occult with exotic interpretations of human history coupled to science fictional accounts of the current world situation. Curiously then neo-Nazism appears increasingly to be a product of the postmodern sensibility than it is of interwar Europe.

Notes

1 For a general history of the phenomenon, see Stanley Payne, *A History of Fascism* (Madison, WI: University of Wisconsin Press, 1995); or from a somewhat different perspective, see Roger Eatwell, *Fascism: A History* (New York: Penguin, 1996).

2 See, for example, Renzo De Felice, *Fascism: An Informal Introduction to its Theory and Practice* (New Brunswick, NJ: Transaction, 1976), pp. 97–107 and Juan Linz, 'Fascism is Dead', in Stein Larsen (ed.), *Modern Europe After Fascism*, 1 (New York: Columbia University Press, 1996), pp. 19–51.

3 The idea of Third World fascism has been approached from various angles; see, for example, James Gregor, *Italian Fascism and Developmental Dictatorship* (Princeton: Princeton University Press, 1979) and Roger Griffin, *The Nature of Fascism* (New York: Routledge, 1991). For a discussion of 'clerico-fascism', see Hugh R. Trevor-Roper, 'The Phenomenon of Fascism', in S. J. Woolf (ed.), *European Fascism* (New York: Vintage Books, 1968), pp. 18–38.

4 Hans-Georg Betz, *Radical Right Wing Populism in Western Europe* (New York: St Martin's Press, 1994) and Hans-Georg Betz and Stefan Immerfall (eds), *The New Politics of the Right* (New York: St Martin's Press, 1998). See, especially, Herbert Kitschelt, *The Radical Right in Western Europe* (Ann Arbor: University of Michigan Press, 1995).

5 Allen Wilcox, Leonard Weinberg and William Eubank, 'Explaining National Variations in Support for Far Right Political Parties in Western Europe, 1990–2000', in Peter H. Merkl and Leonard Weinberg (eds), *Right-Wing Extremism in the Twenty-First Century* (London: Frank Cass, 2003), pp. 126–43.

6 The literature on this topic is now quite substantial. For an assessment, see Peter Merkl, 'Stronger than Ever', in Peter H. Merkl and Leonard Weinberg (eds), *Right-Wing Extremism in the Twenty-First Century* (London: Frank Cass, 2003), pp. 23–46.

7 Christopher Williams, 'Problems of Transition and the Rise of the Radical Right', in Sabrina Ramet (ed.), *The Radical Right in Central and Eastern Europe Since 1989* (College Park, PA: Pennsylvania State University Press, 1999), p. 45.

8 For a discussion, see Helmut Willems, 'Development, Patterns and Causes

of Violence against Foreigners in Germany', in Tore Bjorgo (ed.), *Terror from the Far Right* (London: Frank Cass, 1995), pp. 162–81. For a first-hand account, see Ingo Hasselbach, *Fuhrer-Ex: Memoirs of a Former Neo-Nazi* (New York: Random House, 1996).

9 Ruud Koopmans, 'Explaining the Rise of Racist and Extreme Right Violence in Western Europe', *European Journal of Political Research*, 30:3 (1996), pp. 185–216.

10 Roger Griffin, 'Net Gains and GUD Reactions: Patterns of Prejudice in a Neo-Fascist Groupuscule', *Patterns of Prejudice*, 33:2 (2000), pp. 31–50.

11 Patrick Moreau and Uwe Backes, 'Federal Republic of Germany', in Jean-Yves Camus (ed.), *Extremism in Europe* (Paris: CERA, 1998), pp. 150–76.

12 *Antisemitism World Report 1996* (London: Institute for Jewish Policy Research, 1996), p. 80.

13 For an account of Rockwell's life see Fred Simonelli, *American Fuehrer: George Lincoln Rockwell and the American Nazi Party* (Champaign, IL: University of Illinois Press, 1999).

14 The Southern Poverty Center, 'Active Hate Groups in the United States', *Intelligence Report 97* (Winter 2000), pp. 32–9.

15 Quoted in Jeffrey Kaplan, 'Right-Wing Violence in North America', in Tore Bjorgo (ed.), *Terror from the Far Right* (London: Frank Cass, 1995), p. 56.

16 Yaron Svoray, an Israeli journalist, captures the atmosphere in his *In Hitler's Shadow* (Garden City, NY: Doubleday, 1994).

17 Peter Merkl, *Political Violence under the Swastika* (Princeton: Princeton University Press, 1975), pp. 383–407.

18 Helene Loow, 'White Power Rock 'n' Roll: A Growing Industry', in Jeffrey Kaplan and Tore Bjorgo (eds), *Nation and Race* (Boston: Northeastern University Press, 1998), p. 137.

19 See, for example, Rand Lewis, *A Nazi Legacy* (New York: Praeger, 1991), pp. 1–2.

20 Hasselbach, *Führer-Ex*, p. 168.

21 See, for example, Jeffrey Kaplan and Leonard Weinberg, *The Emergence of a Euro-American Radical Right* (New Brunswick, NJ: Rutgers University Press, 1998), pp. 14–22.

22 See, Charles Higham, *American Swastika* (Garden City, NY: Doubleday, 1985), pp. 121–33.

23 Jeffrey Kaplan, *Encyclopedia of White Power: A Source Book on the Radical Racist Right* (Walnut Creek, CA: AltaMira Press, 2000), p. 171.

24 Niraj Nathwani, 'Atlantic Divide on Fight against Racist Websites', *Equal Voices*, 10:11 (2002), pp. 11–19.

25 *Ibid.*, p. 11.

26 Martin Lee, *The Beast Reawakens* (Boston: Little Brown, 1997), pp. 85–118.

27 Kevin Coogan, *Dreamer of the Day* (New York: Autonomedia, 1999), pp. 532–55.

28 Frederick Simonelli, 'Thriving in a Cultic Milieu: The World Union of National Socialists, 1962–1992', in Jeffrey Kaplan and Helene Loow (eds), *The Cultic Milieu* (Walnut Creek, CA: Altamira Press, 2002), pp. 211–12.

29 The literature here is very substantial; see, for example, Michael Schermer and Alex Grobman, *Denying History* (Berkeley: University of California Press, 2000), pp. 39–97.

30 See, for example, Nicholas Goodrick-Clarke, *Black Sun* (New York: New York University Press, 2002), pp. 213–33.

Part IV

Political parties in the Berlin Republic

11
German party system change

William M. Chandler

Parties provide the primary intermediaries between the citizen and the state. They constitute the principal, if not the sole, channel for elite recruitment and they play vital roles in articulating ideologies and in setting political agendas. For these reasons, parties constitute essential features of the democratic process. Not surprisingly then, changes in this structure carry great meaning for the quality and performance of democracy itself.

Systemic change refers not to the immediate political fortunes of election winners and losers, but rather to the restructuring of competition among parties. This is what fundamentally differentiates party systems over time and one from another. However, problems in identifying such variation often arise owing to the multi-faceted nature and simultaneous functioning of parties as primary agents in parliamentary coalition formation and governance, as providers of organisational infrastructure for the representation and mediation of societal interests, as loyalty networks for their core electorates and finally as activators of broader popular support in the quest for gaining or sharing power.

Although seismic upheavals in patterns of party competition are quite rare (with Italy in the 1990s providing the best recent example), we frequently are likely to sense minor tremors within systems. Assessing the extent of change within a given system involves specifying those conditions that make change likely or unlikely. In general, comparative analysis of party system change has argued that such change depends on two general factors, social cleavages and political institutions. As explored below, to these classic explanations we should add the unusual impact of exogenous jolts.

The extension of mass suffrage meant that parties had to compete for mass electoral support by building membership organisations and establishing solid bases among the previously non-enfranchised. As universal suffrage was achieved, parties anchored themselves on the basis of social class, confessional or regional identities. Social cleavage structures undoubtedly have formed the bedrock for party loyalty, with divisions based on class and religion especially important for the shape of modern European party systems. Over generations, party loyalties 'froze', producing extraordinary stability across party systems in advanced democratic systems.[1] According to the theory of the freezing of party alignments, modernisation and social change do not easily destroy established cleavage bases of party support, but increasingly we have come to question the extent to which modern party systems still express these divisions.

While it is difficult to generalise across party systems about how much change has occurred, in the past forty years we certainly have observed the shrinking of traditional class and confessional bonds, allowing for the partial melting of loyalties and an expanding electoral volatility. This has partially dissipated the holding power of classic ideological and 'milieu' parties. Catch-all *Volksparteien* (people's parties), too, have also suffered erosion in their historic bases of support. Correspondingly, from an organisational perspective, mass integration parties have given way to electoral–professional parties.[2] Such flux notwithstanding, it remains true for most liberal democracies that the core parties spanning the centre-right to centre-left have endured, adapted and, importantly, have continued to be the usual parties of government. In this vein, Peter Mair has cautioned against overstating the extent and impact of new volatility in popular support, in part because much of this shifting has occurred *within* blocs of left and right rather than across them.[3]

Beyond socio-economic, confessional and subcultural divisions, political institutions set parameters for party competition and shape the structure of that competition. Although infrequent, the most dramatic institutional changes occur through regime breakdowns. Subsequent constitutional revisions redefined the exercise of political power through those elective offices crucial to governing. Because these offices are always the prime objects of electoral competition, such constitutional revisions may crucially alter the role of parties and the nature of competition among them. Modern German history presents us with a rich laboratory of such systemic crises.

As Peter Merkl in his numerous writings has always recognised,

German politics is distinctive owing to unique and special conditions, which are the consequence of both a particularly traumatic history and of conscious efforts to avoid the mistakes of the past.[4] Recurrent crises have made democratic stability a German preoccupation in which centrality of parties has been primordial.[5]

The formative phase for German parties followed immediately from Bismarck's 1871 unification of the German Reich. This regime instituted free elections for the *Reichstag* under universal male suffrage, and party organisations developed rapidly. However, the Kaiser, rather than parliamentary majorities, selected and removed his Chancellor, who in turn determined the composition of the government. Without governments being accountable to parliament, parties inherited perverse incentives to solidify their bases rather than to build governing alliances. Thus, lacking a fully democratic system, party competition tended towards fragmentation and polarisation.[6] Parties typically functioned as defenders of economic class interests or confessional subcultures.[7] Most parties remained regionally concentrated. By 1913, only the SPD could claim to be a fully national party.

Defeat in the First World War led to the collapse of the Kaiserreich, the proclamation of the Weimar Republic and the creation of parliamentary democracy. In a revolutionary climate, parties suddenly assumed the primary governing role but without a deep liberal democratic commitment on the part of many influential elites. The Weimar constitution established an exceptionally representative and democratic parliamentary democracy that had to mesh with a highly polarised party system. For the first time, parties themselves governed within unstable coalitions. Pillarised patterns of representation allowed for the perpetuation of an ideological and highly fragmented party competition, and provided the bases for bitter partisan struggle. This proved explosive given the negative post-Versailles atmosphere of reparations and repressed nationalistic resentments. When the stock market crashed in 1929, economic depression devastated Germany. The electoral consequences were immediate. In the 1930 *Reichstag* elections, the Nazi vote jumped from a mere 2.6 per cent to 18.3 per cent. The liberal middle-class parties were besieged and the extremes gained, in a classic expression of Giovanni Sartori's polarised pluralism.[8] Stable governing coalitions became impossible as the regime lurched from coalitional crisis to presidential emergency rule. The tragic effects culminated with Hitler's *Machtergreifung* (seizure of power), which eliminated all party competition for the next twelve years.

Postwar rebuilding and the evolution of party competition

Following unconditional surrender in 1945, the victorious military authorities within their Zones of Occupation controlled the rebirth of parties. In the Soviet Zone, four anti-Nazi parties were licensed, the KPD, SPD, CDU and LDP, but the Soviet military command advantaged the KPD in appointments to key offices. Then followed the forced merger (*Zwangsvereinigung*) of the communists and socialists into a single SED. Once the GDR was founded, the rationale of 'Dictatorship of the Proletariat' provided for the SED appropriation to itself the role of vanguard party within an anti-fascist National Front of block-parties and social organisations. This multi-party facade poorly disguised the concentration of power and the effective exclusion of opposition voices. The SED's monopoly of power relied a *nomenklatura* system of party-book recruitment to all high offices.[9]

In the three western zones, parties were also reestablished under licensing by military occupation authorities, but developed quite differently. Starting at the local level, then in the *Länder*, parties quickly assumed a primary role of rebuilding democracy. This laid the foundation for reestablishing legitimacy and stability. In the 1949 Basic Law, they were accorded constitutional status.[10] Article 21 of the Basic Law defines the positive role of parties and sets limits on anti-democratic formations. The Party Law of 1967 and rulings of the Federal Constitutional Court have subsequently defined the meaning of *Parteienstaat*, which expresses the centrality of parties.

Beyond these constitutional and legal bases of a competitive multi-party system, other crucial institutional effects are found in the electoral system and in German federalism. The Federal Republic's unique electoral law provides for the election of one-half of the Bundestag directly through single-member districts and the other half via party lists. However, this two-ballot system of personalised proportionality is not a mixed single-member district/proportional representation system, because the total party-seat share is determined by the second (proportional) list ballot.

The first Bundestag election in 1949 could be considered the last Weimar election, because it appeared to have recreated the major divisions of pre-1933 Germany. However, by 1953, a new pattern of party competition was taking shape. Simplification was primarily accomplished with the national application of the '5 per cent rule'. Minor parties were coopted by Konrad Adenauer into the CDU and others gradually disappeared. However, proportionality did not lead to renewed fragmentation primarily owing to the 5 per cent share of the vote minimum to qualify for party representation in the Bundestag. The implementation of this rule nationally in 1953 dramatically simplified the party system.[11] In the post-unity era, the three direct mandates (constituency) exception to the 5 per cent hurdle, as well as the possibility of excess mandates (*Überhangmandate*) have had significant impacts on party representation and on shaping governing coalitions. The two-ballot system, by promoting strategic voting via ticket-splitting, has also had important benefits for smaller parties and has affected coalition formation.

Federalism provides for both a division and sharing of power, which allows for a *Land*-level regional voice and corresponding party system variation. This, too, has had a number of consequences for shaping party politics. The *Länder* provide opportunity for new parties to enter the system and have functioned occasionally as testing grounds for new coalition options. Within the policy process, the *Länder* in the Bundesrat may play a direct role, sometimes as a veto player, in blocking or modifying government agendas.[12]

The most basic changes in the party system have involved simplification and convergence. Convergence has been possible by virtue of the transition from class-milieu parties to catch-all *Volksparteien*, of which the CDU/CSU provided the prototype. The postwar establishment of the CDU/CSU as a new party type ranks among the most important of these. The choice not to recreate a Catholic redoubt on the model of the old Centre party allowed the development of a loose catch-all formation spanning the Catholic–Protestant divide and was designed to provide a broad umbrella for various regional groupings and to maximise its share of the electorate. Once in power, Chancellor Adenauer successfully also coopted leaders from many of the existing the minor party formations and absorbed their voters into the CDU/CSU camp. For much of the postwar era, the Christian democrats could claim a natural advantage in support, usually about 5 per cent above the SPD. However, since Kohl's first election as Chancellor in 1983, CDU/CSU federal support suffered a steady, slow erosion, hitting a low point in 1998.

In the 1950s, Adenauer's CDU/CSU, by expanding its base of electoral support, became the dominant party of government. In opposition, the SPD initially sought to retain its self-definition as the party of the working class and to hold on to its Marxist heritage. This strategy meshed poorly in a climate of Cold War division and anti-communism, and the SPD suffered badly in competition against the more dynamic Adenauer party. The prospects of permanent opposition forced the SPD to adapt programmatically and strategically in order to better imitate the CDU/CSU's broad catch-all success. Belatedly, the social democrats achieved their own internal conversion. The SPD's Bad Godesberg programme of 1959 finally rejected the ideological baggage of Marxism and moved toward a more pragmatic social democracy. This meant the acceptance of the mixed economy as well as Germany's place in the Western Alliance and in Europe. This new ideological flexibility made the SPD attractive to the growing middle-class electorate. Convergence with the far more successful CDU/CSU, expressed in Kirchheimer's famous 'waning of opposition' thesis, came to mean inter-party consensus across many value positions.[13]

Simplification and convergence produced a stable 'two-and-a-half' party system in which the FDP remained the third player. Historically, the FDP has always been a classic middle-class party, with strong secular roots and solid support among civil servants, entrepreneurs and the well educated. As a party which usually garnered less than 10 per cent of the vote, it enjoyed a quite remarkable postwar role as a coalition partner of both CDU/CSU and SPD. Its governing influence derived primarily from its pivotal coalition maker role. All three coalition possibilities persisted until the early 1980s, making it a triangular system.[14]

The high point of convergence, during the SPD–CDU/CSU Grand Coalition between 1966 and 1969, left only the FDP in the opposition and gave rise to radical protest on both the left and right. This phase saw the first serious revival of extremism, marked with the partial breakthrough of the neo-Nazi NPD, which in 1969 narrowly missed gaining entry to the Bundestag with 4.3 per cent vote.

When the 1970s introduced a new dynamic of dealignment, this process began to challenge the stability and persistence of party support in most democracies. These changes were rooted in socio-economic and value transformations. Gradual declines in class voting could be traced back to changing occupational structures. Particularly significant was the decline of the industrial blue-collar voter, which posed severe challenges for social democrats. Social democratic socio-economic bastions were always located in secular, urban–industrial centres, and their core electorate remained skilled workers, especially trades union members.

The unionised share of the electorate has also declined over time. This change had dramatic effects on the SPD. Of necessity, it had to appeal to a broad range of white-collar employees as well. For the CDU and CSU, the corresponding challenge was the progressive secularisation of German society and the decline in the number of voters who attended church regularly, particularly among Catholics. The bastions of this most successful catch-all party were diverse, but were concentrated among church-goers, especially Catholics, across the broad middle classes, and especially in the traditional *Mittelstand.* Secularisation eroded the CDU core. In the post-industrial age, the territory occupied by the tertiary white-collar and service sectors, broadly speaking the new middle classes, became the crucial competitive battleground for all parties. Since the late 1960s, the psychological disengagement from parties meant greater voter volatility and greater potential for new parties to challenge the preeminence of well-established political families.[15] The resultant declining strength of partisanship implied an expanding potential for protest politics.

The primary expressions of protest politics were the rise of new social movements, primarily 'green' parties, as well as some populist advances, but these rarely portended comprehensive transformations in party systems. In 1983, with the entry of the Greens into the Bundestag the structure of systemic relations began to shift toward a bipolar model of competition between two camps of right and left and a shift away from the prevailing 'two and-a-half' party system to one of alternation between two blocs. By the late 1980s, some revival of xenophobic nationalism resurfaced, but was temporarily side-tracked by unification.[16] However, the newly opened borders of post-unification Germany encouraged waves of asylum seekers and refugees that provoked a renewal of extremism. From 1991 to 1993, the far right enjoyed regional successes in an atmosphere of insecurity. Importantly, as this issue was defused by policy compromise, far-right support faded.

Unification and the evolution of party competition

The Gorbachev revolution counts as one of those rare, unanticipated exogenous shocks that may reshape democratic politics. The collapse of the GDR and the almost instant unification reverberated throughout German politics and prompted substantial political and policy recalibrations, but party-system effects were felt primarily in the east. SED one-party rule was abolished and a free, competitive, multi-party system was installed with the wholesale transfer of West German party competition into the territory of the former GDR.[17] The fusion of the two German states increased the size of the German population and electorate by one-fifth. However, as Charlie Jeffery has noted: 'Unification brought together a dealigning western electorate with an essentially non-aligned eastern one.'[18]

Established western parties had to sink roots within an eastern electorate, but quickly encountered obstacles to building effective organisations. The GDR's decrepit bloc-party façade, although at first seemingly doomed, left a mixed legacy of activist beneficiaries from the old regime, many of whom had cooperated with the *Stasi.* The bloc parties' feeble organisations lacked competent members ready for recruitment into elected office. Both CDU and FDP faced severe internal clashes between the old guard and younger renewalists, while the gradual exit of older bloc-party members was not matched by the recruitment of a younger *corps.*[19] For the SPD, there was no available partner from the old regime, leaving it at an initial organisational disadvantage. Unification provided no bonus for the Greens, who only after great internal strain eventually merged with its much smaller eastern partner, *Bündnis '90,* whose core was located among the dissident civil rights movements of the GDR. In 1990, the Greens' ambivalent response to unification was translated into the exclusion of their western wing from the Bundestag (also owing in part to the bad luck of a temporary electoral law that disadvantaged them). Oddly, the weaker *Bündnis '90* in the east did elect members, thus keeping the party alive in the Bundestag.

Although the PDS had to adapt itself to competitive pluralism, it enjoyed the advantage of being the only indigenous eastern party. In the 1990 Bundestag elections, the PDS survived thanks to a ruling of the Constitutional Court, which imposed a one-time-only electoral law that created two districts, east and west, in which the 5 per cent hurdle could be passed. This favoured the PDS, which won 11.1 per cent in the east, largely from former SED adherents, but only 2.4 per cent of the vote cast across the entire Federal Republic. Thereafter, the party consolidated itself but has remained vulnerable as an aging, regional party. Its defeat in the 2002 Bundestag elections lent credence to this view.

Renormalisation marked the most recent Bundestag elections. The election of 1998 was a watershed in a number of ways. Most importantly, it produced a governing 'power shift' with the first eviction of a ruling party/coalition directly by the voters. After some sixteen years in opposition and numerous electoral setbacks, the SPD was led by the new Chancellor candidate, Gerhard Schröder, and pursued a conscious strategy of competing for the middle ground. This strategy brought about the first complete right to left transfer of political control in creating a Red–Green majority. Schröder's victory was made easier by the ineffectiveness of Helmut Kohl's overly personalised campaign, but it also had deeper roots. 1998 also marked the last Bonn election and the emotive transition to the 'Berlin Republic'. In terms of party system change, it represented an apparent consolidation of a five-party system federally.[20]

The new left-wing coalition continued to contain within itself unresolved internal tensions, and was initially beset by internal in-fighting, policy gaffes and loss of popular support. Disastrous losses followed in a series of regional and local elections beginning with the February 1999 upset in Hesse. In preparing for the 2002 elections, the Red–Green coalition found itself on the defensive owing to an economic slowdown and high unemployment, but was saved by floods and then by the Bush administration's intention to wage war against Iraq.

For the CDU/CSU, 1998 produced the lowest level of popular support (35.1 per cent) since 1949. Post-election, the CDU, although psychologically down, enjoyed a quick, brief revival in *Landtag* elections. This advance was cut short by the exposure of the Kohl secret party funding scandal in November 1999, which left the CDU in disarray. Turnover in leadership was sudden, especially after Wolfgang Schäuble became implicated and had to step aside in favour of an inexperienced and untested Angela Merkel. The atmosphere of scandal meant a reprieve for the struggling Socialists and Greens, who had not yet adjusted to the role of governing. The CSU meanwhile remained the most stable core of conservatism. In 2002, the rallying of the CDU/CSU behind the candidacy of Edmund Stoiber raised the old question of whether a Bavarian could win a federal election as the party Chancellor candidate. Stoiber's ambitions to be Chancellor candidate surfaced as the prospects of winning increased. His candidacy turned out to be a near-miss failure. Last-minute shifts within the electorate had enormous significance: the 2002 election was the closest election in memory, with just 9,000 votes separating the two major parties. The SPD lost substantial numbers of voters, but retained its claim to being the largest party in the Bundestag. It also benefited from the *Überhangmandate* (excess seats) which meant a net gain for the SPD of 3 seats.

The Greens have always lived with natural internal tensions, but the former 'anti-party party' has undergone significant moderation as pragmatism in the exercise of power has become crucial to power sharing. In 2002, behind the personalised campaign of Joschka Fischer and the mobilisation of anti-war sentiment, the Green advance was decisive to survival of the coalition in the face of heavy SPD losses in the western *Länder*. Fischer's impact as an extraordinarily popular foreign minister showed the power of personalisation even within a party viscerally hostile to the institutionalisation of leadership.

In 1998, the PDS surpassed the 5 per cent hurdle and become a parliamentary *Fraktion*, but the state of its long-term health remained in question, particularly given the internal ambivalence towards accepting unconditionally a market-based political economy. Nor has the PDS been able to overcome the inherent weaknesses of an aging membership and lack of roots in the west. These electoral handicaps clearly surfaced in 2002 when it had to accept a disastrous defeat when it gained only 4 per cent of the vote. The PDS' loss was the SPD's gain: the SPD established a dominant position in the east in 2002, in good part by capturing a chunk of the PDS electorate.

Although one can hardly underestimate the importance of the catch-all *Volksparteien* for the continuity found in the German party system,[21] it also remains true that their integrative capacities have diminished over time. 2002 was the first election since 1949 in which both CDU/CSU and SPD failed to garner over 40 per cent of the popular vote. The tension between the modern versus the traditional wings of the SPD has never been fully resolved and hit a crisis point with a post-election free-fall in popularity. This forced Schröder's hand to move hard for economic structural reforms, against the wishes of the trades unions and the left wing of his party.

In 2002, the most significant development for the structure of party competition was the demise of the PDS in federal politics. Its demise has permitted the consolidation of the Red–Green coalition, a pattern of bi-polar government and opposition relations, a return to a four-party system. 2002 was a bitter defeat for the CDU/CSU, which must still resolve its own internal tensions and settle the leadership question. The FDP has once again shown its survivability, but its uncertain future remains owing to its lack of a stable core electorate.

Assessing a half-century of German party evolution

The first Bundestag election in 1949 opened the possibility of a return to Weimar fragmentation. However, the 1953 installation nationally of the 5 per cent hurdle initiated the processes of concentration and simplification of competition took firm hold. By the 1980s, partial dealignment had loosened up party loyalties, but the basic structure of competition was only partially modified. Looking back over time, we also discover a number of significant trends in the German party system that predate unification, including the changing social bases of party loyalties, the relative decline in party core support and increasing electoral volatility. Many of these changes are artifacts of economic modernisation, social mobility and secularisation. Across Germany, two concentrations of volatile voters have become the object of intense interest for party strategies. One is the expanding new middle-class electorate, where voters tend to be available by virtue of their mobility. The other is the electorate of eastern Germany, among whom, even more than a decade after unification, relatively feeble party loyalty exists, and for whom the major parties imported from the west have provided limited appeal. Both types of voters are likely to be relatively issue-sensitive and susceptible to immediate appeals of party campaigns.

Beyond such broad trends, all German parties have endured new challenges based on new tensions resultant from unification's integration of east and west. Unification also reversed traditional class ties among eastern voters. In 1990, their eagerness and gratefulness for unification initially gave Helmut Kohl a diverse base among blue-collar voters. However, the CDU could not replicate its (western) confessional basis, and in recent elections voting patterns have partially reconverged towards western patterns. The SPD's capture of a large portion of the eastern working-class vote became fully evident, especially in its regional gains in the 2002 contest.

Another essential feature of party system change directly related to unification involves the new regionalism. Pre-unification, the Federal Republic's primary regional divide was north–south. Unification has unavoidably created the east–west divide as a prime factor shaping the evolution of party competition. In the new *Länder*, we have also observed the further demise of both Greens/*Bündnis '90* and the FDP, where a three-party configuration took hold, as the PDS solidified its base as a regional party of protest. While this explains its surprising survival in 1990 and its adaptation in the 1994 and 1998 elections, the consolidation of regional support has not allowed the PDS to purge itself of inherent vulnerabilities. Its aging membership has compartmentalised its appeal. This became fully evident in 2002, which signalled the probable marginalisation of the PDS as a federal party. Even if the east has remained characterised by a regionally distinct party system, in the long run, and even allowing for some *Länder* distinctiveness, its persistence seems unlikely, given pressures towards an integrated national politics. The PDS' decline has also permitted a degree of 'normalisation' with the reemergence of a four-party model of competition. At the *Land* level, two distinct patterns persist: in the east, a three-party system consisting of SPD, CDU and PDS, while in the old west, we observe the persistence of a four-party system.

Significantly, the German party system has continued on its course towards bi-polarity, which has increased the likelihood of coalitional alternatives in governance. From 1994 through 2002, elections have demonstrated an essential bi-polar division. Perhaps the most significant consequences of post-unity party system change involve coalition-building in governing functions. If some deeply ingrained features of party competition persist, coalition possibilities have altered. Greater balance has given the SPD an advantage, as the pivot in several possible coalition scenarios, over the CDU/CSU which normally can count only on the FDP as a coalition partner. Notably in the east, the SPD has joined either grand coalitions or Red–Red coalitions. Elsewhere the SPD has had the possibility of different governing combinations (with the Greens, CDU or FDP).

The reshaping process has also affected the crucial minor parties. Over a quarter-century of organisational development, the Greens have developed their bastions almost entirely within urban areas and amongst non-church-going, highly educated voters. For this reason, we can observe the stabilisation of a reliable Green electorate in west, but not in the east. The Greens' eastern partners, the *Bündnis 90*, grew out of the small civil rights groups and former GDR dissidents and has continued to suffer from a restricted membership and appeal.

The FDP by the mid-1990s seemed to have become, ominously, a party lacking its own social core or regional bastion. Accordingly, its survival came to depend increasingly on loaned votes from a coalition partner, usually the CDU/CSU.[22] In the 1990s, repeated setbacks in *Landtag* elections made its prospects for 1998 look doubtful. Although its crucial pivot function appeared to have been lost with defeat in 1998, the often-predicted demise of the FDP has never happened. Survival allowed the FDP to redefine its own distinctive place in the electorate. With the smashing victory of over 10 per cent in the May 2000 *Landtag* election in North-Rhine Westphalia and its 9.9 per cent share of the vote in the October 2001 Berlin city election, the FDP was back in play. However, new disappointment was not far off with a poor showing in the 2002 Bundestag elections. Party leader Guido Westwerwelle's attempt to portray himself as chancellor material was unconvincing, while the refusal to announce a preference for a coalition with the CDU/CSU may have cost it some crucial loaned voters on the second ballot.

The shock of unification has not facilitated any sustained revival of extremism.[23] Despite anomalous regional instances, like the German People's Union's (DVU) 12.9 per cent share of the vote in Saxony-Anhalt in 1998, the far right has remained splintered and prone to self-destructive tendencies. With highly unstable social bases, these fringe parties remain akin to flash-party phenomena in which surprise success is quickly followed by political collapse. The 1998 Bundestag election and subsequent *Landtag* contests produced no signs of sustained extremism, and 2002 witnessed a halving of support for fringe and extremist groups, from about 6 per cent to 3.9 per cent. This collapse seems remarkable, given vibrant anti-foreigner populism in several neighbouring countries.[24]

Generally, we can confirm Saalfeld's observation of a 'mixed picture of persistence and change … since unification'.[25] Federally the pattern of representation has not changed, with the partial exception of the PDS. If unification delayed the modernising effects of post-industrialism by forcing a reversion back to the materialist politics of economics and jobs, the dramatic changes within the eastern parties and electorate seen in both 1998 and 2002 might more accurately be judged a normalisation. The SPD's 1998 success was particularly notable among post-industrial, new middle classes. This not only reinstated the party's competitiveness, it also fostered a normalisation of class loyalties in the new *Länder* where the SPD gained at the expense of the CDU. The return to traditional and expected patterns of social class alignments in party support became clear in 1998 and 2002, when the SPD captured many of the eastern working-class voters, who the CDU had first won over. Recent elections also demonstrate the exceptional balance of forces and closeness of competition, with the 2002 election being the tightest race in modern history.

Finally, we might recall the many initial predictions of a post-unification refractionalisation, including a resurgence of extremism. In reality, such tendencies have remained weak or non-existent. Even given the shock of unification, scenarios of polarisation and blockage have not been validated. The German party system has often been counted as one of the more stable and predictable in Western Europe. However, at certain points in the years since 1945, this party system has undergone crucially important changes. What is most surprising is that so little appears to have changed since its initial consolidation in the 1950s. In the face of the sudden new strains of unification, the German party system has been both adaptive and enduring.

Notes

1 Seymour Martin Lipset and Stein Rokkan, 'Cleavage Structures, Party Systems, and Voter Alignments', in Seymour Martin Lipset and Stein Rokkan (eds), *Party Systems and Voter Alignments: Cross-National Perspectives* (New York: Free Press, 1967), pp. 1–64.

2 Angelo Panebianco, *Political Parties: Organization and Power*, trans. by Marc Silver (Cambridge: Cambridge University Press, 1988).

3 On 'core' party system change, see Gordon Smith, *Democracy in Germany, Parties and Politics in the Federal Republic*, 3rd edn (New York: Holmes & Meier, 1986); Peter Mair, 'Introduction', in Peter Mair (ed.), *The West European Party System* (Oxford: Oxford University Press, 1990), 1–22; Peter Mair, *Party System Change: Approaches and Interpretations* (Oxford: Clarendon Press, 1997); and Steven Wolinetz (ed.), *Party Systems* (Aldershot: Ashgate, 1997).

4 Peter Merkl (ed.), *West European Party Systems* (New York: Free Press, 1980).

5 Thomas Poguntke, 'The German Party System: Eternal Crisis?', in Stephen Padgett and Thomas Poguntke (eds), *Continuity and Change in German Politics: Beyond the Politics of Centrality?* (London: Frank Cass, 2002), pp. 37–8 and Stephen Padgett (ed.), *Parties and Party Systems in the New Germany* (Aldershot: Association for the Study of German Politics, 1993).

6 Smith, *Democracy in Germany.*

7 Hans-Georg Betz, 'The Evolution and Transformation of the German Party System', in Christopher S. Allen (ed.), *Transformation of the German Political Party System* (New York: Berghahn, 1999), pp. 30–61.

8 Giovanni Sartori, 'European Political Parties: The Case of Polarized Pluralism', in Joseph LaPalombara and Myron Weiner (eds), *Political Parties and Political Development* (Princeton: Princeton University Press, 1966), pp. 137–76 and Giovanni Sartori, *Parties and Party Systems: A Framework for Analysis*, 1 (Cambridge: Cambridge University Press, 1976).

9 Oskar Niedermeyer, 'Party System Change in East Germany', *German Politics*, 4:3 (1995), pp. 75–91 and Peter Eisenmann and Gerhard Hirscher (eds), *Die Entwicklung der Volksparteien im vereinten Deutschland* (Bonn: Aktuell, 1992).

10 Peter Merkl, *The Origin of the West German Republic* (New York: Oxford University Press, 1963).

11 Thomas Saalfeld, 'The German Party System: Continuity and Change', *German Politics*, 11:3 (2002), p. 103.

12 Roland Sturm, 'The Territorial Dimension of the New Party system', in Stephen Padgett (ed.), *Parties and Party Systems in the New Germany* (Aldershot: Association for the Study of German Politics, 1993); Roland Sturm, 'Divided Government in Germany: The Case of the Bundesrat', in Robert Elgie (ed.), *Divided Government in Comparative Perspective* (Oxford: Oxford University Press, 2001), pp. 167–81; and William M. Chandler, 'Federalism and Political Parties', in Herman Bakvis and William M. Chandler (eds), *Federalism and the Role of the State* (Toronto: University of Toronto Press, 1987), pp. 149–70.

13 Otto Kirchheimer, 'The Transformation of Western European Party Systems', in Joseph LaPalombara and Myron Weiner (eds), *Political Parties and Political Development* (Princeton: Princeton University Press, 1966) pp. 177–200 and Steven Wolinetz, 'Party System Change: The Catch-All Thesis Revisited', *West European Politics*, 14:1 (1991), pp. 113–28.

14 Franz-Urban Pappi , 'The German Party System' in Stefano Bartolini and Peter Mair (eds), *Party Politics in Contemporary Western Europe* (London: Frank Cass, 1984), pp. 7–26.

15 On psychological disengagement, see Russell Dalton, 'Two German Electorates?', in Gordon Smith, William E. Paterson and Peter H. Merkl (eds), *Developments in German Politics* (Durham, NC: Duke University Press, 1992), pp. 55ff and Russell Dalton, 'Political Cleavages, Issues, and Electoral Change', in Lawrence Le Duc, Richard G. Niemi and Pippa Norris (eds), *Comparing Democracies* (London: Sage, 1996), 319–42.

16 John Leslie, 'Unification and the Changing Fortunes of Germany's Parties of the Far Right', in Christopher S. Allen (ed.), *Transformation of the German Political Party System* (Providence, RI: Berghahn, 1990) pp. 99–132.

17 Niedermeyer, 'Party System Change in East Germany'.

18 Charlie Jeffery, 'From Hyperstability to Change?', in David Broughton and Mark Donovan (eds), *Changing Party Systems in Western Europe* (London: Pinter, 1999), p. 112.

19 Clay Clemens, 'Disquiet on the Eastern Front: The Christian Democratic Union in Germany's New *Länder*', *German Politics*, 2:2 (1993), pp. 200–23.

20 On the 1998 election, see Wolfgang Gibowski, 'Social Change and the Electorate: an Analysis of the 1998 Bundestagswahl', *German Politics*, 8:2

(1998), pp. 10–32 and Stephen Padgett, 'The Boundaries of Stability: The Party System Before and After the 1998 Bundestagswahl', in Stephen Padgett and Thomas Saalfeld (eds), *Bundestagswahl '98: An End of an Era?* (London: Frank Cass, 1999), pp. 241–50.

21 Gordon Smith, 'Dimensions of Change in the German Party System', in Stephen Padgett (ed.), *Parties and Party Systems in the New Germany* (Aldershot: Association for the Study of German Politics, 1993), pp. 87–102.

22 Christian Søe, 'The Free Democratic Party: A Struggle for Survival, Influence and Identity', in David Conradt, Gerald R. Kleinfeld, George Romoser and Christian Søe (eds), *Germany's New Politics: Parties and Issues in the 1990s* (Providence, RI: Berghahn, 1995), pp. 149–76,

23 Peter H. Merkl and Leonard Weinberg (eds), *Right-Wing Extremism in the Twenty-First Century* (London: Frank Cass, 2003).

24 See Chapter 10 by Leonard Weinberg in this volume.

25 Saalfeld, 'The German Party System', p. 124.

12

The dynamics of party support in Chancellor-democracy: Schröder and his SPD

Clay Clemens

Among the most striking features of Gerhard Schröder's first term as Chancellor was his ambivalent relationship with his own SPD. On one hand, few postwar German chancellors have so frankly asserted independence from, even indifference to, the party that put them in power and sustained them there. In governing style and policy substance, as well as attitude and mere time commitment, Schröder seemingly paid little heed to the SPD. Most colleagues considered their relationship with him as, at best, a form of 'cohabitation'. Yet, he nonetheless enjoyed more than sufficient security from any open party challenge. Fellow Social Democrats either supported or acquiesced in government decisions, even those that conflicted with their traditional preferences across a series of domestic and foreign policy issues.

Schröder's first term thus gives rise to a set of related questions. First, how did his relationship with the SPD compare to that between previous chancellors and their own parties, and how can it best be characterised? Second, to what extent did the elements of the party in fact accept his leadership and go along with government policy in various areas? Third, and most importantly, what factors can account for Schröder's relative security within and support from his SPD?

Chancellors and their parties: a survey of the literature

A small but rich literature has emerged over time on the Federal Republic's chancellorship. Early on, during and immediately following Konrad Adenauer's near-total dominance of political life in the 1950s, analysts generally depicted the postwar system as a 'Chancellor-democracy'. To some this smacked of a quasi-authoritarian leadership cult by which still largely apolitical Germans abdicated their own political role; to others it represented the only way to assure democratic stability. But regardless which view they took, most early analysts who used this label attributed Chancellor-democracy primarily to new, seemingly powerful constitutional protections or resources outlined in Bonn's Basic Law. Such provisions mainly aimed to avert repetition of conditions akin to those of the Weimar Republic, when an overly-powerful head of state, a squabbling legislature and temporary alliances of radicals all undermined chancellorial authority. Under the 1949 Basic Law, the head of government was fully protected from dismissal by a ceremonial President, was less vulnerable to shifting parliamentary majorities thanks to the constructive no-confidence stipulation, was empowered with guideline competence (*Richtlinienkompetenz*) and was endowed with substantial administrative assets.

Notions of a constitutional Chancellor-democracy did not last long. After 1960, it became more widely accepted that Adenauer's own power owed much to political circumstances. As Peter Merkl noted in explaining the old man's survival into the 1960s, these included his unique international stature and 'the plebiscitary character of West German democracy'. Merkl also stressed Bonn's bipolar party system and Adenauer's ability to exploit the balance of interests within his new, heterogeneous CDU in order to stay on top.[1]

In any case, however impressive the chancellorship's Basic Law prerogatives, they seemed less formidable once the Federal Republic's malleable 'semi-sovereign' formative decade passed and a host of new institutional and political counterweights gained in importance, particularly greater demands from within a chancellor's own political party and from its coalition partners. Chancellor-democracy thus seemed less apt in Adenauer's final years, as well as in the much briefer, less lustrous tenures of his Christian Democratic heirs, Ludwig Erhard and Kurt Georg Kiesinger.

Some, like Wolfgang Jäger, favoured junking the term 'Chancellor-democracy' altogether in favour of something like 'coordination democracy', implying that the inherent authority of the Chancellor was little more than that of a moderator among fellow elites within his party and with those of its coalition allies.[2] Others continued to describe the system as a Chancellor-democracy, albeit in a more modest form, implying that the chief executive by no means wielded total authority, but *did* remain the central player in politics and governance. Moreover, they attributed this role less to formal Basic Law powers than broader trends toward the 'personalization of political functions [strengthened by] modern mass communications' as in other major western democracies such as Britain, France and the United States. This development made for a fusion of representative institutions with plebiscitary elements focused on the chancellor, whose 'strong position … as leadership partisan was bound to the party political constellation'.[3]

Certainly it was hard to deny that Bonn's first two Social Democratic chancellors, Willy Brandt and Helmut Schmidt, played the central role in German politics: Brandt ushered in a host of reforms and spearheaded a major change in the Federal Republic's foreign policy; Schmidt governed even longer, managing the German response to a major recession, several domestic crisis and a revival of Cold War tensions. And despite a stumbling start, CDU/CSU Chancellor Helmut Kohl took hold of German politics in the 1980s, led the drive toward national reunification and possessed an unrivalled position in the 1990s, breaking almost all longevity records for a democratic head of government anywhere.

A blend of political factors seemed to help chancellors play this role. As Renata Mayntz noted, a head of government's 'real power would depend largely on the support he [got] from his party and the parliamentary party (and often also from his coalition partner), and on his popularity with the electorate'. But of those related factors, she continued, 'the most important basis of the chancellor's power is his position within his political party'. Indeed, party support may be seen as not merely most important, but as indispensable for cultivating and preserving it. The means for garnering such support includes managing the party's internal organisation – most probably as Federal Chair – or helping shape its programmatic identity. By contrast, 'popularity with the electorate' itself would enhance a chancellor's overall authority only if it brought extra voters to the party at *Land* and national elections, the so-called 'bonus of office' (and sometimes not even then).[4]

Erhard, for example, cared little for internal CDU affairs, did not choose to become its Chair until some years into his chancellorship, and even then continued to count mainly on his own strong standing with voters. Ultimately that 'Chancellor bonus' did not seem to help his party. Some have thus characterised Erhard as one of two charismatic losers, a chief executive whose popularity did not help his authority. Despite being broadly popular with voters, Kiesinger also faced unique constraints in mustering and relying on party support, constraints generated by the unique challenges of having to share power with a co-equal partner in the CDU/CSU–SPD Grand Coalition.

Brandt, by contrast, was a long-time party Chair and someone whose very name was synonymous with modern Social Democracy. Moreover, for many years – most notably in his triumphant 1972 reelection bid – he also enjoyed immense public popularity. The result was considerable SPD support and great authority, making him the first incumbent since Adenauer to vindicate the notion of Germany as a Chancellor-democracy. After the 1972 election, his management of the SPD drifted and his popularity waned, a double blow, making it easier for colleagues to oust him after a 1974 espionage episode.

Helmut Schmidt, by contrast, never took on the Chairmanship of his party and delegated the work mainly to Brandt and Herbert Wehner. He counted on that division of labour and the immense respect he enjoyed among voters of all stripes to shore up SPD support for his government. For years that formula worked despite policy differences with many elements of his party. But with time that arrangement for managing the SPD broke down. And while Schmidt remained popular with the electorate, that personal appeal in time actually undercut him as it seemed to help his own Social Democrats far less than their junior coalition partner, the FDP, which successfully wooed moderate voters who wanted to retain the centrist chancellor while offsetting his own party's left wing.[5]

If Schmidt's fate indicated that personal popularity was not a sufficient condition for party support and chancellorial power, Helmut Kohl's tenure suggested that it was not even an essential one. Even after becoming head of government in 1982, Kohl famously devoted considerable time and energy to managing the CDU, including his power base among party factions and functionaries. That proved sufficient to ensure its support for him and his government even when, as during his first two terms, he was often not popular enough with voters to generate an electoral bonus.[6]

In assessing heads of government, Lewis Edinger noted that each served as either an 'autonomous and authoritative leader … [who] dominates his party and considers it his instrument' or as head of a team of 'coequal party elites' sharing influence over policy (depending on 'personality and style', as well as 'power alignments' within and among the parties).[7] Subsequent analysis expanded on this typology.

Ludger Helms has suggested that Chancellor–party relationships that can be depicted not only as *autonomous* (i.e. with the leader so dominant within the party as to be able to instrumentalise it in his governance), but as *neutral* (neither agent nor master of the party), *dependent* or *detached.* Helms also revives a four-decades-old typology first proposed by Heidenheimer to capture a chancellor's 'dominant style of public presentation':

a) *government* and *party* leader: equal emphasis on both roles, but separation of the two
b) *government* and party leader: more emphasis on the former role, but some on the latter
c) *government* (and party) leader: almost exclusive focus on the former role
d) *government–party* leader: close integration of the two roles.

Helms categorised Adenauer, Brandt and Kohl as autonomous and as falling into categories (a) or (b) – meaning that each enjoyed latitude from his party, but partly because they also devoted enough attention to managing its affairs. By contrast, he rated Erhard, Kiesinger and Schmidt, who all focused more heavily on government affairs, as either neutral or detached and as falling into categories (b) or (c). The lesson seems to be that a chancellor, even a popular one, downplays his party role only at great peril.[8]

Schröder and his SPD: characterising the relationship

Early assessments of Schröder's relationship with his party vary somewhat. Karl-Rudolf Korte has characterised him as a 'presidential' style chancellor, with near-total detachment from his SPD in terms of the leader's own focus and its impact on either his tenure or his government's policy: 'The chancellor is above all head of government and only party leader secondarily … As a populist, Schröder makes a virtue out of the deficit of his lack of closeness to the Social Democratic base.'[9] Helms placed him as somewhere between a '*government* and party leader' (category (b)) and a '*government* (and party) leader' (category (c)), but noted a greater tendency toward the latter, more detached style.[10] Comparisons have been drawn with Schmidt more than any other predecessor.

Schröder and the SPD

To be sure, Schröder was by no means a total outsider, having made his career in the party from a young age. Yet from early on he also proved to be a maverick. As he nonetheless enjoyed success in Lower Saxony and rose to be Minister-President in the early 1990s, he distanced himself even further from long-standing tenets of party policy. His fabled moniker, *Genosse der Bosse* (comrade of the bosses), underscored a growing readiness to flaunt the Social Democratic welfare state and corporatist commitments by working with business leaders to spur investment. Indeed, in 1995 then-party Chair Rudolf Scharping dismissed Schröder as the SPD Federal Executive Committee's spokesman on economic policy for his controversial comment that: 'There is no Social Democratic economic policy. There is no Christian Democratic economic policy. There is only a modern economic policy.' Schröder's bid to become the SPD's Chancellor designate in 1998 pitted him against its Chair Oskar Lafontaine, someone far more closely associated with traditional Social Democracy and beloved of those active in their party organisation. By contrast Schröder 'explicitly cast himself as a [British Labour Prime Minister Tony] Blair-style moderniser, intent on bringing the SPD kicking and screaming into the twenty-first century [reflecting] a deeply ambivalent attitude towards [its] traditions and values'.[11]

In early 1998, the party nonetheless chose him as its candidate, since the more traditionally dependable leaders – Johannes Rau, Lafontaine and Scharping – had all run against Kohl previously and lost. Schröder managed to make his own showing in Lower-Saxony's *Land* elections that winter into a test of his voter appeal and thus won an informal 'internal primary' over Lafontaine. The latter gave up his bid for the nomination, but remained Federal party chair and retained heavy influence over that year's election strategy. A division of labour thus emerged. Schröder ran as a moderate reformer, advocating a 'third way' between traditional Social Democracy and market capitalism. By contrast, Lafontaine ensured that the election programme paid proper respect for SPD orthodoxy, while campaign manager Franz Müntefering shrewdly reconciled these differences, in part by blurring them.

After their triumph in September 1998, this division of labour remained in place, allowing Schröder some, but not complete, latitude. Management of the SPD remained with Lafontaine, who – as Federal

Chair – played a key role in negotiations forming a coalition with the Greens. Indeed on social and economic policy, the new government programme seemed to reflect less Schröder's Blairite third way than the classical Keynesianism of Lafontaine, who also became finance minister with expanded powers in the first Red–Green cabinet.[12] It was an unprecedented arrangement: never before had the Chair of a major party served as a subordinate in a colleague's government.

Since Schröder did not fully control his government at first, classical Social Democratic and/or Green items dominated its agenda from late 1998 until mid-spring 1999. Early on the coalition passed a 'radical liberalization of German citizenship policy', permitting dual passports.[13] The government revoked large portions of a pension reform plan implemented under Kohl, increased child benefits, cut medical coverage payments and lowered the bottom rate of income taxes, making them more progressive.[14] The coalition agreed on negotiations to begin phasing out nuclear energy, and two ecological tax reform measures in 1999. Labour Minister Walter Riester also revised payroll tax waivers for holders of 'small jobs' and limited the definition of self-employment towards strengthening 'the financial foundation of the German welfare state by widening its tax base'.[15] Not surprisingly, most of these items already had fairly broad support from SPD traditionalists and the left. Although the modernisers championing moderate third way policies were less enthralled, they too acquiesced.

Little of this initial agenda reflected Schröder's own preferences. Indeed, many of these early initiatives angered the very business constituency he was hoping to woo as part of his effort to spur employment. They warned him that both the 'Alliance for Jobs' – his scheme for reaching a business-labour consensus on employment – and their participation in talks to phase out nuclear energy could be jeopardised without cuts in both corporate taxes and social spending. Lafontaine's preference for stimulating consumer demand rather than curbing the costs of business also created a potential conflict with the new ECB. Differences over these issues in turn sparked friction in the government's top ranks: Schröder saw his Finance Minister as a loose cannon, while the latter took press criticism of his initiatives as having been fed by the Chancellor.[16] Rather than making for an effective division of labour and greater cabinet discipline, Schröder and Lafontaine's unusual power-sharing arrangement only fed personal antagonism and philosophical differences. The mercurial Saarländer abruptly quit both his party and government posts in March 1999, surprisingly early.

Schröder now had little choice but to advance himself in place of Lafontaine. That month he was formally installed as federal SPD Chair, to be reconfirmed in December. Schröder, rarely seen at party headquarters, made clear his intention to be an absentee Chair. By default, coordination of party and government fell to chancellory minister Bodo Hombach, a chief exponent of his 'third way', and SPD business manager Ottmar Schreiner, a Lafontaine ally. This arrangement also failed. By mid-1999, Schröder was moving Hombach and Schreiner out, and planning to appoint Müntefering, his trustworthy 1998 campaign manager and chair of the powerful North Rhine-Westphalia branch, as the first-ever SPD General-Secretary. Müntefering would be delegated responsibility for managing Federal party affairs – personnel, organisation, strategy and campaigns. In addition, he would meet regularly with Bundestag caucus chair Peter Struck and a newly-named Chancellory Director, Franz Walter Steinmeier, to coordinate discussions of policy. In this new arrangement, Schröder – nominally now Federal Chair – delegated representation of SPD interests and views to Müntefering almost entirely.

Some depicted this approach as a result of strategy, not mere circumstance or necessity. They cited the views of Schröder's top chancellory aides Steinmeier and Wolfgang Nowak. Both argued that their chief was drawing lessons from the loosening of ties between all political parties and their traditional core constituencies, reflected in the ever-growing share of undecided voters. In this view, parliamentary institutions, including parties, simply no longer had the capacity to deal with the problems of modern society and were losing public confidence. Long programmatic discussions were now not merely pointless but could scare off the key, centrist swing voters that their SPD had won in 1998. In place of a reliance on parties, Steinmeier and Nowak contended, modern political leadership needed to construct multiple, loose, temporary networks of key corporate, labour, academic, religious and international elites in order to discuss ways of achieving broad, pragmatic consensus solutions to major problems. Indeed Schröder would become famous for naming bipartisan commissions on key issues – everything from genetic engineering to Bundeswehr reform, immigration and labour market policies.[17]

In any case, the Chancellor plainly sought to minimise SPD interference with his governance. As Chair, Schröder rarely hesitated to forgo consultations and preempt party decisions that could affect his government, such as in voicing his hopes to continue the Red–Green coalition after 2002. Needless to say, he sought complete autonomy on government personnel decisions. This was especially true in terms of ministerial appointments: in his first term he named a record number (seven) of cabinet appointees who were not members of the SPD caucus or in many cases even of the party itself.

Most importantly, the Chancellor-Chair would preserve broad latitude on policy decisions, regardless how often or how much those initiatives might run contrary to traditional party positions. He took over as SPD Chair after having committed postwar Germany to its first outright combat operation, NATO's bombing campaign against Serbia over the latter's ethnic cleansing in Kosovo. Schröder's subsequent support for sending armed forces to Macedonia and – shortly thereafter – Afghanistan, corresponded to what he called a new 'self-understanding' of German foreign policy.

As if to put SPD leaders on warning, in June 1999 the Chancellory published a joint paper on economic policy with Tony Blair's office: it faulted traditional social democracy's failure to take into account the need for private sector job creation, as well as its penchant for heavy regulation and social spending. Later that year, newly named finance minister Hans Eichel produced an austerity programme that would limit pension, jobless and welfare benefits by linking them to inflation rather than earnings. In early 2000, his government pushed through (with the help of Union *Länder*) a major reduction of top tax rates, even offering corporate leaders concessions that they had not initially sought, such as some substantial cuts in the capital gains rate.[18] In early 2001, the chancellor called for reducing jobless benefits for long-term unemployed who refused to take work. Throughout this period his government was working on a pension reform proposal that constituted a 'radical break with past policies and present programmes' of the SPD: it cut benefits and for the first time ever introduced a private component to old-age insurance.[19]

While governing in ways that broke many a party taboo, Schröder made no bones about his remoteness from the SPD's other internal affairs. Unlike Adenauer, who often donned his cap as CDU Chair in order to make partisan attacks on behalf of his government's policy, Schröder rarely spoke in his capacity as SPD leader. For example, throughout the crippling CDU/CSU finance scandal of 1999–2000, Müntefering and others scored political points against their wounded foe, but the Chancellor maintained statesmanlike neutrality, even voicing concern that German democracy might suffer if its largest centre-right party collapsed.[20] Nor did he usually join SPD colleagues in personal attacks on his rival, CSU chief Edmund Stoiber, before or even during the campaign of 2002.

The SPD and Schröder

Given this lack of enthusiasm for his own party, the Chancellor could hardly expect much in return. Throughout his first months, SPD deputies and activists openly attacked his style – the flashy cigars and pricey shoes. His statements on economic policy and support for a war in the Balkans also sparked sharp criticism. Indeed, at the special 1999 conference held to confirm his election as Chair, Schröder conceded his unpopularity and tried passing it off with a small joke, noting that while the party gave him little love, wife Doris provided all he really needed. While pledging not to strip the SPD of its traditional programmatic character, he also openly warned against any division of labour in which the government did the dirty work and the party espoused only pure principles. Otherwise most of his speech read like a government address. Some 76 per cent of the delegates did endorse him, but without enthusiasm.[21]

Throughout 1999 the policies of his government drew SPD fire, especially budget austerity and taxes. When Schröder announced plans to restructure government social programmes, it was stamped 'a break with party programmes' by the Frankfurt Circle and 'a declaration of intellectual bankruptcy' by the Young Socialists (*Jusos*), both left-wing bastions; SPD allies of labour declared 'not with us' and the German Trade Union Federation (DGB) spoke of 'an historically blind defamation of the social state'.[22] Most such critics also blasted his joint statement with British Prime Minister Blair, not merely because its 'third way' redefined social democracy, but because it was worked out between his Chancellory and 10 Downing Street without party involvement. But even moderates like the Chair of the party's strongest district association (western Westphalia's Joachim Poss) joined the left in opposing these innovations. SPD members booed Schröder at *Land* election rallies in September 1999. Rumour had it that his own defence minister Scharping, fresh from an impressive performance during the Kosovo war, was preparing to replace him. As one of the latter's backers put it: 'What can Schröder not do? Get along with the party. What can Scharping do? Get along with the party.'[23] At a December conference, hundreds of local SPD associations proposed changes in party and government policies, demanding higher taxes on corporations and the wealthy. Recent *Land* election setbacks led them to declare that they were not lemmings who would follow him blindly.

The mood improved in 2000, thanks mainly to a rebound made possible by the CDU/CSU's finance scandal, which helped improve the poll ratings for Schröder's party. Still, in April, some forty-five leftwing SPD Bundestag representatives published an open letter criticising him and his domestic policies. For example, evolving government proposals for reforming pension policies drew even more criticism from within party ranks: only nineteen of twenty-seven SPD Bundestag caucus executive committee members and 70 per cent of the deputies backed it in July. Moreover, most elements of his government's pension reform plan found greater favour with the FDP, Union and business than with his own SPD. That autumn, some nineteen Social Democrats openly rebelled against his plan for deploying troops abroad to Macedonia. When Schröder then chose to back US military action against Afghanistan's Taliban, these dissidents joined with Green critics in a *Frondeur* that briefly threatened to bring down his government altogether.

It was not a first for a popular Chancellor to face such constant attacks from with party ranks. Erhard was bedevilled and ultimately ousted by his CDU before serving less than one full term. And while Schmidt lasted eight years, it was all he could do to swim against a tide of SPD resistance on economic, energy and nuclear policy.[24] Yet unlike these 'charismatic losers', Schröder enjoyed relatively speaking a surprising degree of security and support, or at least acceptance, from colleagues. Rarely was he or his agenda in serious jeopardy primarily from within SPD ranks or as a result of the often overt party indifference and resistance.

In terms of job security, Schröder's first term compared favourably with the early tenure of his immediate predecessor. No Chancellor has been universally credited with wielding more control over his own party than Kohl. Yet at least twice during his first two terms, Kohl came close to being dumped by a CDU *putsch*: in spring 1986, amid charges of his involvement in the Flick party finance affair; and more famously in late summer 1989 after firing his popular, long-time General-Secretary. By contrast, at no point in his first term did Schröder come nearly so close to removal by his own party, even when SPD fortunes seemed bleakest. Schröder faced down Lafontaine in early 1999, Klimmt's effort to mobilise party sentiment against economic austerity measures later that year and Scharping's abortive bid to present himself as an alternative Chancellor to unhappy Social Democrats. When in early 2000 some forty-five left-wing Bundestag deputies openly challenged his economic policies, the chancellor quickly dismissed the threat, noting that the SPD owed recent electoral successes to unity behind government policy. These dissenters backpedalled.[25] Schröder also blunted the threat of dissident SPD deputies to undercut his policy or even bring down his government in opposition to its deployment of forces in Macedonia and Afghanistan, although the latter did require taking the most extreme of all disciplinary measures – calling an Article 68 confidence motion in his own government. But no SPD deputies voted against him or his policy, and even had he lost, chances of him reemerging at the head of newly reconfigured government with the FDP or Union were good.

In short, even relative to a predecessor renowned for being in control of his own party, Schröder enjoyed relative job security: at no point did his lack of deep SPD support, intra-party grumbling or even outright moves against him seriously endanger his tenure as Chancellor. Likewise, though he was by no means warmly welcomed when first taking over from the more popular Lafontaine as Federal Chair, Schröder received a steadily rising share of the delegate vote at SPD party conferences: from 76 per cent (April 1999) to 86 per cent (December 1999) and finally to 88 per cent (November 2001). Kohl, by contrast, started out at higher levels early in his chancellorship, but his share dropped to a record low of 77 per cent at the end of his second term. Schröder's was in fact the somewhat more positive trajectory.

To what extent did SPD resistance prove an obstacle to Schröder's policy leadership? Whereas Kohl's general policy preferences were firmly within the traditions of his CDU, with its broadly centrist orientation, Schröder from the start depicted himself as the champion of changes that would ignore or transform traditional Social Democratic principles in many areas. Although rates of passage for *Regierungsvorlagen* (government proposals) in the Bundestag are normally quite high, there is enough variation to indicate that some governments have had more success than others. Brandt's first administration, for instance, had a 75 per cent success rate, mainly owing to a thin majority, although in Kohl's last term, with a similarly narrow margin, he achieved a record 93 per cent. Within this range, the Schröder government's 89 per cent passage rate from 1998 to 2002 is on the high side. At the very least, his government suffered few legislative defeats at the hands of his own deputies. Even Eichel's austerity measures passed in November 1999 without serious SPD resistance. So too did Schröder's 'historic' tax reform. Although his government's pension reform plan received lukewarm backing from the SPD Bundestag caucus in July 2000, by November only ten of 298 members voted no.[26] Attacks on Schily's strict internal security measures did not put them, let alone the government, at risk. Finally, the revolt against sending troops to Macedonia and later Afghanistan also fizzled out. In sum, despite continuous grumbling, and in some cases outright attack, the SPD generally backed its Chancellor: some referred to the party broadly as a 'chancellorial election league', and to the Bundestag caucus as a 'certification stamp for cabinet proposals' (*Stempelmaschine fur Kabinettsvorlagen*).

Schröder and his SPD: explaining the relationship

Why in the final analysis did a Chancellor who made little pretence of seeking to cultivate and build upon a close political or philosophical relationship with his own party organisation nonetheless enjoy its support or acquiescence? Several different dynamics – policy, power and strategy – could be seen at work in this relationship.

Policy dynamics: conversion and conciliation

Did the Chancellor manage to expand support for new ways of thinking about socio-economic and security policy beyond a core of reformists by converting the even larger share who had started out sceptical of or even hostile to his moderation? To some degree, he did. On pension reform, it was not just SPD modernisers, but the left as well, that gradually rejected long-standing principles of Social Democratic policy and came to embrace new, hitherto unacceptable modifications (rather than insisting on variable contribution rates and fixed benefit levels, for example, they now defended precisely the reverse priorities). Likewise, on security policy, it has been argued that a majority of the SPD was willing to break with its long-standing taboo against using German troops abroad, especially after Kosovo, and began to accept that certain desperate humanitarian and even security situations could be resolved only by 'coercive diplomacy', backed by military force.[27]

Party policy preferences did shift in some key respects during that first term. Yet the very persistence of sharp criticism and differences on many issues suggests a less than total conversion. Moreover, any ideational change that took place did not occur in a vacuum. As Hering himself argues, rather than gradually persuading the party to embrace the merits of a new pension policy, Schröder brought it around through a '*coup*'; he used his powers of appointment to marginalise top hard-line defenders of traditional SPD priorities, and then defined his own alternative without prior consultation.[28] Any change of party interest and ideas thus came about more as a result of an exercise of power on his part; put differently, any SPD conversion was more an intervening variable than an independent one in his success with getting its support or acquiescence. Much the same could be said of signs that party leaders and members had been 'converted' on security policy. The real question, then, is how their chief was able to get away with such *faits accompli* that compelled them to adjust their policy stances.

A second possible explanation is that, for all of the sharp divergences, Schröder shrewdly conciliated party critics in enough areas to defuse opposition. Indeed, from the time he became Chair, some observers detected a growing sobriety. As Heribert Prantl pointed out, Schröder was no longer '*Bruder Leichtfuss*'.[29] Schröder developed a knack for throwing party critics a bone just as discontent seemed to peak, especially in areas where he felt the costs could be contained, for example his selection of open critic Reinhard Klimmt as transportation minister, his pledge to rescue the Holzmann firm and his resistance to Britain's Vodaphone taking over Mannesmann. These measures came after a series of catastrophic 1999 electoral defeats. Indeed, by mid-2001 some ardent reform advocates publicly prodded him to stick with his plans for far-reaching change in health care and labour market policies. As the 2002 campaign geared up, Schröder the reformer appeared to discover his partisan credentials. His strong appeal to the traditional streak of SPD pacificism in opposing the United States on Iraq during the 2002 election campaign further mobilised even otherwise critical party supporters.

Such timely concessions helped defuse some anger in party ranks with larger measures like budget austerity, tax cuts, partial privatisation of pensions and labour market reform. CDU/CSU and FDP attacks on the Chancellor for selling out his own agenda indirectly testified to their concern that such a strategy of 'two steps forward, one step backwards' could work. Yet unlike Kohl, whose own neutrality on most major domestic policy disputes made it easier to alternately appease a variety of viewpoints within his Union, Schröder was the chief advocate of modernisation and thus more consistently and openly at odds with trades union elements and the anti-market left. Efforts to propitiate them could not conceal the fact that he and his government were still pursuing major reform measures without broad SPD support.

Power dynamics: cooptation and circumvention

Did Schröder then emulate Kohl in seeking to coopt critics by using patronage powers to cultivate a broad network of personal alliances among party elites, deputies and functionaries as an instrument for both rewarding loyalty and penalising criticism?[30]

To be sure, in 1998 the new Chancellor did bring a number of allies with him from Lower Saxony to Berlin, though most were in the government administration, not high party posts. Even one exception, Peter Struck, was no close associate of the Chancellor and was elected independently by caucus colleagues. Far more critical was Schröder's appointment of Müntefering as the new General-Secretary, whose commitment to SPD unity and success made him a decisive figure. Moreover, Müntefering also chaired the SPD's largest *Land*-level association, that of North Rhine-Westphalia which – along with Schröder's own Lower Saxony branch – had a good chunk of votes at any Federal party conference. It would be hard for critics to undercut the government without making deep inroads into either man's base.

Moreover, there was a potentially broader pro-Schröder faction in the party consisting of those who backed his reform efforts, including a number of new, mainly younger deputies, swept into the Bundestag in 1998. Müntefering treated the forty most junior SPD Bundestag deputies as a discrete group from the outset, hoping to cultivate their support. Thirteen of them, for example, published an open letter endorsing the Schröder–Blair paper on economic modernisation. Müntefering and Schröder's Chancellory quietly encouraged their efforts to form a new faction, 'Network 2010', which on substantive grounds favoured the 'third way'.

But in contrast to Kohl, Schröder neither had a large set of elite-level SPD allies nor made major efforts to cultivate them. He named a record number of outsiders – without party affiliation – to cabinet posts, and developed a penchant for establishing non-partisan commissions to deal with major issues. His patronage powers within the party itself were limited by the fact that a Chair has little *direct* control over many posts. Moreover, whereas Kohl's networks built up over a quarter-century atop the CDU gave him enough *indirect* influence over career prospects within its ranks to make his support or opposition decisive, Schröder's ability to wield such influence was diluted by his long-ambivalent relationship with his SPD, his belated acquisition of the chairmanship, his lack of personal loyalists within party ranks reaching down to regional or local levels and, more generally, his relative disdain for this kind of politics. Few Social Democrats had reason to hope that loyal support for the Chancellor could help their own party careers or reason to worry that criticising, even thwarting, him would damage those personal prospects. As for the Bundestag caucus itself, the reform faction remained a minority and the influence of 'Network 2010' remained limited. Moreover, the party Chair made only modest efforts to extend his network among the SPD's more powerful trade unionists and its anti-market left. Finally, unlike Kohl, he devoted little time or political capital to developing personal loyalties among district- or local-level party functionaries.

If the Chancellor did not win over – or win against – critics, he could alternatively try to circumvent or isolate them. Not long after becoming Chair, for example, he unveiled plans to restructure the SPD as a way of minimising interference with government policy: he reduced or redefined the role of party 'working groups' (*Arbeitsgemeinschaften*) – allegedly as an economy measure.[31] These groups served as a link to broader interest groups or clienteles outside the party; they also constituted an institutional power base for traditional left-wing Social Democrats. Needless to say Müntefering circumvented the Frankfurt Circle and its Bundestag ally, the Parliamentary Left, two longstanding informal factions that would also be bastions of criticism. Finally, he proposed streamlining his own North Rhine-Westphalian SPD and giving it a General-Secretary, thus weakening separate regional party organisations that had served as bastions of traditional Social Democracy. Müntefering also proposed giving all due-paying members a say in the selection of party candidate lists for the Bundestag, and even primary elections in which voters could take part. Finally, Schröder and Müntefering spoke of a need for generational renewal in party ranks. Thus the efforts by Chancellory aides and Müntefering to cultivate 'Network 2010' may be seen as an effort to offset the lingering influence of an older, more hostile, generation of SPD party members who still dominated almost all key party posts.

In personnel as well as structure, Schröder further sought to isolate his critics. As Hering notes, for example, the Chancellor expressly avoided involving Rudolf Dressler, a staunch defender of traditional party policy, in anything to do with pensions reform.[32] At higher levels, he went after rivals, mainly through effective use of the media. In the 1990s, SPD strategists had tried to depict Schröder, Lafontaine and Scharping as a 'troika' like the 1970s leadership trio of Brandt, Schmidt and Wehner. But relations among the younger group were even more bitter than those among their party elders had been. As frictions between Schröder and Lafontaine mounted in early 1999, 'targeted indiscretions' about their disagreements came from the Chancellory, media leaks that many believed triggered the latter's resignation. When later that year, Scharping's success as wartime defence minister during Kosovo fuelled talk of a new challenger to Schröder, the Chancellor reportedly bristled: 'I took care of the one, and I'll take care of the other.' Any hope that Scharping had of becoming a major force in the party as Deputy Federal Chair was undercut by Müntefering's elevation to General-Secretary. Then the Chancellor clipped his Defence Minister's other wing by backing big defence spending cuts. A wounded Scharping was left to flounder along for two years, only to be brutally dispatched just before the 2002 election after some extravagant indiscretions brought him bad publicity.

Yet while many of these efforts to circumvent centres of opposition within the SPD worked, some failed – for example, plans to substantially weaken the *Arbeitsgemeinschaften* and restructure the North Rhine-Westphalian party association. As for Schröder's success in isolating critics by limiting their influence on government policy, he succeeded only with substantial help from the victims themselves: even after breaking with him, all still had real potential for remaining highly troublesome to the Chancellor within party ranks, but ultimately did not – Lafontaine withdrew in pique and Scharping unaccountably self-destructed. Moreover, any success that the Chancellor did enjoy in circumventing or isolating SPD critics still begs the question of how he was able to get away with it.

In sum, policy and power dynamics alone did not generate enough support for Schröder's effort to transform the SPD. Major elements of the party remained sceptical of him and his main goals. Yet while the relative quiet of 'leftists and traditionalists who in numerical terms are still so strong' might well have been 'deceptive' in that they remained unwilling to support a full-scale transformation of their party, they nonetheless also did not use this considerable leverage to block or thwart the government or dilute its policies, even those they disliked.[33]

Strategic dynamics: coalition and voter dependence

Ultimately dependence is the dynamic that best explains SPD acceptance of Schröder's personal and policy leadership. Above all, he counted on making his personal popularity the key to his party's electoral success. In 1998, he had gained the SPD's designation as Chancellor candidate by making his own reelection as Lower Saxony's Minister-President a test demonstration of his ability to bring in voters from beyond the SPD's traditional base. Then, even with his defeated rival Lafontaine still serving as Chair, the campaign that year was based heavily on Schröder's appeal. Once victorious, he missed no opportunity to remind critics of what they owed him. When the left-wing threatened to rebel against his economic reform policies in 1999, Schröder countered: 'They think they won the election. But they didn't at all. *I* won the election.'[34] One brief *coup* against him as early as summer 1999 fizzled out when the Saarland SPD under Klimmt – openly basing a regional election campaign on criticism of his own Federal Chair's economic policies – did even more poorly than expected. It appeared that traditionalist SPD policies did even worse among voters than Schröder's moderation.

Still, he was not yet out of the woods. The first-term low point of his own popularity – with approval of just above zero on a +5/–5 scale – and of SPD fortunes came in the autumn of 1999. Despite his personal appearances on behalf of local candidates, the party did disastrously at municipal elections in its own bastion of North-Rhine Westphalia. Local leaders complained about a perceived indifference to their electoral fortunes; party officials did not even invite him to attend events in the second round of balloting there. And yet the long-ruling Social Democrats still lost.

Schröder's personal approval began rising again in late 1999, thanks partly to the CDU/CSU's financial affair and a drop in unemployment, but also owing to the government's ability to pass bills, even reforms unpopular in the ranks. From that point on, Schröder's popularity never again dipped below +1 on a +5/–5 scale. Some two-thirds of all Germans routinely gave him a positive job performance.[35] Moreover, in polls pitting him against either likely Union Chancellor candidate – Angela Merkel or Stoiber – the Chancellor held a clear, usually double-digit, edge. And the party's fortunes also rebounded: it gained ground in all four 2001 *Land* elections, by common consensus thanks heavily to the Chancellor's image. As Tissy Bruns observed: 'We don't know exactly what the voters who mark an "X" by the SPD are voting for. But we do know who they are voting for: Gerhard Schröder.'[36] This in turn helped him within the party.[37]

Such standing cushioned him against outright opposition to his policies in the autumn of 2001. In the dispute over sending troops to Macedonia, the Chancellor warned SPD caucus dissenters: 'When one can not make use of the responsibility one has, one has to give it up' – widely interpreted as a threat to resign. Later, he even called a confidence motion in his own government to shore up support for government policy on Afghanistan, risking a defeat that might have destroyed his government. Outwardly such threats had little effect: minds were not changed and others charged extortion. Still, Schröder did get dissenters back into line on these votes. None wanted to be blamed for undermining the leader whose personal popularity at that stage seemed to be their best hope for retaining power in Germany's upcoming national election.

To be sure, early 2002 saw some setbacks. The nomination of Stoiber as the CDU/CSU Chancellor candidate generated a brief euphoria for the Union: positive publicity for the opposition nominee coupled with bad economic news briefly narrowed Schröder's huge lead in popular approval. The SPD then suffered a truly catastrophic loss in April 2002's Saxony-Anhalt *Land* election, but that defeat could be blamed mainly on that region's far-left SPD–PDS government. Though Schröder had long planned to make himself the main issue in his party's 2002 Federal campaign, this disaster emboldened him to make such a strategy public. With Saxony-Anhalt's results seeming to bode ill for SPD prospects in September's Bundestag election, Schröder declared bluntly: 'There will be a personalisation of the election campaign. It will be about the question: do you want a Chancellor Schröder to continue, or Herr Stoiber?'[38] And, indeed, the 2002 campaign was built almost entirely around the Chancellor. To be sure, he endorsed the SPD manifesto, but no one detected a firm bond between candidate and party. All talk was of once again finding the centre, which Schröder depicted as the key to success. Left-wing critics again grumbled that they could not recognise any of social democracy in the campaign materials, yet there was no move to replace him. Indeed, despite this ambivalence, they rallied to him – all the more so after his blunt opposition to US policy on Iraq and his well-publicised personal engagement on behalf of East Germans beset by massive summer floods.

There was a second way in which Schroder suborned his party into supporting him despite their obvious frictions on policy, programme and even personality. He made himself far more vital to the continuation of a coalition with the Greens than anyone might have expected from the start. A Red–Green alliance was the natural choice of most Social Democratic voters from 1998 right through the legislative term. Though it is harder to demonstrate coalition preferences of party activists and parliamentary deputies, Dieter Wiefelspütz, one of the latter and himself known to favour a deal with the FDP, conceded an underlying preference for a Red–Green coalition.[39] This preference was even more pronounced among those most prone to criticise or in theory resist Schröder – his party's left wing: although wary of the Green penchant for quasi-liberal economic reform, it had even less desire to ally with the more unequivocally free-market FDP or form a grand coalition with the Union.

Only the Chancellor himself was at first said to be indifferent toward, or even unenthusiastic about, a Red–Green coalition. Moreover, despite coming to depend upon both Foreign Minister Joschka Fischer and Green Bundestag caucus chair Rezzo Schlauch, Schröder did not prove especially attentive to his junior partner's concerns and often brushed them aside.[40] It was evident that he could have governed without too much problem personally atop either a Grand Coalition with his Union rivals or a new social–liberal alliance with Guido Westerwelle's FDP. At times Schröder dropped hints of moving in that direction by appointing prominent Union or Liberal leaders to chair independent commissions, discreetly meeting with them, echoing their policy stance on key issues, lobbying them for votes on initiatives like pension reform and approving (or at least not criticising) *Land*-level alliances without the Greens. Indeed, serious difficulties within his government could trigger hints, explicit or not, by Müntefering, Clement and others that the Chancellor might seek an alternative. Yet in early 2001, Schröder declared his desire to begin the following year's campaign with a commitment to the Greens.[41] SPD moderates like the Seeheimer Circle immediately objected that such an alliance was no 'law of nature' and should not be renewed automatically. Even Müntefering and Clement cautioned against a premature commitment. Schroder could thus 'triangulate', implicitly warning his party's potential dissidents on the left, all unequivocal Red–Green proponents, that their interest lay in continuing to help this government succeed.

In autumn of 2001, the Chancellor again counted heavily on this factor in disciplining critics of his decision to send German troops to

Afghanistan. When the Greens and SPD left wing baulked, he called for a confidence motion under Article 68. It appeared that unless these dissenters changed their minds, he might survive only with Union or FDP support. That prospect fed constant speculation about the likelihood of a new government in Berlin. Addressing members of his party's restive Bundestag caucus, the Chancellor stressed his desire to continue a Red–Green alliance, but added that if backbench critics did deny his government its own majority, he would have to draw the obvious conclusions. Hours later he not only won with SPD and Green backing, but brushed off left-wing efforts to pass a resolution condemning military planning.

At that same party conference left-wing Social Democrats uniformly praised only one element of their Chair's address: his pledge to continue a Red–Green alliance. So relieved were they by their chief's disavowal of a coalition shift that they swallowed several otherwise indigestible policy decisions (ironically, the Greens were key backers of Schröder's economic reforms, and Fischer in particular proved a valuable ally in bringing about his 'new' approach to German foreign policy).

Conclusion: wave of the future?

On one hand, Schröder's style and relative success as Chair of his SPD – despite an openly remote relationship between them – seems counterintuitive as well as anomalous. But on the other hand, perhaps it seems inexplicable only because the most recent standard of comparison was the quite different chancellorship of Kohl, a man who bestrode his CDU like a colossus for a quarter century. Indeed, it is more likely the latter's style and success that will be seen as increasingly unconventional, in large part because it defied the times: Kohl has often been depicted as the last dinosaur of an era when parties could count on firm social bonds between themselves and their voters, support that in his Union's case could even come close to an absolute majority of the electorate. His fate depended mainly on maintaining a firm base within the organisation, and he could get by without broader personal appeal among voters.

By contrast, even in the 1970s, such a 'bonus' was in fact more a necessity for SPD chancellors, whose party was not assumed to enjoy a structural majority in the electorate. But especially as traditional social milieus that had once assured both major rivals more than 40 per cent of the vote each began to decline, the external appeal or pull of a lead candidate grew more decisive: even Kohl in his later years fell back more on his image as 'Chancellor of unity' and his alliance with the FDP than on party management, especially once his CDU extended eastward into territory whose politics and politicians he knew far less well than those of the old Federal Republic. In that light, Schröder's seemingly unorthodox effort to lead and even transform his SPD from outside-in rather than inside-out is less surprising. His express reliance on winning over centrist voters regardless of partisan affiliation more than catering to the faithful, and his emphasis on cultivating networks of interests and organisations outside rather than within his SPD may indeed – as Chancellory strategists suggest – better represent the wave of the future.

Yet if in this approach nothing succeeds like success, nothing fails like failure: near-exclusive focus on leading the party from outside its organisation requires an image of personal popularity and successful governance – something Schröder did enjoy for much of his first term and which thus helped keep his otherwise restive and divided party in line. By contrast, not long after his re-election in 2002, the Chancellor's own image *and* the electorate's perception of his government's performance both plummeted precipitously. Sceptical observers wondered if, with so few other resources to fall back upon, Schröder's standing in the party could survive such a depletion of his chief assets.

Notes

1 Peter Merkl, 'Equilibrium, Structure of Interests and Leadership: Adenauer's Survival as Chancellor', *American Political Science Review*, 56:3 (1962), pp. 634–50.

2 Wolfgang Jäger, 'Von der Kanzlerdemokratie zur Koordinationsdemokratie', *Zeitschrift für Parlamentsfragen*, 35:1 (1988), pp. 15–32.

3 Karlheinz Niclauss, *Kanzlerdemokratie: Bonner Regierungspraxis von Konrad Adenauer bis Helmut Kohl* (Stuttgart: Kohlhammer, 1988), pp. 13–74, 267.

4 Renata Mayntz, 'Executive Leadership in Germany: Dispersion of Power or "Kanzlerdemokratie"', in Richard Rose and Ezra N. Suleiman (eds), *Presidents and Prime Ministers* (Washington, DC: American Enterprise Institute: 1980), pp. 147–8.

5 William Paterson, 'The Chancellor and His Party: Political Leadership in the Federal Republic', *West European Politics*, 4:1 (1981), pp. 13–14.
6 Dieter Roth, 'Das ungeliebte Kanzler: Helmut Kohl im Licht (oder Schatten?) demoskopischer Befund', in Reinhard Appel (ed.), *Kohl im Spiegel seiner Macht* (Bonn: Bouvier, 1990), pp. 285–301.
7 Lewis Edinger, *West German Politics* (New York: Columbia University Press, 1986), p. 155.
8 Ludger Helms, '"Chief Executives" and Their Parties: The Case of Germany', *German Politics*, 11:2 (2002), pp. 146–64.
9 Karl-Rudolf Korte, 'In der Präsentationsdemokratie: Schröder's Regierungstil prägt die Berliner Republik', *Frankfurter Allgemeine Zeitung*, 26 July 2002.
10 Helms, '"Chief Executives" and Their Parties', pp. 154–61.
11 Charles Lees, *The Red–Green Coalition in Germany: Politics, Personalities and Power* (Manchester: Manchester University Press, 2000), p. 83.
12 Michaela W. Richter, 'Continuity or *Politikwechsel*? The First Federal Red–Green Coalition', *German Politics and Society*, 20:1 (2002), pp. 28–9.
13 Simon Green, 'Beyond Ethnoculturalism? German Citizenship in the New Millennium', *German Politics*, 9:3 (2000), p. 119.
14 Christine Margerum Harlen, 'Schröder's Economic Reforms: The End of *Reformstau*?', *German Politics*, 11:1 (2002), p. 66.
15 Stephen Silvia, 'The Fall and Rise of Unemployment in Germany: Is the Red–Green Government Responsible?', *German Politics*, 11:1 (2002), p. 14.
16 Harlen, 'Schröder's Economic Reforms', pp. 64–7.
17 *Frankfurter Allgemeine Zeitung*, 3 June 2001.
18 Harlen, 'Schröder's Economic Reforms', p. 72.
19 Martin Hering, 'Moving the Deadweight of Ideas: The Social Democratic Party and the Reform of Germany's Pension System', Paper delivered at the 97th annual meeting of the American Political Science Association, San Francisco, 30 August–2 September 2001.
20 Interview in *Die Welt*, 17 February 2000.
21 *Die Welt*, 13 April 1999.
22 *Die Welt*, 14 June 1999, 16 June 1999.
23 *Süddeutsche Zeitung*, 17 September 1999.
24 'Schmidt's consensus politics only allowed a policy of the smallest steps. The great tasks of the future – one thinks of the environment or pension finance – were not dealt with'. See Jäger, 'Von Der Kanzlerdemokratie', p. 26.
25 *Die Welt*, 18 April 2002.
26 Hering, 'Moving the Deadweight of Ideas', pp. 26–7.
27 *Ibid.*, p. 3 and Jeffrey Lantis, *Strategic Dilemmas and the Evolution of German Foreign Policy* (Westport, CT: Praeger, 2002), pp. 172–83.
28 Hering, 'Moving the Deadweight of Ideas'.

29 *Süddeutsche Zeitung*, 12 April 1999.

30 Clay Clemens, 'Party Management as a Leadership Resource: Kohl and the CDU/CSU', in Clay Clemens and William Paterson (eds), *The Kohl Chancellorship* (London: Frank Cass, 1998), pp. 91–119.

31 *Süddeutsche Zeitung*, 8 June 1999.

32 Hering, 'Moving the Deadweight of Ideas', p. 15.

33 *Ibid.*

34 *Die Welt*, 30 July 1999. As former SPD official Peter Glotz noted, 'everyone in the party knows that no elections can be won without him, which naturally gives his statements a certain weight'. Interview in *Die Welt*, 18 June 1999.

35 EMNID data cited in *Die Welt*, 12 July 2001.

36 Tissy Bruns, 'Wer würden Sie bestellen?', *Die Welt*, 4 April 2001.

37 Tissy Bruns, 'Die Angst des Kanzlers vor dem SPD', *Die Welt*, 4 September 2001.

38 Cited in ARD, 21 August 2002, at www.Tagesschau.de.

39 *Die Welt*, 20 November 2001.

40 Richter, 'Continuity or *Politikwechsel*', p. 36.

41 *Süddeutsche Zeitung*, 12 January 2001.

13

The PDS and the party systems in unified Germany

David F. Patton

In federal and devolved states, party systems often differ at the national and subnational levels as a result of the specific cultural, economic or institutional features of a region. An example of extreme divergence is that of the British province of Northern Ireland where four major parties compete in a highly polarised party system that bears no resemblance to that of Westminster. Less dramatic examples can be found in the Catalan and Basque regions of Spain or in Scotland or Wales. In Germany, distinctive subnational regional systems exist as well. For instance, the CSU has led Bavaria for decades, while the SPD has governed in North-Rhine Westphalia since 1966. After German unification in 1990, a party system emerged in eastern Germany that differed dramatically from the national party system in terms of size, the relative strength of the parties and the degree of polarisation between its component parts. This chapter examines the changing dynamic between the eastern and the national party systems in Germany and the electoral implications of this dynamic for the PDS, the successor to the ruling communist party (SED) of the former GDR. In so doing, it explores an underdeveloped area in the literature on party systems: namely, the electoral consequences of the interaction between divergent national and sub-national party systems.

In some countries, different party systems at the national and subnational level appear to have minimal impact on one another. In the United Kingdom, for instance, the party system of Stormont remains quite insulated from that of Westminster. The same applies to the *Südtiroler Volkspartei* which has dominated politics in South Tirol since 1948 despite the radical transformation of Italian politics in the 1990s.

The CSU in Bavaria and the SPD in North-Rhine Westphalia each remained dominant in their respective states despite changes in the national party system. In many other cases, though, the relationship between the local and the national system is highly dynamic, with the two systems influencing each other and their constituent parts in important ways.

History shows that the normalisation of relations among parties at the state level may be an important step toward the subsequent normalisation of party relations at the national level. A party widely perceived as disreputable may first become 'fit for government' (*regierungsfähig*) at the state level prior to entering a governing coalition at the national level. There are many examples of this 'stepping-stone effect'. Most notoriously, the NSDAP joined governing coalitions at the state level in Thuringia and Brunswick in 1930 before entering into national government in 1933. In the 1950s, the refugee party (BHE) joined state coalitions in Schleswig-Holstein, Lower Saxony, Bavaria and Baden-Württemberg prior to joining the Adenauer government in 1953. In the 1980s and 1990s, the Greens entered numerous state governments, beginning with Hesse in late 1985, before forging a governing coalition with the SPD in Bonn in 1998. In Austria, Haider's *Freiheitliche Partei Österreichs* (FPÖ) first governed at the state level before joining the national government in Vienna.

Yet other examples suggest that the inclusion of a newcomer party into a state governing coalition can actually hasten its decline rather than serve as a springboard to national power. Inclusion can have a 'fatal embrace effect' or a 'de-mystification effect' (*Entzauberung*). The former results in the loss of an independent, distinct identity once a newcomer party becomes a junior member of a governing coalition; the latter effect follows when a populist party loses much of its appeal among voters after it is faced with the difficult, often unglamorous task of governing. For instance, the BP lost half of its seats in the Bavarian state parliament after four years in state government between 1954 and 1958. Soon after the Schill Party had entered into government in Hamburg in the autumn of 2002,[1] it appeared likely that it would experience a decline similar to that of Hamburg's *STATT Partei* (STATT-Party) in the mid-1990s;[2] namely, it would prove unable to govern effectively, fail to acquire national credibility and disappear come the next legislature period.[3]

Still other examples show that when a party is vigorously excluded from power at the state level, it may never be viewed as fit to govern at the national level. The established parties in the Federal Republic steadfastly refused to include the far-right NPD in state governments in the 1960s or the *Republikaner* and the DVU in the late 1980s and 1990s. All three parties were subsequently rendered irrelevant: they lost support and fell out of the state parliaments to which they had been elected. Nonetheless, it is possible that the established parties may inadvertently generate additional support for a party by appearing to exclude it unfairly. This leads to a 'sympathy and solidarity effect' which occurred in Germany in the 1870s in the case of the Catholic Centre and, as we shall see, the PDS in the 1990s.

While a number of factors contributed to the PDS' electoral defeat in 2002,[4] this chapter explores the electoral implications of the evolving relationship between national and eastern party systems. At a general level, we can identify two broad patterns of interaction between the national and the eastern party systems since unification. The first pattern, characteristic of the 1990s, proved highly favourable to the PDS, which could fully benefit from its unique position as a local 'insider' and a national 'outsider'. As we shall see, the party's competence in local government bolstered its electoral fortunes in 1992–93 which in turn intensified the isolation of the PDS at the national level. This in turn further attracted protest voters to the PDS in local, state and national elections. The second pattern, which emerged by the late 1990s, was much less favourable to the PDS. A 'vicious cycle' gradually replaced the 'virtuous cycle' of the earlier period. The inclusion of the PDS in state governing coalitions after 1998 appears to have cost the party crucial local support in the Federal elections of 2002; the greater acceptance of the PDS in the Bundestag after 1998 made the party less attractive to disenchanted eastern voters.

The following analysis considers each pattern in more detail, focusing first on the party system placement of the PDS at the three levels (eastern local, eastern state and national), then on the dynamic interplay between the three levels and how this interplay affected the PDS' electoral performance, and finally on the 'lessons' drawn by the political parties.

The PDS as a local insider and national outsider: 1992–98

After unification in 1990, a party system with three large parties (CDU, SPD, PDS) gradually established itself in the local assemblies and state parliaments of eastern Germany, while a five-party system that featured two large parties (CDU/CSU, SPD) and three small parties (FDP, Greens, PDS) took shape in the Bundestag. The PDS had distinct niches at the local, state and national levels from 1990 to 1998.

At the local level, the PDS soon became an important, influential and generally accepted actor in eastern Germany. This was to a significant degree a result of its local presence and its extensive contacts to important social groups. With its large and active (albeit aging) membership, the PDS had especially good relations to those interest groups that represented those living in rental units, the unemployed, owners of small garden plots, retirees, former GDR elite and the holders of property that was being legally contested by its former owners. The party also had extensive ties to many small businessmen who had set up their businesses after the fall of the Berlin Wall. Overall, the PDS enjoyed as least as many contacts to groups in civil society as did the SPD or the CDU. Unlike the CDU, whose relations with the churches and business were particularly strong, the PDS' network of contacts revolved primarily around interest groups focused on key social issues such as affordable housing and joblessness.[5]

In addition to its engaged members, the PDS had reform-minded leaders at the local level who energetically tackled the problems of their cities and districts. According to Werner Patzelt:

> [t]here these groups of comparatively young, well-educated elite, who already in the GDR had been willing to shape things (*gestaltungswillige*) and who had been formed by the GDR without being responsible for a system that they had already often been somewhat dissatisfied with even then, now invested their commitment and expertise so convincingly that political capital was accumulated off of whose interest the PDS still lives quite comfortably in local, state and federal elections.[6]

In short, as one author of a local study on the PDS notes, a division of labour soon arose. On the one hand, educated party activists in their forties and fifties, many of whom had previously worked as university instructors in the social sciences, managed the party and determined its political direction. On the other hand, an older generation of members, many of whom were former GDR functionaries, ensured that the party remained active at the grass-roots level.[7]

It was at the local level where the PDS reversed the electoral decline that had set in after the March 1990 *Volkskammer* elections. In the Berlin local elections of May 1992, the PDS won 29.7 per cent of the votes cast in the eastern half of the city. It emerged as the strongest party in several eastern districts, finished just behind the SPD in the formerly East German areas and improved markedly upon the 23.6 per cent of the vote it had garnered in the eastern half of city in the 1990 Berlin state elections.[8] In late 1993, the PDS performed well in the Brandenburg local elections where it increased its share from 16.6 per cent (May 1990) to 21.2 per cent. Berlin and Brandenburg marked the start of a string of election victories that would continue throughout the decade. In the 1990s, the share of the PDS vote rose from 14.3 per cent in the first cycle of local elections, to 19.8 per cent in the second cycle, to 22 per cent by the end of the decade. In contrast, the CDU share stagnated at around 35 per cent, the SPD share rose to 26 per cent where it stagnated and the FDP and Greens all but vanished at the local level in the 1990s.[9]

Wolfram Friedersdorff, a PDS district mayor in Berlin, acknowledges that the importance of local politics to the party's revival in the early 1990s cannot be overestimated. He believes that only through local politics was it possible for the PDS to establish itself in the Federal Republic. The PDS won the support of voters that might have otherwise turned to other forms of protest. By way of its extensive grass-roots engagement, the PDS came into contact with East Germans that were not part of a narrow socialist milieu.[10] After some initial attempts to isolate the PDS at the local level,[11] the other parties soon developed *de facto* a working relationship with the party.

In contrast, the PDS remained isolated in the eastern state parliaments until 1998 when it joined the SPD in coalition in the northern state of Mecklenburg-West Pomerania. The qualified exception was in Saxony-Anhalt, where the PDS in parliament supported a minority SPD-led government between 1994 and 2002. At the start of the 1990s, the PDS had been ostracised in the eastern parliaments. In Saxony and in Berlin, the mainstream parties attempted to keep PDS proposals off the legislative agenda because of the party's unwillingness to remove deputies tainted by a past association with the East German *Stasi*. In Saxony, almost all parliamentarians left the chamber when the PDS parliamentary leader spoke in October 1991, and the established parties refused for a time to consider PDS proposals;[12] in Berlin, the FDP submitted a proposal not to consider PDS initiatives that narrowly failed to secure a majority in the state parliament.[13] The PDS in Berlin struggled to find an audience for its speeches in parliament since, as one observer wrote in late 1991, 'the CDU deputies above all have made a sport of constantly interrupting the ex-communists with heckles'.[14]

By the mid-1990s, the party was encountering less hostility in many of the eastern state parliaments, yet was still kept out of governing coalitions at the state level.

The PDS remained an outsider in the Bundestag. The established parties excluded the PDS from governing coalition; refused to co-sponsor legislation with the party; rejected all PDS parliamentary initiatives; established in 1994 an alternative method of allocating committee seats that would reduce the PDS' presence in Bundestag committees; and empowered the Federal Office of Constitutional Protection to investigate the PDS for evidence that it posed a threat to the constitutional order.

The Christian Democrats, in particular, combined their unwillingness to cooperate with the PDS at the national level with sharp criticism of the party during election campaigns. This peaked in the federal election campaign of 1994, contributing to what Stöss and Neugebauer have described as 'defamation of the PDS in a blind rage'.[15] Chancellor Helmut Kohl called PDS supporters 'communist rabble' and 'red-coated fascists', borrowing this latter term from an earlier speech in which the Social Democrat Kurt Schumacher in 1930 had called the communists a 'red-coated duplicate version of the National Socialists'.[16] Other leading Christian Democrats were no gentler in their language. Wolfgang Schäuble (CDU) labelled the PDS 'the party of the Berlin Wall sharp shooters and henchman assistants (*Gefängnisschergen*)';[17] Theo Waigel spoke of the 'criminal SED/PDS' and a 'cancerous tumour in the democracy';[18] and Peter Hintze warned that '[A]fter Stasi torture, the Berlin Wall and barbed wire, spying and misery, the old SED-communists are luring with racy protest slogans. This is how the PDS cooks its red soup with firewood that it has itself chopped.'[19] Conservative politicians referred to the party as the 'SED/PDS', 'Cadre party', 'ex-SED', the 'SED-Successor PDS' and the 'party of SED-continuation' in order to underscore its communist origins.[20]

No parties in the Bundestag would jointly introduce a bill with the PDS, even if there was general agreement on content. They instead introduced their own legislation, neither seeking nor accepting the PDS as a co-sponsor of a bill. A PDS Bundestag deputy complained in 1992 that 'everything is done in order that our motions do not make it through committee. We would not even be able to carry the motion "Kohl is chancellor"'.[21] The established parties in the federal parliament made no secret of their disdain.[22] According to *Der Spiegel* in 1991.

> Good manners are suspended whenever a deputy from the PDS steps to the podium in the Bundestag. Parliamentarians from all the other caucuses unabashedly slide their chairs across the floor, rustle their newspapers and talk loudly with one another as if there were no speech from the PDS. That is exactly the point to it all. It is to make clear to the parliamentarian outcasts from the SED-successor party that their presence is not valued at all. The newcomers complain that the only ones who listen to them are the 'notorious hecklers'.[23]

Hecklers regularly interrupted the PDS speakers with cutting remarks about their responsibility for the crimes and economic ruin of the GDR.

Consequences

The PDS' strong grass-roots presence and its pragmatic, engaged *corps* of local politicians contributed to the party's revival and acceptance at the local level by the mid-1990s. The party also benefited from its 'outsider' status at the national level. By ostracising the PDS, the only party with a predominantly eastern leadership and electorate, the mainstream parties exacerbated the problem caused by the paucity of East German elites within the political establishment of the Federal Republic. Heidrun Abromeit has referred to a 'representation gap' (*Vertretungslücke*) of eastern interests.[24] This provided the PDS, in the eyes of many eastern voters, with an important function to fulfil in a political system where most top posts were held by West Germans. They wanted a distinctly East German voice to articulate and represent what they perceived to be their distinct interests and identity.[25] Eastern voters turned in ever greater numbers toward the PDS. According to Detlef Pollack, 'the interest of the East Germans in the PDS must be viewed within the context of their attempts to achieve an independent voice given the political realities of unified Germany'.[26] Polls indicated that a number of East Germans were voting for the PDS in order to ensure an 'eastern voice' in German politics, even if they did not share its ideology.[27]

The cold shoulder that the established parties turned toward the PDS in Bonn gave the PDS parliamentary group, led by the charismatic Gregor Gysi, the opportunity to enhance its reputation in the East as an underdog fighting against all odds for eastern interests. To Joschka Fischer (Greens), the PDS willingly became 'the party of martyrs in the East. And in the Bundestag the CDU/CSU set upon Gysi and his troops like a pack of hyenas and before running cameras they then allow themselves to be skinned and boiled in oil like the martyrs in early

Christianity and then they present themselves as the crucified Christ for the people in the East!'[28] Disillusioned East Germans signalled their protest by voting for a party that the mainstream parties viewed as beyond the pale. Following the PDS' surprise gains in the Berlin local elections of 1992, Gysi made just this point. 'CDU, SPD and FDP constantly give off the impression that every vote for the PDS riles them in particular ... The result is that anyone who is particularly dissatisfied with federal or state policies votes for the people that will most annoy those governing.'[29]

The resurgence of the PDS at the local level led to even sharper criticism of the PDS at the national level. The CDU/CSU revived its anti-communist language following the PDS' success in Berlin and Brandenburg in 1992–93. The strong performance of the PDS in the Saxony-Anhalt state election of Spring 1994, followed by the controversial decision of Reinhard Höppner (SPD) to head a Red–Green minority government in Magdeburg to be tolerated by the PDS in parliament, was the backdrop for the CDU/CSU's 'red socks campaign'. In the Federal election campaign of 1994, the CDU/CSU and FDP darkly warned that the SPD was preparing to assume power in Bonn with the help of the PDS ('red socks'). This election campaign made sense in a five-party system in Bonn, where two large parties competed with three small parties, of which one (the PDS) was seen by many West German voters as extremist. The governing CDU/CSU hoped to scare anti-communist West Germans into not voting for the SPD by casting doubt on its intentions regarding the PDS. Richard von Weiszäcker, the former Federal President, criticised the use of the PDS 'as an election campaign club in the hand of one western party to strike at the head of another western party'.[30]

Weiszäcker continued that 'without doubt this resulted in short term successes for one of these two camps, especially since it deeply unsettled the other camp and put it on the defensive. It was of most use though to the PDS itself.'[31] If, as Weiszäcker and others speculate, the 'red socks' campaign actually helped the PDS in the eastern states, then this too was not necessarily a bad thing for the CDU since it deprived the SPD and *Bündnis '90*/Greens of potential voters on the left.[32] Dan Hough writes that 'attempts by western politicians to characterise the PDS as a reincarnation of the SED or as a communist party play into the hands of the PDS, as it is able to illustrate how distant these Westerners are from the political realities in the eastern states'.[33] In short, the 'red socks' campaign, although perfectly logical within the context of the five-party system in Bonn, not only made little sense in eastern Germany, but actually contributed to the resurgence of the PDS within an eastern three-party system. The PDS recorded solid gains in all five state parliamentary elections in the East in 1994 as well as in the federal elections of that year. In short, developments in Bonn, which followed the logic of a five-party system, both affected and were affected by developments in the East, which followed the logic of a three-party system.

In 1998, a similar pattern returned. After state elections in Saxony-Anhalt in the spring, Reinhard Höppner chose to lead a SPD minority government that was tolerated by the PDS in parliament. Once again, the CDU/CSU and FDP ran an election campaign ('red hands campaign') that warned the voters of an SPD–PDS coalition in Bonn. Once again, the CDU lost votes in the East, while the PDS increased its share of the eastern vote to 21.6 per cent. In the following year, the PDS performed extremely well in several eastern state elections, in part owing to the difficulties faced by the SPD–Greens Federal government.

Its exclusion from the Federal government may have helped the PDS in yet another way. Since the PDS had neither cabinet posts, nor good relations to big business or the leading national interest groups, nor significant political influence, it was perhaps less susceptible to scandals. This was, at least, what the PDS repeatedly asserted. In a 1994 letter to Bundestag president Rita Süssmuth, Gregor Gysi wrote: 'it is the case that I speak of the PDS as the cleanest party in Bonn because it participates in no corruption ... I constantly point out in connection with this that it is not solely to our credit, but also a necessary consequence of exclusion.'[34] After a serious scandal in the 1990s involving the sequestering of SED monies in the Soviet Union, the PDS stayed clear of the scandals of the 1990s and the year 2000 that hurt the CDU and SPD at the polls.

'Lessons' learned by the parties

By the mid-1990s, PDS reformers were favouring the formation of SPD–PDS (Red–Red) coalitions at the state level. Several considerations informed their strategy. First, they believed that the PDS' competence and pragmatism at the local level had contributed to its revitalisation. They hoped that by governing at the state level in an equally effective, pragmatic fashion, they would build upon the 'bottom-up' model that seemingly had worked so well at the local level. They hoped to win over new supporters on the basis of their policy making and to depend less upon protest voters and the traditional communist milieu of the GDR. They also hoped that by proving themselves to be capable of governing at the state level, they would attract disillusioned centre-left voters in western Germany who still viewed the party with suspicion.

By the late 1990s, the SPD had begun to warm to the option of SPD–PDS (Red–Red) coalitions at the state level in the East. They hoped to liberate themselves from the position of being a junior partner in CDU-led grand coalitions in a number of states. This constellation had proved damaging to the SPD in Berlin and in Thuringia. Some SPD strategists realised that they might 'demystify' the PDS by bringing it into state government, thereby making it less attractive to protest voters. Finally, by late 1998, it had become clear that the anti-communist campaigns of the CDU were increasingly counterproductive in eastern Germany. The SPD now had less to fear from new 'red socks' campaigns that might arise in the wake of an SPD–PDS state government. The CDU recognised this as well and reevaluated its policy toward the PDS.

A new pattern emerges: 1998–2002

After the elections of 1998–99, the interplay between the eastern and the national party systems developed in a direction that would prove far less favourable to the PDS. At the local level in eastern Germany, the PDS remained an active and pragmatic political force. It continued to hold numerous council seats, participate in local administration and place many mayors. It also found acceptance among the other parties at the local level.

At the state level, the size of the party system remained generally constant. Yet relations between the SPD and the PDS improved within this three-party constellation. By the late 1990s, the PDS was becoming a viable potential coalition partner for the SPD. The first SPD–PDS state government formed in Mecklenburg-West Pomerania in 1998. In January 2002, the second Red–Red coalition arose in Berlin after the PDS had secured 48 per cent of all votes casts in the eastern part of the city. For the first time, the PDS governed a state that included citizens of the old Federal Republic. Had the SPD performed better in Thuringia in 1999 and in Saxony-Anhalt in 2002, it would have probably formed coalitions with the PDS in these states as well.

At the national level, parliamentary relations significantly improved between the PDS and the four established parties which increasingly treated the PDS as a normal party. This was in part because the PDS now enjoyed the rights, privileges and status of a *Fraktion* after clearing the 5 per cent hurdle in the 1998 federal elections. With a few exceptions, it took part like any other party in the affairs of the Bundestag. In April 2000, the CDU/CSU and the PDS together introduced a draft law concerning reparations for slave labourers, marking the first formal cooperation between the two parties in the Bundestag.[35] The tone with which the CDU/CSU greeted PDS speakers in parliament had also softened. For its part, the Schröder government had discovered a new-found interest in the PDS once the party had acquired a say over federal policy in the Bundesrat. Schröder did not hesitate to bargain directly with Helmut Holter (PDS), Labour Minister in Mecklenburg-West Pomerania, over the conditions under which Mecklenburg-West Pomerania would support the government's tax reform in the Bundesrat.

Moreover, the PDS relaxed its strident opposition to government policy, while following a pragmatic course in the Bundesrat. Its parliamentary caucus increasingly refrained from demonstrations of protest. For example, whereas during the Gulf War in January 1991 Gregor Gysi, as the chair of the party group in parliament, had appeared in front of the Bundestag wearing a white arm band and had spoken out strongly against the war, in May 2002 Roland Claus, as PDS caucus chair, would apologise for the fact that several PDS deputies had unfolded a transparency opposing war while President Bush delivered a speech on the floor of the Bundestag. Nonetheless, the four established parties still steadfastly refused to consider a governing coalition with the PDS at the national level, nor would they form a minority government with the votes of the PDS.

Consequences

For two reasons, it seems clear that the interaction between the transformed eastern and national party systems of 1998–2002 harmed the electoral fortunes of the PDS in 2002.

First, the party now received far less of a 'bottom-up' bonus. In fact, whereas its role in local administration had previously enhanced the levels of acceptance in the East, its participation in state governments in Mecklenburg-West Pomerania and Berlin now triggered an appreciable drop in popularity in both states.[36] In Federal elections, the party's share of the second ballot votes cast in Mecklenburg-West Pomerania fell dramatically from 24 per cent in 1998 (its highest overall average) to just 16.3 per cent in 2002. This represented the largest single drop in support (7.3 percentage points) from 1998 to 2002 that the PDS sustained in any of the eastern states. In Berlin, the PDS received 24.5 per cent of the second ballot votes cast in the eastern part of the city on 22 September 2002. This was down from the 30 per cent of votes it had secured in the Federal elections of 1998 and down from nearly 48 per cent garnered in the Berlin state election of 2001. The PDS' overall share in Berlin was 11.4 per cent which was down from the 14.5 per cent secured in 1998 and from the 22.6 per cent garnered in the autumn 2001 state election. In both states, the PDS lost support among previous core followers and among voters who were disappointed with the party's record in state office. The party's failure in Schwerin and Berlin to deliver on its lofty promises to cut unemployment, and to maintain (or even to extend) social benefits, exposed it to sharp criticism on the left. Related factors, such as the corruption charges against Helmut Holter in Schwerin or Gysi's decision to quit the Berlin state government in Summer 2002, complicated matters further for the PDS and made it difficult for the party to generate much grass-roots excitement during the Federal election campaign.

The election results in Berlin and Mecklenburg-West Pomerania were particularly damaging to the PDS because the party failed to win a much-needed third district mandate in either state. This would have allowed them to re-enter parliament without 5 per cent of the national vote. Of the five districts that had appeared as potentially winnable (other than the two in Berlin that the PDS did win), three were in Berlin, one in Rostock and one in Halle. Yet in Rostock, the PDS' share of the first ballot votes cast plummeted 15 percentage points from 33.5 per cent to 18.5 per cent. Likewise, the PDS received a significantly lower share of the first ballot votes cast in the Berlin districts of Pankow, Kreuzberg-Friedrichshain-Prenzlauer Berg, and Treptow-Köpenick. In short, the PDS performed disproportionately badly in those districts where it was governing at the state level.

The Red–Red coalitions in Berlin and in Schwerin also hurt the PDS by making it more difficult for the party to present itself as a credible national opponent of the SPD. The PDS had described itself as the left-wing opposition to Red–Green at its election party congress in Rostock in April 2002. Yet its claim was weakened by its eagerness to govern with the SPD in eastern Germany. For the first time, the PDS faced the difficult task of campaigning as an opposition party at the national level and as a governing party at the state level. Made necessary by the growing tension between the national and the eastern state party systems, this *Spagat* proved especially difficult for the PDS during the election campaign. Differences of strategy among the party leaders complicated matters further.

Second, the position of the PDS within the national party system was now less favourable to the party's campaign efforts in the new Federal states. When the CDU/CSU and FDP did not run another version of the 'red socks campaign' of 1994, the PDS not only had a more difficult time attracting sympathy votes or protest votes, but it struggled to receive any significant media coverage at all. The showdown between Gerhard Schröder and Edmund Stoiber instead dominated the headlines.

The PDS was neither fish nor fowl. While no longer an outcast in the Bundestag, the PDS remained on the outside looking in. Both the SPD and Greens had made it abundantly clear that they would neither form a coalition with the PDS nor be elected on the basis of its votes in the Bundestag. This put the PDS in a difficult position during the campaign of 2002. The voters saw a choice between two rival blocs (SPD–Green and CDU/CSU–FDP). Since most East Germans favoured Schröder over Stoiber, many were reluctant to vote for the PDS which was widely seen as wasting a vote. It seems clear that to at least some East Germans the decline of the PDS, while perhaps regrettable, was the lesser evil to Stoiber becoming Chancellor. Some tacticians in the PDS tried to make their party appear relevant by indicating that it might help Red–Green to power if the coalition needed the votes of the PDS. This offer, however, was frivolous in view of Schröder's refusal to rely upon PDS support to return to office. It also weakened the party's claim to be an opposition party.

Lessons learned?

With the failure of the PDS to re-enter the Bundestag, the size of national party system fell from five to four parties.[37] The emerging dynamic between the national and eastern party systems will probably be even less advantageous to the PDS. In the coming years, the PDS faces the prospects of reduced visibility in national politics. It seems likely that the leadership of the CDU/CSU and FDP will soon pay the

PDS little attention with few West Germans now worrying about Red–Red coalitions in the East. The SPD will no doubt continue its dual strategy of 'demystifying' in the East, while dismissing the option of a Red–Red–Green coalition at the national level.

The PDS has reconsidered its pro-SPD course since the election. This is understandable given that the PDS has received little credit for the accomplishments (however modest) of the coalition governments in Schwerin and Berlin, while its policy record in these governments has disappointed many of its supporters. The Greens in coalition can better escape the 'fatal embrace' of the larger SPD since their issues (e.g. environment, multi-culturalism, same-sex marriages, a more liberal drug policy) are much more clearly recognisable as Green issues, whereas it would be harder for the PDS to do the same since its policy agenda resembles that of SPD traditionalists. Following the Bundestag election, the reform-minded leadership suffered a stinging defeat at the PDS' party congress in Gera in October. A newly elected leadership openly questioned the wisdom of cooperation with the SPD and strove to sharpen the oppositional character of the PDS. Yet unless the PDS quits the state governments in Berlin and in Schwerin, something it is understandably reluctant to do, it will remain bound to the strategy of the party reformers. Moreover, with no other potential coalition partners on the horizon, it is not clear how the PDS could effect societal change without joining forces with the Social Democrats. In any case, polls indicate that since the federal election and the party congress in Gera the level of public support for the PDS has fallen well below that what is needed to rejoin the Bundestag in 2006.

Conclusion

This case study has produced several findings. First, the national and subnational party systems in Germany influenced each other in important ways. Eastern Germany was not South Tirol; rather, the national party system significantly affected the eastern party systems and vice versa. Second, the size of the respective party systems (five-party or three-party), the weight of the parties within the respective party systems (two big and three small or three big), and the degree of polarisation between the mainstream parties and the PDS (high, medium, or low) all affected the interplay between national and sub-national party systems. However, the changing relationship among the parties within a given party systems was particularly significant.

Third, the interplay between party systems at the regional and national levels did not remain static, but rather evolved over time, owing in part to strategic choices and in part to the developing interaction of the party systems. A constellation which was favourable to the PDS in the 1990s, when the party was at once a local insider and a national outsider, gave rise to a decidedly less favourable pattern by the end of the decade. As the PDS gained support in the East, the SPD considered including it in eastern coalitions as an alternative to CDU-led grand coalitions. In hindsight, the electoral high-water marks of the PDS in Mecklenburg-West Pomerania in 1998 (24.4 per cent) and in eastern Berlin in 2001 (47.6 per cent) were probably Pyrrhic victories that resulted in Red–Red coalitions that contributed to the party's defeat in the Bundestag elections of 2002. Likewise, as the PDS became stronger in the Bundestag in the 1990s, it not only acquired the normal rights of a *Fraktion*, but its new-found strength led the established parties to reexamine and normalise their relations with the PDS. This in turn made it harder for the party to present itself as a trenchant symbol of eastern discrimination.

Fourth, at least in the German case, one must consider the dynamic that arises between three distinct party systems: eastern local, eastern state and national. The PDS performed well when it was integrated into the former, yet was excluded at the latter two levels. Once included at both the local and the state level (Schwerin and Berlin), it faced grave new challenges. It would now have greater difficulty winning over disillusioned voters who increasingly viewed the PDS as part of the establishment and hence part of the problem. It would also strike many voters as being a less convincing party of opposition at the national level given its role in the Bundesrat and its relations to the SPD within the eastern states.

Fifth, and finally, between 1992 and 1998 the policy of isolating the PDS at the national and state levels did not produce the desired 'irrelevancy effect'. Instead, it brought forth an unintended 'sympathy and solidarity effect' that helped lift the electoral fortunes of the party. The reasons for this varied. The party pointed to its own political isolation as evidence of the marginalisation and discrimination of the East Germans; its leader Gregor Gysi, who was admired by many East Germans for his pluck, turned out to be highly skilled at publicly presenting his party in a sympathetic light; and finally, and perhaps most importantly, it was difficult to make the PDS appear irrelevant when it was clearly an important political force at the local level in eastern Germany. East Germans had regular contact with PDS activists and many came to value their community engagement. *De facto* cooperation between the mainstream parties and the PDS at the local level had not led either to the 'de-mystification' of the party or to a 'fatal embrace effect'. Instead, the PDS enhanced its reputation of being effective at local governance and steadily improved its share of the votes cast in local elections. In fact, one can argue that the 'stepping-stone effect' was partially borne out during the 1990s. The acceptance of the PDS in local politics helped pave the way for its inclusion in state level coalitions in 1998.

Between 1998 and 2002, the PDS demonstrably failed to use its foothold in the state governments of Mecklenburg-West Pomerania and Berlin as a stepping stone to joining the national government. Moreover, its presence in these very state governments had a 'de-mystification effect'. Many voters in these states grew disenchanted with the PDS in power and either stayed at home or voted for the SPD on 22 September 2002. And once the established parties at the national level had normalised relations with the PDS in the late 1990s, they eliminated much of the 'sympathy and solidarity effect' that had earlier arisen when the party was publicly ostracised. Yet by continuing to reject any coalition with the PDS at the national level, the mainstream parties did generate an 'irrelevancy effect' that proved very costly to the PDS during the election campaign of 2002. Past supporters of the PDS feared they would be wasting their vote, and thereby helping Edmund Stoiber, if they voted for a party that would either remain in the opposition or not enter the Bundestag. This quandary will probably continue to plague potential supporters of PDS in the years to come.

Notes

1 Established by the former judge Ronald Schill, the *Partei Rechtsstaatliche Offensive* (Party of a Rule of Law Offensive, PRO) campaigned in Hamburg on a law-and-order platform that brought the party unexpected success in the port city. In late September 2001, it won nearly 20 per cent of the vote in the Hamburg state elections. It subsequently formed a governing coalition in Hamburg with the CDU and the FDP. Roland Schill, known as 'judge merciless' on account of his preference for tough sentences, became the Minister of Interior in Hamburg.

2 As a populist party of protest, the *STATT-Partei* captured a surprising 5.6 per cent of the vote in the Hamburg state election of 1993. It subsequently agreed to a government of cooperation with the SPD in Hamburg. After a turbulent four years in parliament, the *STATT-Partei* received just 3.8 per cent of the vote and did not cross the 5 per cent threshold needed for reentry into parliament.

3 See 'Eine Partei zerfleischt sich selbst', *Handelsblatt*, 31 July 2002.

4 These included: the sudden decision of Gregor Gysi, a popular PDS politician, to turn his back on politics after it became known in the summer of 2002 that he had inappropriately used frequent flier miles he had accumulated while on state business; the fact that Gerhard Schröder could improve his standing in the East by responding energetically to the floods in the summer of 2002; the popular position of the government on the issue of war against Iraq; the polarising effect of Edmund Stoiber's candidacy that led many East Germans to vote for the SPD in order to prevent Stoiber from becoming Chancellor; the previous inability of the PDS to come up with a new party programme; the lacklustre election campaign run by the PDS; and signs that the East–West cleavage in German politics had lost salience as an electoral issue. For a detailed discussion of the PDS' defeat, see Richard Stöss and Gero Neugebauer, 'Mit einem blauen Auge davon gekommen. Eine Analyse der Bundestagswahl 2002', *Arbeitshefte aus dem Otto-Stammer-Zentrum*, Nr. 7 (Berlin: Otto-Stammer-Zentrum, 2002) and Dieter Roth and Matthias Jung, 'Ablösung der Regierung vertagt: Eine Analyse der Bundestagswahl 2002', *Aus Politik und Zeitgeschichte*, 49–50/2002 (9–16 December 2002), pp. 8–9. For the views of former PDS General Secretary Dietmar Bartsch, see Dietmar Bartsch, 'Die Markenzeichen moderner sozialistischer Politik fehlten', *Disput* 3:1 (January 2003), at http://pds-onlinede/politik/publikationen/disput/view_html?zid=1045&bs= 1&n=12&a.

5 Günter Pollack, 'Die PDS im kommunalen Parteiensystem', in Michael Brie and Rudolf Woderich (eds), *Die PDS im Parteiensystem* (Berlin: Karl Dietz Verlag, 2000), p. 33.

6 Werner J. Patzelt, 'Die PDS nach 2000: Neugeburt oder Fehlgeburt', in Frank Berg and Lutz Kirschner (eds), *PDS am Scheideweg*, Manuscript 20 (Berlin: Rosa-Luxemburg-Stiftung, 2001), p. 6.

7 Lothar Probst, 'Wer ist die PDS? Einblicke in den Alltag einer postkommunistischen Partei', *Frankfurter Allgemeine Zeitung*, 1 September 1997.

8 The PDS recorded approximately the same level of support in East Berlin as it had in the local elections of May 1990.

9 Pollack, 'Die PDS im kommunalen Parteiensystem', pp. 195–6.

10 Wolfram Friedersdorff, interview with author, Lichtenberg City Hall,

Berlin, 13 July 2001.

11 For instance, in anticipation of PDS gains in the Berlin local elections of 1992, the governing CDU/SPD coalition altered the constitution in order that the district mayor be appointed by the majority in the district assembly, rather than by the largest party as had previously been the practice. This change would allow the established parties to prevent the PDS from appointing mayors throughout much of East Berlin.

12 'Rede vor fast leerem Plenarsaal', *Frankfurter Rundschau*, 26 October 1991; and 'LL/PDS wird nicht mehr "geschnitten"', *Sächsiche Zeitung*, 12 September 1992.

13 'SPD stimmt geschlossen mit der Opposition', *Der Tagesspiegel*, 17 October 1992; 'Hammelsprung war notwendig', *Frankfurter Rundschau*, 17 October 1992.

14 Hans-Martin Tillack, 'Pensioniert die PDS!', *Die Tageszeitung*, 24 October 1991.

15 Gero Neugebauer and Richard Stöss, *Die PDS: Geschichte, Organisation, Wähler, Konkurrenten* (Opladen: Leske & Budrich, 1996), p. 222.

16 Neugebauer and Stöss, *Die PDS*, pp. 221–2; Willy Albrecht (ed.), *Kurt Schumacher. Reden-Schriften-Korrespondenzen 1945–1952* (Berlin: J. H. W. Dietz, 1985), p. 64.

17 Neugebauer and Stöss, *Die PDS*, p. 220.

18 Johannes Volmert, 'Die "Altparteien" außer Fassung. Reaktionen und Kampagnen auf die Wahlerfolge der PDS – ein Pressespiegel', in Michael Brie, Martin Herzig and Thomas Koch (eds), *Die PDS: Empirische Befunde & kontroverse Analysen* (Cologne: PapyRossa, 1995), quotations on pp. 177 and 170.

19 'Zitat des Tages', *Neues Deutschland*, 27 June 1994. This quote appeared in *Bild am Sonntag*, 26 June 1994.

20 Ralph Bollmann, 'Mitten in Zehlendorf', *Die Tageszeitung*, 22 September 1999.

21 Dagmar Enkelmann, quoted in Silke Lambeck, 'Karriere in der falschen Partei', *Berliner Zeitung*, 24 November 1992.

22 See Lambeck, 'Karriere in der falschen Partei' and Christian Stoll, 'Rote Raus: Die PDS in Bonn', *Wiener*, 4 (April 1991), pp. 42–6.

23 'Schwer verträglich', *Der Spiegel*, 22 July 1991, p. 33.

24 Heidrun Abromeit, 'Die "Vetretungslücke". Probleme im neuen deutschen Bundesstaat', *Gegenwartskunde*, 42:3 (1993), pp. 281–92.

25 See Dan Hough, *The Fall and Rise of the PDS in Eastern Germany* (Birmingham: Birmingham University Press, 2002).

26 Detlef Pollack, 'Ostdeutsche Identität – ein multidimensionales Phänomen', in Heiner Meulemann (ed.), *Werte und nationale Identität im vereinten Deutschland. Erklärungsansätze der Umfrageforschung* (Opladen: Leske & Budrich, 1998), p. 315.

27 When PDS voters were asked in 1998 why they voted for the party, 27 per cent listed the reason: 'out of protest against predominance of the West in the development of the East'. 'Krenz vor Kohl', *Der Spiegel*, 3 August 1998, p. 32.

28 Quoted in Gregor Gysi, *Freche Sprüche* (Berlin: Schwarzkopf & Schwarzkopf, 1995), p. 103.

29 'Ich bekämpfe DDR-Nostalgie', *Der Spiegel*, 1 June 1992, pp. 36–7.

30 'Wahlkampfkeule PDS', excerpts from Richard von Weizsäcker's address on Reformation Day 1995 in the Brandenburg Cathedral, reprinted in *Blätter für deutsche und internationale Politik*, 12/95 (December 1995), p. 1422.

31 *Ibid.*

32 Bertolt Fessen, 'Ressentiment und Fehlwahrnehmung', *Berliner Debate INITIAL*, 6:4/5 (1995), p. 142.

33 Hough, *The Fall and Rise of the PDS in Eastern Germany*, p. 138.

34 The letter of 26 September 1994 is reprinted in Gysi, *Freche Sprüche*, p. 170.

35 'Antrag von CDU/CSU und PDS', *Berliner Zeitung*, 13 April 2000.

36 This probably did not come as a surprise to the party's leaders. After entering the state government in 1998, the PDS of Mecklenburg-West Pomerania had suffered rare electoral setbacks prior to 2002. In the June 1999 communal elections in Mecklenburg-West Pomerania, the PDS received 21.9 per cent of the vote which was down from the 24.3 per cent garnered in 1994. In the EU elections of 1999, the PDS won 24.3 per cent of the vote in Mecklenburg-West Pomerania, whereas it had received a 27.3 per cent share five years earlier, thereby distinguishing itself as the only state branch in the East to receive a lower share of the vote in 1999 than it had received in 1994. The lacklustre showing of the PDS in Mecklenburg-West Pomerania (and to a lesser extent in Saxony-Anhalt in Spring 2002) suggested that when the PDS left the opposition, protest voters lost interest in the party and its electoral performance suffered.

37 The party has two deputies in the Bundestag and can still exert some influence over Federal policy in the Bundesrat.

14

Elections in the *Länder*, 1990–2002[1]

Arthur B. Gunlicks

Five phases can be distinguished in the development of political parties in the western German *Länder*. The first phase, from 1945 to 1953, covers the period during which older parties were reestablished, e.g. the SPD, and new parties were founded, e.g. the BHE, CDU, CSU and FDP.[2] The second phase, which lasted from 1953 to 1969, saw the developing concentration of parties culminating in the three- (or two-and-a-half) party system of CDU/CSU, SPD and FDP. The third phase, which spanned the period from 1969 to 1983, was a period of three-party dominance, while in the fourth phase, from 1983 to 1990, the Greens emerged as a fourth party. Finally, following a reorientation after unification in 1990, a five-party system has developed at the national level with the rise of the PDS, although the PDS has a special regional character and in *Land* elections has been confined to the new *Länder* and Berlin in the East just as the Greens and FDP have been successful only or mostly in the West.[3]

This chapter describes and analyzes elections in the *Länder* of united Germany since 1990. More specifically, we look at election results in the first elections following unification and, in the twelve following years, at coalition formation, voting turnout and gains and losses in each *Land* since 1990. Finally, we address the complicated question of the relevance of *Land* elections to national politics and Bundestag elections.

Elections in the *Länder*

There were fifty-two elections in the sixteen *Länder* between 1990 and

September 2002 (see table 14.1). Three of them, in the Saarland, Lower Saxony and North-Rhine Westphalia, were in the former West Germany before unification on 3 October 1990. In analysing these elections, I have divided Germany into three general regions: North, South and East. I have included in the North the following five *Länder*: the city-states of Bremen and Hamburg, Schleswig-Holstein, Lower Saxony and North-Rhine Westphalia. The *Länder* of Baden-Württemberg, Bavaria, Hesse, Rhineland-Palatinate and the Saarland comprise the South. The East consists of united Berlin and the five new *Länder*, Brandenburg, Mecklenburg-Vorpommern, Saxony, Saxony-Anhalt and Thuringia.

The North

In the period 1990–92, the SPD had a significant lead in each of the five northern *Länder* except Lower Saxony, where it won only 2.2 per cent more than the CDU. In each election during this early period, the FDP received more than the 5 per cent required for consideration in the proportional representation calculations for seats in the five *Land* parliaments. The Greens also passed the 5 per cent barrier in every *Land* except Schleswig-Holstein, where they barely missed with 4.9 per cent. Far-right parties also passed the 5 per cent barrier in Bremen and Schleswig-Holstein in September 1991 and April 1992, respectively, while 'other' parties ranged from 3.5 per cent in Bremen to 0.6 per cent in Lower Saxony.

During the course of the decade or more after unification, the SPD continued to receive the most votes in all five *Länder*, in spite of a decline in Hamburg, North-Rhine Westphalia and Schleswig-Holstein. The CDU made gains in Bremen, North-Rhine Westphalia and Schleswig-Holstein, but these were minor gains in the latter two. The FDP share of the vote declined in Bremen, Hamburg and Lower Saxony, but it experienced a rise in Schleswig-Holstein and North-Rhine Westphalia, where it did especially well in May 2000. The Greens generally did well until the end of the 1990s, when they experienced a rather significant decline in their share of the vote in all five *Länder* though, unlike the FDP, the Greens still received more than 5 per cent in each election. The far-right parties had limited success, barely missing the goal of 5 per cent in Hamburg in 1993 and 1997 and losing representation in Bremen in 1995 and 1999. 'Other' parties were more successful, especially in Bremen in 1995 and Hamburg in 1993 (*STATT-Partei*),

Table 14.1 Results of *Land* elections, by region, 1990–2002 (%)

	Dates of election	*CDU/CSU*	*SPD*	*FDP*	*Greens*	*PDS*	*Far Right*	*Other*
North								
HB	9/91, 5/95, 6/99	30.7/32.6/37.1	38.8/33.4/42.6	9.5/3.4/2.5	11.4/13.1/9.0	~/2.7/2.9	6.2/2.5/3.0	3.5/12.9/2.9
HH	6/91, 9/93, 9/97, 9/01	35.1/25.1/30.7/26.2	48.0/40.4/36.2/36.5	5.4/4.2/3.5/5.1	7.2/13.5/13.9/8.5		1.2/7.6/6.8/0.8	3.1/9.2/8.9/22.9
LS	5/90, 3/94, 3/98	42.0/36.4/35.9	44.2/44.3/47.9	6.0/4.4/4.9	5.5/7.4/7.0		1.7/3.7/2.8	0.6/3.8/1.5
NRW	5/90, 5/95, 5/00	36.7/37.7/37.0	50.0/46.0/42.8	5.8/4.0/9.8	5.0/10.0/7.1		1.8/0.8/1.1	0.7/1.5/2.2
S-H	4/92, 3/96, 2/00	33.8/37.2/35.2	46.2/39.8/43.1	5.6/5.7/7.6	4.9/8.1/6.2	~/~/1.4	7.5/4.3/1.0	2.0/4.9/5.4
South								
B-W	4/92, 3/96, 3/01	39.6/41.3/44.8	29.4/25.1/33.3	5.9/9.6/8.1	9.5/12.1/7.7		10.9/9.1/4.6	4.9/2.8/1.5
Bav	10/90, 9/94, 9/98	54.9/52.8/52.9	26.0/30.0/28.7	5.2/2.8/1.7	6.4/6.1/5.7		4.9/3.9/3.6	2.6/4.4/7.4
HE	1/91, 2/95, 2/99	40.2/39.2/43.4	40.8/38.0/39.4	7.4/7.4/5.1	8.8/11.2/7.2		1.7/2.0/2.7	2.8/1.9/2.2
R-P	4/91, 3/96, 3/01	38.7/38.7/35.3	44.8/39.8/44.7	6.9/8.9/7.8	6.5/6.9/5.2		2.0/3.5/2.9	1.1/2.2/2.2
Saar	1/90, 10/94, 9/99	33.4/38.6/45.5	54.4/49.4/44.4	5.6/2.1/2.6	2.6/5.5/3.2		3.6/1.4/1.3	0.3/3.0/3.0
East								
Berlin	12/90, 10/95, 10/99, 10/01	40.4/37.4/40.8/23.8	30.4/23.6/22.4/29.7	7.1/2.5/2.2/9.9	9.4/13.2/9.9/9.1	9.2/14.6/17.7/22.6	3.1/2.6/2.7/1.3	0.4/5.8/4.3/3.6
BB	10/90, 9/94, 9/99	29.4/18.7/26.6	38.2/54.1/39.3	6.6/2.2/1.9	9.3/2.9/1.9	13.4/18.7/23.3	1.1/1.1/5.3	1.9/2.2/1.7
MV	10/90, 10/94, 9/98, 9/02	38.3/37.7/30.2/31.4	27.0/29.5/34.3/40.6	5.5/3.8/1.6/4.7	6.4/3.7/2.7/2.6	15.7/22.7/24.4/16.4	1.1/1.1/4.5/1.1	6.1/1.6/2.4/3.2
Sax	10/90, 9/94, 9/99	53.8/58.1/56.9	19.1/16.6/10.7	5.3/1.7/1.1	5.6/4.1/2.6	10.2/16.5/22.2	~/1.3/1.5	6.0/1.7/4.9
S-A	10/90, 6/94, 4/98, 4/02	39.0/34.4/22.0/37.3	26.0/34.0/35.9/20.0	13.5/3.6/4.2/13.3	5.3/5.1/3.2/2.0	12.0/19.9/19.6/20.4	0.6/1.4/13.6/0.0	3.6/1.9/2.2/7.0
Th	10/90, 10/94, 9/99	45.4/42.6/51.0	22.8/29.6/18.5	9.3/3.2/1.1	6.5/4.5/1.9	9.7/16.6/21.4	0.8/1.3/3.9	5.6/2.3/2.3

Notes:
HB: Hansastadt Bremen
HH: Hansastadt Hamburg
LS: Lower Saxony
NRW: North-Rhine Westphalia
S-H: Schleswig-Holstein
B-W: Bad-Württemberg
Bav: Bavaria
HE: Hesse
R-P: Rhineland-Palatinate
Saar: Saar
Berlin: Berlin
BB: Brandenburg
MV: Mecklenberg-Vorpommern
Sax: Saxony
S-A: Saxony-Anhalt
Th: Thuringia

Source: www.wahlrecht.de.

1997 and 2001; indeed, the law-and-order PRO or Schill Party came out of nowhere to receive a record 19.4 per cent in Hamburg in September 2001 and joined the CDU and FDP in a coalition that removed the SPD as a government party for the first time in forty-four years. In Schleswig-Holstein, the Danish SSW also gained votes in 2000, receiving 4.1 per cent, up from 2.5 per cent in 1996 and 1.9 per cent in 1992.

The South

At the beginning of the 1990s there was a balance between Baden-Württemberg and Bavaria with their large CDU or CSU leads, respectively, and Rhineland-Palatinate and the Saarland with large SPD leads. The CDU and SPD were virtually tied in Hesse, where the SPD held a razor-thin lead of 0.6 per cent in the 1991 elections. The FDP passed the 5 per cent barrier in all five *Länder*, as did the Greens except for the Saarland.

The CSU received an absolute majority in all three elections held in Bavaria in the 1990s. The CDU was the strongest party in Baden-Württemberg throughout the 1990s, although it did not achieve a slight plurality in Hesse until the mid-to-late 1990s. The CDU also gained a slight plurality in the Saarland in 1999, but it remained in second place in Rhineland-Palatinate. The FDP gained more than 5 per cent throughout the 1990s in Baden-Württemberg, Hesse and Rhineland-Palatinate, but it fell below 5 per cent in Bavaria and the Saarland in the elections of the mid- and late 1990s. The Greens gained more than 5 per cent in all of the southern *Länder* in or after 1990 except the Saarland, where they were successful only in 1994. The far-right parties did well in Baden-Württemberg in 1992 and 1996, but they failed to pass the 5 per cent barrier in 2001. They received less than 5 per cent of the vote in the other four southern *Länder*. 'Others' failed to gain 5 per cent in all of the elections except in the 1998 election in Bavaria; however, no single 'other' party received 5 per cent in that election to gain any seats.

The East

Elections were held in Berlin and all of the five new *Länder* just after reunification in 1990. The CDU led by large margins in all the new *Länder* except Brandenburg, where the SPD had a sizable lead. The FDP was comfortably above 5 per cent in all six *Länder* and received 13.5 per cent in Saxony-Anhalt. The Greens also received more than 5 per cent in all of the *Länder*. The PDS was a distant third after the CDU and SPD, with a high of 15.7 per cent in Mecklenburg-Vorpommern and a low of 9.2 per cent in Berlin.

But there was great volatility in the East after 1990. The CDU retained a rather stable plurality in Berlin in 1995 and 1999, but it suffered dramatic losses in October 2001. In Brandenburg, the CDU share of the vote declined by over 10 per cent in 1994, but it regained almost 8 per cent in the 1999 election. The CDU share of the vote steadily declined in Mecklenburg-Vorpommern throughout the 1990s, but it gained slightly in the September 2002 election. It received an absolute majority throughout the 1990s in Saxony, while it declined dramatically in Saxony-Anhalt in 1994 and 1998. However, the CDU increased its share of the vote by 15 per cent in the April 2002 election, becoming once again that *Land*'s largest party. The CDU remained the dominant party in Thuringia throughout the 1990s, receiving an absolute majority in 1999.

The SPD started in Berlin with a little more than 30 per cent of the vote in 1990, then declined over the 1990s only to become the strongest party in October 2001 with less than 30 per cent of the vote! It remained the strongest party in Brandenburg throughout the 1990s, receiving an absolute majority in 1994. The SPD's fortunes improved dramatically in Mecklenburg-Vorpommern during the 1990s, and it became the strongest party in 1998 and September 2002. The SPD's share of the vote rose steadily in Saxony-Anhalt, but it lost almost 16 per cent in April 2002, when the CDU became the leading party again. The SPD was weak in Thuringia, receiving a high of 29.6 per cent in 1994 and only 18.5 per cent in 1999. But nowhere was the SPD weaker than in Saxony, where it started with 19.1 per cent of the vote in 1990 and ended with only 10.7 per cent in 1999.

The FDP did well in 1990, receiving more than 5 per cent in Berlin and all five new *Länder*. It benefited especially in Saxony-Anhalt in 1990, when many voters rewarded it for being the party of the native son, Foreign Minister Hans-Dietrich Genscher, who had grown up in Halle before going to West Germany. But in all of the follow-up elections in the mid-to-late 1990s, including Saxony-Anhalt, the FDP failed to pass the 5 per cent hurdle. Only in 2001 did the party win an impressive 9.9 per cent of the vote in Berlin and 13.3 per cent in Saxony-Anhalt.

The Greens also did well on the first round in 1990, winning between

5.3 per cent in Saxony-Anhalt, 9.4 per cent in Berlin and 9.3 per cent in Brandenburg. It gained an even higher percentage in Berlin in 1995, but it lost votes in all of the new *Länder*. It squeaked past the 5 per cent barrier in Saxony-Anhalt in 1994. By 2002 it had seats only in Berlin, where it won 9.1 per cent of the vote in October 2001.

The PDS, which is virtually absent from the scene in the South and has received minimal support in Bremen and Schleswig-Holstein in the North, is one of the three major parties in the East. Indeed, it won second place in several elections starting in the mid-1990s. It tied or came close to tying the SPD for second place in Brandenburg and Saxony in the mid-1990s and in Saxony-Anhalt in 2002. Moreover, the PDS won significantly more votes than the SPD in Saxony. It increased its vote steadily throughout the 1990s in Berlin, Brandenburg, Saxony, Thuringia and, to a lesser extent, in Saxony-Anhalt. Only in September 2002 did its share of the vote decline in Mecklenburg-Vorpommern by a significant 8 percentage points.

The far-right parties generally had little success in the East, but the DVU did win a whopping 13.6 per cent of the vote in Saxony-Anhalt in 1998 and 5.3 per cent in Brandenburg in 1999. However, it received no support in Saxony-Anhalt in 2002. 'Other' parties have not done well in the East. None has been able to pass the 5 per cent barrier.

Coalitions in the *Länder*

The parties to governing coalitions in the *Länder* are more varied than at the federal level (see table 14.2). *Land* electoral results in the North have been characterised by considerable stability (with the exceptions of Hamburg and Bremen), with the SPD the leading party in all five *Länder* (table 14.2) throughout the 1990s and until 2002. Coalitions in the North have also been relatively stable: the SPD changed partners in Bremen, and it added or dropped a partner in Hamburg, Lower Saxony and North-Rhine Westphalia. Only in Schleswig-Holstein did it govern alone throughout the last decade. On the other hand, it was forced out of government in Hamburg by a coalition of the CDU, FDP and PRO following the September 2001 elections.

In the South there has also been general electoral stability in four of the *Länder*, with the Saarland the major exception owing to 10–12 per cent gains and losses by the CDU and SPD, respectively, from 1990 to 1999. In the Saarland, a single-party CDU government replaced the

Table 14.2 Single-party and coalition governments in the *Länder*, 1990–2002

Year	*B-W*	*Bav*	*Berlin*	*BB*	*HB*	*HH*	*HE*	*LS*	*M-V*	*NRW*	*R-P*	*Saar*	*Sax*	*S-A*	*S-H*	*TH*
1990		10/90 CSU	12/90 CDU/SPD	10/90 SPD/FDP/ B90				5/90 SPD/G	10/90 CDU/FDP	5/90 SPD		1/90 SPD	10/90 CDU	10/90 CDU/FDP		10/90 CDU/FDP
1991					9/91 SPD/G/ FDP	6/91 SPD	1/91 SPD/G				4/91 SPD/ FDP					
1992	4/92 CDU/SPD														4/92 SPD	
1993						9/93 SPD/ (STATT)										
1994		9/94 CSU		9/94 SPD				3/94 SPD	10/94 CDU/SPD			10/94 SPD	9/94 CDU	6/94 SPD/G/ (PDS)		10/94 CDU/SPD
1995			10/95 CDU/SPD		5/95 SPD/CDU		2/95 SPD/G			5/95 SPD/G						
1996	3/96 CDU/FDP										3/96 SPD/FDP				3/96 SPD	
1997						9/97 SPD										
1998		9/98 CSU						3/98 SPD	9/98 SPD/PDS					4/98 SPD/ (PDS)		
1999			10/99 CDU/SDP	9/99 SPD/CDU	6/99 SPD/CDU		2/99 CDU/FDP					9/99 CDU	9/99 CDU			9/99 CDU
2000										5/00 SPD/G					2/00 SPD	
2001	3/01 CDU/FDP		10/01 SPD/PDS			9/01 CDU/FDP /PRO					3/01 SPD/FDP					
2002									9/02 SPD/PDS					4/02 CDU/FDP		

Note: key for *Länder* found in table 14.1, p. 304.

single-party SPD government in 1999. There was more electoral stability in Hesse, but the CDU picked up enough votes 1999 to form a coalition with the FDP and replace the SPD/Green coalition. In Bavaria the CSU continued its dominance with a single-party government, while in Baden-Württemberg the CDU changed coalition partners in 1996 from SPD to FDP. The greatest stability of all was found in Rhineland-Palatinate, where the only SPD–FDP coalition in Germany remained firmly in control.

Electoral volatility in the East brought about more changes in government than in the North or South. In Berlin, the CDU/SPD coalition of 1990, 1995 and 1999, was replaced by an SPD/PDS coalition in 2001. Brandenburg went from an SPD/FDP/Green coalition in 1990 to an SPD/CDU coalition in 1999, with a single-party SPD government in between. Mecklenburg-Vorpommern changed from a CDU/FDP coalition in 1990 to a CDU/SPD coalition in 1994 to an SPD/PDS coalition in 1998 and 2002. In Saxony, the CDU governed alone throughout the period following unification, while in Thuringia the CDU governed in coalition with the FDP in 1990, with the SPD in 1994 and alone after 1999. Saxony-Anhalt started with a CDU/FDP coalition in 1990, followed by an SPD/Green coalition supported by the PDS in 1994, which was in turn followed by a single-party SPD government again supported by the PDS in 1998. In the April 2002 election, however, the dramatic change in the electoral fortunes of the CDU and FDP (gains) and the SPD (losses) allowed the CDU and FDP to form a government.

What emerges from this overview is that there are distinctive opportunities available to the parties for coalitions at the *Land* level. The 'promiscuous' SPD has found it possible to join with all of the other parties in the German five-party system, not only with the Greens but even with the PDS in Mecklenburg-Vorpommern and Berlin, the FDP in Rhineland-Palatinate, the CDU in several *Länder*, and an 'other' party (*STATT-Partei*) in Hamburg. The CDU appears to have far more limited options: it can either form a grand coalition with the SPD or a normal coalition with the FDP and/or an 'other' party. The CDU and the Greens are incompatible above the local level; a CDU/PDS coalition is virtually unthinkable at any level. The SPD would probably not be willing to join with the PDS at the national level, but it has never been forced to discuss openly this possibility in the Federal elections since unification.

At the end of 2002 all of these coalitional permutations were in effect: *Länder* governed alone by the CDU, CSU and SPD; *Länder* governed by CDU/FDP coalitions and by a CDU/FDP/Other (PRO) coalition; *Länder* governed by an SPD/Green coalition; one *Land* governed by an SPD/FDP coalition; and two *Länder* governed by an SPD/PDS coalition (see table 14.2). Even though a single-party government is virtually impossible to imagine at the national level, not all of these coalitions would be possible, either. The SPD and the FDP could join in a coalition, as they did from 1969 to 1980, but an SPD/FDP/Green coalition (the so-called 'traffic light' coalition) is unlikely, because of the differences between the FDP and Greens on key issues. It is unlikely that the CDU and SPD would form another grand coalition, as they did in the period 1966–69, unless no combination(s) of large and small parties yielded a majority. It is even less likely that the CDU and Greens could form a coalition, given their different positions on a whole series of issues. It is barely conceivable that the SPD would join in any combination with the PDS, and it is inconceivable that the CDU or FDP would do so. At the national level, then, the most likely coalitions are SPD/Green and CDU/CSU–FDP, with the possibility of an SPD/FDP coalition. This gives the SPD somewhat more flexibility at the national level, while it has a great deal more flexibility than the CDU or CSU at the *Land* level.

Voter turnout

Voter turnout in Federal, or Bundestag, elections has always been very high in comparison to the United States. Since unification, voter turnout has ranged from 77.8 per cent in 1990, when East and West voted together for the first time, to 82.2 per cent in 1998, when the SPD and its Chancellor candidate, Gerhard Schröder, defeated the CDU/CSU and Helmut Kohl. In 2002, voter turnout was 79.1 per cent; the average for four elections since unification was 79.5 per cent. Electoral turnout in the elections for the EP has been significantly lower, although still relatively high by American standards. In 1989, the turnout was 62.3 per cent, in 1994, it fell to 60.0 per cent and in 1999 fell farther to a mere 45.2 per cent.

Electoral turnout in the *Länder* has been very high in some cases, for example, in the Saarland in 1985, 1990 and 1994. However, turnout in 1999 dropped dramatically in that *Land* to 68.7 per cent. Indeed, the trend in almost all of the *Länder* has been downward. Before unification, every western *Land* had a turnout of more than 70 per cent, while every *Land* except Lower Saxony went below 70 per cent in one or more elections after unification. The low points, 54.8 per cent in the East and 56.7 per cent in the West, were reached by Saxony-Anhalt in 1994 and North-Rhine Westphalia in 2000. In the East, only Saxony and Thuringia had voter turnouts of more than 70 per cent in 1990, while by 2002 turnout had declined significantly below that figure in all five of the new *Länder* except Mecklenburg-Vorpommern, which was at least in the high 60s in 2002 (undoubtedly because the election was held simultaneously with the Bundestag election). Thuringia and Saxony-Anhalt had turnouts below 60 per cent in 1999 and 2002, respectively, with Saxony-Anhalt's turnout of 56.5 per cent even lower than the 56.7 per cent turnout in North-Rhine Westphalia noted above.

The especially low turnouts in the national EP elections of 1999, in Bremen, Brandenburg and Thuringia in 1999, in North-Rhine Westphalia in 2000 and in Saxony-Anhalt in 2002 suggest that the trend toward lower turnouts may continue. This trend will, of course, be seen as evidence of growing *Politikverdrossenheit* (disenchantment with politics) by those who see the sky falling in on German politics, and they may be right to some extent. Given the disappointment in both parts of Germany, but especially in the East, over the economic consequences of unification that ran counter to initial expectations, the party finance scandals involving first Helmut Kohl and the CDU and more recently the SPD and FDP, and high unemployment, high taxes, economic stagnation, the growing threat to the welfare state and other issues, it is not surprising that many voters are alienated. On the other hand, these problems are not confined to Germany. Recent voting turnout figures for some of the *Länder* are still well above 60 per cent (71 per cent in Hamburg in 2001), and turnout in the 2002 Bundestag elections was about average since 1990. Voter turnout has been declining in many democratic countries in recent years, and German turnout figures are still very high at all levels in comparison to the United States.

Are *Land* elections 'partial' Federal elections?

As in other federal systems, a recurring question in Germany is the extent to which the elections in the *Länder* reflect more the popular assessment of political developments and policies of the individual

Länder governments or of the Federal government. In the United States one general school of thought centres around the idea that state gubernatorial elections are basically national referenda which express approval or disapproval of the sitting President and his policies, especially in terms of the economy. Another school suggests that voters focus on the performance of the incumbent governor and the state of the regional economy. In any case state contests are affected by news media which focus on national and international events, and the national political parties exercise some influence in the states through their funding and assistance in state campaigns. It also seems clear that evaluations of the president and the national and international environment can lead to a form of referendum voting in the states. On the other hand, incumbent governors, like incumbent politicians in Congress, are not easily defeated.[4]

Rainer Dinkel, who has studied the relationship between *Land* elections and Federal influences, found that in 65 of 67 *Land* elections the Federal government coalition received less support than expected based on Federal election results. He also cited polls showing that public support for the Federal government tended to be higher shortly after and shortly before Federal elections, i.e. the Federal coalition parties were likely to lose votes in the *Länder* especially at midterm. The reduced support was attributable especially to floating voters who expressed their judgment of Federal policies by voting against the Federal coalition in *Land* elections. Lack of support for the Federal coalition might also be seen in the lower voter turnout in *Land* elections. Dinkel did not find, in contrast to some other scholars,[5] that *Land* elections could be seen as a barometer that measured the strength of the Federal government and opposition parties. It is clear, however, that *Land* elections, like EP elections, are barometer elections in so far as they can and do send signals to the Federal government.[6] Dinkel's general conclusion was that both Federal and *Land* politics were factors in *Land* elections.[7]

Dinkel's hypothesis that support for the Federal coalition is higher shortly before and after the Federal elections does not seem to be borne out by the evidence since 1990, in part because of the impact of unification. Prior to the October 1994 Federal election, in which the CDU/CSU won the largest share of the vote, the CDU experienced a decline of 2 per cent in its share of the vote in five of six *Landtag* (state parliament) elections (Hamburg, Lower Saxony, Saxony-Anhalt, Brandenburg and Bavaria). In the three *Landtag* elections held at the same time as the October Federal election, the CDU registered a loss of over 2 per cent in Thuringia, while the SPD made sizable gains in three *Länder* (Brandenburg, Saxony-Anhalt and Hamburg) just before and in one *Land* (Thuringia) at the time of the Federal elections. On the other hand, the SPD lost more than 2 per cent in all four *Land* elections (Hesse, North-Rhine Westphalia, Bremen and Berlin) held in 1995, while the CDU lost more than 2 per cent in only one of these elections. Just before or simultaneously with the 1998 Federal elections, the CDU lost significantly in two *Landtag* elections (Saxony-Anhalt and Mecklenburg-Vorpommern); in the six *Landtag* elections held in 1999, the CDU gained significantly and progressively in five of the *Länder* (Hesse, Bremen, Saarland, Brandenburg and Thuringia). The SPD gained only in the Mecklenburg-Vorpommern *Landtag* election held simultaneously with the Federal elections and then again in the Bremen *Landtag* election held within the year following the Federal elections. But, the SPD lost badly in the four other *Landtag* elections (Saarland, Brandenburg, Thuringia and Saxony) held in the same time period. The PDS made gains in Berlin as well as in Brandenburg, Saxony and Thuringia in the 1999 *Landtag* elections. The far right also made major gains in one eastern *Land* just before (Saxony-Anhalt) and in another (Mecklenburg-Vorpommern) at the time of the Federal elections. The far right also did relatively well in two eastern *Länder* (Brandenburg and Thuringia) a year after the Federal elections. It seems clear that the *Land* election results after the 1998 Federal elections had much to do with national politics, e.g. the shaky start of the new Schröder government, continuing high unemployment especially in the East and at the end of 1999 the party finance scandal that broke out involving former Chancellor Kohl. But it is difficult to relate these events to the timing of the Federal elections.

The CDU experienced declines of 2 per cent or more in three of the five *Landtag* elections held before the Federal elections of 2002. Losses were posted in Rhineland-Palatinate, Hamburg and Berlin. In Berlin, the CDU lost 17 per cent, while only six months later and five months before the Federal elections it gained 17.3 per cent in Saxony-Anhalt. The SPD gained in three of the five *Landtag* elections (Rhineland-Palatinate, Baden-Württemburg, Mecklenburg-Vorpommern) held in 2001, but it lost 15.9 per cent in the Saxony-Anhalt *Landtag* election only months before the Federal elections in September 2002. The PDS lost votes in an eastern *Land* for only the second time since 1990, when it lost 8 per cent in Mecklenburg-Vorpommern in September 2002. The far right, on the other hand, lost in every *Land* election held in 2001 and 2002 and more than 2 per cent in four of six races. The

Greens also experienced a decline in their share of the vote in fourteen consecutive *Landtag* elections between June 1999 and September 2002 – in seven cases 2 per cent or more – but it did better than expected in the Federal elections of 2002.

Four conclusions emerge from these data. First, there are no general patterns or clear trends that can be discerned. Indeed, where there does seem to be a pattern, as in the months following the 1998 Federal elections when the CDU was gaining consistently, the pattern is broken in February 2000 in Schleswig-Holstein following the December 1999 revelations about the party finance scandal surrounding former Chancellor Helmut Kohl and the CDU.

The second conclusion is that the results of the *Landtag* elections are influenced by region. The most obvious example of this is the volatility expressed in the gains of the PDS and the SPD in the eastern *Länder* from 1990 to the end of 2001 and the losses of the CDU and FDP in the same *Länder* during this time. There are, however, two major exceptions for the CDU: Saxony and Thuringia, where the CDU remains the major party. The FDP began a comeback at the end of 2001 and won enough votes to re-enter the parliaments of Berlin and Saxony-Anhalt. The dramatic gains of the far right, especially in Saxony-Anhalt in April 1998, add to the volatility in the East.

The third conclusion is that there is also considerable volatility in the West, but it is more or less confined to the city-states of Hamburg and Bremen. One could add Berlin, which has a majority population socialised in the West but also a large population that lived under communism for four decades. In 1993 both the CDU and SPD lost significant votes in Hamburg, while the Greens, far right, and others gained around 6 per cent each; the CDU gained strongly and the SPD lost in 1997, while all other parties' voting percentages remained fairly stable; and in 2001 the CDU, Greens, and far right lost significantly but an 'other' party, the PRO, won an unprecedented 19.4 per cent. In Bremen in 1995 the CDU and SPD lost significantly, while 'other' parties picked up 10.7 per cent more votes. In 1999, in contrast, the CDU and SPD gained significantly, the Greens lost 4 per cent and the 'others' lost 10 per cent. In Berlin the CDU went from 40.4 per cent in 1990 to 23.8 per cent in 2001, the SPD and FDP moved down and then up again and the PDS started with 9.2 per cent in 1990 and received 22.6 per cent in 2001.

A fourth conclusion is that the popularity of the *Land* prime minister, or *Landesvater*, makes a difference. This can be seen especially in

Saxony in the East and in Rhineland-Palatinate in the West but also in Brandenburg and Thuringia in the East.

The German scholar who is probably most identified with the question of the relationships between federal and *Land* politics, Georg Fabritius, has offered a useful set of hypotheses about federal politics and elections in the *Länder*.[8] First, he suggests that *Land* elections have not been purely *Land*-based since the founding of the Federal Republic (note the results of the *Land* elections in 1999 and then 2000). Like a number of other observers, he notes the federal themes taken up by the political parties in *Land* elections, the appearance of national political leaders in the *Land* during campaigns, the joint membership of *Land* political leaders in *Land* and national party committees and the difficulty voters have in distinguishing between Federal and *Land* politics.[9] For example, the economic conditions in a *Land*, as is generally the case for an American state, have more to do with Federal than *Land* policies, yet the state of the economy can have a powerful influence on a *Land* (or similarly on an American state) election.

The second thesis is that in spite of the influence of federal politics, the themes of *Land* politics are also important. The popularity of the prime minister is a key variable as is *Land* politics, for example, policies regarding schools, teachers and curricula have become major issues over the years. But the popularity of the prime minister sinks when his party at the Federal level is held in lower esteem. Fabritius argues, furthermore, that the 'normal vote' is more likely to be seen in *Land* elections, because Federal elections exaggerate support or opposition. This 'normality' exists especially when there is no protest against federal policies. Like Dinkel, he also suggests that *Land* election results hardly carry over to the next Federal election or vice versa, when the elections do not take place too closely to each other.[10] While there may be some evidence for the hypothesis that the popularity of the prime minister suffers when his party at the Federal level is held in low esteem, a counter example would be the Bavarian election of 1998 which was held only a few months before the Federal election. In this election the prime minister remained very popular and the CSU actually picked up additional votes in spite of the national party's weakness. It also seems clear that the personal appeal of the prime ministers in the eastern *Länder* remains a crucial factor in explaining election results in Brandenburg, Thuringia and Saxony.[11]

Thirdly, Fabritius argues that the degree of Federal influence on the results of elections in the *Länder* varies and is greatest in crisis periods.

Then *Land* elections most clearly have the character of protest elections, where there is a kind of referendum for or against Federal policies. He notes that the chief beneficiary of the protest is not necessarily the major opposition party; instead, it is frequently a protest party or group that may have just formed or been relatively dormant.[12] Examples in the mid-to-late 1960s would be the rightist NPD and the *Außerparlamentarische Opposition* (APO) or extra-parliamentary opposition which consisted especially of radical left students, the Greens from the late 1970s throughout the 1980s, the right-wing *Republikaner* and DVU in the 1980s and 1990s, the PDS in the East in the 1990s and after 2000 and the *STATT-Partei* and PRO in Hamburg in 1993 and 2001, respectively.

Another hypothesis is that *Land* elections are also more likely to take on the characteristics of protest elections when they occur at midterm, i.e. not too soon before or after a Federal election. Here they may be seen as a kind of plebiscite – though an unclear one – for or against the Federal government or, in any case, as a kind of barometer or measurement of the current political climate. Voters can abstain or vote for a different party and still return to their normal party in the Federal election, which also applies to elections for the EP. Thus there appears to be more solidarity with one's normal party in Federal elections.[13] If this is true, though, it seems inconsistent with Fabritius' previous assertion that *Land* elections are the more 'normal' elections. Indeed, a recent empirical study, which otherwise generally confirms Dinkel's and Fabritius' hypotheses lends strong support to the argument that Federal elections reflect more the 'normal' vote.[14]

The final hypothesis is that the 'coordination' between *Land* elections and Federal politics is the result of *Politikverflechtung* (interlocking relations) between and among the *Länder* and the federation and the German party state. Thus the division of power between the federation and the *Länder* does not mean a separation in terms of policies or parties. The thesis of the 'unitary Federal state' is confirmed in *Land* elections. Party images are set by the Federal parties, but there is a strong mutual dependence between the Federal and *Land* parties. Most obviously the *Länder* are closely associated with Federal politics via the *Bundesrat*.[15] This is reflected in a clever CDU campaign advertisement in the 1958 *Land* elections in Hesse:

> *Deine Wahl in Hessenstaat*
> *zählt im Bonner Bundesrat.*

Regierung Zinn stützt Ollenauer,
wählt CDU für Adenauer.[16]

A somewhat related theme to Fabritius' last hypothesis has been developed by Gerhard Lehmbruch, who suggests that there is an incongruence between the German party system and the Federal system. The British parties form a strong party system which leads to majority rule, i.e. the 'Westminster parliamentary system' of strong, disciplined party government under the leadership of the prime minister which largely obviates bargaining between Government and Opposition. The strong German parties, in contrast, are forced to bargain because of cooperative federalism or the *Politikverflechtung* which exists between the federation and the *Länder*; and because of the *Landtag*'s (state parliament) role in selecting the members of the *Bundesrat* (the upper chamber of the German parliament). The German party system, therefore, is unable to provide the kind of party government found in Great Britain, but must, instead, engage in a highly complex system of bargaining and consensus politics. This can and does lead to blockage, which can frustrate decision makers who are held accountable by the public for their political promises. As a result, Federal cabinet ministers try to work with *Land* politicians to support their policies, while the Opposition leaders do the opposite.[17]

In a recent empirical study of the relationship between federal and *Land* elections, Charlie Jeffery and Daniel Hough note that evidence of a cyclical pattern of support for the main political parties and the national level is now commonplace. Examples are midterm congressional elections in the United States and other 'second-order' elections such as the EP elections in the EU member-states.[18] Following a review of the literature and data, and focusing especially on the findings of Rainer Dinkel, Jeffery and Hough conclude that the data for 1949–90 generally support Dinkel's picture of

> *Land* elections as 'subordinate', or second-order elections subject to an electoral cycle whose turning points were set by the rhythm of the federal rather than the *Länder* electoral arenas. Incumbency in federal government was punished, especially at mid-term. The main federal opposition party held up its vote share better, on occasion doing significantly better than expected, while the gamut of smaller parties, apparently benefiting from voter experimentation when less was at stake, generally did well.[19]

Jeffery and Hough also note the importance of voter turnout as a factor in explaining *Land* election results. Turnout is generally considerably lower in *Land* elections, as it is in EP elections, which punishes government parties that fail to mobilise 'their broadly contented supporters when less is at stake', hurts opposition parties less 'as their voters are typically willing to get out and make a point', and reduces barriers to smaller parties, 'especially those capable of mobilising a concerted protest vote'.[20]

When they looked at the data for the period from 1990 to 1998, however, Jeffery and Hough reached somewhat different conclusions. The trend of increasingly lower turnout in *Land* elections since 1990 appears to be associated with reduced support for both the government and opposition parties, so that 'the success of small parties suggests less of an anti-government effect post-unity than a more indiscriminate effect penalising the wider federal party "establishment"'.[21] Jeffery and Hough reserve judgement on the question of whether this means that *Land* elections might have become uncoupled from Federal politics and are no longer 'second-order' elections. They note the relevance of a number of factors, such as holding *Land* elections on the same day as the Federal election and the important role of the personal appeal of the incumbent prime minister. But a brief look at the results of the *Land* elections since 1998 suggests that the relevance of Federal politics is still strong: the CDU opposition made strong gains in all of the *Land* elections in 1998 and 1999, when the SPD–Green Federal government seemed to be floundering, but it lost significantly after December 1999 when the party finance scandal involving former Chancellor Helmut Kohl was revealed. On the other hand, the most recent elections in Hamburg and Berlin suggested that local issues dominated. Thus the larger question seems still to be unresolved. There can be no doubt that Federal politics can have a decisive influence on *Land* elections, but it is also clear that local conditions and personalities can be important and even decisive as well.[22]

Conclusion

For many years observers have noted the north–south electoral divide in Germany's Federal elections. Since the mid-1990s, it has become clear that divide is now augmented by an eastern division. These divisions are reflected in *Land* elections, with the SPD generally stronger in the North, the CDU or CSU stronger in the South and both major parties having to compete more evenly with the PDS in the East. The smaller FDP and Greens are confined largely to the North and South, whereas in the East since the mid-1990s the Greens have won seats only in Berlin and the FDP has crossed the 5 per cent barrier only recently in Berlin and Saxony-Anhalt. Given the strength of the CDU and the relative weakness of the SPD in Saxony and Thuringia, it will be interesting to observe future developments which might result in a North–South gap throughout unified Germany.

The German five-party system – four competitive parties in the North and South (CDU/CSU, FDP, Greens and SPD) and three competitive parties in the East (SPD, CDU and Greens) – means that opportunities exist for a variety of government coalitions. However, not every combination is acceptable to all parties. In the North and South, the CDU can join with the SPD or FDP, but a coalition with the Greens is highly unlikely. The SPD can form a government with the CDU, FDP, or Greens. In the East, the CDU is also limited to the SPD and FDP, whereas the SPD can join with the CDU, FDP, Greens or even the PDS. In any region the CDU and SPD could join with an 'other' party as well, but these parties are always 'flash' parties that come and go and therefore do not form a part of the permanent party system.

There has been a long debate in Germany, as in other federal systems, about the role of Federal politics in regional elections. The evidence presented above does not suggest any general patterns just before or after Federal elections, and where one pattern does exist following the 1998 Federal elections it is clear that it was the result of national developments following the elections. On the other hand, the data do show the relevance of region, in particular the volatility of elections in the East and the electoral strength of the PDS. The data also show the volatility in the city states of Bremen, Hamburg and Berlin, where local conditions are apparently more important than national developments. Finally, the popularity of *Land* prime ministers affects the outcome of elections. This factor is especially relevant in Saxony and Rhineland-Palatinate, but it also applies to Brandenburg and Thuringia. On the other hand, the popularity of the prime minister may not be enough, as can be seen in Brandenburg in 1999 and in other *Länder* in the various regions where economic conditions simply overwhelmed a once popular *Landesvater*.

What seems to emerge from the evidence is that *Land* elections are influenced by numerous factors, depending on the time, place and personalities of the election. In some cases regional or local factors may be decisive, in other cases national events intervene, and in any case the personalities and their electoral appeal can make the difference. While the evidence in this chapter does not address the issue directly, overall it seems fair to suggest that 'it's the economy, stupid', is probably as important a factor as any other.

Notes

1 I wish to thank Melissa Gainey and Daryl Weade for their technical assistance.

2 The CDU, however, had its roots in the old Centre Party (*Zentrum*) and the FDP could be traced back to liberal parties of the Empire and Weimar Republic.

3 Andreas Galonska, *Landesparteiensysteme im Föderalismus: Rheinland-Pfalz und Hessen, 1945–1996* (Wiesbaden: Deutscher Universitätsverlag, 1999), p. 42.

4 Malcolm E. Jewell and Sarah M. Morehouse, *Political Parties and Elections in American States*, 4th edn (Washington, DC: CQ Press, 2001), Chapter 6.

5 For example, Heino Kaack, 'Landtagswahlen und Bundespolitik 1970–1972', *Aus Politik und Zeitgeschichte*, 13/74 (30 March 1974), pp. 4–5.

6 Christopher J. Anderson and Daniel S. Ward, 'Barometer Elections in Comparative Perspective', *Electoral Studies*, 14:1 (1995), pp. 1–14 and Uwe Jun, *Koalitionsbildung in den deutschen Bundesländern* (Opladen: Leske & Budrich, 1994), p. 93.

7 Rainer Dinkel, 'Der Zusammenhang zwischen Bundes- und Landtagswahlergebnissen', *Politische Vierteljahresschrift*, 18:2 (1977), pp. 348–59.

8 Georg Fabritius, *Wechselwirkungen zwischen Landtagswahlen und Bundespolitik* (Meisenheim-am-Glan: Verlag Anton Hain, 1978) and Georg Fabritius, 'Sind Landtagswahlen Bundesteilwahlen?', *Aus Politik und Zeitgeschichte*, 21/79 (26 May 1979), pp. 23–38.

9 Georg Fabritius, 'Landtagswahlen und Bundespolitik', in Hans-Georg Wehling (ed.), *Westeuropas Parteiensysteme im Wandel* (Stuttgart: Kohlhammer Verlag, 1983), pp. 113–16.

10 *Ibid.*, pp. 118–19.

11 Tilo Görl, 'Regionalisierung der politischen Landschaft in den neuen Bundesländern am Beispiel der Landtagswahlen 1999 in Brandenburg, Thüringen und Sachsen', *Zeitschrift für Parlamentsfragen*, 32:1 (2001), pp. 94–5, 123.

12 *Ibid.*, pp. 121–2.

13 *Ibid.*, p. 123.

14 Frank Decker and Julia von Blumenthal, 'Die bundespolitische Durchdringung der Landtagswahlen. Eine empirische Analyse von 1970 bis 2001', *Das Parlament*, 33:1 (March 2002), pp. 144–65.

15 Görl, 'Regionalisierung,' pp. 113–14, 124–5.

16 Translated as: 'Your Vote in Hesse/counts in Bonn's *Bundesrat.*/The Zinn government supports Ollenauer,/so vote CDU for Adenauer.'

17 Gerhard Lehmbruch, *Parteienwettbewerb im Bundesstaat*, 2nd edn (Opladen: Westdeutscher Verlag, 1998).

18 Charlie Jeffery and Daniel Hough, 'The Electoral Cycle and Multi-Level Voting in Germany', *German Politics*, 10:2 (2001), pp. 76–7.

19 *Ibid.*, p. 84.

20 *Ibid.*, p. 85.

21 *Ibid.*, p. 89.

22 Decker and von Blumenthal, 'Die bundespolitische Durchdringung', p. 164.

Part V
Institutional change and policy innovation

15

Post-unification German military organisation: the struggle to create national command structures[1]

Thomas-Durell Young

> The Bundeswehr has no future in its current structure. The present form of military service produces a surplus of manpower altogether, but a shortage of operational forces. Out-dated material diminishes its operational capability and causes operating costs to soar ... The contributions to the internationally agreed tasks assured by Germany's policy-makers cannot be provided by its armed forces.[2]

Since unification, no German institution has been subject to greater organisational review and drawn-out decision making regarding reform plans than has the Bundeswehr. Whilst German unification itself can be accurately assessed as being the successful product of years of patient, but persistent, skilful German diplomacy, the end of the Cold War invalidated many comfortable assumptions on which German national security policy had been based, particularly as it related to the structure and orientation of the Bundeswehr. Equally, the *Bundesministerium der Verteidigung* (BMVg) (Federal Ministry of Defence) has had the unpleasant task of attempting to reform and reorganise the Bundeswehr, despite inconsistent political attention, contradictory policy guidance and problematic annual defence estimates. One explanation for this less than successful restructuring is that defence reform has been all but held hostage to domestic political considerations.[3] What is remarkable is that the post-unification Bundeswehr has been able to reorganise and reorient itself sufficiently to be able to deploy increasingly large numbers of forces outside of Germany and undertake demanding peace-support operations.

For obvious reasons, defence reform has had to be pursued in a political environment still very sensitive to Germany's recent history.

Notwithstanding the Federal Republic's impeccable democratic credentials, the domestic political debate over defence continues to avoid deep discussion of issues that would evoke images of Germany's militaristic past. Two of the most contentious issues have been the continuation of conscription and the basis upon which Bundeswehr planning will be based. As to the former, German officials stubbornly continue to argue its continued relevance, albeit the need for its continuation owing to the 'uncertain nature' of the international security environment is clearly a weak one.[4] Conscription is Janus-like: it provides an important 'spiritual' (*geistig*) function, i.e. providing the institution with domestic legitimacy and public acceptance; it meets a politically not inconsequential physical requirement, i.e. inexpensive personnel in a cash-strapped fiscal environment. Hence, the extreme reluctance of politicians and defence officials to reconsider its contemporary relevance.

Bundeswehr planning during the 1990s was the object of inconsistent political and financial guidance owing to the slow and incremental deployment of Bundeswehr units to peace-support operations. Moreover, financial guidance was inconsistent owing to the lacklustre performance of the German economy during the 1990s. Oscillations in planning ended in 1998 when the new SPD–Green coalition appointed a blue ribbon commission under the leadership of former Federal President Richard von Weizsäcker to examine future requirements of the Bundeswehr. The results of this commission's work were announced in 2000, but the ensuing controversy and debate amongst the Minister of Defence, Chief of Defence (*Generalinspekteur*) and other officials resulted in even further confusion over planning guidance and priorities.[5]

Given the centrality of these two important issues, it is not surprising that they have dominated many analyses of German defence policy since unification.[6] However, what has gone largely unnoticed has been the sea change that has taken place in German national command and operational structures of the BMVg as well as the authorities and responsibilities of the *Generalinspekteur* and the Bundeswehr itself. Largely forgotten has been the measured transition of new command structures of the Bundeswehr from those of the Cold War whereby the execution of command over the Bundeswehr was purposefully decentralised and interwoven into NATO wartime command arrangements. Indeed, there was no more open and physical manifestation of Germany's Cold War 'singularisation' than its limited national command structure. What is remarkable about the post-unification reforms is that they have been carried out despite domestic and international political sensitivities and even impediments caused by widespread linguistic misunderstandings. To place these reforms in their proper context, the new German structures and procedures are all but a given in other NATO countries.

This chapter addresses the post-unification evolution of Germany's national command structures and the evolution of the responsibilities and authorities of the *Generalinspekteur*. It assesses not only the actual reforms that have been effected over this period, but also the sensitivities and perceptions that have made these reforms so challenging. Germany only divested itself of its Cold War command legacies in September 2002, when it created structures and procedures that are in no way dissimilar to those of its NATO allies. However, these reforms were hard won, their eventual adoption was not a given and this at times tortured evolution reflects Germany's continued uneasiness with the use of military force as an instrument of statecraft.

Defence and military institutions: overview

Catherine Kelleher wrote that the Federal Republic's BMVg probably had the 'least to offer in terms of lessons that can be generalized for the organisation of a central defense establishment', largely because it was organised with the explicit aim of not permitting national operational command and control over its standing forces.[7] The Bundeswehr was explicitly created and organised without the capability to exercise operational command and control over joint national military operations of any size or of any significant duration. This unusual condition was owed to domestic anxieties aroused by the past militaristic, cultural proclivities in German armies, combined with the 'influential' presence of a very apprehensive group of new allies.[8] The general consensus among German politicians and allies in 1954 was that there would never again be a *Generalstab* (General Staff).

As a result, within the BMVg, since its creation, the *Führungsstab der Streitkräfte* (Fü S) (Central Staff of the Armed Forces) was not organised to exercise operational command and control over all Bundeswehr services and individual units. This *sui generis* state of affairs was accepted by senior German politicians until unification in October 1990. Germany's incremental participation in peace-support operations after unification made the need to centralise operational command and control increasingly obvious, if not politically appealing. The simple question that has plagued successive governments and defence ministers has been the degree to which this centralisation of national operational command and control should occur, and in which particular organisational form.

The most sensitive issues of civil–military relations in any democracy is located at the crux of the operational command and control deficiencies in the BMVg and the Bundeswehr: How are the armed forces to be 'commanded' and 'controlled' by the civilian authorities? During the Cold War, it had long been assumed that wartime operational command and control of the Bundeswehr (excluding the Territorial Army) would be transferred to NATO commanders operating within the integrated command structure. Following the promulgation of a state of defence by the Federal government, operational command and control over the Bundeswehr, with only some exceptions (e.g. the Territorial Army), would be transferred to NATO commanders. Albeit a major manifestation of singularisation and not without criticism,[9] it was a long-standing constant in German security policy that NATO and its military structure were essential to its national security. NATO commitments discouraged the development of a mature institutional relationship between civilians and military officials; as such the nuances of 'national command' of the Bundeswehr was not treated as a topic of critical interest by successive governments.

This comfortable situation was disturbed in the early 1990s when the Kohl coalition government began its policy of incremental deployment of forces to UN and NATO-led peace-support operations. Germany was strongly encouraged by its allies to contribute forces to meet the demand generated by the explosion in peace-support operations throughout the world. In such military operations short of war, it became immediately obvious to the senior Bundeswehr leadership, if not their civilian masters, that there was a corresponding need to improve significantly the BMVg's capability for exercising centralised operational command and control of the Bundeswehr, as well as providing a national command linkage to Bundeswehr units deployed outside of the Central Region. This need for reform was initially made patently clear as early as the conduct of Bundeswehr humanitarian relief operations carried out in Iran, Iraq and Turkey in the spring of 1991.[10] Key defence planning documents increasingly argued throughout the 1990s that the Bundeswehr needed to be restructured to participate in these types of missions. These documents also noted the concomitant requirement to maintain effective national command and operational command and control structures.[11] Yet, reluctance on the part of political leadership throughout the 1990s and a widespread lingering misunderstanding of the nature of 'command' resulted in full reform being delayed until 2001 and 2002.

Military command: the legal parameters

The precise form of civil–military relations are delineated in the *Grundgesetz* (the Basic Law or German Constitution). The *Grundgesetz* (Article 87b) makes very clear the principle of civilian control over the military. Article 65(a) invests the power of peacetime national command in the Federal Minister of Defence. The Constitution limits the employment of military force solely to missions of defence in Article 87(a). Article 115 defines how a state of defence is enacted by the Bundestag (Lower House) and Bundesrat (Upper House). Article 115(b) stipulates that, upon the promulgation of a state of defence national command of the Bundeswehr is transferred from the Federal Minister of Defence to the Federal Chancellor. As regards to the operational command and control of the Bundeswehr, the *Grundgesetz* is vague. Article 24 states that the Federal Republic may enter into a system of collective security and transfer sovereign powers to intergovernmental institutions (i.e. participating in the NATO integrated command structure). This particular article is often cited by some informed commentators and some in the SPD to claim that the creation of a national operational command and control structure is constitutionally proscribed.[12] The facts state otherwise. Nowhere does the *Grundgesetz* proscribe the creation of a national military command structure.

These constitutional provisions establishing the parameters for national command and the operational command and control of the Bundeswehr are actually not onerous or unusual. Civilian control of the military in a democracy presupposes that national command is invested in senior political leadership whereas responsibility for the operational command and/or control of forces is delegated to military authorities with requisite political oversight. In the specific case of Germany, the important 12 July 1994 Federal Constitutional Court's decision recognising the legality of German participation in peace-support operations further strengthens the argument that there are no onerous constitutional restrictions on the creation of a national command and operational command and control structures.[13] Rather, one could conclude that far from being a constitutionally driven controversy, domestic political sensitivities have impeded efforts at centralising operational command and control in the BMVg.

Language and history

Efforts to centralise operational command and control capabilities in the BMVg or to alter the command authorities of senior military officials have inevitably led to charges that the government was attempting to re-create a *Generalstab*, which would lead *ipso facto* inevitably to the rebirth of German militarism.[14] Given the obvious emotional character of this issue in Germany, political and defence officials during discussions of command structures had to go to great lengths to avoid any misunderstanding of terms if their proposals were to be judged upon their merits. Yet both the terms *Generalstab* and *Generalstabsoffizier* have both pejorative as well as positive connotations in German, let alone being plagued by historical misunderstandings. Concerning the term *Generalstab*, one senior German officer has written 'the working method of the Prussian–German General Staff has been adopted in the German language as an idiom. A very accurately prepared and successfully executed project is frequently rated "general staff-like" (*generalstabsmässig*).'[15] That said, during the 1990s, because of the sensitivity surrounding the term *Generalstab*, a number of compromise titles were floated, some of which produced some 'interesting' linguistic contortions. For instance, one such compromise term suggested in 1993 was to create a *Gemeinsamer Führungsstab der Streitkräfte* ('Joint' or 'Common' Command Staff of the Armed Forces).[16] Fortunately, for the future of German linguistic purity (not to mention common sense), this proposal and others like it have not been accepted.

As regards history, many Germans have a fundamental misunderstanding of their own country's recent past. No matter how defined, there is nothing inherent in the generic functions and responsibilities of a General Staff (or 'Joint' Staff in contemporary NATO terminology) that makes it 'militaristic'. In fact, Kelleher makes the attractive argument that most Germans have a flawed understanding of German civil–military relations since the 1870s that has led to a widespread misconception of the institution and term *Generalstab*. A comparison of civil–military relations with France prior to the First World War, she argues, would show that the influence of the German General Staff did not differ significantly from its continental counterpart. Indeed, during the Nazi era, 'civilian' control over the Wehrmacht was a priority because of the Nazi distrust of German staff officers.[17]

Just as there is domestic political sensitivity surrounding the creation of a national command structure so, too, have German defence officials taken pains not to send signals to their NATO allies that Bonn was uninterested in maintaining its strong participation in the existing integrated military command structures. A too obvious move to create new structures might be perceived as a manifestation of Germany's intent to replace its dependence on Allied structures with solely national ones.[18] The potential political repercussion from such an innovation, particularly during the early 1990s, could have been disastrous. Thus, official German statements on security and defence policy since unification have stressed the continued need and importance of NATO for Germany's security, whilst underplaying the need for structures more in line to support unilateral operations.[19] This line of argumentation characterised early post-unification key defence planning documents (e.g. the *Verteidigungspolitische Richtlinien* (*VPR*) (Defence Policy Guidelines) and the *Konzeptionelle Leitlinie zur Weiterentwicklung der Bundeswehr* (*KLL*) (Conceptual Guidelines for the Future Development of the Federal Armed Forces). Both documents stressed that NATO will remain indispensable to German security, and the integrated NATO military command structure, at least in German eyes, is essential.[20] Moreover, such concerns over possible Allied sensitivities to the creation of a German General Staff are not without foundation.[21]

Public confusion over terminology and historical misunderstandings complicated German officials' efforts to find a politically acceptable solution. The result of this situation produced two implications. First, it took over ten years before a Federal Defence Minister felt sufficiently comfortable to create a national operational planning centre (*Einsatzführungskommando*). Second, it was not until 2002 that such confidence was also manifested in the long-overdue review of the authorities of the *Generalinspekteur der Bundeswehr*. Thus, we may now turn to the sensitive issue of what authority the *Generalinspekteur* should possess in a unified Germany.

Redefining the *Generalinspekteur der Bundeswehr*'s authorities

Since the creation of the Bundeswehr and until recently, the *Generalinspekteur* has acted as the sole senior military advisor to the Federal Minister of Defence and the Federal Chancellor, and has served as a non-voting member of the *Bundessicherheitsrat* (Federal Security Council). Fearful of Germany's recent wartime history and sensitive to domestic and international perceptions of a resurgence in German 'militarism', the founding fathers of the Bundeswehr specifically denied the *Generalinspekteur* any command or operational command and control authority over Bundeswehr units. (This is not unusual in that the Chairman of the Joint Chiefs of Staff is also proscribed by law from exercising 'command' over the US armed forces.)[22] However, he has the independent authority to inspect all units of the Bundeswehr. In consequence, historically, the position has largely been confined to advising the government on military matters and exercising oversight for the development and implementation of force planning in the Bundeswehr. As such, interestingly, even as the Chairman of the *Militärischer Führungsrat* (Federal Armed Forces Defence Council), he has exercised only 'executive authority'. This Council consists of the *Stellvertreter des Generalinspekteurs der Bundeswehr* (Deputy Chief of Staff of the Federal Armed Forces) and the three service chiefs (*Inspekteure*).[23]

There can be no question that the restructuring of the BMVg towards creating a centralised command organisation presented a major challenge to German political and defence officials during the 1990s (particularly across the backdrop of the Bundeswehr's participation in NATO operations in the Balkans, when the need for reforms became manifest). Arguably, the most difficult reform centred upon the relationship between *Generalinspekteur der Bundeswehr* and the Federal Defence Minister as well as his specific authorities *vis-à-vis* the Bundeswehr. Given that 'command' is inherently a political act, the review of the Minister and *Generalinspekteur*'s relationship lies at that most sensitive political–military nexus where there is convergence of civilian national command authority and senior military officials who are vested with responsibility for operational command and control of the armed forces. That a military commander should have the authority to match his responsibility, in order to best serve senior democratic leaders, was a key finding in the congressional enquiry into the failure of the US armed forces during the 1970s and 1980s that resulted in the passage of the Goldwater–Nichols Defense Reorganization Act of

1986.[24] As a result of the experiences gained during Bundeswehr deployments to peace-support operations during the 1990s, it became increasingly clear that the previous Cold War relationship between the Federal Chancellor, the Federal Minister of Defence and the *Generalinspekteur der Bundeswehr* needed to be revisited, particularly *à-propos* the latter's authorities over the Fü S as well as the Bundeswehr itself. Equally important, the operational command and control structures of the three services, as well as the roles played by the three services' Chiefs of Staff *vis-à-vis* the Minister of Defence and the *Generalinspekteur*, had to undergo fundamental revision if Germany were to be capable of exercising the desired degree of national command and operational control over deployed Bundeswehr units.

It would be a mistake to conclude, however, that German sensitivity over a senior military official exercising 'command' of the armed forces stems from the experiences of the twentieth century. The examples of Hindenberg–Ludendorf and the Reichswehr are excellent examples of military institutions that were estranged from German civil society, let alone democratic control.[25] In reality, the issue of democratic civilian control over the armed forces was a perennial issue of debate throught the nineteenth century from the post-1848 reforms in Prussia throughout the Wilhelmine period. These reforms can be best typified as a continuing battle between successive sovereigns' arguments that, notwithstanding 'democratic' reforms in Prussia and later in the German empire, the monarch must retain command over the army. Thus, it is only in the long historical light that one can begin to appreciate the strong institutional opposition that has existed in the Federal Republic to placing command authority in one military official.

Upon the creation of this Bundeswehr in 1955, the obvious solution to this long-standing problem in German civil–military relations was the integration of the Bundeswehr to the greatest extent possible into NATO wartime command structures; the division of command authority among various officials; and universal conscription to ensure that there was a continual influx of democratic influence to prevent the Bundeswehr from becoming estranged from society. However, the important responsibilities given to the civilian defence establishment in 1955 contributed over time to creating ambiguity over which officials possessed which specific authorities. This ambiguity was settled only on 21 March 1970 by then Minister of Defence Helmut Schmidt, who, acting solely upon his own authority, issued an important decree later known as the *Blankeneser Erlass*.[26] Specifically, the decree established 'the formal specification of interacting responsibilities of the political and military leadership in ministerial and governmental affairs'.[27] This pronouncement established the preeminence of the three service *Inspekteure* in exercising discipline and ensuring the combat-readiness of their services. The *Inspekteure* were vested with 'command authority' over their respective services; there was no command relationship between them and the *Generalinspekteur*. As a result, the service chiefs reported directly to the Defence Minister concerning the combat readiness and discipline in their individual services.[28] Again, there was nothing inherently inefficient or in contraction with the basic tenets of democratic civil–military relations. However, with Germany's recent participation in peace-support operations, particularly in the Balkans, it became increasingly clear that a fundamental review of the *Blankeneser Erlass* was needed: the Defence Minister and Chancellor needed political–military advice from a joint perspective which only a Chief of Defence is able to provide. Equally important, but politically less sensitive, was the need to change organisational structures.

Organisational restructuring

These legal, political and organisational conditions impeded the creation of a national centralised command and control capability. Developing a solution that balanced all of these competing claims and demands was not a simple task. Against this backdrop of the need for a comprehensive reform, there were a number of disaggregated efforts on the part of successive defence ministers throughout the 1990s to restructure the Bundeswehr, as well as sustained attempts to reorganise and to reduce the BMVg's unwieldy size and to move critical elements of it to Berlin. The organisational structure of the BMVg, which was dictated by the exigencies of the Cold War, was neither effective nor efficient. Its mere size often proved to be beyond the ability of a single Federal Minister to exercise control over, let alone to allow it to support the national command and centralised operational command and control over deployed Bundeswehr forces. In the early 1990s, the need to reorganise the BMVg was initially impeded when then Defence Minister Volker Rühe decided that Fü S III would move to Berlin and that the Ministry would be restructured and reduced from its unwieldy size of 5,000 military and civilian personnel to a more manageable size (approximately 3,300) by the end of the 1990s.[29] While it was relatively simple to reduce military offices and personnel by transfers to organisations administratively located outside of the BMVg, effecting redundancies of civil servants proved to be extremely difficult given Germany's rigid labour laws. The need for demonstrable personnel reductions also resulted in some creative reorganisation proposals. One such concept was to remove the service staffs completely from the BMVg. A related proposal was the physical and organisational collocation of the service headquarters (i.e. Fü H (Army Staff), Fü L (Air Force Staff) and Fü M (Navy Staff), along with the *Inspekteure* and their respective operational command headquarters. It was even suggested that the *Inspekteure* and the operational service commanders be merged into one position.[30] The primary outcome of such a reorganisation would have been removing the *Inspekteure* from the BMVg and revisiting the *Blankeneser Erlass.* Unsurprisingly, neither reform proposal was accepted. That said, the radical nature of these proposals demonstrated the extent to which senior defence leadership were willing to go given the need to change the BMVg's organisational structure.

On 31 August 1990, Defence Minister Gerhard Stoltenberg issued a directive regarding future Bundeswehr planning which, *inter alia*, signalled the initial formal recognition that operational command and control structures were in need of reform.[31] The first public discussion on this issue was initiated with the initial draft of the *VPR*, floated by Defence Minister Stoltenberg and *Generalinspekteur* General Klaus Naumann in early 1992. This draft recognised the need to establish national operational command and control structures to support the new missions outlined in the document.[32] This was later reiterated in Defence Minister Rühe's published version of the *VPR.*[33] What is not widely known is that preliminary conceptual planning was already underway to ascertain the most appropriate structure in view of prevailing political realities.

One early model for developing incrementally a national command capability was the creation of a *Streitkräfteführungskommando* (Armed Forces Command Headquarters) in Koblenz. The standing complement of the *Streitkräfteführungskommando* was envisaged to be approximately 80–100 individuals. This small joint headquarters would limit itself to planning national joint operations. From the perspective of the BMVg, this proposed joint headquarters would be capable of supporting a wide range of military operations, including directing crisis management. As an interim measure, until the *Streitkräfteführungskommando* was created, existing *Führungsbereitschaften* (Readiness Command

Groups) within the BMVg would be expanded. These modest staffs would be augmented with personnel as needed to manage crises.[34]

Although press reports indicated that Volker Rühe rejected this proposal shortly after replacing Stoltenberg, in fact it was the senior Bundeswehr leadership that chose not to endorse it and directed the appropriate Fü S staff to develop alternative and politically viable proposals.[35] One of the key impediments to a comprehensive solution was the review of both the *Generalinspekteur*'s responsibilities and his relationship to the Defence Minister. *Der Spiegel* traced the proposal to create an expanded national and operational command and control structures to generals' *Grössenwahn* (megalomania), particularly that of *Generalinspekteur* General Naumann.[36] Shortly after taking office in April 1992, Defence Minister Rühe stated that he would support neither upgrading the position of the *Generalinspekteur* nor approve the creation of an expanded national command authority.[37] The subsequent record clearly demonstrates that within a few years, the force of events necessitated an all but *volte face* on this early public *démarche*.[38]

Given these numerous political obstacles, the BMVg was forced to adopt an incremental approach to solving the challenge of national command and centralised control. The subsequent results constituted a series of 'interim solutions'.[39] This was effected at two levels. First, the operational command headquarters of the individual services were expanded to provide improved national operational command and control over Bundeswehr deployments.[40]

From the founding of the Bundeswehr, there had been no army group headquarters above the *corps* level – despite its possession of three large national *corps* during the Cold War. The reason for this *sui generis* state of affairs was that in wartime the three German *Corps* commanders would implement their respective NATO General Defence Plans under the 'command' of their respective army group headquarters (NORTHAG – Northern Army Group, commanded by a British general in Mönchengladbach and CENTAG – Central Army Group, commanded by an American general in Heidelberg). If the German army were to conduct effectively operations outside of Germany, an operational command and control headquarters, similar to those of its sister services, was obviously required. Consequently, the *Heeresführungskommando* (German Forces Command) was established in 1995 at the former headquarters of III Korps in Koblenz.[41] This headquarters was modest and initially consisted of approximately 100 personnel.[42] It was assigned four principal tasks: to exercise operational command and control over the three army *corps* on behalf of the *Inspekteur des Heeres*; to ensure operational readiness of the major combined arms units of the army; to plan for and control the employment of army forces in national and multinational formations; and to coordinate, as stipulated by MC 36–2, all NATO issues concerning the Bundeswehr in Germany.[43] The creation of this headquarters had a significant impact on Bundeswehr operations. For instance, as German army *corps* increasingly became almost exclusively multinational during the 1990s,[44] this command assumed responsibility for providing national guidance (e.g. training objectives and standards) into the operation of Bundeswehr divisions and brigades.[45] Moreover, a new mobile tactical command was created – the *Kommando Luftbewegliche Kräfte* (KLK) (Air Mobile Forces Command) under the *Heeresführungskommando*. The KLK mission is to command deployed German reaction forces (airmobile/air-mechanised task forces) as well as represent German national interests within multinational formations and before foreign governments.[46] Not surprisingly, given the lack of resources, both the *Heeresführungskommando* and the KLK experienced difficulties during their establishment. Defence officials, for example, estimated privately that the KLK was capable of exercising operational command and control only over a two brigade-size task force of approximately 20,000 personnel.

All three service operational headquarters were activated on 1 April 1994, and assumed full command authority over all German forces and territory on 30 September 1994, the day following the final withdrawal of Russian forces from eastern Germany. These headquarters grew in importance not only as they improved operational command and control over their service formations, but as they also became key institutions supporting the exercise of national command by the Defence Minister. The reorganisation of the BMVg and the final redefinition of *Generalinspekteur*'s role remained incomplete throughout the 1990s. Nonetheless, the service operational headquarters provided the necessary national command linkage between the BMVg and Bundeswehr units deployed outside the Central Region. The choice of headquarters for command responsibilities was generally determined by the nature of the mission. Hence, the embryonic *Heeresführungskommando* provided, not without some difficulties, the national command link to Bundeswehr forces deployed to Somalia, including Luftwaffe units. The *Flottenkommando* provided operational command and control over Bundesmarine participation in enforcing sanctions against Serbia and Montenegro in the Adriatic; the *Luftwaffenführungskommando* exercised operational command and control over Luftwaffe humanitarian flights in the former Yugoslavia.

Notwithstanding the creation of three service operational commands, there remained the need to create a central directorate within the BMVg whose mission was to coordinate national command responsibilities in operations short of war or other than war, to provide options to the Federal Defence Minister and to ensure the execution of the Minister's intent. For all of the reasons cited above, it was clear early on in the process that simply creating a large standing *Abteilung* (department) in the BMVg to support the Minister was not feasible. The organisation of a centralised command capability was a two-phase incremental process, demonstrating once again the degree to which civil–military relations in Germany remain sensitive.

To initiate this reform, on 1 April 1993, the Central/Joint Staff of the Armed Forces, Fü S IV (Organisation) was directed to create a small operational staff.[47] Named *Einsatzführung der Bundeswehr* (Operational Command of the Federal Armed Forces), and organisationally referred to as Fü S IV 4, the office became the operations centre of the BMVg for less-than-war missions. One of the more significant implications of this organisational development was that, while the services increased their ability to exercise operational command and control over their forces, national command over these operations became the responsibility of Fü S IV 4. Significantly, this is the first time that Fü S had acquired such a capability. It was also given the important task of coordinating the activities of the military and civilian *Abteilungen* of the BMVg supporting external Bundeswehr deployments. As a result of its development, the *Einsatzführung der Bundeswehr* came to enhance the power of Fü S in the direction and oversight of these operations at the expense of the three services and their *Inspekteure*.

The incremental and evolutionary approach to reforming command structures in the BMVg continued with the establishment of the *Führungszentrum der Bundeswehr* (FüZBw) (Federal Armed Forces Operations Centre) on 31 August 1994.[48] The FüZBw was headed simultaneously by the Director of the *Koordinierungsstab* (Coordination Staff). FüZBw responsibilities included operational planning, operational command and control and acting as the BMVg's coordination centre during operations. The FüZBw was established to manage some of the most fundamental activities of the BMVg, while also serving as the permanent core for the *Koordinierungsstab*. However, given its modest size, it remained dependent upon the staff work of the service operational headquarters. Ties to the previous decentralised command structure produced tensions early in the Centre's existence because the reform left unresolved one important question: would FüZBw issue orders directly to deployed units or via the service operational headquarters?[49]

An interesting aspect of this reorganisation from the perspective of civil–military relations, however, was its impact upon Fü S and the Defence Minister's relationship with that staff. When the FüZBw was established, it absorbed the assets of Fü S IV 4 (*Einsatzführung der Bundeswehr*) and Fü S IV 7 (*Bereitschaftszentrum der Bundeswehr*), which were transferred to the FüZBw; both of these offices were subsequently disbanded. Furthermore, the Director of the FüZBw, a one-star general, gained the right of special access to the Defence Minister, but not the *Generalinspekteur*. This anomalous situation had the interesting result of giving the *Generalinspekteur* the responsibility for the coordination of the BMVg's efforts, whilst the execution of other-than-war missions remained firmly in the hands of the Ministry of Defence. Key elements of the BMVg moved to Berlin in 1997, including the FüZBw *Stabsabteilung* Fü S V which supported the Minister and the *Einsatzführungskommando* in Potsdam. The key implication of this reorganisation was to place national command and operational command and control of the Bundeswehr in other-than-war operations more directly under the Defence Minister's control, but this initially came at the expense of Fü S. The lengths to which Defence Minister Volker Rühe went to isolate national command and operational command and control from the central staff of the BMVg in other-than-war operations reveals the continued anxiety in Bonn to creating anything close to a national joint chiefs of staff. The final painstaking step in creating a normalised command structure was taken in 2001 with the establishment of the *Einsatzführungskommando* (Operational Command Headquarters) at the Henning-von-Tresckow Barracks in Geltow, near Berlin.[50]

There was a pause in organisational reform during the latter part of the 1990s. This pause can be traced to Minister Rühe's reluctance to revisit this sensitive issue as well as the electoral victory of the SPD and Greens in the 1998 Bundestag election. The SPD/Green coalition deferred any major decisions on defence until the completion of a two-year assessment of the future needs of the Bundeswehr undertaken by a blue ribbon Commission led by former Federal President Richard von

Weizsäcker.[51] While it could be argued that the commission's two-year tenure produced stasis in German defence planning, it did conclude that there were clear requirements for improving national command and operational control structures, as well as enhancing the authority of the *Generalinspektur*.[52] The importance of the decision to create the *Einsatzführungskommando* was that it fulfils the important tasks of the joint planning and oversight of military operations. It meant that service operational headquarters would no longer take the lead in national command of Bundeswehr forces on deployment. The newly established headquarters were established strictly along NATO organisational lines and equivalent to the UK's Permanent Joint Headquarters in Northwood.[53] Consequently, Germany is now equipped institutionally to lead either NATO operations or a future EU rapid reaction force headquarters (thereby placing Germany on an even footing with France and Great Britain).[54]

Revision of the *Generalinspekteur*'s responsibilities

Whereas the restructuring of German command structures was largely incremental, the move by successive defence ministers to revisit the responsibilities and assign new authorities to the *Generalinspekteur* can be best characterised as episodic. The initial move to revisit the responsibilities of the *Generalinspekteur* came as a result of the directive of 9 February 1993 that created the *Einsatzführung der Bundeswehr*. This directive delegated to the *Generalinspekteur*, within the context of other-than-war situations, the following new authority:

> The *Generalinspekteur der Bundeswehr* assumes, on the basis of his command authority and in conjunction with the *Inspekteure*, responsibility for all requisite measures for the preparation, culmination and control of deployments. He also assumes, on the presentation of an appropriate decree (*Erlass*), the central administration of humanitarian aid tasks of the Bundeswehr overseas.[55]

Importantly, the *Koordinierungsstab* was subordinated to the *Generalinspekteur*. The implication of this directive was to make the *Generalinspekteur* the key military officer responsible for coordinating other-than-war operations as well as providing the military's linkage with the Minister of Defence. This was a significant development. For the first time, the *Generalinspekteur der Bundeswehr* was placed in the direct line of responsibility for operational command and control over forces between the Minister of Defence and the service operational commands. While not fully invalidating the provisions of the *Blankeneser Erlass*, this directive diminished the influence of the *Inspekteure* from exercising operational command and control over their services' deployed units in less-than-war operations, and thus, in a small but significant way, removed a Cold War manifestation of Germany's singularisation.[56]

The *Blankeneser Erlass* was fundamentally revised in 2002. The von Weizsäker Commission recommended that the authority of the *Generalinspekteur* be enhanced in order to fulfill his responsibilities.[57] However, it was not until August 2002 that Defence Minister Peter Struck formalised arrangements that had evidently already been planned two years beforehand by his predecessor, Rudolf Scharping, and the previous *Generalinspekteur*, General Harald Kujat.[58] The new arrangments have enhanced and clarified the *Generalinspekteur*'s authority: command authority over the three service *Inspekteure*; authority to direct operations, including command over the *Einsatzführungskommando*; responsibility for Bundeswehr force planning; and, finally, the Chair of the *Einsatzrat* (Operations Council). In addition, Fü S will be moved in its entirety from Bonn to Berlin and be upgraded in order the better to support the new responsibilities and authorities of the *Generalinspekteur*.[59] These changes in the *Generalinspekteur*'s authority make it possible to argue that German military structures have finally become 'normal' by NATO nations' standards and its Cold War singularisation has come to an end.

Conclusion

This chapter explained and documented the struggle to create national command structures and procedures that are complementary to Germany's regained national sovereignty since the end of the Cold War and unification. This process has been incremental and not without delays. However, given Germany's past, it is not surprising that government officials were reluctant to move quickly to 'normalise' its defence establishment by creating national command structures. In this respect, the evolutionary approach to developing adequate command structures squares clearly with Hanns Maull's assessment of post-unification German external policy: 'Germany remained committed to the foreign-policy orientation of a civilian power. Nowhere was this more obvious than in its defence and security policies.'[60] Obviously, strong arguments could be – and probably were – made to change these structures in the early years following the end of the Cold War. German political and defence officials could not have been unaware of the potential risks they were taking by not reforming these structures.

There is, however, one key area in the command organisation debate that portends a future policy issue. Although the organisational structures to facilitate the exercise of national command and operational command and control have been changed, senior government officials collectively are still in the process of learning how to conduct these types of operations. As recent experience has shown, peace-support operations can place civil–military relations in a new and complicated context. Thus, the delicate and critical link in the civil–military relationship in the ruling structures of the Federal Republic faces new stresses. There therefore remains a clear need to formulate explicit procedures for executing these operations and to test those procedures in exercises and civil–military simulations well beforehand to determine where problems are likely to arise.

In the final analysis, the evolution of post-unification command structures demonstrates less a manifestation of growing German nationalism, but rather a government still willing to go to great extents to demonstrate that the Federal Republic shares no similarities with past German experiences of militarism and unhealthy civil–military relations. It was not until 1999 that the Bundeswehr implemented its first national joint operations document; even then, the document stresses the coalitional warfare aspects of joint operations.[61] Additionally, the great pains taken to 'invent' a new nomenclature for obviously needed new structures (and the avoidance any reliance upon an (un)modified *Generalstab* to describe them) manifest the extreme domestic political sensitivity surrounding the issue.[62] This sensitivity reflects an abiding concern over how Germany is perceived abroad, as well as how the German public views the Bundeswehr.

Perhaps history will demonstrate that the incremental approach to developing national command structures in order to carry out power-projection missions was indeed a prudent approach. What is clear is that should a German government decide to contribute forces to a western coalition, it can rely upon a national command structure that can execute the necessary sovereign tasks to support such an operation.

Notes

1 The views expressed in this chapter are those of the author and do not necessarily reflect the official policy or position of the Department of the Navy, Department of Defense, or the US government. The author would like to express his sincere gratitude to the following individuals who provided advice and comments on earlier drafts of this chapter: Brigadier-General Dr Klaus Wittmann, i.G., GEA, Lieutenant Colonel Jack Hoschouer, USA (Ret.), Lieutenant Colonel Raymond Millen, USA, and Oberstleutnant i.G. Norbert Eitelhuber, GE AF. Dr Peter Schmidt provided encouragement and crucial assistance in documentation. Daniel Weisbaum ably assisted in some of the finer points of translation.

2 'Gemeinsame Sicherheit und Zukunft der Bundeswehr', *Bericht der Kommission an die Bundesregierung* (Berlin: 23 May 2000), specifically §4.

3 Mary Elise Sarotte, 'German Military Reform and European Security', *Adelphi Paper*, 340 (London: The International Institute for Strategic Studies, October 2001), p. 14.

4 *Ibid.*, pp. 22–8.

5 See *ibid.*, pp. 33–48 and Johannes Varwick, 'Die Bundeswehr reformieren', *Internationale Politik*, 55:7 (2000), pp. 61–4.

6 See John S. Duffield, *World Power Forsaken: Political Culture, International Institutions, and German Security Policy after Unification* (Stanford: Stanford University Press, 1998); Sarotte, 'German Military Reform and European Security'; Wolfgang Schlör; 'German Security Policy', *Adelphi Paper*, 277 (London: The International Institute for Strategic Studies, June 1993) and Geoffrey Van Orden, 'The Bundeswehr in Transition', *Survival*, 33:4 (1991), pp. 352–70.

7 See Catherine McArdle Kelleher, 'Defense Organization in Germany: A Twice Told Tale', in Robert J. Art, Vincent Davis and Samuel P. Huntington (eds), *Reorganizing America's Defense: Leadership in War and Peace* (Washington, DC: Pergamon-Brassey's International Defense Publishers, 1985), p. 82.

8 See Gordon A. Craig, *The Politics of the Prussian Army, 1640–1945* (New York: Oxford University Press, 1955); F. L. Carsten, *The Reichswehr and Politics, 1918–1933* (Berkeley: University of California Press, 1966); and Donald Abenheim, *Reforging the Iron Cross: The Search for Tradition in the West German Armed Forces* (Princeton: Princeton University Press, 1988).

9 Michael J. Inacker, 'Macht und Moralität: Über eine neue deutsche Sicherheitspolitik', in Heimo Schwilk und Ulrich Schacht (eds), *Die Selbstbewusste Nation* (Berlin: Ullstein, 1994), pp. 364–80.

10 The Bundeswehr's deployment to the Middle East was criticised for poor planning and execution by its ombudsman. See *Kölner Stadt-Anzeiger*, 13

March 1992. According to one German press report, during this deployment of 500 Bundeswehr personnel, the command channels of the commanding officer, Major General Georg Bernhardt, had to be routed through twenty-three offices in the BMVg and other ministries. Within the BMVg, for instance, Fü S III 6 (Central Staff – political–military affairs) was responsible for operations in Turkey and Iran, while Fü L III 3 (operational division of the Air Force Staff) controlled Luftwaffe missions in Iraq within the framework of the United Nations. See *Welt am Sonntag*, 1 March 1992.

11 The most important initial policy and planning documents outlining these organisational reforms are: Der Bundesminister der Verteidigung, *Verteidigungspolitische Richtlinien* (hereafter *VPR*) (Bonn: BMVg), 26 November 1992, §49, §50, p. 32; Federal Ministry of Defence, *White Paper 1994*, (Bonn: BMVg), 5 April 1994, pp. 108–18; and Bundesministerium der Verteidigung, *Konzeptionelle Leitlinie zur Weiterentwicklung der Bundeswehr* (hereafter *KLL*) (Bonn: Informationsstab), 12 July 1994, pp. 3–5.

12 Compare Egon Bahr's support for the creation of a new *Generalstab* in order to support humanitarian and peace operations with the scepticism expressed by another member of the SPD, Hermann Sheer. See Egon Bahr, 'Ein Generalstab kein Tabu mehr', *Europäische Sicherheit*, 41:3 (1992), p. 127 and Matthew A. Weiller, 'SPD Security Policy,' *Survival*, 30:6 (1988), p. 522.

13 See Franz-Josef Meiers, 'Germany's "Out-of-Area" Dilemma' and Robert H. Dorff, 'German Policy toward Peace Support Operations', in Thomas-Durell Young (ed.), *Force, Statecraft and German Unity: The Struggle to Adapt Institutions and Practices* (Carlisle Barracks, PA: Strategic Studies Institute, 1996), pp. 7–25 and 71–99, respectively.

14 One of the early charges of this sort can be found in *Der Spiegel*, 6 April 1992, pp. 18–21.

15 See Christian O. E. Millotat, *Understanding the Prussian–German General Staff System* (Carlisle Barracks, PA: Strategic Studies Institute, 1992), p. 7.

16 *Süddeutsche Zeitung*, 2 July 1993.

17 Indeed, the Nazis' fears were justified as it was General Staff Officers in 1938 and 1944, among others, who attempted to assassinate Adolph Hitler. See Kelleher, 'Defense Organization in Germany', pp. 85–6. Craig is far less understanding and forgiving of the passive manner in which most of the senior Wehrmacht leadership acquiesced in Nazi rule. See Craig, *The Politics of the Prussian Army*, p. 503.

18 The German army's all but complete integration into bi-national and multinational formations would argue against such a development. See Thomas-Durell Young, *Multinational Land Formations and NATO: Reforming Practices and Structures* (Carlisle Barracks, PA: Strategic Studies

Institute, 1997), pp. 40–1. Subsequent reform of the army under the June 2000 'Army of the Future Plan' will not significantly alter this condition. See Gert Gudera, 'The German Army – The Bundeswehr: Its Mission, Tasks, New Structure and Equipment Plans', *NATO Review* 47:1 (2002), pp. 53–61.

19 *White Paper 1994*, §410, §604 and §606.

20 *VPR*, §8; and *KLL*, pp. 4–5.

21 The language of the Goldwater–Nichols Defense Reorganization Act explicitly proscribes the Joint Staff from functioning as an 'Armed Forces General Staff'. Following discussions to move offices of the Fü S remaining in Bonn to Berlin, the predictably Germanophobic *The Times* (London) headlined its report 'Germany Reinstates Banned General Staff'. See Title 10, *US Code, Armed Forces*, §155(e); and *The Times*, 5 September 2002.

22 Title 10, *US Code, Armed Forces*, §163.

23 Kelleher, 'Defense Organization in Germany', p. 97.

24 US Congress, Senate, Committee on Armed Services, *Defense Organization and the Need for Change*, Staff Report, 99th Congress, 1st Session (Washington, DC: GPO, 1985).

25 See Carsten, *The Reichswehr and Politics.*

26 The full text of the *Blankeneser Erlass* (21 March 1970) can be found at www.sipotec.net/bundeswehr/org_3_1.html.

27 Kelleher, 'Defense Organization in Germany', p. 94.

28 Federal Minister of Defence, *White Paper 1985: The Situation and Development of the Federal Armed Forces* (Bonn: Federal Ministry of Defence, 1985), p. 168.

29 *KLL*, p. 11.

30 *Ibid.*; and *Der Spiegel*, 2 August 1993, p. 16.

31 *Welt am Sonntag*, 1 March 1992.

32 See Gerhard Stoltenberg, 'Militärpolitische und militärstrategische Grundlagen und konzeptionelle Grundrichtung der Neugestaltung der Bundeswehr' (Bonn, draft document, n. d.), p. 9.

33 *VPR*, §48, p. 31.

34 *Führungsbereitschaften* exist in each of the civilian and military *Abteilungen*, including the Fü S and the *Führungsberetischaft* BMVg (which is comprised of personnel from all *Abteilungen* of the BMVg).

35 *Kölner Stadt-Anzeiger*, 6 April 1992.

36 *Der Spiegel*, 6 April 1992, pp. 18–21.

37 *Der Spiegel*, 20 April 1992, p. 93.

38 See the interview with Defence Minister Rühe in *Stern*, 16 February 1995, pp. 142–5.

39 The phrase 'kleine Lösung' was used by defence correspondent Michael Inacker to typify this approach. See *Welt am Sonntag*, 29 August 1993.

40 The Luftwaffe (Air Force) and Bundesmarine (Navy) had long possessed centralised operational command and control headquarters.

41 A literal translation of *Heeresführungskommando* would be Army Command Headquarters. However, the official translation employed the unassuming term employed for a US army headquarters for US-based army forces. This decision was intended to allay any potential fear (foreign and domestic) of a German *Generalstab* and a resurgence in German 'militarism' signalled by it. See *Die Welt*, 22 March 1994.

42 Erhard Drews *et al.*, 'Das neue deutsche Heer: Zielsetzung, Konzeption, und Elemente der Heeresstruktur 5.', *Truppenpraxis*, 35:4 (1991), pp. 362–5.

43 Fü H IV 1, 'Führungsebene des deutschen Heeres' (Vortrag f. GE/US Heeresgeneralstabs gespräche, 1992), 12 October 1992 and *White Paper 1994*, p. 109.

44 See Young, *Multinational Land Formations and NATO*, pp. 25–36, 40–1.

45 *Welt am Sonntag*, 2 October 1994.

46 See BMVg, Inspekteur des Heeres, *Operational Guidelines* (Bonn: n.d.), pp. 13–14; and StAL Fü H VI, 'Vortragskonzept', unpublished briefing given to US Department of the Army, Washington, DC, 5 August 1993, Part I, §9 and Part II, §7.

47 See Sts/Org 1 – Az 10–02–01 vom 9.02.93, 'Koordinierung des Einsatzes der Bundeswehr für Unterstützungsaufgaben' (Bonn: BMVg), 9 February 1993).

48 The FüZBw became effective from 1 January 1995. See Sts/Org 1 – Az 10–02–01 vom 31.08.94, 'Entscheidungsabläufe im Ministerium für die Einsatzführungs der Bundeswehr im Frieden' (Bonn: BMVg), 31 August 1994).

49 *Frankfurter Allgemeine Zeitung*, 3 January 1995.

50 See 'Ansprache von Generalinspekteurs Kujat zur Indienststellung des Einsatzführungskommandos', Geltow, 9 July 2001.

51 For one of the best descriptions and assessments of the Weizsäcker Commission, see Sarotte, *Germany Military Reform*, pp. 33–9.

52 'Gemeinsame Sicherheit und Zukunft der Bundeswehr', specifically §10. vi.

53 See Richard M. Connaughton, 'Organizing British Joint Rapid Reaction Forces', *Joint Forces Quarterly*, 26:1 (2000), pp. 87–94.

54 See Martin Agüera, 'New Center to Centralize German Military Planning', *Defense News*, 20–26 August 2001.

55 'Koordinierung des Einsatzes der Bundeswehr für Unterstützungsaufgaben'.

56 Note that at least one press report assumed that the government had revised this document. See *Süddeutsche Zeitung* 2 July 1993.

57 'Gemeinsame Sicherheit und Zukunft der Bundeswehr', specifically §10. vi.

58 See the summary of an official press releases, 31 August 2002, at www.bundeswehrforum.de/presse/16–08–2002.html.

59 See *Der Spiegel*, 16 September 2002, p. 18.

60 Hanns Maull, 'Germany and the Use of Force: Still a "Civilian Power"?', *Survival*, 42:2 (2000), p. 69.

61 James P. Thomas, 'The Military Challenges of Transatlantic Coalitions', *Adelphi Paper*, 333 (London: The International Institute for Strategic Studies, 2000), p. 24.

62 See commentary by Karl Feldmeyer in *Frankfurter Allgemeine Zeitung*, 3 January 1995.

16

Evolution of the German Bundesbank: from *Bank deutscher Länder* to regional bank of the European Central Bank

Karl Kaltenthaler

The German Bundesbank is often held up as the standard for success in central banking. It was a central bank that not only kept inflation very low, but also provided healthy average growth rates and relatively low unemployment in Germany in most of the postwar period. The conventional wisdom surrounding the Bundesbank was that the reason that the central bank was able to deliver these types of economic outcomes was because the institution was independent of government control.[1] The literature on the politics of central banking takes it as axiomatic that independent central banks countries pursue price stability-oriented monetary policies.[2] Leaving Bundesbank technocrats to run German monetary policy was the foundation of that policy's success.

It was the experience of the Bundesbank that shaped the structures of the ECB that has come to supplant its monetary policy powers. The decision making structure of the ECB is a near-carbon copy of the Bundesbank. But most important from the perspective of the conventional wisdom surrounding the Bundesbank's policy success, the ECB, like the Bundesbank, was made politically independent and clearly modelled on the Bundesbank example. The Bundesbank, which is now a constituent part of the ECB, came to define the monetary policy making paradigm of Europe's central bank.

Both the Bundesbank and the ECB have consistently followed strict price stability-oriented policies. I argue that policy making independence is a necessary but not sufficient condition for understanding the policy trajectory of the Bundesbank and the ECB. So what other factor(s) can explain the policy orientation of the Bundesbank and the ECB? Aside from autonomy from political interference, the central bankers must have the desire to make price stability the top priority. The source of this desire comes from the economic ideas the central bankers hold about how to produce what society deems the best economic outcome possible. I posit that the Bundesbank's monetary policy orientation, which was adopted by other European central bankers because of its success, was the product of economic ideas produced in Germany during the Second World War and in the immediate postwar period. These ideas came from the Freiburg School of economics and the direct experience of central bankers with Germany's hyper-inflation in the 1920s. These ideas, which were bolstered by monetarist thinking in the 1960s and 1970s, came to define how the Bundesbank and, subsequently, the ECB has approached monetary policy.

This chapter begins by developing an analytical framework for understanding how economic ideas can shape the policy orientations of independent central bankers. It then traces the development of economic ideas that came to shape policy thinking in the *Bank deutscher Länder* (BdL) and then the Bundesbank. The next section addresses how those policy ideas were able to thrive in the Bundesbank because the polices they produced found societal acceptance in Germany. The chapter goes on to explain how the experience of the Bundesbank led to a convergence around Bundesbank-defined monetary policy norms among European central bankers. The chapter concludes with what this study means for our understanding of the politics of central banking.

Alternative explanations of the sources of policy preferences among independent central bankers

Kenneth Rogoff has championed one of the most compelling arguments about the sources of central banker policy preferences: the policy preferences of decision makers in an independent central bank reflect their professional background before they join the central bank.[3] Decision makers in an independent central bank come from the ranks of the financial community and bring with them into the central bank the financial community's general policy preferences for price stability. In contrast, Roland Vaubel posits that decision makers in an independent central bank derive their preferences for monetary policy not from the financial community, but from the general public.[4] He argues that independent central bankers follow the general macroeconomic preferences of their public in order to appear competent to it. Still others argue that politicians play the primary role in determining the monetary policy priorities of the independent central bank,[5] despite the nominal independence of the central bank. Politicians can get the monetary policy that they want, owing to the asymmetry in power resources of the central bank and its political principals. Independent central bankers will not make policy that angers their political principals, because politicians have the power to punish the central bank through control of its resources and its nominal autonomy.

An alternative thesis explaining the policy orientation of independent central bankers is that ideas shape the decision makers' policy choices. The role that monetarism has played in the policy decisions of the Bundesbank and American Federal Reserve, for example, has been well researched.[6] But none of these studies determined the relative importance of ideas compared to other factors in shaping the policy preferences of central bankers. I argue that the ideas that independent central bankers hold about monetary policy are the most important factors in shaping their policy preferences. Why would ideas be more important to the central bankers than simply doing what their potential principals would want them to? Acting as the agent to principals such as politicians, the financial sector, or the general public is not in the best interest of the independent central bank, because independent central bankers seek the following payoffs from their occupation: a sense that they are doing a good thing for society, an image of competence, and organisational independence, which allows then to control their own resources and enhances their prestige.

Acting as an agent for any societal or state principal threatens all three of these payoffs for independent central bankers because of the difference in time horizons and levels of knowledge between central bankers and these potential principals. Politicians, who seek policies that maximise their chances for reelection, have relatively short time horizons defined by the next election. Financial actors also have relatively short time horizons: they are preoccupied with their bottom line rather than the monetary policy appropriate for a particular stage of the business cycle. Independent central bankers, on the other hand, must think about how monetary policy is going to affect the present business cycle and those to follow. Because of the long-term lagged effects of monetary policy, central bankers must be medium to long term in orientation. Making short-term-oriented changes in monetary policy, indifferent to its long-term effects, could degrade the central bankers' reputation for competence.

Independent central bankers also have a strong incentive to avoid being agents of societal or state actors because those actors usually know less about monetary issues than the central bankers. This is particularly true of the public, which has a tenuous grasp at best of what monetary policy is and how it works. This is also true of a great many politicians. While some may have a cursory understanding of monetary policy issues, most do not. Thus independent central bankers have good reason to ignore the policy preferences of politicians and the general public alike. Were central bankers to conform with the preferences of either, they would nonetheless be held responsible for the consequences of a policy misstep. Thus to stay independent and retain credibility, central bankers rely on their own ideas about monetary policy and resist external policy pressures.

Ideas about the goals and tactics of monetary policy serve as road maps for central bankers who try to determine the best way to manage the currency.[7] But it is important to note that the range of ideas available to central bankers is limited. First, their ideas about monetary policy are constrained by the parameters of acceptable policy established by the political context. Once ideas stray outside of the policy parameters set by the financial sector, the public or politicians, the central bankers could be potentially sanctioned, manifested as a loss of prestige or reputation for competence, loss of formal or behavioural independence or loss of tangible job benefits.

The ideas held by central bankers have two plausible sources: the economics profession and experience. Ideas from the economics profession on the conduct of monetary policy will have a role in shaping the way policy makers think as they help frame the interpretation of data and provide policy options. Policy making experience is also a source of ideas guiding the formulation of monetary policy. Ideas derived from policy making experience are likely to be embraced so long as they prove useful in achieving central bankers' goals; ideas derived from academic economics are likely to be 'stickier', but would ideally be adjusted as circumstances require.

Based on the logic presented above, it was the monetary policy ideas developed from experience and the economics profession that not only guided the evolution of German monetary policy after the Second World War, but were appropriated by those drafting the constitution of the ECB.

The origin of monetary policy ideas in postwar Germany

The *Bank deutscher Länder* (BdL), established in March 1948, was the creation of the occupying Western powers. There was a pressing need for a monetary authority to manage the newly created German DM in anticipation of the June 1948 Currency Reform. The new German central bank, modelled on the American Federal Reserve system, was highly decentralised.[8] The Americans wanted a decentralised central bank so as to avoid a potential abuse of central bank powers as had occurred with the *Reichsbank* during the Weimar Republic and the successor National Socialist regime. These German governments had used the *Reichsbank* to finance German war plans and to facilitate the hyperinflation of 1923, which had so destabilised German politics. Thus an independent and decentralised central bank would preclude the misuse of central bank powers that had helped Germany along the path toward totalitarianism.

The institutional blueprint for the central bank was only one of the pressing issues that the Allies and Germans faced when they were attempting to reestablish a functioning central bank. Two other questions arose: Who would run the new central bank? What principles would guide its operations? The answer to the first question was complicated by the Allies' denazification policy which precluded a great number of the *Reichsbank* staff who had been either active Nazis or had worked closely with the Hitler regime. The bulk of the technocratic talent in central banking in Germany was thus politically tainted.[9] So the question arose: Where would the allies and German authorities find experienced and politically untainted central bankers?

The answer to this question was that it would have simply been impossible to find enough experienced central bank staff in the Western Zones of Occupation to staff the BdL. When the BdL was established in 1948, several former Nazi party-members and fellow-travellers were appointed to the upper levels of the central bank's staff. At American insistence, these individuals constituted a small minority of the total, but as the Germans gained control over their own hiring, the proportion of former Nazi party members in the BdL hierarchy grew; by 1968, the proportion had grown to 53 per cent of the BdL's leadership.[10] This seeming continuity of personnel between the Reichsbank and the new BdL could suggest that the central bank was nothing more than old wine in a new bottle. But the BdL was a stark departure from the *Reichsbank* in terms of the guiding principle of monetary policy.

The one overarching principle of monetary policy governing BdL policy was the maintenance of *price stability.* No other policy goal was to encroach upon this priority. Not only was this the stated goal of the central bank, but there also was a strong and pervasive consensus among the BdL staff that the bank's most important mission was the maintenance of price stability in the newly established Federal Republic.

What fostered this fixation on price stability? There are two sources: first, the experience of the central bankers who came to manage the BdL; second, a shift in thinking in the German economics profession. As was noted above, there was a continuity of key personnel between the *Reichsbank* and the BdL. Many of the central bankers in the early days of the BdL had thus been at the wheel of *Reichsbank* when the hyper-inflation of 1923 hit. They had also been in the central bank when it became a willing participant in the National Socialist regime and financed the inflationary Nazi war spending. These two policy lapses devastated the average German: a major proportion of the German populace was pauperised and the hyper-inflation bred extremism in German politics. Thus, even the old hands of the *Reichsbank* who had been hired to steer the BdL saw that a return to inflation in Germany would be an economic and political disaster. They had learned their lesson well by 1945.

The emphasis on price stability also came from change in the German economics profession during the 1930s and 1940s. Traditionally, the German economics profession had been relatively strong supporters of economic nationalism and a strong state role in the economy. They did not support French-style statism, but rather a collusion between the state and industry on behalf of the German nation. The central bank was viewed as an extension of the state to foster national goals.[11]

The disastrous consequences of the hyper-inflation of the 1920s and the experience with the Nazis led a group of German economists, many who had been at the University of Freiburg during this period, to reject traditional German notions of the economy and call for new manner of economic management. This 'Freiburg School' of economics, which was most notably represented by the likes of Alfred Müller-Armack, Wilhelm Röpke, Wilhelm Eucken and Ludwig Erhard, stressed the need for price stability and as little government intervention as possible in the economy. The group also stressed the need for the government to establish clear rules for economic actors and to provide a social safety net for its citizens. While the group differed over the breadth of the rules for the economy and the size of the social safety net, all embraced the axiom that price stability was the *sin qua non* of a stable economy. In fact, all of the Freiburg School prioritised price stability, arguing that a non-inflationary economy would make counter-cyclical intervention by the government unnecessary.[12]

The Freiburg School was very important in the development of the guiding principles of postwar German monetary policy, for two reasons. First, it became the dominant paradigm in German university economics curricula and thus influenced the thinking of nearly all of Germany's economic technocrats educated after the war. Second, the School's theoretically-based emphasis on price stability buttressed the experiences of the older monetary policy technocrats in Germany. There was thus a confluence of theory and experience that moulded a consensus among German monetary policy decision makers that the primary goal of economic management was the maintenance of price stability.

The norm of price stability became institutionalised with the passage of the Bundesbank Law of 1957, which replaced the provisional BdL and established the Bundesbank as the Federal Republic's permanent central bank. Section 1.3 of the Bundesbank Law 'assigned the Deutsche Bundesbank the task of regulating the quantity of money in circulation and of credit supplied to the economy with the aim of safeguarding the currency'.[13] The Bundesbank Law also stipulated that 'without to the performance of its functions, the Deutsche Bundesbank is required to support the general economic policy of the Federal Government'.[14] Thus the German Bundesbank Law mandated price stability as the central bank's primary goal. This provision reflected not only the consensus among the German central banking community about the primacy of price stability, but it also showed that a majority of German politicians supported the notion that the Bundesbank should be an independent central bank with the primary mission of maintaining the stable value of the currency.

It is important to note that no serious challenger came to threaten the postwar orthodoxy among German central bankers, or politicians for that matter, about the primacy of price stability. Statism was discredited by the Nazi experience; Keynesianism never developed a significant following in Germany, making the country relatively unique among the advanced industrialised states. Keynesianism found little favour in Germany because it tolerated both inflation and political intervention in the economy, taboos in the German economics profession and among the postwar policy elite.[15]

While the Freiburg School's emphasis on price stability became the dominant norm among German central bankers following 1945, there were other new economic ideas affecting the theory and practice of German central banking. Monetarism also found resonance among German central bankers, who were influenced by Milton Friedman.[16] Monetarism, which stressed the neutrality of money, suggested that demand management was not only unnecessary but counter-productive. Central bankers, accordingly, would target a non-inflationary rate of growth in the money supply; monetary policy would then be tailored to keeping money supply growth in that target. Monetary policy was thus not about fine-tuning the economy but about hitting the money supply growth target.

Monetarism found a receptive audience among German central bankers. But rather than supplanting the Freiburg School's position on the primacy of price stability, monetarism complemented it. When Helmut Schlesinger, the Bundesbank's chief economist, introduced monetarist tactics into the central bank's repertoire in 1974, the Bundesbank began the practice of monetary targeting.[17] It is important to note that the adoption of monetarism in the 1970s was a pragmatic tool to assist in the task of ensuring price stability. When asked about the role of monetarism in the policy making thinking of the Bundesbank, a Directorate member answered:

> The price stability mandate was what guided us. Policy ideas such as monetarism only mattered in that they were a way to achieve the goal of price stability, which was our mandate. We had a very pragmatic view toward monetarism. The mandate always came before monetarism. We had no set policy rules determined by monetarism, such as advocates like Friedman have called for.[18]

A *Landesbank* (LCB) president added: 'Less than half of the CBC members were convinced monetarists during the 1990s. We were aware that theory and practice did not always match. What was important was that we got the practice right. Price stability always came before money supply targeting'.[19] The adoption of monetarism never signalled a fundamental shift in the scholarly doctrine in German university economic programmes or among the central bank technocrats.[20] In fact, the Bundesbank missed its annual money supply targets about 50 per cent of the time between 1974 and 1999. Despite this poor record, no one inside or outside of the Bundesbank questioned the central bank's commitment to price stability.[21] No one could question the Bundesbank's commitment to price stability, particularly since the Bundesbank defined price stability as less than a 2 per cent annual rise in consumer prices, a very tight definition by international standards.

The ideas about monetary policy that originated among German central bankers and the economics profession in the 1930s and 1940s thus became entrenched in the BdL and then institutionalised in the Bundesbank. Monetarism only complemented and built on these ideas. But all this was made possible because these ideas found general acceptance among the financial sector, the general public and politicians. The ideas of the Bundesbank were possible because they did not meet active resistance from any powerfully organised sector of German society.

The societal setting

The Bundesbank's ideas about monetary policy fitted into the societal context quite well. Despite a few attempts on the part of the German government to sway Bundesbank policy,[22] none got very far and there was never a serious threat to the central bank's autonomy. The most important reason why the Bundesbank enjoyed this degree of autonomy was the financial sector's preferences and the vaguer ideas held by the general public about the undesirability of inflation. With the financial sector and the general public, the two most powerful societal forces in Germany, on its side, the Bundesbank was fairly confident that its policies would not be successfully challenged by the German government.

The financial sector in Germany

The German financial sector is bank-based in nature. This importance of bank's reflects Germany's position as a late moderniser. In the late nineteenth century, German firms required massive infusions of capital to catch up to other countries as industrialisation got under way. Capital markets have not been an important source of direct finance for German firms, banks are the principle source of finance, even when firms seek to raise capital through securities.

Several types of banks operate in Germany, each with different interests in the political economy. One type of bank is the *universal bank*. These banks perform a wide range of services to clients including saving and investment services, such as brokering securities and underwriting equity issues.[23] These universal banks provide the bulk of investment in the German economy and are dominated by the 'big four': Deutsche Bank, Commerzbank, Dresdner Bank and Hypovereinsbank. These four banks have huge stakes in most of Germany's largest firms, not only do they provide the greatest share of the finance, but they also have seats on their boards. For example, the chairman of Deutsche Bank, which owns a 61.66 per cent voting share in Daimler–Chrysler, is a member of the firm's board, giving Deutsche Bank a controlling say in the decisions taken by the car maker. This pattern is replicated by the rest of the 'big three' with almost all of Germany's large and medium-sized firms. Thus a very close symbiotic relationship exists between big German banks and big German industry. The Federation of German Banks (BDB), which represents the universal banks, is one of the most important interest organisations in Germany. However, the 'big four' universal banks want low inflation, but not at the cost of very low economic growth. These banks depend on economic growth to guarantee that firms can service their debt and to make additional profits from the equity stake they have in those firms.

The second major type of bank in Germany is the *Landesbank* (LCB, or state bank), which are owned by the *Länder* and provide financing to them for things such as public works projects.[24] Their role in the German private finance scene is relatively small when compared to the universal banks.

The cooperative banks and *Sparkassen* (savings banks) round out the German finance sector. The cooperative banks are locally organised and provide loans to small businesses and farmers. The savings banks, which are important financial institutions because of the German population's propensity to save, are organised at the local level and do not shape the German corporate scene. The *Sparkassen* control the greatest share of total bank assets in the country. This gives the *Sparkassen*, which represent the direct financial interests of individuals, a rather high political profile. The German Giro and Savings Banks Association (DSGV), which represents the interests of these banks, has a very strong voice on domestic monetary matters. Since German banks are primarily providers of loans and/or are savings institutions, they all have a clear predilection for price stability although it will vary somewhat from savings banks to the big universal banks. But the consensus among the banks that the central bank should maintain price stability and their high degree of political organisation means that the German financial sector is a powerful advocate of a price stability-oriented monetary policy.[25]

What do German central bankers think about the role played by the financial sector in monetary policy making in Germany? I asked the seven Central Bank Council (CBC) members two questions: What role do the views of the financial community play in shaping monetary policy? Why is that the case? All of the CBC respondents concluded that the financial sector was important as a source of information about the economy and its general health was taken into account when making policy, but the short-term wishes of the banks did not drive policy. A representative answer from the six was given by a Directorate member: 'Monetary policy decisions are taken independently from the banks. I would not deny that in some cases the preferences of the banks have played a role. But I would say that in general terms, there is not much bank influence on the central bank'.[26] A *Land* central bank president stated that: 'We do not listen much to the demands of the banks because they are too short-term oriented. To maintain price stability, we have to take the long-term view on monetary policy. If we were to listen to them, we would have to deviate from our mandate and that we won't and cannot do'.[27] Thus, the financial sector seems to have a limited impact on central bank decision making, because of the potential conflict between the short-term needs of the financial sector and the long-term requirements of price stability. Nonetheless, the financial sector has supported the Bundesbank in any disputes it has had with the Federal Government; it would seem that although the Bundesbank may ignore the short-term preferences of the financial sector, the banks strongly support the Bundesbank's general policy orientation.

The German public

The German history of inflation has been an unhappy one. The hyper-inflation of 1923–24 wiped out the savings of most Germans and nearly brought the economy to a standstill. This inflation, which peaked at about 26 billion per cent annually, led to the near complete breakdown of the money economy.[28] Workers could not get to the bank fast enough to cash their pay cheques before they became worthless. In fact, at the height of the inflation, workers were paid several times a day so as to keep some real value in their wages. This is one of the most salient international examples of an inflation that bankrupted a whole generation. While many Germans have no direct memory of either that hyper-inflation or the collapse of the *Reichsmark* after the Second

Table 16.1 Do you agree with the following statement: 'The control of inflation is one of the most important missions of government economic policy'?

	1		*3*		*5*
	Fully agree		*Undecided*		*Completely disagree*
	(%)	*(%)*	*(%)*	*(%)*	*(%)*
US all	56.0	28.0	7.0	7.0	2.0
Born < 1940	69.0	13.0	11.0	4.0	2.0
Born > 1950	44.0	38.0	2.0	13.0	2.0
Germany all	76.0	18.0	5.0	1.0	0.0
Born < 1940	90.0	8.0	1.0	1.0	0.0
Born > 1950	51.0	40.0	7.0	2.0	0.0

Source: Robert Shiller, 'Why Do People Dislike Inflation?', in C. Romer and D. Romer (eds), *Reducing Inflation: Motivation and Strategy* (Chicago: University of Chicago Press, 1997).

World War, the price stability norm is firmly entrenched in German popular culture. It is interesting to note that when many Germans today, even young Germans, talk about monetary politics, they make reference to the days before the Currency Reform and what that did to the life savings of their compatriots.

Table 16.1 shows the breakdown in German and American attitudes toward the government role in fighting inflation.[29] 76 per cent of all Germans fully agree that the government should make price stability one of its most important missions. If one looks at the Germans born before 1940, the number jumps to 90 per cent that fully agree and 8 per cent that agree. This shows a very strong concern for inflation among older Germans but there still seems also to be a continued pan-generational aversion to inflation: 91 per cent of those born after 1950 either agree or fully agree that the government should prioritise fighting inflation.

As compared to America, the Germans' historical experience with inflation has left them with a greater concern with it. If we compare all of the Germans and all of the Americans, we see that 94 per cent of the Germans compared to 84 per cent of the Americans think the government should prioritise fighting inflation. That 10 per cent gap is large enough to show a significant difference in the two publics' tolerance for inflation. The conventional wisdom that the German public is very concerned with fighting inflation is well borne out by this survey data.

What role did the public play in shaping the parameters of acceptable policy for the Bundesbank? I asked the seven CBC members the following questions: How important are the views of the general public in shaping the parameters of monetary policy? Why is that the case?

All CBC interviewees responded that public views on monetary policy were decisive. One Directorate member stated: 'We are there to keep the DM stable. There is the pressure of expectations from the public that guides us … One is given a certain responsibility and it becomes part of one's consciousness. One cannot separate the two. We are constantly under the pressure of expectations.'[30] Two representative responses from Directorate members draw attention to the connection between the importance of public support and Bundesbank autonomy: '[Our image] in the public's eyes is very important. In the end you need the public on your side. An independent central bank must be understood in the public and must in the long run have the support of the public, which is more important than support from the financial community'.[31] And, 'Look, the independence of the Bundesbank was laid down in a simple law, which could have been changed by a simple majority in the Bundestag. And we know about the importance of public support because of the different attacks [by politicians] which happened over the last forty to fifty years against the Bundesbank'.[32] While maintaining price stability gives CBC members a sense of pride, the public expectation that they will always produce price stability supports them politically. It is clear that the public is immensely important to the central bankers in their shaping of monetary policy, not as a source of policy preferences but as political support for the central bank's policy ideas.

The role of politicians

The German public and financial sector have been stalwart supporters of the Bundesbank's monetary policy orientation. What room does that leave for German politicians in determining the monetary policy orientation of their central banks?

It is clear that German politicians had often found the Bundesbank's monetary policy orientation very frustrating. There are myriad examples of conflict between the Bundesbank and politicians over the direction of monetary policy.[33] These conflicts started with the creation of the Bundesbank and have persisted even beyond the creation of the ECB, of which the Bundesbank is a constituent part. What is very important to note about these conflicts is that in nearly every case the Bundesbank prevailed and maintained its policy line.

To determine the power of German politicians over the central bank, I first asked CDU and SPD politicians the following question: How successful were you in influencing the monetary policy direction of the Bundesbank? An official from the CDU replied: 'It is nearly impossible to have any influence over the Bundesbank. The Bundesbank has the general public on its side, which for historical reasons, has a serious fear of inflation. There is almost no room for political influence over the central bank. It is untouchable.'[34] The SPD official showed even greater frustration: 'The Bundesbank has often maintained a policy that we do not agree with. It clearly places employment as a secondary priority. We have criticised the bank for this but it does not really matter. The bank simply has too much public support to budge'.[35] Second, I asked central bankers the following question: What role do politicians play in shaping the monetary policy orientation of the central bank? One LCB president's answer was indicative of the other CBC responses: 'The politicians only have as much say in monetary policy as the public will give them and that is not much. Since 1957 politicians have had the opportunity to change the Bundesbank Law. It would only take a simple vote of parliament. Not only has this never succeeded, it has never been tried. The Bundesbank is an extremely well protected institution.'[36] This seems to show that politicians in Germany have very little say about the direction of the central bank's monetary policy.

The monetary policy ideas of the Bundesbank have found ample support in Germany because of the strong preference for price stability in the financial sector and in the public, but also because of the economic success Germans have enjoyed since the Second World War. The Bundesbank could take credit for keeping inflation low, but also credibly claim that price stability served as a basis for solid growth and relatively low unemployment for most of the postwar era. This record also made the Bundesbank a standard for good central banking around the world. In no place was this more pronounced than with Germany's western European neighbours. The Bundesbank, but most importantly its ideas, came to serve as a model of how to manage monetary policy in both Europe and farther afield.

From Bundesbank to ECB

When the European System of Central Banks (ESCB), also known as the ECB, came into operation in June 1998, it may have seemed to many that the famed German Bundesbank had been relegated to an insignificant bit part in European monetary affairs. The Bundesbank no longer controlled the monetary destiny of Europe, as it had under the European Monetary System (EMS). In fact, the Bundesbank did not even control the monetary affairs of Germany. The ECB ran monetary policy for the EMU, of which Germany was a constituent part. The president of the Bundesbank had only one of sixteen votes on the Governing Council of the ECB. It may have seemed like the end of the BdL/Bundesbank's legacy of monetary policy, but in fact the ECB is, in many ways, an extension of the postwar Germany monetary policy paradigm. While the institutional structure of the Bundesbank is clearly reflected in the ECB, it is the Bundesbank's monetary policy ideas that have made the most important contribution. The structure of the ECB clearly reflects that of the Bundesbank. In fact, in many ways, the ECB is a near-carbon copy of the Bundesbank's organisation. Also, the mandate of the ECB set down in the Treaty on European Union (TEU, Maastricht Treaty) nearly duplicates the mandate of the Bundesbank as laid out in the 1957 Bundesbank Law. But despite all of the obvious institutional similarities between the Bundesbank and the ECB, the two central banks could behave very differently if the ECB's decision makers operated on different monetary policy principles than the Bundesbank, just as the Bundesbank, which was modelled on the American Federal Reserve System, operated on quite different policy principles than its American counterpart for much of the postwar period.

There are clear signs that the ECB adopted the Bundesbank's monetary policy principles. First, the ECB adopted the Bundesbank's definition of price stability, a 2 per cent annual rise in consumer prices. The ECB has also adopted the Bundesbank's monetary targeting strategy, but refers to a reference value rather than a money supply growth target.[37] The difference in wording is not over the principle of the policy, but over pragmatic considerations. While measuring the actual rate of growth of the money supply was difficult in the German sphere, it is even more difficult in the much larger Eurozone. The ECB does not want to tie itself to the word 'target', when measuring that 'target' is such an imprecise affair.[38]

Why was the Bundesbank the institutional and ideational model for the ECB? The most important reason is the success that the Bundesbank had in maintaining price stability and Germany's postwar economic performance. Moreover, the Bundesbank emerged as the *de facto* lead central bank for the EU, largely owing to the anchor role of the DM in the EMS. The subsequent export of German price stability to the rest of Europe, which was viewed by European central bankers as a positive experience for their countries, made the Bundesbank and its practices an attractive model for the ECB. As one member of the ECB's Governing Council put it: 'The Bundesbank was the leading central bank before it dominated monetary policy in Europe. So the experience and credibility of the Bundesbank mattered. The policy and strategy of the Bundesbank was an important contribution to the young institution.'[39] When the ECB's design become an issue for discussion in 1989–91, Europe's central bankers broadly agreed that the Bundesbank's structure and principles provided the best model.

The ideas of the Bundesbank were disseminated throughout the ranks of the EU's central bankers through multiple channels. There was the frequent and sustained contact between the central banks because of the operation of the 'snake' monetary regime and then the EMS. Central bankers spoke to each other often by phone or met to discuss the common management of Europe's monetary affairs. As the Bundesbank was at the centre of both of those monetary arrangements, it facilitated the German central bank's ability to pass on its views on how to conduct monetary policy. The Committee of Central Bank Governors of the EC, which consisted of all the heads of the EU central banks, provided a formalised setting for the exchange views on how to deal with the pressing monetary issues of the day.[40] It had a very club-like atmosphere, where the central bankers could freely debate monetary policy matters and was the perfect place to disseminate ideas about monetary policy.

There were also fora outside the EU, where European central bankers would meet and discuss monetary policy issues, thus allowing the Bundesbank's ideas get a hearing. One of the most important was the Bank for International Settlements (BIS). The BIS, often referred to as the 'central bank for central banks', held annual meetings about monetary policy issues where central bankers could exchange views and be free from the interference of politicians or the press. Another such forum is the G–7 meetings. These were often occasions when central bankers would discuss monetary issues along with the politicians. While less a central banker-only environment than the Committee of Governors or the BIS meetings, it was another place to exchange ideas about the best way to manage monetary policy.

There was thus ample reason and opportunity for central bankers in Europe to take ideas from the Bundesbank; while the Bundesbank became a regional central bank of the ECB, it is by far the most important national component in terms of the influence it has had on the central bank. While the president of the Bundesbank may have a bit more say in the meetings of the Governing Council because of the relative size of the German economy, he would not be a dominant figure in the ECB. The Governing Council must make monetary policy that is appropriate for all of the Eurozone and not for one or a few countries in particular. But it is indisputable that the stamp of the Bundesbank's ethos is very prominent in every monetary policy decision made by the ECB.

Conclusion

This chapter has traced the development of the sources of the Bundesbank's monetary policy since its creation. I argued that the Bundesbank has not been the agent of societal or state principals in Germany, but has been an autonomous entity guided by economic ideas formed in Germany in the 1930s and 1940s. The Freiburg School and the experience of German central bankers with government intervention in monetary policy led to a strong consensus among German monetary policy makers that the maintenance of price stability should be the primary goal of monetary policy. This price stability goal, and the tactics created to achieve it, were supported by both the German financial community and public. While there were some German politicians who disagreed with the Bundesbank's policies and tried to pressure the central bank from time to time, the Bundesbank was never forced to acquiesce in such pressure because of its high degree of societal support.

Although the Bundesbank *has* been relegated to the status of a constituent part of the ECB, its monetary policy ideas have been adopted by the new central bank. The Bundesbank is by far the most influential member of the ECB, because its ideas have shaped policy orientation of the Governing Council. While the ECB is a European and not a German institution, it is managed along the lines of German monetary policy thinking. One can easily argue that Germany's monetary policy ethos has become Europe's way to approach monetary policy issues.

What do these findings mean for our understanding of the sources of policy for independent central banks? First, ideas matter. Central bankers must find policy guidelines somewhere. They can be directed by political or societal principals, but to make policy that way would severely threaten the medium- and long-term prospects for policy. Ideas from experience and the economics profession provide logically based policy guidelines that allow central bankers to avoid making random policy choices.

Second, the findings clearly show that independent central banks *are* political institutions. One of the rationales, perhaps the most important one, for creating an independent central bank is to remove monetary policy from politics. However, an independent central bank cannot afford to be apolitical. The simple reason is because the policies made by these institutions are too important for groups in a polity to not try to influence. Politicians, the financial community and the general public all have an interest in the course and content of monetary policy. Politicians want to shape it to stay in office. Participants in the financial sector want to shape it to maximise profits. The public wants to shape it in order to achieve the highest possible standard of living. The preferences and power of these groups provide the context in which the ideas central bankers hold about monetary policy must survive.

The third and very significant implication of the findings is that independent central banks are not as inherently undemocratic as many would argue. Society constrains independent central bankers: monetary policy makers do reflect what their society wants. Even highly independent central banks cannot contravene the wishes of their society for extended periods of time. Independent central banks may not be the direct agents of societal principals, but they are not institutions that can long work against their wishes. To do so would be an invitation to lose their independence. The Bundesbank is a very good example of a central bank that worked very harmoniously with society in a framework of democratic politics.

Notes

1 The independence of the Bundesbank as a factor in its price stability orientation is a theme of much of the literature on the central bank. See, for example, Rolf Caesar, *Der Handlungsspielraum von Notenbanken*

(Baden-Baden: Nomos, 1981); Deutsche Bundesbank (ed.), *Fifty Years of the Deutsche Mark* (Oxford: Oxford University Press, 1989); Bruno Frey and Friedrich Schneider, 'Central Bank Behavior: A Positive Empirical Analysis', *Journal of Monetary Economics*, 9:2 (1987), pp. 291–315; and Susanne Lohmann, 'Federalism and Central Bank Independence: The Politics of German Monetary Policy, 1957–92', *World Politics*, 50:3 (1998), pp 401–46.

2 Alberto Alesina and Lawrence Summers, 'Central Bank Independence and Macroeconomic Performance: Some Comparative Evidence', *Journal of Money, Credit, and Banking*, 25:2 (1993), pp. 151–62; Alex Cukierman, *Central Bank Strategy, Credibility, and Independence: Theory and Evidence* (Cambridge, MA: MIT Press, 1992); and Sylvia Maxfield, *Gatekeepers of Growth* (Princeton: Princeton University Press, 1998).

3 Kenneth Rogoff, 'The Optimal Degree of Commitment to an Intermediate Monetary Target', *Quarterly Journal of Economics*, 100:4 (1985), pp. 1169–89.

4 Roland Vaubel, 'Eine Public-Choice Analyse der Deutschen Bundesbank und ihre Implikationen für die Europäische Währungsunion', in Dieter Duwendag and Jürgen Siebke (eds), *Europa vor dem Eintritt in die Wirtschafts und Währungsunion* (Berlin: Duncker & Humblot, 1993), pp. 23–77.

5 Henry Chappell, Thomas Havrilesky and Bob Roy McGregor, 'Partisan Monetary Policy: Presidential Influence through the Power of Appointments', *Quarterly Journal of Economics*, 108:1 (1993), pp. 185–218; Thomas Havrilesky, *The Pressures on American Monetary Policy* (Boston: Kluwer Academic Publishers, 1993); and Robert Weintraub, 'Congressional Supervision of Monetary Policy', *Journal of Monetary Economics*, 4:2 (1978), pp. 341–62.

6 Peter Johnson, *The Government of Money* (Ithaca, NY: Cornell University Press, 1998); Ellen Kennedy, *The Bundesbank: Germany's Central Bank in the International Monetary System* (New York: Council on Foreign Relations Press, 1991); and John Woolley, *Monetary Politics* (Cambridge: Cambridge University Press, 1984).

7 There is a growing literature on how ideas have come to affect policy choice. See Judith Goldstein, *Ideas, Interests, and American Trade Policy* (Ithaca, NY: Cornell University Press, 1993); Peter Hall (ed.), *The Political Power of Economic Ideas: Keynesianism across Nations* (Princeton: Princeton University Press, 1989); Kathleen McNamara, *The Currency of Ideas* (Ithaca, NY: Cornell University Press, 1998); and Kathryn Sikkink, *Ideas and Institutions: Developmentalism in Brazil and Argentina* (Ithaca, NY: Cornell University Press, 1991).

8 Kennedy, *The Bundesbank*; David Marsh, *The Most Powerful Bank: Inside Germany's Bundesbank* (New York: Times Books, 1992).

9 *Ibid.*
10 *Ibid.*, p. 156.
11 Christopher S. Allen, 'The Underdevelopment of Keynesianism in the Federal Republic of Germany', in Peter Hall (ed.), *The Political Power of Economic Ideas: Keynesianism across Nations* (Princeton: Princeton University Press), pp. 263–90.
12 *Ibid.*, p. 281.
13 Deutsche Bundesbank, 'The Deutsche Bundesbank: Its Monetary Policy Instruments and Functions', *Special Series*, 7 (Frankfurt: Deutsche Bundesbank, 1989), p. 111.
14 *Ibid.*, p. 115.
15 Allen, 'The Underdevelopment of Keynesianism' and W. R. Smyser, *The German Economy*, 2nd edn (New York: St Martin's Press, 1993).
16 Milton Friedman, 'The Role of Monetary Policy', *American Economic Review*, 58:1 (1968), pp. 1–17.
17 Jürgen von Hagen, 'A New Approach to Monetary Policy', in Deutsche Bundesbank (ed.), *Fifty Years of the Deutsche Mark* (Oxford: Oxford University Press, 1989), pp. 403–38.
18 Interview with Directorate member, 25 July 2000.
19 Interview with LCB president, 17 July 2000.
20 Manfred Neumann, 'Monetary Stability: Threat and Proven Response', in Deutsche Bundesbank (ed.), *Fifty Years of the Deutsche Mark* (Oxford: Oxford University Press, 1989), pp. 269–306.
21 Deutsche Bundesbank, 'The Deutsche Bundesbank', pp. 100–1.
22 See Marsh, *The Most Powerful Bank.*
23 See Smyser, *The German Economy.*
24 Randall Henning, *Currencies and Politics in the United States, Germany, and Japan* (Washington, DC: International Institute of Economics, 1994) and Adam Posen, 'Why Central Bank Independence Does Not Cause Low Inflation: The Politics behind the Institutional Fix' (New York: Federal Reserve Bank of New York, 1993), unpublished manuscript.
25 Posen, 'Why Central Bank Independence Does Not Cause Low Inflation'; Günter Franke, 'The Bundesbank and the Markets', in Deutsche Bundesbank (ed.), *Fifty Years of the Deutsche Mark* (Oxford: Oxford University Press, 1989), pp. 219–66.
26 Interview with LCB president, 17 July 2000.
27 Interview with LCB president, 18 July 2000.
28 Russell Dalton, *Politics in Germany* (New York: HarperCollins, 1993), p. 18.
29 Table taken from Robert Shiller, 'Why Do People Dislike Inflation?', in C. Romer and D. Romer (eds), *Reducing Inflation: Motivation and Strategy* (Chicago: University of Chicago Press, 1997), pp. 1–53.
30 Interview with Bundesbank Directorate member, 10 June 1997.

31 Interview with Bundesbank Directorate member, 28 June 1999.
32 Interview with Bundesbank Directorate member, 29 June 1999.
33 See Karl Kaltenthaler, *Germany and the Politics of Europe's Money* (Durham, NC: Duke University Press, 1998).
34 Interview with Christian Democrat party official, 18 June 1995.
35 Interview with Social Democrat party official, 17 June 1995.
36 Interview with LCB president, 18 July 2000.
37 European Central Bank, *The Monetary Policy of the ECB* (Frankfurt: European Central Bank, 2001).
38 It is important to note that one of the main reasons the American Federal Reserve dropped monetary targeting was because it became next to impossible to measure accurately the size of the money supply in the United States.
39 Interview with ECB Governing Council member, 23 July 2002.
40 Kathleen McNamara, 'Where do Rules Come From? The Creation of the European Central Bank', in Neil Fligstein, Wayne Sandholtz and Alec Stone Sweet (eds), *The Institutionalization of Europe* (Oxford: Oxford University Press, 2001), pp. 1–21.

17

Standort Deutschland revisited

Michael Huelshoff

In January 2003, German unemployment returned to over 11 per cent of the workforce (seasonally unadjusted). In percentage terms, unemployment was at levels experienced prior to the beginning of the first Schröder election campaign in 1998. In other words, four years of SPD rule had done little to correct structural unemployment problems in Germany. This outcome is especially troublesome for a party based in the working classes, and a Chancellor whose first election campaign contained little of substance other than a promise to reduce unemployment.

In this chapter, I explore some dimensions of the SPD's failure to deliver on the core of its agenda, the fight against unemployment, and examine both international and domestic sources of the troubles faced by the German government. While there remains some evidence of micro-level adjustment in Germany – my 'Storm Before the Calm' hypothesis[1] – the continued high unemployment in Germany is the result of failures on the part of the Schröder government to come to grips with its domestic constituents. As a result, high structural unemployment is likely to continue in Germany for some time. To be sure, Germany's economic woes are not caused only by the Schröder government's failures. Yet inaction on structural reform of the German economy, especially reform of labour markets, heightens Germany's sensitivity to global economic problems.

The chapter begins with a short exploration of the problems facing the German economy today, especially as regards unemployment. Second, alternative conceptualisations of *Standort Deutschland* are explored, beginning with a brief overview of the applicability of models drawn from other economic systems. Third, I explore some of the more significant attempts by the Schröder government to address unemployment. The chapter concludes with a discussion of where Germany might go next.

Germany and the world economy

The debate about German competitiveness has a long pedigree. German business resisted policies designed to increase protections for workers and increase economic democracy throughout the history of the Federal Republic. The reasons were varied, but one core argument against the creation of what would come to be called *Modell Deutschland* was the belief that Germany would not be able to compete with high social costs. And competition was crucial: a resource-poor economy must export in order to pay for its raw materials and foodstuffs.

For most of the history of the Federal Republic, the Germans won this battle, and did so with seeming ease. The productivity of German workers resulted in a high and rising standard of living. German goods were and remain in great demand in the world economy. In comparison with other advanced industrial economies, the Germans weathered the recurrent crises in the 1970s and 1980s in the global system with relatively little pain. German unemployment rates remained low and standards of living remained comparatively high. The reasons often adduced in order to explain the ability of the Germans to prosper while other advanced industrial states stagnated have been summarised in *Modell Deutschland.*

While there is a good deal of continuity between pre- and post-Second World War German political economics,[2] the system developed immediately after 1945 leaned heavily toward the market side of what Erhard called the 'social market economy'. It took a number of years for the political and legal elements of *Modell Deutschland* to come into being, including the works councils laws of 1950s and Concerted Action in the mid-1960s. Yet some of the major elements of *Modell Deutschland* were there from the start: peak associations representing capital and labour, the oversight role played by private banks and corporate management via powerful, interlocking boards.[3] As it evolved over the first two decades after the Second World War, *Modell Deutschland* included a compliant political culture, relatively peaceful industrial relations and moderate wage demands, codetermination, a societal consensus favouring both an anti-inflationary policy bias and extensive social safety nets to protect those who suffered under the resulting measures, an export-oriented economy and state, a pluralist and centrist political climate and competent leadership.[4] Also termed 'organised capitalism', 'managed capitalism', 'corporatism', 'policy networks', 'interlocking politics' and 'multiple consensus requirements', *Modell Deutschland* had a strong institutional bias. Yet *Modell Deutschland* was more than a set of institutions – it was also a particular view of how society should be organised, what Peter Katzenstein has called an 'ideology of social partnership'.[5] The strength of the ideational elements of *Modell Deutschland* was demonstrated even at the height of the model's distress, when informal national-level concertation among capital, labour and the government collapsed in 1976. In later years, as the debate about *Standort Deutschland* intensified, analysts turned to lower levels of aggregation and continued to find elements of *Modell Deutschland* at work.[6]

The consequences of *Modell Deutschland* were both positive and negative for German business, workers and the fight against unemployment. On the positive side, the relative social peace that *Modell Deutschland* generated helped to keep the German economy competitive through the 1970s and 1980s. Further, the troughs experienced in the world economy during the period were not as traumatic for the Germans as they were for many workers in other advanced industrial countries. Fewer were unemployed in Germany as a consequence of, for example, the oil shocks of the 1970s than was common in much of the rest of the advanced industrial world, and standards of living continued to grow. German firms remained competitive, largely by trading pay and non-wage compensation for increases in productivity and by moving up the product chain.

Yet trading pay for productivity could be successful only as long as quality differences continued to run in the favour of the Germans, and as long as there was a product line to exploit. The changes in global markets that began in the early 1970s eventually caught up to the German economy. First, the opening of financial markets that accelerated capital mobility meant falling transaction costs for foreign investment. To be sure, German firms had experimented with foreign sourcing during the late 1960s and 1970s, especially in the electronics industry, only to find that levels of product quality associated with German goods could not be maintained in, for example, Latin America. But the combination of changes in production technology that reduced the demand for highly skilled labour and increases in the education levels of workers in developing countries meant that German-style levels of product quality could now be realised in many developing countries. Open capital and goods markets, in this context, caught up much of the world to German levels of efficiency and quality.

Unfortunately, in many key sectors like autos, there was no product line to exploit this time – production of inexpensive cars could no longer be replaced by production of high-quality cars, as that move had already been accomplished in earlier decades. Further, the German economy failed to generate either an entrepreneurial class in the high-tech sector or a vigorous venture capital market to exploit the possibilities opened by the microchip. There was no German Bill Gates. The Schumpeterian squeeze that many other advanced industrial states experienced during the 1970s, and that Germany partly avoided owing to *Modell Deutschland*, added to Germany's growing problem with competitiveness, particularly the rising productivity in key competing economies such as the United States. Now other advanced industrial countries could match German quality. And they were also producing the key inputs that fuelled the boom of the 1990s – the fusion of high technology and the internet.

Thus, while *Modell Deutschland* helped to shield the Germans from many of the intense and painful adjustments that others experienced in the 1970s and 1980s, it also left the German economy badly exposed as markets opened in the 1990s. The costs of *Modell Deutschland*, then, included a degree of ossification in the German economy, represented in the recurrent debates about *Standort Deutschland*. Workers made complacent by generous retirement, health and vacation benefits, to name only a few of the consequences of *Modell Deutschland*, found themselves under assault from global competition. Both the completion of the internal market in the early 1990s and the huge costs of German unification only added to the burden of a social market economy that seemed to be out of synch with much of the rest of the world.

As each wave of global contraction left more and more workers mired in structural unemployment by the late 1980s, voices for re-writing the rules of *Standort Deutschland* began to reach a crescendo.[7] German unification diverted attention from economic reform for many years, but it also added a large number of workers to the structural unemployed category. Indeed, even in the best of times unemployment in the East ran double of that in the West. Such were the conditions inherited in 1998 by the first SPD government in sixteen years.

Foreign models

In the ongoing debate about German unemployment, a series of examples or models from outside Germany have been held up as potential solutions to Germany's economic problems. This is ironic, since it was in the early 1990s that Bill Clinton joined a number of earlier US presidents in making explicit reference to elements of the German social market economy that the United States sought to emulate. Yet today the search is on to modify or replace *Modell Deutschland* with something – anything – that can address the higher and higher levels of structural unemployment in Germany.

In the 1990s, at least three broad approaches received attention, sometimes intermittently: The US, Dutch and European models. The first is what might be called an 'Anglo-Saxification' of Germany – a freeing up of market forces and of firms.[8] Pointing to the success of the United States in generating jobs during the 1990s, many in the business sector and in the conservative political parties called for the deregulation of labour markets – in essence, a dismantling of many of the elements of *Modell Deutschland.*

This approach enjoyed some initial support after the 1998 election. During the 1998 campaign, the SPD called for a reduction in non-wage compensation (employer-paid contributions to pensions, health insurance, etc.) to below 40 per cent of income. These costs, often seen as one of the key constraints on German competitiveness, had risen sharply during the early 1990s, as the Kohl government extended much of *Modell Deutschland* to the east and increased insurance benefits for home health care and nursing home care.[9] This resulted in an increase in non-wage compensation from 36 to 42 per cent of total income during the early 1990s, just as the United States entered its long boom. An increase in the number of unemployed from 2.6 million to 4.3 million was coterminous with the rise in non-wage compensation, and is not fully explainable by the addition of many new and often unemployed citizens in the east.

Schröder's emphasis on cost reduction was a key element of his promise to reduce unemployment. Schröder also based his policy on the argument that workers should decide for themselves how to invest their non-wage compensation. Rather than mandatory contributions at fixed levels to retirement plans, health insurance schemes, and the like, workers would be free to choose where to place a part of their income. They might choose to divert a larger part of their income into increased health insurance or save for future unemployment. Reducing non-wage compensation would lower the burden on business, and easing the rules for investment of these (reduced) funds would increase personal freedom and responsibility.

Unfortunately, the logic behind this scheme was weak. Increased employment could come only if a lowering of employer contributions to the components of non-wage compensation schemes could be negotiated. Only cutting benefits, shifting the burden from employers to employees, or realising cost savings in administration could reduce these costs. Lowering benefits proved quite controversial, as might be expected, and cost savings via increased administrative efficiency were meagre. Shifting the burden to workers was also not acceptable to the trade unions. Lower contributions would also mean less money for individuals to invest themselves over the long term. The only increase in the number of jobs that such a scheme might be expected to generate would be in those sectors into which these funds would flow – insurance, banking, pension schemes and the like – as long as cutting benefits or shifting their financial burden to workers remained controversial. It seems unlikely that this would do much to lower unemployment in Germany, particularly as much of German unemployment is concentrated to the low-skill portion of the labour market. Since negotiation of cuts in benefits was politically costly, it seems that the stimulus expected from decreasing non-wage compensation would at best be modest. Yet the fight against unemployment rested primarily on this policy, and it is not surprising that unemployment dropped only slightly.

One should not forget, however, that the debate about this policy was also cast in terms of reducing the public's expectation of state protection. Many criticised the German worker for being too dependent upon the state for social protection via health care, pensions and the like. It was argued that this complacency was a hindrance in the development of an entrepreneurial spirit in Germany, and that allowing workers to decide how a share of their income was invested would help develop a sense of self-reliance among the working public. One suspects that this might have been the most important consequence of the drive to change non-wage compensation. Thus, Schröder was borrowing directly from the Anglo-Saxon model in his policy to reduce unemployment, even if the chosen policy was unlikely to lead to many new jobs.

The Schröder government failed to deliver. While pension contributions were stabilised, this occurred at a historically high level. Health insurance contributions have increased. And the unemployment contribution cannot sink as long as the number of unemployed remains so high. Thus, the early reduction in non-wage compensation won by the Schröder government, from 42 to 40.7 per cent of total wages, has recently been lost. The government failed not just because it had the wrong idea, but also because it could not follow it through.

Other models have also received attention from the Schröder government. The Dutch experience with unemployment was heavily debated in the late 1990s, in both Germany and in Europe generally. The Dutch model is based in an exchange between capital and labour of wage reductions for guaranteed employment.[10] With corporatist-style wage bargaining and a general social consensus in favour of this exchange, the Netherlands has successfully avoided much of the large-scale unemployment common in other European countries, including Germany.[11] Yet a close examination of the Dutch model suggests problems for its adoption in Germany. First, wage negotiation is much more decentralised in Germany than it is in the Netherlands. Reaching consensus across sectors and regions in Germany would be much more difficult than in the smaller Dutch economy. Further, the Dutch model includes elements that would be difficult to implement in Germany, for both social and financial reasons. The Netherlands has one of the lowest levels of workforce participation by women, thus achieving a marked reduction in the size of the active labour force relative to the population. Implementing such a programme in Germany today is socially impossible. Further reductions in the Dutch labour force have been achieved by an expansive definition of what constitutes 'disability'. Albeit more difficult today than in the recent past, Dutch workers still find it easier to win disability claims that either reduce or eliminate their hours worked per week than do workers in most other advanced economies. Although not as prevalent today as in the 1980s, it is still the case that workplace stress can result in a disability claim in the Netherlands. Disability payments are a significant percentage of former pay, disabled workers have a right to return to a job identical to their job before disability and benefits run for extended periods. The Dutch active labour force is reduced, but the unemployment rate is arguably artificially low. Financing such a programme in Germany would be very difficult. In retrospect, there is increasing evidence that the success the Dutch have achieved in fighting unemployment may well be as attributable to wage concessions as to the various counting tactics noted above. Recent increases in wages, and rising unemployment in the Netherlands, have taken the bloom off the Dutch model.[12]

A final model is Europeanisation. Attempts to pass the fight against unemployment to the European level predate the Schröder government, and have always foundered on the difficulty in developing any scheme that would not both increase the German net contribution to the EU budget and maintain an acceptable level of benefits for German unemployed workers. Yet some of the Schröder government's initiatives at the European level suggest that it sees, or has seen in the past, a European role for combating German unemployment. The Europeanisation of German unemployment policy is bound up in the conflict between Gerhard Schröder and Oskar Lafontaine that marked the first few months of the new government after it came to power. The animosity between Schröder and Lafontaine is well documented. When Lafontaine became super-Economics minister in the new government in 1998, he began a public campaign to bring the Germans over to the French position on a number of issues, including a role for the fledgling ECB in fighting unemployment. As specified at Maastricht, the ECB's primary policy goal was to fight inflation, not unemployment. Slippage in the Phillips curve since the 1970s notwithstanding, it remains largely agreed among economists and policy makers that, in the short run, monetary policy can achieve one but not both of these goals. Tight money policy keeps down inflation, at the expense of growth and jobs. Loose monetary policy stimulates growth and employment, but at the expense of inflationary pressures. The debate between the tight-money Germans and the loose-money French goes back to the Werner Report in 1960s, the first blueprint to create a European currency. Maastricht represented the success of the Germans in this debate, coming hard on the heels of the failure of the German Bundesbank to support the franc during the currency crisis of 1993.

Yet the French did not stop their demands for political control, and loose money, with the signing of the Maastricht treaty. The focus of debate shifted from the rules guiding the ECB to the influence of what was first called Euro-X, the committee of finance ministers of Eurozone members. Again, Germany and France found themselves at odds – until the appointment of Oskar Lafontaine. He called for the ECB to take an active role in fighting unemployment, meaning a reversal of the German position during the debates about the ECB. He also supported the establishment of a European minimum wage and of growth targets. Schröder's appointment of the more moderate Hans Eichel as Economics Minister after Lafontaine's departure in the spring of 1999 seemed to signal an end to German support for a European role in fighting German unemployment, with two major exceptions.

The first was the German agenda during its tenure as president of the European Council. While Oskar Lafontaine remained in the German government for roughly the first half of the period of the German Council presidency, the prominence of the fight against unemployment in the German presidential agenda cannot be attributed to him alone. Indeed, the balance of the German agenda focused upon what was called *Standort Europa*, and its first element was unemployment.[13] The Germans hoped to negotiate a European Employment Pact, national employment plans and a statute to create common rules governing European firms that would have protected major elements of *Modell Deutschland*. The Cologne Summit resulted in a rather weak Pact, more consultation about means to fighting unemployment and no company statute. While some argue that the Summit was a major step on the way toward a European unemployment policy, there is no doubt that this goal remains far distant.

The second exception was the Schröder government's analysis of the consequences of the early weakness of the Euro. After its introduction, the Euro quickly fell from its introduction point of about $1.17 to €1 to as low as 80 cents to €1. In the past, a stable DM had been a notable consequence of the German Bundesbank's tight money policy and a source of pride for German governments. A strong and stable DM also reassured a German public still sensitive to the lessons of 1920s hyperinflation. Yet the Schröder government welcomed the marked drop in the value of the Euro. While out of character for past German governments, support for the falling Euro carried obvious benefits for the German economy. A weak Euro stimulated German exports and hence German job creation. While it is beyond the scope of this chapter to determine what, if any, impact the falling Euro had on falling German unemployment during the 1990s, the conterminous fall in both Eurozone and German unemployment, and the coterminous rise in both during the winter of 2002–3, is suggestive. At the least, the Euro appreciation did little to help the government when unemployment increased in 2002 and 2003.

Thus, there has been a sort of Europeanisation of German employment policy, but it has been both ineffectual and dangerous. Regulating unemployment at the European level has yet to prove effective, and may never have a noticeable impact on Germany's unemployment problems. In the absence of effective domestic reform, relying upon exchange rate policy to dampen unemployment runs the risk of market fluctuations. Markets for currencies are especially sensitive to political developments in the world, as the dollar depreciation and Euro appreciation during the run-up to the Second Gulf War suggests. Without domestic measures, depending upon a weak Euro is akin to riding the proverbial tiger.

In sum, *Modell Deutschland* has not been replaced by borrowing from abroad. The Anglo-Saxon model has failed to offer much help for the German unemployed, mostly because the Schröder government failed to find the courage to risk the political capital necessary to make such reforms work. Even had the government been able to cut non-wage compensation, it is unclear that this would have done much to help the unemployed. The Dutch model cannot fit German institutional, social and financial constraints. European-level initiatives have also failed, foundering upon the perils of effective regional-level cooperation, ECB policy objectives and the instability of international currency markets. In the final section, I explore domestic efforts to address Germany's unemployment, and also find a pattern of political timidity and failure.

Reform of *Modell Deutschland*

If borrowing from abroad has not offered a long-term solution to German unemployment problems, working within the confines of *Modell Deutschland* has also proved ineffectual. Efforts to revitalise broad-scale consultation among capital, labour and the state – the '*Bündnis für Arbeit*' that had first been reintroduced by the Kohl government – failed to gather much momentum. Again, as in the effort to reduce non-wage compensation, many were critical of the government's commitment to negotiation and its ability to get their closest ally, the trade unions, to accept significant changes that would liberalise labour markets. As a result, the Schröder government turned to expert opinion to help generate a consensus for change in the German economy. In this section, I examine the most prominent of these efforts, the Hartz

Commission. As will be seen, the proposals for change in *Modell Deutschland* offered by the Hartz Commission parallel the post-election SPD strategy, especially as embodied in Agenda 2010 (see p. 382).

The Hartz Commission – officially titled The Commission for Modern Employment Services – was created in February 2002 and was given six months to develop specific proposals to help reduce unemployment. The Commission was charged with a detailed examination of the existing labour market problems in Germany, the analysis of academic opinion regarding Germany's problems, discussion with those affected by Germany's unemployment problems and an analysis of the policies of other countries in fighting unemployment. It was also given a specific goal – the reduction in the number of unemployed by 2 million in three years. This would constitute a near-halving of Germany's unemployment rate as it stood at the end of 2002. In accomplishing such a Herculean task, it was charged with the responsibility of developing proposals that balanced 'effort and returns to effort, work should pay, not unemployment'.[14] Further, its recommendations were to bind economically viable solutions to guarantees of social security, a classic *Modell Deutschland* formulation.

The Hartz Commission's report was broad in scope, yet six key elements are discernable. According to its Chair, the key proposal was to create a so-called 'Personal-Service-Agentur' (PSA), a part- and short-time employment agency run by local employment offices. The PSAs are to work with private employment agencies to place the unemployed in jobs paid via unemployment insurance. The goal, the Commission indicated, was the neutralisation of laws protecting workers against termination by creating a market for short-term employment. Unemployed workers who failed to register with a PSA within three to six months of termination would have their unemployment insurance cut. The Commission expected that this would reduce unemployment by 780,000 in three years. Muted support was found for this proposal in the SPD, while the CDU/CSU was more positive – if sceptical of the long-term feasibility of part-time work to resolve Germany's unemployment problems. The unions were split – favouring more employment, but fearing the creation of a two-tier employment market and the possibility that employers would use this to reduce the number of fixed-employment opportunities. Employers, in contrast, favoured the idea of part-time work, as long as the PSAs did not compete with private companies, and as long as part-time workers did not receive the full benefits and wage rates available to full-time workers – in other words, precisely the opposite of the preferences express by the unions.

The second major element of the report was to cut the amount of illegal work in Germany. '*Schwartzarbeit*' would be discouraged by making it easier for the unemployed to declare themselves self-employed, via the so-called *Ich-AG*. Comprehensive taxes would be cut to 10 per cent and regulations regarding self-employment would be relaxed as long as wages remained below €1,500 per month. Unemployment insurance would be pro-rated according to the wages earned in the *Ich-AG* employment. The expected results were a decrease in unemployment of 500,000, with a further 1.5 million illegal workers becoming legalised. This proposal was strongly endorsed by the CDU/CSU, which had put a similar proposal in their campaign programme. The SPD also supported it, but some misgivings were expressed regarding its impact on the skilled trades. This position mirrored that of business. The unions split on the issue of the *Ich-AG*, with IG Metall in support and Verdi against. IG Metall opposed, however, any requirement that the would require the unemployed to declare themselves an *Ich-AG*, and other unions warned that the proposal might encourage even more illegal work.

The third dimension of the plan was a relaxation of the rights of the unemployed to reject employment offers. In particular, young and single workers would be required to accept employment even if it required reasonable relocation, and/or if the position was more poorly paid than the previously held position. Additionally, the burden of proof was to be reversed – the unemployed would be required to demonstrate why they could not accept a position that required relocation or was more poorly paid. The plan predicted that this would result in a reduction of 680,000 unemployed workers. This proposal received strong support from the CDU/CSU, a silent response from the SPD and outright rejection from the unions. As expected, the business community did not feel that the proposal went far enough.

The fourth Hartz Commission recommendation involved a tightening of the relationship between unemployment insurance and social assistance. Unemployment insurance would be distributed in three lump sums during the first year of unemployment, falling to the level of social assistance at the end of the first year. Further, unemployment assistance would end after the second year of unemployment, with social assistance taking its place. The Hartz Commission made no projections regarding the impact of this provision on unemployment.

This proposal, while designed to save money in the face of growing budgetary problems and to encourage individual initiative, proved too controversial during the run-up to the 2002 election. It received support only from the business community.

The fifth proposal focused upon those unemployed persons between the age of fifty-five and the early retirement age of sixty. They constituted 600,000 of the unemployed in the summer of 2002. These unemployed workers are especially difficult to employ, as they are so close to early retirement age. The Commission proposed that these workers be offered a settlement for their unemployment claims – claims that the fourth proposal would have reduced – in exchange for removing themselves from the labour force. The unemployment rate would thus be reduced by eliminating a class of the unemployed from the calculation of the unemployment rate. This proposal received mixed support from the SPD, and CSU Chancellor candidate Edmund Stoiber expressed strong opposition to what were seen as statistical tricks to lower the unemployment rate. The unions were also critical, mostly owing to the potential for reduced unemployment benefits. IG Metall also raised concerns of social exclusion.

The final major proposal focused upon improving the operation of the *Arbeitsamten.* Job-Centres would be created to accelerate finding employment, especially for male heads of households and single parents. This was projected to result in a drop in unemployment of 680,000. This proposal received the full support of the SPD and the CDU/CSU. The unions were also behind the proposal, but expressed fears that by focusing on one class of unemployed (single parent and male heads of household), a two-class system might arise. Business opinion also supported the proposal.

In sum, the Hartz Commission report represented at least a series of steps, some small, some a little larger, towards systematic reform of *Modell Deutschland.* The most significant reforms involved the restructuring of unemployment insurance and social assistance, cuts in these programmes, and a tightening of the pressure on the unemployed to accept employment. These were also the issues that most divided business, labour and the major political parties. Nearly as significant was the proposal to expand the use of part-time work. While it seems unlikely that the Hartz Commission's recommendations would realise the sharp cuts in unemployment that were projected, had it been enacted there is little doubt that the reforms would have constituted a major overhaul of *Modell Deutschland.*

And yet, the Hartz Commission's recommendations were buried in the blizzard of a Federal election campaign, a campaign that revolved around issues unrelated to Schröder's promise in the 1998 to radically reduce unemployment. Yet the substance of the Commission's report informs the Chancellor's post-election economic programme, the so-called Agenda 2010. Agenda 2010 takes a longer-term and broader view of the problems with *Standort Deutschland* than could the Hartz Commission. Yet on issues of employment and *Modell Deutschland*, much of the core of Agenda 2010 is derived from the work of the Hartz Commission.

One of the key similarities is the proposal to link unemployment to social insurance, and thereby to reduce unemployment eligibility and benefits. PSAs and *Ich-AG*s continue to receive support in the new programme, as do mini-jobs and part-time work. Punishments for rejecting job offers are also strengthened in Agenda 2010. But the programme also offers guarantees to workers, especially in codetermination rights. The German system of wage bargaining is relatively untouched in Agenda 2010. Interestingly, the programme also encourages plant-level negotiations to enhance and protect unemployment – official recognition of what I have argued is common in Germany today. In sum, most but not all of the Hartz Commission's recommendations resurfaced in Agenda 2010.

In the spring of 2003, Schröder won strong support for Agenda 2010 from his party.[15] Yet Agenda 2010 has not received as warm a reception in German society. The relationship between the government and the trade unions has been very uncertain. While supporting some elements of the plan, the DGB, for example, was very critical of the focus in Agenda 2010 on cost savings and cuts in benefits.[16] More generally, many analysts view Agenda 2010 as insufficient – too weak to address the structural problems in the German economy. It remains to be seen if the Schröder government can overcome the opposition from its own supporters to push through the programme.

Conclusion

As noted above, in the early 1990s it seemed as if the German economy could reform itself – despite the inability of the political class to come to grips with the elements of a restructured *Modell Deutschland*. As I argued in the late 1990s, reform would have to come from within, and as long as the political parties sparred for short-term position, reform impulses would continue to be found 'on the ground', and not in the theory of *Modell Deutschland* or in the programmes of governments. Indeed, the calls for increased plant-level flexibility in both the Hartz Commission report and Agenda 2010 point to the importance of tackling unemployment from the bottom up.

Yet it is equally as clear that leaving reform to the plant level is unlikely to have a significant impact on the politically most sensitive statistic – the unemployment rate. Also, the sense of crisis and need for reform – strong as it may have been in the early 1990s – has reached new heights. The 'storm' that I predicted was preceding the 'calm' in Germany has been much longer than I expected. At the risk of torturing the metaphor a bit more, the glacial pace and tepid nature of the Schröder reform package leaves one wondering if any incipient 'calm' will reflect real adjustment or simply represent the eye of a hurricane. Can Agenda 2010 (if enacted) leave Germany ready for the next downturn in the world economy?

Responsibility for five years of drift on unemployment rests firmly with the government. Schröder has been criticised repeatedly for his timidity in approaching complex problems. To be sure, the failure of the government to deliver on its core campaign promise of 1998 is not totally the fault of the government itself. Blame can be shared among coalition partners, trade unions, opposition parties and employers. Yet if there was a chance for the German political class to address the structural element of German unemployment, it was after the 1998 election. Schröder's failure to grasp the bull by its horns has only worsened the problem. Adopting foreign models has not proved effective, and the government's capacity to make its partners accept painful concessions has been seldom evident. Even vague threats of resignation have failed to pull together Schröder's erstwhile allies. Will a fully realised Agenda 2010 leave Germany ready for the next downturn in the world economy? It is anyone's guess.

Notes

1 Michael G. Huelshoff, 'The "Storm Before the Calm": Labor Markets, Unemployment, and *Standort Deutschland*', in Andrei S. Markovits and Carl Lankowski (eds), *Democracy and Change in Germany* (New York: Berghahn, 1999), pp. 95–120.

2 Simon Reich, *The Fruits of Fascism* (Ithaca, NY: Cornell University Press, 1990).

3 Andrew Shonfield, *Modern Capitalism: The Changing Balance of Public and Private Power* (London: Oxford University Press, 1965).

4 See Andrei S. Markovits, 'Introduction: Model Germany – A Cursory Overview of a Complex Construct', in Andrei S. Markovits (ed.), *The Political Economy of West Germany: Modell Deutschland* (New York: Praeger, 1982), pp. 1–11.

5 Peter J. Katzenstein, 'West Germany as Number Two: Reflections on the German Model', in Andrei S. Markovits (ed.), *The Political Economy of West Germany: Modell Deutschland* (New York: Praeger, 1982), pp. 199–215.

6 For a review, see Christopher S. Allen, 'From Social Market to Mesocorporatism to European Integration: The Politics of German Economic Policy', in Michael G. Huelshoff, Andrei S. Markovits and Simon Reich (eds), *From Bundesrepublik to Deutschland: German Politics after Unification* (Ann Arbor: University of Michigan Press, 1993), pp. 61–76.

7 See, for example, the concluding comments of Willi Semmler, 'Economic Aspects of Model Germany: A Comparison with the United States', in Andrei S. Markovits (ed.), *The Political Economy of West Germany: Modell Deutschland* (New York: Praeger), Jeremy Leaman, *The Political Economy of West Germany, 1945–85* (New York: St Martin's Press, 1988), especially the conclusion; Graham Hallett, *The Social Economy of West Germany* (New York: St Martin's Press, 1973), p. 83; D. M. Gross, 'The Relative Importance of Some Causes of Unemployment: The Case of West Germany', *Weltwirtschaftsarchiv*, 124:3 (1988), pp. 501–23; M. Hellwig and M. Neumann, 'Economic Policy in Germany: Was there a Turn-Around?', *Economic Policy*, 5 (1987), pp. 105–45; and K. Sauernheimer, 'Die Standortqualität der Bundesrepublik Deutschland', *Fortbildung*, 35:1 (1990), pp. 3–5. A treatment with several contributions pointing out weaknesses in the German economy is William D. Graf (ed.), *The Internationalization of the German Political Economy* (New York: St Martin's Press, 1992). See also Konrad Seitz, 'Die Japanisch-Amerikanische Herausforderung–Europas Hochtechnologieindustrien Kämpfen ums Überleben', *Aus Politik und Zeitgeschichte*, B10–11/92 (28 February 1992), pp. 3–15; Eric Owen Smith, *The German Economy* (London: Routledge, 1994), pp. 515–16; 'Herzog Verlangt Radicale Reformen', *Handelsblatt* (Internet Edn), 28 April 1997.

8 Thomas Eger and Hans Nutzinger, 'The Labour Market Between "Exit" and "Voice": Can the American Model be Applied to Germany?', Inter Nationes Basis-Info 7–1997, Code No. 770Q8816.

9 This led some to quip that Kohl was the best Social Democratic Chancellor that the SPD did not have during the 1980s and 1990s. See Alexander Hagelueken, 'Mehr Kosten, Weniger Arbeit', *Süddeutsche Zeitung*, 30 June 2001, p. 21.

10 A. F. van Zweeden, 'The Netherlands', in B. C. Roberts (ed.), *Industrial Relations in Europe: The Imperatives of Change* (London: Croom Helm, 1985), pp. 159–80.

11 Jelle Vesser, 'Continuity and Change in Dutch Industrial Relations', in Guido Baglioni and Colin Crouch (eds), *European Industrial Relations: The Challenge of Flexibility* (London: Sage, 1990), pp. 199–243.

12 Wolfgang Münchau and Gordon Cramb, 'Debunking the Dutch Myth', *Financial Times*, 18 September 1997, p. 13.

13 For a detailed analysis, see Michael G. Huelshoff, 'The European Council and EU Summitry: A Comparative Analysis of the Austrian and German Presidencies', *Contemporary Austrian Studies*, 10:1 (2002), pp. 92–117.

14 Bericht der Kommission 'Moderne Dienstleitungen am Arbeitsmarkt', *Moderne Dienstleistungen am Arbeitsmarkt* (Berlin, 16 August 2002), p. 5, author's translation.

15 The political debate on Agenda 2010 was rejoined in summer 2003. See Bertrand Benoit's 'Agenda 2010: Schröder in Reforms Plea as Opposition Hardens' and 'Chancellor Faces Bundesrat Battle for Agenda', *Financial Times*, 14 August 2003, p. 2.

16 Bundesvorstand, DGB, 'Das machen Wir! Menschlich modernisieren – gerecht gestalten', May 2003.

18

Tax reforms and *Modell Deutschland*: lessons from four years of Red–Green tax policy[1]

Achim Truger and Wade Jacoby

When the Red–Green (SPD–*Bündnis '90/Die Grünen*) coalition took over the Federal government from the CDU/CSU–FDP coalition in 1998, tax reforms had a very high political priority. And, in fact, the government pushed through an astonishing number of far-reaching tax reforms within a period of little more than two years. This chapter pursues two objectives. First, it presents a short description of the measures taken and evaluates them with respect to tax theory and the German tax reform debate of the 1990s.[2] Second, it explicitly addresses the question whether these tax changes were influenced by the wish to reform *Modell Deutschland*, i.e. whether something substantial was done to change Germany's status as a (perceived) high-tax country and if so, whether the attempt was successful. We show that even though the problem of high taxes might have been many observers and, indeed, also the government's dominant concern, there was much more to the German debate and that this is to some extent reflected in the reforms. The chapter will also ask whether generously cutting taxes was the right thing to do. It demonstrates that under Germany's special economic and institutional circumstances at the end of the 1990s, the attempt to cut taxes led to serious problems for fiscal policy, growth and employment.

The German tax reform debate in the 1990s

At the end of the 1990s the political pressure to reform taxes had become very strong. Criticism of the German tax system had grown

Table 18.1 Tax revenues and social security contributions as percentage of GDP in Germany, the United States, EU–15 and OECD, 1998

	Germany	*USA*	*EU–15*	*OECD*
Total revenue	37.0	28.8	41.1	36.9
Social security contributions	15.0	6.8	11.4	9.6
Total revenue excl. soc.-sec.	22.0	22.0	29.7	27.3
taxes on personal income	9.3	11.7	10.8	10.1
taxes on corporate income	1.6	2.6	3.5	3.3
taxes on property	0.9	3.1	1.9	1.9
taxes on goods and services	10.1	4.6	12.2	11.4

Source: OECD, *Revenue Statistics 1965–2000* (Paris: OECD, 2001).

louder and louder. The reasons for the dissatisfaction were many. Certainly the most important feeling was that German taxes, especially those on personal income and corporations, were too high and lowered the incentives to work, save and invest, and damaged Germany's international competitiveness. High taxes in the *Standort Deutschland* were seen by many as one of the main 'structural' reasons for Germany's sluggish growth and dramatically rising unemployment over the 1990s. This impression was strongly reinforced by the lobbying and press campaigns of German industry. It is, of course, difficult to dismiss such arguments as pure propaganda, as many economists put those arguments forward. Nevertheless, even a cursory look at the 1998 OECD revenue statistics (see table 18.1) casts doubt on the hypothesis that German taxes were too high in international comparison. These figures show that the actual total tax burden in Germany is roughly in line with other advanced capitalist states. In certain categories, the burden is even considerably below EU–15 or OECD averages.

Consequently, beside the dominant 'high-tax' complaints, there was a quieter debate on the structural deficiencies of the German tax system.[3] One critique aimed at the heavy reliance on social security contributions levied on labour, which raised total labour costs and thus lowered employment. Consequently, some called for shifting taxation away from social security contributions and labour to income and consumption, where the burden was comparatively low. A second critique was that corporate income and property taxes were contributing less to overall revenue, as the general wealth tax had been abolished in 1997, and the share of corporate taxes had diminished considerably since the early 1990s. During this period, taxes on labour income and social security contributions were high and rising. A third criticism was the multitude of tax exemptions and allowances. Thus, the revenues in table 18.1 resulted from high rates levied on a narrow base, and there was a call for cutting rates while broadening the tax base. Such a reform would simplify the tax system, make it more transparent, and thus perhaps increase compliance. There were also potential redistributive gains from such a strategy, especially if reforms reversed the ineffectiveness of capital income taxation in general and interest income in particular (owing to tight German bankers' secrecy laws and the fear of capital flight). A fourth prominent reform proposal was the introduction of an ecological tax that would levy (and steadily raise) taxes on fossil fuels in line with their energy or CO_2 content. Such taxes might lower the emission of greenhouse gases or pollution in general, and the revenue could be used to decrease social security contributions. Fifth, the basic tax-free allowance for children and child benefits was an important topic as was the tax splitting in the taxing of married couples, which had come under pressure as it was regarded as unfair and as discouraging married women from labour market participation.[4] Finally, there was the long-standing necessity of redesigning the communal tax system, especially the local trade tax (*Gewerbesteuer*), which had been severely criticised since the 1970s.

In addition to the fact that the call for tax cuts dominated the much more subtle diagnosis just sketched, the debate was also conducted with a sense of urgency. There had not been any major tax reforms since 1990, because German tax and fiscal policy had mainly and understandably been preoccupied with managing German unification.[5] Moreover, the Social Democrats had blocked a major income tax reform proposal of the last Kohl government in the Bundesrat in 1998. Finally, there was the widespread feeling that something had to be done about Germany's economic crisis with low growth and rising unemployment, and an important part of the German public had been convinced that tax reforms/cuts would be the right remedy.[6] Accordingly, the next sections sketch reforms of income, corporate, ecological, property and communal taxes, as well as Germany's unique system of tax equalisation.

Germany's institutional structure and economic situation

Five special characteristics of Germany's institutional structure and economic situation are helpful in understanding tax reforms and their consequences. First, after the Nazis' radical centralisation of state control, occupied postwar Germany opted for a federal structure. Every federal system needs a fiscal architecture to make meaningful its rules and division of competencies. Yet Germany is unusual in that its states, while initially collecting most taxes, cannot set their own rates. And while state *executives*, through the upper house (Bundesrat), have significant influence in setting the uniform rates that prevail across the whole country, state *legislatures* generally have much less – a source of significant tension.[7] Further, the Constitution mandates the need for explicit consent of both houses of the German parliament (Article 105 and 106, *Grundgesetz*). Thus, any time the Federal government's coalition in the Bundestag is in the minority in the Bundesrat, reforms can easily be blocked.

Second, the German tax system is characterised by a high degree of revenue sharing between the different levels of government (*Bund, Länder, Gemeinden*).[8] For example, with respect to the income tax, the Federal government and the *Länder* as a whole currently each receive 42.5 per cent of the revenue and the local communities receive the remaining 15 per cent. There is also a large redistribution from the richer *Länder* to the poorer *Länder* under the so-called *Länderfinanzausgleich* (LFA). Until recent reforms, the states with the lowest tax revenues were guaranteed up to 99.5 per cent of the average tax revenues of all German states. States that generated more tax revenue than the national average could retain only up to about 103 per cent of that average and had to pass on the rest to poorer states.[9] Thus, with the exception of the local trade tax (*Gewerbesteuer*) and the local land tax (*Grundsteuer*), there is hardly any tax competition. High redistribution and revenue sharing means that almost no tax reforms affect the revenue of just one level of government.

Third, the German constitutional court (*Bundeverfassungsgericht*) has always had a very strong influence on tax policy. As will be detailed below, many tax changes in recent years have become necessary because a verdict by the court had called the existing tax law unconstitutional. Many observers increasingly suggested the court exceeded its competence when giving very detailed prescriptions for future tax laws.[10]

Fourth, Germany still has to overcome the fiscal problems of unification.[11] Huge transfers from the West to the East – averaging more than 3 per cent of German GDP[12] – were needed in order to finance the transition to a market economy in the new *Länder*. After the 1990 and 1991 unification boom, with growth rates of more than 5 per cent induced mainly by deficit-financed public expenditure, Bundesbank monetary policy initiated a recession in order to contain inflation. After that, the economy never really recovered and grew at an average annual rate of only 1.2 per cent from 1991 to 1997, with unemployment rising from 5.4 per cent to 9.5 per cent in the same period (see table 18.2).

Fifth, Germany's fiscal policy is restricted by the Maastricht Treaty and even further by the GSP signed as prerequisites of EMU. The 1992 Maastricht Treaty limits the participating countries' government deficit to 3 per cent of GDP. The 1997 SGP calls for balanced budgets or even budget surpluses in the medium term. The Red–Green coalition government had projected that a balanced total government budget would be reached by 2004.[13] Compliance with the Maastricht Treaty and SGP is monitored by the European Commission, and violation may be punished by severe fines. These restrictions placed significant limitations on the new government's room for manoeuvre, a fact that soon spilled over into the headlines. In March 1999, after only five months in office, Finance Minister Oskar Lafontaine resigned, and Hans Eichel became his successor. Lafontaine and his economic advisors were Keynesians and explicitly took into account the macroeconomic aspects of economic policy. Eichel has a much stronger supply-side orientation and soon put consolidation of the budget at the top of his agenda while at the same time pushing tax cuts.

Important tax reforms, 1999–2001

Income taxation (households and families)

Personal income tax reform proceeded in several steps (see table 18.3) with the last two steps still to come in 2003 and 2005.[14] After some smaller changes in 1999, the government implemented two major tax laws, the *Steuerentlastungsgesetz* (Tax Relief Act) 1999/2000/2002 in 1999 and the *Steuerreform* (Tax Reform) 2000 in 2000. The first contained a three-step lowering of income tax rates that was only partly compensated by a broadening of the tax base. The top rate decreased

Table 18.2 GDP growth and unemployment in Germany, 1992–97

	1992	*1993*	*1994*	*1995*	*1996*	*1997*	*1998*
GDP-growth rate (%)	2.2	–1.1	2.4	1.7	0.8	1.4	2.0
Unemployment rate (%)	6.4	7.6	8.1	7.9	8.5	9.4	8.9

Source: OECD, *OECD Economic Outlook No. 72*, Data on Diskette (Paris: OECD, 2002).

from 53 per cent to 48.5 per cent and the basic tax rate from 25.9 per cent to 19.9 per cent, with the basic personal allowance increasing significantly. Altogether, gross projected annual tax relief was €18.4 billion, and after broadening the tax base, there remained a net relief of €12.4 billion.[15] At the end of 1999, Eichel surprised the public with plans for even more ambitious tax cuts, this time without any major broadening of the tax base. The Bundestag consented in 2000 and, by granting some further tax relief for business and high-income earners, the government succeeded in getting the Bundesrat's consent – a serious defeat for the opposition CDU/CSU in the Bundestag. The plan foresaw the basic tax rate decreasing to 15 per cent and the top rate to 42 per cent by 2005. Total projected annual tax relief amounted to a further €16.7 billion, or 4 per cent of total 1998 tax revenue.[16] Table 18.3 gives figures on personal and child allowances plus tax rates for the period 1998–2005 (projected).

Germany has a dual system of child benefits and child allowances. Parents automatically receive *either* the benefits or the allowance; up to a certain income, the child benefits are larger than the tax allowance, but above that income, benefits are smaller, and the allowance is granted. Thus, high-income families actually receive more support per child, which many regard as unjust. The government's policy was strongly influenced by a 1998 verdict from the Constitutional Court that declared unconstitutional tax provisions that gave single parents additional allowances and denied married couples allowances for child-care and education.[17] The government was compelled to abolish the special allowances for single parents. At the same time, child-care and educational allowances for all parents were introduced in two steps. As these would have favoured high-income families, the government also increased the child benefits in three steps. All in all the projected relief for families amounted to €8 billion, or 1.9 per cent of total 1998 tax revenue.[18]

Table 18.3 Important changes in personal income and family taxation, 1998–2005

	1998	*1999*	*2000*	*2001*	*2002*	*2003*	*2004*	*2005*
Basic personal allowance (€/year)	6,322	6,681	6,902	7,206	7,206	7,426	7,426	7,664
Basic tax rate (%)	25.9	23.9	22.9	19.9	19.9	17.0	17.0	15.0
Top rate (%)	53.0	53.0	51.0	48.5	48.5	47.0	47.0	42.0
Child benefits, 1st and 2nd child each (€/month)	113	128	138	138	154	154	154	154
Child allowance (€/year)	3,534	3,534	5,080	5,080	5,808	5,808	5,808	5,808
Child allowance for single parents (€/year)	2,045	2,045	0	0	0	0	0	0
Child care allowance for single parents (€/year)	2,871	2,871	2,871	2,871	2,340	1,180	1,180	0

Sources: Bundesministerium der Finanzen, *Tax Reform 2000 – An Overview* (Berlin: BMF 2000); *Familienförderung bis 2002*, at www.bundesfinanzministerium.de/Steuern-und-Zoelle/Unsere-Steuerpolitik-.482.12191/. htm.

Corporate income and business taxation

More complicated changes have taken place with respect to corporate income and business taxation.[19] The major reform came in 2001 and led to drastically lower rates and a complete switch in the system of corporate income taxation. Before the reform, retained profits and distributed profits (dividends) were taxed at different rates: the retained profits were taxed at 40 per cent (before 1999: 45 per cent), and dividends were taxed at the stakeholder's personal income tax rate. After the reform, tax rates are uniform at 25 per cent. Dividends are still subject to personal income tax, but to avoid full double taxation, only one-half of the dividends is taxed.

Most German companies are unincorporated, with profits subject to their owners personal income tax. Thus, lowering corporate tax rates did not help unincorporated companies, yet it was clear that a similarly drastic lowering of the personal income tax rate was not sustainable. One alternative – to tax profits at a lower rate – was banned by the Constitutional Court. Therefore, in addition to the lower tax rates owing to the reform of the personal income tax, unincorporated companies' local trade tax is credited in a standardised manner against their income tax liabilities, thereby further reducing their tax burdens.

The projected gross tax relief for companies from these reforms amounted to €36 billion, but there was a substantial broadening of the tax base (mainly reduced depreciation). Still, projected annual net tax relief amounted to more than €14 billion.[20] However, one largely unexpected result of the reform must be noted, namely the dramatic revenue losses from corporation tax: whereas corporation tax used to produce an annual revenue of more than €20 billion before the reform (€23.6 billion in 2000), it produced a negative revenue of €–0.5 billion in 2001 and did not yield not much more in 2002.[21] Though the revenue losses can partly be explained by low growth since 2001, a substantial part (one-third to one-half) of the losses stems from a problem in the reform: during a fifteen-year transition period to the new system, corporations can distribute retained profits from earlier years and receive the difference between the old (higher) tax rate and the new one from the revenue authorities.[22] Corporations have done so to an unexpected extent in 2001 and 2002. It is hoped that in future years this effect will diminish. The effect on total revenue is softened a little, since the distributed profits are subject to income taxation, but the net revenue effect is still negative.

Ecological tax reform

One of the core tax reform projects promoted by the Green Party was the ecological tax reform.[23] During the 1990s, detailed plans had been developed, and when the Red–Green coalition formed the government in 1998, it was clear that something would be done. The ecological tax reform implemented is revenue-neutral, which means the revenue from the new or increased taxes on fossil fuels and electricity were transferred to the public pension system in order to lower social security contributions. The switch had two purposes. On the one hand, taxes were to be used as market-based instruments of environmental policy to induce energy and climate-protecting changes in both production and consumption. On the other hand, the lower social security contributions were to reduce the comparatively high tax burden on labour and thus promote employment. Table 18.4 shows the changes in the

Table 18.4 Important tax rates/changes within the ecological tax reform, 1998–2003

	1998	*1999*	*2000*	*2001*	*2002*	*2003*
Petrol (unleaded) (€/1,000 l)	501.07	531.74	562.42	593.10	623.80	654.50
Diesel (€/1,000 l)	317.00	347.68	378.36	409.03	439.70	470.40
Methane (€/1,000 l)	1.84	3.48	3.48	3.48	3.48	3.48
Light heating oil (€/1,000 l)	40.90	61.35	61.35	61.35	61.35	61.35
Electricity (€/MWh)	–	10.20	12.78	15.34	17.90	20.50
Coal (€/1,000 kg)	–	–	–	–	–	–
Heavy heating oil (€/1,000 l)	15.34	15.34	17.89	17.89	17.89	17.89
Revenue (€ billion)	–	4.2	8.7	11.2	13.8	16.4

Note: l = litres.
Source: Bundesministerium der Finanzen, *Mineral Oil and Electricity Taxation within the Ecological Tax Reform* (Berlin: BMF, 2001); author's calculations.

regular tax rates induced by the reform. In order to secure international competitiveness, there are important special allowances for industry and agriculture. Companies in these sectors pay only 20 per cent of the new tax on electricity and of the increases in light heating oil and methane taxes. Industrial firms are also refunded the part of their eco-tax payments that exceeds 120 per cent of the compensating reduction of social security contributions. Even after the increases, German energy tax rates remained well below the EU's highest.[24]

From an ecological point of view, the reform has been welcomed by many as an important first step. On the other hand, several criticisms remain: the tax rates are rather unsystematic and not in line with energy/CO_2 content; they are still too low to induce strong ecological effects; there are too many special allowances for industry. The revenue shift has been only a partial success, as the intended reduction of 1.8 percentage points of the social security rates for 2003 has been missed by 0.7 percentage points.[25]

Property taxation

As can be seen from table 18.1, the revenue from property-related taxes in Germany, at 0.9 % of GDP, is very low. There has been a steady decline over the decades, and during the 1990s two property taxes, the annual wealth tax and the property-related element within the local trade tax (*Gewerbekapitalsteuer*), were abolished.[26] The abolition as well as some changes in the inheritance and gift tax and the tax on land acquisition (*Grunderwerbsteuer*) took place after a 1995 Constitutional Court verdict found unconstitutional the unequal taxation of financial property (higher) and real estate property (lower). In addition, the court judged the annual wealth tax to be justified only under the condition that the total tax burden of the estimated yield from property through the income tax and the wealth tax together did not substantially exceed 50 per cent of that yield (*Halbteilungsgrundsatz*). This latter prescription contributed mightily to the Court's reputation as the 'secret legislator' of German tax policy.

From a distributional point of view, one possible task for the Red–Green government would have been to find legal ways to revive the wealth tax. Though there was the danger of provoking problems with the Constitutional Court, there was certainly some room for that, even accepting the arbitrary aspects of the *Halbteilungsgrundsatz.* A less risky alternative would have been to raise the inheritance tax, which had to be reformed before the end of 2001 in any event. However, as part of its tax-cutting strategy, the government chose not do anything about property taxation, apart from appointing a Commission to find ways to implement a more equal treatment of financial and real estate property within the inheritance and gift tax.[27] The Commission's proposal, which would have produced very little extra revenue (less than €1 billion), was ignored and the existing laws were extended until 2004.

Communal tax reform

The central problem of Germany's local tax system is the trade tax, which is levied on local companies' profits and allows for considerable tax rate variability across the communities.[28] Providing about 11 per cent of total communal revenue, the trade tax is the communities' most important independent revenue source. Most communal revenue comes from state grants, user fees and a 15 per cent share of the income tax. The trade tax has been criticized for more than thirty years, but there still has not been a major reform. The most serious problem is its extreme dependence on the business cycle: in economic upswings, the revenue increases in a disproportionately strong manner, and vice versa in recessions. Since communities' ability to take on debt are very limited, fluctuating revenue leads to pro-cyclical local expenditures. And since communities make up about two-thirds of German total public investment, and since investment expenditure is their most discretionary category, communities increase investment in boom times and decrease investment during recessions. Trade tax thus serves as built in macroeconomic destabiliser.

The Red–Green coalition government, like previous ones, has not reformed the trade tax, though it might well be that from a macroeconomic point of view this might even have been more important than the reform of company taxation. The Tax Relief Act and the Tax Reform 2000 have only added to the communities' fiscal problems, as they are affected by the revenue losses because of revenue sharing.[29] When in 2001 the economy slowed, communities' financial problems worsened and communal tax reform was back on the agenda.[30] The government appointed a Reform Commission in 2002, but communal taxation remains an area in which reform is needed.

Tax equalisation

German unification had forced some hard choices about the LFA system.[31] If the five eastern *Länder* had simply joined the LFA system under the existing rules, redistribution would have had to rise from €1.79 billion per annum to about €10.23 billion. Indeed, if the LFA had remained unreformed, *every* West German *Land* but Bremen would have become a net payer. In response, Bonn and the western *Länder* agreed to put off admitting the new states to the LFA until 1995. Instead, they set up and financed the *Fond Deutscher Einheit* (German Unity Fund). Then as the public finance misery of the eastern *Länder* became more apparent, Bonn responded with a new program, *Aufschwung Ost*, which provided about DM 24 billion in 1991 and 1992 for investment and employment in Eastern Germany.[32] In 1995, Bonn then footed the bill for extending the by-now staggeringly expensive LFA to the five new states. 'Vertical redistribution' from Bonn jumped almost 500 per cent between 1990 and 1995 (from less than 5 billion DM per year in the early 1990s to around DM 25 billion from 1995).[33] Because Chancellor Kohl had made such a commitment to the German Unity Fund, he could not accept a breakdown of the system that paid for it and was thus in a difficult bargaining position *vis-à-vis* the states.

The pattern of minor concessions by current recipients coupled with increased Federal payments was repeated in negotiations in June 2001. Even though only five states now paid into the LFA (while eleven were beneficiaries), the LFA system was extended for the period 2005–19. Two institutional factors shaped the deal: first, the Constitutional Court had ordered the parties to find a more just system in response to a suit brought by Bavaria, Baden-Württemberg and Hesse. Second, if the state governments could not broker a unanimous deal, manoeuvring would shift to the Bundestag, where more parties would be involved and a plurality would suffice. Given the implicit backing of the court, the richer states did well in this deal, achieving a new rule allowing them to keep the first 12 per cent of revenues over the national average plus a cap on their total contribution. Bavaria gained an estimated €204.52 million per year from these new arrangements. Yet, the poorer *Länder* of western and eastern Germany did not lose the benefits they had won during the 1995 negotiations. Instead, when negotiations seemed in trouble, Schröder stepped in with €6.65 billion to compensate the poorer states for the funds the richer would be allowed to retain. Thus, even a poor state such as Bremen will get an additional €35.8 million per year more than under the earlier system. All in all, this was an expensive accord for the federal government.[34]

A brief evaluation of the reforms

To come to some general evaluation of the reforms one can use as yardsticks both traditional tax theory and the German tax reform debate of the 1990s. The first considers only the effects of the reforms actually implemented, whereas the second also considers which of the proposed reforms have been enacted and which have been neglected. Traditional tax theory distinguishes between a tax reforms effects on allocation (incentives and efficiency), (re)distribution and economic stabilisation.[35] From the point of view of incentives and efficiency, the changes have certainly brought some improvements. This is particularly true for the *tax-cuts-cum-base-broadening* elements in the income tax reform, which have certainly reduced excess burdens and raised incentives to work, save and invest. It is also true – with some qualifications – for the ecological tax reform, which provides incentives to economise on fossil fuels and relieves the tax burden on labour. Economists disagree, however, about whether the reform of corporate income tax has improved incentives. Since tax rates have been lowered substantially, it can be argued that international competitiveness has increased. From an efficiency point of view, however, the reforms have certainly failed to reduce the complexity and administrative cost of the tax system.

With respect to redistribution, the measures have a slight bias in favour of high-income households. The government pursued a balanced income tax reform by substantially raising the basic tax-free allowance, yet the substantial lowering of the top marginal rate still leads to less redistribution.[36] It also seems that corporations and companies gained relatively more than households.[37] And since high-income households own more company shares, this also will add to the bias in their favour. Families with children gained substantially through higher child allowances and child benefits, with high-income families gaining absolutely and sometimes relatively more than lower-income families. All in all then, income disparity can be expected to increase.

With respect to stabilisation policy, automatic stabilisers may be slightly weakened as tax progression for high-income earners has been reduced, and there has been a shift to indirect taxes through the ecological tax reform. As to discretionary stabilisation, the tax cuts naturally have expansionary effects, though the tax side must not be seen in isolation from the expenditure side of the budget to determine the total effect of fiscal policy. The timing of the steps so far has been arbitrary in relation to the economys output gap, since in 1999 and 2000 the tax cuts came pro-cyclically as the economy was recovering, while in 2001 they helped stabilise the economy in a counter-cyclical way. All in all then, from a tax-theoretical point of view, the evaluation of the reforms depends on the weights that are attached to efficiency, distribution and stabilisation. Here, some efficiency gains have to be weighed against losses in distribution and stabilisation.

Taking the German tax reform debate of the 1990s as a yardstick, several elements of the debate are reflected in the government's reforms, whereas some others have clearly been neglected. The general pattern points to the characterisation of the reforms as mainly supply-side and/or '*Standort*'-oriented with some distributional and ecological influence.[38] The government has clearly stressed cuts in income and corporate taxation to promote private incentives and international competitiveness. This policy bias is obvious from the governments rhetoric – 'less taxes, higher investment, more competitiveness, more jobs, higher private consumption'[39] – as well as from the measures taken: the substantially lower tax rates were only partially compensated by a broadening of the tax base. The projected annual tax relief for households and companies up to 2005 as compared to 1998 is the largest in the history of the Federal Republic, amounting to more than €48 billion[40] – a figure representing 2.6 per cent of Germany's GDP in 1998 and 11.8 per cent of total 1998 tax revenue (excluding social security contributions). At the same time, there have been no increases in other taxes since the ecological tax reform is revenue-neutral and attempts to revive the annual wealth tax or raise the inheritance tax have been blocked by the government. Indeed, because of its many loopholes, the ecological tax turned into a *de facto* subsidy for German industry. Moreover no serious attempt has been made to make capital income taxation more effective or to touch bankers' secrecy laws. In sum then, the 'high-tax' and the '*Standort-Deutschland*' arguments, which had already dominated the tax reform debate, have to a great extent been translated into Red–Green tax policy, whereas more traditional redistributive and more ambitious ecological goals obviously have not.

Broadening the perspective: effects on fiscal policy, growth and employment

As Chancellor of the first Red–Green coalition government, Gerhard Schröder famously asked voters to judge him on the country's economic performance. Accordingly, the stakes for sparking growth and reducing unemployment seemed very high. As can be seen in Table 18.5, however, the significant reforms detailed above have not led to positive trends in growth. And while the unemployment rate did decline, the Chancellor could not come close to keeping his promise to cut the ranks of the unemployed below 3.5 million.[41] What went wrong? For some, the answers would lie largely in monetary policy, wage policy or labour market regulation, and we would not deny the importance of any of those policy domains.

As we have seen, however, the impetus behind significant changes in tax policy was always the argument that economic improvements would result from lower (and simpler) taxes. There are at least two ways in which cutting taxes might lead to more growth and employment. First, some argue that cutting taxes and decreasing government spending – for example, on the welfare state – may unleash market forces in the long run. In general, the empirical evidence for this claim is unimpressive,[42] but in the case of Germany in the 1990s it is simply doubtful that liberal orthodoxy about cutting government expenditure made much political sense.[43] It would have seemed counter-intuitive to dismantle the welfare state just when it was most needed in the aftermath of unification. Moreover, it seems odd to cut government spending just when massive public infrastructure investments in the East are called for.[44] As a result, the lower tax/lower spending regimen was never fully applied. German total government spending actually rose as a percentage of GDP in the 1990s compared to 1989 by about 2.5 percentage points. This rise was primarily a result of growing unemployment and the investment needs of German unification. If the first proposition is to gain any credence from the German case, clearly this was not the right period in which to test it.[45]

Thus, the more plausible argument for cutting taxes in Germany applies to the short run. Cutting taxes can stimulate the economy via demand side-effects.[46] The logic is that lower taxes lead to higher disposable incomes. If at least part of this income is spent for consumption or investment, higher growth and employment eventually results. From this point of view, expansionary fiscal policy in the form of lowering taxes certainly made sense at the end of the 1990s after several years of low growth and rising unemployment. However, in order to really stimulate the economy via tax policy, it is essential that the expansionary effects of lower taxes are not (over-)compensated by restrictive measures on the expenditure side of the budget. In other words, when cutting taxes it is essential that one is willing temporarily to accept a higher government deficit. This higher deficit need not be permanent and may well be part of a medium-term consolidation process. Once economic growth is restored, tax revenues will eventually rise again, and if expenditure growth is limited, consolidation will result.

Yet in the late 1990s no such deficits were possible in Germany since the Maastricht Treaty and the GSP mandated keeping the deficit below 3 per cent of GDP and running a balanced budget in the near term. Hans Eichel took over the Finance Ministry in 1999 and made budget consolidation his top priority, initiating an austerity programme that substantially diminished the expansionary effects of the tax cuts.[47] Still, the economy recovered, and in 2000 it grew at 3 per cent owing mostly to a booming world economy. Everything might have turned out well if nothing unexpected had occurred. But something did. After several years of robust growth, in 2001 the US economy slowed, and Germany found itself on the verge of recession (see table 18.5). The 2001 reform contained substantial tax relief that was not counteracted by further

Table 18.5 Macroeconomic indicators for Germany, 1997–2003

	1997	*1998*	*1999*	*2000*	*2001*	*2002*	*2003*
GDP growth rate (%)	1.4	2.0	1.9	3.0	0.6	0.4	0.9–1.4[a]
Unemployment rate (%)	9.5	8.9	8.2	7.5	7.4	7.8	–
Deficit GDP ratio (%)	2.7	2.2	1.6	1.4	2.7	3.2–3.7	1.9–3.3[b]

Notes: [a] Estimate by Arbeitsgemeinschaft, 'Die Lage'
[b] Estimate by Arbeitsgemeinschaft, 'Die Lage' (first value) and Sachverständigenrat, *Jahresgutachten 2002/2003* (second value).
Sources: OECD, *OECD Economic Outlook No. 72*, Data on Diskette (Paris: OECD, 2002); Arbeitsgemeinschaft deutscher wirtschaftswissenschaftlicher Forschungsinstitute e.V., 'Die Lage der Weltwirtschaft und der deutschen Wirtschaft in Herbst 2002', in *DIW-Wochenbericht*, 69:42 (2002), pp. 703–55; and Sachverständigenrat zur Begutachtung der gesamtwirtschaftlichen Entwicklung, *Jahresgutachten 2002/2003. Zwanzig Punkte für Beschäftigung und Wachstum*, http://sachverstaendigenrat-wirtschaft.de.

expenditure cuts, and it helped stabilise the economy and prevented negative growth rates. But this planned step was too weak to do more, especially since it was not sufficiently flanked by either an eased European monetary policy or more expansive wage policy.[48]

In combination with revenue losses from the drop in economic activity, the cut also brought the German deficit very close to the 3 per cent limit. An important part of the revenue losses resulted from the reform of the corporate income tax which, as noted earlier, actually produced negative revenue in 2001. With no convincing signs of recovery for 2002, the government saw no room for fiscal stimulation and overall fiscal policy remained restrictive. In order to avoid a formal EU warning, the government committed to further austerity for 2003 and 2004. However, low growth kept tax revenues falling, and it became clear it would be difficult to stay below the 3 per cent limit in 2002 and also balance the budget after further planned tax cuts in 2003 and 2005. When floods devastated parts of eastern Germany and Bavaria in August 2002, the government used the population's feelings of solidarity as cover for postponing the 2003 tax cut until 2004 and levying a 1.5 per cent surcharge on the corporate income tax in order to finance a €7.1 billion recovery program for 2003.[49] Under the circumstances, the Opposition chose not to try to block this in the Bundesrat. At the end of December 2002, the reelected Red–Green coalition government faced unpromising tax projections,[50] and a deficit exceeding the 3 per cent limit in 2002. The EU Commission has subsequently started the formal 'excessive deficit procedure' found in the Maastricht Treaty. This process could result in fines if the government cannot contain the deficit. Prospects for recovery in 2003 were poor,[51] so that in order to meet the Maastricht criteria, the government would once again have had to run an austerity programme in the face of an economic slowdown.

What could have been done to avoid the problems? Obviously, had the Maastricht criteria and the SGP not existed, the problems would have been much less severe.[52] Clearly, the combination forced the EMU member countries into restrictive fiscal policies that significantly limited counter-cyclical options during economic slowdowns in the 1990s.[53] Without the SGP, Germany could have accepted the temporarily higher deficits owing to the combination of lower growth and tax cuts and let automatic stabilisers and expansionary fiscal policy work. As demonstrated by the experience from the beginning of the 1990s in the United States – where deficit:GDP ratios ran to 6 per cent – there is nothing fatal about a deficit ratio temporarily above 3 per cent.[54]

If one accepts the Maastricht Treaty and GSP, which the Red–Green coalition government certainly did, the alternative would have been to provide less generous tax cuts (especially Tax Reform 2000 and corporate income tax cuts) and include some of the redistributive proposals that it ignored in the German tax reform debate, such as increasing the inheritance tax or reintroducing the wealth tax early in 1999 or 2000. With the help of such measures, the deficit:GDP ratio could easily be a full percentage point lower now. It is, of course, difficult to blame the government for not having foreseen the economic slowdown when the official economic experts did not do so either. But even ignoring the revenue side, there were good reasons for such measures from the point of view of increasing the distributive justice of the tax system alone. Of course, such alternative measures would have had to pass through the Bundesrat, and pursuing them would have meant challenging the dominant views in the German tax debate. They would not have been easy to achieve; the point here is that the government did not even try them.

Conclusion: perspectives for future tax policy

It is very difficult to predict future changes in tax policy because the government's post-election reaction to the budget problems has been chaotic with new proposals or revisions presented almost daily. Finally, the cabinet decided to cut spending by about €8 billion, to increase taxes by about €5 billion, and social security contributions by about €7.5 billion in order to keep the deficit ratio below 3 per cent in 2003, and come closer to balancing the budget in the following years.[55] When the tax increases are fully realised, the projected extra revenue will amount to €17.3 billion. Though both higher taxes and lower spending will have adverse effects on growth and employment, the projected tax changes do include some of the measures that had been called for from the distributive and ecological points of view, but had not previously been taken up by the government. Adverse reactions from the media and the public somewhat softened the government's original plans, but still they include a capital gains tax, loosening of the bankers' secrecy laws, a minimum tax on corporate profits, a slight strengthening of the local trade tax, tax increases on fossil fuels that are more in line with energy usage and reduced special exemptions for industry in the existing eco-taxes.[56] In addition, the SPD *Länder* are preparing an initiative to revive the annual wealth tax.[57]

It is, of course, still uncertain whether the new tax legislation will pass the Bundesrat. If it does, the Red–Green tax reforms will substantially improve on the German tax system from both an efficiency and a distributive point of view. Ironically, however, their main intended goal, increasing growth and employment, will almost certainly be missed since the reforms have been ill-timed and not been embedded in a coherent fiscal policy. With binding deficit constraints like the SGP, it is very risky to cut taxes generously, because the expansionary effects from the tax side are always in danger of being (over)compensated by destabilising cuts on the expenditure side. Unfortunately, since the high-tax complaints remain dominant, no political forces in Germany have both the insight and the courage to recognise this enduring structural dilemma. Instead, when Germany sees the next iteration of the 'high-tax debate' (as it surely will), that debate, if translated into policy, will probably produce a growth and employment result as disappointing as the last one.

Notes

1 We would like to thank Eckhard Hein, Stefan Josten, Sven Wilson and Alexander Hartberg for helpful comments and discussions on some aspects of the chapter.

2 This section of the chapter draws on Achim Truger (ed.), *Rot-grüne Stuerreformen in Deutschland: Eine Zwischenbilanz* (Marburg: Metropolis Verlag, 2001) and Achim Truger, 'Rot-grüne Steuerreformen in Deutschland – eine Einführung', in Achim Truger (ed.), *Rot-grüne Stuerreformen in Deutschland: Eine Zwischenbilanz* (Marburg: Metropolis Verlag, 2001), pp. 7–19.

3 DIW (Deutsches Institut für Wirtschaftsforschung), 'Schwerpunktheft Steuerreform', *Vierteljahrshefte zur Wirtschaftsforschung*, 66:3/4 (1997), pp. 281–411; DIW/FiFo (Finanzwissenschaftliches Forschungsinstitut an der Universität zu Köln), *Anforderungen an und Anknüpfungspunkte für eine Reform des Steuersystems unter ökologischen Aspekten, Berichte des Umweltbundesamtes 99/3, Berlin, Teil 1: Das deutsche Steuersystem – traditionelle Ziele, Mängel und Reformperspektiven* (Düsseldorf and Köln: DIW and FiFo, 1999) and Gerold Krause-Junk, (ed.), *Steuersysteme der Zukunft, Schriften des Vereins für Sozialpolitik* (Berlin: Duncker & Humblot, 1998).

4 Bernhard Seidel, Dieter Teichmann and Sabine Thiede, 'Ehegattensplitting nicht mehr zeitgemäß', *DIW-Wochenbericht*, 66:40 (1999), pp. 713–23.

5 Stefan Bach and Dieter Vesper, 'Finanz- und Investitionskrise erzwingt grundlegende Reform der Kommunalfinanzen', *DIW-Wochenbericht*, 68:31 (2002), pp. 505–17.

6 Robert Cox, 'The Social Construction of an Imperative: Why Welfare Reform Happened in Denmark and the Netherlands, but not in Germany', *World Politics*, 53:3 (2001), pp. 463–98.

7 OECD, *OECD Economic Surveys, 1997–1998, Germany* (Paris: OECD, 1999), pp. 76–9.

8 Bundesministerium der Finanzen (BMF), *Bund-Länder Finanzbeziehungen auf der Grundlage der geltenden Finanzverfassungsordnung* (Berlin: BMF, 2002).

9 Differences in tax revenues between the *Länder* result from different economic conditions or income differences among the *Länder*'s inhabitants not, however, from differences in tax rates, as these are uniform across the country.

10 Ernst-Wolfgang Böckenförde, 'Verfassungsgerichtsbarkeit: Strukturfragen, Organisation, Legitimation', *Neue Juristische Wochenschrift*, 1:1 (1999), pp. 9–17 and O. Höffe, 'Wieviel Politik ist dem Verfassungsgericht erlaubt?', *Der Staat*, 38:1 (1999), pp. 171–93.

11 Jan Priewe, 'Zwischen Abkoppelung und Aufholen – das schwache

ostdeutsche Wachstumspotential', *WSI-Mitteilungen*, 55:12 (2002), pp. 706–13 and Stefan Bach and Dieter Vesper, 'Finanzpolitik und Wiedervereinigung – Bilanz nach 10 Jahren', *Vierteljahrshefte zur Wirtschaftsforschung*, 69:2 (2000), pp. 194–224.

12 H. Flassbeck, 'Moderne Finanzpolitik für Deutschland', *WSI-Mitteilungen*, 54:8 (1999), pp. 498–504.

13 Bundesministerium der Finanzen (BMF), *Deutsches Stabilitätsprogramm, Aktualisierung* (Berlin: BMF, October 2000).

14 In the meantime, the tax cut in 2003 has been postponed to 2004. See Bundesministerium der Finanzen (BMF), *Steurreform 2000* (Berlin: BMF, 2000) and Bernhard Seidel, 'Die Einkommensteuerreform', in Achim Truger (ed.), *Rot-grüne Stuerreformen in Deutschland: Eine Zwischenbilanz* (Marburg: Metropolis Verlag, 2001), pp. 21–46.

15 Bundesministerium der Finanzen (BMF), *Steuerreform 2000.*

16 *Ibid.*

17 Irene Dingeldey, 'Familienbesteuerung in Deutschland. Kritische Bilanz und Reformperspektiven', in Achim Truger (ed.), *Rot-grüne Stuerreformen in Deutschland: Eine Zwischenbilanz* (Marburg: Metropolis Verlag, 2001), pp. 201–27.

18 See Bundesministerium der Finanzen (BMF), *Steuerreform 2000.* Plans to formally reduce tax splitting for married couples were not realised, though there is some *de facto* reduction owing to the lower rate. Many argue that the Constitutional Court might ban attempts to reduce splitting and will not allow splitting to be abolished completely.

19 Stefan Bach, 'Die Unternehmensteuerreform', in Achim Truger (ed.), *Rot-grüne Stuerreformen in Deutschland: Eine Zwischenbilanz* (Marburg: Metropolis Verlag, 2001), pp. 47–94; Bundesministerium der Finanzen (BMF), *Steuerreform 2000*; and Bundesministerium der Finanzen (BMF), *Tax Reform 2000 – An Overview* (Berlin: BMF, 2002).

20 Bundesministerium der Finanzen (BMF), *Steuerreform 2000.*

21 Bundesministerium der Finanzen (BMF), *Ergebnis der Steuerschätzung* (Berlin: BMF, November 2002).

22 Sachverständigenrat zur Begutachtung der gesamtwirtschaftlichen Entwicklung, *Jahresgutachten 2002/2003. Zwanzig Punkte für Beschäftigung und Wachstum*, pp. 221–4, at www.sachverstandigenrat-wirtschaft.de.

23 Achim Truger, 'Der deutsche Einstieg in die ökologische Steuerreform', in Achim Truger (ed.), *Rot-grüne Stuerreformen in Deutschland: Eine Zwischenbilanz* (Marburg: Metropolis Verlag, 2001), pp. 135–69.

24 Achim Truger, 'Ökologische Steuerreformen in Europa – wo steht Deutschland?', *WSI-Discussionpaper*, 87 (Düsseldorf: WSI, 2000).

25 This was mainly owing to rising unemployment caused by the slowdown of the world economy.

26 Hans Dietrich von Loeffelholz, 'Perspektiven und Optionen der

Vermögensbesteuerung in Deutschland', in Achim Truger (ed.), *Rot-grüne Stuerreformen in Deutschland: Eine Zwischenbilanz* (Marburg: Metropolis Verlag, 2001), pp. 229–46 and M. Schratzenstaller, 'Steuergerechtigkeit für niemanden. Rot-grüne Steuerpolitik 1998–2002', in Kai Eicker-Wolf (ed.), *'Deutschland auf den Weg gebracht'. Rot-grüne Wirtschafts- und Sozialpolitik zwischen Anspruch und Wirklichkeit* (Marburg: Metropolis Verlag, 2002), pp. 47–85.

27 Sachverständigenkommission Vermögensbesteuerung, *Bewertung des Grundbesitzes für Zwecke der Vermögensbesteuerung* (Berlin: BMF, 2000).

28 Horst Zimmermann, *Kommunalfinanzen: Eine Einführung in die finanzwissenschaftliche Analyse der kommunalen Finanzwirtschaft* (Baden-Baden: Nomos Verlag, 1999).

29 Hanns Karrenberg, 'Die Steuerpolitik der laufenden Legislaturperiode aus städtischer Sicht', in Achim Truger (ed.), *Rot-grüne Stuerreformen in Deutschland: Eine Zwischenbilanz* (Marburg: Metropolis Verlag, 2001), pp. 95–134.

30 Bach and Vesper, 'Finanz- und Investitionskrise'.

31 Wolfgang Renzsch, *Finanzausgleich und die Modernisierung des Bundesstaates: Perspecktiven nach dem Urteil des Bundesverfassungsgerichts* (Bonn: Friedrich-Ebert-Stiftung, electronic edition, 2001); Wolfgang Renzsch, 'Föderative Problembewältigung: Zur Einbeziehung der neuen Länder in einen gesamtdeutchsen Finanzausgleich ab 1995', *Zeitschift für Parlamentsfragen*, 25:1 (1994), pp. 116–38; M. Burchardt, 'Die Praxis des aktuellen Länderfinanzausgleichs und das Problem der Integration der neuen Bundesländer', *WSI-Mitteilungen*, 45:9 (1992), pp. 577–90; M. Hüther, 'Reform des Finanzausgleichs: Handlungsbedarf und Lösungsvorschläge', *Wirtschaftsdienst*, 73:1 (1993), pp. 43–52; and R. Hickel, 'Föderaler Finanzausgleich im vereinten Deutschland nach 1995', *WSI-Mitteilungen*, 45:9 (1992), pp. 563–76.

32 R. Sally and D. Webber, 'The German Solidarity Pact: A Case Study in the Politics of the Unified Germany', *German Politics*, 3:1 (1994), pp. 18–46.

33 Wade Jacoby, 'Financing the Poor Cousins: Reforming the EU Structural Funds and the German *Länderfinanzausgleich*', Paper presented at the meeting of the American Political Science Association, Boston, MA, 4 September 2002, p. 14.

34 The parties also agreed to fund the *Aufbau Ost* program with €156.46 billion over the same period. Thus, the LFA, *Aufbau Ost* and Fund for German Unity will all run until 2019 under the June 2001 deal.

35 Richard A. Musgrave, *The Theory of Public Finance* (New York: McGraw-Hill, 1959); and Harry S. Rosen, *Public Finance*, 5th edn (Boston: Irwin, McGraw-Hill, 1998), Parts 4 and 5.

36 Gerhard Wagenhals, 'Incentive and Redistribution Effects of the German Income Tax Reform 2000', *Finanzarchiv*, 57:3 (2000), pp. 316–32.

37 This, of course, is only a first-round effect since taxes ultimately are always borne by individuals, not by companies.
38 Achim Truger (ed.), *Rot-grüne Steuerreformen in Deutschland: Eine Zwischenbilanz* (Marburg: Metropolis Verlag, 2001).
39 Bundesministerium der Finanzen (BMF), *Steuerreform 2000*, p. 1.
40 Bundesministerium der Finanzen (BMF), *Steuerreform 2000.*
41 In fact, the number of unemployed was over 4 million at the time of the election.
42 Alexander B. Atkinson, 'Conclusions', in Alexander B. Atkinson and Gunnar Viby Mogensen (eds), *Welfare and Work Incentives: A North European Perspective* (Oxford: Oxford University Press, 1993), pp. 289–97 and Alexander B. Atkinson, *The Economic Consequences of Rolling Back the Welfare State* (Cambridge, MA: MIT Press, 1999).
43 Flassbeck, 'Moderne Finanzpolitik für Deutschland'.
44 Dieter Vesper, 'Zum infrastrukturellen Nachholbedarf in Ostdeutschland', *DIW-Wochenbericht*, 68:20 (2001), pp. 293–8.
45 The classic supply-side argument is that a permanent tax cut might increase labour supply as a consequence of falling marginal tax rates. While labour supply may become a long-term problem for the German welfare state, the high numbers currently unemployed diminish the need for a mechanism to increase labour supply.
46 Olivier Blanchard, *Macroeconomics*, 2nd edn (London: Prentice-Hall, 2001), pp. 92, 357, 518.
47 Klaus Bartsch *et al.*, 'Bündnis für Arbeit in schwierigem Fahrwasser. Gesamtwirtschaftliche Entwicklung, finanzpolitische Fehlentscheidungen und Alternativen', *WSI-Mitteilungen*, 52:12 (1999), pp. 805–25.
48 Achim Truger and Eckhard Hein, '"Schlusslicht Deutschland": Makroökonomische Ursachen', *Wirtschaftsdienst*, 82:7 (2002), pp. 402–10.
49 Bundesministerium der Finanzen (BMF), '*Übersicht über den Fonds* "*Aufbauhilfe*"' (Berlin: BMF, 2002).
50 Bundesministerium der Finanzen (BMF), *Ergebnis der Steuerschätzung.*
51 Sachverständigenrat, *Jahresgutachten 2002/2003* and Arbeitsgemeinschaft deutscher wirtschaftswissenschaftlicher Forschungsinstitute e.V., 'Die Lage der Weltwirtschaft und der deutschen Wirtschaft im Herbst 2002', *DIW Wochenbericht*, 69:42 (2002), pp. 703–55.
52 Jan Priewe, 'Fiskalpolitik in der Europäischen Währungsunion – im Dilemma zwischen Konsolidierung und Stabilisierung', *WSI-Mitteilungen*, 54:5 (2001), pp. 273–81.
53 Jan Priewe, 'Vom Defizit zum Überschuss. US-Fiskalpolitik in den 90er Jahren', in Arne Heise (ed.), *USA – Modellfall der New Economy?* (Marburg: Metropolis Verlag, 2001), pp. 103–30.
54 Achim Truger, 'Fiskalpolitik in der EU von 1970 bis 2000: Eine Zusammenstellung und Kommentierung zentraler fiskalpolitischer Indikatoren',

in Achim Truger and Rudi Welzmüller (eds), *Chancen der Währungsunion nutzen – Koordinierte Politik für Beschäftigung und moderne Infrastruktur* (Düsseldorf: Hans-Böckler-Stiftung, 2002), pp. 17–73.

55 Bundesministerium der Finanzen (BMF), *Entwurf Nachtragshaushalt 2002 und Entwurf Bundeshaushalt 2003 vom Kabinett verabschiedet*, at www.bundesfinanzministerium.de/wwwroot-BMF/BMF-.336.15032/Entwurf-Nachtragshaushalt–2002-und-Entwurf-Bunde … htm and Bundesministerium der Finanzen (BMF), *Finanzielle Auswirkungen des Gesetzentwurfs zum Abbau von Steuervergünstigungen und Ausnahmeregelungen* (Berlin: BMF, 2002).

56 Bundesministerium der Finanzen (BMF), *Deutsches Stabilitätsprogramm.*

57 'Und nun noch die Vermögensteuer', *Handelsblatt*, 21 November 2001.

Part VI
The foreign policies of the Berlin Republic

19

The 'German Problem' reconsidered: the impact of unification on the European order

Stephen F. Szabo

The 'German Problem' was the central strategic and political question which confronted twentieth-century Europe. The strategic problem concerned the role of German power within the broader European system of balances and the inability of the major European powers to balance and contain the rising power of unified Germany. Two non-European powers, the United States and the Soviet Union, had to enter the European system in order to create a new equilibrium, one which was quite stable during the forty-plus years of the Cold War.[1] This problem of power was linked to Germany's late unification and geographical setting in the heart of Europe.[2] There was a domestic dimension to the geopolitical one as well. As Peter Merkl noted, 'The Small German solution meant domination of the future German nation state by Prussia, which was likely to lend its own brand of authoritarianism, militarism, Protestantism, and a head start in social and economic modernization to the union.'[3] As Merkl went on to observe: 'Germany's national leadership had made the country's political backwardness in combination with industrial strength into a virtue, a distinctly German path, or *Sonderweg*, to modernization.'[4] This 'democratic deficit' meant that the German problem was not simply a matter of power, geography and history, but also of leadership, political culture and institutions.[5] As Heinrich August Winkler concluded in his study of Germany's way to westernisation: 'It was not the solution of the question of national unity which stands at the beginning of the road to catastrophe, but the failure to settle the question of freedom.'[6]

German unification in 1990 reopened fears of a return of the

'German Problem' as a geopolitical challenge resulting from both a new imbalance within the European system and from the assertiveness of a newly sovereign Germany led by a new postwar generation less constrained both by the Nazi legacy and the transatlantic community. However the 1990s did not confirm these fears. Unified Germany did not seem to follow the expectations of realists who believed that a more fluid international context combined with an increase in national power would lead to a more nationalist Germany. Rather Germany pursued a policy of multilateralist integration in what Merkl called the 'three poles' of its foreign policy – western Europe, the United States and east central Europe/Russia. While it began to enhance its military role, it did so within a multilateral context and generally continued within a modified form of the 'Civilian Power' paradigm.[7]

The academic consensus on the 'German Problem' at the end of the twentieth century was that it had been transformed. Constructivist and neo-liberal paradigms seemed to better explain Germany's role in the new Europe than those of the realists. Thomas Banchoff, in his study of German foreign policy from 1945 to 1995 concluded that the 'German Problem' had been transformed by an institutional and domestic political configuration which constrained reactions to changes in the international environment. 'In contrast to the pre-1945 decades, however, German power is embedded in a dense web of institutions while avowed German interests in a peaceful multilateral and supranational foreign policy rest upon a democratic political consensus.'[8] In a survey of much of the literature on post-unification German foreign policy, Alison McCartney concluded: 'this new international order and Germany's power/position in it are not the most important determinants of actual policy choices. Domestic politics, history and norms also play crucial roles in defining and making choices. As such Germany offers further evidence of the limitations of neo-realist theory.'[9] The 1990s may prove, however, to have been an interregnum between two eras which opened with German unification in 1990 and closed on September 11 2001.

Germany and Europe in the post-9-11 world: the transatlantic dimension

Expectations that the international environment would become more fluid with the end of the Cold War seemed to be dampened by the experience of the 1990s. Banchoff's conclusion was that:

> Germany did not again find itself at the center of a fluid European balance of power. NATO, the European Union (EU) and other European institutions remained the starting points for its foreign policy … The image of sovereign Germany adrift in a shifting balance of power – the thrust of the old German problem – does not reflect European reality at the end of the twentieth century.[10]

However the system had begun to become more fluid even before 9-11, and these trends accelerated in the wake of those events and their aftermath. All the key institutions of German foreign policy, NATO and the EU, are beginning to reflect this fluidity.

NATO is increasingly becoming a collective security rather than a collective defence organisation owing to enlargement, the need to make this enlargement acceptable to Russia and its devaluation by the Bush Administration. Following the invocation of Article 5 of the NATO treaty by the European members of the alliance and the declaration of unlimited solidarity of the Schröder government in September 2001, the Bush Administration decided not to make much use of this newfound support to bring Germany and NATO more fully into the war on Al-Qaeda, but opted to go it mostly alone in the war in Afghanistan.

The American military and political leadership believed that one of the lessons of Kosovo was to avoid another war by committee. While it tried to find missions for its allies in Afghanistan, it was more concerned with tactical flexibility and did not believe that its allies could provide much in the way of a meaningful military contribution. The selectively multilateral phase of the Bush Administration's diplomacy, which began immediately after 9-11, ended with the President's State of the Union speech in January 2002, in which he expanded the war on terrorism and used the term 'Axis of Evil'. German hopes that the Administration would follow a coalition strategy were replaced by renewed concerns about American unilateralism which were prevalent before 9-11.

The leadership in the Pentagon and in the White House openly devalued the importance of NATO as an alliance and seemed to want a more fluid alliance based on ad hoc coalitions of the willing for future operations. The Deputy Secretary of Defense declared that the task would now determine the coalition, not the other way around, and another senior civilian Pentagon official called for 'keeping the myth alive' in regard to NATO. The major enlargement of NATO, which took place in the fall of 2002 in Prague, was another indication that the alliance was seen in Washington increasingly as a political institution for regional collective security and less as a military alliance for collective defence.[11]

This view is deeply unsettling to Berlin, which continues to wish to preserve NATO as the central security institution in Europe. As General Klaus Naumann, the former head of NATO's Military Committee, has written: 'European allies see NATO as a collective defence and crisis management organization, whereas the United States no longer looks at the Alliance as the military instrument of choice to use in conflict and war'.[12] The transformation of NATO reflected a devaluation of the importance of Europe in US defence policy, owing both to the shift of threats to other theatres and to the growing gap in military capabilities between the United States and its European allies. All of this was made clear in the Bush Administration's official statement of its strategy, *The National Security Strategy of the United States of America.*[13] The new strategy clearly states that deterrence and containment were appropriate for the Cold War, but not for the new threats posed by 'rogue states' and non-state terrorist groups, both of which had the intention of possessing weapons of mass destruction:

> In the Cold War, weapons of mass destruction were considered weapons of last resort whose use risked the destruction of those who used them. Today our enemies see weapons of mass destruction as weapons of choice. Traditional concepts of deterrence will not work against a terrorist enemy whose avowed tactics are wanton destruction and the targeting of innocents.[14]

Invoking and revising the concept of imminent threat to contemporary conditions, the United States now claimed the right to act preemptively. This new doctrine marked a shift in declaratory policy from deterrence and containment. New threats did not, it was contended, allow warning or certainty of attack. The United States did not have the luxury of waiting to be attacked but had to move in a preventive manner.

It is not clear how new all of this is. A policy of preemption may have historical precedents and may be no more that a common sense statement that the United States will strike before it is attacked. Had the US government known on 6 December 1941 that the Japanese fleet was preparing to attack Pearl Harbor, it would have taken defensive and even preemptive actions. The first Secretary of Defense in the Clinton Administration, Les Aspin, announced an initiative in December 1993 that left open the option of either a reactive or preemptive mode in dealing with a Saddam Hussein with nuclear weapons.[15]

What is more striking is the stated policy of *preeminence*. The document explicitly states the goal of continued primacy of American power: 'Our forces will be strong enough to dissuade potential adversaries from pursuing a military build-up in hopes of surpassing, or equaling, the power of the United States.'[16] This is a marked shift in official American strategy from one of containing potential enemies and maintaining a balance of power to a new concept of balance in which the United States will be a dominant, benign hegemon because it stands for not only its own interests, but those of a just world order. This seems to imply a strategy based on bandwagoning rather than balancing and rejects an alternative approach which would encourage multiple centres of power to share in global governance. Instead the United States seems to have chosen a 'smothering strategy' designed to prevent the rise of any peer competitor.[17]

Whether this new doctrine of preeminence has any real operational meaning beyond its declaratory view is unclear, but it embodies a 'my way or the highway' approach toward alliances which runs the risk of creating countervailing coalitions against this arrogance and power. It is a one dimensional view of the world which sees terrorism as dominating all other concerns and not only runs the risk of overcommitment of American resources, and a loss of peripheral vision which misses other key challenges, but also downgrades NATO and the transatlantic relationship. While the Administration challenged the alliance to take on new capabilities (highly mobile forces) and roles to deal with this new threat, the Bush Doctrine emphasises the American willingness to go it alone. It also challenges the European NATO consensus that the alliance focus on Europe and the principle that the alliance is a defensive one and replaces it with a view that 'the only option is offense', and that alliances are 'merely strategic assets that are useful depending on the circumstance'.[18]

This shift from the NATO consensus on deterrence and defence is likely to further the growing gap between the United States and the European approach to strategy and further marginalise NATO. The damage done to the relationship during the 2002 German election campaign and its immediate aftermath was unprecedented. The differences which emerged between Bush and Schröder over Iraq reflected fundamental differences in political interests and strategic cultures. The German elite and public would be very uneasy about any serious consideration of the use of military force. Germany's strategic culture since 1945 has been based not upon pacifism, but upon a very limited basis of legitimacy for the use of force by Germany. Germany has consistently followed a policy which has been based upon a balance of power as the basis for peace. Adenauer's policy of strength, Brandt's *Ostpolitik* and Schmidt and Kohl's willingness to deploy intermediate range nuclear (INF) missiles were all based on this key prerequisite, and was backed up by a Bundeswehr of almost 500,000 men and women. Originally the consensus on German rearmament and entry into NATO was based on integration of German forces into a multilateral system and the limitation to defence of NATO territory. During the Cold War, force was seen as a deterrent and the deterrence aspect was modified with the détente component in the Harmel formula adopted by NATO in 1967.

With the end of the Cold War, the definition of the legitimate use of force was gradually expanded by both the Kohl government and then by the Red–Green coalition, to include use of force out of the NATO territorial area so long as it had a multilateral basis for both legitimisation and deployment. The Balkan wars created a new justification for military action based upon humanitarian values, in these cases to prevent 'ethnic cleansing'. The growing Europeanisation of Europe also provided another rationale, namely the need for Germany to make a contribution to a credible European Security and Defence Policy (ESDP). The German public has gone along with these modifications to a strategic culture which moved from one of 'a culture of reticence' to one of limited, multilateral engagement. That a Red–Green government could deploy German forces in Kosovo, Macedonia and Afghanistan was a remarkable achievement, although one which was not more than provisionally accepted within its activist core.

The unilateralism of the Bush Administration and its emphasis upon an early and robust resort to the use of force went against the fundamentals of German political and strategic culture. If the Administration had begun with a multilateral approach focused on the issue of weapons of mass destruction and Iraq's violations of UN sanctions rather than coming to that position in September, much less porcelain would have broken and the summer storm would have been postponed. Yet the concerns about the direction of American policy were there before 9-11 and would probably have grown, albeit more slowly. Yet the fundamental point is that the strategic cultures of Germany and the United States are diverging in fundamental ways.[19] The escalating rhetoric of a potential war with Iraq combined with the German election campaign further divided the United States and Germany.[20]

These developments were manifestations of a deeper structural change which had begun with German unification but accelerated after 9-11. The strategic glue which held the alliance together is much weaker than it was during the Cold War. Germany and Berlin are no longer divided. The US security tie is no longer existential to Germany. As Joseph Joffe put it: 'Alliances die whey they win … Germany no longer needs American strategic protection; at least the rent Berlin is willing to pay for this shelter has plummeted.'[21] A similar trend can be seen in another close ally of the United States, South Korea. Although it remains a divided nation with a threat on its border, a majority of the South Korean public was reported in a poll taken in late 2002 to believe there was little or no chance of an attack from North Korea. As two American correspondents observed, the US – Korean divide 'has deeper roots involving this country's [South Korea] rapid passage to affluence and its perception that its distant ally is heavy handed and insensitive, particularly with regard to North Korea'.[22]

While the Prague NATO Summit in November 2002 endorsed a statement on Iraq, both France and Germany blocked a stronger resolution, which would have supported the use of force. The continued reservations of Germany about playing any role in a possible war on Iraq also offered a glimpse into what the new NATO might look like. Germany has played a central role in alliance strategy since it entered NATO in 1955, and especially after the withdrawal of France from the integrated military command in 1966. It was an indispensable partner to the United States in all major alliance policies and strategies, including the adoption of the strategy of flexible response, the creation of the Nuclear Planning Group, the acceptance of the Harmel Report's modification of strategy to add the détente component to that of defence, the deployment of INF missiles in the 1980s, the enlargement of NATO in the 1990s and the shaping of the new relationship with Russia. However in 2002 it decided to oppose a major American policy initiative, although it softened its opposition with the agreement to take command of International Security Assistance Force (ISAF) in Afghanistan as well as its support of the Rapid Reaction Force. In addition Germany continues to fall further behind not only the United States, but also the United Kingdom and France, in the military field. As the capabilities gap widens, so too will the influence gap.

This estrangement has created new opportunities not only for France to play a mediating role between the positions of Washington and Berlin, but has also given a chance for some of the new members, most clearly Poland and Romania, to play a close supporting role for the United States in this new era. However it is unlikely that NATO can be effective if its central European member is marginalised. If Germany decides to shift closer to the French view on NATO and the United States, this would also have substantial implications for the future of the US role in Europe as well as for the prospects of a more independent European defence.

The new threat of global terrorism may revive the security core of the German–American relationship if the leadership in both countries comes to share a common perception of the threat and agrees on a strategy for dealing with it. This would, however, require a dramatic change in Berlin and a reorientation of security policy from a European focus to a global one. It would also require some consensus on a strategy for the broad Middle East.[23] Barring such an accommodation, Germany and the United States seem headed in different directions in security policy. In any case, for the first time in fifty years the vitality of the transatlantic circle of German policy is now in question

Europe and the German way

The 2002 election campaign also damaged the Schröder government's relationship with its key partners in the EU. While Germany was not substantively isolated within Europe on the question of Iraq, the impact of Berlin breaking with a common European approach unsettled its EU partners and harmed efforts toward a serious ESDP.

More important was the enlargement of the EU decided at Copenhagen in December 2002 and the more fluid EU which will result from it. The Constitutional Convention and the upcoming IGC of 2004 will try to cope with the challenges to institutional coherence of the EU. In the past, the Franco-German engine managed these strains, but that too seemed seriously weakened in the early Schröder years. The imbalance between the two partners which resulted from German unification became more apparent as their views and interests on the question of European construction seemed to diverge after the introduction of the Euro. German leaders, led by Foreign Minister Fischer, continued to favour a more federalist approach while France maintains its preference for intergovernmentalism. The eastern enlargement of the EU also enhanced Berlin's influence and further diminished the importance of the Franco-German axis.[24]

Schröder also made the EU Commission a target during the election campaign and made the size of the German contribution to the EU budget a major issue. In this, he reflected the feeling of the majority of Germans that they were paying more than their share to Europe and had too little influence on the policies of the EU.[25] His post-election concessions to France on the issue of support for the CAP only postponed a crisis over that issue to 2006 as new, agriculturally dependent, member states join the EU by mid-decade.[26]

German military capabilities and commitment to European defence remained weak and threatened the development of a serious European defence force. Within Europe, Germany continued to lag behind the other major powers, France and Britain, in regard to defence spending and capabilities. Bundeswehr reform was begun in the first Schröder term, and the announcement of a new 'Struck Doctrine' early in the second term, which declared that the mission of the Bundeswehr was now solely crisis reaction and no longer territorial defence, was a major alteration in defence doctrine.[27] But the second Red–Green government has few resources and will have to make some difficult decisions regarding defence spending and procurement if it hopes to make the Bundeswehr capable of meeting the new security challenges.

All of this is the context for the new discussion about the German role in Europe raised by Chancellor Schröder's use of the term *deutcher Weg* during the 2002 campaign. While he claimed to have used the term to emphasise a domestic *Modell Deutschland*, its invocation evoked memories of the *Sonderweg*, especially among Germany's European partners.[28] As one commentator noted,

> Historically, the German Way has stood for a separate national way, a going it alone … for a special role which Germany had taken for a variety of reasons … In Schröder's campaign speech of August 5 in Hanover, he moved himself away from the neo liberalism and bankrupt capitalism; he separated himself from the no longer role model US and retreated from unconditional submission to the American foreign and military policy. He looked for a formula to give meaning to his mood, and found a false one. He propagated a Social Democratization of SPD policies with the detour of the German Way.[29]

The evocation of the German Way and the refusal to participate in a war in Iraq, even if sanctioned by the UN Security Council, marked a real break from the multilateralist consensus of German foreign policy. This 'Made in Berlin' approach to both the United States and to Europe reflected a new sense among both the German public and the elite that Germany should take a less sentimental or emotional approach toward its key partners and should say no when its interests clashed with those of its key partners.

A new strategic culture

These changes in the international environment have been accompanied by changes in the political and strategic culture of Germany. The 2002 election confirmed that the Berlin Republic had now replaced the Bonn Republic. This was evident in the role of eastern German voters in the election outcome. Schröder's use of the Iraq issue succeeded in moving enough former PDS voters (along with an appeal to women voters who were also especially concerned by the prospect of a war) to the SPD column to save the election. But beyond this new volatility, the breaking or challenging of a number of taboos were signs of a changing political and strategic culture. Not only was the Bonn tradition of staying as close to the United States as possible shaken, but the primacy of the Franco-German engine and of European solidarity was as well. The challenge of Jürgen Möllemann to the taboo of anti-Semitism and criticism of Israel, while ultimately unsuccessful, was another indication of change, as was the growing treatment of Germans as not only aggressors but also as victims of the Second World War as evidenced in the raising of the issues of the Beneš decrees and the publication of a number of books, including *Krebsgang* by Gunter Grass, which focused on the sufferings of Germans at the end of the Second World War.[30]

This changing self-view coincided with the coming to power of the first fully postwar generation, the 68ers (those shaped by the protests of the late 1960s). Generational change has been one of Peter Merkl's important themes in his work. This is because generational breaks in Germany are the most significant in Europe, not only because Germany is the pivotal state of Europe, but also because Germany has the most perceptible and important breaks among generational cohorts owing to the dramatic breaks in contemporary German history. The current leadership comes from the 68er generation. Gerhard Schröder and Joshka Fischer were prominent activists against the United States in their youth and have shaped a view of America which, while not antagonistic, remains critical of its global role. The leadership of this generation on the left came of age in opposition to US policy, not in support of it as in Kohl and Schmidt's generation. As Rachel Seiffert put it in the *Financial Times*: 'Former Chancellor Kohl's government was very much one of technocrats with socially conservative values. With Gerhard Schröder's SPD, the 68 generation came to power; former student activists, civil rights campaigners, and Baader Meinhof defence lawyers are all present in the upper echelons.'[31] The extent to which Schröder was willing to use criticism of the US Administration in his recent campaign, and the positive response this theme received from much of the electorate, not to mention the more critical references made to the United States by other leading figures in the SPD, indicates the difference between this generation and that of Kohl as well as the changing generational makeup of the public.[32]

Not only do the 68ers have an ambivalent view of America, but their view of Europe is also quite different from that of the Kohl generation. Schröder was the first Chancellor who did not feel emotionally bound to the postwar consensus.[33] His relation to Europe is entirely pragmatic and instrumental, unencumbered by the emotional and historically driven commitment to Europe of both Adenauer and Kohl.

The 68ers have made an impact in the areas of environmental policy and immigration law and they have broadened the growing consensus of the limited and multilateral use of force by Germany. They remain, however, sandwiched between the founder's generation, which shaped the Federal Republic after the Second World War and the Gen Xers and 89ers that will soon follow them (see below). The 68ers were not shaped by major historical events but rather by the prosperity and rapid growth of West Germany. They were a political generation which believed in mass political action and streamed into the SPD as well as creating the ecopax movement and the Greens. Their contribution to the German political culture was the 'killing of the fathers', their revolt against the generation which had collaborated with or actively participated in the Third Reich. This generation of leaders is one which is largely inexperienced in world politics and international economics. They spent most of their careers in opposition during the long reign of the Schmidt and Kohl governments; in many respects they reflect the parochialism of much of their generational counterparts in the United States.

The generation coming behind them, the Gen Xers – or, as Peter Merkl labels them, the third postwar generation – is a transitional cohort. Their views were shaped by the oil crises of the 1970s and the shocks of the 1980s. They were the first to come of age during the 'limits of growth' era, the first since the end of the Second World War to experience lower expectations of growth. Ecological issues and the great missile debate of the 1980s, in both East and West, shaped them. Their image of America was one of Reagan and of a certain US recklessness. They credit Gorbachev not Reagan for the end of the Cold War. When the Wall came down they were more wary in the West of unification than the Kohl generation and in this regard shared the scepticism of Oskar Lafontaine and his generation. The eastern portion of this generation was on the cusp between those who would benefit from unification and those left behind.[34]

The 89ers, in Merkl's category the fourth postwar generation, and those who follow, were shaped by a great historical event, the end of the Cold War and the unification of Germany. They have also come of age in a time of slow economic growth and talk of Germany as the new sick man of Europe. Unlike the 68ers (and partly because of the 68ers) who used the German past against their fathers, this group has a much weaker link to, and feeling of responsibility for, that past. They feel that while the past cannot be forgotten, they should not continue to be held responsible for the crimes of previous generations and that in some respects, the past 'was often used as a pretext for inaction'.[35] They remain concerned about political and social issues and much of their agenda is a postmaterialist one. Yet they are far more sceptical of politics than the 68ers and have not streamed into the major political parties. The SPD and the Greens (although they admire Joschka Fischer) have less appeal for them as they focus their efforts on pragmatic results at the local level, working through personal networks, the internet and NGOs. They are concerned about practical problems, which affect them directly and can be characterised as 'pragmatic idealists'.

This generation came of age during the rise and crash of the German shareholder economy and its tech-driven *Neue Markt.* The youngest segment of this cohort (12–25-year-olds) place greater stress than the two older cohorts on performance, security and power. They also have less interest in the environment than their counterparts in the middle of the 1980s.[36]

These will be the leaders of the new, 'normal' Germany. They tend to be pro-European, with about half wishing that the EU would develop into one state, and to favour enlargement to the East. 'Europe is a reality for the young.'[37] They also regard Germany's new role in a pragmatic way without the old left–right framework. About 42 per cent want to see Germany speak up for its interests in the world more, and a third want to see Germany have more influence. About a third want to maintain current levels of cooperation with the United States with about a fifth each wanting either to decrease or increase it. A clear relative majority supports the international involvement of the Bundeswehr. This is a cohort which does not think of itself as a generation because it does not believe in collective identities. They are more likely to shift with personalities of leaders rather then remain loyal to the same party and may be the precursor of a more volatile Berlin Republic.

What may be occurring in Germany is what is predicted by the interactive model of generational change, which sees social and political change coming from the interaction between generations, with succeeding generations reacting against the values of the previous one so that there is a cyclical nature to social and political change. In this case, the reaction of the younger generations against the 68ers is interesting and may lead to a more centrist and pragmatic Germany once their successors assume power. The more assertive approach to foreign policy, what Schröder called for as a 'new self-confident German foreign policy', finds resonance with the younger generations.

Return of the 'German Problem'?

The increasing fluidity of the international environment combined with the changing ideational context of the Berlin Republic means that many of the constants of the comfortable Bonn Republic are gone, and the Berlin Republic faces, to paraphrase John Foster Dulles, an 'agonizing reappraisal' of its foreign policy options. Does this place the leaders of the Berlin Republic back into a Bismarckian strategy of shifting coalitions and risk reopening the old German question about *Schaukelpolitik*?

The German question has been reopened regarding the centrality of the transatlantic link for the Berlin Republic. Here the longer-term trend seems to be in the direction of a drifting apart of the two former close partners. This drift may turn into an open break and raises questions concerning a German identity which has been so largely shaped by the presence of America. It also raises a danger for Germany that a weakening of its Atlantic ties may raise renewed fears about a Germany unbound in Europe. The American connection reassured Germany's European partners about the restraints on German power. If this tie is substantially weakened, then these old concerns may return, especially among the newer member states of NATO and the EU, especially Poland. The result could be a return of the Bismarckian dilemma if Europe itself does not prove strong enough to provide a new framework for Germany.

Perhaps of more concern is the prospect of a weak and drifting Germany preoccupied with economic and demographic stagnation and the consequential weakening of Europe which would follow. The inability of Germany to serve as Europe's paymaster would have serious implications for the CAP, enlargement and regional development policies.[38] Combined with the inwardness of the current generation of German leaders, the danger signs are abundant that the German question is about to return to centre stage in a new form in Europe.

The German historian Michael Stürmer has written that 'the German Question, put in its crudest form, has always been twofold: To whom Germany belongs, and to whom the Germans owe their allegiance? In 1990 it was in the fine print of the 'Two-plus-Four' agreement that united Germany should continue to be firmly rooted in the European Union … and be the most loyal member of the Atlantic Alliance.'[39] Now that the Atlantic pillar is weakened if not crumbling, what will be the resilience of the European pillar of German policy? David Calleo has posed the German problem in this broader context:

> The Atlantic Alliance assumed Europe to be intrinsically unstable and therefore to require an external balancing power. The European Union assumed that Europe was not irremediably unstable: Europeans in general, and French and Germans in particular, were capable of reconciling their national interests and of harmonizing them into a collective interest with a common institution.[40]

The answer to the new German question rests, therefore, on whether the European construction can and will hold. If Stürmer is correct in his assessment that the European construction is a function of Pax America and of NATO, then the summer of 2002 has opened the stark possibility that Europe, or at least Germany, will become isolated and stagnant and risk being left behind by a dynamic America. However the answer to the question of whether the German question is back is most probably no, because the construction of Europe will continue, not because of historical memories, personal relationships between leaders or emotional commitments to the European Idea, but because of the limits of the European nation-state in the twenty-first-century. Germany remains big enough to raise concerns within Europe about German hegemony, but too small to provide the leadership Europe needs. Despite the difficulties of the Schröder government with the European Commission, it remains committed to a more integrated and federalist Europe. As Günter Verheugen, the Commissioner for EU Enlargement said when asked what the Commission would do if the Irish voted in their referendum against the Nice Treaty, in effect killing enlargement: 'There is no Plan B.' There is also no Plan B for Germany or the other states of Europe outside of a strengthened EU.

The deep Europeanisation of Germany which has transpired since the 1950s is likely to hold and to deepen. The weakening of the Atlantic circle of German policy will have to be compensated for by a deepening of the Franco-German axis as part of the continuing European Project. However, Europe and Germany have entered an especially fluid time in their histories and face pivotal decisions between now and 2010. How they respond to these watershed challenges will determine whether in fact the German question has been 'solved'.

Notes

1 The classic formulation of this interpretation remains that of A. W. DePorte, *Europe Between the Superpowers: The Enduring Balance* (New Haven: Yale University Press, 1979).

2 See David P. Calleo, *The German Problem Reconsidered* (Cambridge: Cambridge University Press, 1978).

3 Peter H. Merkl, *German Unification in the European Context* (University Park, PA: Pennsylvania State University Press, 1993), p. 33.

4 *Ibid.*, p. 34.

5 As Charles Maier succinctly characterised this aspect, 'Does geographic position determine historical outcomes? Poland, also a nation without natural boundaries, caught between powerful neighbors, expanded for two centuries, and then was partitioned at the end of the 1700s, while Germany was largely unified over the next century. Geography cannot explain their different fates.' Charles Maier, *The Unmasterable Past: History, Holocaust and German National Identity* (Cambridge, MA: Harvard University Press, 1988), p. 117.

6 Heinrich August Winkler, *Die lange Weg nach Westen: vom Dritten Reich bis zur Wiedervereinigung, Band II* (Munich: Beck Verlag, 2000), p. 655.

7 The term is Hanns Maull's. See his 'Zivilmacht Bundesrepublik Deutschland. Vierzehn Thesen für eine neue deutsche Aussenpolitik', *Europa Archiv*, 10 (1992), pp. 269–78.

8 Thomas Banchoff, *The German Problem Transformed: Institutions, Politics,*

and Foreign Policy, 1945–1995 (Ann Arbor: University of Michigan Press, 1999), p. 175. See also John S. Duffield, *World Power Forsaken: Political Culture, International Institutions, and German Security Policy after Unification* (Stanford: Stanford University Press, 1998) and Alison McCartney, 'International Structure versus Domestic Politics: German Foreign Policy in the Post Cold War Era', *International Politics*, 39:1 (2002), pp. 101–10.

9 McCartney, 'International Structure', p. 109. See also Volker Rittberger, 'Approaches to the Study of Foreign Policy Derived from International Relations Theories', in Margaret Hermann and Bengt Sundelius (eds), *Comparative Foreign Policy Analysis: Theories and Methods* (forthcoming).

10 Banchoff, *The German Problem Transformed*, pp. 165, 183.

11 Gunther Hellmann, 'Germany's Balancing Act in Foreign Policy', *Internationale Politik* (Transatlantic edn), 3:4 (2002), p. 20.

12 Klaus Naumann, 'Crunch Time for the Alliance', *NATO Review*, 47:3 (2002), at www.nato.org.

13 White House, *The National Security Strategy of the United States of America* (Washington, DC: The White House, September 2002).

14 *Ibid.*, p. 15.

15 Judith Miller, 'Keeping the US No 1: Is it Wise? Is It New?', *New York Times*, 26 October 2002, at www.nytimes.com.

16 *The National Security Strategy*, p. 30.

17 Ted Galen Carpenter, *Peace and Freedom: Foreign Policy for a Constitutional Republic* (Washington, DC: The Cato Institute, 2002), cited in Quentin Peel, 'Caught in the Web of Nation Building', *Financial Times*, 16 October 2002, p. 15. For a broad survey of the intellectual origins of the Bush strategy, see Frances Fitzgerald, 'George Bush and the World', *New York Review of Books*, 26 September 2002, pp. 80–6.

18 G. John Ikenberry, 'America's Imperial Ambition', *Foreign Affairs* 81:5 (2002), pp. 52, 54. See also Judy Dempsey, 'NATO Challenged to Make a Radical Shift in Principles and Practice', *Financial Times*, 21–22 September 2002, p. 5.

19 Gunther Hellmann, 'Deutchland in Europa: eine symbiotische Beziehung', *Aus Politik und Zeitgeschichte*, B48/2002 (2 December 2002), p. 26. 'The two most important members of NATO were in central questions of international politics, from climate change, through the International Criminal Court and to policy toward Iraq, ... marching more decisively than ever in different directions.'

20 While 76 per cent of the German public found German–American relations to be 'good' or 'very good' at the end of the 2002 campaign, 46 per cent opposed the participation of German troops in a war against Iraq, even with a UN mandate, while 50 per cent supported participation with a UN mandate. Only one month after the election, those numbers shifted slightly more in favour of participation with a UN mandate. Confidence

in the SPD's handling of relations with the United States dropped from 41 per cent in September to 34 per cent in October, but with only 27 per cent having confidence in the CDU's policy toward the United States. See Forschungsgruppe Wahlen e.V. Mannheim, *Bundestagswahl: Eine Analyse der Wahl vom 22. September 2002, Bericht Nr. 108* (Mannheim: Forschungsgruppe Wahlen e.V. Mannheim, 2002), pp. 48–9; the Forschungsgruppe Wahlen's figures for the month after the election can be found in *Süddeutsche Zeitung*, 'Der Kanzler verliert seinen Vertrauensbonus', 19–20 October 2002, p. 7.

21 Josef Joffe, 'The Alliance is Dead. Long Live the New Alliance', *New York Times*, 29 September 2002, section 4. p. 3.

22 Howard W. French and Don Kirk, 'Amid Mounting Protests, US–Korean Relations Reach a Low', *International Herald Tribune*, 12 December 2002, p. 4.

23 See Ronald D. Asmus and Kenneth Pollack, 'The New Transatlantic Project', *Policy Review*, 115 (2002), pp. 3–18; Daniel Hamilton, *German–American Relations and the Campaign Against Terrorism* (Washington, DC: American Institute for Contemporary German Studies, 2002); and Peter Rudolf, 'Deutschland und die USA – eine Beziehungskrise?', *Aus Politik und Zeitgeschichte* B48/2002 (2 December 2002), p. 23.

24 See Christian Hacke, 'Die Aussenpolitik der Regierung Schröder-Fischer: Zwischenbilanz und Perspectiven', *Aus Politik und Zeitgeschichte*, B48/2002 (2 December 2002), p. 8.

25 See the *Allensbacher Jahrbuch*, 8, p. 942, cited in Gunther Hellmann, 'Deutchland in Europa: eine symblotische Beziehung', *Aus Politik und Zeitgrschichte*, B48/2002 (2 December 2002), p. 27.

26 Figures from 2001 indicate that Germany payed out about €4 billion more than it received from the CAP, while France received a net gain of close to €2 billion. 'Reform? Forget It', *The Economist*, 5 October 2002, p. 47.

27 Karl Feldmeyer, 'Zum Abbruch freigegeben', *Frankfurter Allgemeine Zeitung*, 13 December 2002, p. 12. The government will still fall at least €5.8 billion short by 2006.

28 See Schröder's interview with *Die Zeit* in 'Am Ende der ersten Halbzeit', *Die Zeit*, 34 (15 August 2002), p. 3.

29 Heribert Prantl, 'Schröder's Rucksack', *Süddeutsche Zeitung*, 8 August 2002, at www.suddeutsche.de.

30 As Gunther Hellmann observed: 'What is more, the children of Hitler's children have, in recent years, even gained moral capital. The increased exposure of murky chapters in the histories of neighboring countries (in contrast to what many observers regard as the exemplary frankness with which the Germans have dealt with their own inglorious history) and the simultaneous discovery that the Germans also suffered in the exodus and expulsions following World War II have put Germans, for the first time,

in a position in which they appear no less moral than others.' Hellmann, 'Germany's Balancing Act in Foreign Policy', pp. 22–3.

31 Rachel Seiffert, 'Generation Gap', *Financial Times Weekend*, 21–22 September 2002, p. 1.

32 'Joschka Fischer was nineteen years old when he threw stones at the police in Stuttgart. In essence the street protesters of then, who are today in the highest positions of government, have repeated their resistance against an American war, organised and directed from the White House and Pentagon.' 'Freund oder Feind', *Der Spiegel*, 30 September 2002, p. 113.

33 Michael Thurmann and Constanze Stelzenmüller, 'Mit Gewehr, aber ohne Kompass', *Die Zeit*, 38 (12 September 2002), at www.zeit.de.

34 See Merkl, *German Unification*, pp. 40–50.

35 Seiffert, 'Generation Gap', p. 1.

36 See the 14th Shell Jugendstudie, 'Zusammenfassung und Hauptergebnisse', *Jugend 2002* (Hamburg: S. Fischer, 2002), p. 3. However, the voting patterns in the 2002 Federal election indicate that the 89ers and the Gen Xers voted more heavily for the Greens and the FDP, while the Christian Democrats were disproportionately dependent on the Second World War generation. The 68ers were slightly more likely to vote SPD and Green. Women of the younger generations were even more supportive of the Greens and the SPD. Young eastern Germans followed similar patterns, although the support for the Greens was much smaller than in the western part of the country. This is consistent with data indicating that the number of postmaterialists in eastern Germany dropped during the 1990s and that materialists exceeded postmaterialists by seven points. The neo-Communist PDS lost support among the young and is clearly a party of the middle-aged and old. See Forschungsgruppe Wahlen e.V. Mannheim, *Bundestagswahl: Eine Analyse der Wahl vom 22. September 2002, Bericht Nr. 108* (Mannheim: Forschungsgruppe Wahlen e.V. Mannheim, 2002), pp. 53–6.

37 *Jugend 2002*, p. 9.

38 Christian Hacke, 'Die Aussenpolitik der Regierung Schröder/Fischer', p. 15.

39 Michael Stürmer, 'Welcome to the German Question, Once Again', draft article for publication in *Die Welt.*

40 Calleo, *Rethinking Europe's Future*, p. 27.

20
Germany and Poland: beyond the past?

Arthur R. Rachwald

Relations between Germany and Poland are dominated by a one-thousand-year legacy forged by conflicts, ethnic cleansings, territorial changes and negative perceptions, as well as long periods of neighbourly relations, ethnic assimilations, economic cooperation and cultural interchange. It is, by and large, a legacy typical of almost any of Germany's European neighbours, a cyclical heritage of conflict and cooperation, similarities and differences, exclusion and closeness. The historical experience of both nations during the twentieth century has been unusually hostile and surprisingly similar. Both people developed into a modern nation-state relatively late in the context of European history; both experienced totalitarianism, foreign conquests and destruction, territorial losses, human suffering, foreign occupation, mass migration and a long struggle for freedom from foreign domination. Except, perhaps, for the most nationalistic, self-righteous and hardheaded Germans and Poles, citizens of both nations must ponder a pragmatic question about the price and the utility of confrontation and contemplate ways to avert another cycle of self-destruction. With the end of the Cold War, Germany and Poland face each other across exactly the same borderline as one thousand years ago, with no winners but instead staggering losses and bitter memories on both sides.

Ironically, the exceptionally bitter German–Polish experience during the Second World War provides the foundation for mutual reconciliation. Following the unprovoked German attack and brutal occupation of Poland that resulted in the death of over 6 million Polish citizens, the war concluded with Germany's defeat and partition. At war's end, the Poles regained the Oder–Neisse (Odra-Nysa in Polish) territories in the west owing to the Russian annexation of more than half of the prewar Polish state. Initially, this postwar period was not conducive to the fostering of a historic breakthrough in bilateral relations. Until 1970, the German claim to the lost territories and the Polish fear of German revisionism saturated domestic political rhetoric on both sides.

But bound by the shackles of the Cold War both nations eventually realised that only through mutual respect, cooperation, understanding and concessions would they ever be able to free themselves from its deadly dynamics. While the German people desired unification and democracy for the communist East German state, the Poles were concerned with security and stability, as well as liberation from the fetters of communism. By the 1970s it became well understood that the German road to unification led through Poland, and that the Polish return to Europe would cross through the united and democratic Germany. These national aspirations and mutual dependence facilitated breaking the German–Polish deadlock on the border issue – that is, the elimination of one of the main impediments toward German unification and the reuniting of Europe. Next to the German–French normalisation achieved in 1963, the wrapping up of the German–Polish dispute in 1990 provided an indispensable precondition for the conclusion of the Cold War. Seemingly both nations have managed to overcome the legacy of the past and are together pursuing the goal of European unity. Moreover, these two nations differ noticeably from their predecessors during the Cold War and the Second World War, as it is now a relationship between a post-unification Germany and a post-communist Poland.

The post-Cold War settlement

At the foundation of bilateral German–Polish relations are the 14 November 1990 'Treaty between the Republic of Poland and the Federal Republic of Germany on the Confirmation of the Existing Border between Them', and the 17 June 1991 'Treaty on Good Neighborliness and Friendly Cooperation'.[1] As demanded by Poland, the sole objective of the first treaty was to finalise the border issue in a single bilateral document, thereby resolving and then removing from bilateral relations the four-decade-long legal dispute over the finality of the Oder–Neisse border.

The border treaty has confirmed the Polish position that the 1945

Potsdam Agreement has effectively transferred sovereignty over the Oder–Neisse territories from Germany to Poland, and that when in 1950 (the Treaty of Goerlitz) the GDR and then in 1970 (the Treaty of Warsaw) the Federal Republic of Germany recognised the border, they acted as successors of the German Reich. Technically, therefore, the November 1990 German–Polish treaty reaffirmed these two previous agreements, as well as carried out a provision of the 12 September 1990 Moscow treaty on the 'Final Settlement with Respect of Germany'. This treaty, which concluded the 'Two-plus-Four' negotiations, advised that united Germany and independent Poland should finalise the border issue in a bilateral agreement. With respect to the German–Polish border issue, the Moscow treaty stipulated, in addition, that the territorial configuration of united Germany should be limited to the borders of the former West and East German states and the city of Berlin, and that the newly established united German state would never assume any territorial claims against its neighbours. Finally, the Moscow treaty specified that united Germany remove from its Constitution any provision inconsistent with the unification treaty.

The treaty has indeed closed the Oder–Neisse border dispute, and it removed one of the main impediments on the road to European integration. It was, in a sense, the final episode of the long chain of hostilities that began on 1 September 1939. However, it did not produce a business-like normalisation between two nation-states. Instead, the treaty has introduced a paternalistic feature into the bilateral relationship, with Germany assuming a moral obligation to assist Poland's attempt to overcome the adverse political and economic effects of both German fascism and Russian communism. Additionally, Germany has assumed responsibility to support Poland's ambition to join NATO and the EU. While German has gained some moral ground, Poland has acquired a powerful ally in Europe.

This special relationship was explicitly codified in the 1991 'Treaty on Good Neighbourliness and Friendly Cooperation between Germany and Poland'. The treaty was designed to accomplish two distinctive but overlapping objectives: to structure bilateral German–Polish relations, and to set up an indispensable new pillar for an unified and secured Europe, similar to the 1963 Elyseé Treaty that normalised relations between Germany and France. In this way, the bilateral relations between Poland and Germany were to become a vital element of the pan-European security architecture, where the level of cooperation between these two states would bear tangibly on the entire process of

European political and economic integration. Thus, using Germany as a lever, Poland's position in Europe has been elevated to the rank of a major continental actor, while Germany has acquired an important international partner and a convenient diplomatic bridge to Ukraine, the Baltic States and even Russia.

This unusually lengthy and elaborate international document defines general conditions for the mutual cooperation in matters of international security. In Article 8, for example, the German side assumed the obligation to press forward the Polish ambition of European integration. In an unexpected sequence of developments, with the end of the Cold War division of Europe, both countries become perhaps the closest, but not co-equal, allies on the continent. More precisely, this extraordinarily close relationship has been accomplished only between the elites of the both nations; the general public's political and social attitudes lag far behind those of their leaders.

To many ordinary Poles, the Germans are still ruthless expansionists, arrogant and self-righteous, and now are employing economic means to achieve the same centuries-old hegemonic ambitions in Europe. Some Polish critics of the treaty are concerned that in light of an immense economic asymmetry between both countries, Poland has ceded some of its sovereignty to its western neighbour, becoming Germany's 'near abroad' in the east. Many Poles are concerned that the Germans still harbour irredentist sentiments, having accepted neither defeat in the Second World War nor territorial losses to their Slavic neighbour. Moreover, some Poles believe that the country has become just a convenient supermarket and a source of an inexpensive labour for Germany. Some Poles are also convinced that the German authorities and public relate to ordinary Poles in a hostile and even aggressive manner.

At the same time, to some Germans, the Poles appear to be disorganised and quarrelsome, less successful in terms of social organization and economic efficiency, as well as responsible for petty crimes and illicit work in Germany. On the grass-roots level, the stereotypes prevail and the mutual daily contacts are still by and large limited to trade and other economic activities. These negative stereotypes are especially evident along the German–Polish border, where the inhabitants of the former East Germany live side by side with the Polish refugees who were resettled there from the eastern Polish territories annexed by Soviet Russia.

But Germans and Poles have learned how to cohabit while preserving distance. A real people-to-people reconciliation has a long and bumpy road ahead. The unfortunate aspect of these mutually demeaning views is that they are no longer rooted in the experience of the Second World War, but reflect instead recently acquired attitudes and perceptions. It is not an 'old' problem that has already been accounted for and settled; instead it is a 'new' problem that may complicate and slow down better understanding between both nations.

The German–Polish treaties, in conclusion, are a historically unprecedented breakthrough in the state-to-state and elite-to-elite relations, but they are only an initial step forward on a complicated and delicate road to reconciliation between peoples. And even on this level, it is possible to detect a disparity of motives for the improvement of the mutual relations. While at the top of the German concerns has been Poland's stability and control of migration pressure from the east, the Polish intentions have been driven by the economic calculations and a smooth ride to Europe. The most sceptical Poles, however, do agree that regardless how unequal and perhaps not entirely free of mutual doubts are the 'special relations' between Germany and Poland, the unquestionable significance of this unprecedented reconciliation between these historical adversaries is in its preemption of 'special relations' between Germany and Russia. The most obvious legacy of the last two-and-a-half centuries is that German–Russian collusion is a sure prescription for a cataclysmic disaster for Poland and other nations of Central Europe. After all, while Germany has evolved into a liberal democratic state, post-Soviet Russia is still an imperial/colonial state ruled by the former communist elite.

German–Polish security cooperation

The contemporary bilateral German–Polish relationship has its roots in Willy Brandt's *Ostpolitik*. It was the first time in over two centuries that Germany redefined its concept of *Mitteleuropa* and the East. In the traditional understanding of this geostrategic term, the East implied Russia, rather than the nations located between Germany and Russia. The logical consequence of this perspective was that Germany and Russia would approach each other over the heads of the CEE nations, and almost always at their expense. At the end of the Cold War, the CEE region emerged from the Soviet occupation as a group of an independent and ambitious states. Germany gave priority to bilateral relations with Poland, the Czech Republic, Hungary, Slovakia, Ukraine, the Baltic States and the former Yugoslavia, rejecting Moscow's repeated attempts to renew the historical pattern of direct cooperation over the heads of those states. Thus, Germany became Poland's gateway to Europe, and Poland became Germany's gateway to the East. With the primary focus on its immediate neighbours, Germany became a regional leader and a role model, rather than posing a threat of hegemonic domination in partnership with Russia.

Designed to restructure the post-Cold War security system in Europe, the 1999 NATO enlargement to include Poland and other central European states was a most significant regional undertaking that featured close German–Polish collaboration. Although the dissolution of the Warsaw Pact was enthusiastically welcomed as an end of the Soviet occupation, Poland found itself, together with its neighbours, in an uncomfortable security vacuum between NATO and the Russian dominated Commonwealth of the Independent States (CIS). Although the key to NATO enlargement was always in American hands, Poland and other central European states needed a continental ally to advocate their case within NATO. Instinctively, the Poles preferred to seek support from France in matters of national security, but because of the limited French commitment to NATO, the volatile track record of Franco-American relations and the rather unexpected lack of French enthusiasm actively to shape post-Cold War developments in central Europe, the Poles turned to Germany for guidance and support of their ambition to join the Alliance.

In principle, both Germany and Poland have favoured a 'broader Europe', encompassing Germany's eastern neighbours and providing them with the same security guarantees enjoyed by the western European states. They have also agreed on a multilateral approach to European security, and eschewed a bilateral option that would require Poland and the other nations in the region to conclude individual security agreements with the western states, including Germany. Without NATO enlargement, Poland and other nations of central Europe would have no realistic alternative to bilateral security arrangements with Germany, thereby reestablishing another *Mitteleuropa* or a satellite-like security system in the centre of Europe. The mutual preference for a multilateral option was also based on the shared assumption that NATO and the strong American presence in Europe were indispensable for the security of the entire continent, and that Germany would not seek another Rapallo or Ribbentrop–Molotov-like bilateral relationship with Russia. This preference also implied that neither the

OSCE nor the UN were effective substitutes for the security guarantees provided by NATO.

Germany's strong support for NATO enlargement to include Poland, the Czech Republic and Hungary was integral to the more general policy of exporting stability.[2] Positioned between Europe's west and east, north and south, Germany is directly influenced by internal developments in Poland and in other states of the region. Better than any other people in Europe, the Germans easily grasped the perils of remaining a 'frontline' state and the risks associated with the visible vacuum of power that followed the demise of the Soviet empire. The integration of Poland within the western political and security community has enveloped Germany in a democratic neighbourhood.

For the Poles, NATO symbolises Western civilisation and the final liberation from the debilitating and humiliating postwar subservience to Soviet Russia. Moreover, membership in NATO has brought Poland under the security system guaranteed the United States, and reduced Polish dependence on bilateral relations with Germany or any other European state. Consistent with the spirit of the 'new Polish–German Community of Interest'[3] as defined by the Good Neighbourliness Treaty, Germany became 'Poland's advocate' in the process of NATO enlargement. Subsequent to NATO enlargement in 1999, Germany and Poland became military allies – perhaps for the first time in history.

The evident similarity of the German–Polish perspective on the strategic imperatives in Europe has engendered rather extensive multilateral and bi-lateral cooperation in this area. Speaking on 18 June 2002 at the Polish Academy for National Defence, Rudolf Scharping, German minister of defence, summarised this harmony of strategic objectives for NATO, defined as:

- a regional alliance which has not turned into a global police force, but will defend its members' vital security interests whenever and wherever it is required to;
- an Alliance which has adopted its military capabilities to the new threats, but continues to have a broad understanding of our security needs;
- an Alliance which has an unmatched military potential, but has learned to accept, to co-operate with and to support other security organisations;
- an Alliance which has uniquely combined its strategic missions of

providing for collective defence and of contributing to co-operative security by reaching out to non-NATO members;

- an Alliance which has become more European while remaining the foundation for transatlantic security co-operation and the institutional link of the United States to European security.[4]

This statement implies that the relations between Germany and Poland have evolved beyond the narrow context of bi-lateralism, and have embedded within the general framework of NATO a broad continental and even global perspective. This is a new and an unprecedented level of teamwork between both nations. In the matters of European security, at least, Germany and Poland have moved beyond the past.

But even in this respect there is an evident difference in perception of the American role within the Alliance. This, in turn, inhibits the mutual understanding of the transatlantic links. There is a growing German tendency to assert a degree of independence from the United States, while the Poles are among the most enthusiastic and uncritical supporters of the United States. When faced with a choice between Berlin and Washington, Warsaw 'yearn[s] for friendship with America but depend[s] on Germany, their most important neighbour and trading partner'.[5] Like many other central European states, Poland is highly apprehensive about any security guarantee provided by other European states, especially France.

Poland's political relevance is partially derived from Warsaw's closeness to United States, the anchor of the international system and the ultimate guarantor of Poland's relevance in European and world affairs. Furthermore, close relations between Poland and the United States provide Warsaw with effective political leverage with Germany, as well as an opening to assume a middleman's role in central Europe. During his summer 2002 trip to the United States, the Polish President Aleksander Kwasniewski received a highly publicised red-carpet reception that included a politically motivated tour of the Midwest to rally some 10 million Polish Americans on behalf of the Republican party. On this occasion, the Polish President stated that Polish foreign policy 'is built on two pillars – Europe, and America's engagement in Europe',[6] meaning that the Poles, unlike the French, perceive European and American security interest as identical. When necessary, however, Poland would balance to its advantage the European and the American ties: Poland may well try to assert a leadership role in central and southern Europe within an enlarged NATO. It is likely, therefore, that German and

Polish regional aspirations may generate frictions between both countries. It is equally possible that even a low level of tension between Berlin and Washington could present Poland with some thorny choices.

Nevertheless, the multilateral framework of German–Polish relations has been conducive to the enrichment of the bilateral relations in the area of military security. In the second half of the 1990s, Germany and Poland, together with Denmark, established a joint military unit called the Northern Corps. This brigade-size unit is stationed in Szczecin – formerly the German city of Stettin. On a rotational basis, the Northern Corps is commanded either by a German, Polish or Danish general. It represents an unprecedented step forward in German–Polish relations, especially in terms of breaking psychological barriers on both sides. For the Germans, it manifests the recognition that Szczecin is a city under permanent Polish sovereignty; for the Poles, the presence of German troops on Polish soil alleviates the paranoia of some future, foreign occupation. Poland has freed itself from regional fatalism and has gained the level of self-confidence and poise necessary for a give-and-take type of international cooperation in matters of regional security, particularly with respect to Germany.

The habit of working together in the spirit of the Atlantic Alliance is best exemplified by the January 2002 German–Polish agreement to transfer 128 Leopard 2A4 tanks and 23 MiG–29 fighters from Bundeswehr to the Polish armed forces for a symbolic price of 90 million Polish zloty, approximately $21.5 million. Delivery of the first 15 tanks to the Polish 10th armoured cavalry brigade in Swietoszow was marked by a Polish–German ceremony attended by Poland's President Kwasniewski and the Defence Ministers of the both states. The brigade is an element of the Allied Command Europe Joint Rapid Reaction Force.[7] This weapons transfer has helped modernise Poland's armed forces and enhanced the interoperability of the Polish military units with NATO.

A high-level political consultation between the leadership of both nations has become a well-established pattern in bilateral relations. Both working and ceremonial visits between the heads of government, the German Chancellor and the Polish Prime Minister, Defence and Foreign Ministers, and various lower-level officials are a daily reality. Examples of these interactions include an 'unimaginable' address by President Kwasniewski to German conscripts and another address by the German Defence Minister to the graduating class of Polish officers. On one such occasion, President Kwasniewski declared 'Poland perceives Germany and the Germans with friendliness and great hope'. He continued that

'Here, in the middle of Europe, where a pan-continental conflict erupted 60 years ago with the Nazi attack on Poland, is a place where we now build European unity. It is we, the Poles and the Germans, who brought about this change.'[8] On the official level, at least, it is expected that Polish–German bilateral cooperation will serve as a model for other central European states to follow, and that the regional relations among Germany, Poland and the Czech Republic will establish the most integrated and prosperous region in Europe. It is also becoming evident that Germany is become increasingly comfortable with assuming a political leadership role in central Europe, acting as a benevolent, understanding, 'soft', and friendly power with well-defined economic as well as political missions that are welcomed and appreciated by its eastern neighbours. Once the element of fear was removed from relations between Germany and its neighbours, Poland's tendency to look for German support in all matters related to its own well-being and to the entire process of European integration has grown to the point where there is now hardly a single domestic or international issue that will not receive a bilateral evaluation.

Another important element for mutual relations is the 'Weimar Triangle'. Established in early 1990s, this forum was designed to bring together members of the French, German and Polish political elite on a regular basis and facilitate informal talks on all issues of mutual concern. Once a year, the presidents of these three states meet in Weimar for a casual exchange of views and an affirmation that good relations among their states are critically important for the integration and stability in Europe. Although the Weimar Triangle is not a particularly influential diplomatic mechanism measured against NATO and EU, it is nevertheless a form of recognition that Poland belongs at Europe's core, that Germany's relations with Poland are equal in importance to German relations with France, and that this bilateral relationship is central to European security and economic progress. In the future, the European 'locomotive' may as well include Poland in addition to France and Germany, as the state of the German–Polish affairs becomes a measure of stability on the entire European continent.[9]

The new *Mitteleuropa*

The progressive improvement in German–Polish relations accelerated the bilateral and pan-European processes of political and economic integration within the EU framework. Germany's commitment to Poland's accession to the EU is explicitly noted in the 1991 Treaty. Poland, on the other hand, placed its expectations on Germany, and the German economic predominance in central Europe became well established immediately after the breakdown of communism. Trade with Germany accounts for 35 per cent of all Poland's exports, Germany is the third biggest foreign investor (after the United States and France), but overall the strongest economic partner of Poland.[10] The task of effecting the westward integration of Poland and other central European nations has been placed on Germany.

Germany has sought to erect a barrier against political instability and demographic pressures from Ukraine, Russia and Central Asia. Simultaneously, Germany welcomed access to 40 million Polish consumers and another 40 million consumers in the rest of central and southern Europe. Germany also assumed that the pro-western transformation in Poland would be rapid and irreversible. Poland, on the other hand, concluded that the German economic miracle would continue into the foreseeable future, giving Germany a decisive role in shaping the enlargement of the EU. Equally important in Warsaw's calculations was confidence in the Polish capacity to exploit the German sense of guilt. From the very beginning, therefore, the German–Polish endeavour to facilitate the eastward enlargement of the EU was founded on numerous optimistic suppositions and expectations concerning the domestic dynamics in both countries and the future course of bilateral relations. In particular, three bilateral and EU-related issues emerged as the most divisive issues during negotiations on Poland's accession to the EU: free movement of labour; a right of foreigners to purchase land in Poland; and the level of EU agricultural subsidies for the Polish farmers.

In terms of a general attitude toward the eastward enlargement of the EU, there is a fundamental difference in approach between Germany and Poland. From the western perspective, the resolution to enlarge the EU is a product of pragmatic, even commercial, calculations. For the Poles, however, the 'return of Europe to Poland', is an act of a historical justice. It is a delayed compensation for President Roosevelt's decision to 'sentence Poland to communism' and occupation by the Soviet Russia, which for forty-five years deprived the country of its independence, the Marshall Plan and a chance to develop along the democratic and free-market patterns. The Poles believe it is not their own fault that they lag behind the nations of western Europe in terms of economic and political development. Instead, they consider their economic troubles as a by-product of the Yalta agreement and believe that the West has a moral obligation to underwrite Poland's accession to the EU.

In addition, Poland – sure of its strategic and economic importance in Europe – assumes, correctly or not, that the EU enlargement process is more important for the EU than it is for Poland, or at least that the enlargement would be meaningless without the inclusion of the largest, the most populous and strategically most significant nation in the region. It is not surprising that the Poles approached the EU accession negotiations with an unexpected degree of 'Euroscepticism', driving an uncompromising bargain on every issue. As an EU Foreign Minister pointed out, the Poles negotiated as if the EU members were expected 'to plead with it to join their club'. Matthew Kaminski summarised the negotiations: 'Poles know the EU can't keep them out and at the same time declare enlargement a success. Warsaw did the minimum to join, and now holds out for even higher subsidies.'[11]

This boldness reflects Poland's confidence that the country possesses a vital strategic position on the continent. With Germany in the political and economic centre of Europe, and with the declining importance of France, Poland's aim is to use its alliance with Germany to secure for itself the leadership role among the CEE states. The process of enlargement is more than just an extension of the EU to the east and south of Germany; it is in essence a restructuring of the continent around Germany that has now returned to its historical central location and responsibilities west and east of its borders. For the nations east of Germany, enlargement is not an act of gratuity or an award for a good behaviour, but a realisation of their rights as European states. The lengthy process of enlargement negotiations had to focus on countless more or less important technical details, but the most contentious issues had an important bilateral German–Polish dimension.

Sources of bilateral discord: immigration and national minorities

A free movement of labour across national borders has been the top German concern. Like almost any other German–Polish issue, the controversy over the movement of labour has some historico-emotional underpinnings, including the immigration of the Polish workers to the Ruhr in the nineteenth and early twentieth centuries, forced labour during the Nazi occupation of Poland during the Second World War and the migration of Polish citizens, of both Polish and German ethnic background, to Germany in the 1980s and 1990s. In general, the German government encouraged the import of inexpensive Polish labour, as wages paid to the Polish workers are up to 70 per cent lower than the earnings of German workers and do not include social contributions. Likewise, Poland looked favourably at this export of labour, since it provided an opportunity to reduce domestic unemployment and the increased flow of hard currency and technical know-how. On the other hand, the Poles objected to the 'brain drain' of the better-qualified workers, as well as the various patterns of discrimination against the Polish workers, including low wages and second-rate working conditions.[12]

The German side, conversely, became apprehensive about the tendency of the Polish workers either to exceed the agreed quotas for the number of Poles allowed to be employed in Germany, or to stay illegally in the country after the expiration of their official contracts. During the 1990s, the number of Poles residing in Germany was growing rapidly at a time when recession had begun to distress the German economy. The impact of cheap Polish labour on the German economy became a hot political issue among the political parties and labour unions in Germany. In turn, the Polish side became concerned that the Schröder government might try to delay Poland's accession to the EU, or at least demand that a transition period be imposed on the free movement of Polish labour into Germany.

On closer scrutiny, the immigration problem was not economic but rather political, specifically the fear of a right-wing domestic backlash similar to the electoral successes of Jörg Haider's Freedom Party in Austria. Immigrants in Germany now account for approximately 12 per cent of the national population. In several larger cities, the immigrant population is as high as 30 per cent, relatively more than in the United States or Canada. Several studies have concluded that the labour migration phenomenon in Europe is already very common, and the enlargement of the Union would not significantly increase the current rate of labour movement across the national borders. The Deutsche Institut für Wirtschaftsforschung (DIW), for example, expects that not more than 1 per cent of the population in the Czech Republic, Poland, Hungary and Slovakia would be inclined to immigrate, and that Germany has the potential to absorb an additional 2 million immigrants, half of them from Poland. Doubtless, some of these immigrants would benefit certain German economic sectors – for example, computers and telecommunications – facing a shortfall in qualified skilled labour. Additionally, it is well documented that maintaining the current level of social benefits and pensions is conditional on preserving the existing proportion between professionally active and retired population. With a negative demographic growth, the solvency of the German social security system depends on the influx of foreign labour.[13] Finally, an orderly movement of labour across national borders would significantly curtail the relatively common German practice of employing illegal aliens, who make no contribution to the social system of the country. This new attitude toward immigrants is evident in the recently enacted legislation, which regulates the eligibility of foreign nationals to compete for employment in Germany.[14]

The German concern over the influx of foreign labour is closely intertwined with the issue of the German minority in Poland and the Polish minority in Germany. The definition of 'ethnic minority' differs significantly between the two countries, complicating the labour issue. According to Polish figures, the total number of Polish immigrants in Germany approaches 2 million. This number includes both 'old' and 'new' immigrants from Poland. Those counted as 'old' immigrants are either descendants of the labourers who settled in the Ruhr at the end of the nineteenth and the beginning of the twentieth centuries, or Second World War prisoners who did return to Poland at the war's end. Those counted as 'new' immigrants are Poles who, for economic reasons, left Poland for Germany between 1980 and 2000. The legal status of these people varies, but in principle, they are considered ethnic Germans. As a result, they have no legal right to claim a minority status that would entitle them to special educational, cultural and political rights, including subsidies from the German and Polish governments. There are some Poles, usually those with a German spouse, who do possess a dual passport and, while they have a right to work and reside in Germany and are obligated to pay taxes, have neither the legal right to German citizenship nor to the vote. It is only this population that the German government counts as 'native Poles', thus reducing the official accounting of the Polish minority in Germany to a maximum of 300,000 individuals.

There is likewise a disparity in the official accounting of ethnic Germans living in Poland. According to the Polish government, there are not more than 500,000 people with German minority status. According to official German sources, the number of ethnic Germans in Poland approaches 300,000. Polish citizens claiming German roots enjoy a privileged minority status that entitles them to direct subsidies from both the Polish and German governments, access to mass media, special offices, schools, parishes and several guaranteed seats in the Polish parliament. In contrast to the German policy on the minority status for Polish immigrants, these benefits provide a strong economic incentive for the German immigrant to claim minority status. In 1993, for example, the German subsidy for the German minority in Poland was DM 46 million, in addition to a direct Polish assistance in the amount of DM 700,000.[15] These subsidies automatically elevated the standard of living of the Germans in Poland to at least an upper-middle-class level. This treatment of immigrants between Germany and Poland remains markedly unbalanced, which in turn fuels social and political tensions between both countries. Additionally these disparities reinforce many historically rooted, negative perceptions. It is not surprising that the Polish authorities are deeply concerned about the embarrassing asymmetry between the legal and economic status of both minorities. They have so far unsuccessfully demanded recognition of the Polish ethnicity in Germany in accord with the Copenhagen Declaration of 1990 and the Convention of the European Council on Minority Protection of 2000.

The minority issue is a divisive factor in relations between the German and the Polish people because it promotes negative stereotypes. Those in Poland claiming German heritage are generally seen as unscrupulous Poles willing to fake German identity for profit. Their subsidised lifestyle is irritating to other citizens of Poland, and it reinforces a cynical German image of Poles as poor and inept. In turn, the Polish view is that Poland's current economic difficulties reflect two centuries of occupation by Prussia, Germany and then Soviet Russia. To underscore the negative consequences of foreign domination, the Poles point to the economic conditions and social problems experienced by the new *Länder*, where despite some $300 billion in subsidies from the Federal government, the economic situation is not significantly better than that in Poland. So while many Poles may recognise the advantages of close economic and political relations with Germany, they are also apprehensive and uncomfortable about the existing situation, looking to the EU and the United States to offset the long-term economic dependence on Germany. Both sides recognise the benefits of close relations in the rapidly integrating Europe, but this political and economic affiliation has yet to evolve into a mutual respect.

The hope on both sides of the Oder–Neisse border is that once a bilateral consensus on minorities is achieved, the minority issues will no longer be a political problem but instead a matter of cultural identity and demographics. In such a scenario, the minority populations will provide a natural and informal people-to-people link between both nations, slowly bringing together Germans and Poles on social and cultural levels. This expectation is not simply optimistic, but also rooted in historical precedent – the 500-year-long period of peaceful coexistence between German and Poles that existed until the consolidation of the Prussian state at the beginning of the eighteen century.

Continuing sources of distrust

While there is certainly an existing level of tensions between Germans and Poles, it is undoubtedly exacerbated by political developments in Germany that are perceived in Poland as manifestations of a nationalistic backlash and irredentism. Most troubling for the Poles is a growing trend in Germany to present the Germans as victims of the Second World War in general, and the forced deportation from the Oder–Neisse territories and former Prussia in particular. Certainly, the Poles cannot deny that the postwar expulsion of the German populations was neither orderly nor gracious; and in his 1995 speech to the Bundestag, Poland's foreign minister has apologised to the German people for the pain caused by displacement. However, this hurried and chaotic eviction of Germans must be placed in the context of Germany's responsibility for its invasion of Poland in 1939, the extermination of over 6 million Polish citizens, the loss to Soviet Russia of almost 50 per cent of Polish territories in the east and the subsequent westward deportation of 5 million Poles from those eastern territories. Thus, when Edmund Stoiber, the CDU/CSU Chancellor candidate during the 2002 national elections, called for a nullification of the Polish and Czech decrees ordering the deportation of Germans and granting to the former residents of East Prussia a right to reclaim their lost properties, the Poles were traumatised for at least two reasons. First, his demand placed in question the entire postwar European order, since the decision to expel the German population from these territories was originally not made by the Poles, but was mandated by the Allies in Potsdam. A potential Chancellor candidate was in effect questioning one of the main pillars of the postwar European settlement. Secondly, Stoiber's statement had a sobering effect on the Polish enthusiasm to join the EU, since under its rules foreigners from other member nations would acquire the right to purchase land in Poland. It fortified Poland's paranoia against the alleged German conspiracy to support Poland's entry to the Union in order to buy what they had failed to conquer.

Although this particular incident was defined as a 'misunderstanding' or dismissed as a 'tempest in a teacup' and quickly expunged from the agenda of mutual relations, it nevertheless made the Poles more aware of subtle changes in the German culture. It now appears acceptable and politically advantageous in Germany to be more assertive *vis-à-vis* other nations, including the United States, as well as to foster a self-perception of a nation victimised by the Second World War.[16] The Poles find this revisionist cultural drift potentially dangerous, as some seventy years ago a similar reinterpretation of the First World War supplied emotional underpinnings for Hitler's popularity and the ultranationalism central to National Socialism's electoral success. In the spirit of historical candour, Poles favour an exploration of the human and material price paid by the German people during and after the Second World War, as long as such debates are not designed to agitate a revisionist cause.

Another worrisome sign of creeping German nationalism is seen in a proposal to resurrect Prussia by merging the *Länder* of Berlin and Brandenburg into one political and administrative unit. Voters rejected this idea in 1996, but it appears now to be gaining popularity not so much as an organizational consolidation but as an incarnation of the Prussian legacy in Germany. For some in Germany, that legacy includes such values as 'honour, duty, progressiveness, efficiency, selflessness, and tolerance', but for Germany's neighbours – France, Austria and Poland, in particular – Prussia is a symbol and a bitter memory of 'militarism, territorial expansion, arrogance and domination' as well as one of the main antecedents of Nazism.[17] It is not surprising, therefore, that in Poland, as in many other European nations, there continues to be a lingering sense of unease with regard to the long-term political prospects of Germany.

This contradictory background of opportunity and fear with regard to Germany drives the Polish assessment of Poland's prospective membership in the EU. While looking to foreign investments and an open access to the west European labour markets, a considerable percentage of the Polish population is troubled by the image of foreigners (by which Poland almost always implies Germans) invading the country to purchase the land. The psychological bequest of the Polish partitions is strongly entrenched in the mentality of Polish farmers and shared by some residents of the Oder–Neisse territories who, after Poland's admission to the EU, favoured a eighteen-year transition period for the sale of arable land to citizens of other EU member-states. As a popular test of patriotism and a diplomatic competence of the government, this issue received an unwarranted level of national attention.[18] The transition period was eventually reduced to seven years in the former German territories and three years in the other parts of Poland, and at the same time rendered inconsequential by numerous exemptions, including an unobstructed right of EU nationals to lease the land. Besides the political and economic benefits for Poland attending EU membership, this willingness to compromise on the land issue signals a cultural *volte face* toward self-confidence and identification with a broader community of nations.

This decision was also facilitated by the decision of the German government to compensate Polish victims of slave labour during the Second World War. During the Soviet period, Poland was not allowed by Moscow to receive reparations from Germany, but after regaining independence in 1989, the country asked for equal rights with other victims of the Nazi regime. After initial hesitation, the restitution process began in 2001,[19] highlighting the principle that the Polish citizens would not be treated differently than citizens of other European states.

But the most important manifestation of German goodwill and understanding toward Poland was the German decision to maintain its high level of agricultural subsidies for the French farmers. This step, which removed the largest single obstacle on Poland's way to the EU, was made at the time when the EU negotiated the direct income support to the Polish farmers both to alleviate their fear of competition with west European agricultural products and to redress their impression of being treated as second-class citizens in a united Europe. Thus, without alienating France and Spain, the support for the Polish farmers will start at 25 per cent of the average Union support during the first year, gradually growing in ten years to approximately 60 per cent of the Union's average during the same period of time. With the cost of living in Poland being lower than in western Europe, this offer guarantees Polish voters' support for accession to the EU.[20] It also meant that a successful enlargement of the Union, in the words of German Foreign Minister Joschka Fisher, would be 'unimaginable' without Poland.[21]

Conclusion

In more than a decade since unification, German policy toward Poland has been guided by the realistic assumptions that, first, the quality of German–Polish relations would have a defining impact on the entire European continent; and second, that a sympathetic understanding of the Polish needs, anxieties and aspirations is required by Berlin. Germany appears to be guided by a blend of a strategic vision and special sensitivities to its eastern neighbour. In these economically difficult times, Germany has used its economic assets to soften Poland's transition to the EU and to overcome stereotypes rooted in the past. Despite occasional nationalistic flare-ups between Poland and Germany, Germany's leadership has greatly facilitated the domestic and international transformation of Poland as it moves back into the European community of nations. Thus, by abandoning its condescending, nineteenth-century, *Mitteleuropa* mind-set toward Poland and other nations of the region, Germany has helped to redefine the meaning of Europe, and has turned Poland from a foe into a friend.

In the future, the burden of history (the 'old' problems) will continue to fade away in bilateral relations between Germany and Poland. Bilateral relations will be conditioned by the new framework provided by common NATO and EU membership. As a result, the relationship between the two countries will have to assume more a business-like tenor, free of emotions, sentimentalities and exceptions from general rules. While Germany would be less paternalistic, understanding and forgiving, the Poles are likely to be more pragmatic, positive and dependable as partners in a united Europe. With the improving quality of the Polish armed forces, the country may in time become a valuable and politically reliable member of NATO. The strongly pro-American outlook of Warsaw may incite frictions with Germany over the American role in Europe and the world; however, as long as German–Russian relations do not become 'special', Germany and Poland will continue their already well-established alliance. The German economic presence in Poland will grow exponentially, while the Poles will continue to advance their political objectives in Europe with a help of 50 votes in the EP and an active participation in all other EU institutions. In the near future, German relations with Poland are likely to move 'beyond the past' and should not significantly diverge from the prevailing patterns of interaction between Germany and other member-states of the EU.

Notes

1 For the detailed examination of both treaties from the perspective of the international law, see Wladyslaw Czaplinski, 'The New Polish–German Treaties and the Changing Political Structure of Europe', *American Journal of International Law*, 86:1 (1992), pp. 163–73 and Anna Sabbat-Swidlicka, 'The Signing of the Polish–German Border Treaty', *Report on Eastern Europe*, Radio Free Europe/Radio Liberty, 1:49 (7 December 1990), pp. 16–19. For an insightful examination of both treaties in context of Polish–German and Polish–Russian relations, see Janusz Stefanowicz, 'Central Europe between Germany and Russia. A View from Poland', *Security Dialogue*, 26:1 (1995), pp. 55–64.

2 Daniel J. Whiteneck, 'Germany: Consensus Politics and Changing Security Paradigms', in Gale A. Mattox and Arthur R. Rachwald (eds), *Enlarging NATO. The National Debates* (Boulder, CO: Lynne Rienner, 2001), pp. 35–51.

3 Roland Freudenstein, 'Poland, Germany and the EU', *International Affairs*, 74:1 (1998), p. 53.

4 Bundesministerium der Verteidigung (BMVg) 'Germany and Poland in a Changing NATO', at www.bmvg.de/archiv/reden/minister/020618_warschau.php, 18 June 2002.

5 'The Mantle Passes from Vaclaw to Alexander', *Economist*, 16 November 2002, p. 47.

6 *Ibid.*

7 Warsaw, *PAP* in English 10:46 GMT 16 September 2002, FBIS, Document ID: EUP20020916000159.

8 President Aleksander Kwasniewski, 'Poland and Germany: Partners in United Europe', 6 March 2002, *Financial Times Information*, in BBC Monitoring Europe.

9 Statement by the German Chancellor Gerhard Schröder, *PAP News Agency* (Warsaw), 18 June 2002, in BBC Monitoring Europe.

10 'Poland, Germany and Czech Republic Doomed to Succeed', *Polish News Company*, 23 November 2001.

11 Stephen Mulvey, 'Euro Leaders Prepare to Make History', *BBC News, World Edition*, 11 December, 2002; and Matthew Kaminski, 'The Polish Blues', *Wall Street Journal on Line*, 11 December 2002.

12 George K. Menz, 'Beyond the Anwerbestopp? The German–Polish Bilateral Labour Treaty', *Journal of European Social Policy*, 11:3 (2000), pp. 258–9.

13 *Rzeczpospolita*, 16 August 2001 and *Polityka*, 25 August, 2001. Also, Johannes Brocker, 'Migration – On Balance Positive', *Janet Mathews Information Services*, 18 June 2001.

14 Monika Mazur-Rafal, 'Goscie Mile Potrzebni', (Guests Welcomed), *Unia & Polska*, 19:94 (5 December 2002), pp. 32–3.

15 *Ibid.* and Jonathan P. G. Bach, 'Germany after Unification and Eastern Europe: New Perspectives, New Problems', Paper delivered at the University Seminar on Post-Communist States, Societies and Economies at Columbia University, 10 November 1998, p. 4. Dariusz Matelski points out that there are five different degrees of 'Germanness' among the citizens of Poland who claim to have German ties: a very small group of the 'real Germans' with unquestionable ethnic credentials; 'Germans with strong documents' that entitle them to a dual citizenship; 'Germans with weak documents', usually the descendants of those who during the Second World War joined the *Volksdeutsch* list; the 'Poles of German origin' who are unable to provide any evidence of the German origin but subjectively feel German; and the 'candidates for the German minority' in Poland, who just wish to join a German minority organisation in Poland. Also, Dariusz Matelski, *Niemcy w Polsce w XX Wieku* (Germany in Poland in the 20th Century) (Warszawa-Poznan: Wydawnictwo Naukowe PAN), pp. 275–6.

16 'Polish/German Relations – Whose Land Is It Anyway?,' *Warsaw Voice* SA, 14 July 2002.

17 'Prussian Blues', *Economist*, 2 March 2002, p. 49.

18 'Europe: A Most Emotional Issue; Polish Land', *The Economist*, 23 March 2002, p. 48. Also, PAP, Polska Agencja Prasowa (Polish News Agency), *Dziennik on-line*, 2003–01–15. The Polish decision is partially motivated by the expectation that in 2011 (that is, seven years after the admission of Poland to the EU in 2004) there will be a very few German survivors of the 1945–47 expulsion still wanting to buy back lost homesteads. In any case, the right to purchase the agricultural land in Poland is limited only to the individuals or businesses, domestic or foreign, interested in its cultivation.

19 'Nearly One Million Nazi-Era Forced Labourers Have Received Damages', *Agence France Presse*, 13 September 2002. Also, Arkadiusz Dawidowski, 'Fight for Indemnities in Crisis', *Zycie Warszawy*, 6 November 1999, p. 4.

20 Speech by Günther Verheugen, Member of the European Commission responsible for Enlargement, printed in *Rzeczpospolita*, 11 July 2002.

21 Quoted in 'Kwasniewski to Make First Official Visit to Germany', *Agence France Presse*, 5 March 2002.

21

Germany and the future of European integration[1]

Emil J. Kirchner

Since 1995, Germany has found itself in the unfamiliar position of being accused on a number of occasions of either breaking or not honouring EU rules and commitments. Not only did the European Commission have a run-in with German authorities over irregular regional aid subventions to its new *Länder*, the privileged status of the *Landesbanken* and the overshooting of the 3 per cent deficit spending under the GSP, partners in the A400 aircraft project also expressed disappointment over Germany's failure to pay its promised share in the project. Relations with France also became troublesome. Besides pushing France for reforms of the CAP, as part of the drive to reduce its EU budgetary contributions, Germany also provoked an awkward showdown with France at the 2000 Nice summit over the number of votes the country should have in the Council of Ministers. To top it all, public opinion surveys at the end of 2002 showed the German public to be the least enthusiastic of the populations in the 'Euroland' zone towards the single currency.

Having been considered a paragon hitherto,[2] what had gone wrong with Germany's EU reputation? It is important to stress that not all of what were seen as German faults were attributable to the Schröder government, but were rather caused by the circumstances in which Germany found itself internally and externally. On the domestic front, the continuation, if not worsening, of economic problems associated with the fall-out of German unification and the absorption of the five new *Länder*, together with the growing number of younger people less coloured by stigmas of the Second World War in German society, have made Germans more inward looking, self-reliant and self-confident.

Chancellor Gerhard Schröder's insistence on a more self-confident and self-assertive Germany fitted this prevailing mood. Externally, there were continued fears on the part of Germany's EU partners that eastern enlargement would disproportionately favour German's interests. On the other hand, there were also pressures on Germany to translate its economic and political strength into greater engagement or commitment in international crisis situations, such as the Kosovo conflict. But there were, and are, also factors affecting German–EU relations that can be more directly linked to Schröder and his coalition partner the Greens. Schröder's more pragmatic approach and the Greens' lukewarm support for European integration were certainly aspects that separated the Red–Green coalition from the Kohl government.

Though adopting a different leadership style, it is important to note that the Schröder government neither broke with previous German commitments towards EU integration nor slowed down in any significant way the process of EU unification. On the contrary, it engaged fully in EU reform and enlargement efforts, and played an instrumental role in the initiation and deliberations of the debate on a EU constitution. The aim of this chapter will be to assess whether Germany's approach and commitment towards the EU between 1998 and mid-2003 has changed significantly. This will be done by examining Germany's contribution towards the debate on the establishment of an EU constitution. In particular, attention will be paid to Germany's role in the EU convention, whose task was to prepare a draft on the EU constitution. But before we turn to this aspect, it is important to examine briefly the EU image the Schröder government has conveyed after coming to power in September 1998.

German–EU relations, 1999–2003

When the Red–Green coalition (SPD and the Green parties) won the Federal elections in September 1998, questions were raised whether this coalition would be as committed to EU integration as previous administrations had been. In the run-up to the 1998 general elections, there had been concerns over remarks by Schröder with respect to the timetable of the single currency, the request for a lowering of the German EU budgetary commitments and the insistence on a more self-confident Germany, which included a stronger pronouncement of its national interest. Equally, questions were raised over the Greens' traditional aversion toward EU political integration.[3] Would this mean a lowering of Germany's normative EU commitments, an end of chequebook diplomacy or a more cost-benefit-oriented Germany?

The new government went on record to promise continuity in EU and foreign policy affairs. This included support for EU reforms, as stipulated in the Amsterdam Treaty, and EU eastern enlargement. While political union was seen as the final goal, unity in social and ecological policy was also seen as a necessary and contingent part of the union. But it also declared a readiness to defend or promote German interests more explicitly and to seek a lowering of its EU budgetary contributions.

In the first half of 1999, the Schröder government was presented with an early opportunity to translate these aims into action and to prove its EU and international credentials. It not only held the Presidency of the EU, but also chaired the WEU and the G–8 summit. The ongoing debate surrounding Agenda 2000, which called for policy and institutional reforms prior to enlargement, presented the German EU Presidency with an opportunity to pursue the dual aim of institutional/policy reforms and enlargement, while at the same time seeking to lower its disproportionately high EU budgetary contributions. However, attempts for a radical CAP reform, including an attempt to renationalise part of the agricultural subsidies, were spurned by French President Jacques Chirac and an agreement had to wait until the autumn of 2002; and, even then, only with the proviso that the reforms would be phased in in 2007.

This contributed to a cooling off in Franco-German relations and coincided with a temporary love-in between Britain and France. Witness to the latter was the St Malo Agreement in December 1998 to enhance EU defence capabilities and to develop a common defence policy, which was further strengthened by NATO-led military operations in Kosovo in the spring of 1999. Yet, Germany contributed to both the development of an EU defence capability and military operations in Kosovo. First, during its EU presidency, especially the Cologne Summit, Germany helped prepare the making of EU defence capabilities and policies. These were officially announced as the so-called 'Headline Goals' at the Helsinki Summit in December 1999, and sanctioned at the Nice Summit in December 2000. Secondly, the Kosovo conflict of 1999 presented Germany with the challenge of participating in a military intervention. By rising to the challenge, it resulted in the first German military engagement since 1945. What was most surprising was that Germany undertook this in the absence of a UN mandate.

It is also true that Germany's style of engagement had changed. Rather than coordinating initiatives with France, which had been the hallmark of previous administrations, Germany either pursued a more independent line or engaged with various EU partners in the pursuit of EU affairs. A case in point was the aggressive push by the former Finance Minister Oskar Lafontaine for tax harmonisation. Most importantly the friendship or personal chemistry that Kohl had developed with other EU leaders like François Mitterrand and Jacques Delors, was largely absent with Schröder. However, it can be said that the EU deals that had bound Kohl and Mitterrand have given way to greater national 'cost-benefit' considerations, not only in Germany but also in most other EU countries. Changing economic and geopolitical circumstances, as well as challenges arising from the war on terror and forging transatlantic relations, have reinforced their national reorientation and have undermined EU collective decision making.

How do these trends correspond to efforts since 2000 to introduce far-reaching EU reforms and to maintain or enhance decision making capacity in an enlarged Union of twenty-five members? A convention, formed in the wake of the Laeken Declaration of the EU Council in December 2001, was tasked with drawing up recommendations for the drafting of an EU constitution. An IGC, scheduled for the second half of 2003, would finalise the text of such a constitution. This convention serves as a good example for examining the stand Germany has taken on key issues of EU reforms and how this position corresponds with the view of other EU partners.

German contributions to the EU convention can be seen in three ways, involving the initiation of the debate on a EU constitution; the role of German political actors in the deliberations of the EU convention; and the impact of German political actors on the output of the convention.

Initiation of the debate

It is interesting to note that one of the most important first steps in the debate for a EU constitution was advanced by German Foreign Minister Joschka Fischer in his speech at Humboldt University in May 2000.[4] At the outset, what was important about this speech was Fischer's insistence on speaking as a private person and not in his capacity as German Foreign Minister, or on behalf of the German government.[5]

Three key points emerge in Fischer's speech. First, Fischer designated as the overall goal of the EU a move to a federation, though without replacing the nation-states, with a division of sovereignty between the federation and member states. The importance of respect for national identities should be maintained and the notion of a 'EU super state' should be rejected. Fischer called for a clear definition of competencies, with core sovereignties to be regulated by the Union, and the remaining competencies left in the hands of the member states, reflecting the principle of subsidiarity. Competencies would thus be clearly defined, both horizontally (for institutions) and vertically (between member states and the EU). Secondly, in institutional terms he advocated two parliamentary chambers: the first consisting of elected members, who are also members of national parliaments; the second taking the form of the US Senate or the German Bundesrat. The first, roughly the EP, should represent 'a EU of the nation-states and a EU of the citizens'. Either the EU Council or the European Commission would be developed into a full-blown EU executive; the Commission president could be directly elected. The EP and governments should exercise legislative and executive power. Thirdly, the constitution should espouse basic human and civil rights, entail a division of powers between the EU institutions, and contain a precise delineation between the EU and nation-state level. With regard to decision making, Fischer suggested moving beyond the Jean Monnet method, by making increasing use of the method of enhanced cooperation. Equally, he called for the expansion of reinforced cooperation between those states which want to cooperate more closely than others, representing a 'centre of gravity'.

Fischer's intervention was quickly followed by official speeches of other EU leaders, notably the speeches given by President Jacques Chirac before the German Bundestag in June 2000 and Prime Minister Tony Blair in Warsaw in October 2000. However, neither Chirac and Blair espoused the federalist ambitions envisaged in the Fischer project, though both their speeches contained ambitions in their own rights. For example, while Chirac called for the formation of a 'pioneer group' to advance EU integration, Blair embraced the idea of the EU as a 'superpower'.[6] In contrast, Belgian Prime Minister Guy Verhofstadt reflected some of the federalist traditions put forward by Fischer. More in line still with Fischer's thinking were two speeches by German

President Johannes Rau in April 2001 and November 2001.[7] He called for an EU federation of nation-states, and also reiterated Fischer's call for a division of powers between member-states and the EU as well as for institutional reform (e.g. enhancing parliamentary powers and creating a Commission president). In contrast to Fischer, he put greater emphasis on the role of the EU Charter of Fundamental Rights in the EU constitution, and on a strengthened role of the Commission as the defender of the Community interest.

Fischer's speech was also followed in official declarations on European policy by the two main German political parties, the SPD and the CDU, in November 2001. Selective items of these proposals and their impact on the drafting of the European convention will be shown below.

Deliberations in the convention

Owing to the initiatives taken by Fischer, Chirac and Blair during May and November 2000, the December Nice European Council called for another IGC to deal with more pronounced institutional reforms. The 2001 Laeken European Council later chose a new method for preparing this IGC. It agreed on the establishment of a convention on the future of Europe, the task of which would be the preparation of a draft EU constitution by mid-2003.[8] This draft constitution would then be finalised by an IGC between October 2003 and June 2004. The EU convention was formally established on 28 February 2002. The Laeken Declaration had set four broad topics for the convention to consider:

- a better division and definition of competencies in the EU
- a simplification of the Union's instruments
- more democracy, transparency and efficiency in an enlarged EU
- the way towards a constitution for Europe.

The participation of Joschka Fischer, as the main representative of the German governments in the second half of the convention proceedings, gave the convention additional clout and credibility, but also ensured that the views held by Fischer and the German government found recognition in the crucial phase of the convention. From a French perspective, a similar argument can be made for the participation of French Foreign Minister Domenique de Villepin. It also facilitated dialogue between the two respective foreign ministers and facilitated the joint Franco-German declaration to the convention

On 15 January 2003, France and Germany jointly published a contribution on the institutional architecture of the EU.[9] The proposal advocated the creation of a 'federation of nation-states' that would realise the three-fold goal of clarity, legitimacy and efficiency. At the core of the proposal was the institutionalisation of a double chairmanship of the EU, namely a democratically legitimised Commission President and a permanent President of the European Council. The European Council would, by qualified majority voting, elect its Chair for up to five years. This President would exercise his or her mandate full-time in order to prepare, chair and stimulate European Council meetings and to oversee the execution of its conclusions. Moreover, the President would represent the Union internationally, respecting the Commission's competences and those of a newly created European foreign minister. However, he would not chair the meetings of the Council of Ministers. The proposed creation of a permanent Council President received stiff opposition from the smaller member-states.

Under the Franco-German proposal, the EP would elect the Commission President with a qualified majority to be confirmed by the European Council. The President would choose his own College, to be approved by the EP and appointed by the European Council.

The Franco-German proposal envisaged a Foreign Minister, who would be a member of the European Commission, but with a special status as one of the vice-presidents. He would be appointed by the European Council and agreed by the Commission President. The Foreign Minister would have the right to initiate activities in the field of CFSP/European Security and Defence Policy (ESDP), and would chair the meetings of the Council of External Affairs and Defence. Decisions in the area of CFSP would be taken generally by qualified majority voting (QMV), whereas unanimity would be required for decisions regarding military or defence matters. In the area of CFSP/ESDP, the proposal recommends the participation of all member-states, but acknowledges that there will be situations when not all member-states are prepared to participate. In such situations, those who so desire should be able to make use of the instrument of 'enhanced cooperation'. Moreover, a common diplomatic corps would assist the Foreign Minister and consist of the Directorate-General of External Affairs as well as a newly established external unit. The latter would compose the external units of the Secretariat General of the Council of Ministers, and reinforced through seconded diplomats of the member-states and the Commission. The common diplomatic *corps* would cooperate closely with the diplomatic offices of the member-states. The existing delegations of the European Commissions would be transformed into delegations of the EU, in order to promote the establishment of a EU diplomatic *corps*.

Overall, the many progressive elements of the proposal reinforced the image of the Franco-German axis as the 'motor' of European integration. However, it also signalled some differences in terms of a more federalist-minded Germany, as expressed in, for example, the powers of the European Commission and the EP, and the extent of QMV.

Impact on the convention

Measuring the impact or influence by an individual actor on a policy making process is never an easy task and can lead to spurious correlations. It is not the aim here to retrace the multi-actor and multi-faceted decision making of the convention. Rather, I compare the final report of the convention, on the one hand, and official German political party declarations, the Fischer speech, German government statements and traditional views held by Germany towards further integration, on the other. The official declarations on European policy by the two main German political parties, the SPD and the CDU, were issued in November 2001. As far as possible, the different German actors will be identified when comparison is made with the text of the June 2003 convention, but sometimes, where it appears that a general German view prevails, reference is made to 'German actors' or to Germany.[10] In the following, the three main areas of German demands on the convention – general aims, institutional questions and policy areas – will be assessed, and where appropriate critical commentary will be supplied on the outcome of the convention.[11] I start with reference to general aims for further EU development, then turn to institutional issues and finish with policy areas. As a complete treatment of all the provisions introduced in the convention would go well beyond the confines of this chapter, only some of the more important instances are selected.

General objectives

As mentioned above, the general objectives of the European convention were to propose solutions for a better division and definition of

EU competences, to simplify the Union's instruments, to promote more democracy, transparency and effectiveness in the EU and to develop a constitution for European citizens. These views were broadly shared by the German actors.

In an effort to produce more clarity and accountability, the European convention proposed that the 'pillar' system, which treated CFSP, and JHA, as special areas of inter-governmental cooperation, would be merged. The 'pillar' structure, with which Germany was never pleased, was first introduced in the TEU largely at the insistence of the United Kingdom. Its eradication was therefore seen as a welcome change.

In terms of majority voting, major inroads were proposed by the convention into areas of acute national sensitivity, with the national veto remaining in only a handful of areas such as defence, taxation and foreign policy, and in the way in which EU nations ratify treaties or admit members. This change was in line with the argument advanced by the German government that, in an enlarged EU of twenty-five members, decision making would become too cumbersome without an extension of majority voting. A 'double majority' system, favoured by Germany as a country with the largest population, would require a majority of member-states, representing at least 60 per cent of the Union's aggregate population (taking effect on 1 November 2009). The convention stipulated that the European Council could change legislative procedure regarding unanimity and could change unanimity to QMV.

The demand by both the SPD and CDU that the Charter of Fundamental Rights, which sets out a range of entitlements from the right to life and human dignity to the right to strike, be made legally binding in the European constitution was accepted by the convention. The convention also recommended that the Union should accede to the European Convention for the Protection of Human Rights and Fundamental Freedoms.

Two points on the future form of the EU raised by the two political parties did receive general rather than specific mention in the convention. One was the vision expressed by the SPD for the United States of Europe to safeguard the cultural and linguistic identity of the people. The other was a CDU reference to the EU as a '*Staatenverbund*', in which member-states would be the undisputed 'masters of the treaties'.

Points on which German actors had not expressed any particular or strong demands, but which can be deemed as acceptable to the overall German view on further European integration, concerned the following convention proposals. A new office of European public prosecutor would investigate cross-border fraud against EU taxpayers, and could initiate legal cases in the courts of member-states. Provisions would be made for voluntary withdrawal from the Union (though countries wanting to leave would have to negotiate exit terms) and for suspension of membership in case of a breach of fundamental values, an issue raised when the far-right Freedom party joined Austria's ruling coalition in 2000.

Institutional and competence issues

With regard to institutional issues and aspects of competences between the EU, national and regional levels, table 21.1 provides a comparison of the main demands by the two political parties and the agreed text of the convention. There was a marked positive correlation between the views of the two major political parties and the recommendations of the convention. In particular, German proposals found recognition by:

- Making the European Council a fully-fledged EU institution, so its decisions can be challenged in the European Court of Justice.
- Creating a new Legislative Council or 'chamber of states' to work in public alongside the EP. It remained unclear however whether it should be a new body or a glorified version of the existing General Affairs Council (GAC).[12]
- Extending the Commission executive power by right and not merely on the decision of the Council of Ministers. There would be a new two-tier Commission: all member states would continue to send a commissioner to Brussels, but only fifteen would be able to vote at any one time. It would also give the Commission President the right to sack a Commissioner.
- Entitling the EP to co-legislate (together with the Council of Ministers) in seventy areas, almost doubling the present number (which is predominantly in the area of the Internal Market). Thus, the EP would be stronger, but whether its powers could be extended to include legislative and budgetary control over big-spending policy areas, such as agriculture, remains to be seen.
- Strengthening cooperation between national parliaments and the EP. Under the convention, national parliaments would have a new role in limiting EU legislation by allowing them, for example, to send to

Table 21.1 Institutions, competencies and separation of powers

SPD	*CDU*	*Convention*
Separation of powers between Commission, EP and Council	Council, EP and Commission receive law-initiating power	Creation of a 'legislative' Council; increase of EP co-decisions; strengthening of Commission's law initiation
Council as federal chamber (Europäische Staatenkammer)		
Commission as strong EU executive	*Commission* as executive, limited in size	*Commission* to obtain greater executive powers; size capped at fifteen
EP to be strengthened through co-decision and full budgetary competences	*EP* and Council share budgetary powers	*EP* shall, jointly with the Council, enact legislation and exercise budgetary functions, and functions of political control and consultation
EP elects *Commission President*	EP elects *Commission President*; College confirmed by EP and Council	EP elects *Commission President*, and confirms College
Clear separation of competences between EU member states, regions and municipalities; no interference in the internal organisation of member states; strengthening of CoR	Clear separation of competences; reorganisation of institutions and procedures according to the subsidiarity principle	Commission to attach a 'subsidiarity sheet' to proposals; 'early warning system' to engage national parliaments, with the right to appeal to the EJC; CoR may appeal to the ECJ

the presidents of the EP, the Council and the European Commission an opinion on whether a proposal complied with the principle of subsidiarity.

The convention text seeks to strengthen the principle of subsidiarity by stipulating that each institution shall ensure constant respect for the principles of subsidiarity and proportionality. It stresses, *inter alia*, that where opinions on a Commission proposal amount to non-compliance with the principle of subsidiarity and represent at least one-third of all the votes allocated to the member states' national parliaments and their chambers, the Commission shall review its proposal. The Commission is to present an annual report on subsidiarity and proportionality. All these provisions reflect German concerns, as does the acknowledgement by the convention to uphold non-interference in the internal organisation of the member-states. However, despite the various aims, there is no clear agreement over the use of the term and this definition is no clearer. The convention merely proposed to include it in policy making. Concerns with subsidiarity and flexibility reflect member-states' anxiety about overcentralisation. But there are differences between the British (unitary state) perception of seeing Westminster and Whitehall threatened and the German (federal state) vision of defending the competences of the *Länder*. While some progress, including from a German perspective, has been made, it remains to be seen how these vaguely defined rules would feature in the future constitutional treaty.

Overall, the convention has taken a number of progressive, if not far-reaching steps, on strengthening the institutional fabric, the nature of decision making and the division of competences (both horizontally and vertically) of the EU. Generally speaking what is envisaged will make the Council of Ministers more efficient, the European Commission stronger and the EP more important. These innovations sit well with the 'federal-minded' Germany. However, the convention has, in some instances, also sowed seeds for more national control over EU developments and introduced greater complexity with the introduction of the two new positions – the Office of the Council President and the European Foreign Minister. Before dealing more specifically with the implications of these two innovations, it is important to consider the policy areas addressed by the draft treaty, especially those over which the two newly created positions are given responsibily.

Policy areas

In the following I explore three clusters of policy areas: economic governance and social Europe; CFSP and ESDP; and JHA. These policy areas have emerged as the most important EU developments since 1995. We will start by considering German demands and convention recommendations in the area of economic governance and social Europe, as outlined in table 21.2.

The provisions of the draft constitution have been mixed from a German perspective. Both the SPD and CDU wanted to achieve a degree of harmonisation of tax rates, while the convention merely considered its 'approximation'. This outcome may be attributed to opposition from

Table 21.2 Economic governance and social Europe

SPD	*CDU*	*Convention*
Harmonisation of corporate tax, tax for capital returns, energy and VAT; uniform capital markets	Minimal harmonisation of taxation: harmonisation of eco-tax	Exclusive EU competence for monetary policy, exclusive member state competence for economic policy • Single representation of the Eurozone in international financial institutions; single spokes-person in international fora • Strengthen Commission's role in the SGP • Systematic involvement of EP in the Open Method of Coordination (OMC); approximation of tax rates
Social order in all of the EU. Return agricultural and re-distributive policies to the national level	Replace Structural and Cohesion Funds by a 'solidarity fund' with stronger burdens on recipient states; only minimal standards in employee protection	• Inclusion of notions of solidarity, equality, equal opportunities and democracy • Promotion of prosperity and sustainable development; promotion of full employment and high degree of social protection • Social matters as an area of shared competence, but better clarification on scope of EU competence • OMC more clearly defined • Recognition of the role of the Social Partners

countries such as the United Kingdom to tax harmonisation, for example. Consequently, only a diluted proposal with very limited progress towards harmonisation (e.g. on the administration of tax fraud) could be agreed upon. On the other hand, given the difficulties Germany had in synchronizing its economic policies, especially labour market mobility, with those of other member-states, and given the difference in approach to economic policy between Britain (*laissez-faire* orientation) and Germany and France (welfare-protection orientation), the decision that member-states would retain competences over economic (as opposed to monetary) policy suited German interests. It could thus be satisfied with the convention's provision that 'the Union shall adopt measures to ensure coordination of the economic, including employment policies, of the member-states, in particular by adopting broad guidelines for these policies'.[13] Though welcoming, Germany was not explicitly pushing for members of the single currency to decide and police economic guidelines and enforce the EU monetary policy without the involvement of states that were not in the Eurozone. Nor was it a strong advocate about Eurozone members appointing a 'Finance Minister' to represent the single currency. Both these points were more French-inspired. A strengthening of the Commission and EP's role in the GSP and the Open Method of Coordination, respectively, reflected German demands generally for greater powers of these two institutions. With regard to social policy, the convention stipulated that the Union might adopt initiatives to ensure the coordination of member-states' social policies. This fell short of SPD demands for a stronger EU role in governing European social policy. Clearly, coordination is not harmonisation, and neither do all the well-meaning references to equality, solidarity and prosperity amount to concrete measures to be taken at the EU level.

With results being mixed on economic and social policy, did German demands fare better on foreign, security and defence policy?

As table 21.3 indicates, the text delivered by the convention is modest in approach. It is more ambitious than the conservative preferences of a sceptical CDU, but falls short of the more progressive preferences of the SPD. The single office of High Representative and External Affairs Commissioner, however, reflects the joint Chirac–Schröder proposal. By and large progress on CFSP is limited. A number of statements by the convention indicate that there are still basic disagreements over a CFSP's aims. To some extent this should not be surprising, given that the work of the convention coincided with the one of the deepest splits

Table 21.3 Common foreign, security and defence policy

SPD	*CDU*	*Convention*
Strengthening of EU responsibility in foreign policy and in development aid policy	'Enhanced Cooperation' and opt-outs are important CFSP must remain outside the first pillar Development of the Rapid Reaction Force into a EU Army as crisis management forces outside the provisions of the Alliance with complementary political and military structures and capabilities	Group together all provisions relating to external action in the Constitutional Treaty Single person in roles of High Representative and Commissioner for External Affairs Creation of specific External Action Council, establishing a focal point within the Commission for all external issues dealt with by the Commission Instruments: joint initiatives, QMV. The EU to have legal personality and thus sign international treaties Single representation of the Eurozone in international financial institutions; single spokesperson in international fora
Comprehensive security concept for CFSP, capacity to act without NATO, EU conflict prevention and crisis management policies	Integration of national military units into EU security structures Military and civil space policy and common armament policy with common acquisition policy (EU Armament Agency)	Expansion of the Petersberg tasks; increase coherence, resources and efficiency in carrying out operations; more flexibility in decision-making and action; response to the terrorist threat via greater solidarity; introduce a solidarity clause; promote enhanced cooperation between certain member states; set up an EU Armaments and Strategic Research Agency

the EU has experienced, namely the Iraq conflict. Partly, it also reflects great determination on the part of member-states to protect national interests and to avoid the erosion of sovereignty in a field where realist perspectives of 'survival' still play a major role, and where distrust often outweighs the element of trust for closer cooperation. The actual statements are mostly bland in nature, entailing general aims, and long-term perspectives, and are short of radical, concrete, or decisive measures, as the following (selective) examples, taken from the working groups of the European convention, demonstrate:

> Member states shall consult one another on any foreign and security policy issue, in particular before taking any action, which is of general interest in order to determine a common approach. Member states shall ensure, through the convergence of their actions, that the Union is able to assert its interests and values on the international scene and show mutual solidarity. They shall refrain from action contrary to the Union's interests or likely to impair its effectiveness.[14]

At best, these are general guidelines rather than specific policies or aims. Similar vague references occur with regard to a common defence policy:

> The common security and defence policy shall be an integral part of the CFSP, providing the Union with an operational capability drawing on national assets civil and military. The Union may use them on missions outside the Union for peacekeeping, conflict prevention and strengthening international security in accordance with the principles of the UN Charter. CFSP shall include the progressive framing of a common defence policy. This will lead to a common defence, when the European Council so decides, not prejudicing the security and defence policy of certain member states and respecting member states' NATO obligations. In the execution of closer cooperation on mutual defence, the participating member states shall work in close cooperation with NATO.[15]

No proposal is made that would commit Britain and France to exchange their seats on the UN Security Council seats in a favour of a single EU seat, an outcome favoured by Germany.

A further restriction contained in the convention text is that CFSP decisions (both foreign and security matters and defence issues) shall be adopted by unanimity in the European Council and the Council of Ministers: 'The European Council may unanimously decide that the Council of Ministers should act by qualified majority voting.'[16] The British and French insistence on national a veto in European foreign policy making undermines Germany's belief that the EU can work effectively on a world stage only if it ends the system where foreign policy has to be agreed upon unanimously. However, the convention accepted the Franco-German proposal for enhanced cooperation, which would allow a group of EU countries to form a mini-defence bloc with common security guarantees. The Belgian initiative of April 2003, involving the French, German and Luxembourg governments, was a step in this direction. This initiative sought to create a separate European military headquarter with its own planning facilities.[17] More needs to be done on common EU defence for it to establish a genuine military character, although the convention's solidarity clause for mutual defence could be instrumental in promoting further common action towards a common defence. This clause stipulates: 'The Union and its members shall act jointly in a spirit of solidarity if a member state is the victim of terrorist attack or natural or man-made disaster.'[18] This clause is linked to developments in JHA, to which I now turn.

As illustrated in table 21.4, agreements reached in the convention in the area of JHA correspond closely to the policy preferences of both the SPD and CDU. Given national sensitivities and traditions in this field, Germany, like most other EU countries, was happy to sign up to the general tenor of the following statements:

> The Union shall constitute an area of freedom, security and justice: (a) by adopting European laws and European framework laws intended to approximate national laws; (b) by promoting mutual confidence between the member states, on the basis of mutual recognition of judicial and extra-judicial decisions; and (c) by operational cooperation between the member states, including police, customs and other services specialising in the prevention and detention of criminal offences.[19]

There is general agreement among member states on the important issues and necessity for stronger cooperation.

This brief survey of German influence over a range of issues offers a generally positive picture, indicating that Germany's preference for progressive integrationist development found recognition in the text of the convention. However, there were also aspects where German demands fell short or were compromised by the counter-demands of other member states, e.g. the position of a Council President. In these areas, a strengthening of the national component in EU decisions can be observed, with a subsequent promotion of intergovernmentalism in EU decision-making. One such key aspect, and one which is potentially laden with controversy, concerns the proposal for a Council President and a European Foreign Minister.

Table 21.4 Justice and home affairs

SPD	*CDU*	*Convention*
Better cooperation of police work, including with accession states; strengthening of EUROPOL Stronger judicial cooperation in criminal law Citizens' right to appeal to ECJ EP control; ensure data protection Stronger cooperation in internal security and immigration	Uniform conditions for asylum seekers In civil law, common legal bases concerning areas of transnational importance	Asylum, refugees and displaced persons as well as visas should be adopted by QMV under the co-decision procedure Approximation in several areas of criminal law by the adoption of minimum rules, as well as approximation in certain aspects of criminal procedure

The issue of presidents for the Council and the Commission

Anglo-French calls for a powerful EU President to bolster the European Council and to be the public face and political driving force of EU integration were also contained in the Franco-German joint declaration to the convention, but involved a compromise solution. Schröder was not opposed in principle to a full-time Council President, as he felt that the current EU presidency, which rotates every six months between different member states,[20] did not work. However, he insisted on balancing the powers of the Council President with the powers of the European Commission, which the German government, in any case, wanted to see strengthened in terms of becoming a real EU government beside the national governments. Thus the Franco-German proposal constituted a compromise between the German wish for a stronger, democratically legitimised Commission president and the French emphasis on the Council as the locus of national preferences. Despite the French concessions regarding the enhanced role of the Commission, the media interpreted this compromise as a French victory, not least because the wording of the proposal differed between the two versions.[21] Thus, the German edition called for a 'strengthening' of the Commission, while the French form merely mentioned its 'confirmation'.

The Franco-German proposal for a Council President, who would chair the European Council and help to set the strategic agenda,[22] polarised EU member-states. Smaller countries, such as the Netherlands and Finland, opposed the introduction of the Council President, and if it were to happen, desired to limit his/her authority as much as possible for fear of big-power domination. The smaller countries, with the exception of Denmark, tended to prefer a supranational solution enhancing the European Commission's role. However, the Franco-German proposal found support from the British government, which was important, as much depends on agreement between the 'big three'. Prime Minister Blair strongly supported the proposed Presidency of the Council, while indicating his concern about the Commission's greater role in economic policy. The proposal for a Council President was also supported by Spain and Sweden. In a spirit of compromise, the presidium of the convention offered a form of wording that might satisfy some of the criticisms from the smaller states. It read: 'The President of the European Council shall ensure the external representation of the Union, without prejudice to the responsibilities of the president of the European Commission and the Minister of Foreign Affairs.'[23]

In practice, it will not be easy to separate the roles and competences of the two Presidents and the Foreign Minister. The latter's task would be to develop and represent a common European foreign policy. The convention states that the Foreign Minister shall contribute through his/her proposals to the development of the CFSP, which he/she shall carry out as mandated by the Council. The Foreign Minister will chair the Foreign Affairs Council. However, the convention also states that the President of the European Council shall represent the Union in the wider world on CFSP issues, chair the European Council, drive forward its work, facilitate cohesion and consensus and present a report to the EP after each meeting.

It these issues, as well many others raised in the convention, which will have to be finalised in the 2004 IGC, where a stark choice will have to be made between moving in a more intergovernmental or supranational direction.[24] In the past, only a combination of the two methods has enabled the Union to make progress towards deepened integration. Excessive moves in either direction could therefore jeopardise the progressive political integration of the EU. Consequently, it remains important to maintain an overall balance between the two.

Conclusion

Germany has had a number of painful experiences since 1990, in both the domestic and external arenas. Domestically it has suffered from anaemic economic growth, high levels of unemployment, the ever-present threat of deflation and a protracted economic and social reform process. These factors have contributed towards a more inward-looking and self-interested Germany. Externally, it has witnessed both the joys and anguishes of engagement in international crisis situations. Joys in that Germany was able to free itself, albeit partially, from the shackles of a pacifist legacy in the Kosovo conflict, and to pursue an expanding engagement in international peace keeping tasks. Anguish in that Germany felt misunderstood over its reluctance to support the United States in the second Iraqi conflict, and over the lack of recognition or appreciation it has received for its contribution in its conflict prevention and peace-keeping endeavours in various parts of the world. This experience has been a sobering one for a country that is still in the process of finding normalcy and an appropriate external role in crisis management involvement. It has also left Germany with two other problems. One is the unenviable task of having to repair the most fundamental rift in German–US relations since 1949. The other is the need to overcome a deep-seated split within the EU caused by the Iraqi conflict,[25] and to breathe new life into a EU faced with the challenges of enlargement, globalisation and the war on terrorism.

There can be little doubt that its new-found independence, geographic position and size factor, together with its economic difficulties, have had an effect on Germany's relations with the EU. But are these sufficient reasons to undermine a long-held dictum that 'all German governments from Adenauer on have almost religiously held to the belief that EU interests and German interests coincide'?[26] Charlie Jeffrey and William Paterson are inclined to say 'yes' to this question. Their argument is that the costs and burdens of unification have stretched the German paymaster role and conditioned its engagement in the EU. Therefore, in their words, 'the parameters of a possible German EU policy today have shifted away from the "congenial embeddedness of the past"'.[27] They claim that a 'tectonic shift' has occurred in which German and EU politics are drifting apart, thereby changing the relation of Germany to the process of EU integration. For William Chandler, 'politically, an unanticipated consequence has been a growing perception of an incompatibility between EU advances in integration and national [German] needs'.[28]

Although there is some truth in these arguments, nonetheless we have to be careful to separate temporary or short-term changes from the continued underlying support for Germany's long-term commitment to greater (mostly federal) European integration. It is true that in the 2002 German elections, both the CDU/CSU candidate, Edmund Stoiber, and Chancellor Schröder voiced partial hesitations and irritation with EU policies that impinged on German priorities. But there are also indications of persistent and long-term commitments. For example, Germany has played a leading role in the process of EU integration, as it has done in the NATO enlargement process.[29] Evidence of a long-term support for the EU can be deduced from the contribution German actors have made to the European convention and the establishment of a European constitution. German leaders and the major political parties have consistently advocated some form of a federalist EU, and can claim to have successfully influenced the outcome of the convention on this point. Equally consistent with a federal model, they were able to influence the convention on a clear separation of competences between the regional, national and EU levels, and on a strengthening of the principle of subsidiarity. Thus, Germany still appears committed to deeper integration and can take some pride in the progressive, if not federalist, steps for further integration advanced by the European convention.

The fear after 1990 that Germany's role in the EU could change because of its central geopolitical position in Europe, its large population and economic strength seems therefore to be unconfirmed. Germany's role in and contribution to the European convention have demonstrated once again that it prefers an even closer EU with further integration, rather than dominance or strident sovereignty claims. There are also indications, such as the joint proposal to the European convention, that the Schröder government is reviving Franco-German initiatives on important matters of European integration.[30] For both countries, as Peter Ludlow suggests, the Iraqi crisis has been a bruising reminder of their limited powers, and therefore encourages them in 2004 'to accept an EU constitution worthy of the name'.[31] On the other hand, one of the positive consequences of the Iraqi conflict has been the development of closer cooperation between Germany, France and Russia, a fact already recognised in the convention text: 'the Union shall develop a special relationship with neighbouring states, aiming to establish an area of prosperity and good neighbourliness, founded on the values of the Union and characterised by close and peaceful relations based on cooperation.'

Overall, German objectives continue to shape the EU in a supranational rather than intergovernmental direction, to ensure that the enlarged EU is a success and to use the EU as a vehicle for transmitting peace and stability to central and eastern Europe, as well as to the wider world.

Notes

1 I would like to acknowledge the assistance of Ms Katja Mirwaldt in the collection of the data for this chapter.

2 For a review of Germany's relations with the European Union, see Emil Kirchner, 'Germany and the EU: From Junior to Senior Role', in Gordon Smith, William Paterson and Stephen Padgett (eds), *Developments in German Politics* (London: Macmillan, 1996), pp. 156–72.

3 Roland Sturm and Heinrich Pehle, *Das neue deutsche Regierungssystem* (Opladen: Leske & Budrich, 2001).

4 Foreign Minister Joschka Fischer, 'From Confederacy to Federation – Thoughts on the Finality of EU Integration', Humboldt University, Berlin, May 2000.

5 To some extent the text of this speech was repeated and further elaborated in a speech given on the occasion of the presentation of the German–British 2000 Award, London, 24 January 2003.

6 Tony Blair, 'Europe's Political Future,' Speech given to the Polish Stock Exchange, Warsaw, 6 October 2000, at www.fco.gov.uk.

7 See especially President Johannes Rau, 'Unity in Diversity: What Political Form for the EU?', Speech delivered on the occasion of the Herbert Quandt Foundation's seventh Europaforum, Hotel Adlon, Berlin, 16 November.

8 The European convention consisted of 105 members: a president (Valéry Giscard d'Estaing), two vice-presidents (Giuliano Amato and Jean-Luc Dehaene), fifteen government representatives of the existing member states, thirty national parliamentary representatives of the existing member states, sixteen members of the EP, two members of the European Commission, and thirty-nine representatives of the thirteen candidate member-states (without the right to vote). In addition, thirteen observers were eligible to attend.

9 Bundeskanzleramt, 'Deutsch-französischer Beitrag zur institutionellen Architektur der Europäischen Union', *Pressemitteilung Nr. 21* (April

2003), at www.bundeskanzler.de–7698.459668/Deutsch-französischer-Beitrag-zur-instiutionel … htm.

10 Not included were the various oral contributions that German representatives of the convention made during the proceedings.

11 The draft constitution is reproduced by Democracy-forum Secretariat, *Reader Friendly Edition of the Constitution* (11 June 2003), at www.democracy-forum@europarl.eu.int.

12 The official text of the convention was that 'The Council of Ministers shall, jointly with the European Parliament, enact legislation and carry out policy-making and coordinating functions', *ibid.*

13 *Ibid.*

14 *Ibid.*

15 *Ibid.*

16 *Ibid.*

17 See Judy Dempsey, 'France and Germany Seek to Water Down European Defence Plan', *Financial Times*, 28 April 2003.

18 Democracy-forum Secretariat, *Reader Friendly Edition of the Constitution.*

19 *Ibid.*

20 For a review of the rotating EU presidency see Emil J. Kirchner, *Decision-Making in the European Community: The Council Presidency and European Integration* (Manchester: Manchester University Press, 1992).

21 Daniel Dombey and Quentin Peel, 'Convention Flak Obscures a Quiet EU Revolution', *Financial Times*, 22 January 2003.

22 The Chair of the different ministerial councils will still rotate between all twenty-five members, and the European Council can decide that a member-state should preside over a Council formation, except foreign affairs, for at least one year.

23 Democracy-forum Secretariat, *Reader Friendly Edition of the Constitution.*

24 Karel de Gucht, 'The European Commission: Countdown to Extinction?', *Journal of European Integration*, 25:2 (2003), pp. 165–8.

25 The divide over the Iraq conflict was most explicit in the declaration by eight European states, in a letter to the *Wall Street Journal* on 3 January 2003, expressing support for a US war on Iraq. This included five existing EU member-states: Denmark, Italy, Portugal, Spain and the United Kingdom.

26 Klaus Goetz, 'Integration Policy in a Europeanised State: Germany and the Intergovernmental Conference', *Journal of European Public Policy*, 3:1 (1996), pp. 23–44.

27 Charlie Jeffrey and William Paterson, 'Germany and European Integration: Beyond the Stable State?', unpublished manuscript.

28 William M. Chandler, 'The Europeanization of National Politics? The 2002 National Elections in France and Germany', Paper presented at the annual meeting of the EU Studies Association, Nashville, TN, 15–17 May 2003.

29 See Simon Bulmer, Charlie Jeffery and William E. Paterson, *Germany's European Diplomacy: Shaping the Regional Milieu* (Manchester: Manchester University Press, 2000) and Henning Tewes, *Germany, Civilian Power and the New Europe: Enlarging NATO and the European Union* (New York: Palgrave, 2002).

30 See, for example, 'Restarting the Franco-German Motor', *Economist*, 18 January 2003.

31 Peter Ludlow, 'Britain's European policy at Crisis Point', *Financial Times*, 27 May 2003.

22

Community breakdown? Germany, NATO and the guns of September

Mary N. Hampton

Germany has been one of the key members of NATO since its accession to the alliance through the Paris Peace Treaty in 1955. From the beginning, the Federal Republic's membership in NATO performed two critical and complementary tasks: it has grounded German security and democratic identity in the transatlantic relationship; and it has provided Germany with security and an avenue of influence through the Alliance. First, the German–US relationship has been the cornerstone of NATO's success during the Cold War and after. That relationship fundamentally changed German interests and identity. From the 1950s onward, the United States specifically strove to forge a positive identity between itself and West Germany, and to set a stable foundation for the growth of democracy in West Germany. These objectives were met with great success and West Germany evolved into a stable western democracy anchored in the European Community and NATO, the core institution of the transatlantic area. Revealing of the success of postwar transatlantic efforts, Peter Merkl reported in 1999 that a majority of Germans, especially those under the age of fifty, believe that Germany was liberated in 1945, as opposed to being defeated. He observed further that Germany now possesses an 'identity imbued with Western-style, liberal democratic values'.[1] Second, throughout the Cold War, not only did NATO serve West Germany's security interests, but Bonn was able to influence the Allied agenda in important ways. Thus, the Federal Republic both benefited from its security relationship and directly influenced the direction of Allied policy.[2]

This dual success story persisted through the period of Cold War collapse and German unification. NATO thrived. However, at the end of 2002, this half-century relationship – the foundation of NATO's success – appears to be under severe duress. German–US relations have not appeared so tattered since the end of the Second World War. In contrast, the evolution of the EU's autonomous ESDP appears ascendant as the focus for pursuing German security interests in Europe.[3]

The purpose of this chapter is threefold. First, I briefly trace the evolution of Germany's role in NATO, in terms of how West German security interests were met and furthered through NATO, and the positive identity that arose between Germany and the United States through the relationship. I then discuss how both aspects of that bargain were maintained into the post-Cold War period, through the first Bush and the Clinton Administrations in the United States, and through the generational and ideological changing of leadership in Germany in 1998.

Second, I explain how and why this once-steady relationship is eroding. On the one hand, the positive identity complex has begun to unravel, and it has done so precipitously during the current Bush and Schröder administrations. Whereas the left-of-centre coalition government led by Chancellor Gerhard Schröder maintained the positive transatlantic identity through the second Clinton Administration, despite many predictions to the contrary, that same government has had more trouble relating to the Bush Administration, and vice versa. The reasons are twofold. First, mutual mistrust has arisen in the relationship. The United States has become increasingly unilateralist and unpredictable in the eyes of many Germans and other Europeans. These perceptions of unpredictability emanate from specific Bush policies, but also from the general trend in US foreign policy away from the Euro-Atlantic core identity that anchored US foreign policy after 1947 and for the first decade of the post-Cold War period in NATO, when questions were already being raised about that centredness. In turn, the Bush Administration openly questioned German behaviour. The 2002 NATO Prague summit revealed the diverging security interests between Germany and the United States and the residual mistrust that followed the 2002 German election where Chancellor Schröder won a narrow victory, in part by taking a strong stand against the Bush Administration's plans to wage war against Iraq. Finally, the erosion can also be attributed in part to a more assertive united Germany, one that is more willing to strike its own position than was true during the Cold War, but sometimes still breeds mistrust among others when it does so.

Second, and relatedly, the unravelling of the NATO relationship is arising from the evolution in Germany of a new security identity that is tied more to Germany's European identity, which clearly emphasises a 'security governance' approach to international conflict, and is housed in the EU rather than NATO. The current Bush Administration's policies are strengthening the pre-existing European impulse to develop its autonomous defence and foreign policy architectures. As I will argue, while the lessons of NATO's Balkan interventions, and especially Operation Allied Force, led Germany and other EU partners to pursue their own security identity more diligently, that process has gained momentum since 2000.

Third, I assess the possibilities for NATO's future and Germany's place in it. It should be noted, for example, that the demise of NATO has been forecast at any number of moments in the years since 1955, such as during the early 1980s when there was transatlantic discord over the issue of stationing US medium-range missiles in West Germany, or even in the 1950s, when President Dwight Eisenhower's decision to focus on nuclear weapons as the Alliance's main military buttress against the Soviet threat led to rancour between Germany and the United States. NATO always survived and German–US relations always rebounded. That may well be the case today. However, a novel combination of factors suggests that Germany's relationship to NATO and the United States has become precarious, and that the cumulative effect does indeed make for an uncertain future.

The rise of trans-Atlantia

The integration of West Germany into the West after the Second World War was considered paramount by policy makers in London and Washington, and by West German policy makers like Chancellor Konrad Adenauer. That process of integration was kindled by the growing Soviet threat, but also by the desire, especially on the part of United States and West German decisions makers, to democratise West Germany and make it a reliable and like-minded democratic ally. The main channels for this integration effort were NATO and the emerging EC.

The process of integrating West Germany into the West and the US-led security order entailed the creation of a sense of positive identity between the new allies. That construction was largely successful and not only facilitated the emergence of West German democracy, but ensured that the West German democratic identity was tied to NATO and to the United States.[4] NATO thus fulfilled a critical political and socialisation role in grounding West German domestic identity as a democracy in the transatlantic relationship.

NATO also performed a traditional alliance role in defending West Germany against the Soviet threat and guaranteeing that security through an extended US deterrent. In this security cocoon, democracy could and did flourish. Beyond that, owing to the liberal institutional nature of the NATO relationship, West German policy makers were able to place their own national interests on the NATO agenda, thereby benefiting even more.[5] For example, West German *Ostpolitik*, constructed largely under and pursued wholeheartedly by Chancellor Willy Brandt in 1969, was at heart a revisionist foreign policy that sought nothing less than the overcoming of the postwar settlement in order to achieve German unification. While the policy struck fear into many western hearts regarding a more assertive Germany, the fact was that *Ostpolitik* was grounded in and justified through NATO's Harmel policy, and through the Allied pledge made to West Germany in 1955 that the Allies would support German efforts at unification as long as they were pursued in 'peace and freedom'.[6]

The success of NATO at the Cold War's end

On an October day in 1989, US President George Bush's foreign policy of wholeheartedly supporting German unification moved German Foreign Minister Genscher to exclaim to his American counterpart, Secretary of State James Baker: 'It's a moving moment for our nation. Thank you for what you've done for Germany since World War II, particularly for Berlin.'[7] Such sentiment regarding US support for unification was expressed by Chancellor Helmut Kohl on any number of public occasions and in his memoirs, and was also expressed in German public opinion. The historic moment, and the US reaction to it, reinforced the relationship of positive identity between Germany and the United States that developed mainly through the NATO relationship.

When Baker reiterated the US pledge to support German unification in a watershed speech in Berlin 1989, he advised NATO to proceed building a 'new trans-Atlanticism for a new era' by developing its identity as a political community of democracies. In the process, Bush called on united Germany to become a 'partner in leadership' alongside the United States.[8] The Bush administration thereby again highlighted fifty years of positive identity formation between the Germans and United States through NATO, and reinforced NATO's role as the anchor for defending and sustaining German democracy.[9]

In fact, the next years of NATO's evolution as a political community in the 1990s once again helped anchor the united and enlarged Germany. Not only did the emphasis on NATO as a political community help ease the alliance past the moment where many were questioning its relevance given the Soviet collapse; NATO was essentially reborn as the key institution in Europe to welcome new democracies into its fold and to defend against any instability on the continent that could arise with the collapse of the Cold War order. While EU security integration and enlargement picked up steam toward the end of the 1990s, NATO continued to fulfil the security needs of Germany and Europe.

The focus on NATO's role as the safe harbour for European democracy promoted German security goals in many ways. First, the rewards of NATO membership and democracy that it enjoyed through its accession in the 1950s enabled Germany to become a beacon of democracy for the struggling new democracies to its east.[10] In fact, NATO enlargement, at least the first round, was promoted by German leaders and was clearly in the national interest. Second, by opening NATO to new members, Germany would find itself surrounded by allies for the first time in history. Third, enlarging the alliance also meant that the new neighbourhood for united Germany was secured through NATO and that any instability in the region potentially aroused by the Soviet retreat and German unification was preempted. In other words, united Germany's security needs were easily accommodated as NATO itself now moved eastward. Fourth, a united Germany was able to carve a niche for itself in the enlargement process by playing an advocacy role for future members such as Poland. Advocating Poland's case for membership allowed German policy makers to enhance their prestige in Poland (and throughout eastern and central Europe), to enable a climate of improving relations between the two countries, to enrich the already emerging trading relationship and to redeem past German behaviour in Poland and throughout the region.

The only downside to NATO's first post-Cold War enlargement was the potential havoc it could play in Germany's relations with Russia. German leaders therefore played a key role in crafting the historic 1997 NATO–Russia Founding Act, which sought to create more transparency and cooperation between Russia and NATO. In short, as had been true throughout the Cold War period, Germany continued to contribute significantly to and benefit from its membership in NATO. As a result, the German consensus that embraced NATO throughout the Cold War actually deepened in the 1990s, and the pivotal German–US relationship remained positive and stable.

The German consensus regarding NATO was further tested and then reinforced in the 1990s through Allied policies regarding instability in the Balkans. From the moment that German leadership angered many in Europe by insisting on recognising Croatian autonomy in 1992, to the actual NATO military intervention into Kosovo in 1999, the transatlantic security relationship was tested again and again by the ongoing crises in the Balkans. The tortured debate about what role the UN and NATO should play to counter the ongoing Serb aggression in the region frayed the Allied relationship in the first three years of the Clinton Administration. The crisis was difficult for Germany as well in that Berlin had to make historic decisions regarding military intervention in general and for 'out-of-area' conflicts in particular. Finally, through the execution of Operation Deliberate Force in Bosnia in 1995, and then Operation Allied Force in 1999, NATO under US leadership made unprecedented military interventions that reaffirmed the Allied commitment to European stability and to democratic values. In other words, the emphasis on NATO as a democratic community was now expanded to reincorporate the alliance's military mission, although this time under revised conditions. The military capabilities of the alliance were tested for the first time, and were invoked to protect human rights and uphold democratic values, as well as to erase instability from the continent. In short, NATO's new set of missions in Europe resonated with the themes raised in 1989 and conformed well to the security interests and political values of Germany and the integrating Europe.

The NATO interventions also helped construct a new domestic consensus in Germany. The Cold War German domestic consensus that basically forbade a national military combat profile gave way in the 1990s to a new emerging consensus that allowed for German military intervention under very specific conditions and always in concert with its democratic allies. German membership in NATO therefore performed the very positive function of allowing the maturing united Germany to take its place on the European stage of great powers without arousing residual fears about a renationalised, aggressive Germany.

On the US side, from the first Bush Administration through President Bill Clinton's two terms in office, continuity was also maintained by the continued anchoring of the American security identity in NATO. Despite the emergence in the 1990s of the United States as the only remaining superpower and the increasingly global reach of its security profile, the transatlantic relationship remained the rhetorical and substantive anchor for US security identity. From Bush's support of German unification and his continued emphasis on multilateralism as the policy of choice for transAtlantic relations, to Baker's Berlin speech, to Clinton's endorsement of NATO enlargement and NATO intervention in the Balkans, the US commitment remained firm.[11] Germany and other European NATO members remained comfortable relying on NATO as the core security architecture in Europe, and on the United States as the leader, owing to Washington's consistent behaviour and signalling of US interests throughout the decade.

NATO unravelling? German misgivings about trans-Atlantia

While I argued that NATO and Germany's commitment to it thrived in the 1990s, there were signs of discord that became manifest after the American Presidential election in 2000. Since that time, the United States has been in the process of delegitimising its half-century role as the leader of the western democratic community of nations through NATO. The newly elected Bush Administration began to unhinge US security policy and identity from its transatlantic foundation and focus on global issues. In so doing, the new Administration accelerated the emergence of an autonomous European security and political identity that was already under way. On the other hand, some Germany observers argue that Schröder's policy of unilaterally and publicly rejecting any participation in a war with Iraq harmed the EU as well as NATO, and left Germany increasingly isolated in both. In any case, the potential unravelling of the half-century transatlantic bargain, or what I have called 'trans-Atlantia', was all too apparent in the German–US relationship by 2002, and was already being played out in the NATO relationship. At the nexus of these developments lies NATO's uncertain future and Germany's eroding support.

Planting the seeds of discord in the 1990s

The apparent continuity of the 1990s also contained the seeds of change in German–NATO and German–US relations. While Germany and the

United States remained committed to NATO in the 1990s, another trend was shaping German security policy and identity. In the wake of German unification and Soviet collapse, the EU was rapidly pushing to complete its integration process by creating a CFSP. Keeping a united Germany embedded in European institutions was a high priority in this process or a way for Europe to 'flee forward'.[12] The Maastricht Treaty of 1992 had already called for the creation of a CSFP. By the mid-1990s, another set of concerns arising from the ongoing Balkan crises fuelled EU efforts to develop a security and foreign policy apparatus and identity. Both the lack of agreement among EU members as to what policy should be pursued in the Balkans, and the increasingly evident technological disparity between US military capabilities and those of the EU states reinforced the desire to strengthen the EU security component. The European drive toward a common security policy was emboldened with the St Malo Agreement of 1998 between Great Britain and France. Significantly, the British joined political forces with the French for the first time in this process to declare that the EU must be able to marshal autonomous European military forces for future military operations on the European continent. The change from previous discussions, and where such forces would be housed in NATO under the European Security and Defence Identity (ESDI), was that the Europeans now invoked autonomy from NATO where such action is deemed necessary.

This process was deepened with the NATO Operation Allied Force intervention in Kosovo during 1999. While the event revealed the success of the transatlantic community being able to act collectively, it ironically also stimulated further the emerging discordant tones on both sides of the Atlantic concerning military capabilities and the direction of NATO policy. Many members of the US Defense Department, and especially members of Congress, renewed long-standing US complaints about Europe's lack of contribution to NATO's military missions. The tenor took a particularly negative tone as many dismissed European military capabilities, particularly in light of the increasingly evident superiority of US technology. Such arguments found even more resonance and sympathy in the current Bush Administration than was the case during the Clinton and first Bush tenures in office.

Reaction to Operation Allied Force aroused negative feelings in Europe as well. The ever-present complaints about US condescension toward Europe and the lack of willingness to credit European members of NATO with the contributions they have brought to the Alliance grew after Operation Allied Force, as did the determination to enhance European security capabilities. What was different between European reactions this time and during previous bouts of doubt during the Cold War was that a consensus was growing for an autonomous European security profile, alongside of, but separate from, NATO. As happened during previous periods when the Europeans appeared to challenge the preeminence of NATO in European security, Washington's reaction was negative until reassured during the 2000 Nice EU summit that the ESDP would be put into play only upon NATO's decisions to sit out a given crisis in Europe. During this period, US Secretary of Defense William Cohen warned of an independent EU making NATO a 'relic of the past'. By the end of the Nice Summit the EU managed to assuage Washington's concerns, and the Clinton Administration left office with the NATO relationship, and especially US–German relations, basically sound.

The growing importance of the EU as an economic unit and as an alternative identity anchor for Germany and other European states must finally be considered. It was clear by the 1990s that the EU was in fact well on its way to creating an economic counterweight to the US, and that the EU was becoming more aggressive politically in working to forge a distinct European identity. The introduction of the euro in 1999 was accompanied by much rhetoric throughout Europe proclaiming the European currency as a counterweight to the US dollar. This was as true in Germany as elsewhere.[13] Because of its role at the centre of European economic and monetary integration, Germany became a much more self-confident, sometimes assertive player in the European and transatlantic contexts. While such developments in the EU were officially welcomed in Washington, voices of resentment were also raised. The chorus of discontent was greatly fuelled by the move by the EU toward the end of the 1990s to move in the direction of security integration.

The current deterioration of the alliance

To understand just how quickly NATO has been declining as the security organisation of first choice in Europe, one need only to consider Thomas Friedman's observation in November 2002, just prior to the second wave of NATO enlargement, that NATO had to be written off as a serious security alliance; instead, the 'old NATO' should be replaced by a serious military alliance that consisted only of three English-speaking countries – the United States, the United Kingdom and Australia.[14] In poking fun at the NATO members, like Germany, who can only occasionally contribute their 'boutique skills' to common threats, Friedman diminishes NATO in a way that would have been dismissed as silly just a few years ago by serious observers of the transatlantic relationship. Such expressions reflect and feed further the current deterioration of the transatlantic security relationship. Behind the recent decline in the transatlantic security bargain lie the trends I discussed above, which remained important and were in fact accelerating. During and after the 2000 campaign and election, the Bush foreign policy team openly challenged the NATO consensus reached in the 1990s. From National Security Advisor Condoleeza Rice's now famous line during the campaign wherein she questioned US troops being placed in the position of peace-keepers walking children to kindergarten, to the Administration policy of trying to reorient NATO's mission away from European regional issues toward US global interests, the Eurocentric foundation of NATO's Strategic Concept and democratic enlargement were being displaced.

The events of 11 September rekindled hope in Europe that the Bush Administration would increasingly approach the global war on terrorism from a multilateralist perspective and that the transatlantic security relationship would again stand centre stage, especially since NATO invoked Article 5 after the attack. The hope was fleeting, for a number of reasons. US Defense Secretary Donald Rumsfeld made clear that the mission would determine the coalition for the United States; the Bush Administration would not allow the coalition to determine or hinder the mission. This was the direct expression of US lessons learned from Kosovo. NATO was too cumbersome; the European allies were so underdeveloped militarily, the United States would in future interventions keep control of the military strategy and operations, and call on coalition partners as needed.[15] The events of 11 September did not mitigate what many Germans and Europeans perceived as growing US unilateralism and arrogance.

Sympathy and empathy for the United States was initially widespread in Germany and Europe in the months after 11 September. The German government was quick to offer sympathy and support, NATO invoked Article 5 and German and other NATO members offered and carried through military and non-military assistance in Afghanistan. Even after the US–German falling out in 2002, the German government went ahead in offering to take over peace-keeping operations in Afghanistan. However, in Europe and Germany, American insistence that 11 September represented the 'guns of September', or the first shots of a long, 'hot' global war on terrorism was met with scepticism and growing public disenchantment with US policies.[16] Germans were particularly resistant to the Bush Administration's efforts to cast US war plans against Iraq as part of the war on terrorism. Instead of viewing US actions toward Iraq as linked to 11 September, the policy confirmed what many in Germany and Europe perceived as the continued unilateralist surge of Bush foreign policy since the 2000 presidential election.

Germany and other European states thus generally acted throughout 2002 to try and stop, or at least delay, a US preemptive war against Iraq. In Germany, such sentiments were expressed in public opinion and at the governmental level, and came to influence the national election. Public opinion polls taken in the 2002 election period showed upwards of 80 per cent of German respondents to be against Germany taking part in any war against Iraq. Polls also revealed that German public concern with terrorism as a major problem registered about 15 per cent, compared to the 82 per cent that worried about the economy.[17] While the CDU/CSU was quick after its electoral defeat to make a domestic political issue of Schröder's hard stance against war with Iraq, and the injurious effect it had on German–US relations, CSU candidate Edmund Stoiber himself played to the German public sentiment against war with Iraq in the waning days of the election.

Growing signs of discord in German–US security relations

The increasingly negative German perceptions of American foreign policy during 2001 and 2002 played out during the final stages of the 2002 German elections. Schröder's criticisms of Bush's policy toward Iraq and his declaration that Germany would not participate in or support a war against Iraq helped him eke out a victory over Stoiber. That such negative public sentiments against US policy existed in Germany and could be mobilised shocked many observers, as did the unprecedented move of a German mainstream incumbent candidate taking a clear stand against US foreign policy. The situation led to acrimony in German–US relations to the point where an American President refused to call the victorious German Chancellor to offer congratulations. Tension between US and German leaders was not unprecedented: tensions had run high between President Jimmy Carter and Chancellor Helmut

Schmidt and there had been a palpable and mutual distrust of Chancellor Brandt by the Nixon Administration. But much was different in 2002. It was not only the level of ill will that made the situation unique, but that it was played out in such a public fashion. It was not clear in 2002 exactly what shared threat perceptions would realign American and Germany security interests. The episode brought into keener focus an already problematical situation in contemporary NATO relations.

Indeed, Schröder's foreign policy stance reflected the new German approach to security and foreign policy that had developed throughout the 1990s and helped form the German consensus regarding military intervention. As German security identity began to find expression through the EU framework, the focus on *security governance* as the proper approach to security problems in Europe and abroad gained ground: where security objectives were best met by first employing a mix of non-military means, and turning to military tools only as a last resort. As shown in NATO's intervention in Kosovo, when military means were employed by necessity, and only after non-military efforts had failed, the objectives included norms and values that transcended narrowly defined national interests: Operation Allied Force was executed in a clear multilateral framework and in concert with Germany's democratic allies.

The German power that has emerged since unification has thus assumed a unique form. The current German domestic consensus regarding power projection continues to reflect sensitivity to the threat perceptions of others and historical lessons learned based on Germany's past misuse of national power.[18] Growing out of and away from the West German culture of reticence that formed the domestic consensus during the Cold War, the current German tendency is to be a willing participant in projecting power capabilities, but only after all non-military avenues have been closed and only for purposes that fulfil 'community' interests. While the German government in the end participated in Operation Allied Force wholeheartedly in 1999, it did so only after months of diplomatic efforts had failed to achieve peace, and even then only after many criticisms had been made regarding the US proclivity to resort too quickly to military interventionism.

Examining the still-forming German security identity during the growing transatlantic tensions that emerged in 2002 shows the same sort of German reasoning. The German government was clear and quick to support the US-led coalition intervention in Afghanistan in the aftermath of 11 September. The rationale given by the

Schröder–Fischer foreign policy team was that a direct attack has been made on a democratic ally and that the terrorist attack was also an assault on the western community of democracies. For example, Ludger Volmer, a Green member of the German Bundestag, and an advisor on foreign policy to Foreign Minister Joschka Fischer, observed in 2002 that changes since 1989 made German participation in military interventions sometimes necessary, and that sovereign Germany owed it to its democratic allies and the rest of the world to participate in military actions that were morally justified and multilaterally pursued, especially when such interventions no longer served the purposes of one bloc against the other, but of greater community good. Thus, Germany was morally obliged to participate in the military intervention in Kosovo against Serb aggression.[19] Finally, Volmer argued that terrorism posed a real threat to Germany and the rest of the world, and that Germany's participation in the US-led coalition against international terrorism was not a flight into militaristic adventurism, but a necessary component of a multi-pronged international effort to fight terrorism, and especially the political conditions that give it rise.

Problems regarding German support for US policy really began to emerge after Bush used the 'Axis of Evil' metaphor, when it became clearer that the US war on terrorism was going to be broadened in its scope and definition based on American perceptions and that the continued use of military power was going to be a policy centrepiece. According to the current German consensus regarding security policy and power projection, emerging US policy appeared overly muscular in the first instance, and increasingly based on narrowly defined national interests that did not pass the test of addressing a direct threat to national security nor had been submitted to evaluation based on collectively agreed-upon 'community' interests or values.

The US–German misadventure became a hot German domestic issue. While the CDU/CSU, still in opposition, made the worsening of US–German relations a wedge issue in domestic politics after the election, the conservative coalition parties were themselves sometimes ambivalent about Bush's Iraq policy during the campaign, especially at the end. For the most part, however, the CDU/CSU called for closer US–German security cooperation during the election and called on Germany to take its rightful place alongside the United States in leadership. Since then, they have made the issue one that accuses Schröder and his government of undermining Germany's most important security alliance and ally. Many critics of the Schröder government have chastised it for basically behaving in a way that casts doubt on German reliability as an ally. Michael Stürmer argues, for example, that Schröder's action not only alienated Washington and undermined Germany's position of influence in NATO, but also spawned the emergence of a new *Entente cordiale* against the unreliable Germany between France and Great Britain.[20] While some observers argue that Germany and France are actually being drawn closer in response to transAtlantic tensions, thereby strengthening EU security identity in the core states, Stürmer claims that the Schröder government recreated German Wilhelminianism, where Germany, through clumsy diplomacy, once again isolated itself in Europe. Christian Hacke also offers criticism, but states the case somewhat differently. He chastises the Schröder government's undiplomatic and clumsy presentation of its reservations concerning US action in Iraq, thereby 'risking the central interest of German foreign policy – the transatlantic relationship with the US'. Yet, Hacke argues that the German way could and should have become the European way, since there really had developed a gulf between US and European perceptions of and approaches to global security issues. Had Berlin properly consulted with and lined up European support, Europe might have presented a front against US unilateralism; instead, 'the Schröder administration has become unreliable and incalculable itself'.[21]

As the domestic debate in Germany concerning its security identity continues, a number of factors will come into play. Not only is NATO's role in addressing German security interests at issue, so too is the very foundation of the positive US–German relationship that has survived for over a half century. The downturn in US–German security relations reflects in part the maturing of German democracy as a sovereign state that is and will be less and less dependent on the United States for its security and for its confidence as a democracy. German democratic identity is increasingly housed in the EU. Moreover, Germany increasingly questions the US social and economic model. Again, this is not a new phenomenon. Doubts about the United States as a social or political model have always found expression on both the German left and right.[22] A number of factors distinguish the current criticisms. First, the lack of the Bush Administration's commitment to multilateralism, which lies at the heart of the transatlantic bargain, is being criticised much more than was true of previous Administrations. Second, Bush's foreign policy has made doubtful Washington's willingness to continue leading internationally according to the postwar norm of the multilateral security governance of the transatlantic community. Third, the many social and political issues that have long divided the transatlantic community, such as the US gun culture, death penalty and energy consumption, are being aggravated by the first two considerations and by a growing perception in Europe that the US democratic model is itself increasingly frayed, a position fuelled by events like the impeachment brought against Clinton and the unsettling experience of the 2000 presidential election.[23]

These increased doubts about American leadership in Europe are mirrored in the United States, with pointed questions about Europe's reliability as a partner for a global America. American accusations about 'Euro-wimps' are not new, but they have been voiced more frequently and by a wider range of policy makers and observers than previously. The recent wave of 'Euro-bashing' has been especially pronounced among those policy makers and pundits who indeed view the United States as a global power that ought not be constrained by the 'Europutians', but rather should compel them either to help the country carry its global burdens or stand aside.[24]

It is revealing that criticisms have been made about the Bush Administration that mirror those leveled at Schröder. Just as Schröder was criticised for being Wilhelminian, or as an unreliable or heavy-handed ally, so too was the Bush Administration. In its pressuring Europe regarding policy toward Iraq and in the Administration's overall dismissal of European contributions to US security interests, some see the Administration as Wilhelminian in the sense that its policies undermined the order that underwrote the transatlantic community. For example, Stephen Szabo argues: 'It is this hubris, which if followed for much longer, will undermine America's global leadership and isolate it in much the way that Kaiser Wilhelm isolated Germany before World War I.'[25]

From community to coalition? NATO's declining role in addressing German security interests and democratic identity

Changes in NATO during the 1990s clearly reflected and met German security interests and domestic values. The priority given to the democratic enlargement of Europe during the senior Bush and Clinton years gave centrality to the German role in Europe. The first NATO enlargement had direct consequences for German security, almost all of them positive. Members of the German government were pivotal in promoting that enlargement. The 2002 NATO summit in Prague revealed the extent to which Germany's position had been diminished through the actions of both the Schröder and Bush administrations. While the German government supported the latest round of enlargement in November 2002, where seven new members were invited,[26] it is clear that the second round had a different effect on the Alliance than the first.

There was little talk of democratic enlargement in the second round, and much less emphasis on the role of NATO as the central organisation for the transatlantic community of democracies in Europe. In fact, the second round of enlargement seems more reminiscent of the NATO enlargement phase of the Cold War when Turkey and Greece were admitted. That particular round was done clearly for strategic reasons in the bipolar competition between the United States and the Soviet Union. Once again in 2002, the Bush Administration talked mostly about the strategic value the new members would bring to the Alliance, particularly the new members' contribution to the global war on terrorism.[27] EU members spoke more of the preparation this round would be for EU enlargement rather than its positive impact on the transatlantic community of democracies. In short, the second round of NATO enlargement into eastern and southern Europe had little to do with the post-Cold War conception of NATO crafted throughout the 1990s. Seen in this light, current NATO enlargement enhances the transatlantic focus of Germany's security policy and democratic identity very little.

It was also made clear at the Prague Summit that the Bush Administration was attempting to push NATO in a direction that many in Washington had long advocated: to go 'out of area' and become a global player, especially in the United States' war on terrorism.[28] The ground was already prepared after 11 September, when NATO invoked Article 5 because of the terrorist attack. After that, the Bush administration continuously attempted to enlist European support for various US policies in the Middle East, including possible war against Iraq. To that end, and to counter EU efforts at developing its own rapid deployment forces, the Bush Administration was instrumental in introducing a NATO rapid deployment force of around 20,000 troops to be used in out of area missions.[29]

There are a number of serious problems with the latest US thrust; US leadership of NATO in the past has in the end resisted the temptation to try and force the Alliance to participate in American global missions. The reason for resisting is important: the European members of NATO, and especially Germany, have not been interested or willing; NATO has always been a regional organisation. Germans are no more ready now than in the past to change that focus, and given the Schröder government's reaction to possible war in Iraq during 2002, perhaps even less willing now than before. What was clear was that the United States, Germany and Europe did not share the same interests 'out of area' in the Middle East, precisely the reason that previous US leaders had resisted pressuring Europe. Where the Bush Administration saw itself as fighting a new global war on terrorism, Europeans worried about Washington's unilateralism or even hegemonic intentions.

Some authors argue that the 'out of area' precedent had already been set with the NATO intervention in Kosovo.[30] While this is technically correct, it misses the point of NATO's evolution and relevance in the 1990s. Through enlargement and the 'open door' policy to democratic enlargement in the European area, the former Yugoslavia was geographically and politically in bounds for NATO attention and action. It is no coincidence that a former republic of Yugoslavia has just been admitted into NATO. Through this evolving process, NATO members developed a shared sense of threat and common security interests. The United States was also thereby able to maintain its influence in the making of European security policy and on the direction of European integration, an objective that is surely still important.

The Prague Summit was celebrated by many in the United States as the beginning of a new sense of relevance for the Alliance in the post-September 11 world. While NATO welcomed new members who were eager to join, it did not construct a new consensus and showcased mostly specific US security interests.[31] In essence, the Bush prescription for NATO appeared very similar to the US approach used in the Middle East after September 11. NATO members would now contribute to US global policies in an *á la carte* fashion, where and when they were able and willing. NATO would therefore begin to reflect more the logic of a coalition than that of a community.[32]

A widespread concern is thus that the United States is increasingly and transparently attempting to use NATO instrumentally as an extension of US national interests, a function for which it was never intended, which past US leaders resisted and that is certain to leave certain European members like Germany more alienated. On the Bush Administration's part, the concern is that Germany and much of Europe is less than supportive of what Washington sees as a global threat to its interests.

Conclusions: whither NATO and German security identity?

NATO is never a finished product; it is always a work in progress. For over a half century, the NATO relationship and the US–German relationship have faltered at times, but always recovered and thrived. This chapter was written during one of the less auspicious historical moments for both relationships and discussed the main factors that led to the fractured consensus of 2002. Any number of trigger events could reinvigorate German–NATO and US–German relations. Regime change in Berlin could move German security interests closer to those being advocated by the United States and projected onto NATO. Likewise, regime change in Washington could refocus the United States back to the transAtlantic consensus of the 1990s. At great risk to internal party cohesion, Schröder could change course in German foreign policy to realign German and US policies. Again, even less likely, the Bush Administration could refocus US foreign policy toward its transatlantic cornerstone. In short, as in the past, circumstances could conspire to reaffirm NATO's resilience and primacy. Whether that will happen, or whether Germany, Europe and the United States have already travelled too far down different paths for NATO to rebound as the solid anchor of transatlantic security, remains to be seen.

Notes

1 Peter H. Merkl, 'Fifty Years of the German Republic', in Peter H. Merkl (ed.), *The Federal Republic at Fifty* (New York: New York University Press, 1999), p. 23.

2 See Mary N. Hampton, 'NATO at the Creation: US Foreign Policy and the Wilsonian Impulse', *Security Studies*, 4:3 (1995), pp. 610–56.

3 For an in-depth discussion of the evolution of the European security identity and policy, see Franco Algieri, 'Die Europäische Sicherheits- und Verteidigungspolitik', in Werner Weidenfeld (ed.), *Europa Handbuch* (Gütersloh: Verlag Bertelsmann Stiftung, 2002), pp. 585–601.

4 See Mary N. Hampton, 'Germany, the US, and NATO: Creating Positive Identity in Trans-Atlantia', *Security Studies*, 7:2 and 7:3 (1998/99) (special double issue), pp. 235–69 and G. John Ikenberry, *After Victory: Institutions, Strategic Restraint, and the Rebuilding of Order After Major Wars* (Princeton: Princeton University Press, 2001).

5 See Hampton, 'NATO at the Creation', and James Sperling, 'Less than Meets the Eye: A Reconsideration of German Hegemony', in Mary

N. Hampton and Christian Søe, (eds), *Between Bonn and Berlin: German Politics Adrift?* (Lanham, MD: Rowman & Littlefield, 1999), pp. 257–76.

6 Hampton, 'NATO at the Creation'.

7 James A. Baker, III, *The Politics of Diplomacy: Revolution, War and Peace 1989–1992* (New York: G. P. Putnam's Sons, 1995), p. 164.

8 *Ibid.*, p. 159.

9 *Ibid.*, p. 172.

10 See Hampton, 'Germany, the US, and NATO'.

11 For example, see discussion by Stephen Szabo, 'Bush II sollte von Bush I lernen', *Die Welt*, 25 October 2002.

12 On the CFSP, see James Sperling and Emil Kirchner, *Recasting the European Order: Security Architectures and Economic Cooperation* (Manchester: Manchester University Press, 1997); Emil Kirchner and James Sperling, 'Will Form Lead to Function? Institutional Enlargement and the Creation of a European Security and Defence Identity', *Contemporary Security Policy*, 21:1 (2000), pp. 23–45; Algieri, 'Die Europäische Sicherheits- und Verteidigungspolitik'; Mary N. Hampton and James Sperling, 'Positive/Negative Identity in NATO and the EU', *Journal of European Integration*, 24:4 (2002), pp. 281–302. On the CFSP and on Europe 'fleeing forward', see Elizabeth Pond, *The Rebirth of Europe* (Washington, DC: Brookings Institute, 1999), esp. p. 182.

13 Among others, see Werner Link, 'Deutschland als Europäische Macht' in Werner Weidenfeld (ed.), *Europa Handbuch* (Güterstoh: Verlag Bertelsmann Stiftung, 2002) , pp. 605–617, esp. p. 611.

14 Thomas Friedman, 'The New Club NATO', *New York Times*, 17 November 2002.

15 This US position obviously caused resentment in Europe. See discussion in Link, 'Deutschland als Europäische Macht', p. 614.

16 I use 'guns of September' in the same way Barbara Tuchman did for 1914: the outbreak of world war.

17 I thank Dieter Roth for sharing these numbers at the meeting of the German Studies Association, San Diego, CA, September, 2002.

18 See Mary N. Hampton, '"The Past, Present, and the Perhaps": Is Germany A 'Normal' Power?', *Security Studies*, 10:2 (2000/2001), pp. 179–202.

19 Ludger Volmer, 'Was bleibt vom Pazifismus – Überlegungen zu einer neuen Weltinnenpolitik', *Frankfurter Rundschau*, 7 January 2002.

20 Michael Stürmer, 'Adieu, Deutschland', *Die Welt*, 4 October 2002.

21 Christian Hacke, 'Foreign Policy of the Schröder/Fischer Administration: Interim Balance and Prospects', translation from *Aus Politik und Zeitgeschichte*, AICGS online, p. 13, at info@aicgs.org.

22 Concern regarding deterioration in German–US understanding can be found in many sources. See, for example, Werner Weidenfeld, *Kulturbruch*

mit Amerika? Das Ende transatlantischer Selbstverständlichkeit (Gütersloh: Verlag Bertelsmann Stiftung, 1996).

23 For example, see Peter Merkl, *A Coup Attempt in Washington? A European Mirror on the 1998/1999 Constitutional Crisis* (New York: Palgrave, 2001). Merkl chronicles the shock that many Europeans felt through the course of Clinton's impeachment by examining the reactions of the European press.

24 See, for example, Charles Krauthammer, 'The New Unilateralism', *Washington Post*, 8 June 2001.

25 Stephen F. Szabo, 'Power and Hubris', *Commentary*, AICGS, at info@aicgs.org. Realists such as John Mearsheimer and Christopher Layne have also criticised what they viewed as the Bush Administration's push toward global hegemony and/or US primacy. See John J. Mearsheimer, 'Hearts and Minds', *National Interest*, 69 (2002), pp. 13–17; and Christopher Layne, 'Offshore Balancing Revisited', *The Washington Quarterly*, 25 (2002), pp. 233–48.

26 The new members will be Bulgaria, Estonia, Latvia, Lithuania, Romania, Slovenia and Slovakia.

27 Henry Kissinger also compares this latest round of NATO enlargement to that undertaken during the Cold War. See Henry Kissinger, 'Die Risse Werden Grösser', *Die Welt*, 1 December 2002.

28 See, for example, Ron Asmus, 'Nur der Präsident kann die Allianz noch retten', *Die Welt*, 21 November 2002.

29 See Kissinger, 'Die Risse Werden Grösser'.

30 See Asmus, 'Nur der Präsident kann die Allianz noch retten'.

31 See Stürmer, 'Adieu, Deutschland'.

32 Henry Kissinger has observed: 'The future of NATO is less dependent on its military structure than on its ability to develop shared political objectives. Therein lies cause for deep concern.' Kissinger, 'Die Risse Werden Grösser', author's translation.

Conclusion

23

Run, Gerhard, Run; or Is the *Reformstau* real?

Peter Merkl

Chancellor Schröder and his Red–Green coalition barely survived the Bundestag elections of 2002. The SPD lost 49 seats as compared to 1998 and, if the Greens had not picked up nine, their majority would have been lost entirely. In 1998, Schröder's coalition had come in on a wave of hopes and ambitions. After sixteen years of an aging Kohl administration, it was high time for a change. Even the Christian Democratic Federal President, Roman Herzog, in his *Reformstau* speech at the Hotel Adlon in 1997, had eloquently called on German society to give itself a '*Ruck*' (jerk) to overcome a long-standing paralysis in reforming major institutions and processes which was widely seen as responsible for lagging economic growth and sky-high unemployment.

There is likely to be disagreement, of course, regarding which of a number of important factors may account most for the Chancellor's 1998 triumph and his near-loss in 2002. His public opinion polls ten days before the 2002 elections had dramatically risen a crucial 5 per cent for the SPD while the CDU/CSU dropped by 4 per cent.[1] But only three weeks after the elections, a majority of 51 per cent indicated they were not satisfied (and only 41 per cent satisfied) with the outcome,[2] a startling sign of a kind of political buyer's remorse. Eight months later, in May 2003, the percentage of remaining SPD supporters dropped as low as 27 per cent (the Greens held steady), while the CDU/CSU stood at 46 per cent, the FDP at 6 per cent. Together, they were a clear majority for the opposing coalition. The performance of the governing SPD and Greens also drew the disapproval of the electorate (measured at –1.5 on a scale of –5 to +5).[3] *Der Spiegel* magazine had already dedicated its election issue to the theme of '*die blockierte*

Gesellschaft' and posed the question: How do our parties, interest groups, and bureaucracy paralyse society?[4] There was also at least one popular book, Rolf G. Heinze's *Die blockierte Gesellschaft* on the same subject; in 1999, Heinze also coedited a book about the transition from the welfare state to the 'competitive state'.[5] His earlier effort was tantamount to a revival of Michel Crozier's *La societé bloquée* (1970) in which the famous sociologist had described the gridlock of French society and suggested ways of getting around it. In the final analysis, we may not be able to resolve the question whether it was the floods – especially in discontented East Germany – the Iraqi war issue (where 46 per cent were against participation in the American 'military adventure' under any circumstances and 50 per cent in favour only with UN Security Council support) or the *Reformstau* (82 per cent proclaimed unemployment to be the major issue) that was uppermost in the minds of German voters on election day.[6] But we can imagine rather different dimensions and perceptions of social realities competing in the voters' minds and, in a hectic election campaign, pulling them hither and yon. Catastrophic floods may teach people to be less resentful of economic neglect. Perceptions of Washington militarism may reawaken long-dormant fears of the days when war meant at first the false hopes of German militarism under Hitler and then being bombed, starved and endlessly humiliated. Long-range failures like the *Reformstau* may have had a hard-to-measure impact in 1998, and again in 2002.

As in German politics, hectic action and competing perceptions of parallel universes of experience and memory also run through the new wave of German avant-garde cinema, such as *Das Experiment, Heaven, Mostly Martha* and *Nowhere in Africa.* Tom Tykwer's movie, *Run, Lola, Run*, initiated the new generation of movies. Lola is a young redhead who sets off running frantically across town to save her lowlife boyfriend, Manni, from his acute money (and worse) problems with a violent drug dealer. Her first run is followed by a second and a third along the same route, always accompanied by pulsating techno music, as she tries to raise from her father and a banking acquaintance the considerable sum Manni owes and has lost on a train. On each subsequent run, the events and encounters change in small but significant ways, reflecting Lola's changing perceptions of reality and creating dramatically different outcomes. In the end, things are *nicht so schlimm* and Manni is safe. Similarly, the Schröder government has barely survived the reelection test of its first four years (as frantic as Lola's on her first run), bedevilled by major failures in promised reforms –

regarding the labour market, health-care, pensions, taxes and economic stagnation. Maybe the *Reformstau* failures were just a matter of perception, not as compelling as we assumed, or only partial strike-outs in the eyes of the electorate. Perhaps a major natural catastrophe temporarily overshadowed eastern German perceptions of less elemental problems such as high unemployment or everyone's fears of being drawn into a bloody war by a group of madmen in Washington. Is the *Reformstau* real, a long-term problem, or just an alarming slogan? If only Schröder would try harder, or run faster to catch up now. In the long run, will Lola–Schröder survive the mortal challenge of his shortfall which raised such intense concerns in Lola, Roman Herzog, the German electorate and, by implication, the EU?

A century of reformism and *Reformstau*

The same civilisation that gave us the word '*Zeitgeist*' with its overtones of being *with* the wave of the future also pays frequent homage to traditional ways of doing things, to the well-established order of the past. Even the non-conformist individual, the *Unzeitgemäße* or *Querkopf*, gets occasional praise in the cultural Feuilleton of great newspapers, and in obituaries and biographies. And there may well be, in any individual or group and at any time, '*zwei Seelen, ach, in meiner Brust*' (two souls in my bosom), as Goethe wrote about Dr Faustus, one perhaps straining toward desired reforms of whatever description, the other attached to the status quo. The alleged *Reformstau* and similar phenomena throughout German history may just reflect moments of inner struggle, like the conflict in the bosom of young Lieschen in Johann Sebastian Bach's *Coffee Cantata* when she is entreated by her father, the '*alter Schlendrian*' (still a common phrase for 'the sloppy old ways'), to let go of the new drug of choice of the 1700s, coffee. He even promises to help find her a husband if only she would abandon the frightful habit – and she sighs '*Ach, ein Mann*' (a husband, yeah) – but the coffee wins out. Whole generations have ogled reforms and yet, at the same time, chosen the comfortable status quo. Perhaps an overview of reformist and traditionalist opinion leaders and tendencies of the last 100 years of German history would put today's *Reformstau* debate in realistic context.

Here is a macro-societal thumbnail sketch, beginning with the turn of the nineteenth century. The Bismarckian empire of 1871 was, at least at first, a remarkable and widely admired innovation, in both its reordering of central Europe and subsequent diplomacy and its clever constitutional construction. It represented all at once the hegemonic power of Prussia, the high status of nobility and military, the remaining particularistic powers of German history and the rising forces of nationalism and democracy. By 1900, however, its burgeoning economic and military power and imperial ambitions had become a time bomb waiting to be triggered by an arrogant leadership, responsible to no one. The all-too-solid Bismarckian constitution strangled all hopes of checking its unelected civilian and military leaders as the country stumbled into the First World War and the era of disintegrating European empires. Along with this ossified political structure, however, industrial development, science and technology, local administration and university learning – witnessed internationally by a shower of Nobel prizes – flourished to an extraordinary degree.[7] On the political left, moreover, a huge, well-organised labour movement had grown up to dream about, and realise, an entire alternative world of socialism and pacifism in contrast to the feudal and corporatist capitalism and militarism of the established order.

When the empire fell at the end of the First World War, it left behind a burnt-out political shell and a stratified society in deep crisis. Paradoxically, the war had also brought a socialist command economy and the ultimate democratic equality: classless death on the battlefield. Millions of deracinated veterans were dreaming either of a Bolshevik revolution in Germany or of seizing power to fight the war all over again. There were also diverse forces of reform and innovation that throughout the brief span of the Weimar Republic battled against the desperate defence of parts of the old society against change. To illustrate with a less-known example, there were major efforts to modernise and streamline the old Federal-State relations of the empire through the Constituent Assembly, the Committee of States and the *Länderkonferenz*, but these efforts were stymied when the Nazi dictatorship took over. Staggering from crisis to crisis, the Weimar Republic proved unable to establish lasting compromises between the authoritarian past and a democratic future: The centre would not hold and, in 1932–33, when the extreme wings of right and left commanded a combined majority, democracy became its own enemy. The reform-minded forces were buried in the end under a jack-booted nationalism that was hell-bent on refighting the war and, this time, winning hegemony in Europe. And yet, once again, the Weimar Republic was a hotbed of cultural and artistic creativity and innovation at the same time that social and political reforms were failing disastrously.[8]

There followed twelve years of brutal, racist dictatorship, half of that time engaged in what ultimately turned into an all-out campaign for racial empire and ended in Germany's total rout and defeat. Yet even here, as historians have pointed out, the Third Reich was not simply a regression into a repressive and retrograde past but also had a curious innovative pride: In the midst of genocide and preparing wars of aggression, the Nazi leadership also viewed itself as being on a trajectory toward a better future.[9] Its aesthetic flights of fancy, particularly a triumphalist architecture shared with Mussolini's fascism and Stalin's rebuilding of Soviet cities, also gave it innovative overtones. In contrast to these paroxysms, it is of course postwar Germany that deserves the closest examination with regard to its balance of reform-mindedness and the open restoration of earlier values and structures. It was right at the end of the Second World War, more than at any time, that many Germans were still in the thrall of Nazi war propaganda at the same time that defeat, occupation and Allied reeducation intruded into their reveries and war crimes trials taught them that horrendous crimes had been committed in their name. The postwar public opinion data unearthed and analysed by Anna and Richard Merritt clearly outline the two souls in the bosom of many a postwar West German[10] and the distance to be overcome between many running Lolas and post-Nazi reality. Many democratic politicians or opinion leaders recoiled from the Nazi horrors with such vehemence that they lost sight of the very limited possibilities of reform and innovation among the ruins and hunger of 1945, including the often rather unenlightened and only superficially denazified and reeducated German citizenry.

In the early postwar years, frequently only a coalition of democratic German elites and Allied reform and reeducation leadership – hopefully with truly altruistic ideas – was capable of overcoming the hidebound traditionalist resistance to reforms, for example among German teachers and civil servants. Different occupation regimes, of course, also had different reform agendas for their respective zones, most strikingly the Soviets who often used force and repression. The three 'D's' (sometimes four), of demilitarisation, decartelisation, denazification and democratisation could be interpreted differently. After 1949, once the Western military occupation had turned over authority to the Germans, with few remaining controls, many of the reforms were abandoned or rolled back. Old cartels came back and many an old Nazi once again occupied a position of influence. At the same time, a conservative, anti-communist coalition under Konrad Adenauer instituted its own reform vision of a democratic, capitalist and constitutional democracy in the Federal Republic of Germany. While West Germans became prosperous, much of the old social stratification seemed to reestablish itself, at least until the powerful new forces of the market and of social mobility began to challenge them. In the GDR at the same time, under the dictatorial control of the communist state party, there was a headlong rush from one coercive reform to the next through the 1950s and 1960s – agricultural, industrial, educational – toward a communist ideal state that was, at least in theory, considerably more purist than its Soviet model.

The years of conservative reconstruction and reform in the Federal Republic ended at about the time of the first serious economic recession, in the mid-1960s. In a few years the economic and political peace of the economic *Wunderkinder* was shattered by extremist movements of the left and right, the extra-parliamentary opposition, student rebellion, the neofascist NPD and finally a major terrorist threat, the Baader-Meinhof and other terrorist groups.[11] It was an era of strident contradictions in which the Christian Democratic hegemony was broken, issue by issue, in public debates. By that time, the opposition SPD had already renewed itself with the 1959 Bad Godesberg reforms and retooled for its entry into power at the national level. In the 1960s, the party acquired more governing experience in a number of states and in the Grand Coalition (1966–69), before taking over in Bonn in 1969 under Willy Brandt.[12] If the ' conservative guardianship' of the Adenauer years[13] had kept many a left-wing politician and intellectual from addressing reforms, they were now free to launch their own kind of modernisation in the midst of domestic turmoil and the reorganisation of West Germany's relations to the GDR and to Eastern Europe. There was a euphoria of planning and reform at all levels in the early 1970s.

Seen in retrospect, the great change of the late 1960s and early 1970s was really a matter of generations, as the first postwar generation, the rebels of 1968, joined the old radicals of the SPD and a changed FDP in place of the first generation of leaders who had often been the product of the 1920s and 1930s. New social movements such as the anti-nuclear energy movement, environmentalists, feminists, new pacifists and various lifestyle movements and citizen initiatives at lower levels strove for visions of a better world. Some of these visions were not very political. Some outpaced the reform-readiness of the government in the midst of daunting terrorist challenges and the great energy crises of the 1970s. For every successful reform there were at least half a dozen setbacks, such as occurred with the feminist struggle against Paragraph 218 of the Criminal Code, and some total failures. This West German reform era finally succumbed to the combined battering of the energy crises of 1973 and 1979. Many ambitious undertakings ran out of money in an era of the 'limits of growth' and the 'end of the social democratic consensus'. Innovations in West German foreign policy, such as the *Ostpolitik* toward the Soviets and the wooing of the GDR also reached the limits of popular consensus and international cooperation: instead of the further pursuit of détente, Chancellor Helmut Schmidt's government arrived at a frantic effort to refurbish the NATO missiles stationed in West Germany because Soviet leader Leonid Brezhnev, instead of disarming, had ringed the Federal Republic with SS 20s capable of destroying it. The reform era was followed, unfortunately, by a string of electoral defeats and a number of leadership changes in the SPD – Johannes Rau, Hans-Jochen Vogel, Oskar Lafontaine, Rudolf Scharping – while the SPD was in opposition.[14]

The age of Margaret Thatcher and Ronald Reagan also witnessed a return to conservative traditions in West Germany, if with a characteristic Christian Democratic twist: while the new Chancellor Kohl and his team fulminated against the alleged SPD *Schlendrian* and out-of-control reforms, they never intended to get rid of the *Sozialstaat* but advocated only minor cutbacks. But Herzog's criticism of the German political establishment and its 'incapacity to reform' was aimed particularly at Kohl and his team.[15] Their reform spirit stressed going back to the *Leistungsprinzip*, but otherwise accepted much of the economic planning and electronic data processing that had begun their long march through the German economy and public administration under Chancellors Brandt and Schmidt. In the midst of major international structural and technological changes, the Kohl Administration in 1982 inherited a crisis situation marked by high public debt, high unemployment and low economic growth rates. In spite of these obstacles and new demands made by the Federal Republic's most important ally, the United States, and a pronounced dislike for Thatcherian deregulation and privatisation, especially on the part of the trade unions, the West German economy was once more rising to prodigious levels by the end of the 1980s, just in time for German unification.[16] As the great upheaval of 1989 was about to surprise West and East, the SPD had been hard at work on the Berlin Programme, a major reform programme signifying the party's absorption of the quality of life issues of many citizen initiatives and new social movements into a framework of social equality, democratic renewal and Keynesianism. It also stressed security and defence policies free of the arms race – the Cold War had not yet ended – and devoted to international cooperation between East and West. It was an exercise in futility and bad timing.

Unbeknown to the West, the East German society and economy had been in a ruinous downturn ever since the oil crisis of the 1970s.[17] As the dictatorship unravelled and Gorbachev's Soviet Union was unwilling to help, the bankrupt system fell like a ripe plum into the lap of West Germany. It was an extraordinary opportunity and triumph for Chancellor Kohl, but also a task beyond anyone's capacity. A plethora of reform efforts and a flood of West German money were unleashed to create a better infrastructure in the East which often left West Germany by comparison looking backward and traditional.[18] At the same time, the East German citizenry was disappointed and resentful because the reforms and subventions (particularly the *Treuhand* efforts to privatise the ubiquitous public enterprises) never managed to deliver completely equal conditions or a sense of pride and respect in the East. To this day, the eastern German economy is depressed, unemployment disproportionally high, civil society anaemic and many towns bedeviled by neo-Nazi youth terror.

Enter Goldilocks politics

It is not easy to capture the tortured story of the political success and failure of Schröder's reform efforts. Should we pretend that it was a simple history: Schröder arrives with plans, gets an electoral mandate and tries to enact these plans? Or should we concentrate on the programmes of the *Neue Mitte* and *post facto* assessments of which of these projects was tackled and more or less accomplished, and which were perhaps waylaid by politics, by open opposition or simple ineptitude? To complicate matters further, the original use of the term *Reformstau* only names broad fields of action. Candidate Schröder was even vaguer when he so famously promised that under his leadership, the government would not attempt 'to make everything different, but would make many things better than before'. His biggest tactical mistake was probably to err on the side of specificity, promising a substantial reduction in the unemployment rate and saying that 'a government unable to cut the number of unemployed back to 3.5 million did not deserve to be reelected' – one of those famous last words he had to swallow four years later when the rate was still at 4 million.

After a long period in the opposition every new Chancellor, of course, wished to present his ascension to power as a major *Wende*, a turning point in the nation's history. The beginnings of Schröder's Red–Green coalition government, however, were particularly uncertain and unimpressive: To start with, it was not at all certain that the SPD, if it won, would opt for the still somewhat unpredictable Greens as a partner. To be sure, as Lower Saxonian governor he had been in a rather harmonious coalition with them, in fact with Jürgen Trittin, his future Minister of the Environment.[19] When the lead was still see-sawing back and forth between SPD and CDU/CSU in August and September 1998, 40 per cent of the voters were still undecided and the pollsters generally expected the race to be very close indeed.[20] The SPD programme of the *Neue Mitte*, moreover, was perceived by many as not much different from that of the incumbents. Many observers also reckoned that if all six larger parties in the running made it into the Bundestag (five did), a grand coalition of the SPD and CDU/CSU would be unavoidable. As late as August 1998, EMNID polls reported that 54 per cent of German adult respondents favored a grand coalition. A month later, this percentage had dropped to 35 per cent.[21] At that time, only 21 per cent preferred a Red–Green coalition, no more than favoured a renewal of the CDU/CSU–FDP government. On election day (27 September 2002), support for a Red–Green coalition had risen to 25 per cent of the electorate – among SPD adherents 46 per cent – but the grand coalition still commanded 28 per cent.[22] Until this question was resolved, of course, a Schröder government could hardly commit itself to a specific programme such as the New Centre.

Once the coalition question was past, the role of Oskar Lafontaine, the earlier Chancellor candidate and party leader, was almost as consequential an obstacle, because he would become the predominant presence in a Red–Green government and determine everyday economic policy. His course was far closer to that of the traditional left and featured the enhancement of social programmes and pensions at the expense of the ubiquitous German subsidies to business, industry, and agriculture – social, not corporate welfare. When he became the Finance Minister of Schröder's new government, it was as if there were two chancellors of which Lafontaine had the broader following in the

SPD. The *Neue Mitte*, presented in a *Wahlsonderheft* of the SPD campaign, could hope for the full commitment of the government only after the surprise resignation of Lafontaine the following spring.

Finally, we should recall that Schröder's choice of the Greens was perhaps only a half-hearted, second choice of the Chancellor who in 1998, unlike in 2002, had been flirting with the FDP, Kohl's unhappy coalition partner. The Greens, riven as usual by internal squabbles and battered by recent missteps – for example over raising the price of gasoline – were in some ways closer to Lafontaine, though they also had disagreements, for instance, with his rather statist tax cut proposal.[23] None of them, of course, saw any merit in Kohl's 1997 tax cut plans which proposed to give special breaks to those earning more than DM 115,000 a year. Wolfgang Gerhardt, the FDP leader, ruled out a Red-Green-Yellow 'traffic light coalition' and his party, after so many decades in office, welcomed a period of regeneration on the opposition benches. The cumulative effect of all these uncertainties was that the time was hardly right for launching the programme of the *Neue Mitte*. The only clear sign emerging from the 1998 elections was that for the first time in FRG history, Germans had voted a chancellor and his party out of office. Heribert Prantl of the *Süddeutsche Zeitung* quoted the hopeful words from Herzog's *Reformstau* speech – 'I am hoping for a renewal of our courage … our creativity' – but the journalist could read no clear direction in either the electoral verdict or the challenge to the new government: 'The voters are still surprised at what they have wrought. Will they rest easier when they see they have not just replaced a lame squad [of leaders] with a blind one? The SPD faces a great challenge, the Greens the greatest task of their young history.'[24]

The reception of the new Chancellor by various German interest groups was less than auspicious: the president of the Federation of German Industry (BDI), H. O. Henkel said rudely he hoped that 'German society would be spared the [bitter] red–green chalice'. H. P. Stihl, the president of the German Chamber of Industry and Commerce (DIHT) similarly expressed his dismay: in his opinion, the Greens were not *regierungsfähig* (fit for governernment). But he did offer 'the justified congratulations' of German business to Schröder, perhaps in tribute to the well-known pro-business attitudes of this former board member of Volkswagen AG. The trade union chief, D. Schulte, declared himself 'very happy' with the new government, probably unaware of the conflicts to come. Congratulations also came from abroad. President Clinton sent his best wishes. Tony Blair, who by that time had been applying his centrist programme with Thatcherite overtones for seventeen months, called Schröder's victory 'a splendid triumph' and attested to 'the enormous capabilities of Schröder'. French Premier Lionel Jospin hailed the 'great success' of the SPD while his health minister, Bernard Kouchner, exulted that 'with Schröder, we can go another step toward a social-policy-minded Europe'. Austria's Chancellor Klima hailed this 'success for a social-democratic Europe' and the Swedish Prime Minister Göran Persson also expressed his pleasure.[25]

With all this support from more or less centrist fellow social democrats, we can take a closer look at Schröder's programme of the *Neue Mitte*, beyond his course as Lower Saxony's Minister President. The new centrist emphasis obviously owed much to Bodo Hombach's book, *The Politics of the New Centre*, and the state-level experiments conducted in North-Rhine Westphalia under Economics Minister Hombach and Minister-President Clement. It was also evocative of some of President Clinton's rhetoric – 'goodbye to the welfare state as we know it' – and the practices of governments in Great Britain, Denmark and the Netherlands. Britain's Tony Blair, however, had started on the heels of the Thatcher revolution, which had demolished the stranglehold of organised labour, and he first won firm control of his own Labour Party by sidelining its old left-wing faction, a feat Schröder was unlikely to accomplish with the SPD.[26] SPD traditions were not only too deeply ingrained, but they had emerged from the bruising ideological battles of the 1970s, the devastating impact of German unification on the party and the post-unification rebound under Lafontaine. Though it featured an active role for the state, Hombach's New Centre was miles from the orthodoxy of what Gerard Braunthal, an American historian of the SPD, described as 'a reformist, state-affirming socialism', based on full-fledged democracy and averse to the doctrinaire, Marxist left and the opportunist right wing.[27] In the early 1990s – while Kohl was enjoying his post-unification surge – the SPD position involved a bit of Keynesianism, a little state intervention, a nod to environmental modernisation and reforms to redress the balance of social inequality and to democratise state and economy.

The essence of the Schröder–Hombach programme is not easy to summarise. The *Economist* had put the debonair Schröder on its cover and asked icily: 'Would you buy a used car from this man?' The prestigious magazine also called the new centrism of the 'third way', as it is known in Britain, 'Goldilocks politics' – not too hot (socialism), not too cold (neoliberalism), but just right. It also likened defining it to wrestling with a life-size inflatable doll: the moment you grab a limb, all the hot air rushes to other parts of the body.[28] Blair's friend Clinton had ventured his first centrist steps into the teeth of the Gingrich landslide which, again and again from 1993 on, tried to remove him from office by impeachment until, finally, the Republican hardliners got lucky with Ms Lewinsky.[29] The sociologist Anthony Giddens had spelled out his idea of the 'third way' rather systematically in his 1998 book, *The Third Way: The Renewal of Social Democracy*, confronting the contemporary dilemmas of globalisation, individualism, ecology and democratisation.[30] His solutions were the 'social investment state', an enhanced role for civil society, cultural pluralism, a democratic EU, global governance and worldwide market fundamentalism. In his later collection, *The Global Third Way Debate*, Giddens succinctly summarised the commonalities of the new centrism in eleven points, including state reform and containment – against intervention in markets or the civil society – a new social contract (including duties and responsibilities), a core role for civil society, a full employment economy, connecting of social and economic policy, welfare reform, environmental protection and egalitarianism (admittedly harder in Britain than in Germany). Capitalism needs responsibility, just as the worldwide financial markets need regulation and not the neo-liberal panacea of universal deregulation.[31] The third way, in fact, might become the 'social model' for the EU.

For Giddens, the emphasis on the principles of equal opportunity, personal responsibility and the mobilisation of citizens and of democratic communities was the path from the [old leftist] redistribution of wealth to the creation of wealth. He pointed to Clinton's not always successful efforts toward fiscal discipline, health-care reform, investment in training and education, 'welfare to work' and the initiatives against crime and for the promotion of democracy abroad. He also mentioned the genesis of the Blair–Schröder paper at an April 1999 Washington meeting with Clinton and the prime ministers of the Netherlands (Wim Kok) and Italy (Massimo d'Alema). This paper celebrated the nearly universal wave, under various labels, of the new social democracy throughout the West and credited it with a renewal of its ideas and modernisation of its programmes, a 'union of social justice … economic dynamism, and the unleashing of creativity and innovation' in society.[32] The Blair–Schröder paper argued for a proactive state, but one that only helps and never takes over the functions of markets and enterprises – the old principle of subsidiarity. The common programme embraced globalisation after a fashion, scientific innovation and progress, investment in human capital, fiscal discipline, supply-side economics, environmental responsibility and the fight against crime and poverty, and all this with emphasis on the EU.[33] At first, their paper caused a big row in Germany where Lafontaine had penned a 'viciously critical kiss-and-tell book', *Das Herz schlägt links.* Hombach was forced out of office. But this proved to be a Phyrric victory for Lafontaine's supporters since it was the Finance Minister and chief of the divided party who soon resigned all his offices in March 1999 and subsequently withdrew from active involvement in German politics.[34]

Lola's second run: German realities

Hombach himself had still made an effort in his book to avoid direct confrontation by accommodating some of Lafontaine's views, according to *New Statesman* reporter Mark Leonard who introduced the English edition of *Aufbruch.* But the *éclat* brought the end of the 'Schrafontaine' phase, to the relief of German industry, the European stock markets and some foreign governments, and cleared the path for the *Neue Mitte.* The next budget (July 1999) already carried its unmistakable markings – the big budget cuts (*Sparpaket*) together with moving the tax breaks from energy to the social payments. This was the moment of Hans Eichel, Lafontaine's replacement, who cut some DM 30 billion in social spending and federal subsidies, to the dismay of trade unions and cabinet colleagues. Given the huge total government debt (DM 1.5 trillion), annual deficits of DM 60 billion and the pressure of the budget limits imposed by the EMU, Eichel had little choice. Blair and Schröder then met in London to pass a manifesto, *Die neue Mitte/the Third Way*, which had been drafted by Hombach and Peter Mandelson.[35] The seeming stumbling of the government and the divisive arguments inside the SPD were widely perceived as a moment of weakness. Fortunately for Schröder, his problems at the time were overshadowed by the unfolding campaign finance scandal of Helmut Kohl and the CDU/CSU.

To come back to the image of Lola's three seemingly identical runs, the pure programmatics are really just the first run, far from the realities at hand. The second run corresponds to the attempted adaptation of the programme to the stubborn facts of German politics and society which indeed differ greatly from Britain and the United States.

Here Hombach had already done a great deal of spadework by breaking down broad principles into many concrete steps and measures that 'might work' in the Federal Republic, so many in fact that we are reminded of Clinton's 'retail politics' of many smaller issues, such as putting 100,000 more police officers on the beat. The most telling examples come from Hombach's efforts to revive German entrepreneurialism in rustbelt North-Rhine Westphalia with a programme to groom 'wannabe' entrepreneurs to take over the thousands of family businesses that had no heirs. Or of overcoming the fears and gridlock surrounding such big reforms as those of the tax system, social security and pensions and health-care with retail measures. 'The failure of all attempts at [tax] reform', Hombach wrote, 'has two causes. One is that the political price to be paid for removing [old] concessions [is] … too high, and [two] the amount of energy needed to break up private sectional interests too great.'[36]

Hombach also called for a New Corporatism to replace Kohl's defunct unemployment initiative and, to the consternation of representatives of German big business, for a return to Ludwig Erhard's 'social market economy', the foundation of the West German 'economic miracle' of the 1950s.[37] 'The greatest political scandal in Germany today is mass unemployment', Hombach wrote and pointed to the official 4.8 million of unemployed plus about another 2 million jobless concealed in training and work programmes in 1998. Three-quarters of the unemployed represented structural unemployment, a legacy of twenty-five years of incomplete recovery from the 1970s crises and a harbinger of rising crime, social dysfunction and the looming collapse of social security. The *Neue Mitte* is sceptical of the old safety net and prefers, instead, images of economic opportunity like the 'trampoline society' where enterprising individuals can succeed.[38] Eastern Germany had been growing at a good pace, faster than the West, when all of a sudden, growth began to sputter in 1996. Now it needed a major entrepreneurial boost to recover economic dynamism – but without the loss of a sense of community and social solidarity.[39]

Der Spiegel heralded the ascent of the new Chancellor with an issue entitled '*Alles wird anders – aber wird es auch besser*?' – a line reversing his cautious words.[40] Briefly describing various initial problems, the magazine resolutely turned toward the public's readiness for reforms: 60 per cent, according to EMNID polls, believed indeed that the SPD could 'do many things better' than its predecessors. If anything, the public thought some extraordinary reforms – like the ending of nuclear energy production and the first changes in immigration and citizenship law – so overdue as to be unremarkable. To many observers, in fact, the pace of innovation on taxes, pensions and health care seemed too slow and timid. Schröder's opponents, on the other hand, were alarmed that significant reductions of social security taxes were to be paid for with some DM 15 billion of eco (energy) taxes, and even more in the future. This change in tax law was also a step toward lowering the unit cost of German labour, one of the highest in the world and a great burden on the labour market and the international competitiveness of German businesses. There was nearly universal support for greater social justice and equality. The most important initiative of the new government was the corporatist *Bündnis für Arbeit*, a major assault on unemployment but no favourite of the employers' associations.[41] Trade unions supported it, although they had opposed Kohl's earlier efforts in the same direction because they proposed to liberalise the rigid labour market by lifting the statutory protections against firing and of the level of sick benefits.[42] Schröder had brought Walter Riester of DGB into the cabinet and there were hopes that the management–labour gridlock could be overcome, just as it had been in Denmark where a Social Democratic government cut the level of unemployment insurance along with the length of the unemployment benefit period.[43]

The Red–Green coalition negotiations also added further reform schemes to the agenda of the *Neue Mitte*, beginning with the eco tax and its consequences for pensions and unemployment insurance. The second was the broadening of social insurance to include categories of work that had not so far contributed or benefited from it. The entire pension system needed to be adjusted, including the addition of an autonomous old-age insurance for women. The otherwise well-established health-care system also had revealed some gaping holes, for example regarding prescription drugs for the elderly and chronically ill, and guidelines for the level of patients' contributions to their own care. Existing long-term care insurance was also considered for extension. A generous programme also aimed at supporting 'family vacation accounts' for parents and female part-time employment. Reforms of public higher education and of the transportation system rounded out the ambitious agenda of the new government.[44] The actual details of the reform plans drew, of course, the opposition of some groups but not nearly as much emotion as had the general theories of the *Neue*

Mitte which in their stark clarity seemed more alarming, just as Lola's first take of Manni's predicament – no matter how erroneous in its perceptions – had deeply alarmed her.

In the midst of the impending move of the Bundestag from Bonn to Berlin and the cacophony of media reactions, we need to look at what the government really might have accomplished in its four years until the 2002 elections. Schröder's first reaction to all this was to wonder whether his turn at the helm was merely ephemeral or would amount to a sea change in German politics, comparable to the rise of Willy Brandt in 1969 who had proclaimed that he wanted to '*mehr Demokratie wagen*' (dare undertake more democratisation). Schröder's tongue-in-cheek formula was '*mehr Volkswagen*', also a light-hearted reminder of his link to the board of the company.

Lola's third run

As the Bundestag campaign of 2002 rolled around, Schröder's Red–Green coalition must have been painfully aware of what reform-minded American presidents have often found out the hard way: four years are a very short period in which to carry out their plans, even with a handsome, comfortable legislative majority and mandate. Much of the first year is spent with recruitment, organisation and overcoming internal splits. In Schröder's case, the resistance of checking agencies such as the Bundesrat and the supposedly friendly trade unions could slow down or even destroy the expected progress. We are reminded of Max Weber's description of professional politics as the drilling of very hard boards; it will require unfailing determination over long periods that may try the patience of ordinary mortals. The weekly, *Die Zeit*, had a long-running series, 'Agenda, Germany', on the reform challenges facing the Schröder government which has meanwhile been published as a book, *Zeit zum Aufstehen* (time to stand up).

The weekly also asked former Chancellor Helmut Schmidt, who had watched Schröder's career with some sympathy and understanding, for formal comments.[45] Schmidt, in his day, had also been personally very popular, but an outsider in his own party, right of centre and eventually rather isolated and set upon by many younger party comrades. Schmidt responded with a list of five 'cardinal tasks' that any German government would have to tackle in order to get the better of the *Reformstau*. He tellingly called his article '*Unkraut jäten und ackern*' (pulling weeds and ploughing the field) and hinted that governments in office are constantly obliged to clean up and keep up the farm, their political and economic system. He rejected the tendency of many of his compatriots to 'complain to foreigners' when the Germans were really better off than they had ever been, with the exception of long-term unemployment, the stagnation of the East, immigration and the country's lagging economic and productivity growth. The former Chancellor was careful to attribute some of the worst problems to Schröder's predecessors, Kohl and his team, for example the high levels of taxes, public debt and unemployment – in the winter of 1997–98, the number of unemployed approached 5 million and all five parties were frustratingly unspecific regarding effective remedies – as well as the state of eastern Germany after Kohl's promises of a 'blooming paradise' there.

Schmidt's five cardinal tasks and suggested remedies began with mass unemployment – 'by far the most urgent task' – and one shared with France, Italy and Spain. Denmark and the Netherlands, by liberalising the labour market, have shown the way, he wrote, as did Schröder's Hartz Commission report, which did not go far enough in its proposals. Firms should not be bound by regional collective contracts – the number of those covered by them had been declining anyway – and state and local government employees need no longer be in lockstep with federal salaries.[46] Since the employers associations, unions and employees themselves opposed such liberalisation, however, German politicians had been afraid to touch these problems. Eastern German stagnation was the second cardinal task, ever since reconstruction came to a dead end in 1996. Growth could be restarted with the Hombachian device of creating 100,000 new entrepreneurs currently discouraged by bureaucratic red tape and such old-fashioned restrictions as requiring a trademaster's certificate (*Meisterprüfung*) to open a trade shop. Despite a decade of enormous subsidies, the eastern German economy still suffers from overregulation and especially from being subject to Federal laws – for instance regarding industry, construction and the labour market – from which it should be exempted for a considerable time.

Three, all-German economic growth and innovation should be particularly encouraged among small and medium enterprises (SMEs), which employ 70 per cent of the labour force. Research and development should be stepped up and restrictive tax rules, such as those regarding auxiliary income (*Nebenerwerb*), should be scrapped. Schmidt also favoured a deregulation of university studies and a reform of

Federal–State relations and finances in the direction of the same principle of subsidiarity that had been in vogue in the EU. He also wished to cut the long list of legislative subjects on which the Bundesrat enjoyed a veto so that the upper house could become less of a partisan brake on the Federal executive. His fourth task was an overhaul of immigration law and the fifth a political grab bag – including, for example, a rekindling of Franco-German cooperation, a reduction in the number of parties and lessening the dependence of the pension system on subsidisation.

Helmut Schmidt's agenda was more or less echoed in many quarters. The election issue of *Der Spiegel*, for example, named four great failings of politics and society that required government action, after reminding readers of a Willy Brandt campaign slogan of thirty years ago: 'If you want to live securely tomorrow, you must fight for reforms today!' The first failing identified was the decline of the German *Sozialstaat* which is barely any longer able to cope with mass unemployment and poverty. The future economic and fiscal consequences of an aging German population also put the future of the *Sozialstaat* in doubt. Elmar Rieger and Stephan Leibfried, moreover, have shown the inherent conflicts between the forces of economic globalisation and the interests of the national welfare state.[47] In the 2002 campaign, both Schröder and his challenger, Edmund Stoiber, promised to reduce the extraordinarily high fringe benefit cost (*Lohnnebenkosten*) that inflated German wages by 40 per cent and burdened both economic growth and the labour market. Other burdens were the growing 'black' labour market – some 5 million untaxed full-time jobs – and unfair tax differences.[48]

Der Spiegel's second crisis was that of public health-care. The basic health insurance system (AOK) is in deep financial trouble; in particular, the drug industry has an aging society's ability to pay over a barrel. Ever-higher costs and less service loom in the future. This may come as a surprise to Americans who have often looked with envy at the far more comprehensive and yet cheaper German system, whose spiralling costs should be more easily controllable from the top down.[49]

The third area in need of thorough reform is the public education system which, in the midst of the information revolution, suffers from outdated educational goals, worn-down school facilities and mediocre results. The international Pisa study revealed embarrassing weaknesses in German education (as have OECD statistics). In reading competence, for example, only 23 per cent of the students were found to meet the test of understanding. Even more embarrassing was the finding that access and student performance in Germany were seriously hampered by differences in the social background of the student, worse even than in the United States. In opinion polls, majorities have agreed that action is needed in all three fields, unemployment, health-care and education. *Der Spiegel* also pilloried the hypertrophy of German bureaucracy – one in fourteen adults works in public employment – and its maintenance of a *Papierstau* of rigmarole and regulation.

Die Zeit identified the great enemies of reform as the drug industry, employers and the unions, especially the civil service unions.[50] But according to editor Josef Joffe, there is also the mantra of the 'consensus ideology' that disarms every effort to tackle the gridlock. The weekly also interviewed Lord Ralf Dahrendorf on the subject of the *Reformstau.* He reminded the reader of an EMNID poll according to which 70 per cent of German adults believe that the country keeps postponing important reforms: 'People are still content [today] but things keep getting worse.' The distinguished sociologist thought that smaller countries like the Netherlands, Denmark and Sweden had had greater success in reforming themselves, because their interest groups were less powerful. His advice regarding German higher education – he once headed the London School of Economics – was to charge more for tuition.[51] When in the 1990s eastern German universities underwent major reforms from their communist antecedents, it was vainly hoped that the contagion of reform thinking might be passed on to the West. Eventually, the ambition to develop a European model of university education and the OECD comparisons sparked some reform activity. Like the Catholic Church – and for similar reasons – universities are notoriously hard to reform. As the wags have it, reforming a university and expecting cooperation from the academic senate is like trying to relocate a cemetery and expecting those interred to help in the planning and execution of the move. Dahrendorf also took a dim view of German (state-centred) federalism and instead advocated giving local governments more resources and responsibilities in social policy.

Both Schmidt and Dahrendorf praised Schröder's belated creation of the Hartz Commission on unemployment, chaired by Peter Hartz, a Volkswagen executive, in February 2002, although Schmidt felt that it liberalised only one-third of the labour market. *Der Spiegel* was less charitable about Schröder's achievements and felt, in particular, that 'after 100 days of creative chaos [in 1998]' the plans to cope with mass unemployment had not been carried out. The promised tax reforms had been postponed, in part because of the catastrophic floods of 2002.

The much-heralded pension reforms still did not change the pension system's excessive dependence on the tax payer. The severe spending cuts introduced by Lafontaine's successor, Hans Eichel, also shocked and alienated the trade unions, a majority constituency of the SPD. Even if Schröder was reelected in 2002, how could he expect to do better in his second term?

Six months after his reelection on 14 March 2003, Chancellor Schröder again addressed the Bundestag, introducing a 'series of bold reforms', part of his Agenda 2010. The *Economist* thought this reform package was on the right track, though a bit painful. As the weekly pointed out, Germany had the slowest growth rate of the twelve Eurozone nations, at 0.2 per cent, and one of the highest unemployment rates, at 11.3 per cent (or 4.7 million unemployed). Germany also had a high bankruptcy rate: some of the biggest banks and many a *Mittelstand* business were floundering. From being a powerhouse of the EU, it had become what some have called 'the sick man of Europe'. The *Economist* described Schröder's reform agenda as 'piecemeal', lacking in details, and leaving aside the important areas of pension, health-care and educational reforms. The magazine also mentioned the deep anger of the left wing of the SPD at the intended cuts in unemployment and sickness benefits. The government proposed to raise $6 billion of its $149 billion deficit by forcing some 20 million pensioners to contribute to their health-care. A long-delayed and now accelerated tax cut of $28.5 billion might stimulate stagnant economic growth while the ubiquitous 'corporate welfare' – tax breaks and state subsidies to certain industries – was to be reduced and government shares of Deutsche Telecom and other assets were to be sold.[52] The Chancellor promised fiscal reforms aimed at helping the country find its way back to the fiscal strictures of the GSP.

Schröder's popularity among his party comrades noticeably slipped in the months after the introduction of this reform plan which, in the area of social security, enjoyed only the support of one out of five (19 per cent) German voters. A plurality (36 per cent) thought his plan was inadequate to solving the problem, while 25 per cent (and 35 per cent of union members) found it 'too far-reaching'. The trade unions actually presented a counter-proposal for encouraging economic growth, a plan that relied heavily on public investment and new indebtedness. But this plan, too, was rejected in the polls by a margin of 2:1, and union members liked it no better. Moreover, in a May 2003 poll, the influence of trade unions itself was considered 'too great' by 45 per cent, 'just right' by 29 per cent and 'too small' by 19 per cent. This attitudinal shift from 1998 is remarkable since at that time trade union influence was judged as 'too great' by only 21 per cent, as 'just right' by 39 per cent and 'too small' by 32 per cent. As for the employers' associations, 38 per cent considered their influence 'just right' in 1998 and 2003.[53]

Wer soll das bezahlen?

'*Wer soll das bezahlen*', revellers chant at Carnival time in the Rhineland, '*wer has das bestellt? ... wer hat soviel Geld?*' (Who is going to pay for this? Who ordered this ... Who has that much money?). It is a refrain that can easily be applied to the looming German federal deficit – well in excess of the GSP – and to the cost of all the necessary and desirable reforms: 68 per cent of the public judges the state of the economy to be '*schlecht*' (bad); only 30 per cent regard it as partly bad and partly good. It was also second on the list of the most important themes of the May 2003 poll, after the unemployment issues and ahead of taxes (or tax increases), pensions and health care. There is a solid majority, especially in western Germany, in favour of cutting unemployment benefits in order to give the unemployed an incentive to seek jobs. But the proposals to close the budget gap by increasing the VAT are spurned by the public that, at best, would accept only a rise in the tobacco tax: 62 per cent would tolerate a €1 increase in the cost of a package of cigarettes, while 36 per cent would not.

The Iraq War and the war against terrorism occupy an ever-more modest place on that same list of 'the most important themes'; by mid-May, it was last among ten themes. The public is well aware, however, of the state of German–American relations: before the confrontations between the Schröder and Bush Administrations, 88 per cent of Germans considered relations 'good' and only 9 per cent called them 'bad'. But after October 2002, only 65 per cent considered relations 'good' and 33 per cent characterised them as 'bad'. After February 2003, German–American relations were considered 'bad' by 65 per cent of the population and only 32 per cent characterised the relationship as 'good'. The early months of 2003, of course, saw massive peace demonstrations in Europe and around the world against America's rush to war. It was also the time of further solidarisation between Schröder and French President Jacques Chirac against the 'warmonger Bush'.[54] *Der*

Spiegel reflected the German–American split with a cover story on the Second World War air war and its 600,000 German civilian casualties, with pictures and narrative about Hamburg, Dresden and Berlin; the next week, the cover story in the magazine attributed the real cause of the war to oil; and a few weeks later, the cover story focused on 'the lonely Chancellor', described as unpopular and unlucky at the nadir of his political career. It described the rebellion in his own party over domestic policies and how Lafontaine was making himself 'available' for a comeback. But it was reported that despite the letter to President George Bush from the 'coalition of the willing', polls from all over Europe, old and new, showed opposition to the war without a UN Security Council mandate running between 65 and 85 per cent.[55] In Germany, 84 per cent of those polled were against military action by the United States and its allies – 94 per cent of SPD and Green adherents 79 per cent of FDP adherents and 73 per cent of CDU/CSU adherents were against military action.[56]

Did Germans express regret at the profound estrangement with the United States? The polls vindicated Schröder's course with 69 per cent, lonely or not, and further demonstrated the declining perception of the United States as a benign ally and friend: when pollsters asked what emphasis German foreign policy should exhibit, only 9 per cent opted for 'rapport with the US', 49 per cent chose 'European solidarity' and another 37 per cent 'moral criteria', which was an additional comment on what they thought of President Bush's course of policy. The question, finally, about which country represented the biggest threat to peace drew the response 'the US' from 53 per cent of those polled. Only 28 per cent named Iraq and 9 per cent North Korea.[57] Large majorities of 62 per cent versus 6 per cent considered the American military action a violation of international law and even larger majorities (84 per cent versus 11 per cent) did not expect the American victory to lead to peace in the Middle East. At the height of the confrontation, 96 per cent of SPD adherents and 57 per cent of CDU/CSU adherents supported the Chancellor. While envoys of the Bush Administration sought agreement with the CDU/CSU leadership (an effort which was widely resented), the latter could count only on the support of a minority of its followers for its position which was at best an anti-war but less confrontational posture towards the United States.[58] With this dramatic confrontation between the irascible President Bush and the German ally, what claims could mere domestic reforms make upon the public agenda in Germany? How could the Germans worry about their

Reformstau when the maelstrom of war and pece had seized their little ship of state? Only when the war was over, and they had been sidelined, could they begin to return to the need for domestic changes.

What they saw after the end of the war in Iraq was most discouraging. As far as the eye could see, there seemed to be unfinished reforms and few organised supporters to set them into motion. By almost any conceivable measure, the enormous pile of reform tasks that the barely reelected Schröder had to tackle in his second term seemed daunting indeed. His mandate, moreover, was much smaller while the resistance, if anything, had increased. Few knowledgeable observers gave him any chance of being reelected in 2006. How, then, could he hope to overcome the looming challenge of the *Reformstau*? He would have to run faster just to stay in place – run, Gerhard, run! 'There is a tide in the affairs of men', the Bard wrote, 'Which, taken at the flood.' But the tide of 1998 has long begun to ebb.

Notes

1 Forschungsgruppe Wahlen e.V. Mannheim, *Politbarometer* (Mannheim: Forschungsgruppe Wahlen e.V. Mannheim, September 2002).

2 Figures from Forschungsgruppe Wahlen, *Politbarometer* (October 2002).

3 Figure from Forschungsgruppe Wahlen, *Polibarometer* (May 2003).

4 *Der Spiegel*, 21 September 2002.

5 Rolf G. Heinze, *Die blockierte Gesellschaft* (Opladen: Leske & Budrich, 1998) and Rolf G. Heinze *et al.*, *Vom Wahlfahrtsstaat zum Wettbewerbsstaat: Arbeitsmarkt und Sozialpolitik in den 90er Jahren* (Opladen: Leske & Budrich, 1999).

6 Forschungsgruppe Wahlen e.V. Mannheim, *Bundestagswahlbericht 2002* (Mannheim: Forschungsgruppe Wahlen e.V. Mannheim, 2002), pp. 42, 49.

7 Jack R. Dukes and Joachim Remak (eds), *Another Germany: A Reconsideration of the Imperial Era* (Boulder, CO: Westview Press, 1988).

8 Henry M. Pachter, *Modern Germany: A Social, Cultural and Political History* (Boulder, CO: Westview Press, 1978), Chapters 13 and 14.

9 David Schoenbaum, *Hitler's Social Revolution* (Garden City, NY: Doubleday, 1966).

10 Anna J. Merritt and Richard L. Merritt, *Public Opinion in Occupied Germany: The OMGUS Surveys, 1945–1949* (Urbana, IL: University of Illinois Press, 1970); Richard Merritt and Anna J. Merritt; *Public Opinion in Semi-Sovereign Germany: the HICOG Surveys, 1949–1955* (Urbana, IL: University of Illinois Press, 1980); and Richard L. Merritt, *Democracy*

Imposed: US Occupation Policy and the German Public, 1945–1949 (New Haven: Yale University Press, 1995).

11 Peter H. Merkl, 'West German Left-Wing Terrorism', in Martha Crenshaw (ed.), *Terrorism in Context* (University Park, PA: Pennsylvania State University Press, 1995), pp. 160–211.

12 Thomas Meyer, 'From Godesberg to the *Neue Mitte*: The New Social Democracy in Germany', in Anthony Giddens (ed.), *The Global Third Way* (Cambridge: Polity Press, 2001), pp. 74–85.

13 Axel Schildt and Arnold Sywottek, 'Reconstruction and Modernization: West German Social History during the 1950s', in Robert G. Moeller (ed.), *West Germany Under Construction: Politics, Society, and Culture in the Adenauer Era* (Ann Arbor: University of Michigan Press, 1996), pp. 413–43. For a more extended treatment, see Axel Schildt and Arnold Sywottek, *Modernisierung im Wiederaufbau: die westdeutsche Gesellschaft der 50er Jahre* (Bonn: J. H. W. Dietz, 1993).

14 Meyer, 'From Godesberg to the *Neue Mitte*', pp. 76–9.

15 Clay Clemens, 'Assessing the Kohl Legacy', in Clay Clemens and William E. Paterson (eds), *The Kohl Chancellorship* (London: Frank Cass, 1998), p. 14.

16 Rebecca Harding and William E. Paterson (eds), *The Future of the German Economy* (Manchester: Manchester University Press, 2000), pp. 127–9.

17 Eckhard Jesse and Armin Mitter (eds), *Die Gestaltung der deutschen Einheit: Geschichte, Politik, Gesellschaft* (Bonn and Berlin: Bouvier, 1992).

18 Thomas A. Baylis, 'Transforming the East Germany Economy: Shock without Therapy', in Michael Huelshoff, Andrei Markovits and Simon Reich (eds), *From Bundesrepublik to Deutschland: German Politics after Unification* (Ann Arbor: University of Michigan Press, 1993), pp. 77–91.

19 *Berliner Zeitung*, 2–4 October, 1998.

20 Elisabeth Noelle-Neumann, 'An Election Day Campaign since 1995', *Frankfurter Allgemeine Zeitung*, 30 September 1998.

21 *Der Spiegel*, 21 September 1998.

22 *Abendzeitung*, 28 September 1998.

23 *Süddeutsche Zeitung*, 2–3 October 1998.

24 *Ibid.*

25 *Abendzeitung*, 28 September 1998.

26 Bodo Homback, *The Politics of the New Centre* (Cambridge: Polity Press, 2000); Tony Blair, *The Third Way: New Politics for the New Century* (London: Fabian Society, 1998).

27 Gerard Braunthal, *The Social Democrats since 1969: A Party in Power and Opposition* (Boulder, CO: Westview Press, 1994), pp. 205–8.

28 *The Economist*, 10 December 1998.

29 Peter H. Merkl, *A Coup Attempt in Washington? A European Mirror on the 1998/1999 Constitutional Crisis* (New York: Palgrave, 2001).

30 Anthony Giddens, *The Third Way: The Renewal of Social Democracy* (Cambridge: Polity Press, 1998).
31 Anthony Giddens, 'Introduction', in Giddens (ed.), *The Global Third Way Debate* (Cambridge: Polity Press, 2001), pp. 5–6.
32 Hombach, *The Politics of the New Centre*, p. 160.
33 Anthony Giddens, *The Third Way and its Critics* (Cambridge: Polity Press, 2000), pp. 163–77.
34 Oskar Lafontaine, *Das Herz schlägt links* (Munich: Econ Verlag, 1999), English translation: *The Heart Beats Left* (Cambridge: Polity Press, 2000); Giddens, *The Third Way and its Critics*, pp. xxiv–vii.
35 *Ibid.*
36 Hombach, *The Politics of the New Centre*, p. 55.
37 *Ibid.*, pp. 74–83.
38 *Ibid.*, pp. 122–37.
39 Harding and Paterson (eds), *The Future of the German Economy* and Maurizio Ferrera, Anton Hemerijck and Martin Rhodes, 'The Future of Social Europe: Recasting Work and Welfare in the New Economy', in Anthony Giddens (ed.), *The Global Third Way Debate* (Cambridge: Polity Press, 2001), pp. 122–9.
40 Translated as: 'It will all be different, but will it be better?' *Der Spiegel*, 10 October 1998.
41 *Süddeutsche Zeitung*, 17–18 October 1998.
42 *Abendzeitung*, 29 September 1998.
43 *Süddeutsche Zeitung*, 2–3 October 1998.
44 *Frankfurter Allgemeine Zeitung*, 19 October 1998).
45 Dieter Wild, *Zeit zum Aufstehen: Agenda Deutschland – was sich ändern muss* (München: Knaur, 2000); see *Die Zeit*, 19 September 2002.
46 Unemployment figures can be found in *This Week in Germany*, 19 May 1999.
47 Elmar Rieger and Stephan Leibfried, 'Welfare State Limits to Globalization', *Politics and Society*, 6:3 (1998), pp. 363–90.
48 *Der Spiegel*, 21 September 2002.
49 Uwe E. Reinhardt, 'Global Budgeting in German Health Care: Insight for Americans', *Domestic Affairs*, 3:1 (1993/1994), pp. 159–94.
50 The two unions are the German White-Collar Employees' Union (*Deutsche Angestelltengewerkschaftskraft*, DAG) and the German Civil Servants' Federation (*Deutscher Beamten Bund*, DBB).
51 *Die Zeit*, 19 September 2002.
52 *Economist*, 20 March 2003, pp. 14, 43.
53 Forschungsgruppe Wahlen, *Politbarometer* (May 2003).
54 *Le Monde*, 20 January 2003 and *Frankfurther Allgemeine Zeitung*, 24 January 2003.
55 *Der Spiegel*, 6 January 2003, 13 January 2003, 3 February 2003.

56 Forschungsgruppe Wahlen, *Politbarometer* (March 2003).
57 *Der Spiegel*, 17 February 2003.
58 Forschungsgruppe Wahlen, *Politbarometer* (March 2003).

Select bibliography

14th Shell Jugendstudie, 'Zusammenfassung und Hauptergebnisse', *Jugend 2002* (Hamburg: S. Fischer, 2002).

Abenheim, Donald, *Reforging the Iron Cross: The Search for Tradition in the West German Armed Forces* (Princeton: Princeton University Press, 1988).

Abromeit, Heidrun, 'Die "Vetretungslücke". Probleme im neuen deutschen Bundesstaat', *Gegenwartskunde*, 42:3 (1993), pp. 281–92.

Albrecht, Willy (ed.), *Kurt Schumacher. Reden-Schriften-Korrespondenzen 1945–1952* (Berlin: J. H. W. Dietz, 1985).

Alesina, Alberto and Lawrence Summers, 'Central Bank Independence and Macroeconomic Performance: Some Comparative Evidence', *Journal of Money, Credit, and Banking*, 25:2 (1993), pp. 151–62.

Algieri, Franco, 'Die Europäische Sicherheits- und Verteidigungspolitik', in Werner Weidenfeld (ed.), *Europa Handbuch* (Gütersloh: Verlag Bertelsmann Stiftung, 2002).

Alleman, Fritz René, *Bonn ist nicht Weimar* (Köln: Kiepenheuer & Witsch, 1956).

Allen, Christopher S., 'The Underdevelopment of Keynesianism in the Federal Republic of Germany', in Peter Hall (ed.), *The Political Power of Economic Ideas: Keynesianism across Nations* (Princeton: Princeton University Press, 1989).

Allen, Christopher S., 'From Social Market to Mesocorporatism to European Integration: The Politics of German Economic Policy', in Michael G. Huelshoff, Andrei S. Markovits and Simon Reich (eds), *From Bundesrepublik to Deutschland: German Politics after Unification* (Ann Arbor: University of Michigan Press, 1993).

Almond, Gabriel, 'Communism and Political Culture Theory', *Comparative Politics*, 15:1 (1983), pp, 127–38.

Almond, Gabriel and Sidney Verba, *The Civic Culture* (Princeton: Princeton University Press, 1963).

American Jewish Committee, 'Perspectives from Berlin on Anti-Semitism', *AJC Briefing Paper* (Berlin: American Jewish Committee, 11 June 2002).

Anderson, Christopher J. and Daniel S. Ward, 'Barometer Elections in Comparative Perspective', *Electoral Studies*, 14:1 (1995), pp. 1–14.

Andert, Reinhold and Wolfgang Herzberg, *Der Sturz: Honecker im Kreuzverhör*, 3rd edn (Berlin, Weimar: Aufbau-Verlag, 1991).

Arbeitsgemeinschaft deutscher wirtschaftswissenschaftlicher Forschungsinstitute e.V., 'Die Lage der Weltwirtschaft und der deutschen Wirtschaft im Herbst 2002', *DIW-Wochenbericht*, 69:42 (2002), pp. 703–55.

Asmus, Ronald D. and Kenneth Pollack, 'The New Transatlantic Project', *Policy Review*, 115 (2002), pp. 3–18.

Atkinson, Alexander B., 'Conclusions', in Alexander B. Atkinson and Gunnar Viby Mogensen (eds), *Welfare and Work Incentives. A North European Perspective* (Oxford: Oxford University Press, 1993).

Atkinson, Alexander B., *The Economic Consequences of Rolling Back the Welfare State* (Cambridge, MA: MIT Press, 1999).

Ausstellung des Bundesministeriums der Justiz (ed.), *Im Namen des Volkes? Über die Justiz im Staat der SED* (Leipzig: Forum Verlag, 1994).

Bach, Stefan, 'Die Unternehmensteuerreform', in Achim Truger (ed.), *Rot-grüne Sturreformen in Deutschland: Eine Zwischenbilanz* (Marburg: Metropolis Verlag, 2001).

Bach, Stefan and Dieter Vesper, 'Finanzpolitik und Wiedervereinigung – Bilanz nach 10 Jahren', *Vierteljahrshefte zur Wirtschaftsforschung*, 69:2 (2000), pp. 194–224.

Bach, Stefan and Dieter Vesper, 'Finanz- und Investitionskrise erzwingt grundlegende Reform der Kommunalfinanzen', *DIW-Wochenbericht*, 68:31 (2002), pp. 505–17.

Bahr, Egon, 'Ein Generalstab kein Tabu mehr', *Europäische Sicherheit*, 41:3 (1992), p. 127.

Bahry, Donna, Cynthia Boaz and Stacy Burnett Gordon, 'Tolerance, Transition, and Support for Civil Liberties in Russia', *Comparative Political Studies*, 30:4 (1997), pp. 484–510.

Baker, James A., III, *The Politics of Diplomacy: Revolution, War and Peace 1989–1992* (New York: G. P. Putnam's Sons, 1995).

Baker, Kendall L., Russell J. Dalton and Kai Hildebrandt, *Germany Transformed: Political Culture and the New Politics* (Cambridge, MA: Harvard University Press, 1981).

Banchoff, Thomas, *The German Problem Transformed. Institutions, Politics, and Foreign Policy, 1945–1995* (Ann Arbor: University of Michigan Press, 1999).

Barnes, Samuel, Max Kaase, *et al.*, *Political Action: Mass Participation in Five Western Democracies* (Beverly Hills: Sage 1979).

Barry, Brian, *Sociologists, Economists, and Democracy* (London: Macmillan, 1970).

Bartsch, Klaus *et al.*, 'Bündnis für Arbeit in schwierigem Fahrwasser. Gesamtwirtschaftliche Entwicklung, finanzpolitische Fehlentscheidungen und Alternativen', *WSI-Mitteilungen*, 52:12 (1999), pp. 805–25.

Blanchard, Olivier, *Macroeconomics*, 2nd edn (London: Prentice-Hall, 2001).

Baun, Michael J., 'The Maastricht Treaty as High Politics: Germany, France, and European Integration', *Political Science Quarterly*, 110:4 (1995/96), pp. 605–24.

Baylis, Thomas A., 'Transforming the East German Economy: Shock without Therapy', in Michael Huelshoff, Andrei Markovits and Simon Reich (eds), *From Bundesrepublik to Deutschland: German Politics after Unification* (Ann Arbor: University of Michigan Press, 1993).

Bergmann, Werner, 'Wie viele Deutsche sind rechtsextrem, fremdenfeindlich und antisemitistisch? Ergebnisse der empirischen Forschung von 1990 bis 2000', in Wolfgang Benz (ed.), *Auf dem Weg zum Bürgerkrieg? Rechtsextremismus und Gewalt gegen Fremde in Deutschland* (Frankfurt-am-Main: Campus Verlag, 2001).

Betz, Hans-Georg, *Radical Right Wing Populism in Western Europe* (New York: St Martin's Press, 1994).

Betz, Hans-Georg, 'The Evolution and Transformation of the German Party System', in Christopher S. Allen (ed.), *Transformation of the German Political Party System* (New York: Berghahn, 1999).

Betz, Hans-Georg and Stefan Immerfall (eds), *The New Politics of the Right* (New York: St Martin's Press, 1998).

Blair, Tony, *The Third Way: New Politics for the New Century* (London: Fabian Society, 1998).

Boarman, Patrick, *Germany's Economic Dilemma: Inflation and the Balance of Payments* (New Haven: Yale University Press, 1964).

Böckenförde, Ernst-Wolfgang, 'Verfassungsgerichtsbarkeit: Strukturfragen, Organisation, Legitimation', *Neue Juristische Wochenschrift*, 1:1 (1999), pp. 9–17.

Bode, Imgo, 'Die Bewegung des Dritten Sektors und ihre Grenzen', *Forschungsjournal Neue Soziale Bewegung*, 13:1 (2000), pp. 48–52.

Brand, Karl-Werner, Detlef Büsser and Dieter Rucht, *Aufbruch in eine andere Gesellschaft: Neue Soziale Bewegungen in der Bundesrepublik* (Frankfurt: Campus Verlag, 1983).

Braunthal, Gerhard, *The German Social Democrats since 1969: A Party in Power and Opposition* (Boulder, CO: Westview Press, 1994).

Breyman, Steve, *Why Movements Matter: The West German Peace Movement and US Arms Control Policy* (Albany: State University of New York Press, 2001).

Bulmer, Simon, Charlie Jeffery and William E. Paterson, *Germany's European Diplomacy: Shaping the Regional Milieu* (Manchester: Manchester University Press, 2000).

Burchardt, M., 'Die Praxis des aktuellen Länderfinanzausgleichs und das Problem der Integration der neuen Bundesländer', *WSI-Mitteilungen*, 45:9 (1992), pp. 577–90.

Burgess, John, *The East German Church and the End of Communism* (New York: Oxford University Press, 1997).

Caesar, Rolf, *Der Handlungsspielraum von Notenbanken* (Baden-Baden: Nomos, 1981).

Calleo, David P., *The German Problem Reconsidered* (Cambridge: Cambridge University Press, 1978).

Canache, Damarys, Jeffrey J. Mondak and Mitchell A. Seligson, 'Meaning and Measurement in Cross-National Research on Satisfaction with Democracy', *Public Opinion Quarterly*, 65:4 (2001), pp. 506–28.

Caniglia, Beth, 'Informal Alliances vs. Institutional Ties: The Effects of Elite Alliances on Environmental TSMO Networks', *Mobilization*, 6:1 (2001), pp. 37–54.

Carpenter, Ted Galen, *Peace and Freedom: Foreign Policy for a Constitutional Republic* (Washington, DC: The Cato Institute, 2002).

Carsten, F. L., *The Reichswehr and Politics, 1918–1933* (Berkeley: University of California Press, 1966).

Chandler, William M., 'Federalism and Political Parties', in Herman Bakvis and William M. Chandler (eds), *Federalism and the Role of the State* (Toronto: Toronto University Press, 1987).

Chandler, William M., 'The Europeanization of National Politics? The 2002 National Elections in France and Germany', Paper presented at the annual meeting of the European Union Studies Association, Nashville, TN, 15–17 May 2003.

Chappell, Henry, Thomas Havrilesky and Bob Roy McGregor, 'Partisan Monetary Policy: Presidential Influence through the Power of Appointments', *Quarterly Journal of Economics*, 108:1 (1993), pp. 185–218.

Christoph Sterzing, 'Deutsche Rüstungsexporte: Politik zwischen Moral und Interesse', in Volker Perthes (ed.), *Deutsche Nahostpolitik. Interessen und Optionen* (Schwalbach: Wochenschau-Verlag, 2001).

Clay, Clemens, 'Disquiet on the Eastern Front: The Christian Democratic Union in Germany's New *Länder*', *German Politics*, 2:2 (1993), pp. 200–23.

Clemens, Clay, 'Assessing the Kohl Legacy', in Clay Clemens and William E. Paterson (eds), *The Kohl Chancellorship* (London: Frank Cass, 1998).

Clemens, Clay, 'Party Management as a Leadership Resource: Kohl and the CDU/CSU', in Clay Clemens and William E. Paterson (eds), *The Kohl Chancellorship* (London: Frank Cass, 1998).

Clay, Lucius D., *Decision in Germany* (Garden City, NY: Doubleday & Co., 1950).

Connaughton, Richard M., 'Organizing British Joint Rapid Reaction Forces', *Joint Forces Quarterly*, 26:1 (2000), pp. 87–94.

Coogan, Kevin, *Dreamer of the Day* (New York: Autonomedia, 1999).

Cooper, Alice, 'When Just Causes Conflict with Accepted Means: The German Peace Movement and Military Intervention in Bosnia', *German Politics and Society*, 15:3 (1997), pp. 99–118.

Cooper, Alice, 'Party-Sponsored Protest and the Movement Society: The CDU/CSU Mobilizes against Citizenship Law Reform', *German Politics*, 11:2 (2002), pp. 88–104.

Cox, Robert, 'The Social Construction of an Imperative: Why Welfare Reform Happened in Denmark and the Netherlands, but Not in Germany', *World Politics*, 53:3 (2001), pp. 463–98.

Craig, Gordon A., *The Politics of the Prussian Army, 1640–1945* (New York: Oxford University Press, 1955).

Crozier, Michel, *La société bloquée* (Paris: Editions du Seuill, 1970).

Cukierman, Alex, *Central Bank Strategy, Credibility, and Independence: Theory and Evidence* (Cambridge, MA: MIT Press, 1992).

Czaplinski, Wladyslaw, 'The New Polish–German Treaties and the Changing Political Structure of Europe', *American Journal of International Law*, 86:1 (1992), pp. 163–73.

Dahl, Robert A., *Democracy and its Critics* (New Haven: Yale University Press, 1989).

Dahlem, Franz, *Weg und Ziel des antifaschistischen Kampfes: Ausgewählte Reden und Aufsätze* ((East) Berlin: VVN Verlag, 1952).

Dahlem, Franz, 'Einige Probleme unserer künftigen Arbeit in Deutschland: Rede vor ehemaligen Häftlingen des KZ Mauthausen', in Franz Dahlem, *Ausgewählte Reden und Aufsätze 1919–1979. Zur Geschichte der Arbeiterbewegung* ((East) Berlin: Dietz Verlag, 1980).

Dahlerup, Drude, 'From a Small to a Large Minority: Women in Scandinavian Politics', *Scandinavian Political Studies*, 11:4 (1988), pp. 275–99.

Dalton, Russell, 'Two German Electorates?', in Gordon Smith, William E. Paterson and Peter H. Merkl (eds), *Developments in German Politics* (Durham, NC: Duke University Press, 1992).

Dalton, Russell, *Politics in Germany* (New York: HarperCollins, 1993).

Dalton, Russell, 'Political Cleavages, Issues, and Electoral Change', in Lawrence Le Duc, Richard G. Niemi and Pippa Norris (eds), *Comparing Democracies* (London: Sage, 1996).

Dalton, Russell, *Citizen Politics: Public Opinion and Political Parties in Advanced Western Democracies*, 2nd edn (Chatham, NJ: Chatham House Publishers, 1996).

De Gucht, Karel, 'The European Commission: Countdown to Extinction?', *Journal of European Integration*, 25:2 (2003), pp. 165–8.

De Felice, Renzo, *Fascism: An Informal Introduction to its Theory and Practice* (New Brunswick, NJ: Transaction, 1976).

Decker, Frank and Julia von Blumenthal, 'Die bundespolitische Durchdringung der Landtagswahlen. Eine empirische Analyse von 1970 bis 2001', *Das Parlament*, 33:1 (March 2002), pp. 144–65.

della Porta, Donnatella, 'Protest, Protesters, and Protest Policing', in Marco Giugni, Doug McAdam and Charles Tilly (eds), *How Social Movements Matter* (Minneapolis: University of Minnesota Press, 1999).

DePorte, A. W., *Europe Between the Superpowers: The Enduring Balance* (New Haven: Yale University Press, 1979).

Der Bundesminister der Verteidigung, *Verteidigungspolitische Richtlinien* (Bonn: BMVg, 26 November 1992).

Der Bundestag und Bundesarchiv, *Der Parlamentarische Rat 1948–1949: Akten und Protokolle*, Band 1 (Boppard-am-Rhein: Harold Boldt Verlag, 1975).

Deutsche Bundesbank (ed.), *Fifty Years of the Deutsche Mark* (Oxford: Oxford University Press, 1989).

Deutsche Bundesbank, *Monthly Report* (Frankfurt: Deutsche Bundesbank, various years).

Deutsche Bundesbank, 'The Deutsche Bundesbank: Its Monetary Policy Instruments and Functions', *Special Series, 7* (Frankfurt: Deutsche Bundesbank, 1989).

Deutscher Bundestag, *Materialien der Enquete-Kommission 'Aufarbeitung von Geschichte und Folgen der SED-Diktatur in Deutschland'* (Baden-Baden: Nomos; Frankfurt-am-Main: Suhrkamp, 1995).

Deutsches Institut für Wirtschaftsforschung, 'Schwerpunktheft Steuerreform', *Vierteljahrsheft zur Wirtschaftsforschung*, 66:3/4 (1997), pp. 289–411.

Deutsches Institut für Wirtschaftsforschung/Finanzwissenschaftliches Forschungsinstitut an der Universität zu Köln, *Anforderungen an und Anknüpfungspunkte für eine Reform des Steuersystems unter ökologischen Aspekten, Berichte des Umweltbundesamtes 99/3, Berlin, Teil 1: Das deutsche Steuersystem – traditionelle Ziele, Mängel und Reformperspektiven* (Düsseldorf and Köln: DIW and FiFo, 1999).

Deutschkron, Inge, *Israel und die Deutschen: Das schwierige Verhältnis* (Cologne: Verlag Wissenschaft und Politik, 1983).

Di Palma, Giuseppe, *To Craft Democracies* (Cambridge: Cambridge University Press, 1990).

Diner, Dan, *Beyond the Conceivable: Studies on Germany, Nazism and the Holocaust* (Berkeley and Los Angeles: University of California Press, 2000).

Diner, Dan, *Feindbild Amerika: Über die Bestädigkeit eines Ressentiments* (Munich: Propyläen Verlag, 2002).

Dingeldey, Irene, 'Familienbesteuerung in Deutschland. Kritische Bilanz und Reformperspektiven', in Achim Truger (ed.), *Rotgrüne Stuerreformen in Deutschland: Eine Zwischenbilanz* (Marburg: Metropolis Verlag, 2001).

Dinkel, Rainer, 'Der Zusammenhang zwischen Bundes- und Landtagswahlergebnissen', *Politische Vierteljahresschrift*, 18:2 (1977), pp. 348–59.

Dorff, Robert H., 'German Policy toward Peace Support Operations', in Thomas-Durell Young (ed.), *Force, Statecraft and German Unity: The Struggle to Adapt Institutions and Practices* (Carlisle Barracks, PA: Strategic Studies Institute, 1996).

Drews, Erhard *et al.*, 'Das neue deutsche Heer: Zielsetzung, Konzeption, und Elemente der Heeresstruktur 5.', *Truppenpraxis*, 35:4 (1991), pp. 362–5

Dubiel, Helmut, *Niemand ist Frei von der Geschichte: Die nationalsozialistische Herrschaft in den Debatten des Deutschen Bundestages* (Munich: Hanser Verlag, 1999).

Duffield, John S., *World Power Forsaken: Political Culture, International Institutions, and German Security Policy after Unification* (Stanford: Stanford University Press, 1998).

Duisburger Institut für Sprach- und Sozialforschung, 'Die Nahost-Berichterstattung zur Zweiten Intifada in der deutschen Printmedien, unter besonderer Berücksichtigung des Israel-Bildes. Analyse diskursiver Ereignisse im Zeitraum von September 2000 bis August 2001' (Duisburg: Duisburger Institut für Sprach- und Sozialforschung, 2002).

Dukes, Jack R. and Joachim Remak (eds), *Another Germany: A Reconsideration of the Imperial Era* (Boulder, CO: Westview Press, 1988).

Dyson, Kenneth H. F., *Party, State and Bureaucracy in Western Germany* (Beverly Hills: Sage, 1997)

Eatwell, Roger, *Fascism: A History* (New York: Penguin, 1996).

Ebsworth, Raymond, *Restoring Democracy in Germany* (London: Stevens & Sons, 1960).

Eckstein, Harry, 'A Culturalist Theory of Political Change', *American Political Science Review*, 82:3 (1988), pp. 789–804.

Edinger, Lewis J., 'Post-Totalitarian Leadership: Elites in the German Federal Republic', *American Political Science Review*, 54:1 (1960), pp. 58–82.

Edinger, Lewis, *West German Politics* (New York: Columbia University Press, 1986).

Edinger, Lewis and Brigitte L. Nacos, 'From the Bonn to the Berlin Republic: Can a Stable Democracy Continue?', *Political Science Quarterly*, 113:2 (1998), pp. 179–91.

Eisenmann, Peter and Gerhard Hirscher (eds), *Die Entwicklung der Volksparteien im vereinten Deutschland* (Bonn: Aktuell, 1992).

Epstein, Catherine, *The Last Revolutionaries: German Communists and Their Century* (Cambridge, MA: Harvard Univeristy Press, 2003).

Eschenburg, Theodor, *Jahre der Besatzung, 1945–1949. Band 1: Geschichte der Bundesrepublik Deutschland* (Stuttgart: Deutsche Verlags-Anstalt, 1983).

European Central Bank, *The Monetary Policy of the ECB* (Frankfurt: European Central Bank, 2001).

Fabritius, Georg, *Wechselwirkungen zwischen Landtagswahlen und Bundespolitik* (Meisenheim-am-Glan: Verlag Anton Hain, 1978).

Fabritius, Georg, 'Sind Landtagswahlen Bundesteilwahlen?', *Aus Politik und Zeitgeschichte*, 21/79 (26 May 1979), pp. 23–38.

Fabritius, Georg, 'Landtagswahlen und Bundespolitik', in Hans-Georg Wehling (ed.), *Westeuropas Parteiensysteme im Wandel* (Stuttgart: Kohlhammer Verlag, 1983).

Ferree, Myra Marx, 'Thinking Globally, Acting Locally: German and American Feminism in the World System', *AICGS Humanities*, 11 (2002), pp. 13–29.

Ferree, Myra Marx and William Gamson, 'The Gendering of Abortion Discourse: Assessing Global Feminist Influence in the United States and Germany', in Donnatella della Porta, Hanspeter Kriesi and Dieter Rucht (eds), *Social Movements in a Globalizing World* (London: Macmillan, 1999).

Fessen, Bertolt, 'Ressentiment und Fehlwahrnehmung', *Berliner Debate INITIAL*, 6:4/5 (1995), pp. 132–44.

Finifter, Ada W. and Ellen Mickiewicz, 'Redefining the Political System of the USSR', *American Political Science Review*, 86:4 (1992), pp. 857–74.

Fitzgerald, Frances, 'George Bush and the World', *The New York Review of Books* (26 September 2002), pp. 80–6.

Flassbeck, H., 'Moderne Finanzpolitik für Deutschland', *WSI-Mitteilungen*, 54:8 (1999), pp. 498–504.

Forever in the Shadow of Hitler: Original Documents of the Historikerstreit, trans. by James Knowlton and Truett Cates (Atlantic Highlands, NJ: Humanities Press, 1993).

Forschungsgruppe Wahlen e.V. Mannheim, *Bundestagswahl: Eine Analyse der Wahl vom 22. September 2002, Bericht Nr. 108* (Mannheim: Forschungsgruppe Wahlen e.V. Mannheim, 2002).

Forschungsgruppe Wahlen e.V. Mannheim, *Bundestagswahlbericht 2002* (Mannheim: Forschungsgruppe Wahlen e.V. Mannheim, 2002).

Franke, Günter, 'The Bundesbank and the Markets', in Deutsche Bundesbank (ed.), *Fifty Years of the Deutsche Mark* (Oxford: Oxford University Press, 1989).

Frei, Norbert, *The Adenauer Era and the Nazi Past*, trans. by Joel Golb (New York: Columbia University Press, 2002).

Freudenstein, Roland, 'Poland, Germany and the EU', *International Affairs*, 74:1 (1998), pp. 41–54.

Frey, Bruno and Friedrich Schneider, 'Central Bank Behavior: A Positive Empirical Analysis', *Journal of Monetary Economics*, 9:2 (1987), pp. 291–315.

Fricke, Karl Wilhelm and Roger Engelmann, *Konzentrierte Schläge: Staatssicherheitsaktionen und politische Prozesse in der DDR 1953–1956* (Berlin: Ch. Links, 1998).

Friedman, Milton, 'The Role of Monetary Policy', *American Economic Review*, 58:1 (1968), pp. 1–17.

Friedrich, Carl J., 'Rebuilding the German Constitution, I and II', *American Political Science Review*, 43:3 and 43:4 (1949), pp. 461–82, 704–20.

Friend, Julius W., *The Linchpin: French–German Relations, 1950–1990* (New York: Praeger, 1991).

Fuchs, Dieter, 'Trends of Political Support in the Federal Republic of Germany', in Dirk Berg-Schlosser and Ralf Rytlewski (eds), *Political Culture in Germany* (London: Macmillan, 1993).

Fuchs, Dieter, 'The Democratic Culture in Unified Germany', in Pippa Norris (ed.), *Critical Citizens* (Oxford: Oxford University Press, 1999).

Fuchs, Dieter and Robert Rohrschneider, 'Postmaterialism and the Electoral Choice before and after German Unification', *West European Politics*, 21:2 (1998), pp. 95–116.

Galonska, Andreas, *Landesparteiensysteme im Föderalismus: Rheinland-Pfalz und Hessen, 1945–1996* (Wiesbaden: Deutscher Universitätsverlag, 1999).

Gardner Feldman, Lily, *The Special Relationship between West Germany and Israel* (Boston: Allen & Unwin, 1984).

Gardner Feldman, Lily, 'The Jewish Role in German–American Relations', in Frank Trommler and Elliott Shore (eds), *The German–American Encounter. Conflict and Cooperation between Two Cultures 1800–2000* (New York: Berghahn, 2001).

Gauck, Joachim, *Die Stasi-Akten: Das unheimliche Erbe der DDR* (Hamburg: Rowohlt, 1992).

Geddes, B., 'A Comparative Perspective on the Leninist Legacy in Eastern Europe', *Comparative Political Studies*, 28:2 (1995), pp. 239–74.

Gedmin, Jeffrey, 'Helmut Kohl, Giant', *Policy Review*, 96 (1999), pp. 37–50.

Germany, Bundesministerium der Finanzen, *Deutsches Stabilitätsprogramm, Aktualisiserung* (Berlin: BMF, Oktober 2000).

Germany, Bundesministerium der Finanzen, *Steuerreform 2000* (Berlin: BMF, 2000).

Germany, Bundesministerium der Finanzen, *Mineral Oil and Electricity Taxation within the Ecological Tax Reform* (Berlin: BMF, 2001).

Germany, Bundesministerium der Finanzen, *Bund-Länder Finanzbeziehungen auf der Grundlage der geltenden Finanzverfassungsordung* (Berlin: BMF, 2002).

Germany, Bundesministerium der Finanzen, *Ergebnis der Steuerschätzung November 2002* (Berlin: BMF, 2002).

Germany, Bundesministerium der Finanzen, *Finanzielle Auswirkungen des Gesetzentwurfs zum Abbau von Steuervergünstigungen und Ausnahmeregelungen* (Berlin: BMF, 2002).

Germany, Bundesministerium der Finanzen, *Tax Reform 2000 – An Overview* (Berlin: BMF, 2002).

Germany, Bundesministerium der Finanzen, *Übersicht über den Fonds 'Aufbauhilfe'* (Berlin: BMF, 2002).

Germany, Bundesministerium der Verteidigung, *Konzeptionelle Leitlinie zur Weiterentwicklung der Bundeswehr* (Bonn: Informationsstab, 12 July 1994).

Germany, Federal Ministry of Defence (Sts/Org 1 – Az 10–02–01 vom 9.02.93), 'Koordinierung des Einsatzes der Bundeswehr für Unterstützungsaufgaben' (Bonn: BMVg, 9 February 1993).

Germany, Federal Ministry of Defence (Sts/Org 1 – Az 10–02–01 vom 31.08.94), 'Entscheidungsabläufe im Ministerium für die Einsatzführungs der Bundeswehr im Frieden' (Bonn: BMVg, 31 August 1994).

Germany, Federal Ministry of Defence, *White Paper 1985: The Situation and Development of the Federal Armed Forces* (Bonn: Federal Ministry of Defence, 1985).

Germany, Federal Ministry of Defence, *White Paper 1994* (Bonn: Federal Ministry of Defence, 5 April 1994).

Gesterkamp, Harald, 'Professionell auf der Weltbühne, verankert in der Region', *Forschungsjournal Neue Soziale Bewegung*, 13:1 (2000), pp. 92–6.

Gibowski, Wolfgang, 'Social Change and the Electorate: An Analysis of the 1998 Bundestagswahl', *German Politics*, 8:2 (1998), pp. 10–32.

Giddens, Anthony, *The Third Way: The Renewal of Social Democracy* (Cambridge: Polity Press, 1998).

Giddens, Anthony, *The Third Way and Its Critics* (Cambridge: Polity Press, 2000).

Giddens, Anthony (ed.), *The Global Third Way Debate* (Cambridge: Polity Press, 2001).

Gimbel, John, *The American Occupation of Germany: Politics and the Military, 1945–1949* (Stanford: Stanford University Press, 1968).

Goetz, Klaus, 'Integration Policy in a Europeanised State: Germany and the Intergovernmental Conference', *Journal of European Public Policy*, 3:1 (1996), pp. 23–44.

Golay, John Ford, *The Founding of the Federal Republic of Germany* (Chicago: The University of Chicago Press, 1958).

Goldstein, Judith, *Ideas, Interests, and American Trade Policy* (Ithaca, NY: Cornell University Press, 1993)

Goodrick-Clarke, Nicholas, *Black Sun* (New York: New York University Press, 2002).

Görl, Tilo, 'Regionalisierung der politischen Landschaft in den neuen Bundesländern am Beispiel der Landtagswahlen 1999 in Brandenburg, Thüringen und Sachsen', *Zeitschrift für Parlamentsfragen*, 32:1 (2001), pp. 94–125.

Graf, William D. (ed.), *The Internationalization of the German Political Economy* (New York: St Martin's Press, 1992).

Green, Simon, 'Beyond Ethnoculturalism? German Citizenship in the New Millennium', *German Politics*, 9:3 (2000), pp. 105–24.

Gregor, James, *Italian Fascism and Developmental Dictatorship* (Princeton: Princeton University Press, 1979).

Griffin, Roger, *The Nature of Fascism* (New York: Routledge, 1991).

Griffin, Roger, 'Net Gains and GUD Reactions: Patterns of Prejudice in a Neo-Fascist Groupuscule', *Patterns of Prejudice*, 33:2 (2000) pp. 31–50.

Gross, D. M., 'The Relative Importance of Some Causes of Unemployment: The Case of West Germany', *Weltwirtschaftsarchiv*, 124:3 (1988), pp. 501–23.

Grotewohl, Otto, *Im Kampf um Die Einige Deutsche Demokratische Republik: Reden und Aufsätze, Band VI, Auswahl aus den Jahren 1958–1960* ((East) Berlin: Dietz Verlag, 1964), pp. 7–8.

Gudera, Gert, 'The German Army – The Bundeswehr: Its Missions, Tasks, New Structure and Equipment Plans', *NATO Review*, 47:1 (2002), pp. 53–61.

Habermas, Jürgen, *Legitimation Crisis* (London: Heinemann, 1976).

Habermas, Jürgen, *The Theory of Communicative Action*, 2 (Boston: Beacon Press, 1987).

Hacke, Christian, 'Die Aussenpolitik der Regierung Schröder-Fischer: Zwischenbilanz und Perspectiven', *Aus Politik und Zeitgeschichte*, B48/2002 (2 December 2002), pp. 7–15.

Hager, Carol, 'Environmentalism and Democracy in the Two Germanies', *German Politics*, 1:1 (1992), pp. 95–118.

Hall, Peter (ed.), *The Political Power of Economic Ideas: Keynesianism across Nations* (Princeton: Princeton University Press, 1989).

Hallett, Graham, *The Social Economy of West Germany* (New York: St Martin's Press, 1973).

Hamdan, Fouad, 'Aufdecken und Konfrontieren: NGO-Kommunikation am Beispiel Greenpeace', *Forschungsjournal Neue Soziale Bewegung*, 13:3 (2000), pp. 69–74.

Hamilton, Daniel, *German–American Relations and the Campaign Against Terrorism* (Washington, DC: American Institute for Contemporary German Relations, 2002).

Hampton, Mary N., 'NATO at the Creation: US Foreign Policy and the Wilsonian Impulse', *Security Studies*, 4:3 (1995), pp. 610–56.

Hampton, Mary N., 'Germany, the US, and NATO: Creating Positive Identity in Trans-Atlantia', *Security Studies*, 7;2 and 7;3 (1998/99) (special double issue), pp. 235–69.

Hampton, Mary N., '"The Past, Present, and the Perhaps": Is Germany A "Normal" Power?', *Security Studies*, 10:2 (2000/2001), pp. 179–202.

Hampton, Mary and James Sperling, 'Positive/Negative Identity in the Euro-Atlantic Communities: Germany's Past, Europe's Future', in *Journal of European Integration*, 24:4 (2002), pp. 281–301.

Hanrieder, Wolfram F., *West German Foreign Policy, 1949–1963: International Pressure and Domestic Response* (Stanford: Stanford University Press, 1967).

Harding, Rebecca and William E. Paterson (eds), *The Future of the German Economy* (Manchester: Manchester University Press, 2000).

Harlen, Christine Margerum, 'Schröder's Economic Reforms: The End of *Reformstau*?', *German Politics*, 11:1 (2002), pp. 61–80.

Harnisch, Sebastian and Hanns W. Maull (eds), *Germany as a Civilian Power? – The Foreign Policy of the Berlin Republic* (Manchester: Manchester University Press, 2001).

Hasselbach, Ingo, *Führer-Ex: Memoirs of a Former Neo-Nazi* (New York: Random House, 1996).

Havrilesky, Thomas, *The Pressures on American Monetary Policy* (Boston: Kluwer Academic, 1993).

Hefeker, Carsten, 'The Agony of Central Power: Fiscal Federalism in the German Reich', *European Review of Economic History*, 5:1 (2001), pp. 119–42.

Heinze, Rolf G., *Die blockierte Gesellschaft* (Opladen: Leske & Budrich, 1998).

Heinze, Rolf G. *et al.*, *Vom Wohlfahrtsstaat zum Wettbewerbsstaat: Arbeitsmarkt und Sozialpolitik in den 90er Jahren* (Opladen: Leske & Budrich, 1999).

Hellman, Gunther, 'Deutchland in Europa: eine symbiotische Beziehung', *Aus Politik und Zeitgeschichte*, B48/2002 (2 December 2002), pp. 24–32.

Hellman, Gunther, 'Germany's Balancing Act in Foreign Policy', *Internationale Politik* (Transatlantic edn), 3:4 (2002), pp. 17–23.

Hellwig, M. and M. Neumann, 'Economic Policy in Germany: Was there a Turn-Around?' *Economic Policy*, 5 (1987), pp. 105–45.

Helms, Ludger, '"Chief executives" and Their Parties: The Case of Germany', *German Politics*, 11:2 (2002), pp. 146–64.

Henning, Randall, *Currencies and Politics in the United States, Germany, and Japan* (Washington, DC: International Institute of Economics, 1994).

Hennis, Wilhelm, *Richtlinienkompetenz und Regierungstechnik* (Tübingen: J. C. B. Mohr, 1964).

Herf, Jeffrey, *Reactionary Modernism: Technology, Culture and Politics in Weimar and the Third Reich* (New York: Cambridge University Press, 1984).

Herf, Jeffrey, *War By Other Means: Soviet Power, West German Resistance and the Battle of the Euromissiles* (New York: Free Press, 1991).

Herf, Jeffrey, 'German Communism, the Discourse of "Antifascist Resistance", and the Jewish Catastrophe', in Michael Geyer and John W. Boyer (eds), *Resistance Against the Third Reich, 1933–1990* (Chicago: University of Chicago Press, 1994).

Herf, Jeffrey, *Divided Memory: The Nazi Past in the Two Germanys* (Cambridge, MA: Harvard University Press, 1997).

Herf, Jeffrey, 'A New *Schlussstrichmentalität*? The Schröder Government, the Berlin Memorial and the Politics of Memory', in Carl Lankowski (ed)., *Germany After the 1998 Federal Elections* (Washington, DC: American Institute for Contemporary German Studies, 1999).

Herf, Jeffrey, 'Abstraction, Specificity and the Holocaust: Recent Disputes over Memory in Germany', *Bulletin of the German Historical Institute* (London), 22:2 (2000), pp. 20–35.

Hering, Martin, 'Moving the Deadweight of Ideas: The Social Democratic Party and the Reform of Germany's Pension System', Paper delievered at the 97th annual meeting of the American Political Science Association, San Francisco, 30 August–2 September, 2001.

Heuss, Theodor, *Der Grossen Reden: Der Staatsmann* (Tübingen: Rainer Wunderlich Verlag, 1965).

Hickel, R., 'Föderaler Finanzausgleich im vereinten Deutschland nach 1995', *WSI-Mitteilungen*, 45:9 (1992), pp. 563–76.

Higham, Charles, *American Swastika* (Garden City, NY: Doubleday, 1985).

Hirschman, Albert, 'Exit, Voice, and the Fate of the German Democratic Republic', *World Politics*, 45:2 (1993), pp. 173–202.

Höcker, Beate, 'Geschlechterdemokratie im europäischen Kontext', *Aus Politik und Zeitgeschichte*, B31–32, 2000 (28 July 2000), pp. 30–8.

Höffe, O., 'Wieviel Politik ist dem Verfassungsgericht erlaubt?', *Der Staat*, 38:1 (1999), pp. 171–93.

Hofferbert, Richard I. and Hans-Dieter Klingemann, 'Remembering the Bad Old Days: Human Rights, Economic Conditions, and Democratic Performance in Transitional Regimes', *European Journal of Political Research*, 36:2 (1999), pp. 155–74.

Hofferbert, Richard I. and Hans-Dieter Klingemann, 'Democracy and Its Discontents in Post-Wall Germany', *International Political Science Review*, 22:4 (2001), pp. 363–78.

Holsti, Kalevi J., *Peace and War: Armed Conflicts and International Order, 1648–1989* (Cambridge: Cambridge University Press, 1991).

Holzhauer, Johanna and Agnes Steinbauer, *Frauen an der Macht. Profile prominenter Politikerinnen* (Frankfurt-am-Main: Eichborn, 1994).

Hombach, Bodo, *The Politics of the New Centre* (Cambridge: Polity Press, 2000).

Horwitz, Gordon J., *In the Shadow of Death: Living Outside the Gates of Mauthausen* (New York: Free Press, 1990).

Hough, Dan, *The Fall and Rise of the PDS in Eastern Germany* (Birmingham: Birmingham University Press, 2002).

Huelshoff, Michael G., 'The "Storm Before the Calm": Labor Markets, Unemployment, and *Standort Deutschland*', in Andrei S. Markovits and Carl Lankowski (eds), *Democracy and Change in Germany* (New York: Berghahn, 1999).

Huelshoff, Michael G., 'The European Council and EU Summitry: A Comparative Analysis of the Austrian and German Presidencies', *Contemporary Austrian Studies*, 10:1 (2002), pp. 92–117.

Huelshoff, Michael, Andrei Markovits and Simon Reich (eds), *From Bundesrepublik to Deutschland: German Politics after Unification* (Ann Arbor: University of Michigan Press, 1993).

Hüther, M., 'Reform des Finanzausgleichs: Handlungsbedarf und Lösungsvorschläge', *Wirtschaftsdienst*, 73:1 (1993), pp. 43–52.

Hyde-Price, Adrian, 'Berlin Republic Takes to Arms', *The World Today*, 55:6 (1999), pp. 13–15.

Hyde-Price, Adrian, *Germany & European Order: Enlarging NATO and the EU* (Manchester: Manchester University Press, 2000).

Ikenberry, G. John, *After Victory: Institutions, Strategic Restraint, and the Rebuilding of Order after Major Wars* (Princeton: Princeton University Press, 2001).

Ikenberry, G. John, 'America's Imperial Ambition', *Foreign Affairs* 81:5 (2002), pp. 44–60.

Imig, Doug and Sidney Tarrow, 'The Europeanization of Movements? A New Approach to Transnational Contention', in Donatella della Porta, Hanspeter Kriesi and Dieter Rucht (eds), *Social Movements in a Globalizing World* (London: Macmillan, 1999).

Inacker, Michael J., 'Macht und Moralität: Über eine neue deutsche Sicherheitspolitik', in Heimo Schwilk und Ulrich Schacht (eds), *Die Selbstbewusste Nation* (Berlin: Ullstein, 1994).

Inglehart, Ronald, *The Silent Revolution: Changing Values and Political Styles among Western Publics* (Princeton: Princeton University Press, 1977).

Inglehart, Ronald, *Culture Shift in Advanced Industrial Society* (Princeton: Princeton University Press, 1990).

International Monetary Fund (IMF), *International Financial Statistics* (Washington, DC: IMF, various years).

Jacoby, Wade, 'Financing the Poor Cousins: Reforming the EU Structural Funds and the German *Länderfinanzausgleich*', Paper presented at the 98th annual meeting of the American Political Science Association, Boston, MA, 4 September 2002.

Jäger, Wolfgang, 'Von der Kanzlerdemokratie zur Koordinationsdemokratie', *Zeitschrift für Parlamentsfragen*, 35:1 (1988), pp. 15–32.

Jansen, Mechtild, 'Nebensache, Detailproblem oder grundlegende Herausforderung', *Forschungsjournal Neue Soziale Bewegung*, 12:3 (1999), pp. 54–7.

Jarausch, Konrad H. (ed.), *Dictatorship as Experience: Towards a Socio-Cultural History of the GDR*, trans. by Eve Duffy (New York: Berghahn, 1999).

Jeffery, Charlie, 'From Hyperstability to Change?', in David Broughton and Mark Donovan (eds), *Changing Party Systems in Western Europe* (London: Pinter, 1999).

Jeffery, Charlie and Daniel Hough, 'The Electoral Cycle and Multi-Level Voting in Germany', *German Politics*, 10:2 (2001), pp. 73–98.

Jeffrey, Charlie and William Paterson, 'Germany and European Integration: Beyond the Stable State?', unpublished manuscript.

Jeismann, Michael (ed.), *Mahnmal Mitte: Eine Kontroverse* (Cologne: Dumont, 1999).

Jesse, Eckhard and Armin Mitter (eds), *Die Gestaltung der deutschen Einheit: Geschichte, Politik, Gesellschaft* (Bonn and Berlin: Bouvier, 1992).

Jewell, Malcolm E. and Sarah M. Morehouse, *Political Parties and Elections in American States*, 4th edn (Washington, DC: CQ Press, 2001).

Johnson, Peter, *The Government of Money* (Ithaca, NY: Cornell University Press, 1998).

Jopp, Mathias, 'Deutsche Europapolitik unter veränderten Rahmenbedingungen: Bilanz–Strategien–Optionen', in Heinrich Schneider, Mathias Jopp and Uwe Schmalz (eds), *Eine neue Deutsche Europapolitik? Rahmenbedingungen –Problemfelder–Optionen* (Bonn: Europa Union Verlag, 2001).

Joppke, Christian, '"Exit" and "Voice" in the East German Revolution', *German Politics*, 2:3 (1993), pp. 393–414.

Jun, Uwe, *Koalitionsbildung in den deutschen Bundesländern* (Opladen: Leske & Budrich, 1994).

Jung, Otmar, *Grundgesetz und Volksentscheid* (Opladen: Westdeutscher Verlag, 1994).

Kaack, Heino, 'Landtagswahlen und Bundespolitik 1970–1972', *Aus Politik und Zeitgeschichte*, 13/74 (30 March 1974), pp. 1–8.

Kaase, Max, 'Demokratische Einstellungen in der Bundesrepublik Deutschland', in Rudolf Wildenmann (ed.), *Sozialwissenschaftliches Jahrbuch für Politik*, 2 (Munich: Gunter Olzog Verlag, 1971).

Kaiser, Karl, *Deutschlands Vereinigung: Die internationalen Aspekte* (Bergisch-Gladbach: Gustav Lübbe Verlag, 1991).

Kaiser, Karl, 'Germany's Unification', *Foreign Affairs*, 70:1 (1991), pp. 179–206.

Kaltenthaler, Karl, *Germany and the Politics of Europe's Money* (Durham, NC: Duke University Press, 1998).

Kamenitsa, Lynn, 'The Process of Political Marginalization: East German Social Movements after the Wall', *Comparative Politics*, 30:3 (1998), pp. 313–33.

Kaplan, Jeffrey, 'Right-Wing Violence in North America', in Tore Bjorgo (ed.), *Terror from the Far Right* (London: Frank Cass, 1995).

Kaplan, Jeffrey, *Encyclopedia of White Power: A Source Book on the Radical Racist Right* (Walnut Creek, CA: AltaMira Press, 2000).

Kaplan, Jeffrey and Leonard Weinberg, *The Emergence of a Euro-American Radical Right* (New Brunswick, NJ: Rutgers University Press, 1998).

Karapin, Roger, *Movements and Democracy in Germany: Conventional Participation, Protest and Violence on the Left and Right, 1969–1995*, unpublished book manuscript.

Karrenberg, Hanns, 'Die Steuerpolitik der laufenden Legislaturperiode aus städtischer Sicht', in Achim Truger (ed.), *Rot-grüne Stuerreformen in Deutschland: Eine Zwischenbilanz* (Marburg: Metropolis Verlag, 2001).

Katzenstein, Peter J., 'Germany as Number Two: Reflections on the German Model', in Andrei S. Markovits (ed.), *The Political Economy of West Germany: Modell Deutschland* (New York: Praeger, 1982).

Katzenstein, Peter, 'The Taming of Power: German Unification, 1989–1990', in Meredith Woo-Cumings and Michael Loriaux (eds), *Past as Prelude: History in the Making of a New World Order* (Boulder, CO: Westview Press, 1993).

Kelleher, Catherine McArdle, 'Defense Organization in Germany: A Twice Told Tale', in Robert J. Art, Vincent Davis and Samuel P. Huntington (eds), *Reorganizing America's Defense: Leadership in War and Peace* (Washington, DC: Pergamon-Brassey's International Defense Publishers, 1985).

Kennedy, Ellen, *The Bundesbank: Germany's Central Bank in the International Monetary System* (New York: Council on Foreign Relations Press, 1991).

Keohane, Robert O., *After Hegemony: Cooperation and Discord in the World Political Economy* (Princeton: Princeton University Press, 1984).

Kielmansegg, Graf Peter, *Nach der Katastrophe: Eine Geschichte des geteilten Deutschland* (Berlin: Siedler Verlag, 2000).

Kirchheimer, Otto, 'The Transformation of Western European Party Systems', in Joseph LaPalombara and Myron Weiner (eds), *Political Parties and Political Development* (Princeton: Princeton University Press, 1966).

Kirchner, Emil, *Decision-Making in the European Community: The Council Presidency and European Integration* (Manchester: Manchester University Press, 1992).

Kirchner, Emil, 'Germany and the European Union: From Junior to Senior Role', in Gordon Smith, Willliam Paterson and Stephen Padgett (eds), *Developments in German Politics* (London: Macmillan, 1996).

Kirchner, Emil and James Sperling, 'Will Form Lead to Function? Institutional Enlargement and the Creation of a European Security and Defence Identity', *Contemporary Security Policy*, 21:1 (2000), pp. 23–45.

Kitschelt, Herbert, 'Political Opportunity Structures and Political Protest: Anti-Nuclear Movements in Four Democracies', *British Journal of Political Science*, 16:1 (1986), pp. 57–85.

Kitschelt, Herbert, 'Left-Libertarian Parties', *World Politics*, 40:2 (1989), pp. 194–234.

Kitschelt, Herbert, *The Radical Right in Western Europe* (Ann Arbor: University of Michigan Press, 1995).

Kitschelt, Herbert (with Anthony McGann), *The Radical Right in Western Europe* (Ann Arbor: University of Michigan Press, 1997).

Klandermans, Bert, 'Mobilization Forum: Must We Redefine Social Movements as Ideologically Structured Action?', *Mobilization*, 5:1 (2000), pp. 25–30.

Klein, Ansgar, 'Soziale Bewegungen bleiben ein bedeutender politischer Faktor', *Forschungsjournal Neue Soziale Bewegung*, 13:1 (2000), pp. 36–42.

Kloke, Martin W., *Israel und die deutsche Linke: Zur Geschichte eines schwierigen Verhältnisses* (Frankfurt: Haag & Herchen, 1990).

Kocka, Jürgen (ed.), *Historische DDR-Forschung: Aufsätze und Studien* (Berlin: Akadamie Verlag, 1993).

Kogon, Eugen, *Die unvollendete Erneuerung* (Frankfurt-am-Main: Europäische Verlagsanstalt, 1964).

Kolb, Eberhard, *The Weimar Republic*, trans. by P. S. Falla (London: Unwin Hyman, 1988).

Koopmans, Ruud, *Democracy from Below: New Social Movements and the Political System in West Germany* (Boulder, CO: Westview Press, 1995).

Koopmans, Ruud, 'Explaining the Rise of Racist and Extreme Right Violence in Western Europe', *European Journal of Political Research*, 30:3 (1996), pp. 185–216.

Koopmans, Rudd, 'Globalization or Still National Politics? A Comparison of Protests against the Gulf War in Germany, France and the Netherlands', in Donatella della Porta, Hanspeter Kriesi and Dieter Rucht (eds), *Social Movements in a Globalizing World* (London: Macmillan, 1999).

Koopmans, Ruud, 'Globalisierung, Individualisierung, politische Entflechtung', *Forschungsjournal Neue Soziale Bewegung*, 13:1 (2000), pp. 26–31.

Krause-Junk, Gerold (ed.), *Steuersysteme der Zukunft, Schriften des Vereins für Socialpolitik* (Berlin: Duncker & Humblot, 1998).

Kreile, Michael, 'Der Wandel des internationalen Systems und der Faktor "Macht" in der deutschen Europapolitik', in Heinrich Schneider, Mathias Jopp and Uwe Schmalz (eds), *Eine neue Deutsche Europapolitik? Rahmenbedingungen–Problemfelder–Optionen* (Bonn: Europa Union Verlag, 2001).

Kriesi, Hanspeter, Ruud Koopmans, Jan Willem Duyvendak and Marco Giugni, *New Social Movements in Western Europe* (Minneapolis: University of Minnesota Press, 1995).

Küsters, Hanns Jürgen and Daniel Hofmann (eds), *Dokumente zur Deutschlandpolitik: Deutsche Einheit, Sonderedition aus den Akten des Bundeskanzleramtes 1989/90* (Munich: R. Oldenbourg, 1998).

Lafontaine, Oskar, *Das Herz schlägt links* (Munich: Econ Verlag, 1999), English translation: *The Heart Beats Left* (Cambridge: Polity Press, 2000).

Lahusen, Christian, 'International Campaigns in Context: Collective Action between the Local and the Global', in Donatella della Porta, Hanspeter Kriesi and Dieter Rucht (eds), *Social Movements in a Globalizing World* (London: Macmillan, 1999).

Lantis, Jeffrey, *Strategic Dilemmas and the Evolution of German Foreign Policy* (Westport, CT: Praeger, 2002).

Large, David Clay, '"A Beacon in the German Darkness": The Anti-Nazi Resistance Legacy in West German Politics', in Michael Geyer and John W. Boyer (eds), *Resistance Against the Third Reich, 1933–1990* (Chicago: University of Chicago Press, 1994).

Larres, Klaus, 'Collapse of a State: Honecker, Krenz, Modrow, and the End of the German Democratic Republic', *European Review of History*, 1:1 (1994), pp. 79–84.

Layne, Christopher, 'Offshore Balancing Revisited', *Washington Quarterly*, 25 (2002), pp. 233–48.

League of Nations, *International Statistical Year-Book* (Geneva: League of Nations, 1930).

League of Nations, *Statistical Year-Book of the League of Nations, 1933/34* (Geneva: League of Nations, 1934).

Leaman, Jeremy, *The Political Economy of West Germany, 1945–85* (New York: St Martin's Press, 1988).

Lee, Martin, *The Beast Reawakens* (Boston: Little Brown, 1997).

Lees, Charles, *The Red–Green Coalition in Germany: Politics, Personalities and Power* (Manchester: Manchester University Press, 2000).

Legrand, Jupp, 'Editorial', *Forschungsjournal Neue Soziale Bewegung*, 12:4 (1999), pp. 2–4.

Lembruch, Gerhard, *Parteienwettbewerb im Bundesstaat*, 2nd edn (Opladen: Westdeutscher Verlag, 1998).

Leslie, John, 'Unification and the Changing Fortunes of Germany's Parties of the Far Right', in Christopher S. Allen (ed.), *Transformation of the German Political Party System* (Providence, RI: Berghahn, 1999).

Lewis, Rand, *A Nazi Legacy* (New York: Praeger, 1991).

Lijphart, Arend, *Patterns of Democracy: Government Forms and Performance in Thirty-Six Countries* (New Haven: Yale University Press, 1999).

Link, Werner, 'Deutschland als Europäische Macht', in Werner Weidenfeld (ed.), *Europa Handbuch* (Gütersloh: Verlag Bertelsmann Stiftung, 2002).

Linz, Juan, 'Fascism is Dead', in Stein Larsen (ed.), *Modern Europe After Fascism*, 1 (New York: Columbia University Press, 1996).

Lipset, Seymour Martin and Stein Rokkan, 'Cleavage Structures, Party Systems, and Voter Alignments', in Seymour Martin Lipset and Stein Rokkan (eds), *Party Systems and Voter Alignments: Cross-National Perspectives* (New York: Free Press, 1967).

Lohmann, Suzanne, 'Dynamics of Informational Cascades: The Monday Demonstrations in Leipzig, East Germany, 1989–91', *World Politics*, 47:1 (1994), pp. 42–101.

Lohmann, Suzanne, 'Federalism and Central Bank Independence: The Politics of German Monetary Policy, 1957–92', *World Politics*, 50:3 (1998), pp. 401–46.

Loow, Helene, 'White Power Rock 'n' Roll: A Growing Industry', in Jeffrey Kaplan and Tore Bjorgo (eds), *Nation and Race* (Boston: Northeastern University Press, 1998).

Maier, Charles, *The Unmasterable Past: History, Holocaust and German National Identity* (Cambridge, MA: Harvard University Press, 1988).

Mair, Peter, 'Introduction', in Peter Mair (ed.), *The West European Party System* (Oxford: Oxford University Press, 1990).

Mair, Peter, *Party System Change: Approaches and Interpretations* (Oxford: Clarendon Press, 1997).

Markovits, Andrei S., 'Introduction: Model Germany – A Cursory Overview of a Complex Construct', in Andrei S. Markovits (ed.), *The Political Economy of West Germany: Modell Deutschland* (New York: Praeger, 1982).

Markovits, Andrei and Philip Gorski, *The German Left: Red, Green and Beyond* (New York: Oxford University Press, 1993).

Markovits, Andrei and Simon Reich, *The German Predicament: Memory and Power in the New Europe* (Ithaca, NY, London: Cornell University Press, 1997).

Marks, Gary and Doug McAdam, 'Social Movements and the Changing Structure of Political Opportunity in the European Union', *West European Politics*, 19:2 (1996), pp. 249–78.

Marks, Gary and Doug McAdam, 'On the Relationship of Political Opportunities to the Form of Collective Action: The Case of the European Union', in Donatella della Porta, Hanspeter Kriesi and Dieter Rucht (eds), *Social Movements in a Globalizing World* (London: Macmillan, 1999).

Marsh, David, *The Most Powerful Bank: Inside Germany's Bundesbank* (New York: Times Books, 1992).

Matelski, Dariusz, *Niemcy w Polsce w XX Wieku* (Germany in Poland in the 20th Century) (Warszawa-Poznan: Wydawnictwo Naukowe PAN).

Maull, Hanns, 'Zivilmacht Bundesrepublik Deutschland. Vierzehn Thesen für eine neue deutsche Aussenpolitik', *Europa Archiv*, 10 (1992), pp. 269–78.

Maull, Hanns, 'Germany and the Use of Force: Still a "Civilian Power"?', *Survival*, 42:2 (2000), pp. 56–80.

Maxfield, Sylvia, *Gatekeepers of Growth* (Princeton: Princeton University Press, 1998).

Mayntz, Renata, 'Executive Leadership in Germany: Dispersion of Power or "Kanzlerdemokratie"', in Richard Rose and Ezra N. Suleiman (eds), *Presidents and Prime Ministers* (Washington, DC: American Enterprise Institute: 1980).

McAdams, James P., *Judging the Past in Unified Germany* (New York: Cambridge University Press, 2001).

McCartney, Alison, 'International Structure versus Domestic Politics: German Foreign Policy in the Post Cold War Era', *International Politics*, 39:1 (2002), pp. 101–10.

McDonough, Peter, Samuel H. Barnes and Antonio Lopez Pina, 'The Growth of Democratic Legitimacy in Spain', *American Political Science Review*, 80:3 (1986), pp. 735–60.

McKenzie, Mary M., 'Competing Conceptions of Normality in the Post-Cold War Era: Germany, Europe and Foreign Policy Change', *German Politics and Society*, 14:2 (1996), pp. 1–18.

McNamara, Kathleen, *The Currency of Ideas* (Ithaca, NY: Cornell University Press, 1998).

McNamara, Kathleen, 'Where do Rules Come From? The Creation of the European Central Bank', in Neil Fligstein, Wayne Sandholtz and Alec Stone Sweet (eds), *The Institutionalization of Europe* (Oxford: Oxford University Press, 2001).

Mearsheimer, John J., 'Hearts and Minds', *National Interest*, 69 (2002), pp. 13–17.

Meiers, Franz-Josef, 'Germany's "Out-of-Area" Dilemma', in Thomas-Durell Young (ed.), *Force, Statecraft and German Unity: The Struggle to Adapt to Institutions and Practices* (Carlisle Barracks, PA: Strategic Studies Institute, 1996).

Meinecke, Friedrich, *Die deutsche Katastrophe: Betrachtungen und Errinerungen* (Wiesbaden: E. Brockhaus, 1949).

Menz, George K., 'Beyond the Anwerbestopp? The German–Polish Bilateral Labour Treaty', *Journal of European Social Policy*, 11:3 (2000), pp. 258–9.

Merkel, Wolfgang, 'The Third Ways of Social Democracy', in Anthony Giddens (ed.), *The Global Third Way Debate* (Cambridge: Polity Press, 2001).

Merkl, Peter H., 'Executive–Legislative Federalism in West Germany', *American Political Science Review*, 53:3 (1959), pp. 732–41.

Merkl, Peter H., 'Equilibrium, Structure of Interests and Leadership: Adenauer's Survival as Chancellor', *American Political Science Review*, 56:3 (1962), pp. 634–50.

Merkl, Peter H., *The Origin of the West German Republic* (New York: Oxford University Press, 1963).

Merkl, Peter H., *Germany: Yesterday and Tomorrow* (Oxford: Oxford University Press, 1965).

Merkl, Peter H. (with Otey M. Scruggs), *Rassenfrage und Rechtsradikalismus in den USA* (Berlin: Colloquium Verlag, 1966).

Merkl, Peter H., *Modern Comparative Politics* (New York: Holt, Reinhardt & Winston, 1970).

Merkl, Peter H., *German Foreign Policies, West and East: On the Threshold of a New European Era* (Santa Barbara, CA: ABC–Clio Press, 1974).

Merkl, Peter H., 'The Women of West Germany', *The Center Magazine* (May–June 1974), pp. 68–9.

Merkl, Peter H., *Political Violence under the Swastika* (Princeton: Princeton University Press, 1975).

Merkl, Peter H., 'The Politics of Sex: Western Germany', in Lynne Iglitzin and Ruth Ross (eds), *Women in the World: A Comparative Study* (Santa Barbara, CA: ABC–Clio Press, 1976).

Merkl, Peter H., *The Making of a Stormtrooper* (Princeton: Princeton University Press, 1979).

Merkl, Peter H. (ed.), *West European Party Systems* (New York: Free Press, 1980).

Merkl, Peter H. (ed.), *West German Foreign Policy: Dilemmas and Directions* (Chicago: Chicago Council on Foreign Relations, 1982).

Merkl, Peter H., 'West German Women: A Long Way from Kinder, Küche, and Kirche', in Lynne Iglitzin and Ruth Ross (eds), *Women in the World: The Women's Decade, 1975–1985* (Santa Barbara, CA: ABC–Clio Press, 1985).

Merkl, Peter H. (ed.), *New Local Centers in Centralized States* (Lanham, MD: University Press of America, 1985).

Merkl, Peter H. (ed.), *Political Violence and Terror: Motifs and Motivations* (Berkeley and Los Angeles: University of California Press, 1986).

Merkl, Peter H. (ed.), *The Federal Republic of Germany at Forty* (New York: New York University Press, 1989).

Merkl, Peter H., 'Forty Years and Seven Generations', in Peter H. Merkl (ed.), *The Federal Republic of Germany at Forty* (New York: New York University Press, 1989).

Merkl, Peter H., *German Unification in the European Context* (University Park, PA: Pennsylvannia State University Press, 1993).

Merkl, Peter H., *The Federal Republic at Forty-Five: Union without Unity* (New York: New York University Press, 1995).

Merkl, Peter H., 'West German Left-Wing Terrorism', in Marilyn Crenshaw (ed.), *Terrorism in Context* (University Park, PA: Pennsylvania State University Press, 1995).

Merkl, Peter H., *The Federal Republic of Germany at Fifty: The End of a Century of Turmoil* (New York: New York University Press, 1999).

Merkl, Peter H., 'Fifty Years of the German Republic', in Peter H. Merkl (ed.), *The Federal Republic at Fifty* (New York: New York University Press, 1999).

Merkl, Peter H., '*Reformstau* über alles: The FRG at 50', *Politik* (Newsletter of the Conference Group on German Politics) (Autumn 1999), pp. 8–9.

Merkl, Peter H., *A Coup Attempt in Washington? A European Mirror on the 1998/1999 Constitutional Crisis* (New York: Palgrave, 2001).

Merkl, Peter H., ' Stronger than Ever', in Peter Merkl and Leonard Weinberg (eds), *Right-Wing Extremism in the Twenty-First Century* (London: Frank Cass, 2003).

Merkl, Peter H. and Kay Lawson (eds), *When Parties Fail … Emerging Alternative Organizations* (Princeton: Princeton University Press, 1988).

Merkl, Peter H. and Leonard Weinberg (eds), *The Revival of Right-Wing Extremism in the Nineties* (London: Frank Cass, 1997).

Merkl, Peter H. and Leonard Weinberg (eds), *Right-Wing Extremism in the Twenty-First Century* (London: Frank Cass, 2003).

Merkl, Peter H. *et al.* (eds), *The Politics of Economic Change in Japan and West Germany: Macroeconomic Conditions and Policy Responses* (Stanford: Stanford University Press, 1993).

Merkl, Peter H. *et al.* (eds), *The Politics of Economic Change in Japan and West Germany: Strategies and Policies of Economic Growth and Security* (London: Macmillan, forthcoming).

Merritt, Anna J. and Richard L. Merritt (eds), *Public Opinion in Occupied Germany: The OMGUS Surveys, 1945–1949* (Urbana, IL: University of Illinois Press, 1970).

Merritt, Richard L., *Democracy Imposed: US Occupation Policy and the German Public, 1945–1949* (New Haven: Yale University Press, 1995).

Merritt, Richard L. and Anna J. Merritt, *Public Opinon in Semi-Sovereign Germany: The HICOG Surveys, 1949–1955* (Urbana, IL: University of Illinois Press, 1980).

Meuschel, Sigrid, *Legitimation und Parteiherrschaft zum Paradox von Stabilität und Revolution in der DDR, 1945–1989* (Frankfurt-am-Main: Suhrkamp, 1992).

Meyer, David, 'How the Cold War Was Really Won', in Marco Giugni, Doug McAdam and Charles Tilly (eds), *How Social Movements Matter* (Minneapolis: University of Minnesota Press, 1999).

Meyer, Thomas, 'From Godesberg to the *Neue Mitte*: The New Social Democracy in Germany', in Anthony Giddens (ed.), *The Global Third Way Debate* (Cambridge: Polity Press, 2001).

Miethe, Ingrid, 'Women's Movements in Unified Germany: Experiences and Expectations of Eastern German Women', *AICGS Humanities*, 11 (2002), pp. 43–59.

Millotat, Christian O. E., *Understanding the Prussian–German General Staff System* (Carlisle Barracks, PA: Strategic Studies Institute, 1992).

Milward, Alan S., *The Reconstruction of Western Europe, 1945–1951* (Berkeley and Los Angeles: University of California Press, 1984).

Mishler, William and Richard Rose, 'What are the Origins of Political Trust? Testing Institutional and Cultural Theories in Post-Communist Societies', *Comparative Political Studies*, 34:1 (2001), pp. 30–62.

Mishler, William, and Richard Rose, 'Learning and Re-Learning Regime Support: The Dynamics of Post-Communist Regimes', *European Journal of Political Research*, 41:1 (2002), pp. 5–36.

Moeller, Robert G. (ed.), *West Germany Under Construction; Politics, Society, and Culture in the Adenauer Era* (Ann Arbor: Univeristy of Michigan Press, 1997).

Moeller, Robert G., *War Stories: The Search for a Usable Past in the Federal Republic of Germany* (Berkeley and Los Angeles: University of California Press, 2001).

Mommsen, Hans, *The Rise and Fall of Weimar Democracy*, trans. by Elborg Forster and Larry Eugene Jones (Chapel Hill, NC: University of North Carolina Press, 1996).

Moreau, Patrick and Uwe Backes, 'Federal Republic of Germany', in Jean-Yves Camus (ed.), *Extremism in Europe* (Paris: CERA, 1998).

Müller, Harald, 'German Foreign Policy After Unification' in Paul Stares (ed.), *Germany and the New Europe* (Washington, DC: Brookings, 1992).

Müller, Jan Werner, *Another Country: German Intellectuals, Unification and National Identity* (New Haven: Yale University Press, 2000).

Musgrave, Richard A., *The Theory of Public Finance* (New York: McGraw-Hill, 1959).

Mushaben, Joyce Marie, 'Anti-Politics and Successor Generations: The Role of Youth in the West and East German Peace Movements', *The Journal of Political and Military Sociology*, 12:2 (1984), pp. 171–90.

Mushaben, Joyce Marie, 'Grassroots and *Gewaltfreie Aktionen*: A Study of Mass Mobilization Strategies in the West German Peace Movement', *Journal of Peace Research*, 23:2 (1986), pp. 141–54.

Mushaben, Joyce Marie, 'Innocence Lost: Environmental Images and Political Experiences among the West German Greens', *New Political Science*, 14 (1986), pp. 39–66.

Mushaben, Joyce Marie, 'Second Class Citizenship and its Discontents: Women in the New Germany', in Peter Merkl (ed.), *The Federal Republic at Forty-Five. Union Without Unity.* (New York: New York University Press, 1995).

Mushaben, Joyce Marie, 'The Rise of *Femi-Nazis*? Women and Rightwing Extremist Movements in Unified Germany', *German Politics*, 5:2 (1996): pp. 240–75.

Mushaben, Joyce Marie, 'Concession or Compromise? The Politics of Abortion in United Germany', *German Politics*, 6:3 (1997), pp. 69–87.

Mushaben, Joyce Marie, *From Post-War to Post-Wall Generations. Changing Attitudes towards the National Question and NATO in the Federal Republic of Germany* (Boulder, CO: Westview Press, 1998).

Mushaben, Joyce Marie, 'What the SPD–Green Coalition Means for German Women', in Carl Lankowski (ed.), *Germany After the 1998 Federal Elections* (Washington, DC: AICGS Research, December 1998).

Mushaben, Joyce Marie, 'Coming to Terms with the Nation: The Political and Literary Voices of Women', in Peter Merkl (ed.), *The Federal Republic at Fifty: The End of a Century of Turmoil* (New York: St Martin's Press, 1999).

Nathwani, Niraj, 'Atlantic Divide on Fight Against Racist Websites', *Equal Voices*, (10:11 2002), pp. 11–19.

Nelkin, Dorothy and Michael Pollak, *The Atom Besieged: Anti-Nuclear Movements in France and Germany* (Cambridge, MA: MIT Press, 1982).

Neugebauer, Gero and Richard Stöss, *Die PDS: Geschichte, Organisation, Wähler, Konkurrenten* (Opladen: Leske & Budrich, 1996).

Neumann, Manfred, 'Monetary Stability: Threat and Proven Response', in Deutsche Bundesbank (ed.), *Fifty Years of the Deutsche Mark* (Oxford: Oxford University Press, 1989).

Newnham, Randall E., *Deutsche Mark Diplomacy: Positive Economic Sanctions in German–Russian Relations* (University Park, PA: Pennsylvania State University Press).

Niclauss, Karlheinz, *Kanzlerdemokratie: Bonner Regierungspraxis von Konrad Adenauer bis Helmut Kohl* (Stuttgart: Kohlhammer, 1988).

Niclauss, Karlheinz, *Der Weg zum Grundgesetz* (Paderborn: Schöningh, 1998).

Niedermeyer, Oskar, 'Party System Change in East Germany', *German Politics*, 4:3 (1995), pp. 75–91.

Nipperdey, Thomas, *Nachdenken über die deutschen Geschichte* (Munich: C. H. Beck Verlag, 1986).

Noelle, Elisabeth and Erich Peter Neumann, *Jahrbuch der Öffentlichen Meinung, 1947–1955* (Allensbach: Verlag für Demoskopie, 1956).

Noelle, Elisabeth and Erich Peter Neumann, *Jahrbuch der Öffentlichen Meinung, 1965–1967* (Allensbach: Verlag für Demoskopie, 1967).

OECD, *OECD Economic Surveys, 1997–1998, Germany* (Paris: OECD, 1999).

OECD, *Revenue Statistics 1965–2000* (Paris: OECD, 2001).

OECD, *OECD Economic Outlook No. 72, Data on Diskette* (Paris: OECD, 2002).

Offe, Claus, 'New Social Movements: Challenging the Boundaries of Institutional Politics', *Social Research*, 52:4 (1985), pp. 817–68.

Offe, Claus, 'Reflections on the Institutional Self-Transformation of Movement Politics: A Tentative Stage Model', in Russell Dalton and Manfred Kuechler (eds), *Challenging the Political Order: New Social and Political Movements in Western Democracies* (New York: Oxford University Press, 1990).

Pachter, Henry M., *Modern Germany: A Social, Cultural and Political History* (Boulder, CO: Westview Press, 1978).

Padgett, Stephen (ed.), *Parties and Party Systems in the New Germany* (Aldershot: Association for the Study of German Politics, 1993).

Padgett, Stephen, 'The Boundaries of Stability: The Party System Before and After the 1998 Bundestagswahl', in Stephen Padgett and Thomas Saalfeld (eds), *Bundestagswahl '98: An End of an Era?* (London: Frank Cass, 1999).

Panebianco, Angelo, *Political Parties: Organization and Power*, trans. by Marc Silver (Cambridge: Cambridge University Press, 1988).

Pappi, Franz-Urban, 'The German Party System', in Stefano Bartolini and Peter Mair (eds), *Party Politics in Contemporary Western Europe* (London: Frank Cass, 1984).

Paterson, William, 'The Chancellor and His Party: Political Leadership in the Federal Republic', *West European Politics*, 4:1 (1981), pp. 3–17.

Patton, David F., *Cold War Politics in Postwar Germany* (New York: St Martin's Press, 1999).

Patzelt, Werner J., 'Die PDS nach 2000: Neugeburt oder Fehlgeburt', in Frank Berg and Lutz Kirschner (eds), *PDS am Scheideweg*, Manuscript 20 (Berlin: Rosa-Luxemburg-Stiftung, 2001).

Payne, Stanley, *A History of Fascism* (Madison, WI: University of Wisconsin Press, 1995).

Peukert, Detlev J. K., *The Weimar Republic: The Crisis of Classical Modernity*, trans. by Richard Deveson (New York: Hill & Wang, 1989).

Pfetsch, Frank R., *Ursprünge der zweiten Republik* (Opladen: Westdeutscher Verlag, 1990).

Phillips, Ann L., *Power and Influence after the Cold War: Germany in East-Central Europe* (Lanham, MD: Rowman & Littlefield, 2000).

Poguntke, Thomas, 'The German Party System: Eternal Crisis?', in Stephen Padgett and Thomas Poguntke (eds), *Continuity and Change in German Politics: Beyond the Politics of Centrality?* (London: Frank Cass 2002).

Pollack, Detlef, 'Ostdeutsche Identität – ein multidimensionales Phänomen', in Heiner Meulemann (ed.), *Werte und nationale Identität im vereinten Deutschland. Erklärungsansätze der Umfrageforschung* (Opladen: Leske & Budrich, 1998).

Pollack, Günter, 'Die PDS im kommunalen Parteiensystem', in Michael Brie and Rudolf Woderich (eds), *Die PDS im Parteiensystem* (Berlin: Karl Dietz Verlag, 2000).

Pond, Elizabeth, *Beyond the Wall: Germany's Road to Unification* (Washington, DC: Brookings, 1993).

Pond, Elizabeth, *The Rebirth of Europe* (Washington, DC: Brookings Institute, 1999).

Posen, Adam, 'Why Central Bank Independence Does Not Cause Low Inflation: The Politics behind the Institutional Fix' (New York: Federal Reserve Bank of New York, 1993), unpublished manuscript.

Priewe, Jan, 'Fiskalpolitik in der Europäischen Währungsunion – im Dilemma zwischen Konsolidierung und Stabilisierung', *WSI-Mitteilungen*, 54:5 (2001), pp. 273–81.

Priewe, Jan, 'Vom Defizit zum Überschuss. US-Fiskalpolitik in den 90er Jahren', in Arne Heise (ed.), *USA – Modellfall der New Economy?* (Marburg: Metropolis Verlag, 2001).

Priewe, Jan, 'Zwischen Abkoppelung und Aufholen – das schwache ostdeutsche Wachstumspotential', *WSI-Mitteilungen*, 55:12 (2002), pp. 706–13.

Rabinbach, Anson and Jack Zipes (eds), *Germans and Jews Since the Holocaust:*

The Changing Situation in West Germany, (New York: Holmes & Meier, 1986).

Reich, Simon, *The Fruits of Fascism* (Ithaca, NY: Cornell University Press, 1990).

Reichel, Peter, *Politik mit der Erinnerung: Gedächtnisorte im Streit um die nationalsozialistischer Vergangenheit* (Munich: Hanser Verlag, 1995).

Reinhardt, Uwe E., 'Global Budgeting in German Health Care: Insight for Americans', *Domestic Affairs*, 3:1 (1993–1994), pp. 159–94.

Renzsch, Wolfgang, *Finanzverfassung und Finanzausgleich: Die Auseinandersetzungen um ihre politische Gestaltung in der Bundesrepublik Deutschland zwischen Währungsreform und deutscher Vereinigung (1948 bis 1990)* (Bonn: Dietz Verlag, 1991).

Renzsch, Wolfgang, 'Föderative Problembewältigung: Zur Einbeziehung der neuen Länder in einen gesamtdeutchsen Finanzausgleich ab 1995', *Zeitschift für Parlamentsfragen*, 25:1 (1994), pp. 116–38.

Renzsch, Wolfgang, *Finanzausgleich und die Modernisierung des Bundesstaates: Perspecktiven nach dem Urteil des Bundesverfassungsgerichts* (Bonn: Friedrich-Ebert-Stiftung, electronic edn, 2001).

Reuter, Ernst, 'Ansprache auf der Gedenkfeier des Bezirksamtes Neukölln am 10. Jahrestag der Vernichtung des Warschauer Ghettos am 19. April 1953', in *Ernst Reuter: Schriften, Reden*, 4 (Berlin: Propyläen Verlag, 1972), pp. 714–21.

Rice, Condoleeza and Phillip Zelikow, *Germany Unified and Europe Transformed* (Cambridge, MA: Harvard University Press, 1995).

Richter, Michaela W., 'Exiting the GDR: Political Movements and Parties between Democratization and Westernization', in Donald Hancock and Helga Welsh (eds), *German Unification: Process and Outcomes* (Boulder, CO: Westview Press, 1994).

Richter, Michaela W. 'From Occupation to Unification: Political Parties and Democratic Transformations in Germany', in *Transformation of the German Party System*, Working Paper 7:8. (Berkeley: Center for German and European Studies, University of California, 1996).

Richter, Michaela W., 'Continuity or *Politikwechsel*? The First Federal Red–Green Coalition', *German Politics and Society*, 20:1 (2002), pp. 1–48.

Rieger, Elmar and Stephan Leibfried, 'Welfare State Limits to Globalization', *Politics and Society*, 6:3 (1998), pp. 363–90.

Rittberger, Volker, 'Approaches to the Study of Foreign Policy Derived from International Relations Theories', in Margaret Hermann and Bengt Sundelius (eds), *Comparative Foreign Policy Analysis: Theories and Methods* (forthcoming).

Rogers, Daniel E., *Politics after Hitler: The Western Allies and the German Party System* (New York: New York University Press, 1995).

Rogoff, Kenneth, 'The Optimal Degree of Commitment to an Intermediate Monetary Target', *Quarterly Journal of Economics*, 100:4 (1985), pp. 1169–89.

Rogowski, Ronald, *Rational Legitimacy* (Princeton: Princeton University Press, 1974).

Rohrschneider, Robert, *Learning Democracy: Democratic and Economic Values in Unified Germany* (Oxford: Oxford University Press, 1999).

Rohrschneider, Robert and R. Schmitt-Beck, 'Trust in Democratic Institutions in Germany: Theory and Evidence Ten Years after Unification', *German Politics*, 11:3 (2002), pp. 35–58.

Roller, Edeltraud, *Einstellungen der Bürger zum Wohlfahrtsstaat der Bundesrepublik Deutschland* (Opladen: Westdeutscher Verlag, 1992).

Rosen, Harry S., *Public Finance*, 5th edn (Boston: Irwin, McGraw-Hill, 1998).

Roth, Dieter, *Zum Demokratieverständnis von Eliten in der Bundesrepublik Deutschland* (Frankfurt: Peter Lang, 1976).

Roth, Dieter, 'Das ungeliebte Kanzler: Helmut Kohl im Licht (oder Schatten?) demoskopischer Befund', in Reinhard Appel (ed.), *Kohl im Spiegel seiner Macht* (Bonn: Bouvier, 1990).

Roth, Dieter and Matthias Jung, 'Ablösung der Regierung vertagt: Eine Analyse der Bundestagswahl 2002', *Aus Politik und Zeitgeschichte*, 49–50/2002 (9–16 December 2002), pp. 3–17.

Rucht, Dieter, 'German Unification, Democratization, and the Role of Social Movements: A Missed Opportunity?', *Mobilization*, 1:1 (1996), pp. 35–62.

Rucht, Dieter, 'The Structure and Culture of Collective Protest in Germany since 1950', in David Meyer and Sidney Tarrow (eds), *The Social Movement Society: Contentious Politics for a New Century* (New York: Rowman & Littlefield, 1998).

Rucht, Dieter, 'Linking Organization and Mobilization: Michel's Iron Law of Oligarchy Reconsidered', *Mobilization*, 4:2 (1999), pp. 151–69.

Rucht, Dieter, 'The Impact of Environmental Movements in Western Societies', in Marco Giugni, Doug McAdam and Charles Tilly (eds), *How Social Movements Matter* (Minneapolis: University of Minnesota Press, 1999).

Rucht, Dieter and Jochen Roose, 'Neither Decline nor Sclerosis: The Organizational Structure of the German Environmental Movement', *West European Politics*, 24:4 (2001), pp. 55–81.

Rudolf, Peter, 'Deutschland und die USA – eine Beziehungskrise?', *Aus Politik und Zeitgeschichte*, B48/2002 (2 December 2002), pp. 16–23.

Rühl, Lothar, 'Security Policy: National Structures and Multilateral Integration', in Wolf-Dieter Eberwein and Karl Kaiser (eds), *Germany's New Foreign Policy: Decision-Making in an Interdependent World* (New York: Palgrave, 2001).

Ruhm von Oppen, Beate, *Documents on Germany under Occupation, 1945–1954* (London: Oxford University Press, 1955).

Rupp, Richard E. and Mary M. McKenzie, 'The Organization for Security and Cooperation in Europe: Institutional Reform and Political Reality', in Mary M. McKenzie and Peter H. Loedel (eds), *The Promise and Reality of European Security Cooperation: States, Interests, and Institutions* (Westport, CT: Praeger, 1998), pp. 119–38.

Russo, Henry, *The Vichy Syndrome: History and Memory in France Since 1944*, trans. by Arthur Goldhammer (Cambridge, MA.: Harvard University Press, 1991).

Sa'adah, Anne, *Germany's Second Chance: Trust, Justice, and Democratization* (Cambridge, MA: Harvard University Press, 1998).

Saalfeld, Thomas, 'The German Party System: Continuity and Change', *German Politics*, 11:3 (2002), pp. 99–130.

Sachverständigenkommission Vermögensbesteuerung, *Bewertung des Grundbesitzes für Zwecke der Vermögensbesteuerung* (Berlin: BMF, 2000).

Sally, R. and D. Webber, 'The German Solidarity Pact: A Case Study in the Politics of the Unified Germany', *German Politics*, 3:1 (1994), pp. 18–46.

Sarotte, Mary Elise, 'German Military Reform and European Security', *Adelphi Paper*, 340 (London: The International Institute for Strategic Studies, 2001).

Sartori, Giovanni, 'European Political Parties: The Case of Polarized Pluralism', in Joseph LaPalombara and Myron Weiner (eds), *Political Parties and Political Development* (Princeton: Princeton University Press, 1966).

Sartori, Giovanni, *Parties and Party Systems: A Framework for Analysis*, 1 (Cambridge: Cambridge University Press, 1976).

Sauernheimer, K., 'Die Standortqualität der Bundesrepublik Deutschland', *Fortbildung*, 35:1 (1990), pp. 3–5.

Schäuble, Wolfgang, *Der Vertrag: Wie ich über die deutsche Einheit verhandelte* (Stuttgart: Deutsche-Verlags Anstalt, 1991).

Schermer, Michael and Alex Grobman, *Denying History* (Berkeley: University of California Press, 2000).

Schildt, Axel and Arnold Sywottek, *Modernisierung im Wiederanfrau: die Westdeutsche Gesellschaft des 50er Jahre* (Bonn: J. H. W. Dietz, 1993).

Schildt, Axel and Arnold Sywottek, 'Reconstruction and Modernization: West German Social History During the 1950s', in Robert G. Moeller (ed.), *West Germany Under Construction: Politics, Society, and Culture in the Adenauer Era* (Ann Arbor: University of Michigan Press, 1997).

Schirrmacher, Frank (ed.), *Der westliche Kreuzzug: 41 Positionen zum Kosovo-Krieg* (Stuttgart: Deutsche Verlags-Anstalt, 1999).

Schlör, Wolfgang, 'German Security Policy', *Adelphi Paper*, 277 (London: The International Institute for Strategic Studies, 1993).

Schmid, Carlo, *Politik als Geistige Aufgabe* (Bern, Munich, Vienna: Scherz, 1973).

Schoenbaum, David, *Hitler's Social Revolution* (Garden City, NY: Doubleday, 1996).

Schratzenstaller, M., 'Steuergerechtigkeit für niemanden. Rot-grüne Steuerpolitik 1998–2002', in Kai Eicker-Wolf (ed.), *'Deutschland auf den Weg gebracht'. Rot-grüne Wirtschafts- und Sozialpolitik zwischen Anspruch und Wirklichkeit* (Marburg: Metropolis Verlag, 2002).

Schwarz, Hans-Peter, *Konrad Adenauer*, vol. 1, (Providence, RI: Berghahn, 1950).

Seidel, Bernhard, 'Die Einkommensteuerreform', in Achim Truger (ed.), *Rot-grüne Stuerreformen in Deutschland: Eine Zwischenbilanz* (Marburg: Metropolis Verlag, 2001), pp. 21–46.

Seidel, Bernhard, Dieter Teichmann and Sabine Thiede, 'Ehegattensplitting nicht mehr zeitgemäß', *DIW-Wochenbericht*, 66:40 (1999), pp. 713–23.

Seitz, Konrad, 'Die Japanisch-Amerikanische Herausforderung – Europas Hochtechnologieindustrien Kämpfen ums Überleben', *Aus Politik und Zeitgeschichte*, B10–11/92 (28 February 1992), pp. 315.

Semmler, Willi, 'Economic Aspects of Model Germany: A Comparison with the United States', in Andrei S. Markovits (ed.), *The Political Economy of West Germany: Modell Deutschland* (New York: Praeger, 1982).

Senatsverwaltung für Wissenschaft, Forschung und Kultur, *Colloquium: Denkmal für die ermordeten Juden Europas: Dokumentation* (Berlin: Senatsverwaltung, 1997).

Shiller, Robert, 'Why Do People Dislike Inflation?', in C. Romer and D. Romer (eds), *Reducing Inflation: Motivation and Strategy* (Chicago: University of Chicago Press, 1997).

Shonfield, Andrew, *Modern Capitalism: The Changing Balance of Public and Private Power* (London: Oxford University Press, 1965).

Sikkink, Kathryn, *Ideas and Institutions: Developmentalism in Brazil and Argentina* (Ithaca, NY: Cornell University Press, 1991).

Silvia, Stephen, 'The Fall and Rise of Unemployment in Germany: Is the Red–Green Government Responsible?', *German Politics*, 11:1 (2002), pp. 61–80.

Simonelli, Frederick, *American Fuehrer: George Lincoln Rockwell and the American Nazi Party* (Champaign, IL: University of Illinois Press, 1999).

Simonelli, Frederick, 'Thriving in a Cultic Milieu: The World Union of National Socialists, 1962–1992', in Jeffrey Kaplan and Helene Loow (eds), *The Cultic Milieu* (Walnut Creek, CA: Altamira Press, 2002).

Smith, Eric Owen, *The German Economy* (London: Routledge, 1994).

Smith, Gordon, *Democracy in Germany, Parties and Politics in the Federal Republic*, 3rd edn (New York: Holmes & Meier, 1986).

Smith, Gordon, 'Dimensions of Change in the German Party System', in Stephen Padgett (ed.), *Parties and Party Systems in the New Germany* (Aldershot: Association for the Study of German Politics, 1993).

Smith, Jean Edward, *Lucius D. Clay: An American Life* (New York: Henry Holt & Co., 1990).

Smyser, W. R., *The German Economy*, 2nd edn (New York: St Martin's Press, 1993).

Smyser, W. R., *From Yalta to Berlin* (New York: St Martin's Press, 1999).

Søe, Christian, 'The Free Democratic Party: A Struggle for Survivial, Influence and Identity', in David Conradt, Gerald R. Kleinfeld, George Romoser and Christian Søe (eds), *Germany's New Politics: Parties and Issues in the 1990s* (Providence, RI: Berghahn, 1995).

Sperling, James, 'Less than Meets the Eye: A Reconsideration of German Hegemony', in Mary N. Hampton and Christian Søe (eds), *Between Bonn and Berlin: German Politics Adrift?* (Lanham, MD: Rowman & Littlefield, 1999).

Sperling, James, 'Neither Hegemony nor Dominance: Reconsidering German Power in Post Cold War Europe', *British Journal of Political Science*, 31:2 (2001), pp. 394–408.

Sperling, James, 'Germany and the Transatlantic Relationship after Enlargement', Paper presented at the German Studies Conference, San Diego, CA, 4–6 October 2002.

Sperling, James, 'The Foreign Policy of the Berlin Republic: The Very Model of a Post-Modern Major Power? A Review Essay', *German Politics*, 13:1 (2004), pp. 1–34.

Sperling, James and Emil Kirchner, *Recasting the European Order: Security Architectures and Economic Cooperation* (Manchester: Manchester University Press, 1997).

Stefanowicz, Janusz, 'Central Europe between Germany and Russia. A View from Poland', *Security Dialogue*, 26:1 (1995), pp. 55–64.

Stoll, Christian, 'Rote Raus: Die PDS in Bonn', *Wiener*, 4 (April 1991), pp. 42–6.

Stöss, Richard and Gero Neugebauer, 'Mit einem blauen Auge davon gekommen. Eine Analyse der Bundestagswahl 2002', *Arbeitshefte aus dem Otto-Stammer-Zentrum*, Nr. 7 (Berlin: Otto-Stammer-Zentrum, 2002).

Sturm, Roland, 'The Territorial Dimension of the New Party System', in Stephen Padgett (ed.), *Parties and Party Systems in the New Germany* (Aldershot: Association for the Study of German Politics, 1993).

Sturm, Roland, 'Divided Government in Germany: The Case of the Bundesrat', in Robert Elgie (ed.), *Divided Government in Comparative Perspective* (Oxford: Oxford University Press, 2001).

Sturm, Roland and Heinrich Pehle, *Das neue deutsche Regierungssystem* (Opladen: Leske & Budrich, 2001).

Suckut, Siegfried (ed.), *Das Wörterbuch der Staatssicherheit* (Berlin: Ch. Links Verlag, 1996).

Svoray, Yaron, *In Hitler's Shadow* (Garden City, NY: Doubleday, 1994).

Szabo, Stephen F., *The Diplomacy of German Unification* (New York: St Martin's Press, 1992).

Take, Ingo, 'Transnationale Allianzen als Anwort auf die Herausforderungen des 21. Jahrhunderts', *Forschungsjournal Neue Soziale Bewegung*, 13:1 (2000), pp. 87–91.

Tarrow, Sidney, 'Europeanization of Conflict: Reflections from a Social Movement Perspective', *West European Politics*, 18:2 (1995), pp. 223–51.

Teltschik, Horst, *329 Tage: Innenansichten der Einigung* (Berlin: Siedler, 1991).

Tewes, Henning, *Germany, Civilian Power and the New Europe: Enlarging NATO and the European Union* (New York: Palgrave, 2002).

Thomas, James P., 'The Military Challenges of Transatlantic Coalitions', *Adelphi Paper*, 333 (London: The International Institute for Strategic Studies, 2000).

Timm, Angelika, *Hammer, Zirkel, Davidstern: Das gestörte Verhältnis der DDR zu Zionismus und Staat Israel* (Bonn: Bouvier Verlag, 1997).

Trevor-Roper, Hugh R., 'The Phenomenon of Fascism', in S. J. Woolf (ed.), *European Fascism* (New York: Vintage Books, 1968).

Truger, Achim, 'Ökologische Steuerreformen in Europa – wo steht Deutschland?', *WSI-Discussionpaper*, 87 (Düsseldorf: WSI, 2000).

Truger, Achim, 'Rot-grüne Steuerreformen in Deutschland – eine Einführung', in Achim Truger (ed.), *Rot-grüne Stuerreformen in Deutschland: Eine Zwischenbilanz* (Marburg: Metropolis Verlag, 2001).

Truger, Achim (ed.), *Rot-grüne Stuerreformen in Deutschland: Eine Zwischenbilanz* (Marburg: Metropolis Verlag, 2001).

Truger, Achim, 'Der deutsche Einstieg in die ökologische Steuerreform', in Achim Truger (ed.), *Rot-grüne Stuerreformen in Deutschland: Eine Zwischenbilanz* (Marburg: Metropolis Verlag, 2001).

Truger, Achim, 'Fiskalpolitik in der EU von 1970 bis 2000: Eine Zusammenstellung und Kommentierung zentraler fiskalpolitischer Indikatoren', in Achim Truger and Rudi Welzmüller (eds), *Chancen der Währungsunion nutzen – Koordinierte Politik für Beschäftigung und moderne Infrastruktur* (Düsseldorf: Hans-Böckler-Stiftung, 2002).

Truger, Achim and Eckhard Hein, '"Schlusslicht Deutschland": Makroökonomische Ursachen', *Wirtschaftsdienst*, 82:7 (2002), pp. 402–10.

Van Orden, Geoffrey, 'The Bundeswehr in Transition', *Survival*, 33:4 (1991), pp. 352–70.

van Zweeden, A. F., 'The Netherlands', in B. C. Roberts (ed.), *Industrial Relations in Europe: The Imperatives of Change* (London: Croom Helm, 1985).

Varwick, Johannes, 'Die Bundeswehr reformieren', *Internationale Politik*, 55:7 (2000), pp. 61–4.

Vaubel, Roland, 'Eine Public-Choice Analyse der Deutschen Bundesbank und ihre Implikationen für die Europäische Währungsunion', in Dieter Duwendag and Jürgen Siebke (eds), *Europa vor dem Eintritt in die Wirtschafts- und Währungsunion* (Berlin: Duncker & Humblot, 1993).

Vesper, Dieter, 'Zum infrastrukturellen Nachholbedarf in Ostdeutschland', *DIW-Wochenbericht*, 68:20 (2001), pp. 293–8.

Vesser, Jelle, 'Continuity and Change in Dutch Industrial Relations', in Guido Baglioni and Colin Crouch (eds), *European Industrial Relations: The Challenge of Flexibility* (London: Sage, 1990).

Vogt, Jochen, 'The Weimar Republic as the "Heritage of our Time"', in Thomas W. Kniesche and Stephen Brockmann (eds), *Dancing on the Volcano: Essays on the Culture of the Weimar Republic* (Columbia, SC: Camden House, 1994).

Volmert, Johannes, 'Die "Altparteien" außer Fassung. Reaktionen und Kampagnen auf die Wahlerfolge der PDS – ein Pressespiegel', in Michael Brie, Martin Herzig and Thomas Koch (eds), *Die PDS: Empirische Befunde & kontroverse Analysen* (Cologne: PapyRossa, 1995).

von Hagen, Jürgen, 'A New Approach to Monetary Policy', in Deutsche Bundesbank (ed.), *Fifty Years of the Deutsche Mark* (Oxford: Oxford University Press, 1989).

von Loeffelholz, Hans Dietrich, 'Perspektiven und Optionen der Vermögensbesteuerung in Deutschland', in Achim Truger (ed.), *Rot-grüne Stuerreformen in Deutschland. Eine Zwischenbilanz* (Marburg: Metropolis Verlag, 2001).

von Rosen, Rudiger, 'The German Financial System after Unification', *Vital Speeches of the Day*, 58:4 (1 December 1991), pp. 114–18.

von Weizsäcker, Richard, *Reden und Interviews* (Bonn: Presse- und Informationsamt der Bundesregierung, 1988).

Wagenhals, Gerhard, 'Incentive and Redistribution Effects of the German Income Tax Reform 2000', *Finanzarchiv*, 57:3 (2000), pp. 316–32.

Walk, Heike and Achim Brunnengräber, 'Von Mobilisierungsschwächen und kosmopolitischen Grössen: NSBs und NGOs', *Forschungsjournal Neue Soziale Bewegung*, 13:1 (2000), pp. 97–100.

Wallach, H. G. Peter and Ronald A. Francisco, *United Germany: The Past, Politics, Prospects* (Westport, CT: Praeger, 1992), pp. 48–9.

Walser, Martin, *Erfahrungen beim Verfasser einer Sonntagsrede: Friedenspreis des Deutschen Buchhandels 1998* (Frankfurt-am-Main: Suhrkamp Verlag, 1998).

Weidenfeld, Werner, *Kulturbruch mit Amerika? Das Ende transatlantischer Selbstverständlichkeit* (Gütersloh: Verlag Bertelsmann Stiftung, 1996).

Weil, Frederick, 'The Development of Democratic Attitudes in Eastern and Western Germany in a Comparative Perspective', in Frederick Weil (ed.), *Research on Democracy and Society: Democratization in Eastern and Western Europe* (Greenwich, CT: JAI Press, 1993).

Weil, Frederick, *The Effects of Diffusion, Nostalgia, and Performance on Democratic Legitimation in Unified Germany* (Frankfurt: Campus Verlag, 2000).

Weiller, Matthew A., 'SPD Security Policy', *Survival*, 30:6 (1988), pp. 515–28.

Weingardt, Markus A., *Deutsche Israel- und Nahostpolitik. Die Geschichte einer Gratwanderung seit 1949* (Frankfurt, New York: Campus Verlag, 2002).

Weintraub, Robert, 'Congressional Supervision of Monetary Policy', *Journal of Monetary Economics*, 4:2 (1978), pp. 341–62.

Wendt, Alexander, *Social Theory of International Politics* (Cambridge: Cambridge University Press, 1999).

Wettig, Gerhard, 'Moscow's Acceptance of NATO: The Catalytic Role of German Unification', *Europe-Asia Studies*, 45:6 (1993), pp. 953–73.

White House, *The National Security Strategy of the United States of America* (Washington, DC: The White House, September 2002).

Whiteneck, Daniel J., 'Germany: Consensus Politics and Changing Security Paradigms', in Gale A. Mattox and Arthur R. Rachwald (eds), *Enlarging NATO. The National Debates* (Boulder, CO: Lynne Rienner, 2001).

Wilcox, Allen, Leonard Weinberg and William Eubank, 'Explaining National Variations in Support for Far Right Political Parties in Western Europe, 1990–2000', in Peter H. Merkl and Leonard Weinberg (eds), *Right-Wing Extremism in the Twenty-First Century* (London: Frank Cass, 2003).

Willems, Helmut, 'Development, Patterns and Causes of Violence against Foreigners in Germany', in Tore Bjorgo (ed.), *Terror from the Far Right* (London: Frank Cass, 1995).

Williams, Christopher, 'Problems of Transition and the Rise of the Radical Right', in Sabrina Ramet (ed.), *The Radical Right in Central and Eastern Europe Since 1989* (College Park, PA: Pennsylvania State University Press, 1999).

Willis, F. Roy, *The French in Germany 1945–1949* (Stanford: Stanford University Press, 1962).

Winkler, Heinrich August, *Die lange Weg nach Westen: vom Dritten Reich bis zur Wiedervereinigung, Band II* (Munich: Beck Verlag, 2000).

Witt, Linda, Karen M. Paget and Glenna Matthews, *Running as a Woman. Gender and Power in American Politics* (New York: Free Press, 1994).

Wittman, Rebecca, 'The Wheels of Justice Turn Slowly: The Pre-Trial Investigations of the Frankfurt Auschwitz Trial, 1963–1965', *Central European History*, 35:3 (2002), pp. 345–78.

Wittmann, Rebecca, *Beyond Justice: The Auschwitz Trial, the Law and the Holocaust* (Cambridge, MA: Harvard University Press, 2003).

Wolffsohn, Michael, *Eternal Guilt: Forty Years of German–Jewish Relations*, trans. by Douglas Bukovoy (New York: Columbia University Press, 1993).

Wolinetz, Steven, 'Party System Change: The Catch-All Thesis Revisited', *West European Politics*, 14:1 (1991), pp. 113–28.

Wolinetz, Steven, (ed.), *Party Systems* (Aldershot: Ashgate, 1997).

Woolley, John, *Monetary Politics* (Cambridge: Cambridge University Press, 1984).

Young, Brigitte, *Triumph of the Fatherland: German Unification and the Marginalization of Women* (Ann Arbor: University of Michigan Press, 1999).

Young, Thomas-Durell, *Multinational Land Formations and NATO: Reforming Practices and Structures* (Carlisle Barracks, PA: Strategic Studies Institute, 1997).

Zelikow, Philip and Condoleeza Rice, *Germany United and Europe Transformed: A Study in Statecraft* (Cambridge, MA: Harvard University Press, 1995).

Zimmermann, Horst, *Kommunalfinanzen: eine Einführung in die finanzwissenschaftliche Analyse der kommunalen Finanzwirtschaft* (Baden-Baden: Nomos Verlag, 1999).

Zink, Harold, *American Military Government in Germany* (New York, Macmillan, 1947).

Index